The type of ink-blot used in the Rorschach Test: a projective technique for studying personality. (See page 557.)

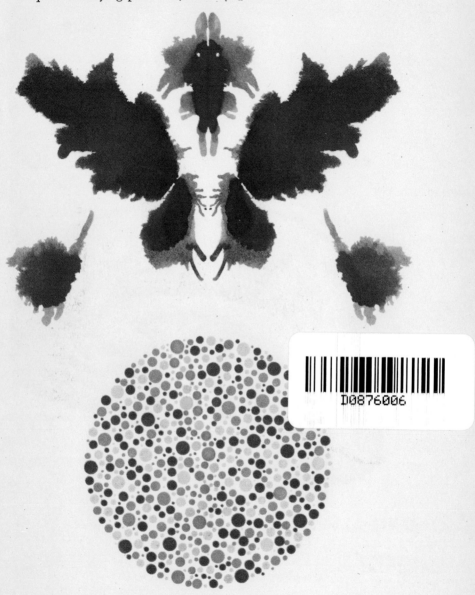

The Jensen test for color-blindness: at ten feet, normal persons see one bar; red-green color-blind see two. Used by special arrangement with Dr. Milton B. Jensen. (See page 259.)

THIRD EDITION

Psychology and life

THIRD EDITION

The Third Edition of *Psychology and Life* has been prepared with the special assistance of:

ROBERT LEEPER, Department of Psychology, University of Oregon, critical consultant throughout the book and contributor to Chapters 9 and 10 on learning and thinking

THEODORE C. RUCH, Head of the Department of Physiology, School of Medicine, University of Washington, contributor to the text of *Illustrated Reference Manual: The Brain and Nervous System*

EDWARD J. SHOBEN, JR., Department of Psychology, University of Iowa, critical consultant on the new material on clinical psychology

In addition, the Third Edition of *Psychology and Life* has had the benefit of unusual cooperation from numerous other teachers and critics in psychology. Specific acknowledgment of their work appears in the Preface and in appropriate places throughout the book.

Psychology and life

Including Illustrated Reference Manual: The Brain and Nervous System

FLOYD L. RUCH Professor of Psychology
The University of Southern California

SCOTT, FORESMAN AND COMPANY
Chicago, Atlanta, Dallas, New York

The drawings in *Psychology and Life*
are the work of Angela Bartenbach
and Seymour Fleishman

Preface

ELEVEN years ago we attempted to create a textbook for the elementary course in psychology which would meet the interests and needs of students without sacrifice of scientific rigor. While the reception of the work through two editions has been most gratifying, these vital objectives are even more attainable today, and we sincerely hope that in the estimation of teachers and students the Third Edition of *Psychology and Life* will reflect this fact.

In the first place, the last eleven years have been years of mature productivity for the science of psychology. Experimental, statistical, and clinical studies have become not only more numerous but also more rigorously defined in method and more explicitly centered around the problems that concern human beings as they strive for personal and social adjustment in a profoundly changing world. These are the problems which most strongly interest the student of today, as of eleven years ago, but today we can make available to him sound scientific studies in place of the exploratory hypotheses and findings which formerly were often the only materials available in these areas. Only if the student feels that psychology is a balanced field—including the study of these important human problems—will he be willing to extend his interest to other, less immediately interesting, aspects of psychology.

In the second place, hundreds of teachers of psychology throughout the country have made their experience with previous editions available to the author and editors of the present one. These have been tabulated, analyzed, and taken to heart. One criticism of paramount importance emerged, and this we have squarely faced—that logical organization had occasionally been sacrificed, and certain other devices resorted to, in the interest of avoiding "textbookishness" and maintaining reader interest. Consequently we have made an all-out effort to tighten up and strengthen both the organization and development, and to insure factual accuracy, while holding the vital qualities that have made this a book about psychology *and* life and for undergraduates.

Four criteria or working specifications were employed systematically in selecting the material for the Third Edition. This was necessary and desirable because it is impossible for any textbook to summarize all the factual data in the field of psychology. The criteria are:

1. Does information on this topic meet a crucial and frequent need of the individual living in modern society?
2. Does this topic have intrinsic interest for the student?
3. Are the facts known? That is, has adequate investigation by clinical, experimental, or statistical methods been performed?
4. Is the material, when not useful or interesting in and of itself, necessary as background for advanced courses?

These questions had to be answered in the affirmative by some combination of the following three: colleagues in psychology; the students themselves; and a cross section of college administrators representing various types of institutions. In common with previous editions, the present one is an attempt to recognize, organize, and interpret the good and the true in the literature of psychology rather than an effort to alter the course in psychology. It is felt, however, that there has been a happier resolution than ever before toward a central core and quality of material meeting the requirements of all types of students.

This is an appropriate point at which to record my gratitude for the many contributions, both critical and creative, of the following editorial consultants who had a part in the shaping of the newest *Psychology and Life:* Arthur G. Bills of the University of Cincinnati; Constance Lovell of the University of Southern California; Ann Magaret of the University of Wisconsin; Robert H. Seashore of Northwestern University; Charles L. Stone of Dartmouth College; and G. R. Wendt of the University of Rochester.

Collaboration to a point nearing co-authorship is to be acknowledged at this point to Robert Leeper of the University of Oregon, who is responsible for the major portion of the new material in Chapters 9 and 10; to Joseph Shoben of the University of Iowa, who aided in the writing of Chapter 12; and to my brother, Theodore C. Ruch, of the Medical School, the University of Washington, who again assumed the major responsibility for the text of the reference manual on the brain and nervous system.

Here, then, is the Third Edition of *Psychology and Life.* I give it to my teacher-friends and associates with particular pleasure because it is a revision which, to a very large degree, they have made.

FLOYD L. RUCH

Contents

PART TWO

Endowment and environment

PART THREE

Knowing our world

PART FOUR

Emotional adjustment

PART FIVE

The individual and the group

PART SIX

Illustrated reference manual: the brain and nervous system

Acknowledgments

The GREATLY EXPANDED ILLUSTRATION PROGRAM of the Third Edition was made possible through the cooperation of many psychologists and special sources. For the most part, professional services are acknowledged in some detail on the page where the illustration appears, while agencies and magazines are listed below. To all, the author and publisher wish to express their appreciation.

2.	*Life* photographer Mark Kauffman, © *Time,* Inc. *(top left);* C. H. Stoelting Co. *(top right);* reprinted from *Look—America's Family Magazine (bottom).*
3.	Acme Photo.
19.	Maze from W. R. Miles, "The High Relief Finger Maze," *Journal of General Psychology,* 1928, volume 1, p. 8; photo from Ewing Galloway, N. Y.
24.	*Life* photographer Herbert Gehr, © *Time,* Inc.
26.	Bettman Archive.
27.	Jerry Cooke—Pix.
30, 36.	Bettman Archive.
37.	Bettman Archive; © Underwood and Underwood.
38.	From *Psychologies of 1925,* Carl Murchison (ed.), Clark University Press, 1926; Bettman Archive.
39.	Iowa Child Welfare Research Station, State University of Iowa.
41.	*Life* photographer Myron Davis, © *Time,* Inc.
44.	Acme Photo; Ewing Galloway, N. Y.; © G. A. Douglas from Gendreau, N. Y.; Acme Photo.
78, 79.	*Life.*
124.	Acme Photo *(top left);* Santa Fe Railway Photo *(top right);* Ewing Galloway, N. Y. *(bottom).*
152.	Robert M. Zingg.
159.	International News Photo *(left);* Irving Browning *(center);* *Life (right).*
171.	*Life* photographer Frank Scherschel, © *Time,* Inc.; Irving Browning *(inset).*
182.	International News Photo.
187, 192.	Acme Photo.
212, 213, 214.	By permission of Dr. L. L. Thurstone and Science Research Associates.
227.	Ewing Galloway, N. Y. *(left);* Keystone *(right).*
250.	*Life* magazine, © *Time,* Inc.
286.	Abrams Aerial Survey Corporation.

287.   Los Angeles *Times;* North American Aviation, Inc.

288.   Acme Photo; Alfred Eisenstaedt—Pix.

289.   Acme Photo.

302.   George Karger—Pix.

314.   International News Photo.

318.   Acme Photo; Jerry Cooke—Pix.

319.   World Republic, Inc.; British Information Service; Acme Photo.

348.   Maze on left courtesy Dr. Robert Leeper; maze on right from Hull Clark, "Differential Habituation to Internal Stimuli in the Albino Rat," *Journal of Comparative Psychology,* 1933, volume 16, p. 260.

383, 384.   Data used by permission of the American Psychological Association.

410.   Underwood and Underwood.

472.   Acme Photo.

497, 500.   From *Principles of Dynamic Psychiatry,* by Jules H. Masserman, W. B. Saunders Co., 1946.

508.   Bettman Archive; *Chicago Daily News.*

517.   *Life* photographer Bernard Hoffman, © *Time,* Inc.

523.   Reprinted from *Look—America's Family Magazine.*

525.   Dr. J. L. Moreno.

540, 541.   Acme Photo.

547.   Official U. S. Navy photograph.

579.   Chicago Area Project *(left);* National Film Board of Canada *(right).*

581.   Acme Photo.

600, 601.   Chicago Area Project.

602.   Acme Photo; National Recreation Association; Chicago *Sun.*

615.   Reprinted from the November 1946 issue of *Fortune* by special permission of the Editors.

618.   Bettman Archive.

656.   Brown Brothers.

682.   Bettman Archive.

683.   Bettman Archive; Library of Congress.

The drawings on the following pages are the work of Seymour Fleishman: 13, 19, 42, 44, 57, 63, 83, 85, 86, 87, 90, 91, 97, 112, 113, 124, 174, 206, 223, 224, 236, 240, 242, 245, 249, 253, 279, 282, 285, 290, 297, 298, 306, 318, 319, 320, 325, 342, 348, 350, 354, 355, 360, 367, 383, 384, 398, 412, 430, 473, 493, 540, 541, 563, 568, 572, 573, 579, 581, 592, 594, 645, 704, 705, 706, 712, 726, 730. The drawing on page 281 is by John E. Schacht.

The drawings on the following pages are the work of Angela Bartenbach: 8, 9, 109, 132, 175, 241, 264, 265, 696, 697, 698, 699, 701, 702, 707, 708, 709, 711, 714, 715, 718, 722, 723, 724, 734, 738.

Thanks are due to Wesley H. Greene, Director, College Film Center, Chicago, for his kind cooperation in showing psychological films on a wide variety of subjects for selection for *Psychology and Life.*

PART ONE

Introduction

The chronoscope, which measures reaction time.

The modern psychologist uses precision apparatus— here, to study the brain waves of the man behind the screen.

A clinical psychologist diagnoses a child's emotional patterns through observing him in a specially designed play-situation.

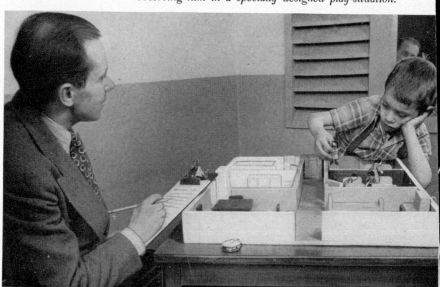

One of the contributions of applied psychology is the measurement of aptitudes. This is one of the Minnesota Tests of Manual Dexterity, used in industry.

Psychology as science

SINCE THE STONE AGE, man has made great advances in his control of physical nature, but he now lags far behind in the adjustment of human nature. For all his great technological advance, he has created a world in turmoil.

Modern science has made discoveries which can give us a world of untold beauty, comfort, and productivity—but which can also be used to destroy the world. Toward what end our ever-increasing knowledge will lead us depends upon many complex factors in political, social, and economic life. In the long run, however, all of them are related to individual human beings. We must face the sober truth that our present knowledge and our present understanding of human relations and individual adjustment are inadequate. Man must gain new knowledge and new understanding of man, and so armed, he must strive for friendly, intelligent cooperation at home and in the international community. And in the process each individual must work out his own personal adjustment to himself and the difficult world around him.

This is the challenge of the present. Where does psychology come in?

Psychology is sometimes defined as "the study of man," but this definition is too broad, for it applies also to biology and to sociology, economics, anthropology, political science, and education. In fact, psychology is rather hard to place with reference to other fields of study. In some universities it is classified with the natural or biological sciences; in other universities it is classified with the social sciences. The truth is that *psychology is partly a biological science and partly a social science, overlapping these two major areas and relating them to each other.*

While all these fields are concerned with the "study of man," each studies him from a different viewpoint. Biology studies human beings as living things that grow, repair their bodies, adjust to their physical environments, and reproduce their kind; it is concerned with the physical processes of existence. As for the difference between psychology and the social sciences, it is sometimes asserted that the other social sciences study men just in groups, and that psychology studies men just as individuals. This distinction was more nearly true in earlier decades. A modern sociologist interested in the problem of crime, for instance, would not make merely a group study but would make detailed case-history studies of *individual* criminals as well. And some of the studies in psychology, such as public-opinion polls, are concerned mainly with *groups* of persons.

The better distinction is this: *psychology is the field which deals with human nature or human activity in general.* It does not seek to understand and explain learning processes, for instance, just with reference to law-obeying or labor-union membership (as a criminologist or an economist might wish to do). Instead, in psychology we wish to get some understanding of learning processes as they might occur in *any* field of human life. No psychologist claims, consequently, that his field ever will contain all the valuable knowledge about human nature. A geologist, similarly, would not know the concrete details about every region of the earth, although he may have a very good understanding of the general processes of rock formation. Such generalized knowledge gives basic understanding of a broad range of phenomena—a basic understanding which can then be applied to specific facts or problems.

OBJECTIVES OF PSYCHOLOGY

ALTHOUGH PSYCHOLOGY THUS OPERATES in a wide field, it has four specific objectives: to contribute to the solution of social problems; to contribute to one's understanding of others; to contribute to an understanding of oneself; and to contribute to the understanding of human experience for its own sake, apart from any practical applications.

Solution of social problems

Psychology is not only a body of knowledge but a way of looking at man. The psychologist believes that man-made institutions can be changed, that man-made difficulties can be overcome. He believes that man is a rational being who can solve his problems and control his destiny by applying scientific methods to human thought, feeling, and behavior. One of the chief aims of psychology is to help solve the problems that arise as people live together in a complex society.

Human happiness grows from the harmonious adjustment of people to the social conditions around them. Sometimes these conditions are satisfactory; far more often they can be improved. Society expects its college graduates to be leaders in community life and to help improve social conditions. There is much for them to do, and a knowledge of psychology will help them do it. Crime, industrial unrest, war, race conflict, international distrust—all these are social problems which keep people from living at their maximum happiness and efficiency. They are all long-run problems which keep the world in a state of disorganization and distrust, and so make another, final, war a real threat. And they are all problems to which psychology can contribute knowledge and recommendations for action.

Understanding others

A better world means a happier world, and a happier world is made up of people who know how to get along both with others and with themselves. Here psychology can make a great contribution to more successful interpersonal relations—which are the foundation of successful intergroup relations.

To work and live harmoniously with others, you must know why they think and feel and act the way they do. Why can some students get very high grades with apparently little effort, while others, no matter how hard they work, barely get along? Are there any inborn differences among the different peoples of the world which explain why their customs and beliefs are so different? What makes a person drink excessively? These are typical of the many interesting problems we see around us all the time. The following chapters will attempt to meet them—to explain why human beings behave as they do.

Naturally one course in psychology will not give complete answers to all such questions. After all, many of the answers are still beyond the scientist. No book, no course, no teacher can give perfect insight into the vagaries of human nature. But as you study psychology, you will be puzzled less often than in the past by what people feel, think, say, and do.

Understanding yourself

Whatever course your life may take—whether you are a businessman or a physician, a scientist or a homemaker, whether you marry, whether you have children—your greatest resource in living is yourself. You as a complex and highly individual personality have many characteristic ways of thinking, feeling, and behaving. The study of psychology cannot give you detailed help in solving the personal problems which you as an individual face in your own particular life situation, for psychology is the study of *general* processes. However, by setting forth some of the marvelous processes which underlie human thought, feeling, and behavior, it will give you new concepts and new facts of human living, which you may then *apply* to your own personal problems. By showing the different ways of adjusting to meet physical, emotional, social, and intellectual needs, it will indicate how you can live in greater harmony both with the world and with yourself.

Understanding for its own sake

Even though the psychologist is interested in putting his knowledge to work in solving social problems, he does not believe that there is any necessary distinction between theoretical and practical knowledge. One of the chief contributions of psychology is understanding for its own sake. Psychology, like every other science, has certain fields which have no immediate practical interest but which are an indispensable foundation to the understanding of natural phenomena. These fields have an intrinsic interest which makes their study rewarding for its own sake.

Moreover, understanding which is sought for its own sake today may be of the greatest practical value tomorrow. The first research into the structure of the atom was not directed at practical applications. Penicillin was discovered by accident during the course of scientific laboratory investigations. The "theoretical" research of psychologists before the war was put to important practical use by the United States Air Force in evaluating, selecting, and training men.

In the social field also, psychological research which now seems to have little practical value is not only interesting in itself but may yield information that will someday greatly increase man's ability to cure his social ills. The research of today in psychiatry, propaganda, and industrial psychology can have great effect on the mental health, public opinion, and labor relations of tomorrow.

But before going on to study in detail some of the many challenging problems psychology has tackled, we must discover how the psychologist operates in his study of man. How does he set about gaining the understanding of human thought, feeling, and behavior which is so essential in the world today? In this chapter we shall examine the true foundation of psychology: its scientific attitudes toward man and its methods of studying him.

MAN AS THE PSYCHOLOGIST SEES HIM

FROM EARLIEST TIMES, people have been interested in themselves and have tried to understand why human beings think and feel and act the way they do. Our primitive ancestors, burdened with superstition and lacking in facts, thought that the human body was inhabited by a demon or "little man," who was sometimes good and sometimes bad but was always the boss of the person's behavior. The primitive explanation of death was that the little man left the body of the big man and did not return. Today civilized people do not believe in a supernatural "little man" as the causal force in human life. However, you do meet some people who believe that the human mind and human experience are too complex and too subtle to be the subject of scientific study.

The modern psychologist does not believe that there is anything in human psychology which is not open to scientific study. He believes that man thinks and feels and acts the way he does because of the interaction between his internal needs and capacities and the outside influences in his environment. There is nothing necessarily mysterious about these needs, capacities, and influences; they are either already known or are presumed to be knowable through scientific research. Human psychology, like everything in the natural world, is essentially a matter of cause and effect.

Although this cause-and-effect may be complex and may be very difficult to discover because of the limitations of our present methods, there is no reason to believe that human psychology is beyond the powers of understanding and scientific method.

Man is an organism

The first concept the psychologist has of man is that he is an *organism:* that is, he is an individual composed of a group of organs which work together to carry on his life activities. This concept, which the

Lemur, gorilla, and man . . . Man is an organism, but one far more complex and far more adaptable than the lower animals . . . both in body structure . . .

psychologist shares with other scientists, is based on his attitude that man can be understood—his thought, feeling, and behavior scientifically explained—just as other natural phenomena can be explained. At one time the weather was believed to be governed by a mystical "law of nature." Health and illness were once considered subject to "nature's way," not to human knowledge and control. And man's thought, feeling, and behavior were ascribed to "just human nature" or to inborn "instincts"—all these, needless to say, being beyond human understanding. Now meteorology and medicine are well-established sciences. But the acceptance of psychology has been slower—partly because the average person feels that scientific study undermines the dignity and importance of man.

The psychologist does not deny the individuality and complexity of every human being. There are innumerable factors operating to make every person feel and think and act the way he does, just as the weather today is not exactly like the weather of any other day. But still there are general principles of human experience which the psychologist can discover and which can help you understand particular things about particular people, just as there are general laws of weather which enable the meteorologist to explain why it is cloudy this particular morning and will probably rain this particular afternoon.

Man lives in an environment

Everyone lives in an *environment,* by which we mean the external surroundings of an organism. Every environment contains many different objects, most of which do not at a particular moment arouse the individual to activity, although there are many objects in the en-

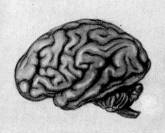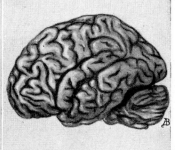

*and in brain, which is man's greatest resource and
the basis of his unique material and spiritual achievements.*

vironment which are potentially capable of arousing him to activity
of some sort. The parts of the environment that do make him react at
any particular moment (or that are capable of making him react) give
off "stimuli."

The word *stimuli* is the plural of *stimulus,* which in Latin means
"goad" and in the strict terminology of physics means "some form of
energy." In psychology the word *stimulus* refers to some form of physical energy acting on cells in the human body—some form of physical
energy which, if it were sufficiently intense, or if the change in its
intensity were strong enough, would arouse nerve impulses from those
cells. For strict usage the word *stimulus* needs to be distinguished from
stimulus object. Thus, a light bulb is a stimulus object, but the light
waves from it which enter the eye of the person and act on the cells in
the retina are the stimuli. When a stimulus is strong enough to make the
organism respond in some way, it is said to be above the *threshold* or
"limen." A similar stimulus which is too weak to produce an observable
response is said to be below the threshold, or "subliminal."

An individual could not exist or develop except in an environment,
and must depend on his environment for the means of satisfying his
basic needs for food, warmth, and so on. Every individual has a complex relationship with his environment, because he is complex, and
because the environment itself is complex—containing not merely the
means for physical sustenance but also people and social institutions
which mold the individual in certain habits, desires, and interests often
known as the "social motives." For example: the average American
requires both food to keep alive (a biological need) and also a feeling
that he is "getting ahead in the world" (a social need). But whether

Man as the Psychologist Sees Him 9

the environment is *physical* or *social,* the individual is always interacting with it in many complex ways.

Man adjusts

The interaction between man and his environment must take some form
of *adjustment,* or attempts at overcoming obstacles to the satisfaction of
biological and social needs. Adjustment can occur in response to either
internal or external stimuli. When you have a tickle in your throat,
you cough to ease the discomfort. When a mosquito settles on your
arm, you slap it away. Both responses are adjustive, but in one case the
stimulus is internal and in the other case external.

The process of adjustment is of basic importance to human life,
whether it is relatively simple (like running from the path of a car)
or complex (like selling insurance to get money to buy food). Human
living is a constant process of adjustment, although that adjustment
may take many forms. For example, when an individual adjusts, he
may either change his environment or change his response to it;
if both are unsuccessful in satisfying his needs, he may try to modify
his needs. But whatever form adjustment takes, it always involves
a complex relationship between the individual's needs, the opportunities the environment provides for satisfying those needs, and the
individual's capacities for making the most of those opportunities.
Such a complex process naturally has a rather complex physiological
basis. To understand it fully, you must become acquainted with *The
Organs of Adjustment.*

The organs of adjustment

The organs of the human body are divided into two chief groups, according to whether they (1) function internally to maintain the individual's
health and growth, or (2) function in the individual's activities in the
environment as he overcomes obstacles to the satisfaction of his needs.
The first group, the *organs of maintenance,* includes the organs of
respiration, excretion, and digestion. The second group, known as the
organs of adjustment, is made up of the receptors in sense organs, the
nervous system, the skeleton, and the muscles. This distinction between
the functions of organs becomes hard to maintain, because, for example, the circulatory system serves in both maintenance and adjustment, and the state of the organs of maintenance influences the success of the person's adjustment activities.

The organs of adjustment include three distinct kinds of bodily
mechanisms: (1) those which receive stimuli; (2) those which produce

changes in the environment or in the organism's relation to it; and (3) those which connect the first two and coordinate the responses of the person as a whole. Because of their importance to psychology, we shall discuss each in turn.

The receiving mechanisms. The receiving mechanisms—such as the organs for seeing, hearing, and tasting—are usually composed of two parts. These are (1) the *receptor cells,* which receive the stimuli coming from within the body or from the environment; and (2) the *accessory structures,* such as the focusing mechanisms of the eye, which help to provide effective stimuli for the receptor cells.

The receptor cells are the most essential parts of the receiving mechanisms, which could not operate without them. They are found in the eye, in the inner ear, on the tongue, in the nose, in the skin, and in the muscles and joints. Of all the various stimuli acting upon each receptor cell, it is sensitive only to certain ones. The cells in the eyes, for example, are not sensitive to sound waves.

The connecting mechanisms. The connecting mechanisms, or *connectors,* are the organs which connect the receptor cells with cells in the organs of response. There are two groups of body structures serving as connectors: the nervous system and the circulatory system.

The more important structure serving this function is the nervous system. In man the connection between the receiving and responding mechanisms is rarely direct, usually passing through the brain or spinal cord. A series of connections or nerve pathways running between the receiving and responding organs is known as a *neural pattern.* (These connections will be discussed more fully in Part Six on *The Brain and Nervous System,* especially pp. 695-713.)

The blood stream also functions as a connecting and coordinating system, playing a highly important role in coordinating the various activities of the body. The effect that an activity has on one region of the body may be transmitted by the blood stream to other parts. For instance, if a muscle of the right arm is exercised to the point of complete fatigue, the other muscles of the body will become tired, because chemical substances produced by exercising the arm muscle are distributed by the blood to all parts of the body.

Part of the coordination accomplished by the blood stream is attained through its distribution of *hormones.* Hormones are chemical substances produced by certain glands known as the *ductless glands* (sometimes as the *endocrine glands*). The term "ductless" is used because the substances secreted by the glands do not pass through a "duct" or tube but pass directly into the blood stream, where they flow to all parts of the body. In sudden fear, for example, a certain ductless gland becomes active and pours its secretion into the blood stream, where it can flow to all the organs of the body. Its action on some of these organs brings about such widely diverse effects as dilation of the iris of the eye, constriction of the blood vessels in the stomach wall, and an increase in the rapidity of blood clotting.

The responding mechanisms. The third group of organs functioning in adjustment are called the responding mechanisms, or *effectors*. These effectors consist of both glands and muscles.

In action, the effectors manipulate both the individual and the world around him, in order to satisfy the individual's needs. For example, if the temperature of the room you are studying in becomes too high for comfort, you may reach out and turn off the radiator. The stimulus of heat has been received by a group of warmth receptors in your skin and nerve impulses thus aroused have been carried through the brain to your arm and hand muscles, which have responded by taking action to reduce the heat.

Or if you get a cinder in your eye, your tear glands secrete a liquid which washes the cinder away. Such a glandular response acts in the same way as the muscular response of your arm, to satisfy the organism's basic need for relief from pain and discomfort.

While the psychologist recognizes that man has all these different types of bodily mechanisms, he does not feel content with the program which physiology follows. He does not assume, in other words, that human activity can be understood, or its laws be determined, by studying the structures and functions of each part of the body separately. He does not work, typically, with the eye alone, or merely with a nerve-muscle preparation, or the like. Instead, he studies the human organism by dealing with it as a complex functional unit. He studies the whole person to find out the laws of perception, motivation, learning, and the like. At the same time, however, his understanding of the processes of the whole person is helped along by interpretations— both from physiology and from psychology—regarding the influences of changes or differences within these several kinds of organs of adjustment.

Patterns of adjustment

Everyone knows that the newborn baby's way of responding to his environment is a great deal simpler, and a great deal less adjustive, than the behavior of the complex, efficient, self-sufficient adult. A psychologist would say that the adult's behavior patterns are more complex than the infant's. In psychological terminology, a *behavior pattern* is a sequence of actions which adjust the organism to a particular situation in the outer world or within the organism itself. Some behavior patterns are very simple indeed, such as coughing or suddenly withdrawing your hand from a hot object, and may occur without full action of the brain. Other patterns are extremely complex, such as solving a geometry problem, which is literally "brainwork." But whether simple or complex, they are essentially the same in that underlying each behavior pattern is a *neural pattern*, which is, as you will remember, a nerve pathway between the mechanism that receives a stimulus and the mechanism that responds to it. As the individual matures, his neural patterns become more complex, thus allowing more complex behavior patterns.

Man functions as a whole

Neural pattern   Behavior pattern   Adjustment pattern

The student should note, however, that in an organism as complex as man, the idea of a single stimulus acting upon a single receptor is an abstraction. Stimuli act in patterns, many at a time. For instance, when you are sitting in the library studying on a warm spring afternoon, you are stimulated in many ways. You see and feel the book in your hand, hear the low voices of two students whispering at the far end of the room, feel the spring breeze blowing in the window, and smell the fresh new grass outside. Yet in spite of all these stimuli acting upon you, you concentrate—with varying degrees of success—on thinking about the words on the page before you. You may be responding to all these stimuli, but you are doing one main thing: studying.

In all of daily life, many activities are going on simultaneously in the human organism, but it behaves as a whole—that is, it does one main thing at a time. Usually the secondary activities support the

Man as the Psychologist Sees Him   13

main activity or at least do not seriously interfere with it; if they do interfere, the organism will suppress or inhibit them. An important thing to realize about every living organism is that normally its activities are integrated into a smoothly functioning whole. *Neural patterns underlie behavior patterns, and behavior patterns unite to form the adjustment pattern of the whole organism. Man functions as a whole.*

Adjustment as a guiding concept in psychology

The concept of *adjustment*—of the individual interacting with his environment to satisfy his needs—suggests a useful way of organizing the subject matter of psychology. Go back and glance over the Table of Contents of this book. You will see that *Psychology and Life* is divided into these main sections:

Introduction
Endowment and Environment
Knowing the World
Emotional Adjustment
The Individual and the Group
The Brain and Nervous System

The first long section, on *Endowment and Environment*, emphasizes the relations between the individual's biological inheritance and his surroundings. It outlines the main factors in heredity and environment that influence human adjustment. It describes the various biological and social needs—the motivations—that underlie human thought, feeling, and action. It acquaints you with some of the emotional needs that present complex problems of human adjustment. And it shows you how people differ in intelligence: that is, in their ability to adjust in new situations.

Knowing the World contains, first, a chapter on "The Sensory Processes"—a detailed discussion of the receiving mechanisms. This is followed by chapters on "Perception, Attention, and Report," "Learning: Its Basic Nature," and "Remembering and Thinking"—that is, on how we organize, retain, and use impressions and ideas in the complex process of adjustment.

The section on *Emotional Adjustment* describes the various ways people have of adjusting to the frustration of emotional needs, outlines the factors that influence emotional adjustment, and shows how psychologists can help emotionally maladjusted people.

The next section deals with *The Individual and the Group*—that is, with the psychology of complex social relationships. It suggests that social problems, which are social blockings of the individual's needs, are subject to human control. It indicates how psychological knowledge can help solve them.

The last section, *The Brain and Nervous System,* gives you a more detailed understanding of the most vital and highly developed of man's connecting and coordinating mechanisms.

Before going on to these particular problems of psychology, however, we must examine the special *methods* psychology uses in examining them. As you know, people have been wondering about human behavior for centuries. Only in the last three-quarters of a century, however, have they studied it by means of scientific operations. The remainder of this chapter will discuss *The Operations of Psychological Investigation, The Methods of Research in Psychology,* and *How the Emphasis of Psychology Has Changed.*

THE OPERATIONS OF PSYCHOLOGICAL INVESTIGATION

IN MEETING its objectives, both theoretical and practical, psychology may execute one or more of the following operations:

  1 Description of the individual's experience.

  2 Prediction of his future experience.

  3 Control of his experience, making use of the knowledge gained by description and prediction.

  4 The statement of useful principles—the organization of psychological knowledge.

It does not matter whether your fundamental motivation in studying psychology is "knowledge for its own sake" or "knowledge for its application's sake." The essence of science is in its special methods of operation, which can be used on both theoretical and practical problems.

Description

Description of the individual's thought, feeling, and behavior is the fundamental operation of psychology: it is essential to the others and comes first in time. Prediction and control in any science are based on accurate description. We must first know what happens under different conditions before we can attempt to predict what is likely to happen in the future. And we must be able to predict before we can direct future events into some desired channel.

Let us choose as a simple example of description the scientific observation and recording of color-blindness. Color-blindness has several varieties, the most common being the *red-green* variety, which exists in a measurable degree in about five in every hundred men. It may be studied and described entirely in terms of behavior, as follows:

If we place red, green, and blue tufts of yarn in a single heap before a red-green color-blind person and ask him to put the different colors in separate piles, he does a seemingly odd thing. He will place all the blues, and nothing but blues, in one pile. However, he will not separate the reds and greens correctly into piles, but will mix them together, sometimes in one pile and sometimes in more than one. The degree of his confusion will depend on the severity of his defect, for color-blindness is not an all-or-none attribute; it may occur in any degree from slight color weakness to total absence of color perception. It is difficult for a color-blind person to give a subjective account of his color sensations—many color-blind persons, in fact, do not suspect their defect. Only through objective description of color behavior can we detect and describe color-blindness as the absence of some of the differences in visual sensation which allow the normal individual to distinguish between "colors."

Psychologists employ two important methods of observing and describing human beings: (1) *introspection* (meaning, literally, "looking in"), which is the observation by an individual of his own conscious states and processes, such as thinking and feeling; (2) *objective observation*, which is observation by others of an individual's overt behavior under various conditions.

Introspection. By introspection, the subject is able to furnish information about psychological processes that might be overlooked by any other method. You can familiarize yourself with the technique of introspection by conducting the following exercise: Think of your breakfast table this morning. Can you "see" the form of your plate? Can you "hear" the sound of silverware against it? Can you "taste" your toast or cereal? Can you remember how the coffee smelled? If you do succeed in calling up these images, how long do they persist? How does the clearness of your strongest impression compare with the clearness of the original perception?

Everyone learns to perform such simple introspections into his own mind. But no one, with any amount of practice, can observe a sensation felt by someone else. This is the first serious limitation on the use of introspection: (1) its results cannot be verified by another person. Furthermore, (2) it is of no use with animals, and it is too difficult to be used with young children, the feeble-minded, or adults who have not been trained in its technique.

Still another important limitation is that (3) many of man's activities are wholly or partially unconscious, and hence cannot be observed by the introspective method, which reports only conscious experiences. The influence of the unconscious is demonstrated by experiments with hypnosis, in which the subject can be given instructions governing his activities which will become effective after he has been brought out of the hypnotic state. He will carry these instructions out in faithful detail, but either will be altogether unable to account for his behavior or will give a false reason for it.

> "We have here a hypnotized subject to whom I say that when he wakes he is to take a flower-pot from the window-sill, wrap it in a cloth, put it on the sofa, and bow to it three times. All of which he does. When asked for his reasons he answers, 'You know, when I woke and saw the flower-pot there I thought that as it was rather cold the flower-pot had better be warmed a little, or else the plant would die. So I wrapped it in the cloth, and then I thought that as the sofa was near the fire I would put the flower-pot on it; and I bowed because I was pleased with myself for having such a bright idea.'" (Moll[1])

To this account we might well add that, commonly, the previously hypnotized person usually feels somewhat foolish and ill-at-ease when he carries out such commands as this. Often he tries to fight off the tendency to carry out the act when he believes it would make him appear foolish to others, but he finds this uncomfortable and, when he has no strong scruples against the action, he tends to invent some reason why he should perform the action, and then eases his state of tension by doing it.

Experiments like this one convince the psychologist of how unconscious attitudes can influence thought and behavior without the individual being able to locate their influence by introspection. In Chapter 13, we shall study the normal process of *repression* by which attitudes become unconscious.

Obviously, the introspective method has distinct limitations. Psychologists supplement it with a second method of observing human beings: objective observation.

Objective observation. The objective method allows one person to observe what another does, not what he thinks or feels. Its first great advantage is that (1) the observations can be verified. The environment in which the act is performed may be standardized in detail or may be systematically described, so that it can be duplicated or recognized by another worker, or by the same worker at a later date. The behavior itself is also described in detail, complicated apparatus often being used to get graphic records of the subject's behavior, records which can be analyzed by several psychologists. Another great advantage is that (2) it permits study of animals, children, the feeble-minded, and the insane, and even the normal subject need not be specially trained in self-observation.

Of course, through the objective method we observe just the individual's behavior, not his mental processes. This is a serious limitation. Some psychologists charge that this method gives us the beginning and end of a response, but skips the response itself.

In a certain sense, of course, this is true. With objective observation we do not observe, directly, any processes of learning, thinking, forgetting, or the like. But it must be realized that even when we use introspective observation, we cannot observe directly all the important psychological processes. A lot of the work of psychology, consequently, consists of using the directly observed facts to infer processes which cannot be seen directly, just as physics uses directly oberved facts to make inferences regarding such things as atomic structure.

Accurate observation of another's behavior demands (like introspection) the development of skill, which is best acquired under the supervision of a trained observer. The casual reports of the untrained observer are frequently inaccurate, for these reasons:

1 Being untrained, he may be unable to differentiate between what he actually sees and what he merely infers.

2 He may not know the past history of the subject observed.

3 He may not be familiar with all the conditions which might be responsible for the behavior in question. Hence, he may fail to note their presence or absence.

4 He may have a personal affection for the subject and a desire to see him in a favorable light; or he may dislike the subject and want to report him unfavorably. This tendency to let what he wants influence what he sees is known as *bias*.

5 He probably has the very human desire to tell a good story.

A revealing example of an inaccurate observer is the father who boasted to a psychologist that his three-year-old daughter could read. When challenged by the psychologist, the father brought out a book of nursery rhymes, opened it to the first page, and said, "Now, darling, read for the nice man." The words tumbled out rapidly and letter perfect. At the end of the first page, the psychologist gently took the book and said to the child, "I'll bet you can't tell me what is on the next page." Proudly the child recited the rhymes on that page with equal fluency and accuracy. The father listened in consternation and reluctantly concluded that the child was reciting words by rote rather than reading them. Clearly, his bias and perhaps his ignorance of the limitations on children's learning progress had kept him from observing the presence of memory as well as intelligence in the child's performance.

All these possible sources of inaccuracy are carefully guarded against by the psychologist when he is conducting scientific observations.

Introspection and objective observation work together. As you compare the two methods of observation, you will notice that they can supplement each other, that they can be used in combination. For example, such a combination was useful for an experiment in which college students learned to trace a finger maze (Husband[2]). Objective records were made of their actual learning progress and then compared with their introspective reports of what learning procedure they used. Thus the experimenters could compare objective performance under different learning procedures.

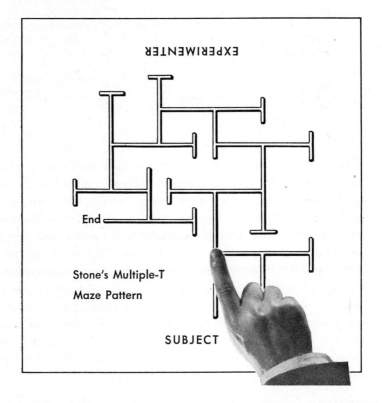

Stone's Multiple-T
Maze Pattern

This experiment was designed to test how fast the subject could learn the true path through a maze, that is, could enter the passages leading out of the maze without entering blind alleys. In this experiment, the maze was made of wires mounted on a smooth board. The subject was blindfolded and his finger was placed on the starting-point. Then he was given a signal to begin exploring the maze to find his way through it. During each trial, he was not permitted to lift his finger from the track. The time required to reach the goal and the number of entries into the "blinds" were recorded for each trial. The best learner was the one who spent the shortest time and made the fewest errors in learning the true path so that he could repeat it in successive trials without error.

As the subjects learned, they were asked to carry on introspections on how they learned. The majority reported that they translated the maze into words—the so-called *verbal* method of learning. They would say to themselves as they traversed the maze: "First you go ahead, then to the left, then ahead, then to the right," etc. Such subjects simply memorized the true path as one would a poem or speech. Other subjects attempted to form a picture of the maze in the "mind's eye": they were called the *visual* group. The third group learned by the "feel" of their fingers and arms: they were called the *motor* (muscle sense) group. Then a comparison was made of the average performances, objectively observed, of the three groups as they were classified from introspective reports. As will be seen from the table, the verbal method was obviously the most efficient of the three.

Method	Number of Subjects Using It	Trials Required to Learn the Maze
Verbal	29	19.5
Visual	4	24.3
Motor	10	44.5

Here you see in operation the two fundamental ways psychologists have of describing human activity. They can gather introspective observations, in which the subject looks inward and reports his psychological experiences, and they can then associate these reports with the external or internal conditions stimulating the subject. Or they can use objective observations, in which they record details of a subject's overt behavior and then relate that behavior to the environmental conditions influencing the subject. Each of these methods has its advantages and limitations, but the two used together give a more nearly complete description than either used alone. Together they have made possible the recent advances in scientific psychology, and together they represent psychology's main approach to the description of human behavior.

Prediction

Now we come to the second operation psychology uses in obtaining and applying knowledge of how people think, feel, know, and act—prediction of future behavior. We have already described how a color-blind person fails to distinguish between different colors, especially red and green. How can we use our description to predict his future behavior in different situations involving color discrimination?

Careful study of hundreds of red-green color-blind subjects has shown that they are ill-fitted for certain occupations. For instance, they make poor aircraft pilots because they cannot tell a red signal from a green one; they are prone to operational errors which endanger their own lives and those of their fellow crew members and which may also destroy valuable equipment or jeopardize the success of a vital mission. But from observations of color-blindness like those we have made, it is possible to predict that sooner or later the defective person will have an accident in situations where safety depends on accurate discriminations between red and green. The United States Army Air Forces reject pilot candidates who are color-blind.

Prediction simply involves the analysis of a given situation to see how a given description—in this case, of color-blindness—applies to it.

Control

Control of human activities, in the sense of applying a sure cure, is likely to be a delicate if not impossible operation. In a matter like color-blindness, however, from knowledge of the limitations of the color-blind person it is possible to reduce the possibility of accidents. For instance, the color-blind person can select work, hobbies, and recreational skills which do not require color discrimination.

The dangers of color-blindness may be controlled even further. The red-green color-blind have been considered in many cities where traffic lights are no longer pure red and pure green. Yellow has been added to the red, and blue to the green, so that the color-blind person can distinguish the lights by their yellow-blue components. These cities need not restrict the color-blind in their driving, because analysis of accident statistics shows them to be as safe as drivers of normal vision.

Adapting a situation to predicted behavior is only one way of obtaining desired ends. The behavior itself must frequently be modified. Here again, automobile driving is a good example. Often automobile drivers with some defect which causes them to have serious and frequent accidents can be "trained around" the defect with such success that they can drive safely. Certain persons have "tunnel vision": that is, they see clearly only in a narrow cone directly in front of their eyes. Very frequently they have accidents at intersections because they do not see the vehicle approaching from one side until it is practically upon them. When a person with tunnel vision has a cooperative attitude toward law and a genuine desire to be a safe driver, he can usually be trained to turn his head sharply to left and right every time he approaches an intersection, so that all oncoming traffic is brought into clear central vision.

Of course description, prediction, and control are applicable to normal as well as abnormal people. Vocational guidance illustrates how these three operations of psychology are applied to the normal person. The first operation, *description*, states the psychological requirements of various vocations: interests, aptitudes, and personality. Then when a person is tested for these requirements, it is possible to make with considerable confidence a *prediction* as to his degree of happiness and success in the various careers. The final *control* of behavior consists in his choosing the most promising vocation and taking the necessary training for it. You will find vocational guidance presented in detail in Chapter 17, for choosing your lifework is obviously one of the most important problems you will ever encounter. Psychologists are learning to make descriptions and predictions of more and more complex aspects of human experience.

Deriving useful principles

Psychologists are not content with just describing, predicting, and controlling human experience. They also strive to *interpret* and *organize* their facts—to evolve general principles of human thought, feeling, and behavior. To do this, however, they must make their descriptions and predictions under carefully controlled, carefully observed conditions and must interpret them according to certain principles of scientific method. It is the special *Methods of Research in Psychology* which distinguish it from ordinary common-sense observation.

THE METHODS OF RESEARCH IN PSYCHOLOGY

PSYCHOLOGISTS have four chief methods of obtaining scientifically valid facts and ideas about human thinking, feeling, and action. These are *The Field-Study Method, The Life-History Methods* (including the day-book method, the case-history method, and the biographical method), *The Clinical Methods*, and, finally, *The Experimental Method*.

The field-study method

The field-study method is the least complex of the research techniques used in any science, including psychology. It consists simply in the investigator's going into the field and making observations; he makes no effort to control the conditions under which he studies his subjects, nor does he need or request cooperation from them. As a matter of fact, field studies usually are most successful when the research worker's subjects are not aware that he is observing them.

Field-study methods are used particularly by the naturalists, those scientists whose chief objects of study are animals. The ornithologist, for example, when he wants to study some species of bird, simply goes into the region which is the bird's habitat and observes the bird's behavior. He does not try to subject the bird to the rigid conditions of a laboratory experiment; he does not need or want the cooperation of the bird beyond its appearing on the scene; and his observations are most rich in detail when his presence is not known.

The writer had some graduate students employ this method of "scientific snooping" in a study of the conversations of fifty college girls and fifty college men. The observers sauntered up to the conversing individuals and listened long enough to get the gist of the conversation without being noticed in particular. The topics were tabulated with the following interesting results:

Topics of conversation among college students

The opposite sex	17%
College studies	12%
Campus activities in general	8%
The same sex	8%
College sports and others	8%
Food and restaurants	8%
Entertainment and amusements other than sports	6%
Professors as persons	6%
Politics	6%
Off-campus news	5%
Cultural interests other than college courses	4%
Miscellaneous	12%

Much use was made of the field observation method in England during World War II to determine how well the morale of the people was holding up. The trained observers, working under the direction of Duff-Cooper, were known popularly as "Cooper's-Snoopers."

The life-history methods

Life-history methods of psychological research involve intensive studies of individuals, usually in the attempt to trace the *development* of the particular form of behavior under investigation. What the psychologist does is to study the factors in the lives of various people which have led up to their becoming criminals, successful physicians, radicals or conservatives, etc. By this study of the antecedents of some specific form of behavior, he hopes to find the *causes* of that behavior. Usually, the life-history method takes one of three basic variations in actual practice—the *daybook method*, the *case-history method*, or the *biographical method*.

The daybook method. The daybook method is most often used in child study. The child's development is carefully watched and records are made of when he first smiled, sat, stood, spoke a word, walked, thus suggesting standards of normal development. As used by child psychologists, the method is a more carefully controlled form of the "baby book" which mothers use to record the high points in their children's growing up.

An elaborate form of the daybook method is employed at the famous Yale Clinic of Child Development, where Dr. Arnold Gesell and his associates have for years kept detailed and accurate records of the development of thousands of children. Here cameraman and stenographer are at work as Dr. Gesell tests a child in a special observation chamber.

The case-history method. In the case-history method, the psychologist gathers data about the previous experiences of a person in an effort to understand better his present behavior. The following case, taken from a psychologist's files, illustrates the method. Sylvia, the subject of the study here presented, sought psychological help because of a speech defect, stuttering, which impaired her social relations.

Preliminary investigation disclosed two facts: the girl had severe feelings of inferiority, and her father was also a stutterer, although his defect appeared only when he was under emotional tension.

> "The stuttering had started at the age of seven or eight with encouragement by the mother, who thought it very cute. Sylvia was the youngest of four children. Two of the children were brothers whose ages were greater than Sylvia's, and they do not appear to have played a significant role in the latter's development. A sister, however, who was just three years older than the patient, had attempted to suppress every aspiration and thought put out by the younger child since her birth. The sister was ably assisted by the mother. This seems to be a reverse of the usual procedure wherein the youngest child is the spoiled and petted member of the family circle. Sylvia had come late in her parents' life as an undesirable luxury, and she early became their device for tension reduction and emotional transference victim. The child promptly developed an inferiority complex, finding in her stuttering a way of attracting attention to herself, and becoming a person of consequence." (Bagby[3])

Sylvia's stuttering, therefore, was seen to be an effect of her feelings of inferiority, which had been engendered by her relationships with her family. Treatment in her case was concerned with the inferiority feelings rather than with her speech, and the stuttering cleared up without direct treatment as the girl became more sure of herself and more willing to accept and assert her own individuality.

Such studies not only give a counselor insight into people whom he is trying to help but also provide a good deal of important information about types of human behavior. Sylvia's case, for instance, contributed materially to knowledge of the causes of stuttering.

The biographical method. The psychologist using the biographical method attempts to ferret out scientifically valid facts and ideas about people from accounts of their lives written by the people themselves or by their biographers. Instead of examining his subjects directly, he reads their biography or autobiography.

> A fine example of this method in psychological research is a study of the life stories of several hundred geniuses. Such evidences of intellectual status as poems written during childhood, and age at learning to read, were compared with the accomplishments of average children. By a somewhat complicated procedure involving such comparisons, the actual degree of intelligence was estimated for some three hundred persons whom the world has called geniuses. Of the entire group popularly thought geniuses, the least intelligent was found to be equal in ability to the average person. The study showed, with reasonable reliability, that the adult whom the world calls a genius demonstrates his superiority in childhood. (Cox[4])

Until the late eighteenth century, a mentally disturbed individual was not treated as a sick person whose illness had its origin in inherited defects or in unfortunate life experiences. Disturbed individuals were thought to be possessed by an "evil spirit," and were often imprisoned or tried as witches (as in the Salem trial above).

The application of scientific study to biographical materials is limited in two significant respects. First, the biographer is not a psychologist and does not always know about or recognize the importance of seemingly trivial incidents in determining development. He may lack information about many aspects of the subject's private life.

In the second place, the biographer's motivation may bias his account. After all, why does a person usually undertake the laborious task of writing a biography or autobiography? The probability is that even though he may strive for a true record, the very fact that he has an interest strong enough to make him write suggests that he may be partial. He is frequently motivated by the urge, recognized or unconscious, to praise or blame his subject. At best, literary biographies are a poor substitute for first-hand study of life development, but they are useful when the subject—because of death or the inaccessibility of the famous—cannot be examined by more direct methods.

The modern clinical psychologist gives scientific tests to diagnose the patient's illness, and treats him by various forms of psychotherapy which we shall consider in Chapter 14. In this hospital at Youngstown, Ohio, a patient is receiving a range of tests, including the Rorschach "ink-blot" test (directly at the patient's left).

The clinical methods

The case-history approach as it has been described here leads to a discussion of the clinical methods, which are among the newest and most interesting developments in psychology.

Clinical psychology has been defined as the ". . . science, technique, and art of employing psychological principles, methods, and procedures to promote the welfare of the individual person for the purposes of optimum social adjustment and self-expression" (Doll[5]). As such it is closely related to medicine and is rapidly establishing itself as a very useful and well-recognized profession.

Of course the psychologist is not equipped to do everything necessary for the easing of man's ills. He is not a physician and has neither the legal right nor the training to treat physical disease or the severe mental abnormalities called *psychoses*. Whenever the question of physical health arises, the psychologist must defer to the doctor; but when physical examination by an M.D. has ruled out organic disease, the psychologist is equipped to go on his own. Following is an example of the daily appointment schedule of a clinical psychologist in a large city, showing the kind of problems with which he legitimately deals.

8:30 A.M. Mr. M., a stutterer, referred by his instructor in a university extension course.

9:30 Mrs. D., a marriage adjustment case, coming because her six years of marriage have been unsatisfactory emotionally and sexually; she was referred by a former client of the psychologist.

10:30 Mr. J., sent for testing by Dr. Jones, a physician. Mr. J. seems to have a nonallergic asthma, and his doctor is interested in having the possibility of emotional factors as a basis for the disease explored through psychological diagnosis.

11:30 Miss T., a vocational guidance case, referred by her college psychology instructor. Miss T. is not much interested in college and would like to leave to go to work, but she is not sure that is wise and would like to know something more about her abilities before deciding.

12:30 P.M. Mrs. Z. and her five-year-old son, Charlie, coming because Charlie is a feeding problem, unduly aggressive toward his parents, and still wets the bed at night. The psychologist devotes thirty minutes to talking with the mother and thirty minutes to a special kind of therapeutic play with the boy on each of the Z.'s visits. They were sent in by a physician who found nothing wrong with the child physically.

2:30 Mr. A., a man who is so afraid of the dark that he refuses all social activity that would take him out after nightfall and feels uncomfortable if he steps into a dark closet without propping the door wide open with a door stop. He picked the psychologist's name out of the telephone directory.

3:30 Philip, a nine-year-old boy who cannot seem to learn to read, in spite of superior intelligence. Philip was referred by an overworked school psychologist who couldn't find time to handle this rather difficult case of nonreading.

4:30 Mr. C., who came in originally saying that he "knew" his health was all right but that he felt tired and lethargic. He thought his feelings of weariness might be connected with some of his worries. When Mr. C. comes today, however, he must be told that his worries and his feelings of tiredness have no connection. A medical report from Dr. Smith, to whom the psychologist sent the client, shows that Mr. C. has undulant fever and must have medical attention.

Often, of course, the psychologist must call in a specialist trained to deal with particular problems. In later chapters, many of these difficulties will be discussed in greater detail.

The experimental method

The psychologist investigates the general processes underlying human thought, feeling, and behavior by experiments as well as by life-history and clinical investigations. Actual experiments in psychology involve rigid control of the factors being studied. To understand clearly the experimental method, which is essentially the same in all sciences, let us take a simple problem: *Which of two commercial fertilizers produces the better yield of corn?*

This question may appear straightforward and direct, but it requires further clarification. What do we mean by "better" yield? Also, are we interested in corn in general or in a particular kind of corn? To be precise, we may reword our question as follows: "Which of two specified commercial fertilizers produces the better yield of a specified variety of seed corn—better yield being defined as the heavier yield?" With the question stated in definite terms, the next step is to list all the factors—*variables*—which influence the yield of corn. This list would include not only the fertilizer but also the chemical composition of the soil, rainfall or irrigation, amount of sunlight, altitude of the cornfield, drainage of the soil, method of cultivation, and depth to which the corn is planted.

Now all the factors or conditions other than fertilizer are to be *held constant*. This does not mean that they are not allowed to operate at all, for obviously the corn could not grow unless they were all present. It does mean that their influence on the corn yield is allowed for by growing the corn in two cornfields which are exactly similar except for the fertilizer used. Thus any difference in the corn yields of the two fields must result from the difference in fertilizer. With all other factors influencing corn yield thus "held constant," the only freely operating factor, the fertilizer, is known as the *independent variable*. Its influence on yield is what we are interested in measuring.

The final influence of this independent variable is measured in terms of a *dependent variable*, such as the number of pounds of corn produced by each experimental field. The dependent variable is sometimes referred to as the *criterion*. Let us suppose that the field which was fertilized with A yielded 10 per cent more corn than the field fertilized with B. Since all other conditions were held constant, we can conclude that fertilizer A is the better fertilizer when weight is taken as the only criterion. Here it is important to note that one independent

Until recently, theories of psychology were not tested by the logic of science. Some eventually proved valid, some not. For example, John Locke, in his Essay Concerning Human Understanding (1690), derived the theory that human knowledge is acquired during life, not composed of "innate ideas"—a theory which became basic to modern science. But his theory of habits as formed by "association" has been shown inadequate by modern research (see p. 328).

variable usually produces more than one effect, even if all other factors are held constant. For instance, fertilizer A might produce a corn different in quality or color from that produced with fertilizer B. It is quite possible that if quality were taken as the criterion, fertilizer B would be judged the better.

The fundamental requirement of the experimental method is that all the factors which produce a given result be held constant, except the one whose effects you are examining. Otherwise it is impossible to tell what influence this one factor has on the situation. For instance, if fertilizer A had been used on a better-drained field than was fertilizer B, we should be in the dark as to which factor caused the difference in yield—fertilizer or drainage.

The ideal of the experimental method can never be completely attained in the social sciences. Psychology can never expect the precision of physics or chemistry, which do not study living organisms. For one thing, it is difficult to locate and measure all the factors operating in a complex human situation, and then to find two groups exactly the same in these factors. For another, experimental procedure often involves endangering or interfering drastically with the natural development of the subject.

Both these difficulties of the experimental method are indirectly responsible for the surprise of the visitor at the psychological laboratory when he is shown the caged white rats and other animals. People usually think of rats as belonging to biology rather than to psychology. Why does the psychologist study animals? There are at least three answers to this question:

Today the psychologist tests his theories by experiment. This picture is taken from Dr. Jules Masserman's Principles of Dynamic Psychiatry *(©W. B. Saunders, 1946). It shows the experimental situation in which Dr. Masserman tests with animals various clinical theories of human emotional behavior. Such cooperation between clinic and laboratory has progressed in recent years and will be discussed more fully in later chapters on* Emotional Development.

1 The experimental method often demands either interference with the daily routine living of the subject, or regimentation of his experiences to the point where he either refuses to participate or is unable to do so. Then an animal must be used as subject.

2 Many of the experimental techniques employed by the psychologists involve danger to the subject. One of the most fascinating studies in psychology is on how particular functions are localized in definite parts of the brain and nervous system. A fundamental technique of study is to remove some part of the brain or nervous system from a normal subject and then observe any changes in his behavior. If, for instance, a certain area of the brain is removed and blindness follows, the scientists can infer that vision is probably associated with that area. Quite naturally, man objects to having his brain tampered with, even for science, and so—except when injuries, disease, or accidents necessitate such operations—scientists turn to animals for such experiments.

3 A further advantage in studying animals is their simplicity compared with man. There are not so many variables which have to be held constant in order to isolate the effect of the one variable the scientist is interested in. Often a particular kind of behavior can best be studied in simple animals, where it is easier to observe than in such a complex animal as man. There is obviously danger in arguing from animal to man because of differences in their structure, capacity, behavior. Nevertheless, men and animals are enough alike in many fundamental ways to permit cautious interpretations of human behavior from animal behavior.

The Methods of Research in Psychology 31

Despite all its difficulties, the experimental procedure is psychology's best method of deriving principles of human behavior. Since it can use objective observation, it has the great advantage of all objective method: both behavior and the conditions surrounding it are either standardized or accurately described so that the observations can be checked or repeated. Finally, it has the advantage given by its own special logic: it can ascertain the influence of a single factor in a complex situation. Moreover, it may also, as we have seen on page 20, use the method of introspection, with all its attendant advantages.

The logic of all scientific research

The human organism as well as the plant organism is affected by many interacting forces and events. A person's behavior at any given moment depends on his whole past training, his physiological condition, his behavior the moment before, the nature of the present environmental stimuli, and many other variables. The independent contribution that any one variable makes to the total effect can be inferred only when it acts alone. For if all variables but one are kept from operating unequally—are "held constant"—then any change in the person's behavior must have been produced by the only shifted variable. Much of our everyday thinking about human behavior is naïve in failing to employ the logic of science: to recognize and hold constant all other variables than the one whose effects are being examined. Let us consider two much-quoted claims of how just one variable, heredity, has had a predominant influence in family histories. In both cases, you will see that the other important factor in human development, environment, has been completely neglected as a possible influence on the lives of these people.

1 A study made of the families of eminent scientists revealed that their relatives stand a far better than average chance of distinguishing themselves in science (Brimhall[6]). Certain superficial thinkers have concluded from this study that scientific ability is inherited. This would assume, however, that only one variable, scientific heredity, is operating in all these families. Actually, of course, the relatives of great men of science share scientific environment as well as scientific heredity. Their unusual scientific ability shows the importance of environment as well as of heredity.

2 Another striking failure to recognize more than one variable is found in the mistaken inferences drawn from the histories of the Juke and Edwards families (Walter[7]).

So outstandingly successful is the Edwards family that it is frequently used to illustrate the importance of good heredity. Up to the year 1900, a total of 1394 descendants of Jonathan Edwards, the eminent divine, could be traced, and their lives and contributions to society carefully studied. Let us examine some of the statistics. (The descendants not listed were either women or successful citizens whose careers were less spectacular but were entirely respectable.)

College graduates...................... 295
College presidents...................... 13
Physicians 60
Clergymen 100
Officers in army or navy................. 75
Authors and writers.................... 60
Judges 30
United States Senators.................. 3
Criminals 0

Now let us contrast this distinguished family history with the less inspiring history of the Jukes. Max Juke was a shiftless, illiterate, drunken backwoodsman who has given the world some 540 known descendants. This is the record of some of them:

Paupers 310
Convicted criminals 130
(Seven were murderers)
Learned honest trade 20
(Ten of these did so in prison)

Over half the female descendants were prostitutes. It is estimated that up to the year 1877 the known members of this socially ineffective family had cost the state of New York more than one and one-quarter million dollars. The end was not then in sight, nor is it yet.

This remarkable contrast between the Juke and Edwards families has often been used as an argument by those who advocate controlled breeding as a means of improving the human race. To the uninitiated, it would indicate unmistakably the powerful force of heredity in human behavior. However, the student should note that the study does not take into account the different *environments* of the two families. Thus it fails to follow a fundamental rule of science: control, or at least allow for, the influence of all variables but the one whose influence is being examined. What the study does not show is that the Edwards family had good heredity, but it also had good environment—that the Juke family had bad heredity, but it also had bad environment. Thus it is impossible to tell whether heredity or environment was responsible for the Jukes' low degree of social efficiency and the Edwards' high degree of social efficiency. (Cf. Scheinfeld[8])

Many psychological experiments set up two situations or groups of individuals—each containing a different *degree* or condition of the independent variable, which is the factor or characteristic of particular interest to the investigator. One group, the *experimental group*, is unusual with respect to this characteristic. The other group represents the "normal" or usual set of conditions, and is called the *control group* (or control situation). The control group must be identical with the experimental group in all but the condition of the one independent variable.

For instance, suppose an experimenter wants to discover whether removing diseased tonsils will raise the intelligence. In this case, the condition of the tonsils is the independent variable and intelligence is the dependent variable. First he selects for study two groups of children which are alike in intelligence and in all important respects which might affect intelligence, and both of which have diseased tonsils. Then the tonsils are removed from one group—the experimental group. Then he compares the intelligence of the two groups. If the intelligence of the operated group does not go up, he concludes that removing diseased tonsils has no effect on intelligence. If the intelligence of the operated group does go up, then he concludes that removing diseased tonsils does have an effect on intelligence.

The logic of science, as outlined in this section, applies to all scientific research and would help greatly if applied more widely in our thinking about most important topics. It must be emphasized that in psychology, research produces valid results in proportion to its use of this rigorous kind of thinking about the problem under investigation. This is true regardless of the method of study applied. Field studies, biographical studies, clinical studies, and experimental studies can reach useful conclusions only if the logic of science underlies them all.

Statistics in scientific research

Because scientists are almost never able to control perfectly all the factors that affect the specific variables they are studying, they tend to think in terms of general tendencies and general probabilities rather than in terms of individual cases. This is particularly true for the psychologist, whose subject matter is both complex and difficult.

The reason for this is plain. Investigations of human activity frequently impose serious inconveniences on people and frequently are impossible under decently civilized conditions of life. For instance, to answer the problem of the relative effects of heredity and environment mentioned before, it would be necessary ideally to take individuals with identical heredities and raise them from birth in different environments. Since the only people having identical heredities are identical twins, the logic of scientific research would demand that several pairs of identical twins be separated at birth and brought up under very different and known environmental circumstances. Since most parents of twins would naturally object to such a procedure, it is impossible to use scientific logic in dealing with this problem.

In consequence, psychologists fall back on the science of *statistics*, an application of mathematics, which establishes methods for collecting, organizing, and interpreting data quantitatively. By statistical methods, the inadequacies of research conditions can be, in large measure, compensated for. The statistical treatment of data will indicate trends in the data and the mathematical probability that various conclusions have of being sound. Moreover, when it is impossible to hold certain conditions constant in the investigation of some problem, it is sometimes possible to achieve the same goal by using statistical techniques to hold the variables *statistically constant.*

Suppose that a psychologist is asked to determine the effects of chronological maturity on ability to teach school. Ideally, a comparison of teaching ability should be made between two groups exactly alike in all respects except age. That is, their training and intelligence (and that of their students), the difficulty of their courses, and their desire to teach well should all be identical. If all these factors could be rigidly controlled, it would be safe to infer that any differences in teaching ability that the psychologist might find were the results of differences in age.

Actually, of course, it would be extremely difficult to find groups that could be so perfectly *equated* or *matched.* There are statistical procedures, however, by which the research worker could make allowances for any differences other than those of age and thus hold their effects fairly constant in analyzing his data. By using statistical tools, he could study groups that were not perfectly matched and still come to rather reliable conclusions about the effects of age on teaching ability.

In Chapter 15 we shall examine some of the statistical procedures that psychologists use in measuring and comparing different aspects of human thought, feeling, and behavior. Statistics, therefore, is a particularly important part of the scientist's equipment and is especially important for the psychologist, who must deal with human variables that are not easily controlled.

HOW THE EMPHASIS OF PSYCHOLOGY HAS CHANGED

As MAN'S KNOWLEDGE of himself progressed, psychologists began to develop certain fundamental generalizations. These generalizations eventually crystallized into definite ways of regarding man, which in turn suggested particular methods of study. Sometimes, however, the methods suggested the fundamental generalizations. Out of this interplay of methods and principles rose definite psychological "schools" or "isms" which in time came to be fairly distinct from each other in three ways: first, in the problems studied; second, in the method of study; and third, in the theories developed.

The early study of man

As you know, man's first primitive concept of psychology presupposed a "little man" who was thought to be the causal force in human activity. Later in human history, the Greek philosophers, notably Plato and Aristotle, became interested in the *psyche* or "soul" as the central agency in human experience. Their theories were based on casual observations, with no systematic attempt at a scientific method of observation and description. They began a long tradition of philosophical interest in the human mind which was continued through such philosophers as Descartes, Hobbes, Locke, Hume, James Mill, Herbart, and Leibnitz in the seventeenth, eighteenth, and early nineteenth centuries. Although the activities of these philosophers were not experimental, they were related to modern psychology in that they were directed at an understanding of human mind and experience.

Thomas Hobbes (1588-1679)

In the early nineteenth century, there developed a flourishing school of experimental physiology which was destined to have great influence on the still nonexistent science of psychology. Discoveries about the brain and nervous system stimulated inquiries into the physiological basis of human thought, feeling, and behavior—inquiries which employed the experimental method of the natural sciences. Johannes Müller, for instance, demonstrated the neural basis of vision, and E. H. Weber and Gustav Fechner worked in the new field of psychophysics, concerning themselves with the nature of the relationships between stimulus intensity and sensation intensity. Until the late nineteenth century, then, philosophy and physiology were the two alternative approaches to the study of what we now know as psychology.

The structuralists

The first school of psychologists, the structuralists, was formed about 1879 by a development from philosophy on one side and physiology on the other. Wilhelm Wundt and his followers, who later included E. B. Titchener, sought to justify psychology as a separate science by pointing to conscious experience as its unique subject matter. They held that the human mind is composed of elementary mental states, such as sensations, images, and "feelings," which are directly observable through introspection. The name "structuralist" came from their claim that complex experiences are constructed from these mental elements much as the chemical compound is constructed from the basic chemical elements. They applied the experimental method to the study of sensation, seeking to discover the *physiological bases of various types of conscious experience.* Here for the first time psychologists defined a problem rigorously and then set about investigating it through careful empirical observation. Most important, here for the first time psychology was established as a separate branch of science.

Wilhelm Wundt
(1832-1920)

The functionalists

The functionalists broke away from the structuralists about 1900 because they were not satisfied with studying the mental elements revealed through introspection and their physiological bases. They also wished to study *the value of mental experience in adjusting the individual to his environment.* That is, they were interested in behavior as well as in conscious experience. John Dewey, the famous American psychologist, philosopher, and educator, had this conception of psychology. The functionalists began to use the objective method in order to study the learning process, for learning is one important means by which the individual adjusts to his environment. They, like the structuralists who came before them and the behaviorists who came after, thought of the human being as composed of units. For the structuralists these units were mental states; for the functionalists, they were both mental states and stimulus-response acts, which have value in adjustment.

John Dewey
(1859-   )

The behaviorists

The behaviorists became convinced that the introspective method has fatal limitations for revealing the nature of man. They were certain that consciousness could not be accurately studied at all and decided to discard it from their scientific work. Some of them even denied the existence of consciousness merely because one person cannot observe it in another. Instead, they turned to man's *overt behavior,* which they studied through the objective method. The behaviorists made much use of the methods and results of the physiologists; their greatest con-

tribution to psychology is their work on *conditioned reflexes*, which will be discussed in later chapters.

The behaviorists attracted considerable attention in the United States during the period immediately after World War I, under the leadership of Watson, Hunter, Dashiell, and others. Most psychologists, however, felt that conscious and unconscious experience should not be neglected by psychology, no matter how difficult the study might be. For this reason, thoroughgoing behaviorism was rather short-lived in the United States and never dominated popular thought in Europe outside of Russia (where Pavlov did his physiological studies).

John B. Watson
(1878-   )

The psychoanalysts

The school of psychoanalysis came into existence around the turn of the century, under the leadership of Sigmund Freud, the famous

Viennese physician and psychiatrist. The emphasis of psychoanalysis is on *the unconscious mental processes*. Freud held, as do his followers, that the great driving forces of humanity are unconscious systems of ideas or cravings. According to this school, these wishes or urges are never felt directly in consciousness, although from earliest childhood they influence behavior in numerous indirect ways.

Sigmund Freud
(1856-1939)

Psychoanalysis started as a means of discovering the cause and cure of the personality defects which arise from these unconscious drives. As therapy, it employs a set of techniques for making the patient bring the unconscious part of his personality into consciousness and learn to control its workings. It was later expanded from therapy to explanation of cultural phenomena. It is, however, decidedly limited as a school. There are many traditional problems in psychology about which it has little to say, such as the nature of perception, thinking, intelligence. Moreover, it relies entirely on the clinical method, neglecting experimental verification of its theories.

Alfred Adler, one of the better-known members of Freud's school, split off from it and founded his own school. While retaining many Freudian concepts, he emphasized as one of the main human drives, not unconscious sexual urges, but unconscious attempts by the individual to adjust to feelings of inferiority.

The Gestaltists

The word *Gestalt,* meaning "pattern" or "configuration," is brought directly into English from the German. It indicates the emphasis that the Gestaltists place on the influence that the whole pattern of behavior or experience has on a part of the pattern. The Gestalt school has grown up as a well-motivated protest against the assumption that mind or behavior can be viewed as constructed of single elements. It believes that the *whole* of experience or behavior is far more important than its *parts* —that just as a house is more than a certain number of bricks, so is an act more than a group of reflexes, and a conscious experience more than a group of elementary sensations, feelings, and images.

Kurt Lewin
(1890-1947)

This school was founded by Wertheimer and is best known in the United States through the teachings of Köhler, Koffka, and Lewin (all these men were exiles from Germany). Gestalt experimenters use introspection as well as the objective methods of the behaviorists.

The following chart organizes the facts about the chief schools of psychology.

SCHOOLS OF PSYCHOLOGY

Name	Main Topics	Methods	Leaders	Approximate Date of Origin
Structuralist	Sensations	Introspection	Wundt, Titchener	1879
Functionalist	Behavior (especially learning)	Introspection; observation of behavior	Angell, Dewey	1900
Behaviorist	Stimulus-response; animal behavior	Observation of behavior	Pavlov, Watson	1914
Psychoanalyst	Mental disorders; unconscious processes	Clinical investigation	Freud, Adler	1900
Gestalt	Perception, memory	Introspection; observation of behavior	Wertheimer, Koffka, Köhler, Lewin	1912

How the Emphasis of Psychology Has Changed 39

These various schools should not be regarded as hostile camps; such divisions can be most constructive as long as they represent convenient divisions of labor and do not retard the progress of psychology by stimulating "interdenominational" quarreling. Nor do all psychologists fall into one or another of these divisions. This book presents materials from all schools, without attempting to label each fact or principle as coming from a particular one. Although their methods and interpretations may differ, all share the fundamental aim of psychology: the understanding of man or some aspect of his behavior and experience.

CHAPTER 2

The management of learning

The Prerequisites to Learning

Avoiding Cloudy Thinking

Efficient Study Procedures

Examination Techniques

L EARNING IS A COMPLEX PROCESS which requires careful analysis and management. Almost everyone can improve his ability to learn if he comes to understand some of the problems and processes involved in efficient learning—whether or not he has been consciously aware of having study difficulties. Of course many students are quite aware that they do have particular difficulties, and seek guidance.

The chart on page 42 shows the study difficulties that were reported by a group of 171 students at the University of Minnesota who sought special training in studying (Bird and Bird[1]). There were 115 first-term freshmen and 56 second-term freshmen and sophomores in the group. Of course these students were obviously having more than average difficulty, since they had to ask for special help, and thus are not representative of all students. Nevertheless, the chart is interesting because of its indication that time and college experience did not seem to help the students much in mastering some of these problems. Notice that many of the problems were reported by almost the same percentage of second-term freshmen and sophomores as first-term freshmen. Evidently these particular problems do not smooth themselves out automatically as the student becomes used to college life.

This chart indicates, in short, that college students have a strong need for study guidance and for knowledge of the many ways that

41

psychologists have developed in their efforts toward improving learning efficiency.

Study difficulties of college students seeking help

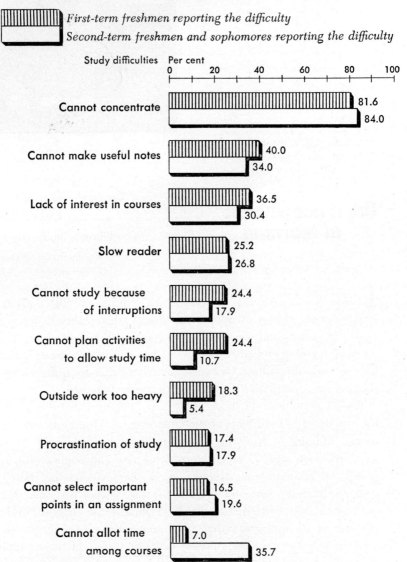

First-term freshmen reporting the difficulty

Second-term freshmen and sophomores reporting the difficulty

Study difficulties	Per cent
Cannot concentrate	81.6 / 84.0
Cannot make useful notes	40.0 / 34.0
Lack of interest in courses	36.5 / 30.4
Slow reader	25.2 / 26.8
Cannot study because of interruptions	24.4 / 17.9
Cannot plan activities to allow study time	24.4 / 10.7
Outside work too heavy	18.3 / 5.4
Procrastination of study	17.4 / 17.9
Cannot select important points in an assignment	16.5 / 19.6
Cannot allot time among courses	7.0 / 35.7

Data from Charles Bird and Dorothy M. Bird. *Learning More by Effective Study.*
© D. Appleton-Century Co., Inc., 1945, page 24.

In recent years, psychologists have performed many experiments to find means of helping students study more efficiently. Students have learned how to study by scientifically tested methods, and then have been examined to see if their learning efficiency has increased.

In one successful how-to-study experiment, there were two groups of students. During the quarter preceding the experiment, Group I had only 25 per cent of its students doing passing work and Group II had only 27 per cent of its students doing passing work. Then for one quarter, Group I was given special instruction in the methods of learning, while Group II was given none. During this quarter, the per cent of students doing passing work in Group I rose from 25 to 70—so that 45 per cent more students were doing passing work. The per cent of passing students in Group II rose from 27 to 34—that is, only 7 per cent more students were doing passing work. Obviously Group I had a faster rate of improvement than Group II because it had received special instruction in study methods. Not only was this special instruction in the methods of learning immediately fruitful, but the beneficial effects had not been lost by the end of the quarter following the one in which the training was given. The special-help group still showed marked improvement over the group of students who had been left to flounder by themselves. (Pressey[2])

Sometimes, unfortunately, the effects of "how to study" instruction are only temporary or are limited to the students who have higher ability at the outset (Edmiston[3]). When this occurs, it usually means that the individuals concerned have not cared to be good students, for interest and enjoyment are not only the *results* of more efficient learning—they are also the *prerequisites*. In order to manage your learning well, you must make the material meaningful according to your interests and must be interested enough in what you are learning to train yourself in good study procedures.

THE PREREQUISITES TO LEARNING

Studying is a complex process which requires the best possible working conditions. You cannot learn at your top effectiveness unless you know how to concentrate and unless you are a skilled reader.

Concentration

Paying attention, like any other behavior, can be changed through learning. You can help yourself to maintain voluntary attention by keeping several important factors under control:

1 An efficient daily routine.
2 The proper study environment.
3 Motivation in learning.
4 Emotional attitudes toward learning.

An efficient daily routine. Any activity in progress sets up in us a tendency toward further activity of the same kind. You can take

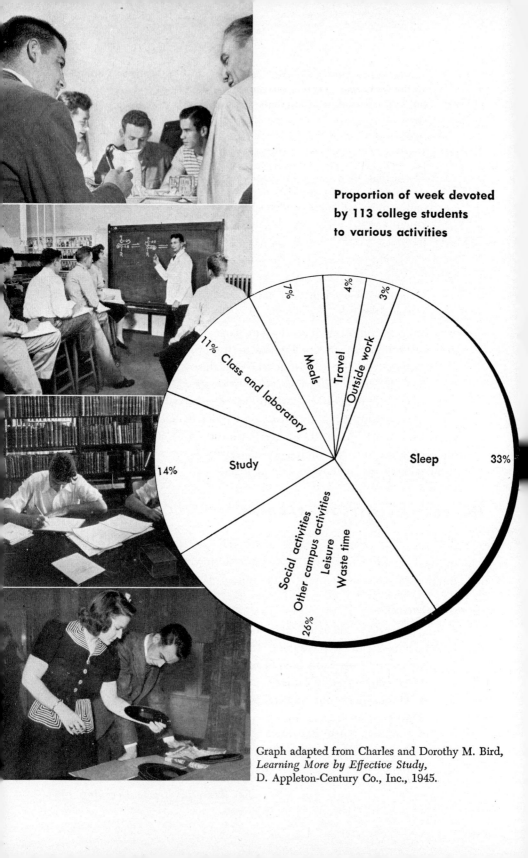

**Proportion of week devoted
by 113 college students
to various activities**

7%

4%

3%

11% Class and laboratory

Meals

Travel

Outside work

Study

14%

Sleep

33%

Social activities

Other campus activities

Leisure

Waste time

26%

Graph adapted from Charles and Dorothy M. Bird,
Learning More by Effective Study,
D. Appleton-Century Co., Inc., 1945.

advantage of this motivation in helping yourself concentrate on your studies. You should work while you work and play while you play. An excellent way of helping yourself do this is to prepare a guiding program for your day which includes all activities—whether lecture, laboratory, student activities, recreation, meals, sleep, or just plain loafing. Do not make up a schedule so unreasonably severe that you could never follow it.

One good way of making up a realistic schedule that fits your habits and study needs is to discover and analyze how you actually spend your time now. If you keep an accurate record for one week, hour by hour, of how you spend your time, you will probably be surprised to discover that you actually spend less time studying and more time in aimless time-passing than you ever realized. Students who enter college directly from high school often find it especially difficult to arrange their time efficiently. There are no demands made on them except a few hours of classes a day, no compulsory "study periods," no parents to remind them of their "homework." Suddenly being freed of outside pressures to study is frequently hard to become adjusted to.

While drawing up an accurate schedule of how your time goes may be bothersome—and will probably contain some unpleasant surprises— it is worth while in the end. It can not only be a real revelation as to just how you are spending your time at college, but it can show you just how much time you have—apart from sleep, meals, transportation, classes—to spend on studying and recreation. Knowing this will help you make a deliberate choice as to how much time you will spend on your studies and how much on recreation, and you will no longer be victimized by a faulty sense of time and an inability to manage what time is available.

In drawing up your schedule for the future, you should take into account as many facts from this chapter as you can—remember, for instance, to adjust your study periods to the kind of material you are learning. You may be helped, too, by the chart on page 44 showing how students distribute their time. Then after you have your schedule drawn up, keep to it, but do not be discouraged by occasional deviations.

Following such a schedule gets you in the habit of studying at definite times, and so will enable you to get your work done regularly. Thus you are able to concentrate harder while you are studying, for you know that your free time is sure to come. Moreover, you are untroubled by distracting feelings of worry over all the work you have not yet done. The student who is behind in his work is often kept from making the most of the time he has left by the discouraging feeling that he cannot possibly get through. You will also be able to enjoy your loafing and recreation because you will not be troubled by guilt feelings over assignments left undone.

The proper study environment is one of the prerequisites to effective concentration on studying. Work done in a noisy environment takes much more energy than work done in a quiet environment. When you study, turn off the radio and keep yourself out of earshot of social conversations. Your roommate or your family should understand if you insist in a friendly but firm way that you do not want to be disturbed while you are studying. However, you have no right to expect the cooperation of others if you interrupt them while they are trying to concentrate or if you insist on working in a social environment like a student lounge.

One of the best ways of keeping yourself from distracting influences is, if possible, to keep your social environment separate from your working environment. Many students concentrate best in the college library, although they still find that it takes some determination to refrain from talking to their friends and looking out the window. Students who study in their rooms often find it best to have a certain chair or desk where they do most of their work. But wherever you choose to study, the essentials to controlling distraction are quiet and the freedom from social temptations.

Motivation in learning. A very important factor determining the student's ability to concentrate on his work is his interest in learning the material before him. There are many complex factors that determine how much interest and drive the student brings to the learning situation. Among these factors are his early intellectual experiences in the school and home, the amount of encouragement he received in reading books and following intellectual interests, his whole emotional relationships with teachers and fellow students, and the life-goals that are approved in his family and community. These are the factors that determine whether the student comes to college anxious to explore many fields of learning and willing to put his studies ahead of social and athletic activities, whether he is interested in learning for its own sake or for the degree or job it may bring him, whether he comes to college because he wants to learn or because it is the "thing to do" in his home group. But even for students whose home and school life before college has not been conducive to the development of intellectual pursuits, college can be a time of expanding interests and intellectual stimulation.

The student who has an immediate interest in the material before him usually finds it easy to concentrate. Many students, however, are able to concentrate on their college work not because of any deep intellectual interest in their courses but because they feel that success in college will bring them success in later life. This consideration is a sadly limited one, but it is very realistic, for the record you are making in your studies right now will be either an asset or a liability for many years to come. It will be the basis for the granting or withholding of honors; it will be consulted by prospective employers in deciding whether you will be given an opportunity. Several studies have shown that the person who succeeds scholastically also succeeds in later life (Gifford,[4] Nicholson,[5] and Tunis[6]). While there is a very serious limitation on these studies in that their only criterion of success is money earnings, they do explode the popular student superstition that the so-called "grind" does not do well in the business world.

Do not jump to the unwarranted conclusion that the good students succeeded in later life simply *because* they were good students. There is no implication that high scholarship causes high earnings later. It may well be that both high scholarship and high earnings result from high basic intelligence, a desire to succeed, and a willingness to put work ahead of pleasure. But employers who have good jobs to offer are coming more and more to consider the school records of applicants, and being a good student will certainly increase your chances of finding an opportunity to demonstrate your ability. Moreover, it has been shown (Young[7]) that there is no relationship between scholarship and the number of friends and acquaintances possessed by each student, nor between scholarship and social success.

All the evidence makes it quite clear that studying at college, contrary to popular belief, will not blight the student's life either during or after college. The best-adjusted student will combine other activities with his studying, but he will put studying first and will train himself to concentrate on attaining his working objectives.

Be sure, of course, that your working objectives are attainable. Your long-run goals do not always provide adequate motivation for the task before you. So when you study, set yourself some short-run goals which will bring you immediate satisfaction. For instance, resolve to translate one page of French before getting up to stretch or talk to a friend. Attaining this subgoal strengthens your resolve to attain the next. This process will eventually bring you to your main goal: all the pages are translated and the assignment is prepared. It will also help you concentrate on material which is not compellingly interesting.

An active attitude in learning helps to build up motivation in the study situation. You will find this easier if you relate what you are studying to your own special problems and beliefs and if you try to grasp the general principles rather than learn by rote. Also, a physically active attitude—a firm posture—helps many students concentrate, although experiments show that any tendency to excessive physical relaxation should be avoided during active study.

> In one of these experiments, subjects were asked to exert a mild muscular tension while learning (Bills[8]). The tension was produced by gripping an instrument known as the hand dynamometer, a device designed to test the strength of grip. Of course the subjects did not attempt to maintain their maximum grip. The results showed that those subjects who maintained a little muscular tension during learning were the most efficient in learning and in recalling.
>
> Another experimenter found that self-induced muscular tensions were more helpful to the poorer learners than to the good ones (Stauffacher[9]).

Emotional attitudes in learning. Sometimes it happens that a student really wants to succeed in his studies, has the intelligence necessary for success, tries to follow all the correct methods of learning, but "just can't concentrate." The trouble may lie in excessive daydreaming which makes his mind wander from his work. Or it may be in feelings of anxiety or depression which keep him from giving his whole attention. In such cases, the student is probably suffering from some emotional frustration which keeps him from working at full capacity. He should then realize that he is having adjustment difficulties, and if he cannot work them out for himself, he should seek the expert help of a clinical psychologist, who will help him locate the source of his inability to concentrate. Most students, however, can overcome inability to concentrate by using some of the psychological facts we have just encountered—plus a little old-fashioned determination.

Skill in reading

Reading ability is something which can be acquired through hard work and the elimination of inefficient habits (Lauer[10]). People vary greatly in their inborn ability for reading, but they probably differ even more in the extent to which they have developed their inborn ability.

If you were a seasoned manuscript editor, capable of reading twenty-five thousand words per hour (the equivalent of some sixty pages of an ordinary book), this section would be of little value to you. Most students, however, will be able to improve their reading skill.

Good eyesight is the first essential to effective reading. If you suffer from a headache, smarting or burning eyes, or a feeling of tension around the eyes following a period of reading, you should consult an eye specialist for a thorough test of your vision.

For **proper illumination,** read in diffused or indirect light rather than in the harsh glare of an unshaded globe. Your eyes will not become tired so fast, and you will be able to sustain clear vision for a longer period (Ferree and Rand[11]). In choosing a study lamp, remember that the pupil of the eye adjusts to the *average* light, so that a dark field with a few bright lights causes more eyestrain than a bright field that is uniform. When there is a circle of light on your book with the rest of the room in darkness, you will develop eyestrain.

The brightness of the light is not so important as its uniformity (Tinker[12]). In fact, the human eye is remarkably able to adjust to widely differing levels of intensity, although most people prefer light of medium brightness (Ferree and Rand[13]). Once you have a uniform lighting with no glare spots, your own observations of your comfort are a safe guide in telling you how bright the light should be.

The color of light, as well as its uniformity, is an important factor in rapid, effective, comfortable reading. Natural daylight of uniform intensity is easiest on your eyes. After this come yellow, orange, and red, while blue and green are decidedly hard on your eyes (Ferree and Rand[14]). A word of warning: the color of light is not indicated by the color of the bulb; you must ask your dealer the color.

The role of eye movements in good reading. Some books that discuss the question of how to study efficiently still contain the suggestion that you can improve your reading efficiency by trying to improve your eye movements in reading. This suggestion is made because the original research in this field showed a considerable difference between the kinds of eye movements made by good and by poor readers. The difference in their eye movements was then assumed to be the cause of the difference in their success as readers.

In reading a line of print, you see the words by fixating your gaze on one spot at a time, by moving your gaze quickly to another spot about an inch or so along the line, then to another spot, and so on. You see only while your eyes are fixated. Regardless of whether you are a good or a poor reader, most of your reading time is spent in these fixation pauses, and only a minor fraction in shifting from one fixation point to another. However, the eye movements assume different patterns depending on whether you are a good or poor reader.

When the good reader is perusing familiar material, his eye movements proceed in a regular, methodical way across each line, then make a return sweep to a point near the beginning of the next line, and so on. But the poor reader, even when he is reading familiar material, makes more pauses per line, often makes more regressive movements to parts of the line he has already covered, and is less accurate in his return sweep to the beginning of the next line. These facts were early demonstrated by careful experimental studies made with ingenious photographic apparatus. They led at first to the conclusion that the poor reader's difficulties must lie in his inefficient eye movements. Accordingly, efforts were made to improve reading ability by teaching better eye movements. Sometimes, indeed, this is what is needed, and improvements can then be made in this way. But as more has been learned by research in this field, less and less emphasis is being placed on the role of eye movements in good reading. Two discoveries have contributed to this change of emphasis:

1 It has been found that when expert readers are reading material that is difficult for them, they make more fixations and reversal movements than in reading familiar material.

2 It has been found that the people who learn most from *reading* material once are also the ones who learn most from *hearing* it read to them once; the people who learn an average amount from one reading are those who learn an average amount from hearing it read, and so on.

In other words, the crucial factors that govern speed and understanding in reading are such things as vocabulary mastery, familiarity with the ideas presented, and ability to grasp complex concepts.

Silent reading. You may have noticed that children, old people, and foreigners just learning English often mutter or whisper when they are reading. So do many poor readers. Lip movement lowers the rate of reading and distracts you from the full significance of what you are reading. If you observe this habit in yourself, practice to overcome it. It is true that even a good reader makes some small movements of the vocal apparatus, but they are so reduced that they are not perceptible to the naked eye and do not interfere with good reading.

AVOIDING CLOUDY THINKING

AN IMPORTANT FACTOR IN SUCCESSFUL COLLEGE WORK is, obviously, the ability to think logically. This ability is dependent not only on intelligence but also on training, especially if it is training which emphasizes the *application* of principles of logic to the particular problems and materials with which the student is confronted. In this section, we shall consider some of the common kinds of cloudy or crooked thinking which must be avoided in the interest of better management of learning—both in college work and in the many forms of learning that go on outside formal education.

Common causes of cloudy thinking

The all-or-nothing dichotomy in characterization. One feature of cloudy thinking is that it is all-or-nothing. For example, we cannot make the statement that "criminals are cowards," because certain acts of criminals require extraordinary bravery; furthermore, the worst criminal is law-abiding most of the time (Metfessel[15]). Other examples will be discussed all through this book. They will include the popular tendency to think in terms of stereotypes, or rigid preconceptions which are applied to all members of certain national, political, occupational, or racial groups, whether or not they actually hold for most members of these groups or for only a few who are then said to be "typical." In most areas of human life, certain characteristics can be found in degrees rather than in all-or-nothing amounts.

Failure to get all the facts. Before you accept and quote opinions you read in books, magazines and newspapers, or hear over the air, you should make an effort to determine their authoritativeness.

Scientific writing requires constant checking against the logic of science discussed in the preceding chapters, and supporting facts must be carefully examined. In more popular writing, the logic must be sound but the author need not give the full details of evidence as he would in a scientific work. In this case it is especially necessary to check on the standing of the author. Each recognized profession has some official society which makes an attempt to guarantee the ability and honesty of its members, and a good writer will usually be affiliated with one of these societies. If the author claims respect on the basis of membership in some scientific society, make sure that it is a bona-fide organization by looking it up in *Scientific Societies of the United States* (Bates[16]). Make sure too that he is writing in the field of his earned reputation; for example, a physician—no matter how well known he is in his own field—may or may not have sound ideas on religion, politics, or economics. When an author is writing outside his own field, test him as you would any other amateur; make him give the evidence before you accept his statement.

Learn how to read the newspapers. We have all heard someone say, "It's true all right; I saw it in the newspaper." Many of us have not yet outgrown such blind acceptance of newspaper authenticity. The accuracy of the newspaper account suffers from many possible sources of error. In the first place, there is the factor of speed. Newspaper reporters work under great pressure at all times. They might prefer to stop to check details for accuracy, but they have to "make a deadline."

Another important influence in the editing of news is unconscious bias. The editor and publisher usually associate with large property owners and others of high income. Their values tend to be the same as those of their advertisers. Such persons may be beyond bribery and intimidation, but they might still slant the news in the direction of the interests of the "owner group" and against, for example, organized labor. But it is also true that publications controlled by labor unions slant the news in their own direction. In reading a newspaper it is well to note how the same story is handled by papers of different bias. The truth about a strike in a large steel mill will probably lie somewhere between the account given by a labor paper and one owned by politically conservative publishers.

Pleasantness and the desire to believe. Numerous studies by psychologists have shown that people tend to forget unpleasant facts faster than they forget pleasant ones (see p. 371). Charles Darwin was so well aware of this fact that he made a particular effort to find and record evidence which was negative to his theory of evolution, because he was afraid that otherwise he would forget these distasteful facts. Do not trust your memory, especially with regard to facts or suggested solutions which are unpleasant. They are more elusive than the things that you prefer to believe. Experiment has clearly shown that belief is determined by desire to believe, regardless of the evidence for or against the truth of a series of propositions.

> A set of thirty issues in various fields of human interest was drawn up and presented to a large number of subjects. The subjects were then asked to indicate the degree of their belief or disbelief in them. After the ratings of the strength of belief or disbelief had been completed, the subjects rated the degree to which they desired the propositions to be true or not true. The results showed that actual belief and desire to believe run hand-in-hand, regardless of the nature of the evidence (Lund[17]).

Just before America entered World War II, another experiment was conducted on the connection between belief and desire to believe. The results closely confirm the experiment showing that people tend to believe what they want to believe regardless of the evidence.

> In this experiment, a large number of items were selected from newspapers and magazines such as *Time* and *Life*, items which these had characterized as rumor or propaganda. The subjects were asked to

indicate whether they considered them true, false, probable, or improbable. Five judges decided upon which response to a question most favored the Allied position. If the rumor as it stood favored the Allies, it was considered that the pro-Ally response would be "true"; if it favored the Germans it was considered that the pro-Ally response would be "false." Some sample propaganda items and their pro-Ally scoring appear below:

It is now clear that at least 10 of the 26 German midgets who worked in the Lilliputian Village at the New York World's Fair last summer were capitalizing on their small size to conceal their real activity, spying on the United States for the German government. (True.)

Germany has recently changed to the construction of submarines on the production-belt plan, at a rate of one per day, thus putting her well ahead of the British destruction-rate, and raising to a new high the danger to Britain's lines. (False.)

To provide an indication of attitude toward the belligerents, an attitude-test was included in the questionnaire. This was made up of questions drawn largely from *Fortune* surveys (for November and December 1939, and January 1940). Here is a sample of the questions:

"What do you think the United States should do?
Fight with the Allies now.
Fight with the Allies if they are losing.
Send supplies to the Allies but not to the Germans.
Sell to both sides cash and carry.
Give no aid to either.
Help Germany."

The questionnaires were scored according to the "pro-Ally" interpretation of each statement. The score for each individual was thus the number of pro-Ally interpretations of rumors which he accepted as True or Probable. For the group of 226 subjects, the *average* number of pro-Ally interpretations for the 25 rumors was found to be 13.13. However, the group displaying strong pro-German attitude accepted a mean of only 4.2 out of 25 pro-Ally suggestions, while the strongly pro-Ally group believed 18.2 rumors favorable to the Allies. These results indicated a close relation between attitude and acceptance of propaganda (Coffin[18]).

Failure to consider all possible hypotheses. In the study of the Jukes and Edwards families, the experimenter failed to consider the hypothesis that environment had any bearing on the social achievement of the two families, although the data to prove such a hypothesis were readily available. A similar example of cloudy thinking is the popular hypothesis that a person's intelligence can be judged simply by looking at his eyes. Actually, you might find that people base their judgments of another person's intelligence on the total impression they receive from the person (from dress, carriage, and manner of speaking). Thus another and more probable hypothesis would be that intelligence is judged through the effect of the total person.

Such attempts to explain facts under a single hypothesis are very characteristic of cloudy thinking. It is not generally recognized that most of the facts one collects through research, reading, or conversation may be explained and unified in terms of several hypotheses. The scientist or critic examines all the facts which may have a relationship to those he is interested in, and decides which of all these relationships are most likely to be worth further study. He constructs a hypothesis about these relationships, and then proceeds to test it against his selected facts. If he fails to recognize all possible hypotheses, he reduces his chances of discovering the true relationships.

Failure to consider all data. In the examples mentioned above, the error in thinking was the failure to consider more than one hypothesis as a possible explanation for existing data. Part of the reason for this failure was that certain aspects of the situation were not taken into account. The false conclusion from the Jukes and Edwards family histories arose because only part of the available information about these families was taken into account: their records of achievement and the fact that the individuals in each family had common heredity. The neglected fact was that these individuals had common environments. Thus the failure to recognize all the data limited the number of hypotheses considered. It is also true, however, that the concentration on one hypothesis led to the failure to recognize all the facts.

The failure to recognize all the facts about a situation is very common in all our thinking. When food prices first started to mount during the worst of the postwar inflation, newspapers and radios carried reports of the number of persons in the country suffering from vitamin deficiencies, and the explanation given was that, because of the high prices, American families were no longer able to buy enough food of the right sort. Two facts were not taken into consideration: first, that even during normal times there are many families who are too poor to buy necessary foods; and second, that even people with sufficient incomes often lack vital information about nutritional requirements. It is obvious that not all the vitamin deficiency could be explained by high food prices.

Changes of methods of measurement will bring changes in results. A change of method of observation may result in error, as in the following:

> Crime statistics show that the number of arrests is greatest near the beginning of the year. This could mean that more crimes are committed

during this period; on the other hand, it could mean that law enforcement is more strict at that time. Let us take another example. You have often heard that the rate of insanity is increasing during modern times. Is the true rate of insanity increasing, or is it merely that the modern physician is better able to detect insanity when it is present?

We must be certain that the method of revealing the material in question has not changed before we can conclude that the fact itself has changed.

Mistaking correlation for causation. The fact that two things go together (are *correlated*) does not prove that one causes the other. There is, for example, a positive correlation between the number of times people go to see a physician and their intelligence scores. This does not mean that bright persons are more sickly than the average person, but that seeing the doctor is a health precaution taken more often by the intelligent than by the less intelligent person. When two sets of factors seem to influence each other, make sure that they are not both being influenced by a third set of factors.

The use of technical terminology. Ideas are often as easily carried by simple, short, and clear words as by more complicated terms, and often technical terminology covers up a basic lack of clarity of thought. The following is "a parody, but not a very gross one" of the modern habit of substituting long technical words for meaningful English. Here is a beautifully simple passage from Ecclesiastes:

> "I returned, and saw under the sun, that the race is not to the swift, nor the battle to the strong, neither yet bread to the wise, nor yet riches to men of understanding, nor yet favor to men of skill; but time and chance happeneth to them all."

And here it is translated into modern scientific jargon:

> "Objective consideration of contemporary phenomena compels the conclusion that success or failure in competitive activities exhibits no tendency to be commensurate with innate capacity, but that a considerable element of the unpredictable must invariably be taken into account." (Orwell[19])

There is nothing really wrong with words such as these, provided they do not lull you into the belief that you understand them when you really do not—and provided that you make sure that they do mean something.

Assuming things with the same name to be the same thing. If you are not careful to distinguish between words and ideas, you will sometimes let the word overrule the idea.

For example, the word *fatigue* is properly defined as a chemical condition in the tissues which is caused by working and which in turn lowers the ability to work. In the case of mental work, too, such as adding or memorizing, there is a lowering of efficiency after a period of work, but it appears long before any sufficient chemical change is noted. This also is called *fatigue*—"mental fatigue." The fatigue in these two cases is entirely different. In fact, the latter should not be called fatigue: it is really boredom, for nervous tissue does not fatigue. The fact that people speak of "brain fag" is a good example of the false concepts engendered by calling two different things by the same name. This is one of the most frequent types of error in loose thinking.

Checking your thinking and opinions

Some thinkers go wrong because they accept the first solution that is suggested without going to the trouble of testing it against the known facts. One good way to protect yourself is to give your solution to some other person for criticism. If you cannot convince an intelligent, interested, and open-minded person that your solution is right, there is probably something wrong with it that deserves further thought. Another useful way to check yourself is through logic.

Many of the principles studied in formal logic are so technical that students often think they are employed only by the highly trained thinker. Actually, all through everyday life we make extensive use of syllogistic reasoning. Usually, of course, we do not state our syllogisms in full form; we state merely one of the premises from which we draw the conclusion, and often put the conclusion first. For example, you may hear a person say, "I don't believe the government ought to pay for the education of medical students, because that would be socialistic." This argument represents an abbreviated syllogism, with one of the premises taken for granted. Stated fully it would run:

> All socialistic measures are bad.
> Government subsidizing of medical students would be socialistic.
> Therefore government subsidizing of medical students would be bad.

This example indicates how people can come to faulty conclusions because they fail to state their premises fully and to define their terms carefully. For example, we might ask this person what he means by a "socialistic measure," and he says that he means some enterprise which the government runs but which could be handled by private management. We then ask him whether he believes that the government should return all schools, fire departments, and parcel-post carrying to private hands. He will probably come to see then that he does not really accept the first premise, which he left unstated—that is, he does not really believe that all socialistic measures (as he has defined them and as the term was used in his argument) are bad. But if he believes that some governmental enterprises are bad and some good, then obviously he is judging them on some other basis than mere government ownership, and he must discover what that basis is.

The purpose of formal logic is to study such syllogistic reasoning to find the rules whereby one can determine whether a conclusion follows legitimately from the stated premises. However, much cloudy thinking occurs because people accept premises which are faulty or which they have not thought through (such as the first premise above), rather than because they argue falsely from them. Psychologists consequently have been concerned with several problems beyond the area of formal logic, such as pleasantness and the desire to believe.

Another question of interest to psychologists is whether there are any devices or intellectual tools by which people may more safely and accurately draw the appropriate conclusions from the given premises. One such device is to translate each statement in terms of letter symbols.

> In some cases a symbolic presentation of an argument gives appreciable help in checking the soundness of a conclusion. One experiment on the use of the syllogism (Wilkins[20]) found that more than half the subjects marked this syllogism as valid:
>
> > *All Mongolians have slant eyes.*
> > *The Chinese have slant eyes.*
> > *Therefore, the Chinese are Mongolians.*
>
> Notice that the conclusion is correct but that it does not follow from the two premises. When the syllogism was stated in terms of letter symbols which themselves carried no meaning of a specific sort, the subjects made only half as many errors. However, the experimenter's final conclusion was that this device of translation into abstract symbols is not generally much help in checking the logic of a syllogism. As she said, "Most items increase in difficulty as the material is changed from the familiar to the symbolic . . . , but a few items representing very common fallacies are much less difficult in symbolic material than in familiar."

An even better method of checking opinions is by means of *graphic* (diagrammatic) representation.

> Let us draw a diagram of the relationships in the Mongolian and slant-eye problem, using the letter symbols set up in the discussion of that example.
>
> The area within the large circle represents B, or *slant-eyed people;* the area in one of the smaller circles lying within the larger one represents A, or *Mongolians.* The relationship

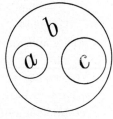

of the two circles shows that Mongolians are slant-eyed people. Circle C, representing *Chinese,* must also fall within the area B, which contains all slant-eyed people. Notice that the directions are complied with when this is done. A (Mongolians) might or might not coincide with C (Chinese) and still satisfy the conditions stated in the syllogism.

EFFICIENT STUDY PROCEDURES

CLEAR THINKING, concentration, and skill in reading are essentials to effective learning. But even students who possess these basic prerequisites often do not study at their top efficiency because they lack the knowledge of certain study procedures which have been worked out through careful experiments. How well you learn what you read depends upon your efficiency in *Making Material Meaningful,* in recognizing *The Facts about Learning "Transfer,"* in *Practicing Active Self-Recitation,* and in *Spacing Your Learning Efforts.*

Making material meaningful

Meaningful material is easier to learn than the same number of nonsense units. Many studies in psychological laboratories have served to establish the proof of this proposition.

> In one study, groups of students were asked to read specially prepared articles averaging 1100 words in length. They read the material carefully twice, which is just about the way the average student prepares his daily assignments. Some of the subjects were tested immediately after reading the material, some after twenty-four hours had passed by, and the rest at the end of a two-day period. The subjects were tested both for rote memory of specific facts and for comprehension of the essential thoughts. In the test of rote memory, the students had to label as "true" or "false" statements which were given in the exact words of the text. Comprehension was tested by having the students label the truth or falsity of statements which were related to the ideas in the passage but were not in the original words. The results for the two types of tests showed that the students lost practically nothing in idea-comprehension over the two-day period, whereas they declined significantly in their memory of specific facts. (English, Wellborn, and Killian[21])

The obvious implication for the student is that he will learn more easily and remember for a longer time material that really makes sense to him. If you learn what you are reading as so many meaningless statements, you may eventually be able to recite a good share of it in parrot fashion, but it will never become a real part of your mental equipment and will soon be lost.

There are many ways to make material meaningful. Here are some of them:

1 Survey the assignment as a whole.
2 Relate new facts to old problems.
3 Cross the boundaries between courses.
4 Draw up a summary in outline form in your own words.
5 Avoid using memory "crutches."
6 Look for the general principles.
7 Learn by doing.

Survey the assignment as a whole. In taking up all or part of a book as assigned, it is wise to look over the table of contents of each chapter before you start reading it. Then read over the assigned materials as rapidly as you can before starting intensive study. Do not try to remember any of the details, and do not linger over any part you cannot understand. The purpose of this first reading is to give you a general idea of the master plan of the material—what topics are discussed and how they are related to each other logically. Students sometimes feel that this first skimming is "superficial" or "a waste of time." They feel they must work through the material right from the beginning, understanding and memorizing as they go. Actually, this first quick survey will save you time in the end, for it will put the details into perspective. You will get an idea of what is important and what is unimportant, and the details will be easier to remember because they will take on meaning in relation to the whole. After the initial quick skimming should come a slow, thoughtful, and selective reading. And last of all, a final quick reading of the by now well understood material will insure reasonable retention of the materials studied.

Relate new facts to old problems. In your notebook, list problems of pressing interest to you. When you encounter a new material, ask yourself how this should affect your attitude or action on some problem or belief. How, for example, should your study of various peoples in history affect your attitudes toward "foreigners"? When you learn in your social science courses about the desperately poor living conditions of millions of Americans, do you begin to wonder if our free-enterprise economy is working as well as it might or if something can or should be done to make it work better?

Also, strive to relate facts to personal problems. How does some fact in psychology help you choose your lifework? How does another fact better enable you to control your temper?

Cross the boundaries between courses. One of the weaknesses of American education is the practice of breaking up the whole field of knowledge into more or less watertight compartments. This effort is both absurd and unworkable, because truth is unitary. Any attempt to distinguish sharply between closely related fields of knowledge is bound to be arbitrary and confusing. For instance, you, as a student of psychology, are concerned with a subject which has important relationships with every other branch of learning. Keep asking yourself how the facts before you relate to the materials of another course. For example, the chapter on industrial psychology later in this book will give you some of the psychology behind labor problems. As you read this material, try to relate it to some of the economic issues in labor problems that you may have discussed in your social science courses.

Draw up a summary in outline form in your own words. Any book contains much illustrative matter that is not absolutely essential. Interesting examples are introduced to keep the style from becoming too heavy and to drive home some fundamental point. As you read, prepare a summary of the essential material only, neglecting the anecdotes and illustrations, which tend of themselves to stick in your mind. In writing your summary, emphasize the principles illustrated. But above all else, make the summary in your own words. No amount of copying sentences lifted bodily from a text will help you learn so much as preparing your own summary will. In writing a summary, you will discover which parts you understood thoroughly and which topics require more study. Moreover, if it is carefully prepared, the summary can be used for review, so that at examination time you will not have to reread the whole discussion, including the incidental material. You will have the most important principles drawn up in easy form for review.

One reason for taking notes in your own words is that if you are going to remember and retain the material, it will *have* to be in your own words. When you try to remember a concept in the vocabulary and style of another person, this calls for a huge feat of memory. Unless you are a wonderful memorizer, you will fail. Note-taking gives you a permanent record for review and also helps make lectures or reading assignments meaningful—provided the notes are intelligently taken. The following principles of good note-taking may seem obvious, but they are neglected by many students whose study procedures are otherwise quite efficient.

First of all, good notes are readable. Don't hurry your writing so much that your notes become illegible. Notes are meant to be read when they are "cold." You can develop a set of simple abbreviations to eliminate much of the mechanical labor in note-taking. Set down a series of suggestive phrases which will be meaningful later. Make key statements in your own words. Remember, though, that your notes will be useless if they are not understandable later—to you, if not to anyone else.

Second, good notes are accurate. Notes properly taken can be referred to in the absence of the original publication. After you have taken notes, be sure to check them against the original to make certain they are accurate. If they are not, using them merely strengthens your errors. If you encounter a statement in your reading which you do not understand, take it down in your notes, but mark it with a question mark in parentheses and investigate it later.

Third, good notes are complete—and complete on the spot. Efficient study involves learning to take notes in final form during the lecture. These should be written in ink for permanence. Time spent in review can be used more profitably in making new organizations of material, rather than rewriting notes taken in class.

Fourth, good notes contain full bibliographic references. Remember that the ideas you gather in reading or from attending a lecture belong to some other person. You must be sure to label their source correctly. There are many forms of bibliographic reference, but the complete one must contain the author's name and initials, the title of the book or article, the publication date and edition, the publisher's name.

It is well to remember that there is no one correct outline for a given set of facts. The outline is for your use now and in the future. Its form will be determined by your needs and your interests.

Avoid using memory crutches. Students often invent elaborate means for remembering facts for examinations. The language student may remember the position of words on the vocabulary list; the anatomy student may remember that two important bones both begin with *o*.

While memory crutches can sometimes help temporarily in retaining arbitrary facts until usage has lodged them firmly in mind, one of their basic defects is that they usually employ accidental connections which are as hard to remember as the original fact itself—or harder. Moreover, they obviously are not based upon any meaningful generalizations, which as you know are more easily remembered than arbitrary facts. They are to be relied upon only when no real meaning can be derived from a series of arbitrary facts or dates.   .

Discover the general principles early. Learning is much easier if you succeed in discovering the general principles—in establishing relationships between facts.

It has been shown (Waters[22]) that learning the correct method without understanding the principle involved is of little value in learning how to solve either a fairly simple problem or a more complicated one of a similar sort. Understanding errors which are specific to the problem at hand will aid you in the solution of that problem but will not carry over to other similar ones. Hearing a short statement of the principle in advance will help decidedly in learning, but the statement must be general enough to fit all related cases if it is to be of value in guiding your efforts toward unaided solution of similar problems.

Before you start off in a learning project, listen carefully to any general statement your instructor makes about the material at hand. If he does not give you any very clear idea of the principles involved, do not just plunge ahead in confusion—ask him to tell you the basic ideas you should keep in mind as you study the material or work out the problem.

Learn by doing. If you drive an automobile, you will have noticed that when you are at the wheel in traveling a new road, you learn that road much better than you would if someone else were driving. In the same way, you cannot learn French grammar by hearing someone explain it—you must practice writing French sentences. And no speech teacher can do more than tell you the principles of effective delivery—then you must practice yourself. In other words, guidance should consist in showing you the right path, not in carrying you along it.

If you are having study difficulties, do not wait to have your fears confirmed by your examination grades. Consult your instructor, or your college psychologist or college study clinic if available. They can help you analyze and overcome your study difficulties.

The facts about learning "transfer"

There was a period in American educational practice when authorities defended the doctrine of formal discipline, urging that the student study certain subjects because of their supposed "strengthening" effect on the mind. Latin, Greek, and mathematics were favorite subjects. These subjects were supposed to be "logical"; therefore, their study should make one's mind logical, and of course, a logical mind can master almost anything. This belief in such a *transfer* of training went unchallenged for a long time, but eventually it was questioned. In the first crude studies of the problem, the defenders of formal discipline seemed to prove their case, but later investigations showed that their experiments were unscientific in failing to account for all the variables in learning.

One typical early study appeared to establish the fact that the study of Latin actually does make it easier to acquire a command of English writing (Harris[23]). A group of students was divided into several sections, according to how many years of Latin they had taken, and then the average grade of each section was computed:

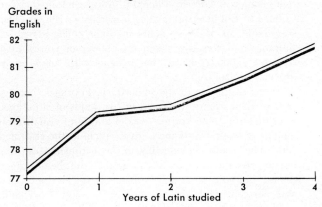

Relationship between years of Latin studied and grades in English

What is wrong with this picture?

Data from L. H. Harris. "A Study in the Relation of Latin to English Composition." *School and Society*, 1915, Volume 2, page 252.

It is clear from the graph that the students who had studied Latin were slightly better in English composition than those who had not, and that the more years of Latin they had taken, the better were their grades in English. But this study does *not* demonstrate that taking more Latin *causes* a student to do well in English. One of the fundamental rules of experimental method has been violated. No attempt was made to hold standard the initial ability of the students. There is every reason to believe that those students who elect Latin are, in general, more intelligent and are better learners in all subjects than those who avoid it. Since Latin has the reputation of being a difficult subject, students who are lazy or dull avoid it. We are not justified, therefore, in taking these data for evidence that students who have studied Latin will as a result do better in other courses. Rather, the choice of Latin and the higher grades in English are variables which depend on a third variable: intelligence. Probably students who take Latin do better in English than those who do not take Latin because they are more intelligent to begin with.

The only proper technique in experimenting upon this problem of transfer of learning consists of using two groups of subjects who are equal in all characteristics likely to affect their performance in the given experiment. Among these would be age, sex, intelligence, previous experience, interests, and ability to do the task in question. One group is subjected to the type of training presumed to have formal disciplinary value, while the other group is given no such training. Finally, the two groups are tested in a new task to see if the trained group is superior.

One such properly controlled experiment was conducted to determine the degree of transfer of training resulting from the study of descriptive geometry. The experimental group contained 326 students in the College of Engineering at the University of Illinois. The control group was made up of 78 students in other colleges who did not receive training in descriptive geometry. Those of you who have taken descriptive geometry know that it deals with solids or objects in three-dimensional space.

, At the beginning of the semester in February, both groups received tests of their ability to reason in two kinds of situations. One test was in arithmetic; the other test was in ability to visualize objects in space. Similar reasoning tests were given again at the end of the semester in June. The results showed that in the arithmetic test, the group trained in geometry did not gain any more than did the untrained group. But in the test of ability to visualize objects in space, the trained group gained 43.5 per cent while the untrained group lost 5 per cent.

Thus it is quite clear that the study of descriptive geometry did not "strengthen the mind" in so far as ability to do arithmetic division was concerned, but did improve the ability to think about objects in space. (Rugg[24])

This carefully controlled study showed that the mental training involved in learning a subject carries over to new learning material only if the new material involves similar skills. Hundreds of such experiments have by now been conducted to determine the limits of transfer of training (Hamley[25]). This whole subject is too complicated for detailed treatment here, but the strong indications are that transfer effects are too small to justify learning one subject which is useless of itself in the hope that it will help with something useful (for instance, learning Latin solely because it is supposed to help in the learning of French). If you want your learning to carry over from one field to another, you should concentrate on the basic methods and techniques of learning.

Practicing active self-recitation

When you feel that you have mastered a certain paragraph or page, close your book and ask yourself questions about what you have learned. Then open the book and check your own summary for errors and omissions. This attempt to recall actively what you have just read is known as *self-recitation*. At first you may have difficulty in knowing what questions to ask yourself, but eventually you will become skilled in picking out the important problems the author wants to raise and in finding the answers to them. For instance, after reading the section in Chapter 1 on methods of *Description* in psychology, you might have stopped and asked yourself: "What is the difference between the method of introspection and the method of objective observation? What are the advantages of each? the disadvantages?" You might even have scribbled down the answers to each of these self-questions—though *in your own words,* not the words of the book.

This attitude of self-questioning may seem very difficult and very time-consuming when you first try it, but you may find later on that you agree with the findings of how-to-study experts at the University of Minnesota:

"Most students agree after becoming expert in the recitation method that the method yields the following advantages: better preparation for examinations and class discussions; more thorough learning; greater interest in the subject; and more specific concentration, with resulting alertness and the checking of daydreams. Subjectively, these students find their work more satisfying as self-confidence increases and as they enjoy the security which mastery affords. A large number of students are pleased because the method saves time. They take the long view of the method. They insist that review periods are not agonizing drawn-out sessions but occasions when they can rely on their outlines and sense their grasp of the field." (Bird and Bird[26])

"One student writes, 'In using this method I find I have greater interest in my work since I know I have done it well, and this makes me interested in the work for itself. In being able to wish that I would be called on, and desiring to make a good record for the day, I become more and more interested in the recitation classes and no longer dread them, and I do not need to bluff.' . . . A slightly different note is struck when one student writes, 'The method of recitation discouraged me at first and I felt like going back to my old method; but when I went to class the next day and heard the teacher ask the same questions I had written in my own notebook I felt that all my work was not in vain.'" (Bird and Bird[27])

The important psychological advantage of this method of study is that you are practicing the very behavior you will be graded on later. You are forcing yourself to think—to solve problems and to organize your material. The exact proportions of reading and self-recitation which should be used in learning will depend to a very great extent upon the nature of the material—whether it consists of general principles to be comprehended or of specific items to be learned verbatim.

Some material that college students encounter does have to be learned verbatim. In beginning languages, there are vocabulary lists; in history, there are names, dates, and places; in zoology, the names of nerves, blood vessels, and bones. Psychological experiment has clearly shown that when the material to be learned consists of specific items for memorization, the best results are obtained by spending over half the study time in active recitation (Gates[28]). You can either ask yourself questions or ask some friend to test you on the list of items you have learned. Then go back and concentrate on those you got wrong.

Much material that a college student wants to learn is not of the verbatim type; in history, literature, and psychology he reads long assignments which he must understand and translate into his own words. In such subjects, concepts are developed at length, trends are described, many examples are set forth—but only certain definitions, dates, principles need to be remembered verbatim. It has been shown (Peterson[29]) that when the material is full of ideas and concepts to be grasped and remembered, the proportion of time spent in reading should be *greater* and the amount of time in recitation *smaller* than for verbatim material. But the active questioning of the self-recitation method can still be very helpful to you in mastering principles and ideas. It is one of the most valuable of all the methods of learning.

Spacing your learning efforts

Besides having to discover the most effective study methods, the learner frequently must decide how he will distribute the time he has to spend on studying. Suppose that you have one hundred hours in which to study a particular subject, to learn the lines of a play, or to perfect yourself in some relatively simple motor act. You could study or practice ten hours a day for ten days; or you could work one hour a day for one hundred days. Many other variants are possible: two hours a day for fifty days, or a half-hour per day for two hundred days, and so on. All these schedules involve the same total amount of time devoted to study. But some of them involve *distributed practice* (short, well-spaced learning periods), while others involve *massed practice* (long, concentrated learning periods). Which of them will allow the greatest and most permanent improvement per unit of time?

Factors in spacing your learning efforts. The factors underlying the superiority of a particular learning schedule are very complex. We can discuss only some of the more important ones:

First of all, there is the "warming up" period. You do not start right in to work the very moment you sit down at your desk. In the first place, your materials must be brought out: the book opened and placed in a good position, the pencil sharpened, or the pen filled. Perhaps you broke off some interesting activity to start preparing the lesson. This is not easily done, and there will be a period during which thoughts unrelated to study continue to pass through your mind. All this preparation takes time, but once it has been made, it need not be repeated during a particular study period. Obviously, the longer the study period, the smaller the proportion of it that is lost in getting started.

Another factor is of course the forgetting which follows learning. If the practice periods are placed too far apart, even though they be of ideal length in and of themselves, the total schedule will not be an efficient one.

It is also obvious that the most interesting activity becomes boring if indulged in for too long a period at one sitting. You can't keep your mind on even your most interesting subject if you force yourself to study it for hours on end with no letup. A certain degree of variety, introduced by changing from one subject to another, serves to keep your interest fresh.

A fourth and very important factor to keep in mind in spacing your learning effort is the kind of material being learned. Does it consist of arbitrary items to be memorized verbatim or of ideas or principles whose meaning must be grasped? This factor we shall take up in more detail.

Spacing verbatim learning. Psychologists have shown that distributed practice—short, frequent periods—is most effective in learning material verbatim.

> A classic experiment of thirty years ago (Starch[30]), recently verified (Henry and Wasson[31]), compared four different methods of using two hours of time in memorizing a code. One group of subjects practiced for ten minutes twice a day for six days; a second group practiced twenty minutes once a day for six days; a third group practiced forty minutes every other day for six days; and a fourth group practiced two hours at one sitting. The ten-minutes-twice-a-day and the twenty-minutes-once-a-day groups learned most effectively and were about equal in efficiency. The group which practiced two hours at one sitting was least efficient of the four, while the group which practiced forty minutes every other day was intermediate.

This study shows that for verbatim learning, distributed practice appears to be more efficient than massed practice. When the subject matter involves rote learning, break your study periods up into shorter ones. Even when studying any subject to get the broad principles and relationships, you will encounter at the same time certain detailed facts or names to be remembered. Check these items in the margin so that you can find them easily later, but do not stop to attempt to memorize them at the moment. After you have read the material for its general significance, go back and prepare a list containing the items to be committed to memory. Carry this list about with you and study it intensively for several periods of fifteen minutes distributed throughout the day—using, of course, more time in active recall than in passive reading.

Spacing the learning of ideas. When subject matter is interesting and meaningful, the superiority of distributed practice declines or may even disappear. The student might well study such material for an hour or two at one sitting, especially in his first attempts to grasp the general ideas and relationships presented.

> Unfortunately, there is a dearth of well-controlled experiments to determine the best length of study periods when interesting and meaningful material is to be learned. A close approach to the fundamental problem is seen in the work of a psychologist who investigated the problem of massed versus distributed practice in solving puzzles (Cook[32]). Psychologically, puzzle-solving is very similar to the study of mathematics and similar logical material which the college student has to learn. It was found that massed practice is very much superior to distributed practice in this type of meaningful learning. However, the superiority of the massed practice over the distributed practice declines as learning advances and the principal insights and understandings have already been accomplished.

For learning ideas and principles, the best procedure seems to be: massed learning followed by distributed learning. In general, it can be said that when the study subject is one which is meaningful and full of opportunity to see new relationships, you can well afford to spend as many as two hours at one sitting. Thus you have time to grasp, organize, and question yourself on the material, without your train of thought being broken before the ideas are really mastered.

EXAMINATION TECHNIQUES

Every student has to take examinations. Whether he dreads them as a crisis to be got through somehow or accepts them calmly as just part of the semester's work—whether he fails or does very well or just barely gets through—depends on many factors. One important factor, which he cannot control, is of course his inherited ability to learn. But there are many other factors which determine whether he does his best according to his ability, and which he can do much to control:

1 Accepting examinations as helps, not ordeals.
2 Learning with the intent to remember.
3 Accomplishing the original learning efficiently.
4 Frequent review.
5 Discriminating review.
6 Review adjusted to the type of examination.
7 Planning examination answers.
8 Avoiding disturbing emotions.

Accepting examinations as helps, not ordeals

Examinations have often been criticized from the standpoint of mental hygiene. Certain educators have felt that they should be eliminated because they give the individual a taste of failure and hence lead to feelings of inferiority. This objection is debatable. Perhaps adjustment to failure is something that we all have to learn, for no one can be successful all the time.

While examinations can harm the student if they cause him to work for grades rather than for useful understanding of himself and the world about him, they can be a great help to him if he recognizes that examinations perform some useful functions.

First of all, they provide a good opportunity to coordinate work. We all need something to give us a little push now and then. The examination is valuable because it forces the student to review and organize the material in his mind, as he should do anyway but often would not bother to do otherwise. If the examination helps us organize what we learn, we should not worry too much about its artificial nature as an incentive.

Second, they are a means of grading performance. There are many situations where rewards must go only to the abler students. Entrance to college or to advanced work (such as medical school), tuition scholarships, and student loans cannot be available to everyone. Since judgments of ability must be made, they are best based on fair and objective examinations—rather than on unreliable personal impressions or favoritism. For instance, examinations are necessary to protect society from dangerous and costly incompetence. Would you like to be operated on by a surgeon who had never shown his ability by passing a rigorous "State Board"? If you were an employer, would you hire an accountant or an engineer because he just happened to apply for the job? Most employers require proof of your ability, and examinations are a good means of demonstrating it.

Examinations are also an excellent indication of ability and progress. The sincere student is pleased to do well on an examination because the examination stands for something. The grade itself is valueless, but it symbolizes mastery of a subject matter or skill. If used properly, examinations can diagnose the individual's strength and weakness. They tell which subjects are in line with his interests and abilities, and they can be very helpful in selecting a vocation, as we shall see in Chapter 17. They can also give the student an idea of how well he is learning what he set out to learn. They warn him if he is not doing well or if he is not improving, and they give him a well-earned sense of pride if they show that he is increasing his knowledge. Remember, however, that *the examination is just an indicator, not a goal.* Your learning is more important than the grade you receive on your learning.

The student who does his best on examinations is the student who determines to get the most out of them.

Learning with the intent to remember

As you study, keep reminding yourself that you are going to be called upon to use what you are learning, in an examination if nowhere else. The intent to remember definitely improves your ability to remember.

> In an early study, a small group of college students were asked to memorize the Chinese equivalents of English words (Boswell and Foster[33]). In one phase of the experiment, the subjects were instructed to memorize for permanent retention. In the other phase, the subjects were told to memorize for temporary retention. The same amount of time was spent in memorizing, but when instructions were to memorize for permanent retention, both immediate and delayed recall were superior.

Learning with a purpose seems to be the most effective learning.

Accomplishing the original learning efficiently

One way of making sure that you will remember what you learn is to distribute your original learning effort over a long period of time. Of course, you must space your learning effort according to the type of material. For instance, you will forget less if you do your verbatim learning a little at a time, and your learning of ideas and principles in longer stretches. You will also remember more if you have made the materials meaningful as you learned them, so that they do not consist of so many disconnected facts and half-understood ideas, and if you have maintained an active, self-questioning attitude which made what you studied a permanent part of your understanding and interests.

In short, the most intensive pre-examination review of what you have learned will not enable you to remember much if you have not learned much in the first place or have not learned it efficiently. Many students apparently do not understand that the word *review* means "viewing again." All too often, their so-called "review" consists of viewing the material for the first time. Last-minute efforts to cram into your mind materials that should have been assimilated slowly over a period of weeks or months will not enable you to do your best on an examination. Your original learning must be accomplished efficiently.

Frequent review

The task of the student does not end with mastering his material perfectly for the moment. He must be able to remember it until examination time—and longer, if he wants his education to be more than a series of momentary impressions. His learning is really complete only when the subject matter has become so much a part of him that he uses it effortlessly in solving problems which come up in daily living. Then and then only can he say that he has "learned"; up to that time he has merely studied. The important thing to remember is that you will forget what you learn unless you either review it or use it.

> To show how quickly learning may be forgotten, a study was made of how well the students in a typical college course knew the subject matter nine months after the course was over (Eurich[34]). At the end of the nine months, the average score of the class had fallen to a score which 97 per cent of the same class had surpassed at the close of the semester's work. (It is interesting that those students who knew the most at the end of the semester tended to remember the most.)

If you have no opportunity to use your learning in daily life, frequent review will serve to bring it back. Most of what you forget is forgotten right after you have learned it. From this fact we can readily infer that an immediate review would be highly desirable, and experiment shows that our inference is correct.

> One experiment clearly shows that immediate review makes for more permanent retention of meaningful materials. In this study, a class lecture was given to one group of students who didn't review immediately after the lecture, and also to a group who took an immediate five-minute review test. The first group recalled only 24 per cent of the items on a quiz given after a period of six weeks had elapsed. But in the review group, the amount of recall after six weeks was 36 per cent— that is, 50 per cent better than the nonreview group. (Sones[35])

Many teachers are adopting the practice of conducting a short review quiz at the end of each class meeting. This procedure enables the student to determine his weak points for further study. Moreover, the fact that there is a quiz facing the student causes him to assume a more active attitude toward the material of the day's discussion. These factors together not only increase learning but also strengthen retention. The wise student takes advantage of a free period following a lecture to review what has been said that day before the material "gets cold," and he reviews frequently between examinations, rather than "cramming" at the last minute. Here the importance of wise planning of time is obvious.

Discriminating review

You learn many things you need not remember. When you review, emphasize the points that are the most important or the most difficult. You can save yourself time and effort if you keep a list of the difficult points in your assignments as you read through them. Points which are difficult at first are likely to be under-learned, and hence easily forgotten. If you keep a list of your difficulties, you can use it for extra review.

It is obvious that you should also make a special effort to review the main ideas emphasized throughout your lectures and readings. Many students do not know how to pick out the main ideas, however. One way to begin is to go through your text and make sure you are familiar with the importance and interrelations of the chapter and section headings. Review the terms and statements which are emphasized either by italics or by the wording of the text. Intelligent underlining of your text will help you here—if it is underlining that you did yourself (rather than inherited from the previous owner of your book) and if it is underlining that concentrates on the most important ideas. Read over any summaries at the end of the chapters, and if the author has provided questions for review, make sure that you can answer them.[*] In going over your class notes and reading notes, underline in colored pencil the most important principles set forth. Then try to see how they are interrelated, and make sure that you can recall the important detailed facts, dates, names which support these important principles.

Self-questioning can also prove extremely useful in selecting material for review. Many students are very successful in picking out the questions that they would ask if they were the instructor—often, the questions they choose appear on the actual examination. After you

---

[*]Question-summaries for review of *Psychology and Life* are provided in the accompanying workbook, *Working with Psychology.*

have drawn up a list of such questions, practice answering them—either mentally reciting the answers or writing them out in outline form.

If you can obtain examinations from previous years—either from official files or from students who have taken the course—make part of your reviewing consist of answering the questions in full. Write your answers out, and you will discover many of your weak spots and so will be able to select materials on which you need special review.

One important prerequisite to discriminating review which is often neglected by the student is making sure that he understands just what ground he should cover in his review. Usually the instructor will announce what part of the course or textbook the examination will cover, but if he forgets, ask him.

Review adjusted to the type of examination

Most colleges today give two kinds of examinations: the *essay examination* and the *short-answer examination*. Each of these has certain characteristics which you should keep in mind as you review your material.

The *essay examination* tests your ability to organize and interpret your learning. It requires that you not only memorize the details of what you have learned but also be able to make them meaningful. Often it requires that you explain how the facts and ideas of the course are applicable to problems in other courses and in everyday life.

In preparing for an essay examination, you should not be satisfied with verbatim learning: make sure you understand the general principles, ideas, and trends; make sure, too, that you are familiar with the details, for you must be able to support your essay discussion with solid facts. Since the essay examination is mainly a test of your ability to discuss ideas intelligently, you will often find that it covers only a few areas of the course, although it covers those few exhaustively. However, do not become discouraged from your efforts to review all the materials of the course, for you never know which area the instructor will choose to examine you on.

In preparing for a short-answer test, you should keep in mind that it will test you more on your knowledge of facts than on your ability to organize and interpret facts. For a short-answer examination, you should be particularly well-acquainted with names, dates, places, scientific terms, and the statements of important ideas and principles. Do not make the mistake, however, of neglecting to make this material meaningful. In recent years the short-answer examinations have been skillfully developed to test reasoning ability and thorough understanding of principles and their applications. Remember, too, that the coverage of the short-answer examination is very broad; so be careful to leave no part of the course unstudied.

Before you start reviewing for an examination, ask your instructor what type it will be. Usually he can tell you. But if for some reason you are in doubt as to the type of examination you are going to have, prepare for an essay type. Experiment has shown that students who are instructed to study for an essay examination succeed equally well on both types, while students who are instructed to study for an objective and then take an essay examination are handicapped (Meyer[36]). The reason is that students who expect essay examinations prepare differently from those who expect objective ones (Meyer[37]). If they expect an essay examination, they make the material meaningful so that they are in a position to handle essay and objective examinations equally well. But if they expect an objective examination, they usually pick out isolated points and memorize them, so that they are ill-equipped for the logical analysis required by the essay examination. Of course this method of preparing for the short-answer examination is not always very effective because, as we have pointed out, modern short-answer tests are skillfully designed to test the students' grasp of meaning. The basic procedure in both cases should be to understand the general ideas and relate the specific facts to them.

Planning examination answers

Be certain that you understand all the questions before starting to write; if you do not, ask for an explanation. You must get an overall view of the examination if you are to divide your time properly and make the right emphases in your paper. Also, some examinations allow you a choice of questions, and you cannot choose intelligently unless you see all the questions in perspective. Notice the time suggested for answering each question and obey faithfully, for here is a strong indication as to how much weight the instructor will give each question in determining your final grade.

As you first read through the questions, you will of course find that some seem "easy" and some "hard." Many students find it helpful to jot down an outline of their ideas on each question while the ideas are still fresh in their minds. Then if the ideas on later questions are forgotten during the concentration on earlier ones, they can be easily recalled from the brief scribbled outline. Most students also find it helpful to answer the easier questions first. As they write on the material they know best, they not only gain in self-confidence but often get ideas on how to answer the more difficult questions (such ideas should of course be jotted down immediately on a separate piece of paper). As you tackle the more difficult questions, try to work out one important idea at a time, and many of the missing facts and ideas will come to mind—moreover, this procedure will also prevent your answering the question in a confused way.

One final technique for planning a successful examination paper has been suggested by how-to-study experts and is passed on here:

> "One feature of planning time in the essay examination deserves more attention than it usually gets. Time should be planned for checking all answers before the examination officially closes. This final review should not be left to chance; rather it should be provided for as carefully as the time given to each question. At least ten minutes of an hour test, and approximately twenty minutes of a two-hour test, should be reserved for the checking of answers and for the correction of misstatements and slips of the pen. Occasionally, with the aid of this kind of review, additional information or better ways of expressing ideas come to mind. An essay examination may be lifted from the class of ordinary to excellent performance by the effort expended calmly before Fate, in the person of the instructor, sits in judgment." (Bird and Bird[38])

The student who writes feverishly until the last minute may impress his fellow-students as being so full of ideas that he is certain to do well. Nevertheless, studies show that the most successful student is likely to be the one who plans his examination beforehand so that he has plenty of time to cover and review his answers (and may even be through writing a little early).

Avoiding disturbing emotions

Fear and excitement in an examination usually come when the student knows that he cannot give the right answers or cannot give them quickly enough. Obviously the best way to keep your head in an examination is to come as well prepared as possible—and to come with a good night's sleep behind you. Disturbing emotions are closely related to physical condition: staying up all night trying to study makes you physically exhausted and thus not only slows up your thinking but also makes you more subject to unfavorable emotional reactions in the examination situation.

However, it may happen that a student is well prepared for an examination, has had a good night's sleep, knows all the best examination strategy—and then just "blows up" when he sits down to write.

If this happens frequently, it usually means that he has some unconscious attitude toward competitive examinations which keeps him from performing as well as he is able. Like the student who cannot concentrate, he will probably benefit by the help of a clinical psychologist or psychiatrist in overcoming his emotional upsets on examinations.

While most students do not experience such disturbing emotional reactions on examinations that they need a psychologist's help, they can benefit from the psychological principles of learning discussed in this chapter. Psychologists know that a large number of people never realize fully the potentialities for achievement given them by their heredity. No matter what your innate ability to learn, you are probably not making the most of it. If you really want to improve the management of your learning resources, you can.

PART TWO

Endowment and environment

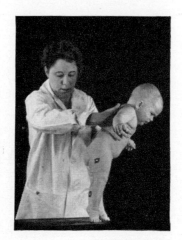

LEARNING (?) *to walk. Through a combination of practice and maturation, the reflex stepping movements of the newborn child develop gradually into the mature walk shown in the last picture. Note the changed relations between parts of the body (indicated by marks on the body) as the muscles mature and strengthen and as balance and coordination improve.*

CHAPTER 3
Nature and nurture: how we develop

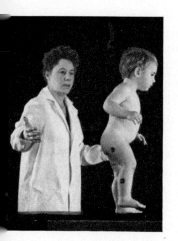 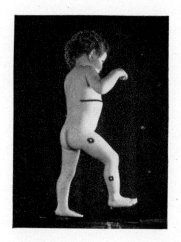 

The Mechanics of Heredity

Maturation Before Birth

Maturation After Birth

How Maturation and Learning Interact

T HE OLD-FASHIONED dirt farmer and the modern experimental botanist both are aware that the plant is the joint product of seed and soil. Poor seed, even if planted in the richest soil, will produce a poor plant. Conversely, the best of seed will not produce a healthy, vigorous plant if it is placed in barren soil.

Just as the plant is the product of both seed and soil, so is the human being the product of one group of factors called *heredity* and of a second group called *environment*. To understand human behavior, you must understand how both heredity and environment control the development of the organism.

Development is a product, not a sum, of heredity and environment. This might be written as a simple algebraic formula:

$$T \times H \times E = \textit{Level of development}$$

H (heredity) is a factor which determines how high a level of development a given E (environment) will bring about. Correspondingly, E is a factor which determines how effective a certain H will be in influencing development—all in a given amount of T (time).

If any term in the above formula were reduced to zero, their product, level of development, would become zero, for you will remember from algebra that anything multiplied by zero gives zero for a product. This is just another way of saying that heredity alone is meaningless and so is environment alone. Both are important in determining your development, and development takes time.

The influence of heredity is not restricted to the early part of life. It does not manifest itself at one particular time in the life of an individual. It is not an actor who says his lines and leaves the stage, but rather a director whose influence is felt throughout the life-drama. Heredity is active in guiding the development of the individual from the moment of conception to the instant of death itself.

Up to the time of birth, the human being has little opportunity to learn, so that his development is mainly the product of growth steered by heredity—maturation. At birth, he begins to learn from his environment. However, behavior following birth is not all learned. Some behavior not present at birth comes into being later through maturation. A number of essential nervous, muscular, and glandular structures in the human body are not ready to function at birth; some are not ready until years afterward. And until these essential structures are mature, no stimulus will be effective in producing the behavior for which they are responsible.

> One very good example of maturation is the voice change occurring in all normal boys at the age of puberty. The boy's voice becomes lower because of a thickening in his vocal cords, a thickening produced by certain alterations in the working of the ductless-gland system. However, the change in pitch is not entirely smooth and harmonious, as the hoarsely squeaking or unexpectedly failing voice of the adolescent boy testifies. While the low voice which finally develops in the adult male is not present at birth, it is just as much determined by maturation as if it were. Observation of boys who have grown up out of touch with other boys shows that even in the absence of knowledge of this change, the characteristic voice change takes place at adolescence. It is not, therefore, something that is learned by imitation of other boys but is the result of maturation of structures.

We must, then, expand our conception of *maturation*—to include development which comes after birth in all normal individuals of the species, as the result not of learning but of bodily changes determined by heredity acting over a period of time.

You see that the influence of heredity on human development is expressed through maturation, with the environment supplying stimuli which set off patterns of response already prepared by maturation.

However, the environment also provides situations which are conducive to the person's *learning*—that is, to his adopting new behavior patterns or altering old ones.

All through life, learning helps shape our interests, attitudes, and reactions. As soon as the infant comes from the uterus, where he has neither need nor opportunity to learn, he begins to alter his innate behavior patterns through contact with the environment. The learning process interacts with the maturation process to make you the person that you are. The net effect of the interaction depends upon *The Mechanics of Heredity, Maturation Before Birth, Maturation After Birth,* and *How Maturation and Learning Interact.*

THE MECHANICS OF HEREDITY

Heredity is the process by which certain substances in the sperm and egg determine the characteristics of the individual they produce. The study of the substances and chemical reactions which constitute the physical basis of heredity properly falls within the boundaries of biology. But the knowledge gained by research in that field greatly clarifies many problems in psychology, and it is worth while to have some familiarity with the essential concepts regarding the mechanics of heredity.

What can we inherit?

You have all heard of a pregnant woman who religiously went to concerts or read "uplifting" literature in order to make her unborn child musical or literary. You may even have heard of a parent who had some inherited physical defect corrected by surgery and then thought that his child would be unable to inherit that defect. And it is often said that a man who comes to be "money mad"—perhaps as the result of an early environment of poverty—will have "money mad" children.

These are just additional cases where science shows popular belief to be misguided. These particular misconceptions are based on the now-outmoded theory of "the inheritance of acquired characteristics." Modern scientists know that the learning which occurs during our life and the bodily changes that occur outside our reproductive organs are not passed on to our children. They distinguish between the *germ cells* in an organism, which give rise to sperms or eggs, and the *body cells,* which give rise to the bodily organs, the bones, the skin— in short, to all the different parts of the body except those which directly transmit inherited characteristics.

Much more research will need to be done before we can say more exactly whether the reproductive cells can be influenced at all by conditions occurring during the life of the parent. It is not out of the realm of possibility that the chemical conditions existing during the person's lifetime (as a consequence of diet, disease, use of drugs, or heavy smoking) *might* cause some changes of the contents of the reproductive cells, since there is nothing that would shield them from general chemical conditions existing in the body of the person. But participation in music and participation in business, for example, do not create different chemical states in the body and so do not influence the reproductive cells in different ways.

One work on heredity draws the following conclusions:

> "Among psychologists in general the belief prevails that of the various factors involved in producing personality, the likelihoods of their being influenced by heredity are as follows:
>
> *Most likely to be influenced by heredity:* Basic abilities, such as intelligence, speed of reaction, motor skills, sensory discrimination, etc.
>
> *Less likely to be influenced by heredity:* Temperamental traits, such as emotionality, alternation or evenness of mood, activity or lethargy, and other characteristics in which gland activity is conceivably involved.
>
> *Least likely to be influenced by heredity* (if at all): Attitudes, stylistic traits, beliefs, values and other such characteristics in which training or conditioning are clearly major factors." (Scheinfeld[1]) *

You may wonder why children are often very different from their parents and other relatives even in the characteristics which are "most likely to be influenced by heredity." This "why" of heredity can best be approached by explaining the "how."

How we inherit

At the moment of conception, two living germ cells (sperm and egg) unite to produce an individual. Within both sperm and egg are found twenty-four minute rodlike structures called *chromosomes*. (The word means "color bodies" and was given these structures because they stain a dark color when treated with certain chemicals.) Many lines of evidence converge to show that chromosomes play a very important —almost an all-important—role as bearers of hereditary traits. They are the materials which influence the development of the fertilized ovum as it unfolds into an individual organism. How this is done is still mostly unknown.

---

*From *You and Heredity,* copyright, 1939, by Amram Scheinfeld, published by J. B. Lippincott Company.

It is known, however, that within each of the chromosomes a child receives from each parent are many still smaller parts called *genes*. Each microscopic gene carries some of the real determiners of heredity. That is to say, each gene is composed of some substance, or contains some structure, which is absolutely necessary to the development of some trait of body or behavior. The whole heredity of the individual consists of many traits, each determined by a gene, a pair of genes, or a group of genes.

The fertilized egg from which the child develops contains forty-eight chromosomes. We may say for purposes of simplified discussion that half the child's chromosomes come from the mother and half from the father (although genetic studies have established that male children actually receive twenty-five chromosomes from the mother and twenty-three from the father). Thus, despite popular belief, the child does not inherit more characteristics from the parent of his own sex, and numerous measurements of inheritable characteristics in parents and children support this fact.

In the lower organisms, plants especially, it is possible to determine by carefully conducted experiments the exact chromosome and gene involved in the hereditary transmission of a particular trait. In man, however, the process is so complex that there is little hope of accomplishing a similar result. Whereas in the lower animals certain traits seem to be determined by single genes, most human traits are apparently determined by a large number of genes. Therefore it is not possible to account for one particular

The baby comes from

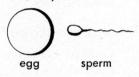

egg   sperm

Within the egg
and sperm lie the

chromosomes,
24 in each.

Within the
chromosomes

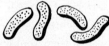

are the tiny genes.

As the egg and sperm
unite into one cell,

the combination of
genes constitutes the
inherited chemical
determiners—
the heredity—
of the child.

characteristic through tracing one particular gene as it meets other genes—the procedure used with insects and plants. But although the study of human heredity is still in its infancy, it can explain certain puzzling facts.

Why we are like and different from our relatives

Curiously enough, the power of heredity in determining the individual's characteristics is manifested by both the resemblances and the differences that people show in inheritable traits.

Psychologists have developed some special methods for studying the resemblances and differences between individuals of varying degrees of biological relationship. The first step, of course, consists of measuring the trait under investigation in some convenient unit: to compare height, we use inches; to study resemblance in some psychological ability, we use scores on mental tests.

The second step is to find some means of measuring the degree of resemblance in the particular trait in question. Psychologists have found that degree of resemblance may be conveniently expressed in terms of a *coefficient of correlation*. A coefficient of 1.00 means a perfect resemblance, and a coefficient of 0 means no resemblance at all (for further discussion, see Chapter 15).

It has been demonstrated that the degree of resemblance between the intelligence and height of two individuals depends upon the closeness of their biological relationship. The chart on page 85 is based on a number of studies (Burks,[2] Conrad and Jones,[3] Merriman,[4] and Lauterback[5]). It shows the resemblance usually found between individuals in both intelligence, (as measured by the Stanford-Binet Test) and physical height (as measured at the same age). As you can see, the correlation is lower—that is, the degree of resemblance is less—as the biological relationship becomes more remote.

This fact is virtually common knowledge. We all know that there are often striking resemblances between parents and children, and between children of the same parents. Yet we all know too that there are often striking differences among them—differences, such as in hair color and eye color, body build and glandular functioning, which cannot easily be attributed to differences in environment. We often forget this fact when we speak of the influence of heredity on psychological characteristics. We speak as though heredity ought merely to create resemblances between parents and children. But the truth is that *there is also the possibility that heredity will operate to produce differences among relatives.*

How individuals of varying degrees of biological relationship resemble each other in intelligence and height

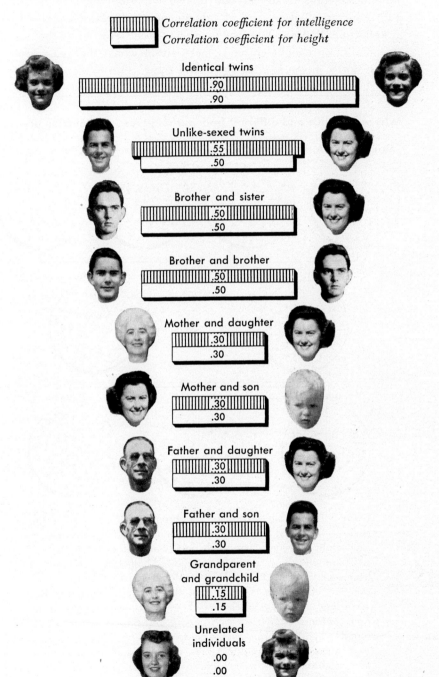

Correlation coefficient for intelligence
Correlation coefficient for height

Identical twins
.90
.90

Unlike-sexed twins
.55
.50

Brother and sister
.50
.50

Brother and brother
.50
.50

Mother and daughter
.30
.30

Mother and son
.30
.30

Father and daughter
.30
.30

Father and son
.30
.30

Grandparent and grandchild
.15
.15

Unrelated individuals
.00
.00

The fact that relatives both resemble and differ from each other in inheritable traits is largely due to two important facts of heredity: (1) reduction division, and (2) dominance and recessiveness.

Reduction division. After the ovum has been fertilized by the sperm, it contains forty-eight chromosomes, within which the genes are located. But each sperm and egg, as you know, contributes only twenty-

---

Why we are like and different from our relatives . . . Reduction division

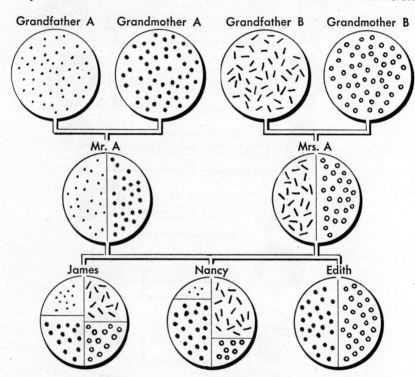

Every individual has 24 pairs of chromosomes in most of the cells of his body. Through reduction division he transmits to each child only one from each pair. Consider the hypothetical "A" family. Both Mr. and Mrs. A received half their chromosomes from each parent. Their children all receive the same proportions of chromosomes (half the 48) from each parent. But according to the laws of chance, they will receive different selections *within the 24 from each parent,* and thus will receive different proportions from each grandparent. The proportions most likely to occur are found in James, who draws about equal numbers of chromosomes from each; less likely is the case of Nancy; and very improbable, though not impossible, is the case of Edith.

four chromosomes to the new individual, through a special cell division within the fertilized egg—the *reduction division*. Therefore each parent contributes to the child only half the chromosomes (and genes) he received from his parents, and each child is likely to receive a different combination of chromosomes. The situation just with respect to the parents and grandparents is illustrated below:

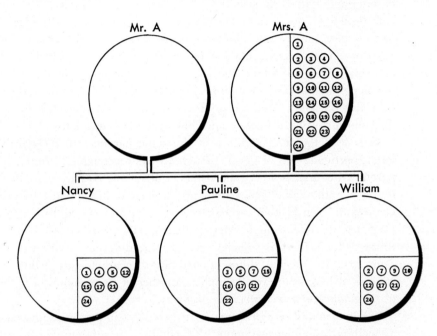

The children receive from each grandparent not only different *proportions* but also different *selections* of chromosomes. For instance, even though Nancy, Pauline, and William all receive eight chromosomes from Grandmother B (via Mrs. A), they may receive different particular ones (indicated, for convenience, by numbers). Since each chromosome contains genes different from the genes of the other chromosomes, each child will be both like and different from his siblings, parents, and grandparents (and from other more distant relatives not shown here).

Only in the case of identical twins are there identical chromosomes, and then only because such twins develop from the same egg, which has split in two.

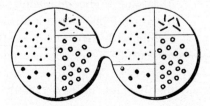

This *reduction* in the number of chromosomes (and consequent selection) is accomplished in one of the last cell *divisions* which produce the reproductive cells (the sperm cells or ovum). This special cell division has been termed the *reduction division,* and is different from any other cell division which occurs in the development of the individual, in the following way:

In other cases when cells divide—as to promote body growth—each chromosome within the original cell is duplicated in each of the new cells produced. But in reduction division, each of the new cells which is formed gets merely one chromosome from each of the twenty-four *pairs* of chromosomes contained in the preceding cell. Furthermore—and this is very important—the selection in each pair of chromosomes is independent of the selection in the other pairs of chromosomes. The diagrams on pages 86-87 make clear the significant role of reduction division in causing likenesses and differences among relatives.

Thus it is that two children of the same parents can receive different particular sets of genes, though always receiving half from each parent. Of course, brothers and sisters or other relatives are more likely to receive the same genes than are unrelated individuals, but the chances of even brothers and sisters receiving exactly equivalent sets of genes are infinitesimal. Merely through the process of reduction division, then, there is sufficient reason why different children of the same parents receive different hereditary characteristics. But the process of heredity is very complex. Another of its phenomena is that of *dominance and recessiveness of genes.*

Dominance and recessiveness. That heredity can produce differences as well as resemblances among the members of a family is also due to an interesting relationship among the genes which are inherited from each parent. As you know, inherited characteristics are produced by genes given to the individual by both his parents. Sometimes these genes have the same effect, as when the child receives only genes for black hair. But in other cases, the genes are determiners of different characteristics—as, for instance, genes for blond hair and genes for black hair.

When only one of an opposing pair of genes takes effect in the child, it is said to be *dominant,* and the ineffective gene is said to be *recessive.* If the gene for a particular trait is dominant, it will result in a child with that trait no matter what kind of gene it is united with. A recessive gene, however, must join with one just like it in order to take effect. This process can be further understood by reference to the diagrams on pages 90-91.

At the present time we do not know exactly how many cases of dominance occur in the human being. Many traits, however, are definitely known to be dominant. Among these are some types of skin and brain cancers, drooping eyelids, cataracts, certain muscular troubles, white forelock ("blaze"), baldness (dominant in men only), and dwarfism. Many less dramatic traits are probably also dominant, but they are less easily observed and traced.

There are also many recessive conditions, such as taste-blindness, a rare type of complete color-blindness, some types of visual and hearing defects, certain kinds of paralysis, some neuritis, albinism ("dead white" skin with pink eyes and white hair), possibly certain types of insanity and epilepsy, and one rare and atypical form of feeble-mindedness known as amaurotic family idiocy.

If two parents produce an amaurotic idiot child, the odds are that of all the brothers and sisters in the family, three fourths will carry the gene and that one fourth will show idiocy (cf. the distribution of genes as explained on page 91). It is the one half of the children who carry the gene in recessive form but do not display idiocy who suggest the terribly complex problems posed by any "sterilization of the unfit" program. Should the children who are not idiots be sterilized because there is a chance that they may mate with someone who also carries a recessive gene for idiocy and so produce idiot children?

Although maturation is not an obvious thing like color-blindness, albinism, and idiocy, *the rate and extent of maturation are evidently limited by heredity*. The detailed proofs of this statement are very complicated, but we can accept the statement as a working principle subject to revision.

In this section, we have seen how heredity can determine some of the individual's physical and psychological characteristics. In the next section, we shall see how heredity operates over a lifetime, through the process of maturation.

MATURATION BEFORE BIRTH

EVERY HUMAN BEING before he is born lives in an environment—the mother's womb—which can have little effect on his development through stimulation. It is constant from day to day and so gives him no opportunity to learn new responses. Since this is the case, development up to the time of birth must be attributed largely to maturation. Accordingly, the clearest evidence of how the individual develops through maturation alone is obtained by studying the infant both in the uterus

Dominance and recessiveness can be illustrated by tracing the inheritance of a condition known as "taste-blindness." There is a certain chemical substance which tastes bitter to about 70 per cent of all people while the other 30 per cent cannot taste it at all. The best evidence indicates that a person's ability or lack of ability to taste this substance is inherited—i.e., it is dependent upon the possession of certain genes.

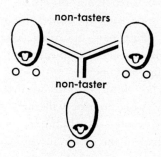

If both parents possess only "non-taster" (○ ○) genes, the individual can receive only non-taster genes and will not be able to taste the bitter chemical.

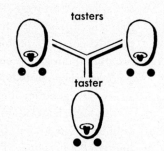

If both parents possess only "taster" (● ●) genes, the offspring will be a "taster" since he receives only taster genes.

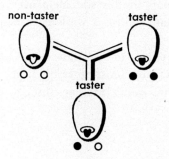

However, a person who receives a taster (●) gene from his taster (● ●) parent and a non-taster (○) gene from his non-taster (○ ○) parent will also be able to taste the substance. This relation is described by saying that the taster gene is *dominant* over the non-taster gene, which is said to be *recessive* to the taster gene.

and just after birth, before it can have learned from its environment. In later chapters of the book, we shall be discussing all the many ways by which the individual learns from the environment after birth—in this section we shall study the unlearned equipment of *The Unborn Child* and *The Newborn Child:* that is, we shall summarize the effects

Now suppose that two such persons—each bearing both taster and non-taster genes, but each able to taste the substance—marry and have a family. Each parent will contribute only one taster or non-taster gene to each child.

1 2   3 4
● ○   ● ○

1 3   1 4   2 3   2 4
● ●   ● ○   ○ ●   ○ ○

As you can see, the mother may contribute either $\overset{1}{●}$ or $\overset{2}{○}$, and the father may contribute either $\overset{3}{●}$ or $\overset{4}{○}$. (The genes are numbered for convenience; there is no difference between the two dominant genes or between the two recessive genes, but the number will show from which parent they came.) There are four possible combinations of genes for a child of these parents. He might get $\overset{1}{●}$ and $\overset{3}{●}$; he might get $\overset{1}{●}$ and $\overset{4}{○}$; he might get $\overset{2}{○}$ and $\overset{3}{●}$; or he might get $\overset{2}{○}$ and $\overset{4}{○}$. Notice that each child of this couple has one chance in four of receiving two dominant genes, two chances in four of receiving one dominant and one recessive gene, and one chance in four of receiving two recessive genes.

Because $\overset{1}{●}$ and $\overset{3}{●}$ are dominant, a child receiving any of the first three combinations would be able to taste the chemical substance. A child with the fourth combination would not be able to taste the substance, even though both of his parents could, because he has received two recessive genes. Here you see how dominance and recessiveness can produce differences as well as resemblances between parents and children.

of maturation up until the time of birth, before the effects of maturation and of learning begin to interweave. In this way, we shall become acquainted with the endowment the child has with him when he enters the complex environment outside his mother's body. Then in the next section we shall go on to study *Maturation After Birth*, investigating the bodily structures which, as they become mature after birth, result in new forms of behavior.

The unborn child

The human fetus (unborn child) can respond to stimulation long before it is born, but it has no direct contact with the outside world and thus has little opportunity to learn from it.

The living human fetus is ordinarily not available for scientific observation. In certain circumstances, however, it is necessary, as well as permissible under our laws and morals, for the physician to interrupt the normal process of development within the uterus and to deliver the fetus prematurely. Fetuses delivered in this way provide valuable information about innate behavior.

> One of the first systematic investigations of the behavior of the unborn child was carried out in Europe (Minkowski[6]), and later followed up and verified in this country (Hooker[7]). Fetuses delivered surgically at from two to eight months following conception were studied.
>
> Since a general anesthetic was used in some cases, the fetus was more sluggish than normal, and perhaps otherwise different. But the study situation was abnormal in still another way: When the fetus is in its place in the maternal uterus, its blood stream is fed by that of the mother, and oxygen and food materials constantly pass from the maternal circulation to that of the fetus. For the prematurely delivered fetus, however, this mutual connection is broken.
>
> Although scientists have not been able to examine a normal fetus in its normal environment, they can make allowances for any abnormalities in the fetus which is prematurely removed from the mother.

The general method of study with prematurely delivered fetuses is, first, to observe the unstimulated fetuses, and then to give them various types of stimuli and note the responses they are capable of making. Such responses to stimuli are then known to be innate, not learned.

A recent series of motion pictures of the fetus has been of extreme value in cataloguing and interpreting its reactive equipment (Hooker[8] and Gesell[9]). Here we can follow the development of the human fetus from the fourth week after conception to its full term of thirty-eight weeks when, on the average, natural birth takes place. The motion-picture studies, and others, show that the unlearned activities of the mature human fetus are of two basic kinds: (1) spontaneous movements and (2) externally stimulated movements.

Spontaneous movements. Movements of the head, trunk, and limbs are "spontaneous" in the sense that they occur when no external stimulus is applied. The head turns from side to side; the arms and legs draw in and thrust out. The movements are slow and irregular, involving several joints at once, and often several members of the body move at the same time. This sluggish, irregular, widespread movement is aptly described as *mass action* or as *irradiation* (raying out).

Externally stimulated movements. When the skin of the fetus is stimulated with a brush, either by friction or by pressure, the responses are more jerky than are the slow, spontaneous movements, and they, too, show gross irradiation. The motion-picture series below shows a generalized response to a specific stimulus.

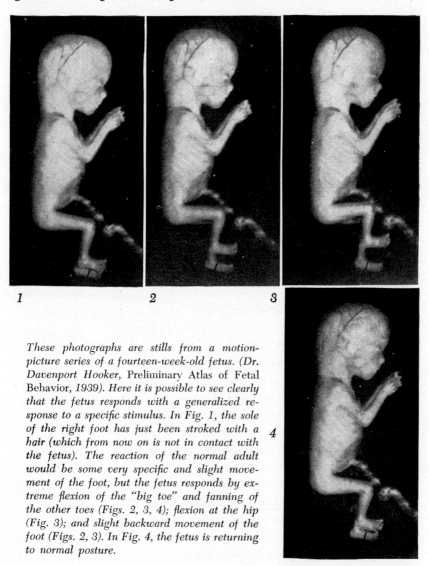

These photographs are stills from a motion-picture series of a fourteen-week-old fetus. (Dr. Davenport Hooker, Preliminary Atlas of Fetal Behavior, 1939). Here it is possible to see clearly that the fetus responds with a generalized response to a specific stimulus. In Fig. 1, the sole of the right foot has just been stroked with a hair (which from now on is not in contact with the fetus). The reaction of the normal adult would be some very specific and slight movement of the foot, but the fetus responds by extreme flexion of the "big toe" and fanning of the other toes (Figs. 2, 3, 4); flexion at the hip (Fig. 3); and slight backward movement of the foot (Figs. 2, 3). In Fig. 4, the fetus is returning to normal posture.

Some responses to stimuli are quite specific. A touch applied to the lip arouses the response of opening and closing the mouth: probably the beginning of the more complex pattern of sucking. Touching the eyelid makes it contract. Also, it is possible to arouse another specific response by moving the whole body into various positions in space, without changing the relationship of the arms and legs to the rest of the body. In response, the fetus makes balancing movements, turning the head and moving the arms and legs.

These observations demonstrate that the human fetus, like any organism, makes spontaneous movements and also responds to stimulation. However, its behavior is very simple and is of course far from adequate in adjusting to the complex outer world. This inadequacy is due to two factors: physical immaturity and also lack of opportunity to learn. Complex adjustment requires learning from the environment as well as innate reactions, and the fetus, while probably to some degree able to learn, has little opportunity to do so because of the few changes in the external stimuli it receives.

The fetus can learn but has no opportunity. Although opportunity to learn in prenatal life is so very limited, it has been demonstrated that simple learning can occur in the womb. One experiment established a learned or *conditioned response* in several human fetuses still in the uterus, during the last two months before birth (Spelt[10]).

Here for the first time you meet the extremely important concept of conditioning, which will appear time and again in your study of psychology. Before you can understand this particular conditioning experiment, you must understand the logic of all conditioning experiments. You must know that every conditioning experiment involves four elements: (1) adequate stimulus, (2) original response, (3) neutral stimulus, and (4) conditioned response.

(1) There is an *adequate stimulus,* namely, a stimulus which is adequate to produce a certain response. In this particular experiment, a fetus had been observed to move parts of its body as an innate response when a loud sound was made just outside the mother's body. That is, the sound was an adequate stimulus to produce (2) the *original response* of movement. Every conditioning experiment also involves (3) a *neutral stimulus,* which cannot under ordinary conditions produce the original response, as can the adequate stimulus. In this experiment, a vibrator applied to the mother's abdomen over the uterus was not adequate to cause the fetus to move—that is, it was neutral.

Now during conditioning, the adequate stimulus and the neutral stimulus are presented to the subject at approximately the same time.

At first the given response is made only to the adequate stimulus, but eventually the response will be made to the neutral stimulus when it is presented alone. The individual's new response to the originally neutral stimulus is then called (4) a *conditioned response*.

The conditioning experiment with fetuses worked in just this way. During the experiment, the sound was made outside the mother's abdomen just as the vibrator was applied to it. The purpose of the experiment was to see if the fetuses would ultimately come to move in response to the vibrator alone—then they would have learned to make a response they did not make innately. The result was that the fetuses moved in response to the vibrator alone after an average of one hundred applications of sound-plus-vibrator, although individual differences in learning ability were noted.

This experiment, while not yet confirmed by other workers, strongly suggests that under certain conditions fetuses can learn to make new responses if new stimuli are presented. Even before birth, the human being possesses his most valuable resource—the capacity to learn.

The newborn child

By studying the responses the newborn child makes to various stimuli, psychologists have determined that prenatal maturation gives the child sensory receptors which enable him to receive many different stimuli. The newborn baby definitely does react to his environment. His reactions are inadequate to satisfy his basic needs; for instance, he cannot obtain food or shelter. The infant will need adult care for a long time to come, but despite his helplessness he is aware of a good deal of what is going on around him and inside him.

During the past couple of decades the study of infant behavior has taken enormous strides, and many research institutes have been organized for this purpose. In some of the studies the conditions surrounding the child must be so carefully controlled and standardized that the investigator knows all the external (if not internal) stimuli which are acting on the infant. Thus when he administers any additional stimulus he can isolate its own particular effect on the child's total behavior.

Such complete control of all variables is essential to the experimental method, even though it is not possible in the hospital or home. Many research institutions, however, contain special observation chambers so well controlled that no chance blast of air, no unexpected flicker of light, no unwanted variation in temperature or humidity, no unbidden noise can possibly enter. These chambers are equipped with a special recording apparatus which automatically registers the amount and kind of body movements made by the baby as he responds to the stimuli around him and to those applied by the investigator.

All the studies of infant sensitivity to stimuli operate on the principle that although the newborn baby cannot tell us what he does or does not feel, he *can* make a muscular response to stimulation. Therefore studying sensitivity to stimulation also means studying muscular response. But there is one important limitation. It is true that if a child makes a muscular response to a stimulus, then he is surely sensitive to it. But the converse is not true: that is, if the child fails to make a muscular response to a stimulus, this does *not* mean, necessarily, that he is insensitive to it. It may just be that his nervous and muscular systems are not yet able to make a response.

With this important limitation in mind, then, let us see how well the newborn infant receives and reacts to stimuli.

Sensitivity to sound. Even before birth, human infants respond to loud noises transmitted through the abdominal wall of the mother. About twenty-four hours after birth, or as soon as the fluid in the ear has drained out, loud sounds will cause most babies to cry. Moreover, there is evidence that young infants have some pitch discrimination.

> One experiment has shown that tones of varying pitch produce varying reactions in infants between two and four weeks of age (Morgan[11]). Tones of high pitch tended to stimulate activity, while those of low pitch tended to soothe the infants who were crying and to lessen activity in the others. Since the high and low tones produced different responses, we conclude that babies from two to four weeks of age have hearing equipment sufficiently developed to permit some discrimination between tones.
>
> Another experimenter (Stubbs[12]), working with babies under ten days of age, was able to confirm these results in part but found that the differences between responses to low and high tones were not nearly so great as indicated by the previous experiment.

Another interesting test proves the acuteness of infants' hearing. Incidentally, it is similar to the experiment performed to discover whether fetuses can learn, for it, too, involves conditioning.

> When the sole of a baby's foot is tickled, the typical baby responds by extending his great toe and fanning out his little toes, an innate pattern which is found in most babies (it is called the *plantar reflex*). He makes no such toe response to a nearby sound. However, a normal-hearing child can be brought to do so through the conditioning process.
>
> If the sound is repeatedly presented at the same time that the sole of the foot is tickled, the child of normal hearing will eventually give toe responses to the sound alone. That is, if the neutral stimulus (the sound) is repeatedly presented at the same or nearly the same time as

the adequate stimulus (tickling), the neutral stimulus (sound alone) will become adequate to elicit the toe responses. If the conditioning is successful, then it is known that the child is not deaf, for he *does* respond to sound, though by his toes rather than by crying or any direct response. One baby was thought to be deaf because he failed to react visibly to sounds which seemed very loud to adults. Happily, the child was not deaf, for he did respond to sound in the conditioning experiment. (Aldrich[13]) This general process is shown below:

An infant learns through conditioning

1. Original condition

Infant fans out his toes when the sole of his foot is tickled.

Infant makes no toe response to the sound of a buzzer.

2. Conditioning

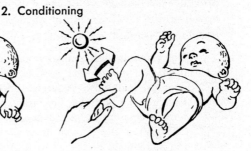

Infant's foot is tickled and the buzzer is sounded at the same time.

This is repeated until—

In the meantime,

a control baby keeps on making the toe response only when its foot is tickled and not at the sound alone.

3. Learning is accomplished

A new response has been acquired: the infant has been conditioned to fan out his toes at the sound alone.

Sensitivity to light and color. The visual sensitivity of the newborn child is revealed by the fact that the pupil of his eye contracts in bright light and enlarges in dimmer light. The response of the eye to light is absent at birth but develops rapidly and becomes quite efficient by the thirty-fourth hour following birth (Sherman and Sherman[14]; Sherman, Sherman, and Flory[15]).

Experiment has shown further that infants as young as fifteen days can discriminate between various colors in different combinations.

> Color filters were arranged so that two colors could be projected upon a screen above the infant's head as he lay on his back. They were projected in such a way that one color appeared to be surrounded by the other. When the filter was moved, the center color seemed to move within the field of the other color. The infants could discriminate colors, for they moved their eyes in following the moving color stimuli. Control experiments showed that the discriminations had not been made upon the basis of a difference in the brightness of the two colors, or of some mechanical aspect of the experimental situation. (Chase[16])

Sensitivity to odors. Sensitivity to odors, the *olfactory* response, is seated in receptors well back in the nostrils. During prenatal life and for a day or so after birth, the nasal cavities are filled with fluid which prevents the passage of air. As soon as the nasal cavities are dried out, however, the newborn infant clearly shows that he can make a well-developed response when he is stimulated by a variety of odors.

> One experimenter stimulated newborn babies (aged three hours to ten days) by forcing their nostrils full of gentle puffs of air laden with odorous materials: sassafras, citronella, pyridine (burned wood), lemon, violet perfume, turpentine, and asafoetida. All these seven different odors produced a definite response of increased bodily activity. The greater the concentration of the odorous substance, the greater the increase in bodily activity. Air with no smell produced some increase in general activity, but not so much as the faintly scented air. (Disher[17])

Sensitivity to taste. The sense of taste of the newborn baby also seems to be well developed. In the infant, the area containing these taste organs is greater than in the adult. The baby has taste organs on the inside surfaces of the cheeks, on the lips, and in the larynx, although he has the greatest number on the tongue. Psychologists applying citric acid, salt, sugar, and quinine as taste stimuli to newborn infants have elicited reactions in as high as 86 per cent of the applications (Pratt, Nelson, and Sun[18]). Remember, too, that the lack of response in the other 14 per cent does not necessarily mean that these infants could not taste. These workers also found some evidence of infants' making differential or discriminatory reactions to taste stimuli. Tastes unpleasant to the adult produced defense or rejection movements of the tongue and lips of infants, pleasant-tasting substances being accepted.

Sensitivity to movement. The muscles, tendons, and joints of the adult contain minute sensory receptors which respond to body movements. These responses give the individual *kinesthetic* sensations, i.e., sensations of bodily movement. These sensations are the basis of our muscular coordination; if we cannot judge accurately how our bodies are moving, we cannot control our motor responses to the world around us. Experiments have shown that the bodily responses giving rise to accurate kinesthesis or muscle sense develop rapidly in infants during the first few hours of life.

> When the tiny infant is pushed on the chin, he will make defense movements with his hands. One experimenter counted the number of unsuccessful movements the baby makes before touching the hand of the experimenter. Success increased rapidly with age. Babies younger than 21 hours of age made no successful responses; babies 50 hours of age required (on the average) fifty trials; and babies about 12 days old, only about four trials. However, this test is not a perfect measure of growth of kinesthesis, as other factors, such as recovery from the effects of birth, increase in muscular strength, and development of the sense of touch, would contribute to the greater success of the older infants. (Sherman, Sherman, and Flory[19])

Sensitivity to pain. Newborn infants definitely respond to pain, although they are not so sensitive as at a later age.

> In one series of observations (Sherman and Sherman[20]), the legs and faces of a group of infants were stimulated by needle pricks. It was found that no infant at birth responded to single pricks. However, when the stimulus was applied a number of times to get a summation or additive effect, all the babies, even those under five hours of age, responded to stimulation on the face. The experimenters, of course, were careful to discontinue their stimulation as soon as it was clear that the response to pain was present, i.e., when the babies struggled or cried.
>
> Although the newborn child is relatively insensitive to painful stimuli, his sensitivity increases rapidly during the first few days of life. In babies ranging from half an hour old to 5.5 hours old, an average of 6.5 needle jabs in the head area were required to produce an avoidance response. At 35.5 to 40.5 hours only 1.7 such stimulations were required to produce a response. After 41 hours only one stimulation was sufficient.

Although the neonate is less sensitive to pain than is the older child or the adult, investigators are agreed that some pain sensitivity does exist. This fact is useful in the early detection of some forms of idiocy or extremely low intelligence which are characterized by almost complete insensitivity to pain.

Sensitivity to other stimuli in the skin is present from birth. The newborn infant does respond to variations in the temperature of his milk, for the frequency of sucking reactions decreases as the temperature varies above or below normal (Jensen[21]). Also, as we have seen, stroking the sole of the foot will cause toe movements. These and many similar reflexes show that numerous receptors in the skin are sensitive in infants only a few hours old.

So far in our discussion of the newborn child, we have been concerned with his *ability to receive stimuli*. But it is impossible, as we have seen, to separate the stimulus side from the response side in describing the infant's behavior. Response is the criterion of sensitivity, and sensitivity to stimulation is required in the arousing and guidance of a response. We will look now at the response side of the infant's behavior, at *what he does* when he receives stimuli—that is, what adjustive equipment he has to meet his needs.

The feeding responses enable the neonate to orient his head toward the nipple and to make the other movements necessary to ingesting milk. As long ago as 1667, Samuel Pepys noted in his *Diary*, so familiar to the student of English literature, that a touch on a waking infant's cheek will cause his head to turn as his mouth opens to grasp the finger. This early observation has been verified and expanded by a series of later investigators, one of whom concludes:

> "At birth the mouth is superior to the hand in what might be called directed activity and definiteness of function. Upon proper stimulation the mouth can both open and close and with the aid of head and neck movements institute a strenuous search for the stimulating object."
> (Halverson[22])

Once the head has become oriented to the nipple, sucking and swallowing are the remaining feeding movements of importance. The sucking movements, present at birth, increase greatly in strength during the period right after birth. They are elicited by touching the lips. Swallowing movements are present at birth and appear to be stimulated by the presence of liquid in the mouth.

Sucking in the human infant affords an excellent example of how the human organism does one main thing at a time. When sucking starts, other activity decreases (Jensen[23]), and when sucking, the infant requires three times as strong an electrical stimulation to produce crying as he does at other times (Wolowik[24]). The biological value of this natural ability to concentrate on feeding should be obvious.

Defense reflexes. The human being at birth has many *reflexes*—that is, simple, automatic ways by which he responds to stimuli. These occur in the absence of opportunity to learn and serve to protect the individual against too much of the wrong kind of stimulation. Noteworthy examples are closing the eyelids in response to intense light (which might injure the retina); spitting out unpleasant-tasting substances; jerking free the hands and limbs when they are restrained; and withdrawing a member of the body which has been painfully stimulated.

The grasping reflex. The strength of the grasping reflex of the neonate has never failed to impress the adult observer. There are two overlapping phases in the development of grasping in the neonate (Halverson[25]). The first is closure of the hand in response to light pressure of the palm. The second is gripping or clinging when the tendons of the fingers are pulled. The closure reflex, which is very strong at birth, disappears in sixteen to twenty-four weeks, but the gripping reflex remains longer. There is some evidence that the grasp of the left hand is slightly stronger than that of the right, while right hand shows greater motility.

Locomotor movements. The newborn baby is powerless to move from place to place but is capable of creeping movements elicited by pressure on the soles of the feet. In response to this stimulation, the baby, placed in a prone position, thrusts out one or both feet, followed by pushing movements of the arms which tend to raise the body from the ground. At the same time the body bends at the waist from side to side alternately. These movements may be aroused during the first four months of life but disappear later (Peiper[26]). They have no relation to the walking movements which are learned later, except perhaps that any movement serves to exercise and strengthen muscles.

Speech responses. Even during the first half year of his life, the infant makes many prelinguistic speech sounds. Among these are *m, n, g, h, w, r, y, o, oo, a.*

Notice that the infant does not make the consonant sounds *z* as in *buzz, s* as in *hiss, p* as in *top, t* as in *tom,* and *b* as in *ball.* Why is this? Try making these sounds yourself. What is the difference between the *n* as in *nga* and the *s* as in *hiss?* Remember that the baby's mouth differs from yours in having no teeth and in having weaker lip muscles. This list of primitive sounds will become longer when the teeth have appeared to make possible the *fricatives,* such as *z* and *s,* and when the muscles have become strong enough to supply the tension needed for the *explosives,* such as *b* and *p.*

Infants the world over make these same simple sounds, yet as adults they all speak very different languages. Obviously, it is learning that makes the difference. The child learns to associate certain combinations of sounds that his mother makes with certain objects around him—for instance, the sound of "Dad-dy" becomes associated in his mind with the father because it is made every time he appears. Then through trial and error the child learns to make the same combinations of sounds his mother does. Thus through learning, some primitive sounds of the prelinguistic period are organized into the conventional language of the particular society in which the individual lives, while other sounds produced in infancy are dropped.

It is not only the speech responses of the newborn child, however, which are organized by learning in the environment. From the time the child enters the physical and social environment of the world outside his mother's womb, all the innate responses we have just studied are modified and organized until they form part of the complex body of learned reactions found in the mature adult.

The newborn child can learn. That the human infant can learn even during the first ten days of life has been strongly suggested by certain conditioning experiments. The ability of human infants to learn during the first days and weeks of life has been studied by a number of workers. Although they have not demonstrated conclusively that human infants can learn permanently during the first few days after birth, there is no doubt that stable new adaptive responses to feeding do appear by the end of the first postnatal month of life. Another study (Wenger[27]) came to the conclusion that conditioning is possible during the first few postnatal days. However, such modification of behavior is unstable and transitory, perhaps because newborn babies spend a great deal of time in sleep or stupor and hence are not reactive.

Another experimenter (Kantrow[28]) established stable conditioned sucking responses in a group of human infants ranging in age from 44 to 117 days. Her results were much more clear-cut than were those with the younger infants in the study above.

This work indicates that infants are capable of learning under certain conditions and that learning can be a potent factor in changing the behavior of human infants.

All these studies of the newborn baby have shown that he is already engaging in adjustive reactions to his physical world. Energies and forces, such as light, sound, and pressures, are not passively endured by even so young a creature. The baby does something about the stimuli which act upon him: he cries and grasps and makes defense movements and sucks and moves about vigorously. Of course such responses are highly inadequate by adult standards, but, although he has much to learn and has far to develop physically, the newborn baby is beginning to interact with his environment.

MATURATION AFTER BIRTH

MUCH OF THE INFANT's difficulty in adjusting to his environment is due not only to his lack of learning but also to the immaturity of his muscles, nervous system, and glands. You remember that underlying every behavior pattern is a pattern of connections between the receiving mechanisms and the responding mechanism. Not only do the child's receptors become more sensitive as he grows older, but there are changes in another two of his important mechanisms: the nervous system and the ductless glands. Moreover, his muscles become stronger and more able to respond. This section will discuss, in turn, *Maturation of Muscles, Maturation in the Nervous System,* and *Maturation in the Ductless-Gland System.*

Maturation of muscles

Often the failure of an organism to show some pattern of behavior can be explained by its lack of sufficient muscle maturity. With maturity comes strength, and strength is essential to the performance of certain response patterns. The three-day-old human infant cannot walk because his muscles are too weak to support the weight of his body. However, he can execute pretty fair walking movements if the weight of his body is supported by some outside agency.

The increased strength of muscles as the organism grows is a result of the increase in size which maturation brings. It should not be thought, however, that maturation is the only factor determining muscle strength; exercise is necessary to develop the cells to their fullest size and strength. Careful experiments have shown that activity strengthens a muscle through increasing only the *size*—not the *number*—of muscle cells (Morpurgo[29]). At birth, the infant possesses his full quota of muscle cells; after birth, they can only become larger.

Maturation in the nervous system

The nervous system is made up of billions of tiny cells which connect with receptors, effectors, or other nerve cells. After the child is born, two important changes occur in his nervous system: (1) There is an increase in the size of his brain. (2) There is an increase in the complexity of the neural patterns which connect his receiving mechanisms and his responding mechanisms.

Increased brain size. Just as an increase in the size of a muscle gives a rough indication of an increase in its strength, so does an increase in the size of the brain give us an even rougher indication of its increased capacity to function. Take, for example, the cerebellum, which is the part of the brain which controls the coordination of movements necessary for balance in sitting, walking, and manipulation. At about the fifth month after birth the cerebellum starts to grow very rapidly in relation to the other parts of the brain, and it continues to grow rapidly until the child is about eighteen months old. During this period the infant sits up, crawls, and walks—functions which depend heavily upon coordination, and thus upon the cerebellum.

More complex neural patterns. The full number of nerve cells is present in the human infant at birth, but age brings, through the growth of new branches, an increase in the possibilities for neural connections. Whether these branches will be used depends upon what happens to the individual. Age brings an increase in the richness of potential connections; opportunity determines the extent to which they will be used.

Maturation in the ductless-gland system

The third great system of structures influencing the development of behavior is the system of ductless glands, or endocrine glands, as they are often called. You will remember that these are glands which secrete certain chemical substances, called *hormones*, directly into the blood stream. The hormones have important effects on bodily development. For example, the change of voice at adolescence is due to the functioning of a hormone from the male sex glands.

The endocrine system is composed of glands whose development is controlled to a large extent by heredity. Responses of the endocrine glands can, however, be changed through learning (emotional conditioning), a fact which has much significance for the understanding of how emotional behavior grows.

Endocrinology is an extremely complicated subject, and the experts are not in complete agreement as to the number of endocrine glands. However, the following glands have now been widely recognized: the *pituitary*, the *thyroids*, the *parathyroids*, the *adrenals*, the *thymus*, the *pineal*, the *testes*, the *ovaries*.

So far, scientists have discovered the functions of these glands mainly by observing what happens when these functions fail: that is, by studying diseased persons. From such study, however, can come knowledge of the positive roles that the endocrine glands play in normal adjustment. (They play a very important role in growth and maintenance also, but this is not the psychologist's main concern.)

The pituitary. Attached to the underside of the brain and lying right in the center of the head is a small structure known as the pituitary body. It secretes many different hormones, some of great importance to body maintenance. Here we shall be concerned with two important effects it has on man's adjustment:

1 It secretes a hormone which promotes bodily growth.

2 It secretes several "middle man" hormones which activate other ductless glands: the sex glands, the adrenal glands, and the mammary glands.

The growth hormone. Proper functioning of the pituitary is very important to normal growth. This fact is clearly shown by the abnormal conditions resulting from different kinds of malfunctioning, including dwarfism, giantism, and acromegaly.

An early deficiency of the pituitary growth-hormone in the blood stream causes *dwarfism,* the underdevelopment of the bones of the body which results in an adult midget. Excess secretion early in life produces *giantism.* During the period of oversecretion, a person can reach the height of as much as nine feet. Then secretion declines, usually leaving the individual strong in appearance but in reality much weaker in muscles and in sexual drive than the average man. When early treatment has been neglected, about the only thing such a giant can do is to place himself on exhibit at a circus side show or in a medical museum. Fortunately, modern surgery can remove some of the excess glandular substance, thus preventing giantism.

Like giantism, *acromegaly* results from an oversecretion of the growth hormone in the pituitary gland. But unlike giantism, it results from oversecretion starting in later life. And while giantism is an overgrowth of the whole body, acromegaly is an overgrowth of only certain portions of the skeleton. It may cause enlarged hands, arms lengthened until the fingers reach knee level, heavy jawbone, greatly expanded chest, and bent back; a person suffering from acromegaly suggests the unscientific but descriptive term "gorilla man." Acromegaly is often accompanied by various symptoms of mental disease or, at least, of inadequate personality. These arise in part from an inescapable consciousness of deformity and consequent feelings of inferiority, and in part from the direct effects that pituitary unbalance has on the nervous system and on the sex glands.

The "middle man" hormones. One whole group of secretions of the pituitary acts directly on other ductless glands and so might be called the "middle men" of the endocrine system. These hormones affect the functioning of the thyroids, the adrenals, and the sex glands, which will be described a little later in this section. One of them also controls a number of organs and behavior patterns related to motherhood. It has been called the "mother-love" hormone because in animals it brings about an increase in the activities of maternal love.

> In one experiment, normal young female rats made little maternal response to baby rats and nest-building materials placed in their cages. But when they received a few doses of this hormone, dramatic changes occurred: their mammary glands swelled and produced milk; they built nests and adopted not only baby rats but the young of other species.

The role of this hormone in the emotions and behavior of the human female has not been directly investigated.

Some popular writers have certainly overemphasized the importance of the pituitary as the kingpin of personality and temperament. Further research is needed to discover how the functioning of the pituitary affects the development and fluctuations of normal personality.

The thyroids. The thyroid glands are located in the neck at either side of the "Adam's apple." They produce hormones which have many complex effects on (1) the development of intelligence; (2) the rate at which the body functions; (3) sexual and physical development; and (4) emotional condition.

Inadequate thyroid secretion during childhood causes delay in physical development and the attainment of sexual maturity. In later life, insufficient thyroid secretion makes some people become fat and sleepy; others become depressed in mood, dissatisfied with life, and suspicious and distrustful of their associates. People with too much thyroid secretion typically become irritable and thin, perspire freely, and frequently have trouble sleeping.

The parathyroids. The parathyroid glands are two or more pairs of small bodies located in or near the thyroids. Their hormone mainly regulates the amount of calcium in the blood, and has a quieting influence on the body; their removal causes convulsions and death.

The adrenal glands. The two adrenal glands are located near the kidneys. Each consists of two parts: an inner core, the *medulla;* and an outer layer, the *cortex.* There is no known physiological relationship between these two parts, so that they are really like two separate glands.

The medulla regulates bodily changes during emotion. During such emotions as fear there is a secretion from the medulla called *adrenin,* which brings about vast bodily changes, such as in blood flow, pulse, and stomach activity.

The cortex regulates general body activity and masculinity. *Over-activity* of the cortex produces both heightened body activity and an accentuation of masculine physical and behavior traits, such as growth of beard and masculine sex interests. This condition, known as virilism, may occur in people of either sex, although it is of course more easily recognized in women. The "bearded lady" of the circus is either a fake or the victim of a too-active adrenal cortex.

With *underactivity* of the cortex, blood pressure falls and the individual loses sex interest, becomes weak and flabby, feels tired, shows lack of psychological control, and dies prematurely. These later effects have long been known to medicine through observation of cases in which the adrenal cortex is destroyed (known as Addison's disease).

Thymus. The thymus gland is located in the chest and, like the pineal gland described below, is little understood. Since it is large in infancy and childhood and tends to atrophy or disappear after puberty, it is thought to hold back sexual development during childhood. Further support for this theory is the fact that when thymus-gland substance is fed to tadpoles, the normal change from tadpole to sexually mature frog is retarded.

The pineal gland. The pineal gland is attached to the underside of the brain, above and behind the pituitary. Its functions are obscure at the present time, and its study has been more or less neglected. It is definitely known, however, that its functioning is related to sexual functioning. Fragmentary knowledge indicates that it has some control over maternal activity in the female, and that it (like the thymus) holds back sexual development in the male.

The testes. From the very beginning of recorded history and literature, the testes of the male have been regarded as the source of virility. In many cultures the practice of castration, or surgical removal of the testes, has been known from earliest times. The eunuch thus produced in early childhood has been valued both as a singer, because he retains the high voice of childhood, and also as a guardian of harems, because he fails to develop sexual interest and capacity.

There is some evidence that the male sex hormones, the *androgens,* produced by the testes, are present even before puberty, when sexual development is normally accelerated. But whether or not the male hormones are active before puberty, it is definitely known that at puberty they are the vital factors in sexual development. Dramatic evidence of their importance is provided by males in whom they are lacking; at the normal period of puberty these males do not develop the characteristics of the adult male.

The personality as well as the body is profoundly influenced by the hormones produced by the testes. Castrated males develop into timid persons, lacking initiative and enterprise, disinterested in romantic love, and lacking in sexual appetite, although their intelligence does not seem to be affected adversely. These symptoms can be dissipated by the artificial administration of male sex hormones.

The ovaries. It has long been recognized that the secretions of the female sex glands, the ovaries, are essential to sexual development. When the human female suffers loss of the ovaries in childhood, the usual adolescent changes fail to occur. These ill effects can be counteracted by administering female endocrine substances, one type (the *estrogens*) controlling menstruation and the other (*progestin*) controlling changes in the uterus. These hormones have complex effects on the psychological life of women (see pp. 136-139).

While endocrinology is a relatively new science, it has discovered some of the vital effects that the ductless glands have on physical and sexual development and on mental outlook (see p. 109). Unfortunately, the role of the hormones in the development of the normal person has yet to be charted with any exactitude. For example, knowledge of how the endocrine glands interact with each other and with various organs of the body will require decades of patient research.

HOW MATURATION AND LEARNING INTERACT

For years there has raged a long, futile controversy over the question of whether human beings have inherited "instincts" which govern their thought, feeling, and behavior. Gallons of printer's ink have been spilled as psychologists, educators, and philosophers have lined themselves up into the "yes" camp and the "no" camp. The "yes" camp has drawn up lists of dozens of human "instincts" ranging from the "maternal" to the "cleanliness" to the "war" instinct. The "no" camp denies the validity of the whole concept.

These so-called "instincts" will be discussed more fully in the next chapter. For the present, suffice it to say that as in most controversies, the root of the difficulty lies in the failure to define terms. In fact, for a long time psychologists were unwilling to employ the term "instinct" because of the general lack of agreement as to just what it meant. More

The ductless-gland system

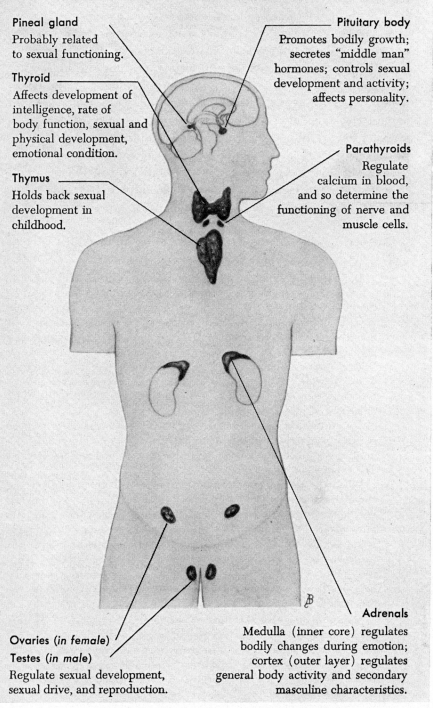

Pineal gland
Probably related to sexual functioning.

Thyroid
Affects development of intelligence, rate of body function, sexual and physical development, emotional condition.

Thymus
Holds back sexual development in childhood.

Pituitary body
Promotes bodily growth; secretes "middle man" hormones; controls sexual development and activity; affects personality.

Parathyroids
Regulate calcium in blood, and so determine the functioning of nerve and muscle cells.

Ovaries (*in female*)
Testes (*in male*)
Regulate sexual development, sexual drive, and reproduction.

Adrenals
Medulla (inner core) regulates bodily changes during emotion; cortex (outer layer) regulates general body activity and secondary masculine characteristics.

recently, however, psychologists are becoming more willing to use the term—with the following understanding as to its meaning:

An *instinct* is a relatively complex behavior pattern which has been produced, at least primarily, by maturation rather than by learning. Sometimes such instincts do not appear in a full-fledged manner when the opportunity first is presented for them, because (1) the bodily organs required for such activities are not sufficiently mature (as the nerve connections in tadpoles for swimming, or the wing-muscles of birds for flying); or because (2) certain glandular conditions have not yet developed (as in the mating responses of rats or the setting responses of hens). In such cases, since the body has had abundant time to mature, the instinctive behavior is often displayed in surprisingly elaborate and complete fashion upon the first occasion when it is possible.

Our best demonstrations of "instincts" come from studies of how animal behavior develops.

> *Maturation in tadpoles.* In one experiment, frog eggs were placed in a solution of chloretone, an anesthetic which stops all responses to stimuli but does not interfere with normal growth. These animals could develop through maturation but not through learning, since stimulation is essential to learning. They were in effect developing in a psychological vacuum.
>
> Tadpoles in a control group were kept under the same conditions of temperature and light as the experimental group but were allowed to swim freely in pure water. Thus they were exposed to the joint influences of maturation and stimulation.
>
> The problem is this: In tadpoles, do the behavior patterns involved in swimming arise through maturation alone? Are they innate? Or must some practice occur to bring them to a point of perfection? The experiment gave the answer.
>
> When the normal animals—those exposed to both maturation and stimulation—had reached the stage of free swimming, the experimental individuals were lifted from their anesthetic solution and placed in pure water. The interesting thing was that the experimental tadpoles swam just as well as the normal ones (when accurate allowance was made for the time required to "thaw out" from the anesthetic). Thus the ability of tadpoles to make swimming movements is one that develops through maturation in the absence of learning prior to the test period. (Carmichael[30])
>
> *Maturation in rats.* The second experiment studied still another behavior pattern which is not functional at birth but matures later in the absence of opportunity to learn. Male rats were reared in isolation until the age of sexual maturity. Until the day they were to be tested for the presence of instinctive sexual behavior, they had never seen another animal. At the age at which normal rats have reached

full sexual maturity as indicated by their engaging in mating behavior, the males reared in isolation were placed in cages with sexually receptive females which had had previous sexual experience. Almost immediately the isolated males engaged the females in typical mating behavior. The observer did not notice any important differences between the behavior of the normal and isolated rats. (Stone[31])

These experiments have made striking verifications of the fact that *in animals, maturation can cause behavior patterns to emerge in practically complete utility with very little previous stimulation or learning.* These behavior patterns may truly be called "instincts." *In man, instinctive behavior is very rare.* In man, maturation and learning interact—that is, both capacity and practice are important in performance.

Capacity, practice, and performance

Although the concept of instinct as an all-or-none pattern of behavior is useful in the study of animals, it is not particularly valuable in explaining and describing human behavior and motivation. In man, as we have just seen, behavior determined solely by maturation is extremely rare.

But while psychologists find that maturation is never entirely responsible for human performance, they know that it plays a very important role. Therefore they replace the concept of an all-powerful "instinct" with the fundamental concept of innate *capacity* or readiness for any skill or ability, as determined by the degree of maturation.

There is a definite relationship between innate capacity to learn (degree of maturation), practice, and performance. For one thing, capacity can be measured only through performance. Moreover, the status of maturation in any skill determines and limits capacity to learn from the environment and apply past learning to new problems. One fundamental principle of maturation is that *performance in man is the product both of innate capacity and of practice (learning).* Without practice the individual cannot perform; and without innate capacity the individual cannot perform.

The relative importance that capacity and practice have in determining an individual's performance is contingent upon the nature of the task. Some tasks depend heavily on innate capacity; others depend heavily on learning. For instance, the ability of a small child to play baseball is determined to a considerable degree by maturation. However, the skills involved in writing a philosophical treatise are probably acquired largely by learning. Skills in reading, writing, formulating values, and complex reasoning are mainly a product of training. Remember, though, that neither maturation nor learning is all-important in any of the more complex human activities.

Psychological experiments have isolated the developing child from certain parts of the environment, the parts which teach special skills. These experiments prove the validity of the concept of maturation as

—Learning and maturation

An interesting experiment has been conducted to determine the relative influence of practice and maturation in the motor skill of ladder-climbing. The subjects were children 24 to 36 months old, and were divided into two comparable groups: the *practice group* and the *isolated group.* The procedure was as follows:

THE PRACTICE GROUP

The practice group was allowed to climb a 2½-foot ladder to a table of interesting toys which were varied so that their novelty was an incentive for climbing the ladder. Then

. . . for twelve weeks the practice group was allowed to practice climbing the ladder, with toys frequently changed to maintain interest. And

. . . at the end of the twelfth week, it had acquired considerable ease and skill of performance.

a factor which combines with learning to increase the complexity of human behavior. One of these studies is described and illustrated below, and clearly demonstrates an important principle of maturation which is essentially derived from the fact that performance is the product of both innate capacity and practice.

THE ISOLATED GROUP

The isolated group was kept away from any opportunity to learn to climb a ladder, but did, of course, practice other habits (such as walking) which have something in common with ladder-climbing in that they involve muscular strength and coordination. Then

... at the end of twelve weeks the isolated group was given a table full of toys which could be reached by climbing a 2½-foot ladder, under the same conditions as governed the practice group. The result was that after thirteen weeks ...

... both groups were identical in ladder-climbing skill. The isolated group had caught up with the practice group because *at a later stage of maturation less practice is required to achieve a given level of performance.*

(J. R. Hilgard, "Learning and Maturation in Preschool Children," *Journal of Genetic Psychology*, 1932, 41, 36-56.)

This principle may be stated thus: *At different stages of maturation, differing amounts of practice are required to achieve a given level of performance. The greater the maturity, the less practice needed.* Exactly how long the opportunity to learn can be withheld without producing a permanent loss in capacity to respond to training is unknown; it probably varies with the skill involved.

The method used in this experiment reveals the problem facing psychologists who want to investigate the relative roles that maturation and environment play in various human activities. The ideal is to hold one of these variables "constant" while investigating the effects of the other, but since human beings have no ways of behaving which are entirely dependent on either capacity alone or learning alone, it is difficult to separate the two factors. Moreover, they cannot treat a human being like a tadpole or a rat—that is, we cannot anesthetize him, or otherwise rear him in a psychological vacuum, in order to test the relative influences of maturation or environment on his behavior. But they can isolate him from certain learning opportunities in the environment and then examine him to see what influence maturation alone could have on his performance. This was the method used in the ladder-climbing experiment, and it can be used even in the case of language, which is a highly complex and socially significant type of behavior. And with language, maturation operates in the same way to permit different performances at different stages of maturity. In the following experiment, the influence of different rates of maturation on performance was controlled by using identical twins as subjects.

At the age of twenty months, identical twins—"T" and "C"—were completely isolated from the other and from the social group. Twin T was given very intensive vocabulary training for a period of five weeks. This training consisted in showing the child objects and getting her to name them. If she failed, she was corrected. To make certain that the child was actually reacting to the objects themselves, she was given directions to pick up certain ones named by the teacher.

Twin C was treated quite differently during this period. She was carefully isolated from any opportunity to acquire language. Words were not spoken in her presence. The persons who took care of her were careful not to speak even to one another in her presence. For a period of five weeks this child was completely isolated from all language influences.

At the end of the five-week period the isolated Twin C was given four weeks of the same type of training that Twin T had received earlier. It was found that Twin C, who was by now, of course, more mature than her mate had been at the start of her training, profited more quickly from the same kind of practice. Twin C, in fact, began to acquire new words earlier in the training period, and she had on each corresponding day of her training period a vocabulary greater than her twin's had been. Her training was discontinued one week sooner, after four instead of five weeks. On her last or twenty-eighth day, Twin C's vocabulary was greater by seven words than Twin T's had been on the twenty-eighth day of her training, and it was almost as great as her twin's had been after thirty-five days' training. The results of the experiment indicate that although training can speed the growth of learning, it cannot transcend the limits imposed by the stage of maturation the individual has attained. (Strayer[32])

Further proof of this principle is an observation on Hopi children, which indicates that learning is only a small factor in determining the age at which walking begins.

The Hopi Indians have a custom of placing their infants in a device which restrains movement. Since some mothers do not follow this tribal custom, it is possible to find groups of babies that have not been restrained. If learning were the big factor in determining the age at which walking begins, the unrestrained group should walk earlier than the restrained, who have had much less practice. However, careful observations show that both groups begin to walk at the same time. (Dennis and Dennis[33])

While it is true that greater maturity *usually* means better performance in any skill, there is a "golden age" when each skill can most easily be developed. One experiment in behavior development, extending over several years, was concerned with this very problem of whether certain skills can best be developed at certain ages (McGraw[34]).

This experiment was an intensive study of nonidentical twin boys, Johnny and Jimmy, who from their third week of life were subjected to enormously different training in athletic skills. Johnny, physically inferior to Jimmy at birth, was stimulated and helped in physical exercise of all kinds, and was encouraged to be self-reliant in overcoming obstacles. Jimmy, however, played unhindered, with no special training either in motor skills or in self-reliance. Periodically they were compared with each other and with a group of normal children serving as controls.

These observations showed that maturational readiness was constantly interworking with the effects of practice. For instance, it is interesting to note that *both* the twins took a few steps alone when nine months old, although Johnny had had practice in stepping movements from twenty days. Also, while Johnny could roller-skate and swim successfully by the time he was sixteen months old, it was not until he reached nineteen months that his intensive training in tricycling suddenly produced marked progress. Evidently, his nervous system was mature for roller-skating earlier than it was for tricycling.

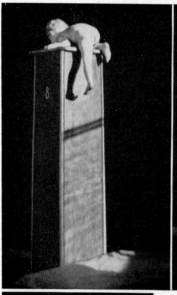

A striking difference between the experimental twins, Johnny and Jimmy, was obvious in their behavior in jumping and climbing off stools. Johnny had begun to receive daily exercise in turning off these stools when he was nine months old, and by the time he was sixteen months old was fearless and happy in the activity—above, at 21 months, he drops easily off a 63½-inch stool. Jimmy, on the other hand, received no special training in the activity and was very fearful of it—he would clutch the edge of the stool, cry, and refuse to jump off, as in the photograph at left. Interestingly enough, Jimmy was afraid of stools only 7½ inches high, so that in analyzing his poor performance it is not easy to separate the relative roles of physical maturation, athletic training, and emotional conditioning. (Photographs from *Myrtle B. McGraw*, Growth: A Study of Johnny and Jimmy, *D. Appleton-Century Co., Inc., 1935*)

By the time the twins were twenty-two months old, Johnny was very proficient in such skills as roller-skating, swimming, and tricycling. Of course, these were feats which Jimmy, who had no special training, and who lacked his brother's courage and initiative, would not even attempt. Then when the boys were twenty-two months old, Jimmy was given two and a half months of intensive practice in the same activities that Johnny had been trained in. Here again the importance of maturational readiness was evident. For in some activities, such as tricycling, Jimmy accomplished an easy performance in a shorter time than Johnny had taken at an earlier age, when his neuro-muscular mechanisms were not mature for that particular activity. But in roller-skating, Jimmy definitely was the poorer, evidently because he was at a later stage of development, when his attention could be more easily distracted. And in general, the practiced Johnny was consistently superior to Jimmy in courage and muscular coordination. Evidently those first twenty-two months of practice had been at an advantageous stage of development.

When the twins were about two years old, the training was stopped and they were returned to their home. Since then, they have been examined in these same performances at intervals varying from six weeks to two months. When they were six years old, their behavior development was reported in a systematic follow-up study (McGraw[35]). As far as is known, they have had little or no practice in either tricycling or skating since their early training in the laboratory. Yet these two skills seem to have deteriorated at different rates. Both boys showed deterioration in roller-skating, in which their greater height was a handicap, and neither showed deterioration in tricycling, in which bodily changes are apparently not so important a factor. This is further evidence that motor skill is definitely influenced by the stage of bodily development.

Since Johnny is still superior to Jimmy in physical courage and skill, this study seems to indicate that the first two years are a very rewarding time to encourage children in athletic feats, although different skills have different stages when they can most easily be developed. Jimmy's greater maturity never enabled him to catch up to Johnny all the way, and in fact was a definite handicap in some skills, such as roller-skating.

This experiment suggests that *for any given activity in life, there are certain "critical periods" when the individual is most susceptible to benefit from practice.*

Individual capacity for learning

The whole question of the relation between innate capacity and learning is of great social importance. It is a central problem facing educators and employers who must decide on which individuals are likely to improve most with instruction and training. For if training helps reduce the differences in performance due to differences in innate capacity, then it is reasonable to expect that, with training, the person of mediocre capacity can catch up with the person of greater capacity.

Actually, the evidence shows that the same amount of training only increases the difference between performances of people of different capacity. That is, if *A* has greater capacity and greater skill than *B*, and both are given the same additional training, *A*'s skill will come to surpass *B*'s by an even greater margin. *For every individual, there is a limit set by maturation to the degree of perfection he can attain by practice in any given activity.* Thus it is extremely important that, when learning opportunities are scarce, they be given to the persons of greatest initial capacity, who are best able to profit by them.

In a large group of individuals of the same chronological age, some will be more mature than others. Suppose each one is given the same motivation to practice some standardized task until the point where practice brings no further improvement—that is, the point where each individual has done the best he can. This point will be at a high degree of skill for the more mature, and at a low degree of skill for the less mature. The subjects have arranged themselves in a certain order of ability which further practice will not change materially (Wells[36]).

However, it is very important to remember that *the difference between the performances of individuals, given equal practice, is greatest in skills which are mainly a matter of inherited underlying capacity.* When the differences are due mainly to environmental training, they are usually reduced under conditions of equal practice.

For example, boys are usually better than girls in taking apart or putting together mechanical gadgets, not because their innate mechanical ability is any greater but because from toddler age they are encouraged to play with trucks and tinker-toys rather than with dolls and tea sets. Given a little practice, the average girl becomes as good as the average boy at this type of performance. (In fact, so far as is known, the differences between the sexes in performing most skills are due much more to differences in the opportunity to learn than to differences in innate capacity.)

Although everyone's maturational status is limited, psychologists have discovered many times that few people reach the very peak of performance within the limitations of their maturational status. Most human beings are content to come to rest at some point below their maximum potential performance. Exceptions will be found in outstanding musicians and athletic champions, who not only have great innate capacity for their particular skills but have devoted enormous periods of practice to developing that capacity to the fullest. For the less outstanding person, the lesson is that although he may have limited ability, he probably has not developed it as far as he can.

Greater capacity makes for faster progress. Another principle useful in guiding educational policy is that the person of higher maturational status reaches a particular point of mastery or skill with less practice than does the one of lower maturational status. Moreover, he continues to improve in performance longer in point of time. In other words, *practice only seems to increase the differences in performance between individuals of different maturational status.*

> College students participated in one extensive experiment designed to test this principle. Two hundred and fifty of them were divided into four groups, each performing a different task related to reading skill. When each group began to practice its particular task, there were naturally some individuals who made a better performance than others—partly because of differences in prior opportunity to learn, and partly because of differences in maturational status. The interesting thing was that the more practice each group had, the greater grew the differences among the performances of its members. That is, the superior students improved at a much faster rate than the poorer students. (Anastasi[37])

Differences in ability to improve are found not only in designed experiments but all through life, for it is always true that individuals do not mature at the same rate. Indeed, it is a matter of common observation that children who are superior to the average at one age will as time goes on increase their margin of superiority over average children of their own age. Backward children, on the other hand, develop at a slower rate and so drop further and further behind.

What about the way people's performances vary with their age? Here a general statement can be made to the effect that *maturation follows an upward course from conception to some point which we can call the "prime of life," and then declines.* The exact age at which maximum development is attained depends upon the nature of the behavior under consideration. Simple performances attain their maximum early in life; complex ones grow more slowly. A young child walks about as well as he ever will, but his ability to talk (as measured by the size of his vocabulary) increases fairly steadily until middle age. Many other skills which are complex and improved by practice seem to improve up until the "prime of life" in the early twenties. But beyond the point of prime, increases in age seem to bring losses in ability to improve with practice: that is, in ability to learn. These losses in learning ability are not important between the ages of twenty and forty-five or fifty years, but as the individual enters old age, learning becomes more difficult. The age cycle in learning ability will come up again in Chapter 10 on *Learning: Its Basic Nature.*

The status of learning ability at any particular time depends not only upon the person's age but also upon what is to be learned. *Pres-*

ent indications are that a person does not have the same innate capacity (*maturational status*) for all skills. The details of this complex and interesting problem must be saved for discussion in Chapter 15 on *Individual Differences and Their Measurement*.

For the present, then, experimental evidence has established some fundamental principles of how practice and innate capacity interact to produce performance—principles that help us understand why individuals differ in skills and accomplishments.

1 Through maturation, behavior patterns in the lower animals can emerge in practically complete utility with very little previous stimulation or learning from the environment. In man, however, such innate behavior or "instinct" is very rare.

2 Performance in man is the product both of innate capacity (maturation) and of practice (learning).

3 At different stages of maturation, differing amounts of practice are required to achieve a given level of performance. The greater the maturity, the less practice needed.

4 For any given activity in life, there are certain "critical stages" of maturation when the individual is most susceptible to benefit from practice.

5 For every individual, there is a limit set by maturation to the degree of perfection he can attain by practice in any given activity.

6 Practice only seems to increase the differences in performance between individuals of different maturational status.

We are saving until later chapters any full discussion of the principles that

7 Maturation follows an upward course from conception to some point which we can call the "prime of life," and then declines.

8 Present indications are that a person does not have the same innate capacity for all skills.

The kind and amount of learning an individual accomplishes will naturally depend not only upon his capacity but also upon the kind of environment he lives in. If his environment presents few new situations, very little learning will take place. Nor will much learning take place in an environment that fails to reward the individual when he makes an appropriate response to a new stimulus situation. From birth, individuals differ from one another not only in heredity but in the learning opportunities presented by their different environments.

The next chapter, on *Motivation*, will show you how the environment influences the learning of social behavior and moral values. All through life, the environment influences the total development of the individual as he makes a gradual change from a newborn infant, whose only responses to stimulation can be crying and ineffectual muscular movement, to a mature adult, whose reactions to his environment are as complex as we all know. One influence in this change is nature and the other is nurture.

CHAPTER 4

Motivation:
biological and social

Drives

Appetites and Aversions

How the Derived Motives Develop

O NE OF THE MOST IMPORTANT and fascinating fields of psychology is the study and description of the internal conditions—the underlying human motives—which influence people to behave as they do. Knowledge of human motivation is basic to our understanding of ourselves and others, and thus to better management of human relations, and will be our concern in this chapter.

When we do not know why someone behaves as he does today, we are not able to predict what he will do tomorrow, and so we will not have any successful way of dealing with him when tomorrow comes. When all we know about a person's behavior is the external stimulus situation, our description of his behavior cannot be complete, our prediction of his future behavior will be extremely inaccurate, and our attempts to influence him will be unsuccessful. To understand why a person behaves as he does in any particular situation, you must know what external situation he is in—but you must know more than that. You must also understand his internal situation, which plays an extremely important role in arousing and directing his behavior.

We are all familiar with the way in which the same external stimulus can produce several different responses because of differences in the accompanying internal situation. For instance, if your roommate asks you to go to the movies, you may turn him down if you are very tired or have a lot of studying to do, but you may agree enthusiastically if you are bored or are so hot that you want to escape into an air-conditioned theater. A psychologist would say you had different motives in the same stimulus situation. *Motives* are the internal conditions operating within a person to influence his reactions to external stimuli. Every activity is made possible by the internal conditions within the organism which direct it toward certain goals. A motive serves to direct behavior in two ways: (1) by causing one external stimulus pattern to win over competing ones; and (2) by causing the individual to seek external objects not present to the senses at the time.

For example, an adult experiencing strong hunger crosses the street to enter a familiar restaurant known to serve good food, although by so doing he has to sacrifice his desire to get in at the beginning of a movie he particularly wants to see. His motive in crossing the street is to obtain food which will relieve his hunger. It involves seeking a nonpresent object and suppressing reactions to competing stimuli. Any motivated act is complete when the goal is reached. The *goal* is some substance, object, or situation which is capable of banishing the persistent internal stimulations. (The goal is sometimes referred to as the "reward" or the "incentive.") Motives not only influence a person's behavior in a certain situation but also affect the way he perceives that situation, as is illustrated on page 124.

The motives or internal conditions which direct our responses to external stimuli may be divided into three groups: *biological drives, appetites and aversions,* and *derived motives* (usually social). What the derived motives are and how they operate is a matter of the greatest importance (and of the liveliest debate); but full understanding requires first an understanding of the biological drives and the appetites and aversions on which our derived motives rest.

DRIVES

Although the terms "drive" and "motive" are used interchangeably by some psychologists, others (including the writer) restrict the term *drive* to the motives based on bodily needs. The drives are observable from birth and are present even during fetal life, although normally at that time they are automatically satisfied by the mother's body.

How our motivations
influence what we see

*Four people in this railroad station could have this same scene
before them, and yet each one could see something different because
of his own special motivations. A stranger in the city would
quickly locate the Travelers' Aid. A woman seeing her husband
and child off on a trip would "have eyes only for them." A
person waiting for an incoming train would watch the announcement
board with great interest. And a little boy would, of course, be
fascinated by the big shiny train.*

It is interesting that the intensity with which drives are felt is
roughly proportionate to the length of time that man can stand to have
them thwarted. We can go several days without water and several
weeks without food; but we can go only a few minutes without
breathing and still live. And introspective evidence indicates that the

strength of the sensations aroused by the various drives at their height comes in just that order. Air hunger (as experienced in suffocation) is most intense; then comes thirst; then comes hunger.

The drives which have been recognized and studied include the needs for food (including a variety of specific substances), water, oxygen, rest, sleep, warmth when cold, cooling when hot, relief from pain, and relief from visceral tensions. We shall discuss each of these needs in turn.

The hunger drive

All the biological drives are of utmost importance in keeping people alive, well, and happy. Remarkably enough, however, they are by no means thoroughly understood, and investigation needs to be pushed forward if we are to have an ever-increasing understanding of the bases of human motivation. Of all the drives, the development of hunger has received most study and can well be considered first.

What is the stimulus in hunger? What makes people feel hungry? Elemental as this question may seem, this is still somewhat of a mystery. From our own introspections we assume that hunger consists of a mass of sensations coming from the stomach. As you will see, definite changes in the condition of the stomach do occur as time passes, and certain of these act as stimuli to produce the sensation of hunger which we feel and report. But is the stomach the only source of the sensations of hunger? Let us examine the evidence.

Understanding of the mechanism of hunger has been advanced through the combined efforts of psychologists and physiologists, who have performed various types of observations on the behavior of the empty stomach. They have definitely shown that stomach contractions set in when the stomach is empty, that is, when the person feels "hungry."

> One group of physiologists employ a very interesting device to study stomach behavior (Cannon[1] and Carlson[2]). A sack of thin rubber with a rubber tube, connected in such a way as to form an airtight system, is swallowed by the human or animal subject. The experimenter then adjusts the position of the sack by manipulating the rubber tube until the sack comes to a position at the upper end of the stomach. The sack is then inflated until it comes in contact with the walls of the stomach. The free end of the tube is connected with a recording device which makes a graphic record of any change of pressure in the stomach balloon. This apparatus is shown in the illustration following.
>
> Subjects are trained to swallow the balloon and sit comfortably for hours while continuous records of their stomach behavior are taken.

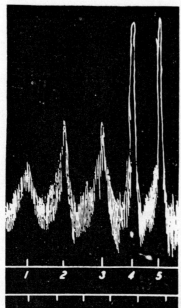

Dr. Anton J. Carlson, professor emeritus of physiology at the University of Chicago, demonstrates the famous stomach-balloon apparatus. (This picture was specially posed for Psychology and Life.*) As the empty stomach contracts, it presses in on the balloon, and makes the stylus (pen) move up and down on the revolving drum. The subject, who cannot see the record, presses a key to indicate when he is experiencing stomach contractions. This record covers a five-minute period. At point 1, mild hunger was reported; at 2 and 3, stronger hunger sensations; and at 4 and 5, sharp pangs. (Record from Anton J. Carlson and Victor Johnson,* The Machinery of the Body, *University of Chicago Press, 1941, p. 292.)*

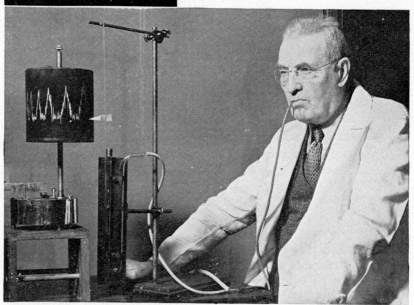

Two types of stomach behavior are distinguishable from the records: that which has to do with digestion; and that which occurs at the moment that acute hunger is introspectively reported. These latter movements, the hunger contractions, are the ones which are of interest to us in our study of the hunger drive.

Particular attention is given in the work of these physiologists to the origin and strength of stomach contractions in relation to the period of time which has elapsed since last eating. They found that the contractions do not occur immediately after eating, when only the regular churning movements of digestion are observed. But as the stomach empties, the hunger contractions set in. They appear about every hour and a half at first but come more frequently as time without food progresses. At first they are faint and do not always lead to conscious sensations, but they become stronger and stronger with the passing of time.

But this work does not tell all the story of the nature of the hunger drive. It leaves many things unexplained. Evidence that empty-stomach contractions are not the only source of the hunger drive is found in more recent experimental work.

One worker compared normal rats with rats from which the entire stomach had been removed. The startling thing was that the animals without stomachs showed hunger in practically the same way that the normal animals did. They learned a maze when food was the reward just as efficiently as did the normal controls; they were equally active as feeding time approached. The only difference was that the operated rats became hungry oftener, which is understandable since they had less food-storage capacity and hence had to stock up oftener. (Tsang[3])

Further evidence has been obtained in experiments on rats in which the nerves carrying sensory messages from the stomach to the brain had been severed. Rats surviving the surgical operation ate as frequently as the normal animals and were otherwise similar in the outward evidences of the hunger drive. (Bash[4] and Morgan and Morgan[5])

This evidence indicates clearly that stomach contractions are not necessary to the operation of the hunger drive. Two alternative hypotheses suggest themselves: (1) that the contractions are one source of the hunger drive but not a necessary one; and (2) that stomach contractions are merely a by-product of some basic condition in the physiological economy of the hungry organism and have no essential role in the hunger drive—although they are a useful sign or signal of hunger. This second hypothesis can never be tested, since it is impossible to design an experiment which would allow stomach contractions to operate in the absence of all other bodily conditions which might be the basis of the hunger drive: that is, to allow the stomach to contract while holding the rest of the body "constant."

Other findings suggest that the hunger drive is chemical in origin.

Blood transfused from the body of a starving dog to that of a recently fed one will cause stomach contractions (Luckhardt and Carlson[6]). Another worker (Tschukitschew[7]) has discovered that the effect on the recipient's stomach depends on whether or not the donor's stomach was active at the time, suggesting a stimulatory and depressant hormone.

These experiments will have to be carried much further before we can definitely say that hunger has a chemical basis. For the present, the study of the origin of the hunger drive is still in its beginning stages.

The wisdom of the body. Man and the lower animals have not one general food hunger but many specific hungers. Interestingly enough, they seem to satisfy these hungers in a nutritionally adequate way, as has been shown by several "cafeteria" experiments in which the subjects were allowed to choose whatever particular foods they wanted to satisfy their general hunger.

> A "cafeteria" situation was set up for three newly weaned babies eight to ten months of age. Two of the infants were allowed to select their foods for a period of six months; the third for a full year's time. An assortment of raw and plainly cooked foods was placed before the infants in dishes and glasses of standard sizes. The pattern of arrangement of the solid and liquid foods was haphazard and was changed from meal to meal. Each infant was permitted to eat with his fingers, and no attempt was made to teach manners during the course of the observations. Everything was left to the child to decide. The results show that the subjects made wise choices of food. They gained normally and showed no signs of nutritional disorders. Especially striking is the behavior of one child who had rickets at the beginning of the experiment. Rickets is a defective bone development which can be cured by a vitamin in cod-liver oil. This child showed a marked liking for cod-liver oil at the beginning of the experiment but gave it up when the rickets had disappeared. (Davis[8])

There would seem to be an inherent "wisdom of the body" which causes organisms to select from a group of foods, all of which are good for them, those foods which are best for them.

In these experiments the available foods were all harmless. How well can the human individual select only edible foods from a collection of both harmful and poisonous foods? This is a question which cannot be answered at present. Only further experimentation will supply us with the missing details. The fact that animals survive in regions where poisonous weeds grow proves that some form of bodily wisdom does protect the organism. At times, however, both animals and human beings eat injurious substances; evidently the wisdom of the body is not complete.

In man especially, still another fact must be recognized. His motives may be so much changed by learning that this innate "wisdom of the body," if it is present, is often overruled by his learned preferences. Thus the Japanese people have suffered extensively from the dietary disease of beriberi, even though this can be prevented very easily by eating unpolished rice or brown rice rather than polished rice. But since their tradition has stressed the idea that the polished or white rice is more fit for human food, this learning has governed their food choices. In our own country we have seen the same phenomenon in the preference for white bread rather than whole wheat bread, which contains some valuable food elements lost in the "refining" process. In some ways, then, learning from the social environment counteracts the "wisdom of the body."

Effects of the hunger drive. Psychologists have shown that hunger contractions directly increase both mental and physical activity.

In one experiment with human beings, the stomach-balloon apparatus was kept in place for long periods with continuous recording of periods of contraction and no contraction. At times when the subjects were having contractions and also at other times, they were asked to squeeze the hand dynamometer (which measures the strength of the grip), were given intelligence tests, and had their gross bodily movements measured. The results showed quite clearly that the human being can squeeze harder, gets a better score on a mental test, and is more active physically during periods of stomach contractions than during periods of quiescence.

The subjects also went to sleep with the apparatus in place. They were awakened at intervals—sometimes during the contractions, sometimes between—and asked if they had been dreaming. In general, the evidence indicated that more dreaming occurred during periods of contraction than during quiescence. This finding explains the efficacy of drinking warm milk or taking some food just before going to bed, to prevent dreaming and disturbed sleep. (Wada[9])

A somewhat similar series of experiments indicates that stomach contractions may increase the rate of learning.

White rats were taught to avoid an electric shock by jumping when a signal was given. They were not given food as a reward for jumping, but they were given an electric shock whenever they failed to jump. Rats were selected for this study because it is possible by means of a surgical operation to bring the rat's stomach outside the body wall, where its contractions can be readily observed by the experimenter. A record was made of the number of trials each rat took to jump at the signal. Then these learning records were compared for the two groups of rats: one learning during hunger contractions, and the other learning when no contractions were taking place. This comparison showed that the rats with contractions learned much faster than the rats without contractions. (Elliott and Treat[10])

From these experiments we can see that the presence of hunger contractions seems to facilitate learning even when there is no reward of food.

The thirst drive

Many interesting experiments have been performed to discover the essential condition giving rise to the thirst drive—to determine whether it derives from the dryness of the throat tissues or from other factors.

In one of these experiments eighteen rabbits were deprived of water for seven days. At the end of this period, twelve of these eighteen rabbits were injected with a drug which increases the flow of saliva and thus moistens the mouth and throat. Notice that the amount of water in the bodies of the twelve injected animals was not increased, so that they had no more water than the other six. But when water was offered, only two of the twelve injected animals drank, whereas the six control animals drank copious amounts. (Pack[11])

At first sight, these results would appear to support the idea—derived from people's introspective reports of how they feel when thirsty—that the thirst drive originates in dryness of the mouth and throat. More recent work, however, indicates that the story is not quite so simple—throat dryness is not the only factor in thirst.

1 One experiment may be discussed in two parts. The first part did support the idea that throat dryness does play some role in thirst. In this first part, the esophagus of dogs (the tube leading from mouth to stomach) was brought out to the surface of the body. Thus the water drunk by the animals could not reach the stomach or have other access to the tissues of the body. But in spite of the fact that the water was not moistening any part of their bodies besides the throat, these dogs did not drink any more eagerly than normal dogs. Reducing throat dryness seemed to relieve thirst.

However, the second part of the experiment indicated other factors in thirst besides throat dryness. Here water was placed directly into the stomach of the dog without passing through the throat and mouth. When the dogs were permitted to drink *immediately after* water was placed in the stomach, they drank as much as they would have if their stomachs had not been directly watered. That they still felt thirsty indicates that sheer weight of water in the stomach cannot be the sole determinant of thirst—if it were, the animals would not have drunk after their stomachs had been filled with water. However, there was a significant development: if the animals were not allowed to drink until *fifteen minutes after* water was placed in their stomachs, they did not drink at all. The experimenters suggest that the pituitary may have some effect on this delayed slackening of the thirst drive. However that may be, this whole second part of the experiment leaves little doubt that there are other factors in thirst besides dryness of the mouth and throat. (Bellows[12])

2 Another experiment pointing to this same conclusion has been made with dogs again used as subjects. It was noted that when the dogs were given a chance to drink, they would always drink an amount sufficient to make up the deficit of their water-supply. But since the

throat of the dog would be moistened immediately with the first swallows, the accurate adjustment of behavior to body needs could not be explained by the concept that thirst depends entirely on dryness of the throat. (Adolph[13])

Exactly what all the factors in thirst are—exactly how the lowered water level of the body sets up the thirst drive—still remains to be discovered. It is known, of course, that thirst very definitely does serve as a drive. Rats will learn a complicated maze when water awaits the successful run and can be obtained in no other way. Men in great thirst will go to extreme lengths to obtain water. In fact, the thirst drive is probably less intense only than air hunger and it ranks in importance with food hunger as one of the needs man must always make provision for.

Air hunger as a drive

One of the most basic needs of the human body is air. Yet the need for air is relatively unimportant as a motive in everyday life. This is simply because air is usually easy to get, and therefore air hunger is rarely experienced.

When, as in suffocation, the supply of oxygen is cut off, carbon dioxide increases in the blood stream. It is thought that air starvation becomes a drive to behavior through the action of carbon dioxide, which not only stimulates receptors in certain blood vessels but also acts directly on a nerve center in the central nervous system.

When oxygen starvation occurs in an atmosphere free from carbon dioxide—as at mountaintops or in high-altitude flying—a peculiar and often fatal sort of drunkenness or confusion comes on. The person loses control and may shout, fight, or burst into tears. Memory is impaired, the senses function poorly, and paralysis is common, especially of the legs. Yet the person feels confident of his abilities and fails to realize how serious his condition is. There is some evidence that partial oxygen starvation brings out certain basic emotional reactions usually held under voluntary control.

Fatigue as a drive

We all know how desperate the need for rest can become, yet the physiology of fatigue is so complex that very little is known about it. The chemistry of the blood is altered in several ways as the result of prolonged exercise, including an increase in the concentration of lactic acid in the muscles and blood. Presumably this condition stimulates the nervous system directly or activates certain receptors.

Tired people go to great lengths to obtain rest. Rest brings a readjustment of the body and a cessation of the persisting stimuli which cause consciousness of fatigue and efforts to rest.

Sleepiness as a drive

Sleep, like rest, is an important need of the body, but it too is still not very well understood. It is not known, for instance, what or how many sensory receptors (if any) are active when we feel sleepy and search for a place to sleep.

Certain drugs, such as chloroform and ether, produce a relaxed condition resembling sleep and suggest that its basis may be chemical. While not much is known of the chemistry of sleepiness, nerve and brain centers may be directly stimulated by chemical conditions within the body. The muscles are also affected, for one of the outstanding conditions bringing about sleep is a general relaxation of the body.

But whatever the chemical factors in sleep, it is definitely known that sleepiness can be caused by injuries to certain parts of the brain, which may be the nerve centers controlling the need for sleep. And besides all these physiological theories of sleep, there is also a theory which explains this need as a conditioned (learned) response.

Here is a vital area of human activity that is barely charted out and is yet to be explored by the scientists of the future.

Warmth and cold as drives

Everyone everywhere is affected by the weather. Clothes, houses, sports, agriculture—and sometimes, it is even said, temperament—are affected by how hot or cold the climate is. No one can dispute the importance of warmth and cold as drives. Just what is their physiological origin?

First of all, there are some receptors in the skin which are sensitive to contact with warm objects and others which are sensitive to cold. In addition, there is one portion of the brain, the *hypothalamus* (shown in the diagram), which responds directly to the temperature of the blood flowing through it. This center is vital in our adjustment to warmth and cold.

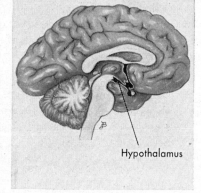

Hypothalamus

The temperature of the human body is regulated by a complex mechanism that balances heat loss against heat production. Thus two temperatures are involved: the amount of heat in the surrounding environment, as well as the heat produced by the body itself. Our bodies obviously lose less heat to their surroundings on hot, humid days than on cold days.

When the body is cold—that is, when external temperature falls below about 57°—bodily activity is stimulated. Increased secretion of thyroxin and adrenin helps bring about this increased activity. Increased muscular activity takes place; the blood pressure rises. Blood is driven from the surface of the body to the deeper tissues, where it will not be exposed to the cold air. The reaction to heat is pretty much the opposite. When external temperature is raised, bodily activity slows down. The arteries at the surface of the body dilate, thus exposing a greater volume of blood to the air for cooling. The circulation rate is increased.

All these automatic bodily changes act in various ways to keep the temperature of the body tissues fairly constant at about 98°-99° F., no matter what the temperature of the environment. But besides these automatic adjustments to warmth, there are of course many things we deliberately do to keep our bodies at a comfortable temperature. Electric fans, air conditioning, ice water, palm-beach suits—oil burners, hot drinks, and fur coats—all are familiar results of man's drives to adjust to warmth and cold. And all are indicative of the importance—and social ramifications—of these drives.

Pain as a drive

To serve most effectively as a drive, pain must be prolonged and not too strong. If you touch a hot iron accidentally, you draw back your hand. This is a simple, specific, already-organized response: the *withdrawal reflex*. The localized pain of brief duration is not, properly speaking, a drive any more than all stimuli are drives. But suppose that even after you have withdrawn your hand the burn continues to smart and you go to the doctor to get it dressed. Here pain is serving as a drive.

Pain has an important biological significance in that most harmful situations produce pain as well as injury. The desire to avoid pain and to protect others from pain has been one of the important motivating forces in the history of man. An excellent example is the search for better anesthetics which is going forward now. Pain touches the lives of all of us, and we pay homage to the medical men who discover and administer anesthetics which prevent needless pain. In recent years the science of anesthiology has taken its place beside surgery, obstetrics, and other branches of medicine.

Visceral tensions as drives

When the bladder and lower colon become distended, receptor cells in their walls are stimulated and produce drives. These drives ordinarily have little significance, as obstacles to their relief are seldom imposed, but they have all the essential characteristics of the other physiological drives: (1) They may be defined as the conditions surrounding some bodily need; (2) they grow out of the physiological state of our tissues; (3) they stimulate the sensory receptors and thus the brain and nervous system; (4) they produce by this stimulation a restless activity which continues until the physiological tissue needs have been supplied.

APPETITES AND AVERSIONS

Appetites and aversions are other internal conditions that arouse, sustain, and direct activity. Like the drives, many of them are the product of maturation; that is, they are present at birth or appear later in life in the absence of opportunity for learning. The appetites and aversions direct human behavior in exactly the same way as do the basic physiological drives. They cause the individual to seek and avoid certain stimulus objects and situations. However, the forms of stimulation chosen and avoided are not vitally related to the life, growth, and continued activity of the individual. They appear to be liked or disliked for their own sakes, apart from their utility in satisfying physiological needs.

Psychologists are not entirely agreed upon the items to be included in this list of inborn likes and dislikes, nor are they agreed upon what to name them. Probably the most satisfactory terms are *appetite* if the object is willingly encountered or actively sought, and *aversion* if it is actively avoided. The practical difficulty in surveying our inherited likes and dislikes lies in finding out which were actually determined by heredity and maturation and which by learning. For example, the Chinese have been brought up to like musical combinations that the trained European ear finds unpleasant; and people who have heard nothing but jazz all their lives find classical music boring.

But despite the difficulty of locating the inborn appetites and aversions, we all know that people continue to seek what they feel to be pleasant and to avoid what they feel to be unpleasant. There are many stimuli which produce pleasant conscious experiences and are actively sought. Among them are musical notes as opposed to noise; certain colors and color combinations, tastes and flavors, smells; and stimulation of the sex organs.

The sexual appetite

The sexual appetite is second only to the hunger drive in its implications for social living, although, unlike the satisfaction of hunger, sexual activity is not actually essential to keeping a person alive. Most modern physicians and psychologists believe, however, that sexual relief is conducive to the highest level of physical and mental health.

While our society does not place elaborate restrictions or taboos upon the food-taking behavior of its members, sexual expression is very closely governed by law and firmly rooted conventions. Greater deprivation makes the sexual appetite more insistent than hunger and other drives which are not so likely to go unsatisfied. Chapter 12 will discuss in more detail the important relation between sexual activity and emotional development.

Scientists are still trying to find the exact location of the internal controls in the sexual appetite. They do know for certain that the intensity of the sexual urge is dependent upon the chemical condition of the blood. Observations of both animals and human beings show that the strength of the sexual drive is profoundly influenced by the presence or absence of certain internal secretions. The most important of these internal secretions is that produced by certain cells found in the reproductive organs: the ovaries of the female and the testes of the male. As you already know, the individual loses much of his sexual appetite when his sex glands are removed by operation at any early age.

In discussing the chemical and neural patterns underlying the sexual appetite, it is necessary to treat one sex at a time because the differences between them are many and complex. The male sex drive will be considered first because it has a simpler physiological basis.

Sexual appetite in the male. As you learned in Chapter 3, the sexual development of the male is steered by (1) the *androgens*, which are hormones secreted by the testes, and by (2) certain "middle man" hormones secreted from the pituitary. In the normal male, the supply of androgens appears to be relatively constant, or at least fails to show the monthly periodic cycle followed by women.

Adult men who are castrated through accident or disease retain for years their ability to perform the sexual act, although there is usually some decline in the strength of the sexual appetite. (This fact has obvious implications for the frequently offered proposal that adult sex criminals should be castrated to prevent repeated offenses.) But young boys who have been castrated never attain sexual maturity either in body build or behavior. Experiments have shown that a similar state of affairs exists in birds (Carpenter[14]) and in white rats (Stone[15]).

Destruction of the pituitary body of the mature male rat is followed by a very rapid decline of copulatory behavior (Wiesner and Sheard[16]). You will remember that the pituitary creates two "middle man" substances that affect sexual functioning: one that acts directly on the testes and thus on the supply of androgens; and another that stimulates the adrenal cortex, which in turn secretes a hormone that accelerates sexual maturation in the male. Here again we see the overlapping of functions in the endocrine system.

With normal development, these various forces seem to operate at a relatively constant level, and the sexual appetite of the male therefore remains fairly stable over time. It is, of course, subject to general physiological conditions such as fatigue, and to various psychological factors.

Sexual appetite in the female. The sexual appetite of the female is much more complex than that of the male. It is therefore not surprising that the endocrinal basis underlying sexual appetite in the female is also much more complex.

It is necessary at this point to review briefly the function of the ovaries. These two small organs are the primary sex tissues of the female, and are responsible for the secretion of the principal female sex hormones: the *estrogens,* which control the sex drive, and *progestin,* which is important in pregnancy. Each of these hormones comes into prominence at a different time in the woman's sexual cycle.

The estrogens are secreted into the blood stream each month at the time of *ovulation:* that is, at the time when a mature egg cell is released from the ovary and slowly makes it way down the *oviduct* (literally "egg-conductor"), a tube leading from the ovary to the uterus. The brief time when the egg is in the oviduct and uterus is the only time that a woman can become pregnant, and it lasts only a few days during the month. In the adult female, ovulation occurs about halfway between the beginning of two menstrual periods.

Progestin is secreted *after* ovulation. Every month around the time of ovulation, the uterus and the ovary undergo certain changes which are essential preparations for pregnancy, even though fertilization obviously does not always occur. Just before ovulation, the uterus prepares to receive a fertilized egg; its lining thickens and becomes engorged with tiny blood vessels and gland formations. And in the ovary a yellowish structure is produced which projects from the surface of the ovary like a half-submerged yellow pea. It is this little structure, called the *corpus luteum,* which secretes *progestin,* the hormone important in pregnancy.

The fate of the uterus lining and the corpus luteum each month depends upon the occurrence or nonoccurrence of pregnancy:

1 If pregnancy does not occur, the corpus luteum reaches its maximum development in about two weeks after ovulation, and then a process of absorption begins which takes about two months and leaves no trace other than a tiny scar on the surface of the ovary. Also, about two weeks after ovulation, the thickened lining of the uterus sloughs off with moderate bleeding; this takes about four days, known as the *menstrual period.*

2 If pregnancy does occur, the uterus remains in a condition favorable to the development of the fertilized egg. It does not slough off its thickened lining; that is, the woman does not menstruate. Also, the corpus luteum continues to exist in its fully developed stage for about six months, maintaining an active production of progestin.

What is the relation between the times when estrogen and progestin are secreted, and the cycle in female sexual appetite? For one thing, it is definitely known that the estrogens control the female sex drive. This relationship is most clearly noticed in the lower mammals. At ovulation, when the blood stream becomes enriched with estrogens, the female animal loses her previous disinterest in the male and becomes highly receptive or aggressively suggestive in her sexual behavior. This behavior is known as "estrus" or "heat" and is a signal that the female animal is in a condition of readiness for pregnancy.

In the human species, however, observed sexual receptivity is not at its height during ovulation. The evidence indicates that *conscious* sexual desire is at a peak during the second day after the end of menstruation and then declines (Davis[17]). It reaches its lowest ebb during the period of ovulation, or at the mid-point between two menstrual periods. It then rises to a new high just prior to the onset of the next menstrual period. Thus the human female, unlike the other female mammals, experiences her lowest sexual drives at the only time she can conceive—at ovulation, midway in the cycle—and her highest at times when she cannot conceive—just before and after menstruation.

Why such a difference should exist between the female of the human species and the female of the lower mammals is not yet known. One very simple but quite possible explanation lies merely in this: Most women keep a rough record of when they may expect the next menstrual period to start. Since it is a period in which they do not expect to engage in sex relations, and since it is a longer period of abstinence than most young married women report as occurring at other times, they have a tendency to seek sex relations before that menstrual period gets under way. In the same manner, after such a period of deprivation, the motivation is stronger than it would be otherwise. Any arbitrary interference with the sex activity of a person which thus was definitely scheduled might be expected to produce an increase in sexual appetite before and after the expected deprivation.

Another explanation is based on the fact that modern woman lives in a highly restrictive society and has been exposed to many cultural traditions, teachings, and misteachings. There is good reason to distrust her consciously directed behavior or introspectively observed interests, for it is possible that she represses her sexual desires at the time of ovulation. Even though modern woman's *conscious* reactions of a sexual nature are out of phase with the physiological cycle, her *unconscious* and therefore more natural behavior may be just as much in phase with her physiological rhythm as is true of the lower animals.

An extremely revealing study has shown that a direct relation does exist between unconscious sexual reactions and the cycle in which ovarian hormones are secreted.

> This study is the work of two physicians: one a medical doctor, one a psychoanalyst. The doctor analyzed the vaginal secretions of a group of women who were undergoing the psychological treatment known as psychoanalysis, and thus was able to chart the menstrual cycle. The other, a psychoanalyst, performed elaborate analyses of the dreams these women reported, which would reveal their unconscious rather than consciously reported sexual attitudes, and charted their menstrual cycle according to their unconscious sexual attitudes. Each physician made his own chart of the menstrual cycle (and hormone secretion) by using his own data without reference to that of the other. The two independently prepared graphs—one based on psychology, one on physiology—coincided almost perfectly.
>
> Around the time of ovulation, while the women were under the dominance of the estrogens, their unconscious problems centered around heterosexual relationships. This condition resembles that in the lower animals, in which the estrogens play their basic role in bringing about sexual activity in the female.
>
> Just after ovulation, the dominance of the estrogens was beginning

to yield to the progestin, the pregnancy hormone produced by the corpus luteum in preparation for pregnancy. Here a brief state of unconscious conflict was noticed: the patients were irritable and flighty. During the third stage, the uterus is preparing for pregnancy and there is marked secretion of progestin from the corpus luteum. Then the women's unconscious interests turned to themselves and centered about their bodily comfort, instead of being directed at sexual activity, which could not cause pregnancy at this stage of the cycle. (Benedek and Rubenstein[18])

Thus in women's unconscious life there is the expected psychological cycle running in phase with the physiological, with both cycles under hormonal control. The interesting question, still not fully answered, is why women's conscious sensations of sexual interest should run a cycle counter to that of both their hormones and their unconscious interests.

Homosexuality and the endocrines. A homosexual is a person whose sexual appetite is directed toward members of his own sex. The *latent* ("hidden") homosexual does not consciously recognize his homosexual urge and does not engage in overt homosexual acts. The *overt* ("open") homosexual recognizes his condition and frequently does practice homosexual acts.

It has been estimated that about 5 per cent of each sex are potentially or latently homosexual but only about 1 per cent are overtly homosexual (Rosanoff[19]). If these figures are correct, they indicate that of the 5 per cent of the population who could become overt homosexuals, only 1 per cent do become so. What determines the sexual direction of the other 4 per cent? In fact, what influences cause people to direct their sexual appetite toward one sex rather than another? Two important influences seem to be present: the physiological factor of endocrine balance; and the social-psychological factor of learning.

To what extent is endocrine balance involved as a factor in homosexuality? No final answer has yet been reached, but some significant experiments with animals indicate that the sexual activity of animals can be greatly changed by alteration in the endocrine balance. The picture is not nearly so clear in the case of human beings. Usually, though not invariably, the active male homosexuals have a decidedly masculine body build, while the passive male homosexuals tend to be feminine in appearance, body build, and particularly in manner. The relationship between anatomical characteristics and homosexuality is very slight, however, and how much of it is endocrinal in origin and how much results from learning is not known.

Various surveys suggest that passive male homosexuals have a higher estrogen-to-androgen ratio in their bodily chemistry than do normal males. However, attempts to treat homosexuality in men through the use of endocrine therapy have been rather disappointing. In fact, there are almost as many clinical reports of apparent failure as of apparent success (Glass and Johnson[20]). And endocrine therapy has not been more effective with female homosexuals than with male. In fact, only one thing stands out clearly from the numerous assays of the relation between endocrine balance and human sexuality. It is definitely established that each sex has *both* "male" and "female" endocrine elements, the balance between them varying from time to time in any one person.

That endocrines determine the sexual adjustment of the lower animals is convincingly clear. But the situation becomes confused and conflicting in the sexual behavior of human beings. For one thing, the line between "normal" heterosexuality and "abnormal" homosexuality is very hard to draw. Sexuality, like many other human traits, is not an all-or-none characteristic. There is no one group of traits that is the exclusive property of all females, no one group of traits that is the exclusive property of all males. Just as each of us has within him both male and female hormones, so each of us has both "masculine" and "feminine" traits. Moreover, many of these traits are learned from the social environment (a fact which will be discussed more fully in Chapter 12).

It is interesting to note in conclusion that from babyhood through childhood, males and females are relatively alike in body build, voice, behavior, and interests. However, they become rapidly differentiated from the age of puberty and remain so until late middle life. Then, as old age creeps on, sex differences tend to disappear: older men speak in a higher pitch, become less aggressive and more womanlike in manners; older women lose their femininity, grow hair on the face and upper lip, lose their rounded curves, and become angular and more masculine in form. These changes through life are undoubtedly a result of the waxing and waning of the sex glands. In sexual development, as in many other areas of human life, maturation and learning interact.

Other appetites in man

The human appetites, aside from sex, have not been so well surveyed and catalogued as have the drives based on tissue needs. This is because they are less essential to life, and because they are so readily influenced by training that it is not entirely clear whether they are inborn appetites or social motives. In fact, some psychologists feel that the category of appetites is not necessary, and place some of them under drives and some under social motives. The following list is far from complete but will serve to illustrate further the concept of appetites.

Musical tones. Various observations show that people respond differently to high and low musical notes. You will recall in this connection that the young human infant cries when he hears high notes and smiles or coos when he hears low notes. The young baby, of course, lacks the muscular strength and coordination to get out of hearing of the unpleasant high notes or to get closer to the pleasant low ones, but there is no doubt as to the difference in his response. And his response must be innate, since learning cannot be called upon to explain this preference in babies who have had no opportunity to learn. Another inborn preference is for tones as against noises.

Colors and color combinations. Psychological experiments indicate that color appetites appear in the absence of opportunity to learn and continue to develop all during life through the interaction of maturation and learning.

> One study of color appetite was made with three-month-old babies, who could not yet have been socially conditioned to prefer some colors to others. As the children lay in their cradles, two sheets of paper of exactly the same brightness were held before their eyes: either a sheet of gray paper and a sheet of colored paper, or else two sheets of different-colored paper. Appetite for color was measured by the amount of time the infant spent looking at one piece of paper as compared with the other. The papers were placed far enough apart so that the experimenter was rarely in doubt as to which piece of paper was being looked at. The results were that the babies showed more interest in the colors (yellow, blue, red, and green) than in the gray. The differences in interest shown in the various colors were so slight that we cannot be sure whether color preferences exist in infants of around three months of age. But it is very clear that color is more interesting than gray even to so young a baby.
>
> This study was not confined to infants, for individuals were tested at age levels from eight months to adulthood. Pairs of colored disks were held up before older babies, who were told to "get the ball." It was noted which of the two balls they preferred, preference being defined as pointing to or attempting to touch the disk. The results showed clearly that for preschool children red was the favorite color, with the position of yellow, green, and blue alternating at different ages. From grade school on, blue displaced red as the favorite. Interestingly enough, the preference for yellow seemed to decline with age. (Staples[21])

In the human adult, there is no good method of separating the influences of inherited appetite for colors from the influences of acquired tastes, but it would be difficult to understand the preferences of young babies on any other than an innate basis, for the simple reason that infants have not yet had an opportunity to learn to prefer one color to another.

Tastes and flavors. Appetite for food does exist in the absence of general hunger drive, as is shown by the way people reach for a sweet at the end of a heavy meal and use seasoning and flavoring. Apparently appetite is largely the result of certain factors in our inherited nature which make some things taste good and others taste bad.

Here again we must contend with the fact that human adults show preferences which have been influenced by learning as well as by maturation. Study has shown, however, that likes and dislikes for different tastes are apparently present at birth—that is, are innate.

> A study has been made of the reactions of one thousand newborn infants to sweet, salt, sour, and bitter substances. Their reactions were positive to sweet and salt, and definitely negative to bitter and sour. The criterion of positive reaction was contented sucking, and that of negative response, discomfort reactions. (Peterson and Rainey[22])

Smells. You will recall the study in Chapter 3 which leaves no doubt that the newborn baby reacts more to smells than to air. The odors which aroused reactions were not less injurious than air; they were not produced by the needs of tissues for food materials; and they were not learned. Therefore, we may tentatively include such reactions in the repertoire of inborn human appetites (or aversions).

To summarize: the appetites have very much the same function in directing behavior as do the basic physiological drives. The organism will persistently seek to maintain the pleasurable gratification of an appetite and will explore his environment seeking it when it is absent.

The role of the aversions in adjustment

First, what are some common aversions, or inborn dislikes? This may best be discovered by reviewing the preceding discussion of appetites, for an aversion is a negative appetite. This discussion indicated that even newborn babies have an appetite for low musical tones and an aversion for high notes. As for taste, sweet and salt are accepted but bitter and sour are actively rejected: in other words, there is an appetite for the first two and an aversion to the second two.

From the point of view of adjustment, the aversion is much less important than the appetite, for the simple reason that it is usually comparatively simple to avoid an unpleasant stimulus situation merely by moving away from it. There are an infinite number of simple responses which will remove the organism from the presence of the stimulus which arouses aversion. In the case of an appetite, however, behavior must be much more precise and more definitely organized to achieve its goal. For example, a young boy will run an errand in order to earn money with which to buy candy which will taste good when placed in his mouth—a complicated chain of reactions. The same boy might, of course, work equally hard to avoid having an unpleasant-tasting substance thrust into his mouth. The point is that the first situation is frequently encountered in life, and the second is seldom encountered and if encountered is easily overcome. But even though the aversions are not among the strongest of our motives, nor among those most important to life, they can be—as we all know from our own daily experience—a source of great annoyance. Putrid smells, loud or screeching traffic noises, bitter medicine have all aroused aversion in most of us at one time or another (more complex aversions are probably not inborn).

Drives, appetites, aversions—all these are inborn; they have a biological origin, they are basic. But obviously there are many forms of human motivation besides these direct biological reactions. After all, what possible bearing do stomach contractions have upon the motives we see around us every day? What is the relationship between physiological needs and such motives of man as his curiosity about the world in which he lives, his political and religious beliefs, his capacity to kill and to love, his patriotism, and his ambition to make money? The relationship is very complex, as you will see in the following section.

HOW THE DERIVED MOTIVES DEVELOP

Complex motives and simple bodily needs seem far apart. Yet these motives grow from bodily needs just as the adult grows from the child, with old, simple forms taking on complexity and variety. This process of development is a complicated one, with social influences and inherited bodily structures working in combination to make the individual feel intellectually curious or content to read dime novels, make him seek or withdraw from outstanding success, make him a solicitous or indifferent parent.

Just how do the biological tissue needs develop into complex motives? It is instructive in this connection to study the rise of the exploratory motive.

The exploratory motive

The exploratory motive has no single, definitely recognizable physiological basis. When an animal is put into an unfamiliar situation, it moves restlessly about, examining each nook and cranny of the new surroundings. What is the physiological foundation of this "curiosity"? The present evidence indicates that the *exploratory motive* is simply an expression of all the drives, appetites, and aversions that happen to be present at the moment the organism is put into the new situation. For instance, the hungrier a rat is, the more actively and thoroughly it will explore. Conversely, in a satiated animal, there is little sign of exploratory activity, or of any other activity, for that matter.

Exploratory patterns are made up of simple habits which have worked in the past in time of need—that is, they are learned ways of achieving satisfactions. When a need arises in an unfamiliar situation, the habit patterns of moving, looking, sniffing will be brought out. The fact that rats explore only an unfamiliar situation has so impressed some writers that they have been led to postulate some mysterious "instinct" for which no physiological basis has ever been found or seems likely to be found. The simple truth apparently is that the rat explores a situation only until it learns where the various rewards or reliefs are located. Stimuli which do not lead to relief of the drive tension are ignored after a time. Thus even a hungry animal would not explore his already familiar cage, which he knows from past experience has no bits of food in the corners, but he might explore any new situation until he discovered that it contained nothing to satisfy him. The exploratory motive in the lower animal seems, then, to be no more than the expression of all or any of his physiological tensions.

The exploratory motive in man must be to a great degree like that in the lower animals. As soon as the baby is able to creep about, he will do so whenever he is "restless," i.e., seeking satisfaction of some need. Even if the exploration brings no more substantial reward than the welcome attention involved in the mother's rescuing her child from real or imagined danger, the child will consider exploration worth while and will repeat it.

In man, *curiosity* is the subjective experience that goes with exploration, just as the sensation of hunger goes with searching for food. However, curiosity merely accompanies the activities of search; it does not cause those activities.

As the child develops, his curiosity in the world about him develops or fails to develop depending upon his environment. If the exploratory behavior of a child—whether through direct looking or through asking questions—is frustrated and discouraged by the adults in his life, curiosity stagnates. But if curiosity and exploration are encouraged, they become highly developed.

For example, the scientist who spends years of patient research to discover the answer to some theoretical question does so partly because he has grown up in an environment that rewards exploration with social approval. In later life his scientific activities come to bring satisfaction for their own sakes and may have little direct relation to the need for social approval. Many a scientist has worked hard for years on some difficult problem, with little hope of recognition to keep him going. But in early life, the rewards that exploration brings are very important in determining whether a person will develop curiosity and in what direction his curiosity will turn.

When a ten-year-old boy centers his exploratory activity on a chemistry set, this interest in molecular formations and chemical reactions obviously does not have a purely physiological basis. Of course, the boy's generalized exploratory drive was originally centered on bodily needs, and he may even have inherited scientific talent from a chemist father. But the most important factor here is social approval, which is represented for the boy in the abstract study of chemistry. Perhaps the boy first became determined to study chemistry during the course of encouraging conversations with his chemist father, whose approval he wants, or with his pretty young science teacher, on whom he has a "crush." Their words of praise and affection have a positive meaning for him, as later on the high-school chemistry prize or perhaps a Guggenheim fellowship will bring him satisfaction in his scientific exploration. Yet the words, the printed certificates of merit, the award from the research foundation have little value in themselves but represent other satisfactions. That is, they represent social approval to the boy who receives them, and they are the means by which his exploratory interest in chemistry is aroused and maintained.

Now let us see just how substitute—or *symbolic*—rewards can encourage the development of drives, appetites, and aversions into complex social motives.

Symbolic rewards

Words, ideas, acts, situations, or objects are called *symbols* when they represent or suggest other words, ideas, acts, situations, or objects. The fact that symbols can take on reward value is an important factor in the organization of drives and appetites into derived motives.

Let us study in detail how symbols can come to act as rewards. To take a simple and familiar example: people who own dogs know how words can come to take the place of action in the life of a dog. There are simultaneous applications of praise-words-and-food, of scolding-words-and-whipping. As a result of this conditioning, the dog comes to react to harsh words from the master by cringing and cowering in the same way that he originally reacted to physical punishment. Kind words come to serve as rewards just as the food and petting originally did, and they produce the same elation. Words have become symbolic: that is, through conditioning, they have come to represent feelings, objects, or situations not immediately present.

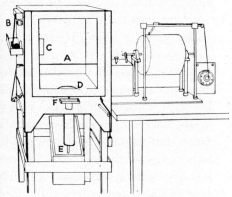

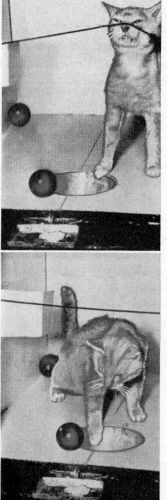

Token-reward habits in animals. *This cat has learned to press a string with his head or paw in order to get a ball (as at upper left). He will then spend the ball in the "cat slot-machine" (as at lower left) in order to open the glass door and secure the salmon in the pan in front of the door. The drawing shows the box in which cats are trained. First, the cat presses string A, which releases rubber balls from the container B. The balls fall into the box through the opening at C, and the cat must roll them into the funnel at D. The balls fall through the funnel, striking the switch E which opens the door of the box, so that the cat can get the salmon located in the little pan at F. The drum at right will record all responses. (Photographs from the film by Dr. Karl U. Smith, The Acquisition of the Token-Reward Habit in the Cat; drawing courtesy of Dr. Smith.)*

Other animals besides dogs show this significant phenomenon of conditioned or symbolic reward. Psychologists have been able to train both cats (Smith[23]) and apes (Wolfe[24]) to work for a token which could later be exchanged for food. Once the animals had been taught the symbolic reward value of the token, they would work as hard for it as for the food itself, as the illustration opposite shows.

Certainly if symbols can take on such reward value in the lower animals, the same process is to be expected in man. Even babies definitely can learn by conditioning, as you will recall from the experiment in which nursing babies were conditioned to make sucking responses when a buzzer was sounded. In the same way, they are conditioned to react to voices and eventually to words as representing or suggesting the satisfaction of bodily needs. All through infancy, the mother's voice is heard murmuring affectionately as she responds to the child's crying and relieves him of pain, wet, hunger, and thirst or gives him the pleasurable sensations of fondling and caressing. There is a close association in the child's mind between the satisfaction of his drives and the sound of his mother's voice. Then as he grows older and starts to play with other children, it sometimes happens that he is hurt by some plaything or is bullied by an older child. Here again the mother sets things right, at the same time speaking words of love and sympathy. Under these conditions the mother's voice *symbolically* takes on the reward value of purely physiological relief. The mere sound of it calls up sensations of love and satisfaction.

Working for social approval

Symbols, then, can serve as substitute satisfactions for dogs, apes, and children. That is, words and objects which are of themselves incapable of satisfying drives and are not originally sought for their own sakes can be associated with real rewards and eventually come to acquire their own power to satisfy human drives. Now let us see how symbolic reward operates as the child grows to maturity.

Symbolic reward and the maturing child. Once the mother's voice has come to represent to the child the love and satisfaction he naturally wants, then it has acquired great power to influence his behavior. The child soon learns that maternal approval goes with certain kinds of behavior and that disapproval goes with others. He finds that when he does the right thing, he receives the satisfactions of love and tenderness—if only in words—that go with maternal approval; that when he does the wrong thing, he receives disapproval and may be punished. He comes to think of things as "bad" or "good" according to his mother's reactions, and he changes his behavior to conform to her standards.

The mother's or father's words and tones often check the child from doing things he very much wants to do, like taking the biggest piece of cake. But the words and tones of approval may also be connected sometimes with things that he does *not* want to do, like setting the table or clearing the sidewalks of snow. It usually happens to some degree, therefore, that the person comes to have some conflicts over this matter of approval and disapproval—that is, he doesn't know whether he wants "his own way" or his parent's approval. In some persons this conflict may result in *negativism*—it is as though they had learned to want the things forbidden or disapproved, and had learned to be averse to the things demanded of them or for which they are given praise. The unwise parent can destroy much of the tendency to seek for social approval by demanding too often that the child sacrifice his own inclinations in order to gain the parent's approval.

At first, symbols of social approval are significant for the child and influence his behavior only when they come from his mother, his nurse, or anyone close to him who satisfies his needs. Later, the stock of symbolic ideas, words, objects that influence his behavior grows from cross or kind words to the many symbols that abound in social life: flag, slogans, discussions of political or social reform, philosophical ideas. As he grows from childhood, he comes to desire the approval of the society as a whole, or at least of the particular social group to which he belongs.

Another very important development is that the individual comes early in his childhood to desire not only approval from his family, not only approval from society, but also approval from himself. The desire for self-respect and the desire for social approval can both be traced to the conditioning afforded by early training. The average individual accepts the standards of the society in which he lives, and applies these to himself, because they have been the basis for his parents' approval or disapproval.

The development of interests. Social conditioning is very important in the development of our interests and values. The term *interest* is usually used by psychologists to mean a pleasurable feeling which accompanies some activity in progress. In everyday words, a person has an interest in something if he likes to do it—whether it is stamp-collecting, fishing, debating, or dancing.

For example, you may possess the complex group of native abilities that is necessary to being an accurate marksman, but you may have been taught by your parents or teachers that it is cruel to shoot animals. Then you will feel that hunting will bring you only disapproval, and the chances are that you will not become interested in it as a sport. On the other hand, if you possess hunting abilities and if you grow up among people who approve of hunting as a sport or as a way of getting food, then the chances are very strong indeed that you will develop a keen interest in hunting.

The development of values. Social approval is an important influence, as has been indicated, not only on our interests but also on our values. This word *value* is frequently used, but needs precise definition. The psychologist would say that the human goals on which motivations center may be classified according to the importance they have in our lives, that is, according to their *value* to us. If a goal seems well worth attaining, we say that it has a high degree of value. When it seems scarcely worth attaining, we say its value is small. If it is something to be avoided, we say it has a negative value.

Everyone has a system of values, which is determined largely by his early environment. For example, one child might grow up in a home in which money making is valued above all else and might accept the values of his parents, whose love and respect he desires. Another child who comes from a family which admires self-sacrifice and public service will probably have the same values. Of course, there are children who become alienated from their parents and home, for one reason or another, and who seek the approval and adopt the values of persons outside the home. An adolescent who all his life has rebelled against his parents will probably acquire new friends whose values and interests he accepts. This does not contradict the fact that our values are developed by a process of learning from others with whom we associate.

The home is the great conditioner of human values and interests— working together with the school, church, movies, trade unions, clubs, and many other social institutions. These institutions interact with the prevalent interests and values and ways of behaving to make up a people's way of life.

The derived motives

Thus we have passed from the simple physiological drives to the more complex derived motives we see around us every day. No one knows how many derived motives there are because they overlap and merge into one another by imperceptible degrees. A tentative list might include patriotism, attitudes toward foreigners, the desire to make money, religious values, respect for parents, desire for social reform, and intellectual curiosity. There are many interesting questions to be answered about such derived motives. Are they found only in man—or are they characteristic of animals too? Have they a direct biological basis?—are they innate? Are they the same the world over? To answer these questions, we turn first to the study of animal behavior and then to the derived motives of people outside our own particular culture.

Social behavior in the higher animals. Man's social behavior can easily be compared with careful studies of social behavior in chimpanzees. Here, for example, is a description of group loyalty in chimpanzees.

> "If one chimpanzee is attacked before the eyes of the group, great excitement goes through the whole group. It will happen that . . . one punishes a wrong-doer with a heavy blow. The moment one's hand falls on him, the whole group sets up a howl, as if with one voice. . . . It is strange how convincing, one might say full of moral indignation, this howling . . . sounds to the ear of man; . . ." (Kohler[25])

Apes will also share food with each other; surely this is socially motivated behavior.

> In one study, pairs of chimpanzees were put together in adjacent cages. One member of each pair was given food or a food-token which he had previously learned to use in food-vending machines, and then watched to see if he would reach it across to the other ape. It was found that food-sharing did occur, and that it was definitely determined by the social relationships among the apes, rather than by strictly physiological or environmental factors. (Nissen and Crawford[26])

Just a partial list of all the social motives that can be seen in chimpanzees includes gregariousness, loyalty to group, dominating over or submitting to another person, competitive acquisition of belongings, sharing with and soliciting from others, and working with others toward a common goal.

Such social behavior in animals has sometimes been thought to indicate that the social motives are inborn in the higher animals, and are therefore presumably inborn in man (Tolman[27]). Against this theory of inborn social motives in animals is the fact that many socializing influences act upon laboratory animals which are reared in cages in the presence of human beings as well as other apes. Also, it is probable that in the higher mammals, especially, much social behavior is taught to the young animal by the mother. The social behavior of animals could as easily be learned as inborn.

Man's derived motives are not inborn. To say that the derived motives are inborn in man is to return to the "instinct" theory of human nature. As was pointed out in the last chapter, man has very few behavior patterns that emerge complete as the result of heredity rather than environment—very few, that is, in relation to the sum total of human activities. In fact, most human activities are based on social motives, which are determined largely by the particular things approved or disapproved in the environment in which the person happens to be born and raised. Of course these social motives are based on biological drives shared by all humans, but the way they are organized into derived motives depends on the particular environment. A person will be selfish or generous, will believe in Jesus or in tree spirits, will be interested in making money or in working for better government, according to the attitudes and behavior that he has all his life heard called "good" or "bad."

One of the most dramatic evidences that complex social motives are not inborn, but the product of social environment, is their complete absence in human children who have grown up in the wilderness. Recently a book has been written about "Kamala," an eight-year-old girl who was found in India living in a den of wolves, where she had apparently been raised since infancy. Some light may be thrown on the theory of the "gregarious instinct" by the report of two kindly missionaries who adopted her and a younger girl, "Amala," also found in the wolves' den, and tried to nurse them back to human ways. This is how the wolf-child reacted to the other children in the missionaries' orphanage:

> "The social behavior of Kamala bore the impress of wolverine ways and prejudices. The younger children tried to allure and entice her to play, but to no avail. She would sit aloof in a corner for hours at a stretch, her back to the children, her face to the wall, bestowing only forced or furtive glances on her well-meaning, would-be companions.
>
> "Toward Amala alone she showed a semblance of companionship; toward others a mixture of shyness and aggressiveness. If approached she assumed a fierce expression and even showed her teeth.
>
> "But among the infants in the orphanage there was one named Benjamin who crawled about on the floor. For awhile it looked as though his quadrupedal status would have a socializing effect. Here was a chance for a palship; but on December 31, 1920, before the new year could begin, Kamala (and Amala too) scratched and bit Benjamin so severely that he never would approach them again. A month later they bit one of the orphan girls, and then escaped into the compound where it took much beating about in the bush to find them." (Gesell[28])

If these creatures had any inborn social motives, they remained well hidden from the people who found the children and tried to establish social contact with them.

Man's derived motives are not universally the same. People often describe as "universal" those motives which only our particular society

Students of human nature, from the eighteenth-century philosophers onward, have often speculated about what man would be like if raised without human education. This situation is shown in the startling case of Kamala, the Indian child who lived in a wolf den until nine years of age. When first found, she crawled on all fours, ate like a wolf, prowled around howling at night, and was unresponsive to human companionship. Only through long and patient handling (as at left) did she progress toward social behavior. By the time of her death at seventeen, she walked erect, spoke fluently, and showed emotional interest in the people around her.

encourages and approves. This is somewhat like generalizing about all trees from one particular variety of maple found in eastern Vermont. Of course certain organic drives are found in the whole human species, like the drives for food, water and air, and so apparently are certain inborn appetites and aversions. But the derived motives—including of course interests and values—are largely a product of the environment.

That derived motives are determined by the particular social environment, that they are not necessarily universal characteristics of mankind, has been demonstrated by many studies of other kinds of culture than the ones we are familiar with in America and the rest of the modern Western world. Many of these peoples live on a crude material level, but their social systems are often highly complex. Anthropological studies yield dramatic evidence of the diversity of man's derived motives.

For instance, in the United States today, we place great importance on private property. We accept the fact that some people have much more than others, and we honor the man who has accumulated a great deal of wealth. This valuation of private property is frequently said to result from man's "acquisitive nature." Interestingly enough, however, this attitude toward material things is far from universal in human society. Some peoples have land and canoes which are shared by the whole community. Others have possessive attitudes, going far beyond ours, with every rock and tree being "owned" by someone. The attitude toward property varies from people to people. The Melanesians, for instance, consider it very greedy if a person who finds something does not share it with others (Klineberg[29]).

Many people believe that war is inevitable because man is "naturally aggressive." It is true that the physiological changes which occur during anger indicate that there may be an organic basis for aggressive behavior. However, aggressiveness can find many other adequate outlets besides destruction and killing. The Eskimos are only one of several peoples who do not wage aggressive war and who do not have any understanding of its meaning or purpose. Among the Eskimos, aggressiveness between individuals is expressed not in physical combat but in a formal duel of words, the better speaker being judged the victor. In other societies, quarrels are fought to their conclusion as the antagonists give goods to each other; the one whose goods give out first is considered the loser. Whether or not aggressiveness has an organic innate basis, the form that it takes can be greatly modified by the social approval given to different outlets for it (Klineberg[30]).

HOW THE DERIVED MOTIVES DEVELOP IN ANOTHER CULTURE

What causes individuals to develop their characteristic motives and behavior patterns?
This question may be difficult to answer by looking only at our own society.
First of all, our way of living seems so natural and so familiar that we may be blind
to the basic trends and causal factors that an outside observer would detect. And
second, it is scientifically unsound to generalize from knowledge of one culture
about the development of derived motives in all cultures. Two social anthropologists,
Gregory Bateson and Margaret Mead, have published a photographic analysis of
"Balinese Character," which they obtained during two years of intimate study of a
Balinese community. This rich and complex culture may seem bizarre to Americans,
but it yields valuable understanding of how the basic human drives are modified
into the many different ways of living found all over the world.

The mother-child relation is in
Bali, as in most other cultures,
basic in the formation of the
child's attitudes toward people.
The custom is for the mother to
frustrate the child in a way that
seems as cruel to us as the custom
of spanking seems to many non-
American people. For example,
she often stimulates a temper
tantrum in her child by "borrow-
ing" another baby and holding
it in the presence of her own.
Her child's natural jealousy at first
results in rage, which the mother
does not respond to in any
relevant way. The mother at up-
per left, with the "borrowed
baby" on her hip, is laughing
at her son's rage. Eventually,
Balinese children learn to with-
draw from emotional give-and-
take with other people because
they learn that it will only bring
them pain. The little boy at cen-
ter left has already learned to be
unresponsive to the "borrowed
baby" situation. In later years,
this "awayness," as the Balinese
call it, develops many manifesta-
tions. At lower left a mother and
daughter both display the form
of withdrawal which a Balinese
may temporarily assume in the
midst of any social situation
where he feels emotionally
unsafe (often he falls asleep).

The Balinese are fond of large, busy groups where emotional contact with people is "safe," because limited, and where they can withdraw emotionally without being noticed. They are also fond of rote work because it permits daydreaming. At right is a group at work on the preparation of food, which combines group activity with rote activity.

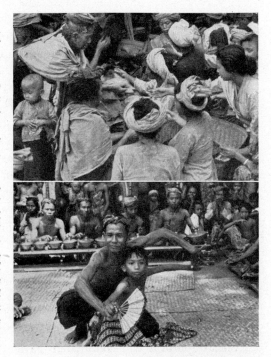

The basic form of learning in Bali is by rote rather than by understanding and (in keeping with the fundamental tendency toward withdrawal) often demands only passive participation from the learner. Here a child is being made to perform the correct movements for the formal dance, which is climaxed by a deep trance, the most extreme form of withdrawal.

Another outstanding feature of the Balinese is the unpleasant emotion connected with eating meals. They avoid eating in public if possible, and if others are present, they turn their backs on each other, hunch over their food, and eat as quickly as possible, as in the photograph at right. Some observers have commented that their attitude resembles the attitude in our society toward elimination. It is thought to arise from the child's earliest feeding experiences, shown at right, below. Usually he is fed while lying helpless on his back in his bath, and the food is forced into his mouth despite his crying and discomfort. Here the social conditioning of the hunger drive is obvious. (Photographs courtesy of New York Academy of Sciences, Gregory Bateson, and Margaret Mead.)

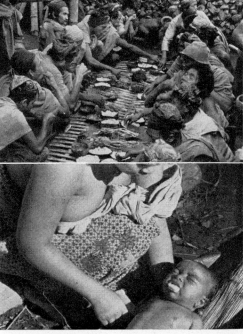

How the Derived Motives Develop 155

The fact that man's derived motives differ among different peoples is due to the fact that they are not inborn. They have no direct biological basis, but are the result of experience in whatever social environment happens to surround the individual. Every child, no matter what his race or country or nationality, is born with a fairly clean slate as far as his derived motives are concerned, although his biological drives and appetites are fixed by maturation. It is social approval or disapproval that later shapes his organic drives into complex motives. This fact is discouraging, in that each child at birth cannot possess all the long-accumulated wisdom of his people; but it also presents an opportunity and a challenge. In order to change certain attitudes and ways of behaving, we can change the learning situation that our society provides for educating children at home, school, movie, and church.

We have seen how social approval is the determining factor in the direction of man's motivation; let us see now how social approval maintains its power to influence people.

How social approval keeps its power—or becomes modified

Social approval will continue to have reward value only as long as it remains associated with the relief of basic bodily needs. We will continue to love our parents or our community only if they satisfy our wants. Should it become apparent that they are failing to provide the things we need and want, the desire for their approval may eventually decline. A mother who consistently neglects her child will not be loved or looked to for approval. In the same way, a society which encourages a man to be self-supporting and self-respecting and then does not give him an opportunity to earn a living may make him feel that in such a "rotten world" he no longer cares what anyone thinks of him. The Great Depression of the 1930's brought great physical misery, but it also drove many men and women into deep disillusionment. These disillusioned people then lost their respect for the social codes; some took to liquor and crime, while others gave up all efforts at self-respect.

A person desires the approval of society as a whole only when he is in sympathy with the prevalent attitudes and ways of behaving. While the criminal does not try to win approval of an honest society, he works for social approval as much as does the honest man—the only difference is that he wants the approval of a small group whose private codes run counter to the prevailing social codes, not the approval of society as a whole.

How does it come about that a person may disapprove of the prevalent social attitudes? The answer, in a democracy, is that there are many groups which hold perfectly legal, but quite different, codes of behavior. People may be radical or conservative, may accept or reject the established standards of morality, may hold that Jews and Negroes are to be persecuted as "inferior races" or are to be respected as equals. People within these subgroups react with approval or disapproval to certain words, ideas, acts, or situations, and they condition their children and others with whom they come in contact to react in the same way.

These subgroups within a society can often become strong and openly challenge the attitudes and behavior that have long received the stamp of general "social approval." The challenge may come in the area of religion, morality, or economic philosophy. The new attitude may be accepted by a large group of people, and yet there may be no adjustment in the formal laws and institutions, which then lose their motivating power. For example, long before repeal of the prohibition against liquor, many people were openly expressing their disapproval of society's disapproval of alcoholic drinking.

The fact that some people break away from accepted social standards can be a force for evil or for good. A serious problem today is the large number of citizens who feel that society is not being run as it should be and that their lives are somehow purposeless and empty, but who are completely cynical or hopeless about any changes occurring and are willing to let "them" run things "their way." On the other hand, when the subgroups resort to violence and intimidation of voters, the outcome is even worse. In a democracy, peaceful change by majority decision is basic and is surrendered only in extreme emergencies. If the shortcomings of a social order cause dissenting subgroups to undertake legitimate social reorganization, the end effect is good: orderly dissenting behavior can produce desperately needed social reform.

The great political leaders and social and economic reformers are acute students of human motivation. The experienced senator, for example, has a practical understanding of some of the social motives, the interests and values and attitudes, that concern man as a "political animal." He knows why the Republicans are against a certain bill and the Democrats for it. But knowledge of human motivation is not confined to politics. The modern teacher makes learning more interesting and thus easier by relating it to the students' interests and needs. The employer is called upon to make frequent application of his knowledge of human motives; today efforts are made to satisfy the employee's basic psychological needs in order to preserve industrial peace. The advertiser appeals to the sexual appetite when he photographs his product along with a girl in a bathing-suit, and he counts on the prestige effect of society women to sell the cigarettes they endorse. The wise mother knows that it is easier to appeal to the need for approval than to resort to force. We all appraise almost unconsciously the drives and appetites and interests and values that make people act the way they do. Whether we appraise them well and to good effect is another question—and one of the principal reasons for an interest in scientific psychology.

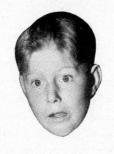

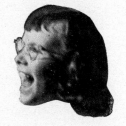

CHAPTER 5

Emotions:
inner springs
of action

Ways of Looking at Emotion

Emotions in Daily Living

Interpreting Emotional Expression in Others

Controlling Our Emotions

LITERATURE IS RICH in vivid presentations of the various nuances and combinations of the basic human emotions. Emotions are the stock in trade of the poet, dramatist, and novelist, who skillfully portray not only the emotions of the characters but also the situation that evokes those emotions. But however stirring and revealing literature may be, it is not a systematic, objective source for understanding emotion. A novelist's work may illuminate a given person or situation; it cannot compete with more technical knowledge as the means of understanding cause-and-effect relationships and emotions as a whole.

WAYS OF LOOKING AT EMOTION

IF YOU WERE ASKED to define "emotion" you might be somewhat at a loss. The dictionary will tell you that the word *emotion* comes from the Latin verb *emovere*, which means "to stir" or "upset." And common sense will tell you that the word means a strong feeling or agitation of some kind. But we all know, too, that emotions are very complex.

An *emotion* is a process which plays a particularly dynamic or energizing role in a person's life. As with other types of motives, it is a

Ways of Looking at Emotion 159

process which arouses, sustains, and directs activity. It is distinguished from physiological motives, however, by being dependent on the organism's psychological processes of representing or realizing *the significance of the situation.* For example, the pain which you feel when the dentist strikes a nerve is a relatively simple motive and is eased as soon as he ceases drilling; your emotional reaction as you sit waiting for the dentist to begin is dependent upon no such simple factors but upon your complex psychological processes of perception and thinking which represent what you think the dentist is going to do. And so it is with all emotions in contrast with bodily drives —both serve as motivation, but emotions are relatively much more complex.

In order to meet the complexity of the emotions, it is necessary to look at them sometimes from one viewpoint and sometimes from another. These viewpoints arise from our basic definition of emotion, and from the way emotion functions in human life. Some ways of looking at emotion are as follows:

1 In terms of the stimulus or external situation which arouses the emotion.

2 As conscious experience, revealed by introspective reports.

3 As unconscious experience, revealed by both experimental and clinical studies.

4 In terms of the observable external and internal reactions which make up the emotion (that is, in terms of behavior patterns).

5 As helps or hindrances.

6 As drives.

Since these different ways of looking at emotion form the basis for understanding this complex human experience, we shall consider each of them in turn.

Emotions from the stimulus point of view

Mere knowledge of the external situation confronting an individual does not always permit accurate prediction of what emotional response he will make. To you a particular person could be an object of affection; to someone else, an object of disinterest or dislike. If two people find themselves in the same external situation, one may react one way and the other a different way, because of their past experience with the situation.

An emotion-provoking stimulus situation need not be a matter of action—it may be just a spoken word or phrase. As the child grows up and learns to use and understand more and more words, these words take on emotional connotations for him. Some words become pleasureful, some disgusting.

You have already learned how the desire for social approval conditions the child to react positively or negatively to certain symbols. If every time a child does something of which his mother does not approve, she frowns and says "bad," the word "bad" will come to have the same significance for behavior that the frown has. If the word "bad" is reinforced with a slap or with the removal of some desired toy, its value as a conditioned stimulus will be increased. Through the use of language it is possible to make children fear things that do not even exist. No child or adult in his right mind has ever seen a "bogeyman," yet foolish parents still—successfully—use this method of frightening children into obedience.

Of course, different words produce different degrees of emotion. One psychologist read a list of one hundred words to a group of fifty subjects and measured (by a method described on p. 417) the degree of emotion displayed by each subject (Smith[1]). He then averaged the degrees of emotion showed by the fifty subjects at the different words. The table shows the strength of response provoked by the five most effective and the five least effective words on the list. Note that the response to the word *kiss* was almost five times as violent as the response to the word *swim*.

Five most effective words		Five least effective words	
Stimulus word	Response	Stimulus word	Response
1. Kiss	72.8	96. Give	16.7
2. Love	59.5	97. Flower	16.1
3. Marry	58.5	98. Pond	15.5
4. Divorce	50.8	99. Pencil	15.4
5. Name (of subject)	48.7	100. Swim	14.2

However, words are just one kind of the infinite variety of symbols that can arouse an emotional response. For instance, people feel solemn when they stand before a monument to a dead soldier because the monument represents his suffering and sacrifice. And they feel momentarily happy when they see the jolly figure of Santa Claus, representing all the fun and excitement of Christmas. The above experiment is just a formal demonstration of a principle with which you are familiar from its operation in all the world around you, a principle which is highly relevant to a study of emotions from the stimulus point of view. This is the principle that people make emotional responses not only to a direct stimulus, but to symbols—that is, to things representing or suggesting that stimulus. But whether the stimulus is direct or symbolic, the important fact is that emotion must always be considered as a response to a stimulus.

Emotions as conscious experiences

Emotions are not just overt reactions to stimuli, but are also conscious experiences. People may be more interested in what the other fellow does than in what he experiences, but they are at least greatly interested in their own conscious experiences. A human being devoid of all his emotional life would become a robot, and no normal human being doubts the reality of emotion as a conscious experience. When you act angry in an exasperating situation, you *feel* angry. The method of introspection has been employed by psychologists, especially in the past, to analyze or identify some of the components in emotional experience. Thus, psychologists have made detailed reports of what visceral (internal bodily) strains they feel and of their intensity and localization, as well as of all the sensory and other conscious elements of the total experience.

Introspection has its limitations here because the introspections of different individuals must be reported in exactly the same language if they are to be directly comparable. This is hard to do, since it is difficult to give specific names to subjective phenomena. There would not be words enough to describe all conscious emotions even if they could be clearly separated. The method of introspection should not be neglected, however, for it is the only way to understand the consciousness of others. The experimental psychologist in searching for patterns of emotion uses the introspections of his subjects as basic data.

One alert psychologist arranged to have a psychology student who had been trained in introspection record her subjective experience upon receiving a "telephone message of importance." Her report follows:*

> "I received a telephone call and was told of my election to Phi Beta Kappa.
> "My mind seemed to be a 'blank,' that is, there seemed to be no ideas present, at least at first. Then there were kinaesthetic and organic sensations in the head as blood seemed to rush to head. I was hot all over and hands were moist—great emotion of joy. Organic sensations in chest, breathed fast, then it seemed as though I must say something to somebody. Want to 'burst' with such an emotion of joy and as always, I couldn't keep it to myself. Head became cooler and I tried to reason with myself in terms of snatchy verbal ideas to see

*This quotation used by permission from *Psychology of Feeling and Emotion*, by C. A. Ruckmick, © 1936, McGraw-Hill Book Co., Inc.

that I must calm down a little. Left my hairdresser and felt so good that I wanted to run. Exhilaration and still also joy.

"Met two girls in hallway who knew about my election. I was so glad to be able to talk to someone. It seemed almost as though I should weep—literally 'weep with joy.' Ideas a little confused and almost forgot to say anything. Then I asked about my friends. Organic sensations in abdomen, chest, and head due to feeling so good that all was tight and strained. Later there was relaxation and a completely worn-out feeling." (Ruckmick[2])

Undoubtedly the behavior and physiological changes accompanying the subjective sensations this girl so vividly describes could have been accurately recorded by some objective means. But only introspection can reveal one important aspect of emotion: the conscious experience that makes emotion meaningful to the person undergoing it.

Emotions as unconscious experiences

Many psychologists do not consider that emotions need to include conscious awareness of reactions to stimuli. They believe that through a process called *repression*, a person can eliminate conscious awareness of both the stimuli and the responses in emotion if they cause him psychological pain. This process will be discussed more fully in Chapter 13, but you have already met an experimental example of how an unconscious idea can influence conscious behavior and attitudes: the hypnotized subject (p. 17) was governed by an idea he was not aware of. In the same way that ideas can be unconscious, emotional reactions can be unconscious. People's external behavior, and even their internal physiological responses, are often influenced by emotions of which they themselves are entirely unaware. Psychoanalysts believe that many painful emotions experienced during childhood are very early repressed from consciousness but continue to influence behavior and adjustment all through life. Unconscious emotions play an important role in bodily functioning and disease (see pp. 172-177).

Emotions as external and internal reactions

In emotions two kinds of physical responses are involved: external and internal. Although the external features of emotion are much easier to observe than the internal, they by themselves do not constitute the emotion.

External response. The external responses of bodily and facial muscles play a direct role in moving physical objects of the environment (hitting an enemy with fist or missile) and in influencing other members of the social group (smiling, scowling, laughing).

The description of human emotions on the basis of external response is not at all perfect, and any classification is somewhat arbitrary. However, it is helpful to consider emotional responses in four categories: destruction, approach, retreat, and stopping of response.

Destruction. In anger, attack is the typical behavior. An angry animal or an uncivilized man makes a physically destructive attack—he throws himself upon his enemy, biting, scratching, choking, hitting, spitting, snarling, according to his species. But in civilized man, the attack is more often symbolic. Words take the place of blows; physical injury gives way to sneering words which attempt to lower the prestige of the enemy in the eyes of his fellows. The end result of anger is, nevertheless, essentially the same in man and beast—real or symbolic destruction.

Approach. In pleasant emotions the essential response is approach. The biological function of approach to the stimulus object is to permit further stimulation. Elation is essentially an approach reaction which follows success in any activity—or which anticipates success, as the confident athlete becomes elated before an important contest.

Retreat or flight. Fear typically involves flight. Flight from a dangerous situation may often be the best adjustment. The flight may be physical or symbolic. Suppose that in crossing a street you hear a horn honk and look up to see an automobile bearing down upon you. You run! Physical flight of this sort is typical even of civilized man when confronted with a dangerous situation which will not respond to treatment by words. But in most of civilized life we "retreat" through words—through apologies, compromises, flattery, or discussion of the emotion-producing situation.

Stopping of response. Gloom (in more severe form called "grief") does not involve destruction, approach, or retreat. In such emotion the response is a widespread stopping of usual responses. In the extreme form the individual refuses to respond to some of the most potent of stimuli. There are patients in mental hospitals, for example, who are too sad to eat and who must be forcibly fed.

Gloom and grief are not altogether unadaptive, however, since these emotional states serve to attract the attention of the individual to the thing that is wrong in his life and may motivate him to do something about it. For example, a very successful lawyer whose active and profitable practice had caused him to neglect his family was literally prostrated with grief when his adolescent son was shot and killed by the police while attempting to escape arrest in a stolen car. But after a brief period of total incapacity, the lawyer became active in securing funds to support the efforts of an institute to study and control juvenile delinquency.

The emotion of gloom corresponds to the "closed for repairs" condition of a retail establishment or the "down time" of machinery which is being repaired. In the long run, gloom is adaptive because it tends to re-establish effective functioning of the individual.

Internal response. The other kind of physical response involved in emotion is the vast complex of visceral (or internal bodily) responses. The activity of the adrenal glands is well understood, and there is mounting evidence for the involvement of the thyroids and pituitaries in the complex of internal response.

If you could look directly into the blood stream of the person suffering any violent emotion, you would discover that the medulla of the adrenal gland was pouring its secretion, adrenin, into the blood stream in excessive amount. This secretion, traveling through the blood stream to the various parts of the body, is responsible for many characteristics of strong emotion. Under its influence the liver releases stored sugar into the blood; chemical changes occur which cause the blood to clot more quickly. Blood pressure rises in strong emotion; the pulse beats more rapidly and more vigorously; the air passages into the lungs enlarge to admit more air. The pupil of the eye enlarges so that more light may enter. Sweat breaks out all over the body, particularly on the inner surfaces of the hand. The temperature of the skin may rise or fall several degrees. All these changes are one evidence of that close connection between body and mind which is the special study of psychosomatic ("mind-body") medicine. They help explain, for instance, why, as you will see later, a person under emotional stress can develop painful physical symptoms which are not pretended but are a product of the internal responses of emotion.

Our emotions as drives

There is no sharp line setting off the emotions from the physiological drives previously discussed. Both are motivational in character—that is, both serve to arouse, direct, and sustain activity. If you are on the beach for several hours, your thirst can lead you to seek drinking-water; but your emotionalized anticipation of thirst can also lead you to bring along a thermos-bottle.

When you anticipate some drive, and when you react emotionally to some situation, the emotional reaction is of course reflecting some previous reactions which you actually have had. But in such cases it is difficult to decide whether the reaction has more the character of an emotional reaction or of a bodily drive. It is probably best to regard it as an emotional reaction, because its continuance depends upon some complex brain processes whereby the person represents to himself the nature of the situation which may be expected. With bodily drives, on the other hand, the continuance of the state of motivation depends not upon such continuing mental processes but upon some continuing stimulation or chemical condition of a relatively simple sort.

Emotions, like drives, intensify and direct the reaction to some external stimulus. In fact, the social importance of emotion is its effect on the way an individual behaves toward the objects and people of his physical and social environment.

EMOTIONS IN DAILY LIVING

Some of our emotions are very intense, like those experienced when our lives are in danger; others are less strong but provide variation and coloring for our experience. Some merely add to the joy or displeasure of our everyday living; others are capable of having a tremendous effect on the efficiency of our activities.

Emotions as helps and hindrances

Even when very intense, emotions can either help or hinder us in various ways.

Emotions can prepare for action in an emergency. Under the impetus of emotion, men and animals are able to perform feats that would be impossible for them under normal conditions. In three ways emotion helps the individual cope with an emergency situation:

First: in strong emotion a person is capable of action over a longer period of time than would be possible if he were entirely calm. One successful track coach never allows his milers to run more than three laps of the four in practice. He paces them to a winning time first on one lap, then on two, and finally on three laps. He depends upon the excitement of the actual track meet to carry the runner through the last lap and, in fact, to supply the burst of energy needed for the final sprint which may determine who wins the event.

A second effect of strong emotion is the capacity for a momentary exertion of one's maximum strength. An excited man once carried a small safe across a room in a burning building and threw it out the window. Later, after his excitement had subsided, he found himself barely able to budge the safe. Combat veterans report similar experiences of sudden bursts of strength and endurance.

The third effect of strong emotion is that of rendering the individual insensitive to what would normally be excruciating pain. A college football player went into three successive plays with a dislocated knee-joint which made his right leg completely useless and which under less excitement would have caused him unbearable pain when moved or touched. Shortly after the player was taken out of the game, he fainted from agony and exhaustion.

Emotion can upset our patterns of response. Although emotions are of adaptive value in such emergency situations as these, upon other occasions they can be distinctly disadvantageous. Our finer and more complex performances are impaired by very strong emotion. The tennis player or baseball pitcher who "loses his head" in a game is lost. The effect of strong emotion on ability to execute well-learned verbal responses is illustrated by stage fright. Violent emotion is even more destructive to original thought. The person who can "think on his feet" is fortunate, though his gift may be emotional control rather than unusual intelligence. A very intelligent person may become temporarily stupid when he is under emotional stress.

Emotions as foundations of living. You may have heard or read of people who prefer to "live dangerously"—that is, live in constant emotional upswings and downswings—rather than pass through existence in "cowlike content." This is an extreme view which can lead to much unhappiness. But still there is no denying that emotions do make our lives richer and fuller with the variety and subtlety, excitement and quiet pleasure they give to existences that may be outwardly dull and routine. If unhappy or unbearably strong emotions are not preponderant, no one wants to abolish the complex processes that are given the name of "emotions."

There is social as well as personal value in emotion. Without the feelings of mother love, children would not be adequately cared for and educated, and the social group would either be unable to pass on its traditions and knowledge from one generation to another or would die out altogether. Without pleasure in work of some kind, the physical means of subsistence would be neglected. Without aesthetic pleasure, art would die. Without curiosity, science could not exist. People incapable of emotion would not experience the party loyalty, patriotism, and intense interest in social reform that underlie political life today. Their religious services, if they continued to attract the public at all, would probably become academic, factual lectures in comparative religion rather than a beautiful and moving emotional experience. And so it goes through all the areas of social life. Emotion is an essential foundation of living.

Everyday emotions

To gain some notion of the nature of emotional life from day to day, fifty-one men students were asked by the writer to report the emotions of fear, anger, worry, annoyance, jealousy, shame, elation, and dejection which had been consciously experienced during the preceding typical week. All these emotions play a vital part in our lives. The following indicates the number of men reporting each of these emotions as having been experienced during that week:

Worry	46	Fear	31
Annoyance	43	Dejection	29
Elation	35	Shame	22
Anger	34	Jealousy	15

Apparently, the strong emotions of anger and fear are less important in daily living than the nagging worries and petty annoyances which beset us.

Worry and fear. Worry is essentially a fear reaction attached to a future event which may or may not take place. Worry usually comes in the evening during the study period, and the same is true of fear. Worry typically lasts two or three hours, according to students' reports, and is more often experienced during the middle of the school week than on weekends, when students tend to relax and "take their minds off their troubles." Fear is of shorter duration, but it also tends to occur more frequently during the week. The most commonly reported subject of fear and worry was failure in courses. Many college students report that they become so emotional in an examination that they forget simple facts, dates, and formulas that have been thoroughly studied. Sometimes, of course, these reports are mere alibis through which the student hopes to be excused for failure or to be granted an extra chance. In other instances, emotional blocks certainly do occur.

> In one extensive study, pupils in the ninth grade were asked for reports on their emotional experiences at the close of each of four examinations in mathematics. There was no definite tendency for the good students, as measured by grades in the examinations, to be more or less emotional in the examination situation. Individuals who showed the most emotion, however, were more variable in their examination marks. The emotional group averaged about the same as the calmer group, but showed more tendency to get high grades on one examination and low grades on the next. (Hastings[3])

More violent fears—the fears of soldiers in battle—are clearly revealed in the answers to 4504 anonymous questionnaires distributed to 1985 flying officers and 2519 enlisted fliers of World War II (Shaffer[4]). All these men had had extensive combat experience. The following table shows the per cent of men reporting these symptoms:

"During combat missions did you feel"	% reporting "often"	% reporting "often" or "sometimes"
A pounding heart and rapid pulse............	30	86
Feeling that your muscles are very tense.......	30	83
Being easily irritated, angry, or "sore".........	22	80
Dryness of the throat or mouth..............	30	80
"Nervous perspiration" or "cold sweat"........	26	79
"Butterflies" in the stomach.................	23	76
Feeling of unreality, that this couldn't be happening to you	20	69
Having to urinate (pass water) very frequently..	25	65
Trembling	11	64
Feeling confused or rattled.................	3	53
Feeling weak or faint	4	41
Right after a mission, not being able to remember details of what happened.................	5	39
Feeling sick to the stomach.................	5	38
Not being able to concentrate..............	3	35
Wetting or soiling your pants..............	1	5

This tabulation represents a fair scale for the severity of the fear reaction in the average person. All normal persons have encountered in everyday life fear-provoking situations strong enough to give one or more of the symptoms at the top of the list; few of us have shown any as violent as those at the bottom of the list. It is very striking here that emotion involves the whole person—"body" as well as "mind."

Annoyance and anger. Annoyance is a mild form of anger. It, like worry, is also likely to occur in the evening and is usually directed against some other person. It is typically of short duration, lasting on the average about twenty seconds. When it passes, it leaves no noticeable aftereffects.

Anger has about the same characteristics as annoyance except that it lasts much longer and is more intense. Anger in college students has been extensively investigated in two interesting studies.

> In one investigation, students at Oregon State College kept an accurate record of their anger outbursts during a week's time (Meltzer[5]). The results were found to agree with similar ones previously obtained with a group of girls at Barnard College (Gates[6]). The technique used was constant for the two investigations, so that comparisons are valid.

The number of outbursts of anger was found to range from none to fifteen a week. Men averaged 39 per cent more outbursts than did women. There was little difference between sorority and nonsorority women in frequency of reported anger, and there was practically no difference between men living in and outside fraternities. Thus there is no evidence from this study that living in a "house" produces a better emotional adjustment than does the life outside.

There were some interesting differences between organized and unorganized students in the days of the week when they were most susceptible to anger. Monday and Tuesday were the days of most frequent outbursts for the organized men and women, and Friday and Saturday were calmest. The independent men and women, however, were more easily angered on Saturday than on Monday. This difference in the days when the organized and unorganized groups were most susceptible to anger suggests that the thwarting of desire for social activity may play an important role in anger. Over the weekend, the organized groups engage in social activities not enjoyed by the independents. Presumably the dances and parties of the fraternity and sorority groups lessen the emotional tension which is built up throughout the week so that they are less susceptible to emotional outbursts on weekends than during the week. The independents, however, may be more subject to outbursts on weekends because they do not have such an emotional outlet. It is interesting that for all students Sunday was freer from outbursts of anger than any other day.

Outbursts of anger were much more frequent during the hour before a meal than during the hour following. This result indicates that an organic tension will predispose a person to anger, while the contentment which follows a meal is conducive to peace of mind and tranquillity. Anger occurred more frequently during periods of tiredness or sleepiness, when emotional control is low, than at other times.

Of all the outbursts, 51 per cent were brought about by the thwarting of self-assertion by other persons; 35 per cent were elicited by the thwarting of self-assertion by things; about 6 per cent of the incidents grew out of thwarted organic activities; and the other 8 per cent occurred in complex situations which could not easily be analyzed.

The results of the Oregon study, taken as a whole, illustrate that, in our culture at least, anger is a social affair primarily—a reaction to frustration by persons rather than things—and that organic tensions predispose one toward it. Certain rules of behavior are suggested by these studies of anger in college students. Do not attempt to settle a difficulty when you are tired, sleepy, or hungry. During the week, provide yourself with some interesting activities to permit the relaxation of tensions which mount at that time.

Jealousy. Jealousy is a combination of anger and dejection which is not frequently reported by college students. This fact may have its explanation in the natural reluctance to admit experiencing an emotion which is generally considered undesirable. In the author's study of the fifty-one college students, jealousy, when it came, was reported as occurring like worry during the hours of the evening when students tire of studying. It is interesting that somewhat fewer than one half of the men students who reported emotions of jealousy attributed them to frustration in love. Failure to excel other men in sports, scholarship, or activities was a somewhat more frequent cause of jealousy.

Exciting entertainment. Modern life provides certain exciting amusements which arouse very violent emotions and are decidedly injurious to the mental and physical health of the individual, particularly to that of the growing child. Many psychologists are convinced, for example, that the excessive emotional excitement engendered by witnessing too-thrilling movies can only be bad for the child.

As a part of a general program to study the effects of motion pictures on growing children, observations were made on the degree of emotional excitement in children witnessing movie thrillers (Dysinger and Ruckmick[7]). Films which have very little effect upon adults are sufficient to set the heart of the adolescent racing. In general, boys are most affected by scenes of conflict, while girls are more susceptible to emotional excitement produced by love scenes. Excitement built up by sensational motion pictures may bring about visceral upheaval which does not subside for more than twenty-four hours.

Thousands of American children spend every available moment at the movies. Their emotional participation seems to be much greater than that of adults, perhaps because they lack the experience which keeps adults aware that "it's only a movie." The excitement these children are experiencing can provide a healthy emotional release, but psychologists agree that it should not be too prolonged or too frequent, for the sake of emotional health.

It is by no means clear that the motion pictures are greater offenders than the radio and the comic sections of our newspapers, yet the sponsors of radio programs, the producers of motion pictures, and the publishers of newspapers are not entirely to be blamed. They are merely satisfying what they feel to be a popular demand. They are decidedly receptive to any communication from parents showing that there is also a demand for saner and less stimulating materials for the entertainment of children. It lies within the power of parents to reduce this important source of emotional excess in everyday life.

Moods in daily living

Usually an emotion is fairly brief, although some of the subjects in the Oregon State College study (pp. 169-170) reported outbursts of anger lasting as long as two days. Such long-drawn-out emotions, whether anger or some other emotion, are usually called *moods*.

Our moods vary with the day of the week and the hour of the day as well as with the season. Two surveys of the moods of male college students agreed essentially in finding that students feel bluer during the first and last half hours of the day than at other times; that they feel lower on Mondays than on any other day of the week; and that happiness of mood is highest in spring and summer, lower in the fall, and reaches the bottom in January, February, and March. (Springer and Roslow,[8] and Cason[9])

Another investigator followed the course of moods of twelve workingmen to see how moods were related to working efficiency throughout an entire year. He found that there was a definite periodicity or fluctuation of mood which could not be accounted for on the basis of environmental changes or apparent physical condition. The cycle of change from trough to trough ranged from three to nine weeks among the twelve subjects, but in no case did the length of the cycle for a given person vary from his own average by more than a week. (Hersey[10])

The implications of these findings for daily living are simply that we should expect daily and seasonal fluctuation in our moods and should not worry when they occur. If, of course, the fluctuations come too fast or if the difference between crest and trough is extreme, the individual should consult some competent psychologist or psychiatrist.

The role of the emotions in disease: psychosomatic medicine

Medical authorities have long agreed that illness and uncontrolled emotionality go together and that health and happiness are parts of one pattern (Weiss[11] and Perry[12]). Now many of them insist that actually, illnesses are very often caused by faulty emotional patterns. One physician, for instance, points to evidence indicating that persistent and repeated emotional disturbances may so overstimulate the alimentary tract that organic lesions develop. It is his belief that uncomplicated peptic ulcers—that is, open sores on the stomach wall which are unresponsive to medical treatment—are probably always of nervous origin and that psychotherapy is always needed to cure them (Kaplan[13]). Is his contention true? Is there an emotional factor in peptic ulcers?

One interesting experiment on this problem took 52 patients showing the characteristic symptoms of peptic ulcer, and divided them into two groups. The first group of 32 patients was the experimental group. They were trained daily for six weeks in the restraint of worry, in discussion, effort, and self-suggestion. The control group of 20 patients was trained for six weeks in nonpsychological subjects. Both received standard diet under medical supervision.

After only three weeks of training, 31 patients in the experimental group were free from pain and discomfort, and 26 of these remained symptom-free after the end of the treatment. All 20 of the patients of the control—or psychologically untreated—group were made free from symptoms as a result of diet and medication, but within two weeks after the expansion of diet, symptoms recurred in 18 cases out of the 20. Not only did the psychological training aid in the initial relief of symptoms, but it aided in keeping the patient in good health after the training was completed. (Chappell, Stefano, Rogerson, and Pike[14])

Two doctors working at the Mayo Clinic (Wolf and Wolff[15]) have reported an interesting case of a peptic ulcer which was due to the patient's emotional life. The subject with whom they worked was a laboratory assistant at the Mayo Clinic, a man of fifty-six who at the age of nine had swallowed scalding-hot clam chowder. As a result of the burn, scar tissue had filled up his esophagus (the tube leading from mouth to stomach). After the accident he could not take food in the usual way but had to feed himself through a surgically produced fistula, or opening made through his abdominal wall into his stomach. He put his food directly into his stomach after it had been chewed to start digestive juices flowing and to permit him to enjoy the taste of his meals. This condition, so unfortunate for the patient, was most fortunate for science since it permitted the physicians to make direct observations of what happened in the stomach when the subject was at ease emotionally and when he was emotionally upset.

They found that under normal emotional conditions, acid in small amounts was continuously secreted with occasional periods of increased flow and increased concentration of blood in the walls of the stomach. The stomach contracted vigorously from time to time. When the subject reported feelings of withdrawal—as in the emotions of fear and sadness—the acid secretion in the stomach was inhibited, the contractions stopped, and the mucous membrane of the stomach paled as the blood concentration tended to decrease. When the emotions he reported were those of anger and resentment, observation of his stomach activity showed that the acid flow increased, that the mucous membrane flushed as blood concentrated still more heavily there, and that the stomach contractions increased in frequency and vigor. All these stomach changes resulting from anger made the mucous membrane particularly liable to erosion, so that the stomach wall itself was left unprotected. The result was that hemorrhages started from such trifling stimuli as the contractions of the stomach itself or from the scratching of partly digested food particles. Once the hemorrhage had begun, the wound was subject to irritation from the acid gastric juices, and a peptic ulcer was well under way. These processes are clearly shown in the illustrations below and on the opposite page.

Changes in gastric physiology associated with feelings of hostility

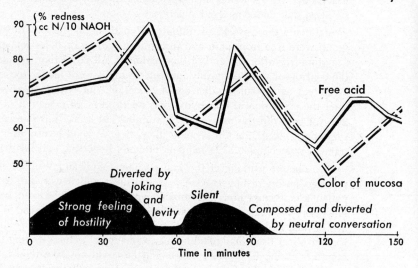

(After Stewart Wolf and Harold G. Wolff, *Human Gastric Function*, © Oxford University Press, 1947, p. 137.)

The graph above was drawn from observations made one morning on the patient whose stomach was open for scientific study. He came to the laboratory feeling bitter resentment and hostility, having just been through a very humiliating experience. The incident was discussed with him in an unsympathetic manner for the first half hour, resulting in an increase in hostility as well as an increase in stomach acidity and a heightening of redness in the mucous membrane. Then an attempt was made to divert him, which succeeded in partially relieving his hostility and abating the stomach acidity and high color of the mucosa. After another half hour the conversation was dropped, and the patient lapsed into silent brooding; again the acid content of the gastric juice rose, as did the amount of coloring in the membrane. Finally he was diverted again, and this time his emotions were completely dispelled and his stomach conditions returned to normal.

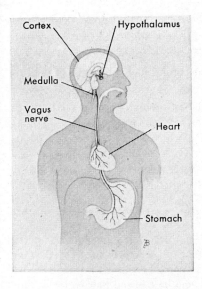

Peptic ulcers have been successfully treated by severing the vagus nerve, an important link between the stomach and the cerebral cortex. The vagus nerve runs down from the medulla, innervating the heart and stomach. It controls the secretion of gastric juices which is caused by nervous stimuli (secretion is also stimulated chemically by the action of food when it reaches the stomach). Overstimulation of the vagus nerve can cause secretion of gastric juice before the food enters the stomach, and this premature secretion seems sometimes to cause ulcers. When the stomach branch of the vagus nerve is cut, the nervously caused gastric secretion is stopped without damaging the necessary secretion from chemical causes.

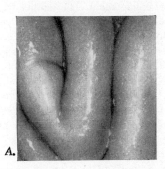

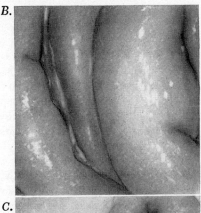

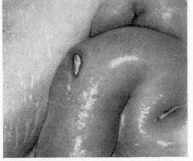

A. *Normal mucosal folds of the stomach while individual is feeling secure and contented. (Approx. actual size)*

B. *Same folds, engorged with blood when the individual is suffering hostility and resentment. (Approx. actual size)*

C. *Small punched-out ulceration induced by the hyperactive supply of gastric juice on the engorged mucosal folds. (Approx. actual size)*

After Stewart Wolf and H. G. Wolff, *Human Gastric Function,* © Oxford University Press, 1947, p. 223.)

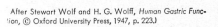

It seems quite likely, then, that the physical disease of peptic ulcer has its origins in emotional stresses, which produce overactivity of the stomach and thus lead to hemorrhage and ulcer formation.

This kind of research, of which there has been a great deal (Weiss and English[16]), has indicated that a certain amount of our slang, known among doctors as "organ language," is more physiologically accurate and less metaphorical than we might think. Such phrases as "It broke my heart," "He hasn't the guts for it," and "I was really griped" seem to be quite literal expressions of the facts with which psychosomatic medicine deals. The following case of "A Youth Who Was 'Griped'" is illustrative:

"Born in Connecticut of Methodist parents, he was raised in a small Massachusetts city. The family consisted of a kindly father, congenial with the boy, a domineering mother on whom the boy was very dependent during his childhood, and a younger sister. The medical history reveals little except that the boy was 'high strung' at the age of eleven. School years were successful and at graduation he started 'keeping company with' a Protestant girl whom his mother knew and liked. This went on for three years while he learned a trade and held his first job. At the age of twenty-one he realized that he really cared little for the girl and broke off the engagement. The mother was irate and scolded him endlessly, and the patient reports that this 'griped him like hell.' He revolted, went with a new crowd, and became engaged to a Catholic girl. During these months he first noticed constipation; later on he began to have abdominal cramps and frequent bowel movements with mucus. Because of these symptoms he came to the Out-Patient Department of the . . . Hospital, where he was treated. . . . Therapy consisted of atropine, to relax the spasm of the intestinal smooth muscle, and discussion to make him understand his psychological impasse. The parents were also interviewed. Symptoms ceased, the girl was accepted by the parents, and the boy has only had one recurrence of the mucous colitis, a short attack after an automobile accident that led to a lawsuit.

"The [patient's] life chart clearly shows the temporal relationship between social and medical data. . . . That problem . . . can be simplified down to the brusque statements that *the boy had nerve enough to oppose a domineering mother but didn't have the guts to see it through without medical help.*" (Cobb[17])

Other parts of the body besides the organs of digestion and secretion are susceptible to diseases arising from emotional stresses. Strong psychological components often are found in such respiratory illnesses as asthma; such heart and circulatory disorders as high blood pressure and neuro-circulatory asthenia (weakness of the nervous and circulatory system); and such skin troubles as urticaria. In fact, one medical man who has made a close study of emotional factors in disease estimates that about half of all patients going to physicians have illnesses precipitated largely by prolonged emotional disturbance (Margolis[18]).

Modern medicine, recognizing those facts, has begun to stress the need to treat sick people as total personalities, taking into account their emotional difficulties as well as their physical symptoms (Hinsie[19]). Physicians no longer dismiss as hypochondriacs patients whose illnesses are related to their emotional problems. Up-to-date clinics now include a psychiatric examination as a routine part of their procedures.

Although it is extremely difficult to distinguish cause and effect, physicians are coming to realize that emotional strain can also very definitely work against success in treating organic diseases such as tuberculosis, heart diseases, diabetes, and epilepsy. The effects of uncontrolled emotional outbursts are particularly bad in tuberculosis, since the patient must not engage in vigorous physical exercise and is thus denied an important means of working off his emotional tensions. The quality of nursing care is of extreme importance in treating psychosomatic illnesses since the nurse, in close contact with the patient, can do much to maintain a calm and cheerful mood in him.

A patient who has emotional problems needs a solid program of mental hygiene as well as the purely organic treatment. He must be taught how not to fall into emotional disturbances which are injurious and avoidable. And he must be helped in adjusting himself, his ambitions, and his activities to his illness. Chapter 14 will discuss some of the techniques of psychotherapy (mental healing) and readjustment which the psychologist and the physician together have worked out to help the person with emotional problems. For a detailed discussion of *How the Nervous System Functions in Emotion,* see pages 732-741.

INTERPRETING EMOTIONAL EXPRESSION IN OTHERS

IN POPULAR THOUGHT we have been inclined to believe that every emotion has some highly distinctive facial and vocal expression, and that the emotional reactions of other persons may be identified mainly by these cues. The psychological research on this problem has indicated that there actually exists a rough accuracy in the identification of emotion by such cues. It is worth knowing about these studies in order to guard against overemphasizing or underestimating the degree to which these cues serve as means of communication.

Patterns of facial expression

If the average person is asked whether he can tell how other people are feeling by the expression on their faces, he will probably say "Yes." It is interesting to see what psychologists have discovered about the ability to recognize what patterns of facial expression accompany what emotion.

Facial expression of emotion in babies. Two independently conducted experiments have shown that even very young children apparently show facial expressions of emotion which can be distinguished from one another.

One much-quoted experiment investigated the extent to which emotions of babies can be identified on the basis of facial expressions alone. A group of college students were shown motion pictures of emotional reactions in babies. They were specifically told that only four situations with their accompanying emotions were included: *hunger* due to deferred feeding; *fear* aroused by sudden dropping but with no pain involved; *pain* from being pricked with a needle; and *anger* aroused by restraint of movements of the head. The observers were shown several sequences of moving pictures of the babies' responses but were not told what the stimulus situation was for each sequence. The table shows how well the students could judge the emotions of anger and fear:

Actual emotion shown by babies	Percentage of judges calling it:				
	Hunger	*Pain*	*Anger*	*Fear*	*Don't know*
Anger	18	23	*31*	18	10
Fear	21	19	27	*30*	3

Notice that anger was correctly identified by only 31 per cent of the students and fear by only 30 per cent. However, since there were only four emotional situations from which the students could choose, they had a one-in-four or 25 per cent chance of judging the emotion correctly by sheer accident. Thus for both anger and fear, the percentage of correct identifications of the emotion was somewhat—but not very much—greater than would occur purely by chance. (Sherman and Sherman[20])

In another experiment, sixty-eight college students who were enrolled in a class in child training attempted to identify emotional expression in a ten-months-old baby. Each student was given a set of twelve descriptions of emotion-provoking situations and was asked to match the picture and the situation. Chance matching of photograph and situation would have resulted correctly in 8.3 per cent of the cases. The results revealed, however, correct matchings in 47.4 per cent of the cases, which is 5.7 times better than chance alone would account for. (Goodenough[21])

This evidence certainly indicates that it is possible to make rather accurate judgments of facial expressions in babies—what about in adults?

Facial expression of emotion in adults. In normal social conversation, we are able more or less successfully to follow the effects that our words have on the other person by carefully observing his face—which serves as a barometer of his emotion, perhaps giving warning that our words are too strong, or else reassuring us that our listener is not displeased. There are, however, significant limitations on our ability to tell emotion from facial expression. While the professional actor can register emotions which will be interpreted with a high degree of consistency, the facial expressions of the ordinary person cannot be judged so accurately, although they are easier to judge than the expressions of children.

Two psychologists have worked in succession to find out whether the emotions reported by normal human beings are accompanied by definite and easily recognizable facial expressions.

In the first experiment (Landis[22]), twelve women, eleven men, and one boy served as subjects. Each was stimulated by smelling a bottle of ammonia, falsely labeled syrup of lemon; looking at pornographic pictures; cutting the head off a living rat or seeing it done; receiving a severe electrical shock; looking at pictures of people with skin diseases; telling a lie.

After each stimulus was presented, photographs were taken of the facial expression, and the subjects were asked to give their introspective report as to what emotion had been aroused in them. Evidence that real emotions were evoked was yielded by the outcries, profanity, and other exclamations of the subjects. Stimulus situations arousing disgust, anger, astonishment, and sexual excitement were frequent enough to permit detailed analysis of the accompanying facial expressions.

The experimenter reported that the photographs showed no evidences of facial expressions characteristic of a particular emotion. However, it appears that he was looking only for obvious and easily recognizable patterns of facial muscles.

When another psychologist several years later analyzed the same photographs looking for more subtle patterns of facial expression, he found that some definite patterns could be made out (Davis[23]). Certain facial expressions seemed to go with some emotions more frequently than with others. For instance, his analysis of the pictures showed smiling in cases of reported pain in only 7 per cent of the observations, while smiling occurred in 60 per cent of the emotional responses reported as sexual. Also, a particular muscle group of the face was found to be involved in only 3 per cent of the cases of reported sexual emotion but in 50 per cent of the cases of reported pain. From this we can conclude that *there is a tendency for certain muscles or muscle groups to be involved in one particular emotion which are not involved in another.*

This second analysis also showed that situations the experimenter judged to be similar caused the subjects to show a high degree of similarity in their facial expressions. For example, the situation of listening to classical music gave rise to facial expression patterns which bore very little resemblance to any other patterns except those assumed when listening to jazz. Three situations involved crude sexual stimulation: viewing photographs of artists' models; looking at pornographic pictures; reading case histories of sexual problems. All three gave rise to emotional responses which tended to a very high degree to involve the same facial muscles. It is interesting to note that the facial expression pattern assumed while looking at pictures of loathsome skin diseases closely resembled those which occurred in the three sexual situations; material suggesting romantic love gave different patterns of facial expression.

The work of these two psychologists when taken together shows us that while no all-or-nothing patterns of facial expression are to be found in each of the emotions, there is some tendency for certain muscles to be involved more frequently than others in the facial expression of a particular emotion. And the fact that recognizable facial patterns could be found proves that, although individual differences are great, there is a central core of common elements which can be isolated. However he may do it, there is no doubt that the adult can with fair accuracy judge emotions from facial expressions, indicating that there are definite facial patterns which accompany emotional patterns.

The studies just described were concerned with facial expressions displayed under carefully designed experimental conditions. Another interesting experiment has been performed to discover whether people display recognizable facial patterns of emotion in actual life situations.

To investigate the judgment of facial expressions of emotion aroused naturally under conditions of everyday life, the psychologist selected fourteen candid-camera photographs from back issues of picture magazines and had two sets of lantern slides made from them. The slides of one set included everything in the original picture. The second set contained only an enlargement of the face selected for study. The slides containing the facial expressions alone were submitted to psychology students, who were instructed to judge the person's emotional reactions. Since the photographs were taken from picture magazines, and since the subjects were not questioned as to the actual emotions they were experiencing, the actual emotions they were feeling could not be known. All that could be determined from asking the students to judge the emotions was how closely their judgments agreed with each other, rather than how accurate they were. However, the fact that the judges did agree that the expressions were different indicates that different facial expressions do accompany different emotions.

The first group of ninety students was shown the first set of slides, containing the facial expression alone, and asked to indicate in writing, "What emotion is being experienced by this person?" A record was then made of their answers. A week later these same students judged the expression again but this time in its original setting. Then a list was made up of the terms they used most frequently both times and was given to a second group of sixty-five students from another campus. On being shown the first set of slides, this group was asked to indicate which term of the list best represented the facial expression shown. (A new term could be inserted if none on the list seemed appropriate.) They were then shown the second set of slides as soon as the first interpretations had been made and were again asked to choose an appropriate term from the list drawn up of the first group's reactions.

Interestingly enough, there was a marked similarity between the two judgments of each group, indicating that they could discern the emotion underlying a given expression from the face alone, without knowing the situation. Moreover, the two groups of students agreed fairly closely on their judgments. That there was not extremely wide variation in judgment within each group is shown by the fact that in no instance was an expression predominantly judged as among the unpleasant emotions interpreted as "joy" or "happiness." (Munn[24])

This study clearly indicates that there are facial expressions which accompany different emotions and which can be distinguished from each other.

The eyes vs. the mouth as revealers of emotion. In discussing the facial expression of emotion it is worth while to examine the popular belief that the eyes are "the windows of the soul." What do psychologists have to say about the relative importance of the eyes and mouth as revealers of emotion?

One psychologist (Dunlap[25]) took pictures of college students who had been subjected to different types of stimulations, arousing different types of emotional response. The "judges" were instructed to examine them and select from a list supplied by the experimenter the term most accurately describing each facial expression. The list of terms included *pleased, annoyed, interested, despondent, tired, resentful, disgusted, angry, frightened,* etc. After the pictures as a whole had been identified, copies of them were cut in two, separating the eyes and the mouth. The parts were then interchanged in various combinations. "Pleased" eyes were coupled with the mouth of the same person expressing pain; eyes showing pain were combined with the mouth of the same person showing pleasure. The two new photographs were then mounted below fresh, unmutilated photographs. These were given to a class of fifty men, who were asked to label the mutilated pictures to show which most resembled the complete picture in emotion expressed. It was found upon analyzing the data of this experiment that the majority of the judgments were made on the basis of the mouth. Of the two mutilated pictures, the one showing the same mouth expression as the original was generally judged to be more similar to it than was the one showing the same eye expression as the original.

Further understanding of the eyes versus the mouth as revealers of emotion is contributed by another recent study (Hanawalt[26]). The upper half alone and the lower half alone of faces showing twenty posed emotional expressions were projected separately on a screen. The subjects, college undergraduate women, were asked to identify from the half-face what emotion was portrayed, and then from the full face. The identifications were, of course, attempted without any knowledge on the part of the students as to what the stimulus situation actually was. This method is illustrated below:

In their studies of facial expression of emotion, Dr. Hanawalt (cf. above) and Dr. Munn (p. 180) both worked with the picture at left above. Here we can see their different methods at a glance. Dr. Munn showed the judges first the picture of the total situation and then the picture of the full face alone, and asked them to judge what emotion the man was feeling. Dr. Hanawalt showed the judges first the upper face alone, then the lower face alone, and then the whole face (these were cut out from the original picture).

As might be expected, this experimenter found that the students made many more incorrect identifications from the half-faces than from the full faces. Similar results were obtained with twenty unposed candid-camera shots, many taken from *Life*.

Interestingly enough, neither the lower half nor the upper half of the face was consistently superior in expressing emotion in recognizable patterns. However, the lower half was consistently more revealing in the expression of happiness and mirth, while the upper half was more revealing in the expression of fear and surprise. Suffering, love, interest, anger, determination, and contempt showed no superiority of one half over the other as measured by the number of correct identifications. Happiness was the most easily determined emotion and contempt was the most difficult.

All these psychological studies on the facial expression of emotion lead to certain definite conclusions. Apparently different emotions are accompanied by facial expressions which can be recognized in both adults and babies, although the emotional expressions of babies are harder to read than those of adults. Long association with a particular person acquaints us with his peculiarities of emotional expression and makes his face easier to read. On the question of which part of the face is more "expressive"—the upper (eyes) or lower (mouth)—psychologists find some tendency for the mouth to be more revealing of emotion, although there is also evidence that their relative importance depends upon the particular emotion being portrayed.

In general, we can say that the face is a useful source of information about what people are feeling. Every one of us in all our many personal contacts learns to judge with more or less accuracy the kind of emotional situation we are either participating in or watching from an audience.

Interpreting emotion from the voice

No discussion of emotional expression is complete without some mention of the role of the voice as used by both children and adults. If an observer is unable to see the subject and is ignorant of the stimulus situation, can he identify an emotion on the basis of vocal expression alone?

Babies' crying as clues to their emotions. What does the baby's cry tell us about what he is feeling? The answer seems to be "not much."

One of the studies of accuracy in interpreting facial expressions was accompanied by an experiment to determine the possibility of recognizing a baby's emotion by his cry. The judges in this experiment were medical students, nurses, and graduate students in psychology. They were out of sight of the babies at all times, but only a thin screen separated them from the baby whose emotion they were judging, so that they could easily hear his crying. The stimuli employed were, as before, deferred feeding (hunger), dropping (fear), restraint (anger), and needle prick (pain). The results show that the judges were not at all accurate in determining why the babies were crying. Only 6 out of 19 identified cries of hunger correctly; only 1 out of 22 judged fear correctly; only 2 out of 23 for anger; and only 5 out of 19 for pain. (Sherman and Sherman[27])

The results of this study on how accurately superior adults can tell from a baby's cry what type of stimulus situation he is reacting to are rather disappointing. However, they do not prove the nonexistence of innate patterns of vocal response which are specific to each stimulus situation arousing unpleasant reactions. They may merely indicate the inability of adults to analyze the emotional crying by "naked-ear" methods. Elaborate analysis of voice photographs might reveal unmistakable patterns.

You may wonder why a mother is usually quite accurate in telling why her baby is crying. We must conclude with these investigators that her greater accuracy is due to the fact that the mother has logical expectations as to the probable cause. If, for example, feeding time is near and the baby cries, she would conclude that the crying is due to hunger.

The vocal expression of emotion in adults. The adult human voice is even richer than the face in varieties of emotional expression. The rising inflection means questioning, doubt, incredulity: "What! Leaving so soon?" The rising and falling inflection shows sarcasm: "What a smart idea *that* was." A slow, dragging monotone expresses defeat and dejection: "I lost my job today." Rapid, staccato speech with much variation of pitch—as in the football announcer—suggests excitement. Suddenly lapsing into a slower, softer, lower voice is a trained speaker's trick for heightening drama and excitement.

In anger there is an increase in vocal pitch and loudness of the voice which is undoubtedly inborn. The widespread increase in body tension causes more tension in the vocal cords, producing greater loudness and higher pitch. Quavering and stuttering, inborn expressions of fear, are imitated by the actor who wants to convey the feeling of fear to the audience.

Vocal vibration during fear is somewhat akin to the *vibrato* of the singer—that is, the rhythmic pulsation of pitch and intensity of the human voice around a central tone. In both singing and speech, the vibrato as a language of emotion has no specific, unchanging symbols or medium of expression; its effect is to intensify the effect of other expressive movements and sounds (Tiffin and Seashore[28]). But unlike other forms of vocal expression, it does not help us identify the emotions that other people are feeling.

Detecting emotion from internal changes

As you know, emotion may be regarded not only as external but also as internal responses to stimuli. Internal responses are not easily visible and their study requires the use of special instruments and special experimental methods. What evidence do they give of clear-cut visceral (internal bodily) changes appropriate to particular emotions?

> One experimenter took records of breathing, pulse rate, and blood pressure in a group of fourteen men and sixteen girls of college age subjected to various emotional situations. These situations included, among others, the reading of a short-short story with a surprise ending; seeing a large bull snake which was "accidentally" allowed to escape; and being subjected to pistol shots, loud blasts from an automobile horn, and sudden flashes of light. There were also brief motion-picture scenes of bathing beauties; a beautiful mountain scene; a stagecoach holdup and other Western super-thrillers; and the lengthy embrace of two lovers. The films were new to the students, and many of them were scenes cut from commercial films by the censors as too stimulating for public consumption.
>
> The visceral changes in the students were easily noted for every different situation and its acompanying emotions. The time required to breathe in, divided by the time spent in breathing out (inspiration-expiration ratio), dropped in response to disgusting situations and rose in response to stimuli which gave rise to noble sentiments. This result showed most clearly in the realm of sexual stimulation. Sexual emotions of the cruder sort were accompanied by a drop in the inspiration-expiration ratio, while stimuli which gave rise to sentiments of idealized love produced a rise in the inspiration-expiration ratio. Fear-provoking situations also showed a lowering of the inspiration-expiration ratio. Changes in the rate of the pulse beat were small but tended in the direction of increased action during disgust and crude sexual stimulation. Breathing was shallower in disgust than in fear. In extreme fear the inspiration-expiration ratio increased, breathing became deeper and more variable, and the heart alternately went faster, then slower. Witnessing scenes of lingering embraces produced highly variable changes within the same subject, who seemed to alternate between the type of change that comes in undergoing the experience of beauty and that which comes in disgust. (Gaskill[29])

One recent summary of the more important literature on the subject comes to the conclusion that fear, anger, and elation have recognizably different physiological patterns of response (Arnold[30]). As such evidence slowly unfolds, we become more and more convinced that each separate emotion has its own underlying pattern of response, both internal and external.

Visceral changes are involuntary. The visceral responses in emotion differ from the external responses in a very important manner. The internal components of emotion are not ordinarily subject to voluntary control. Practice before the mirror, if diligently executed, will eventually bring considerable voluntary control of the facial muscles. Some athletes, for example, strive never to show emotion or exertion, no matter how exultant they may be over victory or how depressed by defeat. These people, like the gamblers of the Old West, pride themselves on their "poker faces." But even the poker-faced individual is unable to control the widespread internal upheaval in emotion. This fact is taken advantage of in the use of the "lie detector."

The lie detector is no mysterious mind-reading machine. It is simply a collection of instruments to measure the intensity of the various visceral emotional responses which occur as the subject is questioned on various topics.

The skilled liar learns to tell a story which, although untrue, is logically coherent. It "sticks together." He learns to control the muscles of his face and body so completely that the observer can see no outer change in response to any accusations. He literally learns to lie without flicking an eyelash. The control of the visceral responses, however, is another story—for no human being has yet learned to suppress completely all the inner manifestations of emotion.

Consciousness of guilt engenders a vague fear reaction. Consequently, anything which is true of fear in general is true of this sense of guilt. Certain questions produce emotion; others do not. By analyzing the nature of the questions in relation to the degree of emotion they produce, the skilled operator of the lie detector is able to determine the suspect's guilt or innocence.

There are several varieties of lie detectors, each designed to measure some combination of physiological responses. In the type of apparatus shown on the opposite page, the band around the subject's chest moves in and out as she breathes; it is connected with the front of the apparatus and causes the right-hand stylus (pen) to move on the record, showing rate of respiration. The cloth band around her arm is to measure blood pressure; it too is connected with the apparatus and causes the left-hand stylus to move. The electrode on her hand measures the electrical (galvanic) responses in her skin; it is connected with the back part of the apparatus, and finally with the middle stylus.

In the Chicago Police Scientific Crime Detection Laboratory, Paul V. Trovillo
demonstrates the polygraph, or lie detector, which was developed by the laboratory.
(An office employee poses as the "criminal.") This apparatus measures
respiration rate, blood pressure, and galvanic responses (see p. 186). However,
lie detectors do not always record this same particular combination of physiological
responses. For example, the record below shows respiration (top) and blood pressure
(bottom). It is the record of a subject innocent of one offense but guilty of another.

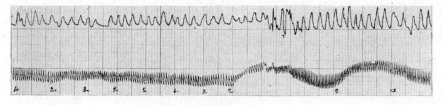

This subject was examined concerning the theft of $5000 from the bank in which he
worked as a junior clerk. For the first seven questions, which were concerned with
the $5000 theft or with some neutral items, he showed general nervousness
but no specific reactions. Then came question 8: "Have you ever taken any money
at all from the bank?" The sudden physiological changes are shown above; the
subject first made a denial, but followed it twelve seconds later with an admission that
he had pilfered some stamps. Question 9 was: "Except for the stamps, have you
taken anything else from the bank?" Again there was a violent physiological
response, and after a preliminary denial, the subject admitted that he had pocketed
some change he found on the floor of the bank. The person guilty of the $5000
theft later confessed. (Record courtesy of Mr. Fred Inbau.)

Interpreting Emotional Expression in Others   187

How accurate is the lie detector? Can a man who understands it "beat the game"? Most psychologists are convinced that the lie detector is fully as accurate and dependable as other traditionally accepted lines of evidence. For instance, the experience of the lie-detector experts at Northwestern University may be summed up as follows: The instrument's findings are confirmed by other evidence or by confessions in 82 per cent of all cases studied. In 17 per cent of the cases the findings of the instrument are neither confirmed nor denied by other evidence. In only 1 per cent of the cases has the lie detector been proved to be absolutely wrong, and in this small group practically all "errors" have arisen from giving the guilty man the benefit of the doubt.

Because of the fact that the lie detector is still new, it has not been admitted as evidence by a great many courts, although the number which accept its report are increasing. Probably the greatest value of the instrument at the present time is in the gathering of evidence which is admissible in court and in narrowing the field of search by eliminating the innocent suspects from further investigation. Its greatest interest to the psychologist is its dramatic revelation of the internal bodily changes which are the involuntary accompaniments to emotion.

CONTROLLING OUR EMOTIONS

Students sometimes expect psychologists to be able to tell them in one easy lesson—or chapter—how to avoid some of the emotional upsets that are the experience of every normal person. No one goes through life without various disturbances, major and minor; you have learned in this chapter about some of the investigations psychologists have performed showing the importance of emotion through all of daily life. But expecting the psychologist to provide a simple formula for controlling emotion is expecting too much.

The psychologist's insight and understanding can, however, be valuable as general guides to the problem of emotional control. He can provide you with some hints on how to control the occasional outbursts of fear, anger, and other violent emotions which are our inborn reactions to emergency situations.

Basic techniques of emotional control

Correcting the external situation, if possible, is after all one good way to control your emotions. Emotional reactions, you will remember, do not come just out of thin air—they depend on *your representation of your life situation*. That representation, in turn, depends upon what the real situation is. For example, if a person is worried that he may have an accident when driving, it may be that he needs to have the brakes of his car adjusted, or increase his skill in driving. If he is worried that he will lose his job in the next economic depression, he should try to increase his competence so that he will be too valuable to be discharged. In other words, his emotional reactions are partly a product of the situation, which can be changed more easily than can his reactions to the situation.

Increasing the ability to deal with life situations is often just as necessary as changing the situation. For example, a young girl's emotional problem may arise in connection with social situations; in that case, making a deliberate effort to learn to dance, to converse easily, and to meet people well will increase her social facility and thus ease the emotional problem. Or a young parent who becomes easily upset when something goes wrong with his child should make a systematic study of infant care, so that he will be able to deal more readily with all the occurrences that now arouse fear and insecurity. A person's emotional reactions depend very heavily upon the adjustment techniques at his command, and these adjustment techniques can be improved through careful, realistic thinking.

Correcting the interpretations of some situations. An emotional reaction is a product of the brain processes whereby the individual represents to himself the nature of the situation he is in. For example, a student may feel humiliated when he asks a question in class and the professor brushes him aside and implies that his question is irrelevant, rude, or stupid. Actually, his question may be valid and to the point, so that instead of accepting the professor's rejection he should reinterpret the situation. He should realize that the professor has emotional problems also, that he may feel his prestige threatened by a question which he cannot answer or which exposes some omission or error in his teaching. And the professor, in turn, should reinterpret the situation by realizing that one sign of the successful teacher is the ability to arouse enough interest in the students so that they assume a questioning attitude, and moreover, that his prestige with the students will actually be increased if he answers their questions directly and modestly, instead of trying to brush them aside. Such a reinterpretation of a situation—that is, re-evaluation in the light of reality—often goes far to reduce the emotional problem, although it is very difficult to achieve and requires honest and courageous thinking. In some cases, the individual may need the help of an objective, friendly outsider, . like a teacher, minister, or psychologist.

Facing the emotion. Some people unwisely attempt to avoid emotion by refusing to admit that the emotion exists. Psychologists working for the British Government observed the emotional behavior of people huddled together in bomb shelters during air raids, and found that admitting fear when in serious danger helps keep that fear from becoming intolerable. In wartime both soldier and civilian must learn, despite their very natural fears, to carry on in the face of danger. The person who boasts of not being afraid when there is real danger is placed under a double load of fear. He not only fears the real danger confronting him but also fears that his bluff will be called and that he will show his fear after boasting that he is unafraid. He has created another emergency situation over and above the original danger which was outside his control. Such added sources of emotional tension can be avoided by facing the fact that the situation is dangerous and that you are afraid, or that a financial or family difficulty is a real source of worry.

Practical devices for emotional control

Sometimes the situation is too immediate and urgent to permit the application of the basic techniques of mental hygiene outlined above. In such instances, the following devices have some value.

Engaging in activity. When a real emergency situation cannot be avoided, activity usually helps to relieve the emotional strain. Keeping busy can be very effective in combating gloom and depression, in allaying anger and fear. The old ideas of whistling to keep your courage up, running around the block to relieve anger, and similar devices are psychologically sound. Work is another good solvent for many moods and emotions. Attempts to work off an emotional condition are most effective when the activity is in and of itself valuable. In battle, for example, any kind of activity is valuable in reducing fear, but digging a slit trench is especially effective because it not only removes part of the emotional tension but makes the situation safer and thus removes part of the source of the emotional tensions.

Of course the difficult situation will usually continue no matter what your activity, but even though it still arouses your emotion, that emotion will have been partly "worked off" and you will be better able both to control your emotion and to set about finding ways of improving the emotion-provoking situation.

Humor. The ability to see the humor in a situation has saved many an awkward moment in the classroom or in social life. There is something about laughter which sweeps away annoyance, worry, jealousy, and even disgust, which dispels timidity and takes the rough edge off the too-aggressive act. Laughter is especially effective in overcoming fear. The well-known ability of the American GI to "wisecrack" was an important ingredient in his morale and fighting spirit.

All kinds of companionship—humorous or otherwise—are a great source of emotional release and comfort to the person suffering unbearably strong anger, fear, grief, or worry. It must be remembered, however, that every person has his own individual emotional reactions and must find his own ways of controlling them.

In this chapter, we have discussed the many different ways of looking at emotion, have learned what psychologists have to say about the important role the emotions play in everyday life, and have become acquainted with the problems of discovering what emotions other people are feeling. Emotions are a fundamental and intricate basis of human life. They are indeed our "inner springs of action."

CHAPTER 6

Intelligence

O NE OF THE PHRASES most frequently used to describe a person is that he is "intelligent" or "not very intelligent." Classified ads often read: "Intelligent young man wanted for. . . ." When a couple sets out to adopt a child, they always specify that the child must be "intelligent" and they inquire into the intelligence of his parents. The whole concept of intelligence is one of the most complex and interesting in life and in psychology. In this chapter we shall discuss what psychologists mean by *intelligence,* how it is measured, and what factors in heredity and environment go into determining it.

Intelligence, as the term is used by psychologists, includes all the abilities through which knowledge is acquired, retained, and applied to the solution of a problem. It includes abilities in perception, memory, imagination, judgment, and learning. In other words, *a person's intelligence is his capacity to make use of his past learning in adjusting to new situations for which he has no ready-made, previously practiced response.*

This definition is admittedly broad, and the various kinds of intelligence are admittedly difficult to determine with exactness—in fact, they are still in process of determination. Psychologists have developed measurements for at least certain forms of intelligence in an individual, however, by putting him in new problem situations and then observing how quickly and accurately he adjusts as compared with other individuals in his age group. These problem situations are scaled in difficulty according to a person's age and are known as *intelligence tests*. Today the intelligence test is not yet fifty years old, but it has already become an important means of informing an individual about himself so that he may plan his life and predict the probable outcome of his various efforts. The intelligence test today is used in business and industry as one basis for hiring or refusing to hire. It is used in the schools to classify pupils into slow-learning and quick-learning groups. And the experiences of both World Wars have left no doubt that a thoroughgoing, scientific intelligence-testing program is essential in mobilizing an efficient military force.

LEVELS OF INTELLIGENCE

PEOPLE who have extremely high intelligence are called *geniuses*. Those with very low intelligence are called *feeble-minded*. Some people are extremely uneven in their intellectual development, but most people are about average in most of their abilities. The following cases illustrate three levels of intelligence and one case of uneven development of intelligence.

While careful study of these cases can leave no doubt that people differ widely in mental ability, it should be kept in mind that the differences are always in *degree*, not in *kind*. A cup of coffee is different in kind from a cup of tea, but a strong cup of coffee is different from a weak cup of coffee only in degree. And so it is with intelligence: people are not intrinsically different in the kind of mental abilities they possess, but only in the degree to which they possess them.

Kenneth Wolf, a case of very superior mental development

"Kenneth Wolf, 11, expects to have his Ph.D. in chemistry when he is 16. He will probably get it, too. At Cleveland's Western Reserve University he leads mathematics and organic chemistry classes full of students years older than he is. His classmates at first kidded him relentlessly, especially about girls, but finally Kennie told them off: 'The subject of girls becomes interesting only when the body matures,' he explained. 'Mine hasn't. It will later.'

"Kennie was kicked out of grade school because, said the principal, 'he disrupted the class, asked too many questions, volunteered too many answers.' Dean C. William Huntley of Western Reserve, a child psychologist, decided that college was the place for the boy. On I.Q. tests Kennie scores about 182, which means that his 'mental age' is about 20. When he entered college last autumn his fellow students regarded him as a repulsive little smart aleck. Since then he has become less offensive to them. He is still enough of a small boy to raid the sugar jar in the chemistry laboratory. But when he was questioned about his chemistry, Kennie answered, 'We're running the oxidation sequence on methanes. Little work with the aldehydes and ketones.'

"Kennie's intellectual, Russian-born parents are both leftish lawyers. During World War I, Father Wolf defended Eugene Debs and other 'seditious' characters. Little Kennie first amazed his parents at four months—by speaking a whole sentence. Just after his first birthday he tackled a first-grade reader. When he was 22 months old, his mother heard a Liszt air coming from downstairs. She thought Kennie had started the player piano, but she found the baby pounding out the melody himself.

"Since then music has overshadowed even chemistry as Kennie's greatest interest. 'I suppose there are eleven compositions now I'd be willing to claim,' he admits. His symphony has never been played: 'It's not necessary. I can hear it.' After he gets his Ph.D., he hopes to study with Composer Paul Hindemith. Kennie is now the only outsider allowed to attend rehearsals of the Cleveland Symphony Orchestra." (*Time*[1])

Harry Parker, a man of average intelligence

Harry Parker got through high school without too much difficulty. He did well in his commercial courses, but made such low grades in his academic subjects that he barely graduated with his class. Upon completion of his high-school course he remained at school, taking post-graduate work in Business English and Mathematics.

Parker's family owned a cabinet and furniture shop, so for three years after leaving high school he worked for his father as a cabinet maker. But after the war started in December, 1941, he went to work in a defense plant as a stock clerk. He liked the work and was in line for a promotion when he was called into the service. After completing basic training, Parker was placed in the Quartermaster's Corps because he had done well on his clerical ability test. Upon graduation he was assigned to an overseas unit and spent two years in North Africa.

Soon after his discharge from the Service, Parker obtained his present job as shipping clerk in a large bookstore. Now he is in charge of classifying and putting new books in the proper sections and has two men working under his direction. He earns $50 a week and hopes to save enough to purchase his own bookstore some day.

Parker is very fond of swimming and during the summer he spends his weekends at the beach. He occasionally reads popular magazines, especially the picture magazines, but otherwise his reading is confined to the headlines of the newspaper, the sports page, and the "funnies." He enjoys radio programs that are "not too highbrow" and spends many of his evenings with friends listening to favorite programs. The rest of his entertainment consists of movies and church events.

When asked as part of a standardized test procedure to tell why wood and alcohol are alike, he stated that alcohol comes from wood. When asked why a poem and a statue are alike, he stated that they both are antiques. (Veterans' Guidance Center[2])

Little Abbie, a case of feeble-mindedness

"Admitted to the New Jersey Training School for Feeble-Minded Boys and Girls . . . at the age of eleven, Abbie was small for her age, left-handed and awkward. She always put the *same foot* forward when going up or down stairs; she knew her letters but could not read; she could count to ten; she knew some color and form; and she sang a number of hymns that she had learned at home. Her sight and hearing were normal, and she was fond of play. Among Abbie's more unfavorable characteristics were a bad memory and a poor power of imitation. She was gluttonous, untidy, untruthful, sly, and profane.

"Three months after her admission she could thread a needle and sew on buttons, could dust and rub floors a little, had learned to read *A man ran* and *I see a man* (sometimes), count to twenty, and, with help, could do such number work as this:

$$
\begin{array}{ccc}
1 & 2 & 3 \\
+1 & +1 & +1 \\
\hline
\end{array}
$$

"For ten years she went to school. 'For ten years . . . her teachers struggled heroically to give her the mastery of *something*.' Little less than marvelous is the optimism and faithfulness of those teachers! We see them struggling on month after month, not in that perfunctory way born of discouragement or conscious failure, but with that courage and cheerfulness which comes from grasping at every straw of encouragement, of progress, of fancied improvement. Had these teachers become discouraged, we would have to admit that perhaps the result might be due to that fact. But there is no sign of giving up in all these years. Within the last few months, however, there has appeared the feeling that Abbie has reached her limit. She will be twenty-two years old before long.

"Today she is still small for her age. She can braid corn-husks a little; can make a bed; can iron an apron; cannot count the cost of three one-cent stamps and three two-cent stamps, with the stamps before her; cannot repeat five figures or a sentence of fifteen words; defines only in terms of use ['What is an apple?' 'You eat it.']; can read a few sentences, spell a few words and write about twenty-five words from memory; knows the days of the week, but not the months of the year; and does not know how many fingers she has on both hands." (Woodrow[3])

The R—— boy, a case of uneven development

An interesting case has recently been reported which shows how the abilities that make up intelligence can be developed to very different degrees in the same person. This is the case of the 29-year-old "idiot" who is able to name the day of the week on which any date fell within the last 30 years. Although spastic paralysis makes this "idiot" unable to do many things that babies of a year and a half can do and may account for his low "mental age" on tests of performance, his mind in many ways has developed to a level found among children from six to nine years of age. Unable to walk or talk, he answers questions by nodding or shaking his head. His vocabulary and his ability to remember numbers and to handle simple arithmetic problems were found equal to that of children in the first or second grade.

His feat of naming the day of the week of any date is not based on any extraordinary mathematical ability, but on his unusual talent for visualizing something that he has once looked at for a long time. The patient is reluctant to give away the secret of his special ability, but a clue was obtained from the fact that he not only could tell that November 27, 1930, was on a Thursday, but that it was printed in red on the calendar. To test the theory that he was *visualizing* the calendar page, a calendar was prepared for 1945, a year with which he was not already familiar. Three colors were used on the dates at random. Two days later, after correctly giving the week day of certain dates, he seemed startled when asked the color of the number. When told to look at it again, he looked to the ceiling, his usual custom, and gave the correct response. Then he not only gave the day of the week, but told whether it was printed in red, blue, or black for practically all the twelve dates chosen.

The fact that he could name the colors on the calendar indicated that he had actually memorized the appearance of the calendar pages, and had probably not mastered the formal principles on which the calendar is constructed. The ability to visualize with such clarity is known as *eidetic imagery* (see p. 393).

Another test was made on the boy when he was shown a series of pictures in a children's workbook for periods of 15 to 30 seconds each. For purposes of comparison, tests were made in the same manner on four other subjects—two psychologists and two children of superior ability, ages nine and eleven. Of the 57 questions asked concerning the pictures (including numbers of various items and colors) the percentage of his correct answers was higher than the percentage of any of the other four subjects. Tested six months later on one of these pictures, the patient gave five correct responses out of six, and the one wrong response had been answered incorrectly when first tested. The other subjects of the experiment claimed that they could not remember any of the details of the picture. So here we see one ability developed far beyond all the others which go to make up intelligence. (Roberts[4])

You have now become acquainted with the various levels of development: a genius, an average person, a case of feeble-mindedness, and one case of uneven development. It is to measure just such different degrees of intelligence that the intelligence test has been devised.

THE DEVELOPMENT OF INTELLIGENCE TESTS

IN THE YEAR 1904 the Minister of Public Instruction of France formed a commission of medical men, educators, scientists, and public officials to study the problem of how to teach the feeble-minded children in the public schools. There was a great deal of useless talk by the pompous members of the commission, but the important work was done by Binet, a scholar of the young science of psychology, and Simon, an elderly physician, who held the first step to be measuring intelligence.

The Binet tests of general intelligence

Binet prepared a test of intelligence which was tried out in 1905. It contained problem situations which were selected with extreme care and which could be accurately scored. These problem situations were varied in nature, were little influenced by the type of the child's environment, and stressed judgment and reasoning rather than mere rote memory.

The concept of the M.A. Binet expressed the results of his tests on feeble-minded children in terms of the age at which normal children could make the equivalent score. For example, if a particular defective earned a score on the test which was earned by the average child of five years, the feeble-minded child was said to have a *mental age* (M.A.) of five years—no matter what his actual age was. This method of defining the unit of intelligence was so convenient that Binet later arranged his various tests in mental age levels.

Binet's extensive use of intelligence tests showed conclusively that intelligence exists in an infinite series of degrees. There are no real lines of demarcation setting off one intelligence group from another. The very bright and the very dull are simply extremes in a continuous distribution. There is no sharp break between the very dull, the dull, the average, the bright, and the very bright.

Binet's final scale (1911). The tentative scale of 1905 passed through a process of revision and standardization which finally culminated, in 1911, in a set of standards arranged by age levels (Binet and Simon[5]). You can get a good idea of what the Binet scale is like if you know what is expected of a normal person at different ages. Below are a

The Stanford-Binet test. *To test the child's memory, the examiner strings together beads of various sizes, as the child looks on. Then he pulls them off the string, and she is asked to restring them in the same order. (From the film* Testing the I.Q., *by Dr. G. M. Gilbert and Prof. Henry E. Garrett, world rights owned by International Film Bureau Inc.)*

few of the items on the original Binet test, without any of its later revisions.

AGE 3 Points to nose, eyes, and mouth.
Repeats two digits.
Gives his family name.

AGE 5 Counts four coins.
Repeats a sentence of ten syllables.

AGE 7 Shows right hand and left ear.
Names four colors—red, green, blue, and yellow.

AGE 9 Defines familiar word in terms superior to use, i.e., shows how it is related to other ideas.
Recognizes value of nine pieces of money.
Gives the names of the months in order.

AGE 12 Uses three given words in one sentence.
Gives sixty words in three minutes.

ADULT Gives three differences between a president and a king.

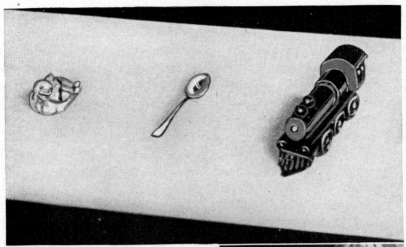

In another part of the Stanford-Binet test, the examiner lets the child look briefly at three (or more) objects; then he covers one of them up while she is not looking; then she uncovers her eyes and tells him "which one is under the box." Although children frequently regard this as a game, the increase in the number of objects naturally increases the difficulty of the task. (From Testing the I.Q.)

The Stanford revisions

The next important step in the development of intelligence tests was made by L. M. Terman of Stanford University, who tried out on about a thousand children the materials which Binet had used, along with others gathered from various sources or invented by himself. With much painstaking effort he arranged the tests into mental age levels and published in 1916 the Stanford Revision of the Binet Tests, which remained for twenty years a standard instrument in clinical psychology, psychiatry, and educational counseling (Terman[6]). These items cannot be reproduced in detail because of the danger of destroying the value of the items for testing. It can be said, however, that they are similar to the ones from the original Binet scale listed above.

In 1937 Terman and Merrill published a new revision of the Binet tests (Terman and Merrill[7]), for in the course of twenty years, certain defects and limitations had become apparent in the 1916 scale.

For one thing, the scale was not applicable to adults. The tests were too easy, especially for the superior adults, and the scoring for adults was incomplete and gave misleading ratings. Moreover, the scale did not provide adequately standardized tests for very young children. But the most serious defect was that the scale existed in one form only. There are many times when a psychologist questions the reliability of a given test score because of unsatisfactory testing conditions (such as fear or sullenness on the part of the subject) or because it does not seem to be consistent with other findings. For example, when the case history shows that a child has received consistently high grades in school, the psychologist questions a low test performance. And often the psychologist wishes to determine whether mental deterioration has occurred. Since a child cannot be tested at too close intervals with exactly the same form of test, an alternative form—one which is similar in nature but differs in specific content—is of great value.

The 1937 revision was standardized on more than three thousand cases and was aimed at correcting the difficulties or defects of the former scale:

1 The test has been extended at the upper limits of the intelligence scale, so that differentiations can be made among adults of superior intelligence.

2 Provision is made for the testing of children as young as two years of age. Below the age of five years, where mental growth is very rapid, sets of tests are provided at half-yearly intervals, others at yearly intervals.

3 The scale now contains two forms of equal difficulty and of comparable material, so that retesting is made easier.

Performance tests

The Stanford-Binet test is probably the most widely used of the intelligence tests because it correlates so well with grades in school and hence is invaluable in predicting a child's school progress and planning his curriculum and promotions accordingly. However, it is predominantly a test of verbal intelligence, although it does measure other abilities also. Thus for a deaf child or for a child of foreign parents who does not come from an English-speaking home, the Stanford-Binet often does not give a fair indication of his intelligence.

Therefore it has been necessary to develop certain tests called *performance tests*, in which hand reactions are substituted for verbal reactions on the part of the person being tested, and in some of which even the presentation of the test items is accomplished without the use of speech on the examiner's part. This kind of test includes such tasks as form boards: boards with recesses into which the individual must fit blocks of the proper size and shape as quickly as he can. Also in common use are picture-completion tests, in which the individual looks at part of a picture and grasps the whole so that he can tell which one of several parts will fill in the blank to make the most sensible whole picture. From the scores obtained in such performance tests, it is possible to derive the mental age of children. One of the best known tests of this type is the Arthur Point Scale of Performance, which is designed to test children from the ages of three to fifteen (Arthur[8]). (Items from this test are shown on pp. 202-203.)

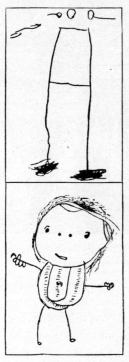

One well-known type of performance test for children involves the measurement of intelligence through drawings. For example, the drawings at left were done by two kindergarten children, the one above by an American girl aged 5 years, and the one below by an American girl aged 5 years 1 month. Although these two children were almost exactly the same age, there are great differences in the accuracy and detail of the two drawings, differences which reflect the differences in their I.Q.'s.

In scoring the drawings, the psychologist counts the number of items present (head, legs, arms attached to body, eyes, etc.). Thus the drawing above is given a score of 7, which is known from experience with thousands of children to represent the mental age of 4 years 9 months, and which is then translated into an I.Q. of 95. The child whose drawing is below is given a total score of 13; her mental age is 6 years 3 months; and her I.Q. is 123. (Reprinted by special permission from The Measurement of Intelligence by Drawings, *by F. L. Goodenough, © World Book Co.)*

For work with older children and retarded adults, most clinicians use another performance test, the Cornell-Coxe Performance Ability Scale. This is very similar to the Arthur Scale, and in fact includes many of the same tests. In addition, it includes tests such as picture-arrangement, in which the subject is required to arrange a series of pictures so that they make a sensible story; and digit symbol, in which the subject is required to code a series of digits into symbols according to a key (Cornell and Coxe[9]).

The items below and on the opposite page are part of a nonverbal scale for measuring the ability of young, deaf, or non-English-speaking children (from the Arthur Performance Test, Revised Form II, Psychological Corporation, 1946.)

Directly below is part of the Healy Picture Completion Test II, which measures thinking or reasoning ability. The subject must look at each picture and then fill it in with the block containing the missing item (C. H. Stoelting Co.).

The Wechsler-Bellevue test of intelligence

Because the Binet-type scales and the performance scales described above were designed primarily for children, they have not been too effective in measuring adult intelligence. The Wechsler-Bellevue test combines the verbal and performance tests into one test designed primarily to measure the intelligence of adults. This test was standardized on adults, so that an adult's intelligence is derived by comparing his score with the scores of other adults his own age. Since the test is set up in two parts—verbal and performance—his verbal intelligence, performance intelligence, and general intelligence can all be obtained. The verbal section includes tests on information, comprehension, vocabulary, similarities between words, arithmetic, and digit span (in which the individual is tested to see how many digits can be repeated after the examiner has first said them). The performance section uses the picture-

Below is the Seguin Form Board Test (Arthur Revision), which tests reaction speed on a simple problem-solving task. At right is a Porteus Maze, which measures the subject's ability to make a clear plan, then follow it through without false moves (as used in the Porteus Maze Test, Maze Test and Mental Differences, Smith Printing and Publishing Co., 1933, *and in the Arthur Point Scale).*

completion test, the block design, the puzzle tests, the digit-symbol test, and the picture arrangement (Wechsler[10]).

At this time it is generally recognized that this test gives the most valid intelligence scores for adults of any test now developed. It is widely used in clinical work.

THE CONCEPT OF THE I.Q.

AT FIRST Binet made no attempt to state why a child was feeble-minded or to predict a child's mental status at a future date. He was content to describe the child's mental status at the time of testing. But as the results obtained from use of the Binet tests accumulated, and as more and more children were tested and retested at later dates, it was seen that the child who was, for example, only one year retarded at an early age would be still more retarded at a later age. The amount of mental retardation (as measured in mental age units) increases as the child becomes older. If a child has a mental age of 3 when he is 4, his mental age will be only 6 when he is 8. Thus, although the mental and chronological ages maintain the same relation to each other (3/4 = 6/8), the total amount of retardation increases from one year to two years. (How many years will this child be retarded mentally when he is 12 years old chronologically?)

Early in the history of intelligence tests, psychologists adopted the practice of stating the relationship between mental age (M.A.) and chronological age (C.A.) as a ratio: that is, dividing M.A. by C.A. (Stern[11]). This ratio gives a figure for any given individual that remains more or less constant over a period of years. Thus it is possible to compare individuals of differing ages, or the same individual at different ages. This concept, which we call the *Intelligence Quotient* (I.Q.), was adopted by Terman for use in the Stanford revision of 1916.

Computing the I.Q.

The formula for the I.Q. is very easily written as M.A./C.A. $\times$ (100). Translated into everyday language, this formula means: Divide the mental age of the subject (as obtained by the tests) by his chronological age, and multiply by a hundred. The multiplication eliminates fractions and decimals, making I.Q.'s expressible as whole numbers.

Let us take an example of the calculation of the I.Q. William is 10 years and 2 months of age to the nearest month, and his mental age is 12 years and 2 months. What is his I.Q.? First we change his mental age into months—giving 146. Chronological age converted into months gives us 122. The next step is simple division: 146 divided by 122 equals 1.20 ("rounded off" to the nearest hundredth). We eliminate the decimal point by multiplying by 100. The resulting figure of 120 is William's I.Q.

If a child is of average intelligence, mental age and chronological age are the same, making M.A./C.A. equal to 1 and I.Q. equal to 100. If the individual is of above-average intelligence, his mental age is greater than his chronological age: The top of the fraction will be bigger than the bottom, as in the case of William, described above; M.A./C.A. will be more than 1; and the I.Q. will be more than 100. In a below-average child, the M.A. will be less than his C.A.; M.A./C.A. will be less than 1; and the I.Q. will be less than 100.

As previously indicated, it was possible on the 1916 Binet scale to obtain somewhat questionable mental ages for adults, but no really valid means were provided for computing the I.Q.'s of adults. The relation of M.A. to C.A. is constant up to the age of 13. But after the age of 13, mental age increases more slowly until at about the age of 16 it levels off and remains about the same. This means that M.A. is constant while C.A. increases, so that I.Q. declines. Therefore the divisor (C.A.) must be "corrected" in order to obtain an I.Q. comparable to those obtained at earlier ages. Since this "correction" is too complex to calculate every time the test is given, Terman and Merrill have in their 1937 edition provided a table for finding I.Q.'s.

Many men and women who served in World War II know their Army or Navy General Classification Test Scores but not their I.Q.'s. Although the Army and Navy used different scales, it is possible to translate either into an I.Q.

To change a Navy G.C.T. score into an I.Q., employ the following formula: I.Q. $= 100 + (1.8$ [NGCT Score $- 50]$). For example, if your NGCT Score was 73, you would first subtract 50 from 73 to get 23. You would next multiply 23 by 1.8, getting 41.4. Finally, you would add 41.4 to 100, giving your estimated I.Q. of 141.

If you know your Army General Classification Score, use the following formula: I.Q. $= 100 + (.9$ [AGCT Score $- 100]$).

The I.Q. shows rate of mental growth

It is apparent by now that the I.Q. is a convenient way of showing the rate at which mental age increases with chronological age in a given individual. If you know the rate at which an individual is growing mentally and if you know his present chronological age and mental age, it is possible to predict with a striking degree of accuracy what his status (mental age) will be at some specified chronological age in the future.

For instance, if a girl of 6 has a mental age of 8, then you can compute her I.Q. as $96/72 \times 100 = 133$. Assuming that her I.Q. remains constant, what will her mental age be when she has reached a chronological age of 10?

What does a given I.Q. mean?

Trained psychologists, as well as teachers and physicians dealing with problem cases, have associated certain I.Q. values with certain general pictures of adaptive behavior. For the beginning student who has not had this practical experience, the numbers mean little. Even if he is told that a man's I.Q. is 75, he probably has no clear picture of what such an individual can and cannot do.

How I.Q.'s are distributed among the population. One way in which the beginning student in psychology can get some impression of the meaning of the various I.Q.'s is to consult the frequency distribution shown in the graph below. (This graph is based on the 1937 revision of the Stanford-Binet tests.) Remember that the average I.Q. is 100. Half the people fall below 100 I.Q., and the other half come above it.

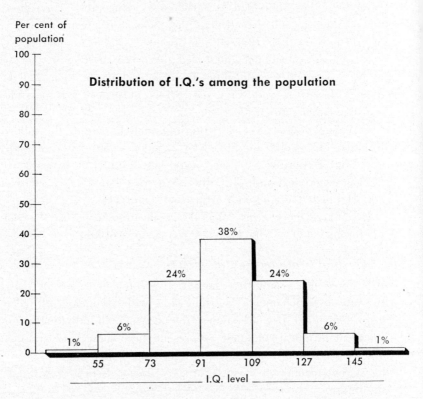

You will notice from the graph how heavily the population is concentrated around the average—that is, around the average score of 100. Note that the total I.Q. range is divided equally into subranges of eighteen points each. The middle range from 91 to 109 (which is classified as the "average" range) contains 38 per cent of the population. The rest of the population falls symmetrically on each side of the middle range into groups that contain 24 per cent, 6 per cent, and 1 per cent of the total.

Meaning of I.Q.'s in terms of general behavior. Another way of getting acquainted with the meaning of I.Q.'s is to see how people of different I.Q.'s behave and what they can do. To examine this, let us start at the bottom and work up.

The feeble-minded, about 2 per cent of the population, are roughly classed into three grades. The lowest form of feeble-mindedness, *idiocy*, has an I.Q. range from 0 to 25; the next grade, *imbecility*, from 26 to 50; the highest grade of feeble-mindedness, *moronity*, from 51 to 70. In the 70's there is a band of doubt where some individuals are feeble-minded and others are not. And in the final analysis, the definition of feeble-mindedness is a social one. People who, because of low intelligence, are not capable of conducting their affairs without supervision are called feeble-minded. The exact intellectual level below which an individual cannot shift for himself will depend upon the complexity of his environment and the problems of adjustment that it presents, as well as upon the training he has received.

Idiots (I.Q.'s ranging from 0 to 25) never learn to avoid the common dangers of life. They would soon die if not cared for by others. Many of them never learn to dress themselves or to say even a few simple words. Some never learn to sit up, and remain in bed all their lives. If you can imagine a human adult who has learned no more than an average two-year-old baby, you have a good picture of the human idiot.

Imbeciles (I.Q.'s ranging from 26 to 50) learn to talk a little. They can even learn to do simple work, such as ditch-digging and mopping floors, under close supervision. They are not able to understand the value of money and cannot be permitted to live outside an institution or away from the close supervision of their families. The imbecile attains a mental ability ranging from that of an average three-year-old to that of an average seven-year-old child. On the basis of the behavior described in the report of little Abbie, one would judge that her I.Q. must have been in the 40's, which would place her in the upper part of the imbecile group; her mental age when mature was about six years.

Morons (I.Q.'s ranging from 51 to 70) can learn to read and write and can perform certain types of routine factory work. As adults, they have the intellectual capacity of average children aged from seven to ten years; they cannot be expected to go beyond the fourth or fifth grade in school. If left to themselves, they usually run afoul of the law, for they are incapable of recognizing the moral obligation to repay debts or to settle for goods bought on credit at a store. Adult morons have normal drives and emotions but lack the capacity of the more intelligent person to foresee the consequence of their emotional behavior—for example, the frequency of illegitimate motherhood is highest among moron girls. Many morons become juvenile delinquents, prostitutes, professional toughs, and petty thieves. It must be pointed out, however, that by no means all such people are morons. As you will learn in Chapter 16, low intelligence is only one of the many possible factors in illegal behavior.

Studies have shown that the average I.Q. of different occupational groups increases as the economic standing of the different occupational groups improves, although it is important to remember that within every group there is considerable variation in I.Q. In general, it can be observed that the great group of average people like Harry Parker includes most but not all of the carpenters, the plumbers, the telephone operators, and the garage mechanics, for example. Above them in I.Q. are the competent business and professional men and women, some as high as Kenneth Wolf.

College graduates probably average close to 120 I.Q. In one large Midwestern State University, the average I.Q. of all students enrolled is 115. College training requires intellectual ability well above average; thus only a relatively small percentage of the population can be expected to profit from higher education. This fact has definite implications for social planning. That higher education is available to only a small percentage of our youth is fair or unfair not on the basis of how many or how few get to go to college but on the basis of how students are selected—of whether the available opportunities are given to those most able to profit from education.

The most significant and dramatic demonstration of the meaning of high I.Q. is still under way. But it is a drama that can be read through the second act at least. For nearly twenty years, Terman followed the fortunes of 1300 individuals representing the cream of the crop of some 250,000 California school children tested in 1922. Each of these subjects had an I.Q. of 140 or more; the average I.Q. for the group was 150 (Terman[12]).

In 1940, a follow-up survey was conducted to see how well these individuals have succeeded in life. These results leave little doubt that the intelligence test measures something vitally important to successful living. Here are the facts:

1 The death rate is much lower than that of the control group used for comparison. This explodes the old notion that bright children are sickly and that a strong back goes with a weak mind.

2 The insanity and suicide rates are lower than those of the general population. This fails to support the legend that "genius is akin to insanity."

3 The divorce rate of the gifted group is lower than that for the state of California as a whole.

4 Ninety per cent of the gifted group entered college; of these, about 93 per cent graduated. This showing is about forty times higher than the standard for the country as a whole. Their college grades and honors were higher than those of the average college student.

5 The gifted were far more active in student-body affairs, as shown by election to office and activity points score.

6 The earnings of the gifted group far excel those of the general public of the same age. Not one of the group was on the relief rolls during the depression, even though many finished their schooling and were just starting in life when it hit. At age thirty, their average earned income was $250 a month or twice the national average at that time. A dozen of the men (or 2 per cent of the group) earned more than $10,000 per year. Only one tenth of 1 per cent of the general population achieved such high earnings. Terman also tested the offspring of his gifted group. The average I.Q. of the three hundred offspring tested was 127.

Since this average score of 127 is considerably lower than the average I.Q. of 150 which the gifted group had, it needs some word of explanation. Especially is some explanation needed since the children of these gifted parents probably have unusually good social environments which would operate to some extent to make their I.Q.'s more comparable to those which their parents had as children. Several factors must be remembered here.

First, the gifted parents had married husbands or wives who were, on the average, of somewhat lower I.Q. than themselves. After all, they selected their spouses on other qualities in addition to intellectual qualities, and even had they desired to marry persons of equal I.Q., other factors being equal, such mates would be hard to find. Thus, each child was the product of heredity from two parents, only one of whom, usually, was of very high I.Q.

Then further, as we noted in Chapter 3, it must be remembered that heredity operates to produce not merely similarities, but also differences, between parents and their children. Through reduction division each child gets only half of the chromosomes which each parent had.

Finally, both as a result of reduction division and as a result of the presence of recessive genes that sometimes can express themselves through new pairings, the child might possess quite different hereditary traits from those manifested by either parent.

The occupational hierarchy in I.Q. In a later chapter, you will see in greater detail how the population becomes stratified in the various occupations according to intelligence level. The table on page 632 gives the typical I.Q. range in several representative occupations. It must be emphasized, however, that *these occupational groups include quite a wide diversity of I.Q.'s.* The range of I.Q.'s in professions like accounting or the law is smaller, because only persons of high I.Q. can enter such occupations. But in occupations like auto repairing or clerking in stores, persons of low, average, and high I.Q. may be found.

Will coaching raise the I.Q.? It is not uncommon to hear laymen speak of intelligence as something which results mainly from study or specialized training. One experiment will suffice to indicate the limits of "coachability" of the Stanford-Binet test performance.

> This experiment employed three groups of school children taken from Grade 2 in two schools which were in similar neighborhoods and which had pupils of similar ability. At the beginning of the experiment all three groups were tested by well-trained examiners. Then followed two weeks in which one group (the control group) was given no special treatment and had no contact with the tests; the second group was coached on the items of the Stanford-Binet test, with the correct answers given to them and explained in detail; the third group was given instruction on how to answer questions of a similar nature. At the end of the two weeks the three groups were again tested. The test was administered again after three months in which none of the groups received any training, and still again after a year of no training, and their I.Q.'s on each retesting were compared with their I.Q.'s on the original test. The final conclusions were these:
>
> 1 Taking the Stanford-Binet tests will cause the child to do slightly better the next time he tries, even without coaching.
>
> 2 Coaching on the identical materials of the test causes a decided increase in the I.Q. obtained immediately after the coaching, but this increase is not permanent.
>
> 3 Coaching on similar materials causes a moderate increase in obtained I.Q., an increase which is only temporary. (Graves[13])

There is nothing in the results of this experiment to indicate that there is any appreciable coaching effect in the proper use of the Stanford-Binet tests. The tests are usually administered at least six or eight months apart—more often, a period of years elapses between them. Also, in administering the test a psychologist does not tell the child which answers are right and which ones wrong, so that this factor of symbolic reward could not cause the child to remember the right answer. Moreover, identical items are not used in successive tests.

You should keep in mind that the increases in test I.Q.'s brought about by coaching do not indicate that the actual intelligence was increased. Coaching introduces an error in a test result but does not affect the mental age level of the subject. The coaching effect is exactly like that produced by putting a piece of ice in a feverish patient's mouth immediately before the thermometer is inserted. The ice will change the thermometer reading, but it will not alter the patient's temperature. Coaching will temporarily and slightly raise an intelligence-test score but it will not raise intelligence.

TOWARD A NEW CONCEPT OF INTELLIGENCE

Binet regarded intelligence as a general ability to adjust in a problem situation. That is, he felt that all specific abilities—self-criticism, judgment, reasoning, learning, abstract thinking, word usage, and even musical ability—were manifestations of a general power or strength of the mind (Binet and Simon[14]). Numerous correlational studies have shown beyond doubt that Binet's definition was an oversimplification. Some traits usually included in "intelligence" are completely independent of each other. That is, a person can be "intelligent" in one field but not in another, indicating that there is not a "general" intelligence which includes all abilities.

An attempt has been made to reconcile the concept of intelligence as a general ability with the fact that there are special abilities which are independent of each other. A British psychologist (Spearman[15]) introduced his basic concept of intelligence as composed of a general factor which he called G and a long series of special factors which he called s_1, s_2, s_3, etc. Any given ability or performance was thought to be composed of a certain amount of G plus one or more s's. The various abilities of man are made up of differing amounts of G, plus differing amounts and kinds of s's.

Recently, this general or G factor has been given a new interpretation. The psychologist Thurstone has proposed a conception of intelligence as composed of a series of specific or primary abilities that vary considerably among individuals (Thurstone[16]). In any one individual, these abilities have relatively low positive correlations—correlations which can be explained by a general intellective factor that may be similar to G. Unfortunately, these primary abilities can be located only by means of a very complex and laborious statistical procedure known as *factor analysis*. Efforts to develop test situations which involve only one of the abstract primary abilities have not often succeeded. About twelve primary abilities have now been isolated and named by the Thurstone group. Some of these are briefly described and illustrated below.

Ability to calculate is of course basic to many professions, and can be measured quite specifically. The subject is given a number code drawn up after the numerical system of the ancient Mayas. Below are numbers 0 to 19:

0 ∪	1 •	2 ••	3 •••	4 ••••	5 ▬	6 •̄	7 ••̄	8 •••̄	9 ••••̄
10 ═	11 •̄═	12 ••̄═	13 •••̄═	14 ••••̄═	15 ═	16 •̄═	17 ••̄═	18 •••̄═	19 ••••̄═

Numbers 20 and over are expressed by putting symbols on top of each other. They can be translated into our numbers by multiplying the bottom symbol by 1, the top symbol by 20, then adding, as follows:

$$\text{••̄} \times 1 = 7$$

$$\begin{aligned} \text{•̄} \times 20 &= 120 \\ \text{••̄} \times 1 &= \underline{7} \\ &\quad\ 127 \end{aligned}$$

The subject, after studying these examples, is asked to make the calculations necessary to translate these symbols into arabic numbers:

••• ▬			•• ••••═		
•• •̄			••̄═ ∪		
•••̄═			•̄ ••••═		

Verbal ability is the ability to deal with relationships expressed through words. It is found in high concentration in vocabulary tests, such as the following:

1. JUVENILE _____ AWKWARD	YOUTHFUL	DEPENDENT	BASHFUL
2. FAMOUS _____ FLUVIAL	RENEWED	FAITHFUL	RENOWNED
3. OVERT _____ RICH	OPEN	TRIFLING	QUIET
4. WANTON _____ GAINFUL	UNRESTRAINED	EXTENSIVE	SOFT
5. REMOTE _____ INIMICAL	DISTENDED	SPARSE	FAR
6. POTENT _____ GAY	THICK	TIRESOME	STRONG

Fluency exists in all sense departments and is measured in terms of how far the stimulus pattern can be disarranged and reduced but still supply the individual with the needed clues. In this test of word fluency, the subject is asked to name the following pictures, with words which all begin with the letter *P:*

The mutilated pictures and words given below test the subject's ability to recognize the whole pattern from seeing its parts, no matter how disjointed they may be:

Memory is the rote memory as measured by recall and recognition methods. For example, the examiner may hold up before the subject a series of cards on each of which is printed a person's name: *Robert Harvey, Edith Gray, James Johnson,* etc. After the subject has viewed them all for a few seconds each, he is given the last names one by one and is asked to choose the right first name from a selected list.

Visualizing is the ability to think about the relationships among objects in three-dimensional space. The high-scoring individual is able to grasp what a situation will be like after specified changes have been made. It can be tested by seeing how long it takes the subject to tell whether these hands are right or left hands:

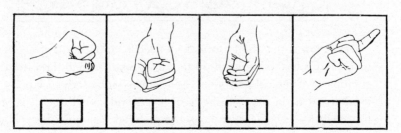

Perceptual speed. Another of Thurstone's primary abilities is rapidity in noting a particular design or element and picking it out from among a group of similar but not identical elements. In the following groups, pick out the two items that are exactly alike:

Induction (reasoning) is the ability to examine a series of facts or data and find the generalization or principle that runs through the series. The data can be expressed in a variety of symbols such as pictures, numbers, letters, direction of lines, etc. In the following example, the subject is to show that he has discovered the correct principle by naming the object that is unrelated to the rest:

Deduction is the ability to make a specific application of a principle given and is tested by means of the *syllogism*, a formal three-step presentation of a logical argument. Since many subjects can label a conclusion as true or false on the basis of general knowledge, it is best to use arbitrary terms or even nonsense material. Examine this syllogism:

All neutrotropes are panchloric.
All isoblasts are neutrotropes.
Therefore, all isoblasts are panchloric.

Does the third statement follow logically from the first two?

The foregoing list of primary abilities is not universally accepted; other workers would omit certain of these and add others. But it does serve to illustrate the goal toward which the factor analysts are working in their attempt to isolate the elements in intelligence. This approach is still in its experimental and formative stage, and there are few studies of the practical significance of these abilities in everyday living. What does seem very clear is that *intelligence is not one all-round ability but a group of abilities.*

CONSTANCY OF THE I.Q.

IF THE I.Q. remains constant, it is possible to predict the future mental status of an individual on the basis of a test of intelligence made in childhood. The advantages of such predictions are obvious. Early in the life of a bright child, his parents can lay plans for his future without fear that their high ambitions will be thwarted, at least by his lack of intelligence. The parents of the child of average intelligence can plan that child's occupational future accordingly and can guide him into some line of work in which his moderate intelligence will not predispose him to failure. In the case of the feeble-minded child, authorities can with confidence place him in an institution.

Since prediction is possible only if conditions remain constant, the constancy of I.Q. is a question of fundamental importance, which involves two important problems. First: how does I.Q. change when conditions remain the same? Second: what factors determine the constancy of I.Q.?

How does I.Q. change when conditions remain the same?

We shall examine here studies that have been made on individuals ranging from feeble-minded to very superior. Except for tests on very young children (with whom there are special testing difficulties), the universal conclusion is that the I.Q. does remain essentially constant when conditions remain the same—that is, when health, type of education, home situation, etc., do not change markedly.

I.Q.'s of the feeble-minded. Let us first examine the evidence with regard to the constancy of the I.Q. of children who are feeble-minded or who are of decidedly inferior intelligence.

A study has been made of the constancy of I.Q. in a group of 441 feeble-minded (Minogue[17]). These children were tested upon admission to an institution and were retested later at intervals of from two to ten years. If the I.Q. had not changed more than five points, it was regarded as constant. (A change of five I.Q. points is not very significant when you consider that the lowest grade of idiot has an I.Q. of practically 0 and that the highest I.Q. is at least 200. Differences of five points in an observed range of 200 must be regarded as remarkably small in the measurement of something as complex as intelligence.)

The result was that 72 per cent of the feeble-minded children *remained constant* in I.Q.; 5 per cent *gained* in I.Q.; and 24 per cent *lost* in I.Q. (The greatest single gain was 21 points; the greatest single loss was 23 points.) This means that the feeble-minded children showed losses more often than gains after a period of several years in the institution.

If I.Q. declines, as it did in most of these children, it can mean only that M.A. is not growing fast enough to keep the same ratio to C.A. as before. Although most of the losses were slight, they would seem to indicate that in most cases institutional life was less effective in developing intelligence than was the home life of the children prior to their admission to the institution. It must be remembered, however, that the M.A. of the feeble-minded individual reaches its maximum at an earlier age than does that of the normal or average individual. Since M.A. stops increasing while C.A. continues to advance, the traditionally obtained I.Q. of the feeble-minded person declines as he grows older. That is, a child of five with an M.A. of three-and-a-half has a higher I.Q. (67) than he will have when he is seven with an M.A. of only four and an I.Q. of 57. This, of course, would occur even in the best environment, and must be borne in mind in evaluating the data given above, as well as the following study of changes in I.Q. in a more representative group.

I.Q.'s of a wide range. One study analyzed the changes of I.Q. of 1183 individuals with I.Q.'s ranging from 80 up to very superior.

These individuals were retested under constant conditions at variable intervals up to six years. The results were that various subgroups of the total group showed average differences between the testings ranging from 0.1 to 5.0 I.Q. points, according to the length of time elapsing between tests.

Since, as you know, a maximum average variation of 5.0 I.Q. points cannot be regarded as significant, the only possible conclusion is that the children's I.Q.'s did not change significantly on the average. Moreover, the average change that did occur in I.Q. scores seemed to result from the children's retaking the same test (this study was made before alternative Stanford-Binets were provided). The largest average difference—of 5.0 I.Q. points—occurred in groups repeating the test within 3 months, and seemed to result largely from practice on specific test items. The smallest average difference—a tenth of a point—occurred in groups where 60 to 72 months elapsed between tests. The superior children gained slightly, while the duller children (as you might expect) lost in I.Q. between tests. (Cattell[18])

The results reviewed here give us no hope that early feeble-mindedness is something which a child will "outgrow." In fact, these results indicate that bright, average, and dull children alike do not change significantly in I.Q. And they are typical of those obtained by more than a dozen studies based on thousands of subjects.

Confirmation of the relative constancy of the I.Q. is found in a very comprehensive study in which 1106 children were tested and then retested one or more times.

The children in this study were cases referred to a Child Study Department because of unsatisfactory school adjustment, including behavior problems as well as poor achievement. The children varied in age from about six-and-a-half to twelve-and-a-half years at the time of the first testing. The average amount of I.Q. change found in retesting was 5.08 I.Q. points. Despite the fact that approximately half of the children were placed in special classes where their difficulties would receive special attention from well-trained teachers, there was a tendency for the lower I.Q.'s to decline slightly. Nevertheless, the relative constancy of the I.Q. was established once more. (Hirt[19])

Closely similar results were obtained by another study in retesting a group of juvenile delinquents. (Mann and Mann[20])

I.Q.'s of the very superior. A recent, comprehensive, and convincing demonstration of the constancy of high I.Q.'s as measured by the Stanford-Binet tests is reported in an aspect of the long-run study of gifted children (Terman[21]). In 1922, at the time of the first testing, the group was in the upper one half of 1 per cent of the total population. Six years later, and again eighteen years later, tests suitable to adults showed a majority of the subjects in or close to the upper 1 per cent of the general population. This finding gives little support to the popular belief that bright youngsters are in danger of "burning out" mentally later in life.

I.Q.'s of the very young. Exceptions to the general rule that I.Q.'s remain essentially constant are I.Q. determinations made upon very young children. The bulk of the available evidence indicates that children who are under four years when tested the first time will show an average difference of ten I.Q. points on a follow-up test coming two or more years later (Goodenough and Maurer[22]). Similar evidence is given by a study in which children aged two to five-and-a-half years when first tested were retested ten years later (Bradway[23]). These results show that verbal items are more dependable and the performance items less dependable in predicting the I.Q. that will be obtained ten years later. Here it seems quite possible or even probable that the main shifting is a result of the fact that, at the lower years, the Stanford-Binet test (or the others now available for such small children) is measuring other factors—such as rate of physical maturation and amount of muscular dexterity—besides the kinds of factors measured by tests with older children.

What factors determine the constancy of I.Q.?

There are two possible hypotheses that may account for the high degree of constancy observed in the I.Q. *First hypothesis:* that I.Q. depends upon the quality of the individual's environment and will remain constant as long as his environment remains the same. *Second hypothesis:* that I.Q. depends upon the heredity of the individual and is constant because the heredity of the individual does not change. The problem of determining the roles played by these two factors is necessarily complex, but its importance in social living is so great that we are more than justified in inquiring into it. After all, if we are to improve the intelligence of the human race, we must understand the factors which determine its development.

The cloud of controversy which often befogs the study of the relative effects that heredity and environment have on human behavior grows out of a failure to define the issue—or, more properly, to define the *issues.* It is obviously impossible to state once and for all whether human behavior depends more on heredity or more on environment. The balance may go one way for one trait of intelligence, another for a particular personality trait, and still another for a trait of morality. This section will find a fairly definite answer to the question of whether heredity or environment has more influence on intelligence—more specifically, intelligence as defined by the Stanford-Binet tests. To determine in turn the effect of each of two variables (heredity and environment), it is necessary to hold one of them constant while the other varies.

We shall examine in turn the evidence on the problem given by each of these approaches:

Keeping heredity the same, varying environment:

    1 Comparing identical twins in different environments (p. 219).

    2 Comparing the same individual in different environments (pp. 220 to 222).

Keeping the environment the same, varying heredity:

1 Comparing the closeness of relationship between foster-child I.Q. and home factors, with the closeness of relationship between real-child I.Q. and home factors (pp. 222 to 225).

2 Comparing unrelated children in same environment (p. 225).

Heredity the same, environment different. Our first procedure is to study the influence of heredity apart from environment. The first way to hold hereditary factors constant while varying environment would be to study a large number of identical twins, the members of each pair being separated at birth and sent into foster homes ranging in quality from the poorest to the best. The quality of the homes entered by the members of each twin pair would be determined purely by chance, so that the quality of the environments of the identical twins would not be correlated. Thus heredity would be held constant while environment was varied.

After an interval of years had elapsed, these twins would be subjected to many kinds of psychological tests and measurements. The scores of each twin would then be compared with the scores of the other twin. Finally, the answers to our various questions about the relative influence of heredity and environment would be judged from the degree of similarity between the members of the twin pairs. For we know that since the heredity of identical twins is identical—and therefore constant from one to the other—the only variable would be environment. Therefore, any differences between the twins in a pair—anything less than perfect correlation of their test scores—would have to be attributed to environmental influences.

As yet no scientific-minded dictator has appeared who would cause identical twins to be separated for purposes of psychological study. But we can and will examine a study (Newman, Freeman, and Holzinger[24]) of nineteen real-life cases of identical twins who happened to be reared apart through adoption into different foster homes. Although these cases are few, they do permit the tentative conclusion that identical heredity seems to be a powerful factor in keeping the I.Q.'s of identical twins close to each other in spite of separate environments.

The average of the differences between the members of each of the nineteen twin pairs is 8.2 I.Q. points. This difference is only slightly larger than the average of the differences between two tests on the *same* individual made at intervals of several years. That is, the intelligence test scores of identical twins reared apart (sometimes in similar and sometimes in different environments) are almost as similar as two scores on the same person and are nearly as similar as those of identical twins reared together. Obviously, identical heredity is a factor operating systematically to determine in a very real way the development of similar intelligence.

The other way of studying heredity alone is to observe what happens to the I.Q. of the same individual when he is placed in different environments. Two general types of study have been made along this line: one analyzing I.Q. changes in children placed in foster homes; the other analyzing I.Q. changes in children attending nursery schools. These studies are important because they indicate the extent to which changes in economic status and education can affect I.Q.

Now let us examine the actual evidence given on this heredity-and-environment question, first, by the foster-home studies, and second, by the preschool studies.

1 One foster-home study observed the changes in I.Q. in a group of 74 children after they were removed from an orphanage to superior and to inferior foster homes (Freeman *et al.*[25]). Their average residence in foster homes was four years. The results show that children removed to superior homes gained an average of 5.3 points in I.Q. scores, while those removed to inferior homes gained only 0.1 point. Thus the difference between living in the poorer homes as compared with the better was sufficient to account for a difference of five I.Q. points between the average amounts gained by the two adopted groups. The results also seem to indicate that the poorer homes were no more stimulating to intelligence growth than the orphans' home, since they brought no increase in I.Q.

The better homes, however, brought some increase in I.Q. The increase may even have been greater than the test results indicate. This is because the original (1916) Stanford-Binet Scale was a little too difficult at the upper ages included in this study, having been standardized on children in school, who are somewhat superior to the general population of children that age because some of the slower pupils have dropped out. Allowing for this, we are safe in concluding that the effect of the better environments was an increase in I.Q. of *about nine or ten points,* not just five.

2 Another much-quoted study of environmental influence on I.Q. is interpreted as being in line with the study just reviewed. Babies whose mothers' family backgrounds were inferior in intellectual level, occupational level, educational achievement, and socio-economic status were placed in foster homes superior in all these respects (Skodak[26]). Practically all the babies were illegitimate. At the end of one year of residence in the foster home, the I.Q.'s of the adopted children had increased an average of 5.7 points; by the end of two years, the average increase was *9.8 points.* No further increases occurred, the deficit in development due to poor environment apparently having been met by this time. (Skodak and Skeels[27])

From these studies we can say that removing dull children to good foster homes does seem to make an improvement in their I.Q.'s, an improvement which is limited by their inherited capacity.

Several valuable investigations have been conducted which suggest some conclusions about the effect of preschool training or nursery-school training on I.Q.

1 One of these studied a group of 600 children from decidedly superior homes to see how participating in the activities of a preschool would affect the I.Q. level (Wellman[28]). These data show that the stimulating environment of the preschool was responsible for an average increase of about *15 I.Q. points*.

2 A similar experiment—in which twenty-eight children were measured before and after one year's experience in another preschool of high quality—showed average changes ranging from *2 to 7 points* for various age groups. (Goodenough[29])

3 In still another study, the subjects were a group of twenty-seven children between the ages of thirty-five and sixty months (Barrett and Koch[30]). These children, who were to enter the nursery school of an orphanage, were matched with "control" children on the bases of sex, chronological age, intelligence, and institutional experience. The control group did not attend the nursery school. The nursery-school group gained in I.Q. from an average of 92 to an average of 113 (or 21 I.Q. points) over a period of nine months; the control group, from an average of 93 to an average of 98 (or 5 I.Q. points). Allowing for the 5-point increase, which probably would have occurred anyway, we can say that the preschool environment caused *about a 16-point average increase* in the I.Q. of the school group.

The number of cases in each of these last two studies above is too small to support a confident conclusion. However, combining the two sets of results gives an overall average increase of *about 10 I.Q. points* in preschool environment, a figure we can view with greater confidence.

4 A three-year study was undertaken to determine, under controlled conditions, the effects of preschool education on the I.Q.'s of underprivileged children of average and below-average intelligence. The children were in residence at a soldiers' orphans' home, a state institution designed for the care of dependent and neglected children. Children of preschool ages were divided into two groups: one preschool and one control group, matched on chronological age, mental age, I.Q., sex, nutritional status, and length of residence in the orphanage. The preschool and control group experienced the same life and routine, except that the preschool group spent several hours a day at the preschool building, where a variety of stimulating activities took place. Over the longest period (approximately 20 months) the preschool children gained 4.6 points in I.Q., while the control group lost 4.6 points. Thus in the end there was a difference in the I.Q.'s of the experimental and control groups of *9.2 I.Q. points* (Skeels, Updegraff, Wellman, and Williams[31])

A pertinent consideration in evaluating the results of all these studies concerns itself with changes in the willingness of the subjects to take an intelligence test. It seems likely that children in preschools and foster homes are more highly motivated to cooperate in taking tests. Perhaps some of the difference attributable to the superior environment can be accounted for on this basis (McHugh[32]).

In looking back over these foster-home and preschool studies, we see that the differences between good and bad environments in foster home or school can produce maximum average differences of around *ten I.Q. points* between experimental and control groups. However, there is a wide variation in the differences actually found in the different studies, one study showing differences as small as two points, and another showing differences as large as sixteen points. Can the same differences be expected regardless of the age at which the environmental changes are made?

> To throw light on this question, an analysis has been made of the case histories of 100 children who were each given the advantages of a good foster home for four years. The age range at time of entrance into the foster home was from 3 to 14 years, and the I.Q. range was from 70 to 130. Analysis shows that any advantageous effects on I.Q.'s obtained by transferring children from an inferior to a superior environment occurred when the change was made *before the age of 6*. There was an average increase of 6.6 I.Q. points in a group of 30 children who were 6 years old or younger when adopted; an average increase of only .7 I.Q. points in a group of 40 children who were 7, 8, or 9 years old when adopted; and an insignificant decrease in a group of children who were 10 to 14 at adoption. (Reymert and Hinton[33])

From this and other similar studies you can clearly see that any advantage of improved environment will be greatest if the child is young when under its influence.

All these studies of the effects of foster homes and preschools on I.Q. allow us to conclude that *the I.Q. can be changed to some extent by environment, but still retains considerable constancy even when environment is markedly changed.*

Environment the same, heredity varying. This section will show just how powerful the environment can be in determining the intelligence of adopted children. The procedure used is that of comparing the correlation between I.Q.'s and environmental ratings for the foster-child group, with the correlation between I.Q.'s and environmental ratings for the group of children living with their own parents. In the last section, we watched to see how a child's I.Q. would change after he was placed in a foster home. Here the reasoning is as follows:

If the quality of the environment in foster homes correlates positively with the intelligence of the adopted children who have lived in them for a long time, and if the original correlation between the quality of the children's heredity and the quality of the foster-home environments was zero, we can conclude that the new correlation between the foster homes and intelligence is due to the effect of environment. In other words, if babies are adopted into foster homes of high or low quality regardless of the quality of the babies' heredity, the correlation between the quality of the home and the quality of the babies' heredity would be zero. If the correlation between the quality of the environment and the intelligence of the foster children increased after a period of residence in the foster home, that increase would be due to the change in environment. Moreover, after making full allowance for the effect of environment on the intelligence, we can assign the remaining influence to heredity. (The detailed solution of this problem involves a statistical technique which is quite beyond the background of the beginning student.)

1 One study of the effect of heredity and environment on intelligence showed the correlations between I.Q. and various other factors in a group of foster children and in a control group made up of children

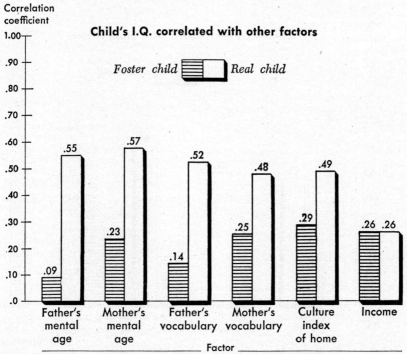

Correlation coefficient

Child's I.Q. correlated with other factors

Data from B. Burks, "The Relative Influence of Nature and Nurture upon Mental Development." *Twenty-Seventh Yearbook of the National Society for the Study of Education*, 1928, 27: Pt. 1, p. 285. Quoted by permission of the Society.

living with their own parents (Burks[34]). These correlations are given in the chart on page 223. You will remember that a correlation of +1.00 means a perfect resemblance, and one of 0 means no resemblance at all.

Compare the correlations between foster parent and child with those of parent and own child. Notice that father's mental age, mother's mental age, father's vocabulary, and mother's vocabulary are all more highly correlated with I.Q. in the case of real children than in the case of foster children.

Through use of a statistical procedure far too complicated to be described here, the conclusion was reached that individual differences in total heredity account for about 80 per cent of variations in intelligence, differences in environment accounting for the remaining 20 per cent.

2 Another attempt has been made to determine the relationship between intelligence of children and the respective factors of heredity and environment (Leahy[35]). Two groups of children were used in the investigation. One group consisted of the biological offspring of the parents with whom they lived. The other group was made up of children who were adopted into foster homes before the age of six months, and who were five to fourteen years of age at the time of the study. In this latter group it was assumed there could be no relationship between the quality of the heredity of parents and that of the adopted children.

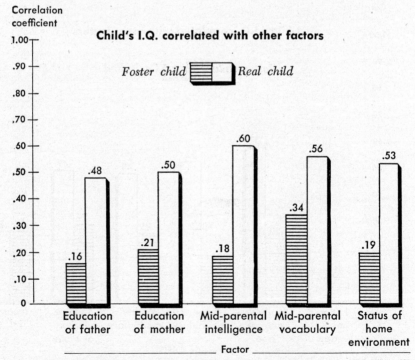

Child's I.Q. correlated with other factors

Foster child ▦ ▢ Real child

Factor	Foster child	Real child
Education of father	.16	.48
Education of mother	.21	.50
Mid-parental intelligence	.18	.60
Mid-parental vocabulary	.34	.56
Status of home environment	.19	.53

Data from A. M. Leahy, "Nature-Nurture and Intelligence," *Genetic Psychology Monographs,* 1935, XVII, p. 282.

To make the two groups comparable, each child in the adopted group was paired with a child in the other group on the basis of the real or foster parents' intelligence-test scores and on the basis of objectively measurable environmental factors, such as occupation and educational status. The correlation between the intelligence of the biological parents and the intelligence of their children must be accounted for on the basis of the *combined effects* of parental heredity and environment of the home. In the case of the foster-parent foster-child combinations, the correlation must be accounted for on the basis of the influences of *environment alone*. The correlations obtained are shown on page 224.

In this chart "mid-parental intelligence" is the average of the intelligence-test scores of the two parents; mid-parental vocabulary is, similarly, the average of the vocabulary scores of the two parents. By comparing the size of the correlation coefficients for the parent-child combinations of the two groups, it is possible to calculate the contribution of measurable environment. Notice that the correlations between real parents and real children are much higher for all the traits studied than are the correlations between foster parents and foster children. In other words, parental heredity plus environment of the home contributes much more to the determination of the intelligence of the children studied than does environment alone.

Still using the method of varying heredity while holding environment constant, it is interesting to examine some data showing the degree of relationship between biologically unrelated children reared in the same home.

According to one calculation (Freeman *et al.*[36]), the correlation between the I.Q.'s of unrelated children reared in the same home is .34. This is appreciably lower than the correlation of .50 found between the I.Q.'s of real brothers and sisters reared in the same home. In the latter case, both heredity and environment contribute to the similarity in intelligence.

Again there is evidence that similar environment has less influence on I.Q. than similar heredity.

But before accepting as final the results of the above studies, we might well inquire into the effect of consciousness of adoption upon the intellectual development of the foster children. Does consciousness of adoption create a barrier between foster parent and foster child which does not exist when there is a blood tie? This question must be left open at the present time, for there is no evidence that will answer it one way or another.

There is another important fact to bear in mind in appraising the relative effects that differences in environment and in heredity have on differences in intelligence or any other mental trait. This is the fact that heredity does not consist wholly of the traits observable in a child's parents. The parents' genes, which they pass on to the child, include determiners for many more traits than they themselves visibly possess —these determiners are the recessive genes. Thus to judge a child's mental heredity by his mother's I.Q. and his father's I.Q. is to leave out of account all the genes which have been transmitted to him from many generations of his ancestors but which do not happen to be visible in the parents. While environment acts only during the life-time of an individual, hereditary influences reach back of the parents into the far-distant past. These pre-parental influences are bound to be a tremendous force in determining intelligence.

These "foster-child real-child" comparisons strongly indicate that common heredity alone, even without common environment, is a factor that works rather strongly to produce similar I.Q.'s. Common heredity plus common environment works even more strongly. Of the two, common environment apparently makes far the less important contribution.

Environmental factors causing uneven development of intelligence

As you know, intelligence is not just one general ability but a complex bundle of abilities. So far we have discussed the hereditary and environmental influences on the *general level* of I.Q. What about the influences on special abilities?

A very interesting study has been made comparing first-grade students in two New York schools in their performance on the Stanford-Binet examination. The two schools differed widely in that the children attending them were drawn from the opposite ends of the social and economic scale. Group A was made up of 140 children from a school situated in a crowded slum area where the children had been subjected to all the evils of the depression practically from birth. Foreign languages were spoken in the majority of these homes. Group B was made up of 114 first-grade children from a school located in a superior residential section in upper Manhattan. In addition to the Stanford-Binet examination, a Goodenough drawing test (a nonverbal intelligence test) was administered to each child individually in the two groups.

The average Stanford-Binet I.Q. for Group A was 101.8, and for Group B the average was 115, a difference of 13.2 points. However, this difference may have been partially due to the fact that the two groups differed in language experience. On the Goodenough drawing test, the average score for Group A was 103.4 and for Group B, 108.2— a difference of only 4.8 points.

In specific abilities, it was found that Group A, made up of the underprivileged children, showed relative superiority in counting and handling money and in sensory discrimination. Group B showed relative superiority on tests which involved sentences, digits, rhymes, and stating the essential similarities and differences between concrete objects. A good social and economic background, with its greater opportunities for stimulation and development, gives a child an advantage in using his inherent abilities on verbal intelligence tests. The children from the slums were more preoccupied with money, which was scarce in their hands, and had developed their sensory discrimination by dodging automobiles as they played in the street traffic. (Saltzman[37])

In short, each group of children lived in an environment which caused some of their abilities to develop more than others. These pictures of middle-class and slum environments suggest why—as the Saltzman study has established—one leads to superior verbal abilities, the other to superior sensory discrimination.

SPECIAL FACTORS IN INTELLIGENCE

Psychologists know that the very general factors—heredity and environment—are not the only ones to take into account in explaining the development of intelligence. There are several other special factors which have a bearing on intellectual development. Likewise, there are many factors which have no bearing on intelligence at all but which have been commonly considered to have some.

Intelligence and birth order

It has been found that first-born children are slightly inferior in I.Q. to those coming later in the family (Steckel[38]). This conclusion was reached after comparing the scores of 5928 pairs of siblings. Since there is no known hereditary mechanism accounting for this fact, it must be attributed to environmental effects, probably to the fact that the younger children are stimulated by and compete with the older ones. The difference is too slight to have practical significance.

Month of birth and intelligence

The astrologists of old preached that the stars influence our destiny, and many people still believe it. For example, if you were born in September, you were said to be more intelligent than the average. If born under Venus, you should be happy and gay—if under Saturn, false, envious, full of debate and law.

A number of studies have analyzed the intelligence-test scores of large numbers of individuals grouped according to their month of birth. A few such studies have shown consistent superiority in intelligence-test scores of individuals born in a particular month or season. One study showed that individuals born in the warm months of May, June, July, August, and September were slightly superior, on the average, to those born in the cold months of December, January, February, and March (Held[39]). The difference between the averages was 1.5 I.Q. through high school (an insignificant difference, however). Two hypotheses have been advanced to explain this difference.

First, it is quite possible that a selective factor influences the results in favor of children born in warm months. Amount of schooling will influence the level of the I.Q. upward a few points at any given C.A. Children born in the summer months are more likely to enter school in September and follow through the grades in regular order. Children born in cold months come of school age at mid-term or after; hence they are a little older upon entering school and, at a given age, have a little less schooling and hence a little lower I.Q. This hypothesis has not yet been proved but should be kept in mind as a possible explanation of the relation between month of birth and I.Q.

An investigation has been made which seems to prove another hypothesis: that children born in the warm seasons (and conceived in the cold winter months) might be superior because they have more intelligent parents, as shown by the fact that they plan births.

> Physicians agree that babies born in the warm summer months have a better chance to get a healthy start in life than do those born in the cold months. The months of birth of 3275 children were tabulated by parents' occupation. In the upper-income groups, the birth rate is higher during the warm months. On the average, the children of upper-income groups are brighter than children of the lower-income groups. Since seasonal variation in birth rate was not found among the children of poorer parents (who were presumably less likely to plan the births of their children), it was concluded that superior intelligence of parents rather than seasonal influence was responsible for the higher intelligence of children born in the warm-weather months. (Goodenough[40])

A similar study of 3361 British births decides against the hypothesis that season of conception influences intelligence, and in favor of the alternative hypothesis that intelligence influences the season of conception. (Roberts[41])

All in all, there is no scientific confirmation of the popular belief that the month or season of birth influences I.Q.

Race and intelligence

The problem of the possible superiority of one race or nation over another has been one of emotional controversy both in the United States and in the totalitarian countries abroad. We like to think we are better, or that our family is better, or our school, church, state, nation, or race is better than others. This will-to-believe sometimes leads us into strange and unconvincing attempts to explain facts. For example, in one study it was found that Indians are faster than whites in reaction time. One reviewer, full of the "white supremacy" complex, argued that this result was just one more proof that the white race is one of supermen—they have a greater capacity for inhibition.

A more common evidence of the racial superiority complex is the belief that Negroes, Orientals, American Indians, and other "races" are innately inferior in intelligence to people of lighter skin. What does the psychologist have to say on this question? First of all, he says what other scientists do: that the whole idea of race is a very cloudy one. As you will see in Chapter 18, it is difficult to mark off clear distinctions between the groups of mankind.

But the psychologist also has some specific comments to offer on this important question of whether the average person of one skin color is born less intelligent than the average person of another skin color. Many investigators have given intelligence tests to members of different races. But there are two main difficulties that stand in the way of a final decision on the question of whether there is "racial superiority" in intelligence—difficulties which make impossible the exact measurement and comparison of the intelligence of different races and nationality groups.

First, since it is obviously impossible to compare all Americans with, say, all Chinese, an investigator must measure the intelligence of a representative sample of each group. Here arises the possibility of errors of selection. Do we have a true cross section of all the elements in the parent group? Are the immigrant Chinese studied in the United States typical Chinese? How does the investigator find "average members" of different "races" to test for purposes of comparison?

The second great difficulty of testing racial intelligence is that there must be adequate control of all the significant variables—of all the factors other than innate intelligence which might influence the results of the test. The most important of these variables are:

1 *Language.* It is obviously unfair to expect people to do well in a test which is not in a familiar language.

2 *Physical environment.* One paper-and-pencil test given to Samoans, which was the nonlanguage or performance type, gave misleading results because the children had never seen pencils.

3 *The subjects' habits of performance.* An appreciation of some of the difficulties encountered by examiners while testing the "red man" can be garnered from the following instances of the influence of tradition: it was considered very bad form to answer a question while anyone who did not understand it might be present; there was such a strong desire for certainty that guessing was unthinkable; and to do anything hurriedly was regarded as "bad manners" (Klineberg[42]). In other societies where there is strong community spirit, natives never understand that the test is not a common venture to be discussed in a meeting and solved cooperatively.

4 *Culture and the test items.* Because of the different social experience of different groups, it is difficult to devise test items that will reflect the subjects' intelligence instead of their lack of certain kinds of experience. For instance, an investigator giving the Binet test to a child in a rural community asked this question: "If you went to the store and bought 6 cents' worth of candy and gave the clerk 10 cents, what change would you receive?" One child answered: "I never had 10 cents and if I had I wouldn't spend it for candy, and anyway candy is what your mother makes." (Pressey[43]) In order to make a fair comparison between different racial groups, each must be given tests which are of the same difficulty and which contain test items on subjects familiar to the examinees. It may be necessary, then, to adjust the form of questions given to one group in order to fit the experience of other groups. Such an adjustment involves a delicate logical issue, since there can be no way to determine the point at which changing the form of the item seriously affects its content, which should be constant in both tests.

The difficulties of testing the intelligence of different racial and national groups have been dramatized by the scientific history of some studies on the "superiority" of the "Nordic race"—a belief which has widespread support. Although many North European peoples have clung to this belief since long before the rise and fall of the Nazis, no scientific investigation has ever supported it. One investigator, working with the Alpha and Beta tests of recruits inducted during the First World War, inferred that differences in performance were related to national origin. When the foreign-born were classified according to the country of their birth and when these scores were combined into the so-called Nordic, Alpine, and Mediterranean groups, it appeared that the prevalent notion of Nordic superiority was justified (Brigham[44]). In a later publication, nevertheless, the investigator reversed himself and showed wherein his earlier interpretation was at fault. This is a notable example of scientific integrity. In the years intervening between his first and second reports he concluded that the method he had used was so unreliable that he found he could not use it to demonstrate a relation between intelligence and racial or national origin. (Brigham[45]) Unfortunately, the original study is more widely known than the recantation.

In general, we may say that the whole problem of whether there are *inherited* racial differences in intelligence is one which is far from solved. Some investigators have the belief (cf. Klineberg,[46] Benedict,[47] Freeman[48]) that these differences are not entirely inherited but are due in large part to differences in environment and would probably disappear if all races lived in comparable environments. However, their belief has never been conclusively proved because of all the difficulties of testing racial intelligence.

For the present, the important facts about the comparative intelligence of different groups are these:

1 Although our present testing procedures reveal differences in the average intelligence of different groups, there is considerable overlapping between groups. In other words, the most intelligent members of one group are more intelligent than the least intelligent members of other groups.

2 Favorable environment does contribute significantly to the determination of I.Q. in all ethnic groups thus far studied. (But whether the influence of environment accounts for the differences between the average I.Q.'s of different groups has not been definitely determined.)

3 The various degrees of intelligence are found in all groups, just as (you will see in Chapter 18) the various physical characteristics of mankind are found in differing degrees in all groups.

Intelligence and health

There is an outstanding example of wishful thinking to be found in the popular belief that the child who is superior in intelligence is inferior in physical health. People like to feel that nature balances things out—good mind against poor health. Numerous studies on this topic show that such a belief is false.

> An intensive study has been made of the health and physical characteristics of a large group of children of high I.Q. (Terman *et al.*[4.]). The superior children were compared with the mentally average group and were found to be better on the average in every desirable trait. The children of average intelligence suffered from more physical illnesses and possessed more bodily defects than the superior.

This series of observations is consistent with the general hypothesis that superior heredity is a factor in both superior mental and superior physical development.

Malnutrition and intelligence. How does malnutrition affect I.Q.? In any attempt to deal with this relationship, one must be on guard to see that all experimental variables are in hand. For example, it is well-established that poor children on the average are less intelligent than children of well-to-do families—who, incidentally, are better fed. Now suppose it were found that the underfed children in a public school were less intelligent than those who showed no medical symptoms of malnutrition. This would not necessarily mean that poor diet causes poor intelligence. This lower intelligence of the undernourished children could result from poor heredity or from lack of intellectual encouragement at home, not necessarily from poor nourishment.

There is only one way of obtaining a dependable answer to the question of whether or how nourishment is related to intelligence. This is to take a group of malnourished children and see if their intelligence changes with their nutritional condition. Numerous studies have been conducted on this important problem but with negative results. The conclusion from them all is that correcting a condition of malnutrition will make the individual more active and happier, but it will not raise his I.Q. (Schwesinger[50]).

Glandular imbalance and intelligence. As you learned in Chapter 3, the endocrine glands produce chemical substances which profoundly affect both physical growth and personality development. The exact relationship between intelligence and these internal secretions is a complex problem which we are still only beginning to solve.

> One line of investigation has attempted to discover the relation between hypothyroidism and intelligence. You will remember from Chap-

ter 3 that hypothyroidism is a condition resulting from too little thyroid secretion in the blood. (If it exists in an extreme degree from birth or an early age, it is called "cretinism.") Severe hypothyroidism causes the sufferer to become lazy and dull in manner, and has serious effects on intelligence. When a once-healthy thyroid gland fails to deliver an adequate supply of thyroid secretion, intelligence declines. And in cretinism—when the thyroid supply is cut off early in a child's life— intelligence does not develop adequately at all.

To see whether such a loss in intelligence would be regained, the mental development of a group of hypothyroid cases was followed during a course of treatment in which thyroid was supplied to the body from outside sources (Bronstein and Brown,[51] and Brown, Bronstein, and Kraines[52]). The patients under thyroid treatment lost their dull appearance; their physical condition improved; they became vivacious and animated in their behavior. But their I.Q.'s were not increased in the average case. There were, however, such large individual differences in the amount of I.Q. change that the investigators did not consider their findings as conclusive evidence in either direction. Moreover, one case in which the treatment was started at two years of age and continued over a period of four years showed an increase in I.Q. from 50 to 60 and remained at this level. And the treatment was irregular enough to suggest that greater increases might have been found had the treatment been more consistent.

While these studies indicate a relationship between thyroid deficiency and lowered intelligence, there is no adequate evidence that disorders of the pituitary have an adverse influence on intelligence (although they do have a harmful effect on social behavior in many instances). In fact, there is evidence that patients with pituitary deficiency (*Fröhlich's syndrome*) are actually superior in intelligence to the average (Schott[53]).

The effect of diseased tonsils and adenoids. How often has the family doctor assured the worried mother that Johnny will do better in school when his infected tonsils or adenoids are removed? Unfortunately, such a doctor is overoptimistic, as careful experiments have demonstrated.

In one study, twenty-eight children whose tonsils or adenoids were diseased were matched with another similarly afflicted "control" group. One afflicted group was operated on in the usual manner; the other was permitted to go unoperated. Retests at the end of six months showed that the mental ages of the operated group had not increased above those of the unoperated group. The retests were given long enough after the operations so that any temporary weakening effect of the surgical manipulation would have disappeared. (Rogers[54])

Similar negative results were obtained in another, equally well-controlled, experiment (Lowe[55]). Combining the results of both these studies leads to the conclusion that there was an average increase of 2.2 I.Q. points in the operated group as against an increase of 4.1 in the unoperated. This smaller increase in the operated group is not enough to suggest that the removal of diseased tonsils actually lowers the I.Q., but it does reveal very clearly the essential falsity of the opposite conclusion. Although operations on tonsils or adenoids may have other beneficial effects, they will not raise the I.Q.

Cerebral syphilis and mental deterioration. It is a well-recognized fact in every mental hospital and clinic that syphilis can attack the nervous system and brain and bring about lowering of intelligence. The writer once observed the progress of this disease in an army officer of superior initial intelligence. As happens in rare instances, all attempts of the physicians to arrest the progress of this disease failed. Over a period of one year, the patient fell two years in mental age. In this connection, it is interesting to note that the deterioration was "spotty." That is to say, the patient lost far more in certain test abilities than in others. His ability to define words was less affected than his ability to solve simple problems in geometry. Deterioration continued rapidly for two more years until the patient's death.

Such a condition is, of course, most unusual as compared with the many other factors in heredity and environment that influence the complex bundle of abilities we call "intelligence." These abilities are determined by many factors in the person's inherited structures which interact with what he learns from his environment. Measuring intelligence—and measuring the factors that influence it—is one of the most challenging and important problems of psychology. In this chapter we have seen how the concept of "I.Q." developed and we have examined its limitations. We have also discovered the important influences that heredity has on I.Q. and have seen how environment can operate within certain limits to influence I.Q. Future work in psychology will doubtless find out much more about this whole question, for it is vital in many decisions which must be made through all of daily life—by the social worker in placing children for adoption, by the young person at school or work, by the employer in hiring, and by the educator in adjusting learning programs and in distributing scholastic opportunities and rewards.

PART THREE

Knowing our world

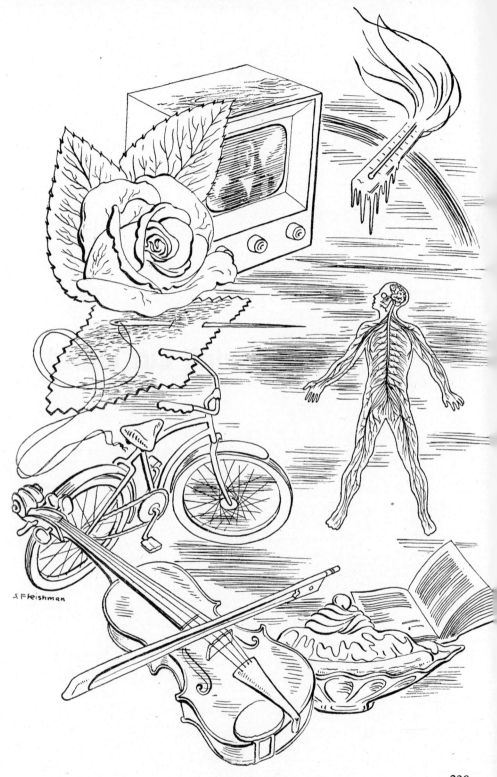

CHAPTER 7

The sensory processes

AT EVERY MOMENT OF YOUR LIFE you are responding to some sort of stimulus. You hear people speaking and you answer them. You feel the hunger contractions of your stomach and go to the icebox. You see an automobile coming and you make coordinated movements of your head, legs, torso, and arms in order to reach the sidewalk within a safe margin of time.

All these responses, and the thousands like them that make up the pattern of our lives, are made possible through the cooperative action of several sets of sense organs. Psychologists do not know yet exactly how many different kinds of sense organs man does possess, but one thing is certain—there are more than the traditional five of seeing, hearing, touching, tasting, and smelling which keep us aware of our environment. There are also sense organs which tell us about ourselves: one group informs us about the positions and movements of various parts of our bodies; still others keep us aware of the condition of our internal organs and so give rise to the many drives (sex and hunger, for example) which have been considered in the chapter on *Motivation*.

The senses to be considered in this chapter—*sight, hearing, touch, body position and balance, smell,* and *taste*—work in different situations and in different combinations. Distant objects are usually perceived through sight, hearing, and (to a lesser extent) smell, while touch acquaints us with objects in direct contact with our bodies. Complex objects and situations usually become known to us through stimuli to several senses. For instance, at the "first night" of a play, you see the stage scenery and the attractively dressed people, you hear music and low voices, and you smell a faint medley of perfumes.

The human being is remarkably adaptive. No one sensory department is absolutely essential to life or even to the enjoyment of life. Blind people learn to read with their fingers; color-blind people often do not even know of their defect; deaf people find much comfort in reading; people who lack a sense of taste or smell can find many other fields of enjoyment. Since several sets of sense organs work together in telling us what is going on inside and outside our bodies, no one set is all-important and different sets can substitute for each other in the process of adjustment.

The human body is full of activity. Most of the sense organs of the body are being stimulated effectively much of the time. Even when you are asleep, for instance, the sound waves in your environment will cause your eardrums to move back and forth, and the further processes in the ear cause an arousal of nerve impulses from the ear to the central nervous system, just as when you are wide awake and are listening intently to the noise.

It is very possible or even probable that much of this incoming nervous activity is "lost" or inhibited within the central nervous system. However, even when you are asleep, if there is a strong and unusual noise in your environment, you are likely to twist and turn to some extent. So, as this simple example shows, even when you are not conscious of your response, and even when you have no conscious sensations, it is still possible for the three essential steps in an ordinary response process to occur:

1 Some *receptor cells* or sensory cells are stirred into activity by stimuli to which they are especially sensitive.

2 Nerve impulses then are carried by the main *connecting mechanism* of interest to psychology—the nervous system.

3 These nerve impulses finally arouse activity in the *organs of response* or *effectors*—the muscles or glands of the body.

Our concern now is with the first important stage of adjustment: receiving stimuli from within our bodies and from the world around us. Without our sense organs we would be completely unable to adjust, for we would be cut off from any knowledge of ourselves and the world around us. It should go without saying that life without sight and hearing would be difficult at best; that life without smell and taste would lose much of its gusto; and that faulty senses of body position and balance would impair the easy and accurate movements which are necessary to all our daily activities, from tooth-brushing to tennis. In this chapter you will discover how your sense organs work, what can go wrong with them, and how important they are in adjustment.

THE SENSE OF SIGHT: THE EYE AND HOW IT OPERATES

VISION HAS ALWAYS been regarded as man's most precious gift. Joseph Addison, the brilliant eighteenth-century essayist, once said:

> "Our sight is the most perfect and most delightful of all our senses; it fills the mind with the largest variety of ideas, converses with its objects at the greatest distance, and continues the longest in action without being tired or satiated with its proper enjoyment."

People take sight so much for granted that they sometimes fail to appreciate its value until it is lost, temporarily or permanently. So different is life without vision that the people who train Seeing Eye dogs prepare for the job by wearing blindfolds for a month so that they can better understand how a blind man feels and reacts.

The permanently blind learn to compensate to some extent through the finer training of their other senses, but they never reach the point where lack of vision is not a handicap. This does not imply that the blind are excluded from all lines of work. In fact, blindness is an asset in certain activities, because it removes distractions and permits more profound concentration.

When the psychologist studies sight, he must consider both *Visual Acuity* (sharpness of vision) and *Color Discrimination*. We shall go into both these aspects of vision, considering their neural basis and the defects which can arise in them. But first, we must study the organ which operates in both kinds of vision—the human eye.

The human eye

Our eyes are as complicated as they are useful. To understand how they work, you must consider both physics and physiology. The eye can be considered both as a remarkably sensitive instrument and as a hard-working bodily organ. In terms of the small amount of light required to activate it, the human eye is better than photographic film.

Under certain conditions, the human eye can see a match flame two hundred miles away. But not only is the eye very sensitive to light— its ability to see small objects is equally startling. Careful tests have shown that the human eye can perceive a thin wire whose diameter is equal to 1/500,000 of the total field of vision.

The eye and the camera compared. Before we can go further, we must have a working knowledge of the human eye, which is essentially like a camera. Study the pictures which show cross sections of a simple camera and a human eye, with the corresponding parts indicated. Notice especially that each has:

1 A sensitive surface upon which an inverted picture of the outer world is projected—the film in the camera, the retina in the eye;

2 A lens for focusing the rays of light on the sensitive surface;

3 An adjustable opening to regulate the amount of light allowed to enter—in the eye it is called the pupil.

The eye also has an auxiliary device for controlling the direction in which it is "pointed" and held in place; these are the three pairs of muscles with which we "roll the eyes." And the eye, of course, contains fluids that are lacking in the camera.

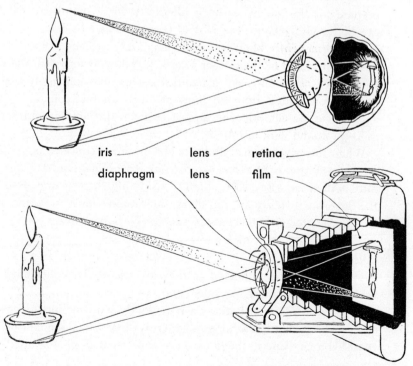

iris   lens   retina

diaphragm   lens   film

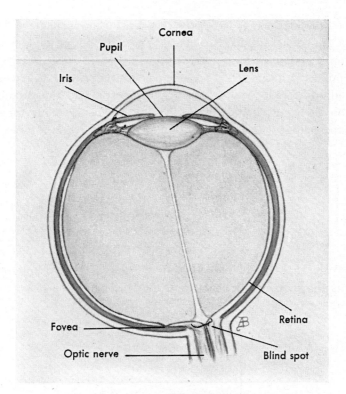

Cross section of the human eye

How we receive visual images. An image in the outer world is "seen" as a pattern of light. The light passes first through the *cornea* (a protective covering), and then through the *pupil,* an opening which changes in size in order to regulate the amount of light that enters the eye and thus influences the brightness of the image. After this adjustment by the pupil, the light rays making up the image penetrate through the *lens,* an oval-shaped structure which focuses the light rays onto the sensitive surface of the *retina.* The new impulses aroused in the retina are then transmitted to the brain through the *optic nerve.* In the picture on page 240 it looks as if this image is upside down, but actually there is no "right" or "wrong side up" to the brain. The nervous connections are such that this "inverted image on the retina" yields the correct conscious experience and the correct muscular adjustments of reaching or whatever action seems appropriate to the person. Learning helps to make our visual-perceptual processes more precise; but no peculiar problem of learning enters into vision beyond those involved in hearing or other sensory fields.

Bringing images into focus. The lens of the human eye differs from a camera lens in that it is elastic. The rigid lens of the bellows camera must be moved back and forth to change the focus in order that the projected image will be sharp and distinct. But the lens of the eye adjusts rapidly and automatically according to the distance of the object being viewed. When the muscle fibers circling the lens relax and permit it to flatten out, the lens is focused on a faraway object:

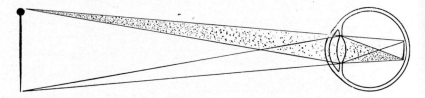

When these muscles contract, they cause the lens to bulge, increasing its thickness at the center and thus bringing near objects into focus on the retina:

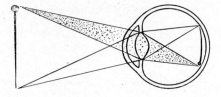

In reading, which is looking at a near object, the eyes eventually become tired and strained and can even produce headaches. Then looking into the distance rests the eyes and allows the lens to assume its resting shape.

How visual excitations travel to the brain. When a pattern of light, or image, stimulates the sensitive receptor cells of the retina, it sets up a chemical reaction. This reaction in turn is communicated to the next nerve cell in the retina, and so it progresses in a chain leading back eventually to the brain. These chemical reactions in the nerve cell, or *excitations*, travel at about 150 miles per hour. They occur with a frequency that depends upon the threshold of the receptor and upon the strength of the light stimulus. The stronger the light, the sooner the "explosions" follow each other. However, a stronger light does not cause the "explosions" to be bigger—just to come in more rapid succession. This fact is often expressed by saying that each cell works according to the *all-or-nothing principle* (see pp. 704-705)—that is, it either reacts with full intensity or it does not react at all. We all know that a sensation becomes stronger as the stimulus becomes stronger—this is because more receptor cells are caused to respond more frequently, not because each one responds more violently.

From each receptor cell in the retina, a chain of nerve fibers leads back to the visual area of the brain. This is located in the *occipital* area at the back of the brain (see the color plate at the beginning of the book). These connections are explained in detail on pages 719-721. For now it is sufficient to say that each point in space is ultimately "projected" upon the surface of the visual area of the brain. That is, every point in space reflects light to corresponding visual receptors in the retina, and this pattern of stimulation is carried by nerve fibers to the brain, where a corresponding pattern of cells is activated.

Seeing by day and by night

The retina of the eye, which corresponds to the film in the camera, is made up of various layers of cells. The significant cells for vision are the cones and the rods, which are located in the retina. The *cones* are effective in the daytime, when the eye is adapted to light, and produce sensations of hue and of brightness. The *rods* are effective only at night, when the eye is adapted to the dark, and are capable of producing sensations of white, grays, and black—that is, of brightness—but no hues.

There are more than seven million cones in the human retina. These are packed closest together in the very center of the retina, the *fovea*, where there are no rods and where images are clearest. The reason why an object can be seen most clearly during the daytime is that, since the cones operate in all but very dim illumination, we can use the fovea, which gives us the clearest images. At night, however, when there is little light and we are using our rods to see, we must look to one side of an object in order to see it, so that the image does not fall on the fovea and the image is not so sharp.

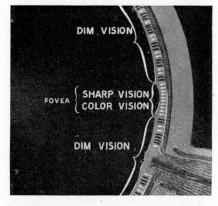

From *Eyes and Their Care*, Encyclopaedia Britannica Films, Inc.

All eyes, including a cat's, are alike in that none of them can see in complete darkness. The human eye, however, can adjust remarkably well to changes in the strength of lighting—provided that the new strength is within the range of possible vision. If you hold a piece of white paper in direct sunlight you can still see printing on it, although such strong reading light is uncomfortable for all eyes and is even injurious for some. People are capable of seeing under illumination only seven-billionths as strong as ordinary daylight, provided the eyes are properly prepared.

The process which prepares the eyes to see under low illumination is known as *dark adaptation*. It requires about half an hour of complete darkness after the last use of the eyes in bright light. Discrimination between hues becomes less keen as the level of illumination falls. In the dark-adapted eye, hue discrimination disappears completely, for the color-sensitive cones cease to function and the "color-blind" rods take over the job of seeing. This change-over from the cones to the rods occurs when the level of illumination falls to about the degree of illumination provided by a full moon.

As the eye becomes adapted to dark, sensitivity to red is lost first and to blue and green last. This is known as the *Purkinje Effect* and accounts for the way the hues at the short-wave end of the spectrum seem to become brighter at nightfall. (The color spectrum at the end of this book shows that red and yellow have the longest waves, with yellow and green following, and blue on the short-wave end.)

During the war the air-raid wardens used blue flashlights—an extremely ill-advised practice because blue is seen better than any other hue by the dark-adapted eye of observers under blackout conditions. A similar error was made by the Navy during the first months of World War II, in providing blue lighting on ships. Fortunately, the error was discovered rather promptly and red lighting was substituted.

There is another advantage in the use of red light, beyond its comparatively low visibility to the enemy observer. The rods of the eye are almost entirely unaffected by red light. Consequently, it is possible to use red light in reading charts and still maintain the eye in the condition of dark adaptation which is so necessary to accurate night observation. When it is not convenient or necessary to employ red light at night—as, for example, in the interior of a ship—special red goggles may be worn which will maintain the eye in a condition of dark adaptation and yet will permit the individual to play cards or read in a lighted room. Thus the lookout does not have to wait in darkness for a half-hour period, prior to going on watch, in order to get used to seeing in the dark.

Night vision can be aided through the use of night binoculars, which magnify objects in the same way that ordinary binoculars do. Tests conducted by the Army Air Forces indicate that magnification of five times is best for most observers (Chapanis[1]). Any greater magnification reduces the field of view so that it offsets the advantage of greater clarity.

Eye movements

Eye movements are of two kinds: jump and pursuit movements. When the eye is looking at any motionless material, careful photographs reveal that it makes a series of jumps—it jumps, then stops, then jumps again. Thus, the eyes, as you know, stop a few times in reading a printed line. Exploration of distance by an eye movement is nearly equivalent to pacing the distance with measured strides. Just as we can tell the length of a room by pacing it off, so can we tell the distance between any two *fixed* points by "pacing it off with the eye."

But in following *moving* objects the eye glides in pursuit movements. One general rule of clear vision operates both in reading and in following moving objects—the eye sees best when the image falls on the dead center of the retina. The eyes must move in unison with a moving object to retain this condition, and that is why they are said to be in "pursuit" of the object.

The sweep movements of the eyes are easier in the horizontal plane than in the vertical. This is fortunate because we more often have to judge the movements of objects coming from the side than the movements of objects coming from above. That is, we have to dodge automobiles more often than airplanes.

An interesting indication of the greater ease of side-to-side as compared with up-and-down eye movements is seen in the results of tests of young babies. One psychologist determined the average age at which external objects first aroused pursuit movements of the eyes (Jones[2]). Side-to-side movements appeared at 58 days, up-and-down movements at 65 days, and round-and-round at 78 days. It is quite clear that the side-to-side movements are more "natural" in the sense that they are perfected earlier in life.

There is an optical illusion which may be the result of the greater difficulty of the up-and-down as compared with the side-to-side movements. Look at the cross in the figure. Which line is longer? Now take a bit of paper or a ruler and measure them. Were you right?

THE SENSE OF SIGHT: VISUAL ACUITY

V ISUAL ACUITY literally means "sharpness of vision." It is measured *either* by the smallness of an object which can be seen at a standard distance, *or* by the greatest distance at which a standard-sized object can be seen.

Measuring visual acuity

You may have heard vision described as 20/20, 13/20, 20/10, or some other mysterious combination of numbers. These are merely ways of expressing visual acuity in terms of the size and distance of the object you can see as compared with the normal or "standard" person.

The most common form of test for visual acuity is the chart of test letters. Usually the chart is placed twenty feet from the subject of the test and given standard illumination. A *normal eye* is defined as one which at twenty feet can read block letters of a certain size—a size set by oculists after testing millions of eyes. It is described as "20/20" in both the Army and Navy classification systems.

The following table compares the Army and Navy standards and explains their meaning in terms of the "standard" or normal eye.

Army Standard	Navy Standard	Explanation
20/40	10/20	½ normal (Must stand half as far as normal to read letters of a given size.)
20/30	13/20	⅔ normal (Must stand a third nearer to read.)
20/20	20/20	NORMAL (Can read at twenty feet what normal person can read at twenty feet.)
20/15	20/15	1⅓ normal (Can read at a third greater distance than normal.)
20/10	20/10	2 times normal (Can read at twice the normal distance.)

The block-letter charts, although widely used, are unsatisfactory because they can be "cheated" under certain conditions. Certain people memorize the letters; other make lucky guesses. Another complication is that the letters differ in legibility. And of course this test is difficult to give to the person who has never learned to read because it involves naming the letters.

A more satisfactory test of visual acuity is made with the Jensen Grids, shown in the following figure. Grids of different angles are presented at standard distances and the subject is asked in each instance to tell whether the lines point up, down, right or left, etc. By systematic exploration, the tester determines the distance at which the person can see the direction of the lines, and then expresses it as a ratio to the "normal" distance, just as in the above table on page 246.

The Jensen test of visual acuity

Used by special arrangement with Dr. Milton B. Jensen.

The neural basis of visual acuity

Visual acuity is greatest in the fovea of the central retina, where the cones are packed most tightly together. It is best under good light, which is capable of stimulating the least sensitive cones as well as the most sensitive.

The size and shape of an object in the external world determines the size and shape of the pattern of receptors stimulated on the retina. If we are to "see" an object, at least three separate receptors must be stimulated. And if we are to "see" a line, at least two receptors must be stimulated. Thus it might appear that the eye would be capable of seeing only those objects which produce images on the fovea long enough to stimulate two or more receptors. Since the cones are an average of about .0001 inch apart, one might think that the image of an object would have to be at least .0001 inch long in order to be visible. However, in certain circumstances the normal eye can see objects that produce images which are only one-eighth as great as .0001 inch in one dimension provided they are great enough in the other dimension. Understanding of how accuracy of observation can apparently surpass the physical limits of the eye, and how three-dimensioned objects can be seen by a retinal surface, involves the study of perception (which will concern us in the next chapter).

From each cell of the fovea, separate nervous connections exist between that cell and the central nervous system. The foveal cells, in other words, are on a one-party line. When impulses come in from such a cell there is the anatomical equipment for relating the impulse to the exact cell stimulated. But with the cells found farther and farther toward the outer edge or periphery of the retina, more and more of the retinal cells are linked together with individual neural cells in the optic nerve. Some of these outlying cells, as one might say, are on a 200-party line instead of a one-party line. Just as with a telephone, there is no mechanism in such a case for telling which of the cells is instigating the nervous impulses coming over such single optic-nerve cells. This fact has important bearings on the different visual acuity of different areas of the retina.

In order for a person to see that two dots are separate dots rather than just a continuous mark, what is required is that an inactive or unstimulated functional unit must lie between the retinal areas stimulated by light from the two dots. In the fovea, with its one-party lines, the two points of stimulation need to be only as far apart as the diameter of a foveal cell. In the outlying parts of the retina, with so many retinal cells connected to one branching cell ultimately connected with the brain, all of such a group of cells are one functional unit. To distinguish different points of stimulation, therefore, the points of light falling on the outlying parts of the retina must be separated by a much greater distance. This is the main reason why one cannot see fine details out of the side of the eye.

Visual defects

There are a variety of visual defects which are of interest to the student of psychology. Some of these can be corrected only through professional care. Others cannot be corrected at all. Still others can be adjusted to or compensated for, once the nature of the defect is realized.

Blindness. Aside from removal of the entire eyeball, blindness can be caused in the following four ways: (1) thickening of the lens and/or fluids of the eye; (2) destruction of the retina; (3) destruction of the nerve pathways from the retina to the brain; (4) destruction of the visual centers in the brain.

Destruction may occur in many ways, although injury from wounds or accidents and the effects of poison and disease are the most frequent causes. Injury may be permanent, causing incurable blindness, or it may be temporary, causing intermittent blindness. Migraine, for example, can produce partial and temporary blindness.

Whatever the particular cause of blindness, it presents a grave adjustment problem. The blind person not only has difficulty earning a living but must guard against becoming emotionally as well as physically dependent on others, and must keep himself from excessive self-pity. Emotional as well as physical adjustment is involved in blindness: here again man functions as a whole.

Near-sightedness. Near-sightedness, or *myopia*, is caused by too great a curvature in the lens of the eye. Because the lens bulges out too far, the image comes in focus slightly in front of the surface of the retina and produces fuzziness:

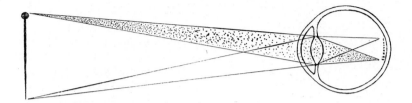

The near-sighted person holds paper work close to his eyes in an attempt to improve the focus. Near-sightedness is usually corrected by wearing glasses. Since the external muscles of the eyes have some influence in determining the length of the eyeball and hence the distance of the retina from the lens, an unorthodox school of sight correction through muscular exercises has grown up. However, most medical specialists have not yet accepted this method.

Far-sightedness. In far-sightedness, or *hyperopia*, the image comes into focus behind the retina. This difficulty may arise because the lens is inflexible and cannot bulge out for close vision, or because the muscles controlling its shape are too weak:

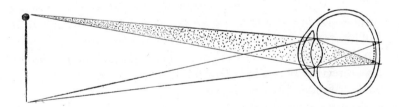

Thus the far-sighted person can see distant objects well, but nearby objects are blurred—he often holds his newspaper at arm's length in an effort to make a near object seem distant. This condition, too, is readily correctable by glasses, and possibly through eye exercises.

Old-sightedness. Old-sightedness, or *presbyopia*, is a special condition of far-sightedness due to the hardening of the lens which comes on with old age. It also may be corrected by appropriate glasses.

It is possible to estimate rather well a person's age on the basis of how close he can hold printed matter to his face and still read it. Hold this book in front of your eyes and move it closer and closer while a friend measures its distance from your eyes. When you have determined the blur point beyond which the printing becomes illegible, read the distance in inches and check against the following chart (Boring[3]). (This chart applies, of course, only to people who are neither far-sighted nor near-sighted.)

Age of reader	Distance of blur point from eyes
10	under 3 inches
20	under 4
30	under 5.5
40	under 8.5
50	under 15.25
60	under 39 or more

Notice that the rapid change starts at around the fortieth year—when life begins for the oculists, optometrists, and lens manufacturers!

Astigmatism. Astigmatism is caused by irregularities in the lens or cornea of the eye, so that part of an object viewed will be in focus and part will be blurred, as you can see in the illustration on page 251 of how an astigmatic person may see the world.

Double vision. Double vision, or *diplopia,* is caused by a muscular imbalance which permits a point in space to fall on noncorresponding parts of the two retinas, so that two slightly different images are transmitted to the brain. It can be caused not only by an inherent weakness of certain muscles, but also by excessive drinking of alcohol, by a variety of poisons, and by diseased conditions. You can produce double vision in yourself by looking at some point on the wall while pressing one eyeball gently but firmly enough to move it out of its usual position. This condition is usually cured by clearing up the source of poison or through the use of muscular exercises under the direction of a physician, for in this case medical practice does make considerable use of exercises.

Scotoma and tunnel vision. The word *scotoma* means "blind spot." All persons have a blind spot in each eye at the point where the optic nerve enters the retina (shown on p. 241). Normally we are not aware

Normal   Near-sighted   Far-sighted

of this blind spot because it has always been there and because other portions of the retina enable us to see very well without it. Such a normal blind spot is not regarded as a scotoma. However, certain conditions—such as excessive use of tobacco and alcohol, and overexposure to light—produce temporary or permanent blind spots which seriously interfere with vision. Scotoma also accompanies some diseases, including migraine; it may arise when the retina itself is injured or diseased; or it may originate in the optical tract leading from the retina to the brain, or in the brain itself.

A caution about using sunglasses is in order here. Every year some twenty million pairs of dark glasses are sold in the United States for the avowed purpose of providing eye comfort and protection against the sun. Despite this fact, each summer shows an increasing number of patients coming to eye specialists complaining of blind spots, along with inflamed and swollen eyes. (Kisker[4])

It is becoming quite apparent that sunglasses acquired and worn without benefit of the specialist's skill are likely to do more harm than good. Cheap sunglasses, like any other piece of colored glass, will cut down the intensity of the sun's visible rays, but they do not filter out the invisible and harmful infra-red rays. In fact, by reducing the intensity of the visible rays, sunglasses actually thwart the protective mechanism by which the eye normally protects itself against glare. This mechanism is the pupillary reflex, or the familiar constriction of the pupil of the eye in response to bright light. The sunglass, moreover, affords a false feeling of security and encourages the wearer to overexposure. A very safe rule with regard to the wearing of sunglasses is to avoid them except on a physician's prescription.

Tunnel vision is a concentric narrowing of the field of vision, so that the external world is seen as through a tunnel or pipe. The individual with tunnel vision is forced by virtue of his restricted visual field to make abnormally large head and eye movements in order to bring different parts of the environment within his field of vision, just as a man with a telescope swings himself around to sweep the horizon with

Astigmatism   *Double vision*   *Tunnel vision*

From *Eyes and Their Care*, Encyclopaedia Britannica Films, Inc.

The Sense of Sight: Visual Acuity 251

his instrument. Formerly, tunnel vision was thought to be exclusively a symptom of an emotional disturbance known as *hysteria* (see p. 501), but it is now known to be produced also by a complex of factors similar to those producing scotoma.

THE SENSE OF SIGHT: COLOR DISCRIMINATION

THE NORMAL PERSON can discriminate different colors from one another with much finer distinctions than he can name. In fact, more than 350,000 colors can be distinguished from one another by the person of average vision. This ability to distinguish color is the second important aspect of vision. In this section we shall consider *The Qualities of Color, Combining Colors, Color-Blindness,* and *The Receptor-Cell Basis of Color Vision.*

The qualities of color

In making distinctions between one color and another, a person (or an animal, for that matter) discriminates on one or more of the three qualities of color: *hue, saturation,* and *brightness.*

Hue. The normal person sees some berries as blue and some berries as black; some neckties as red, some as green. In so doing, he discriminates between these colors on the basis of the different *lengths* (or *frequency*) of the light waves reflected from those objects.

Saturation. The normal person can also distinguish between hues on the basis of their saturation, even if they are the same color. Saturation is a matter of the degree to which a hue is "a good strong red" as contrasted with pink, or "a good strong blue" as contrasted with a pastel blue. The saturation of a color is determined by the *complexity* of the light waves emanating from an object. If the light waves coming from an object contain not only the light waves which would produce some one hue but also some other light waves which, by themselves, would produce a gray, the person will report that the color is less "saturated" than would otherwise have been the case.

Brightness. The normal person can also discriminate between colors on the basis of their relative brightnesses. The brightness of a color is influenced by several factors. One of these is the intensity of the light waves involved. For instance, when you hold an object under a brighter light to look at it, you cause, at least temporarily, an increase in the apparent brightness of the color.

Another important fact is that the brightness of the colors we see depends upon whether we see them with our rods or with our cones

—that is, whether we see them by day or by night. The cones, used in daylight vision, are more sensitive to yellow light than to blue and green, so that even when the physical intensity of various pure lights is the same, the yellow seems to be the brightest. But when the rods are in use—in light so dim that you can see merely different degrees of gray, not different hues—the objects which yield the sensations of lightest gray are not the yellow objects but the objects that are reflecting mainly the wave lengths of blue and green. This is the *Purkinje effect* mentioned on page 244, and is one of the facts which led scientists to the realization that the human retina contains two fundamentally different sorts of receptor cells.

Progressive brightness

The color solid is a means of showing how colors of different hue, brightness, and saturation are related to each other. The fact that color has three dimensions means that you have to make a figure which has three dimensions: that is, a color solid. The figure represents the three dimensions of color sensations as the axis, radius, and circumference of a double cone, which is like one megaphone placed on top of another, mouth to mouth.

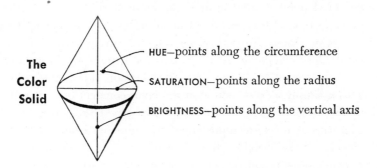

The Color Solid

HUE—points along the circumference

SATURATION—points along the radius

BRIGHTNESS—points along the vertical axis

1 A line running up and down through the center of the color cone is called the axis. Extreme white is at the upper end of the axis running through the color cones, since white is the brightest

visual sensation possible. Black is at the bottom of the axis, for black is the least bright possible. On this line between white and black are found all the grays.

2 While brightness runs up and down the axis, hues are symbolized as points around the circumference—that is, around the color circle.

3 Degrees of saturation are marked off as points between the axis and the circumference, with the axis representing zero saturation.

The basic characteristics of color explain why the color solid is symbolized by this double-megaphone shape. First, it so happens that the very brightest and the very darkest colors are the least saturated. So at the top and bottom of the axis (the brightest and darkest points), the degree of saturation is right at zero—that is, it is at the axis. This accounts for the way the color solid tapers down to a point at the top and bottom. Also, the highly saturated colors are of medium brightness. So at the mid-point of the up-and-down brightness axis, the colors are far away from the zero saturation point at the axis. This accounts for the wideness of the cone at the center.

All combinations of hue, saturation, and brightness are thought of as lying within the boundaries of this double cone. Suppose, for example, that you want to find a dark red of low saturation—a "washed out" maroon. First you locate red as a point *around* the color circle where the two "mouths" of the cones meet. Then to find the point of darkness, you move *down* the cone to a point where if a round "slice" could be removed all the colors would contain the same rather low amount of light: here you find red of appropriate darkness. Then with your red point located around the edge of this darkness "slice," you move *in* toward the zero point of saturation at the center, stopping at the point where the dark red is at the "washed out" saturation you want. One such device is shown in color at the end of this book.

The color plate at the end of this book shows the color wheel. This is simply a cross section of the color cone cut out (at right angles to the axis) midway between the two tapered-off ends of the cone. The various hues are represented by segments around the rim of the wheel. (Hues found in the spectrum—that is, hues which are components of sunlight—are tied together by a rim drawn in a solid line; purples, which are not found in the spectrum but must be produced by combinations of spectral lights, are shown by a rim in broken line.) This color wheel is necessarily simplified; actually, the colors gradually merge into each other around the wheel. Also, they become grayer toward the center of the double cone, which represents gray of medium brightness and, like all grays, zero saturation.

Combining colors

What happens when two hues are combined, that is, when lights of two hues are combined?

Combining lights and combining paints. We must first make clear the distinction between the combining of lights and the combining or mixing of paints. In the discussion to follow, you should keep in mind that the laws of light mixture are sometimes the same as, and sometimes different from, those of paint and dye mixing.

When colored lights are mixed, they are added to each other to give the new result: for instance, yellow light plus blue light gives gray light. However, the mixing of colored paints works not by addition but by subtraction and in some instances gives different results. For instance, when yellow paint is mixed with blue paint the result is green. There are many different wave lengths reflected by both yellow paint and blue paint besides those which give rise to the sensations of yellow and blue, respectively, and among these are the wave lengths which cause us to see green. When the yellow and blue paints are mixed, all the wave lengths are absorbed ("subtracted") by the paint except those which give rise to green.

As you study the laws of color combination, you will frequently meet statements that seem to contradict what you know about color mixture. For instance, you know that the artist considers red, blue, and yellow as his "primary" colors: that is, as the three colors which cannot be derived from any other color, and which when mixed in different proportions can produce all other colors except white and black. The "primary" colors of light mixture, however, are red, blue, and green.

Another kind of "primary" color may be demonstrated on the color wheel at the very end of this book. As you look at these hues, some seem to be more "real" or "fundamental" than others; that is, you cannot break them down into two or more component hues. The yellows and the blues, the greens and the reds, seem somehow more stable than the oranges and the purples, the yellow-greens and the blue-greens. No matter how long or how hard you look at the yellows, blues, greens, and reds, they resist analysis into anything else. They seem to be ultimate and irreducible in consciousness. In the orange, however, you can see red and yellow; in the purple, red and blue; in the blue-green, blue and green; and in the yellow-green, yellow and green.

These four stable irreducible hues are called "psychological primaries," because we cannot analyze them into secondary elements through self-observation. They should not be confused with the three primary colors of the artist's pigments. However, psychologically primary red is not found in the spectrum of daylight, but is produced by adding psychologically primary blue to the red of the spectrum (Dimmick[5]).

Our discussion of color combinations will cover: (1) the laws of color (light) mixture; (2) simultaneous contrast effects; and (3) negative and positive after-sensations.

The laws of color mixture. There are two simple laws which describe the results of mixing lights which are of the same brightness but of differing hue. All can be illustrated on the color wheel.

Law I. All hues opposite each other on the color wheel combine to produce gray. Examples of such combination are yellow fused with purple-blue; purple fused with yellow-green; red fused with blue-green. Two colors which combine to give gray are *complementary colors.*

Law II. All other hues fuse to produce different hues or blends. Examples of this type of mixing are found in the following combinations and results: red fuses with yellow to produce orange; red with blue to produce purple; red with green to produce yellow; blue with green to produce blue-green. You notice that in each case the two hues combine to give a hue which lies between them on the color wheel.

To find the results of the mixture of any two colors, refer to the color wheel. Merely draw a line from one of them to the other. The mid-point of the line will show you the hue that results when these two colors are mixed in equal proportions. For example, the center of the line passing from yellow to purple-blue falls at the hub, G. And we have just seen that these two complementary colors fuse to give gray. The mid-point of the line connecting red and blue falls in the purple sector—indicating that purple is, as we saw above, the result of combining red and blue in equal proportions. The degree of saturation of the resulting combination can also be determined roughly from the color wheel if the saturations of the colors being combined are known. For instance, green and red mix to give yellow of low saturation. On the color wheel a line connecting the green and the red runs through the yellow sector but toward the center—where, as you remember, saturation is zero.

When the hues are not mixed in equal proportion, the resultant hue and saturation correspond to some point beyond the mid-point of the line, a point determined according to the difference between the amounts of each color used.

The color wheel, since it is a cross section of the color cones, contains only two of the three "dimensions" of color: hue and saturation. It can summarize only the facts of the mixture of hues of differing saturation. When the third dimension of brightness is added, the problem becomes more complex. When a hue of low brightness is mixed with the same hue of high brightness, the result is the same hue, but of intermediate brightness. The same is true of black and white, which combine to give gray.

Simultaneous contrast effects. If you place a strip of gray paper on a yellow background, you will observe that the gray becomes slightly bluish. If you place the same gray against a blue background, it will take on a yellowish cast. The apparent change of hue that occurs in gray when its background color is changed is known as the phenomenon of *simultaneous hue contrast*. The color that gray appears to take on is always the complementary hue of the color in the background (remember that two complementary colors when blended give gray). *Brightness contrast effects,* similar to those of hue, can be simply produced. A gray band which runs through a field of white seems darker than the same gray band running through a field of black.

All such contrast effects are called "simultaneous" because the original hue (or brightness) and the contrasting hue (or brightness) are seen by the eye at the same time, side by side.

Negative and positive after-sensations. "After-sensations," as the name implies, are so-called because the secondary color sensation follows the original color sensation.

If you gaze long and hard at a bit of yellow paper, not allowing your eyes to waver, you will notice that the borders of this yellow paper commence to take on a bluish tinge. The yellow itself seems to fade—to lose saturation. After these effects are quite clearly observable, turn your gaze on a piece of clean white paper and you will see on it a patch of blue—which is complementary to the original yellow. This is called a *negative after-sensation* because you see a hue complementary to the hue of the original. A negative after-sensation will mix with an actual sensation to give results which can be predicted through the laws of color mixture.

For example, you have seen that the negative after-sensation of yellow is blue. If that blue is projected upon a piece of red paper, the red of the paper and the blue of the negative after-sensation will combine to give purple. This fact represents a source of error in situations calling for the matching of colors. The chemist and the dye-maker must arrange the conditions of their comparisons of samples in such a way that after-sensations will not affect their judgment. To do this, they must know which colors are complementary.

Positive after-sensations—of the original rather than the complementary hues—also occur after an interval of stimulation. Gaze at an electric light for a time and then blank it out with a piece of paper. For a short time the original light will appear to glow yellow before your eyes.

Another contrast effect is produced by looking intently at a surface of a particular hue and then gazing at a surface of complementary hue. In this case the second hue is seen as more saturated than would normally be possible. In fact, the fullest saturations are obtainable only by first looking at a light of complementary hue.

Color-blindness

How the color-blind see colors. The essential difference between color-blind and normal persons is that colors which appear to be different to the normal person appear as the same to the color-blind. Color-blindness exists in varying degrees from what might be called "color weakness" to complete color-blindness. In the latter, which is very rare indeed, different colors are all seen as degrees of gray.

Color-blind persons frequently do not know that they suffer a defect of vision unless they have been tested and informed of the result. They see all the objects that other persons see, and they have learned to call those objects by the same names that others use. The color-blind sometimes show unconventionality in dress. Many men whose mothers or wives pick out the ties they are to wear with particular shirts and jackets are probably color-blind. And now and then someone may reveal his defect by a chance remark, such as: "It's so hard to see ripe strawberries on the vine. They look just like the leaves!" To the red-green blind person, both the berries and the leaves look yellowish-gray. John Dalton, the eminent but color-blind British chemist, who discovered his defect and described it in 1794, stated that blood looked to him "not unlike the color called bottle green." Today color-blindness is a definite handicap in chemistry, where laboratory experiments often require precise discrimination between colored solutions.

The fact that people cannot be relied upon to discover whether they are color-blind, and the fact that many who know they are will not answer a direct question honestly, have caused several kinds of color-vision tests to be developed. Since most of these tests are set to yield a pass-or-fail mark, they give the impression that color vision is present in a person on an all-or-nothing basis. The truth of the matter is that people vary from strong color vision through many degrees of color weakness to complete color-blindness.

Testing for color-blindness. One of the simplest tests of color vision is the yarns test, in which the subject is asked to match yarns on the basis of color. (See p. 16.) The red-green blind person, for example, is detected when he throws red and green tufts of yarn into the same pile. This test, although simple, is subject to error because the yarns differ from each other in brightness as well as in hue and may be matched on that basis. Also, the yarns fade and lose saturation, which adds to the difficulty of keeping the test standard. (Another and more satisfactory variant of the matching test makes use of metal chips coated with nonfading plastic paint.)

The best brief and simple tests of color vision require the subject to tell what he sees on a color plate made up of large and small dots which may vary in brightness, hue, and saturation. The dots are so arranged that different patterns are made up of dots which seem to "belong together." One well-known test of this type was developed by Dr. Milton B. Jensen, and is shown in color at the beginning of this book. This plate is to be read at ten feet distance in uniform but not direct sunlight. Normal people see one bar pointing between 11 and 12 o'clock; the red-green color-blind see two hands, one pointing between 11 and 12 and the other pointing between 6 and 7 o'clock. The totally color-blind see neither of the two hands.

The explanation is that the two hands contain dots with a small amount of blue in them. This is so slight as to be overlooked by the normal person, who therefore sees one green bar only. The red-green blind person, however, sees the blue in both bars and sees only yellow in the background. Thus the figure appears to have two bars. The totally color-blind person, unable to see red, yellow, green, or blue, sees the plate as completely free of bars.

Another type of test, the Ishihara test, is built on the principle that the color-blind person can distinguish red from green only if they differ in brightness. He is confronted, for example, with a plate containing a red figure 8 against a green background. The left half of the 8 is of the same brightness as the background and he does not see it. But the right half differs in brightness, and so he sees it and reads the plate as a 3.

The classification of color-blindness is far from perfect now. The principal defect in current systems is that they fail to measure and express the various degrees of color-blindness in sufficiently fine categories. The standard procedure, which is of great practical usefulness, is to consider that there are two kinds of color-blindness: *total color-blindness* and *dichromatic color vision*.

Total color-blindness. Total color-blindness is extremely rare, occurring in one among forty thousand people. To date, only a few dozen such cases have been described in scientific literature. Totally color-blind people see all colors as shades of gray, white, and black. Their defect arises because they lack cones in the retina. This shows itself in the fact that they are usually completely blind in the fovea, or the very center of the retina, which is the area of greatest color sensitivity. This peculiarity causes them to shift their gaze in examining an object in order to keep the image from falling on the blind foveal area. It is believed that the retina of the totally color-blind eye possesses no cones whatever and has to depend upon rods for daylight vision.

Dichromatic color vision. The word *dichromat* comes from two Greek words: *di* meaning "two" and *chroma* meaning "color." A *dichromat* is a person who is blind to two colors: red and green. But not only does he fail to see reds and greens—he also fails to see the colors into which red and green can be blended: orange, yellow-green, blue-green, and purple. He does see yellows and blues in all their degrees of saturation and, of course, white through all shades of gray, to and including black. Obviously such a person suffers a severe limitation of visual ability in comparison with that of the normal person.

Can color-blindness be cured? During the recent war, a high premium was placed upon good vision as a qualification for military service. Many an otherwise qualified man was turned down by the Army Air Corps, by Naval Aviation, and by other specialized services because of color-blindness. Interestingly enough, well-authenticated cases have been reported in which a candidate who had failed the color-vision test on his first try passed it later on after engaging in various programs of diet or exercises or combinations of both. When the evidence is carefully examined, however, it reveals that the real improvement did not come in ability to distinguish colors but in ability to pass the color-vision test.

> For instance, what about the claim that Vitamin A can cure color-blindness? The answer is that Vitamin A does improve visual acuity and night vision, and so it is possible that some of the second-trial successes following the taking of Vitamin A are accounted for on the basis of increased visual acuity which pushed the borderline case over the line. For visual acuity as well as color vision is a factor in passing the tests used by the Army. Vitamin A was thus not a cure for color-blindness but for an inability to pass the vision test as a whole.
>
> Another factor which has to be considered in appraising the stories of success following failure on the color-vision tests is the fact that

some examiners are more lenient than others. Two doctors do not agree perfectly in interpreting the results of an examination for color vision. In fact, the experience of the Civil Aeronautics Authority with civilian pilot candidates is that fifty per cent of those failed for inadequate color vision by the first examiner are passed by the second examiner working independently (Viteles[6]).

A third complication is the fact that practice in taking the test may improve ability to pass the test without seriously changing the basic ability to see differences in hues.

One of the tricks employed by certain ignorant or unscrupulous "color-vision trainers," who have sprung up all over the country, makes use of the phenomena of simultaneous and successive color contrast. It is possible with a red-green color-weak retina to bring up the saturation of the red by staring for a while at green, its complementary color, or its near complement. You have learned that one of the plates of the Ishihara test is seen by the normal eye as a red figure 8 against a green background. To the red-green blind person, part of the 8 cannot be seen and hence the figure is read as a 3. By gazing at the green background for a time and then moving suddenly to the figure, he can make the red come up in the crucial part, so that the figure will be legible as an 8.

Another device of the color trainers is to have the subject memorize what he "should" see on the plates. He will remember, for instance, that what he sees as a red 3 on a green background is actually a red 8 on a green background.

Present evidence indicates that we had better restrain our enthusiasm for "cure" of color-blindness until careful research has revealed more about its causes.

The receptor-cell basis of color vision

Several lines of evidence point to the *cones* as the necessary and only instruments of color vision: (1) While rods respond to light, the light is always seen as lacking hue; obviously they alone could not distinguish between hues. (2) Colors are perceived *only* when the intensity of illumination is high enough to bring the cones into action. (3) Color is perceived best when the central portions of the retina (containing only cones) are being stimulated. (4) Another piece of evidence is the relation between the way the cones and rods are distributed on the retina and the ability of these different parts of the retina to distinguish hue. Cones alone (with no rods) are found in the central part of the retina, which is blind to light under conditions of dark adaptation but can distinguish hues. In the intermediate region of the retina, rods and cones are found together.

As you know, the physical basis of the hue of any light is the length of the waves making up that light. But just how receptors are tuned to these different wave lengths—that is, how we perceive color—is still unexplained. Several different theories have been advanced, but none is completely satisfactory.

THE SENSE OF HEARING

Hearing may be somewhat less important in effective living than vision, but it is still very important. In music, in conversation, and in most occupations—in fact, through all of everyday life—hearing plays a vital role.

The physical basis of sound

The physical stimuli for hearing are successive waves of crowded-together and scattered-out air molecules. If you pluck the string of a musical instrument, it will start to vibrate, or move back and forth. As it moves in one direction it crowds the air molecules together in front of it and knocks them in the direction of its movement. Those molecules soon collide with others and send them on (just as when you have a row of dominoes set up in a line you can topple the whole row by tapping the first domino in the line). Then, when the string moves back the other way, it leaves a partial vacuum behind it—an area in which there are fewer molecules. These molecules also are in movement, as the molecules of the air almost always are, and their movements send off another "wave" following the first one of crowded-together molecules. The general movement in the air brings in molecules, too, behind the vibrating swing, and when it returns in its original swing it once more, therefore, sends out another wave of compression or *pressure front*. Sound "waves," then, travel through the air, not in any up-and-down fashion (despite the way that sound waves are often symbolized diagrammatically), but as expanding or enlarging "spheres" of alternate compression and rarefaction spreading out from the source of the sound. (These alternating pressure areas are diagrammatically represented on p. 290.)

Low sounds are made, for example, by the long, heavy strings on the piano. One of these strings might vibrate back and forth only about 32 times a second. For such a low note, the distance between the middle of one compression wave and the next, as the *pressure areas* move through the air, would be about 35 feet. The greater the contrast between the degree of crowding-together and scattering-out for the two parts of the sound wave, the more intense or loud will be the sound produced.

When you hear a sound, especially a musical tone, you are conscious of more than what pitch it is and how loud it is. You are also aware of the quality or *timbre* of the sound. For instance, "Yankee Doodle" sounds different on a violin and on a flute, even if each plays in the same range of pitch and with equal loudness. To understand what gives tones their particular timbre, you must understand the nature of noise and of overtones.

Noise is a sound produced when the fundamental pitch of the sound wave is complicated by irregular disturbances in the air striking the ear. Throw a stick of wood on the floor, then on a table, then on the seat of a chair. Observe that each object it strikes produces a different sound, in which it is hard to distinguish any pitch or rhythm. But if you listen carefully, you will observe that the noises vary in *pitch*. Each noise has a fundamental frequency of vibration which gives it its essential pitch. Although the irregular noise components may be so great that one has difficulty in hearing the fundamental pitch, accurate analysis will always reveal its presence.

Overtones are tones which are sounded along with the fundamental tone produced by a source of sound. In a violin, for instance, each string will vibrate as fractions of its length at the same time that it is vibrating as a whole. That is to say, a wire four feet long will vibrate as a four-foot wire and will be producing the fundamental pitch. At the same time, it will be vibrating as two two-foot wires, each such vibration producing other tones far less audible than the fundamental. And to a much less extent, it will also be vibrating as four one-foot wires, with these sounds even fainter still. These overtones (or "partials," as they are sometimes called) are included in the whole experience of the tone, and are of great importance in determining its timbre.

It is the nature and relative strength of the overtones and irregular noise in a sound which determine its timbre or quality. Musical instruments vary in the number and loudness of overtones they produce and consequently in the timbre of their tones, even when producing notes of the same pitch. The notes of the organ have many harmonizing overtones, and its tones are correspondingly full and rich, while trumpet tones are raspingly hard because many of the tones produced are ones that clash, producing noise. The tones produced by two different players on the same instrument will frequently vary in timbre. This is especially true on an instrument such as the violin, where the slightest difference in the fingering or use of the bow will cause a difference in the way the string divides to produce overtones and will thus cause a variation in the sound produced.

The human ear

The overall structure of the ear. As is shown in the diagram below, the outer ear consists of the external shell (1) and the auditory canal (2), which leads into the eardrum (3). Sound waves travel through the auditory canal until they strike the eardrum, which vibrates in response and in turn activates the three small bones of the middle ear: the hammer (4), the anvil (5), and the stirrup (6). The mechanical motions of these bones cause the muscular attachments of the stirrup to press against the oval window (7) of the inner ear, pushing the membranous window in and out. Movements of the oval window cause pressure fronts to travel through the cochlea (8), in which they are transformed into nerve impulses and travel through the auditory nerve (9) to the brain.

Cross section of the human ear

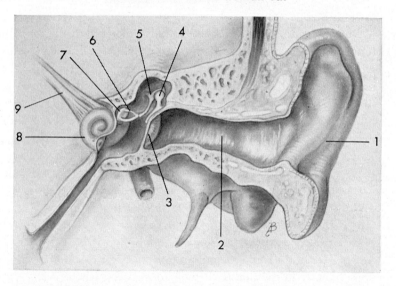

A detailed view of the cochlea is shown opposite. Pressure fronts travel up the vestibular canal (8a) and back down the tympanic canal (8b) of the cochlea, which is actually one long liquid-filled coil. The basilar membrane (8c), which separates the tympanic from the cochlear canal (8d), contains the auditory receptors. The receptors lie on the organ of Corti (8e), the hair cells of which project up into the liquid which fills the cochlear canal. These cells connect with the sensitive nerve endings, which run along the center of the cochlea and out into the cochlear branch of the auditory nerve.

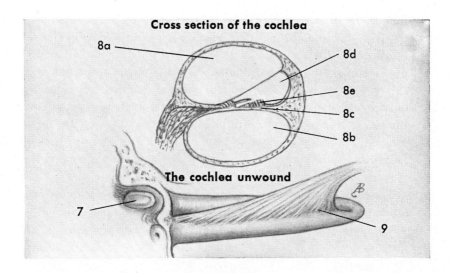

Cross section of the cochlea

8a

8d

8e

8c

8b

The cochlea unwound

7

9

Pressure fronts into nerve impulses. Let us examine in greater detail the manner in which physical motions of a liquid are transformed into nerve impulses. The short fibers in the narrow end of the basilar membrane, near the *wide* end of the cochlea, bulge in response to pressure fronts of high frequencies in the adjacent liquid. The long basilar fibers near the *narrow* end of the cochlea move in response to vibrations of low frequencies. This activity of the basilar membrane in turn induces bending of the hair cells of the organ of Corti. Their bending excites nerve impulses in the fibers associated with the hairs, and these impulses travel through the auditory nerve to the thalamus, from which they are directed to the auditory center of the brain (these connections are illustrated and discussed on p. 722). The complex theories as to how physical amplitude and wave length are translated into psychological intensity and pitch are beyond the scope of this book.

Sound elements in the human voice

Human speech is complex. It contains both tones and noises. The tonal element in human speech is furnished by the *vocal cords*, which are folds of membrane located in the Adam's apple, or *larynx*. The larynx is situated at the upper end of the windpipe and produces sound through vibration of the vocal cords. As air rushes out of the lungs, it sets these cords into vibration and thus produces either high- or low-pitch tones, depending upon the degree to which the cords are under tension at the moment. The tones thus produced are modified as the air passes through the various resonating cavities of the throat and head. Specific consonants and vowels are produced as the lips, tongue, teeth, jaw, and palate modify the sound. For example, explosives (like *b* and *p*) are produced when air is suddenly allowed to escape from the mouth, and the fricative sounds (like *s* and *z*) are produced by the hissing of the air over the tongue and teeth.

Intelligibility of different sounds. Since accurate communication is of particular importance in wartime, much research was devoted during the recent war to the problem of selecting words which are the most intelligible to most persons under most conditions. No word has been found that is 100 per cent intelligible, but some have reached the 96 per cent mark (Boring[7]).

The following table lists nine words, of which the intelligibility over a telephonic system ranges from 10 per cent to 90 per cent:

agree 90%	*tower* 60%	*ranch* 30%
equal 80%	*court* 50%	*bimbo* 20%
puppy 70%	*creak* 40%	*voile* 10%

Tests of intelligibility are best made by pronouncing the list of words over the communication system or by unaided voice, and then asking the subjects to write down what they understand the word to be.

Letters of the alphabet are frequently used in military codes as well as in business and industry. Experience shows that isolated letters of the alphabet are frequently not heard correctly. For example, *b, c, d,* and *t* are easily confused. A great deal of research has been done to find out what words to use as explanation of code letters. The very best ones are still subject to wartime secrecy regulations and cannot be printed in this book, but some good ones are: *a* as in *Adam; b* as in *baker; c* as in *Charlie; d* as in *dog; e* as in *easy.* Digits as well as words differ in intelligibility; for instance, tests of the sort used with other words have shown that *zero* is better than *oh* or *ought* or *nought;* and that *ni-yen* is better than *nine* but *nyner* is still better.

Voice quality. Human voices vary from individual to individual and from time to time in the same person. We label the voices of others as crude or cultured, as pleasant or unpleasant. We are even justified in classifying voices as intelligent or stupid, for experiments have shown that intelligence can be judged on the basis of voice (Michael and Crawford[8]). People's voices, like musical instruments, vary in timbre. Some voices are full and mellow, others thin and rasping; still others are characterized by a nasal twang. Timbre, as you have seen, is determined by the overtones. In the human voice, these are produced in the resonating cavities of the throat and head. Training in speech can improve the way these cavities are used and thus improve voice quality.

Deafness

Deafness is, of course, a great handicap in working and everyday life. The physician whose hearing is poor cannot be expected to diagnose a heart disorder accurately on the basis of a stethoscopic examination. Curiously enough, however, statistics show that the hard-of-hearing are safer automobile drivers than those of normal hearing, probably because they realize their handicap and are more careful than the average driver.

Moreover, the deaf person is more completely cut off from human conversation than is the blind one, for conversation with the deaf is usually a slow and laborious process requiring no small measure of patient kindness. Not only does the deaf person fail to hear—he often loses his ability to talk after prolonged deafness. Without the ear to guide the work of the muscles of speech, the ability to speak de-. teriorates and is eventually lost completely. The hard-of-hearing, like the blind, have an emotional as well as a physical problem. Contact with other people is difficult for them: they not only must make a great effort to hear what is said, but they must put up with the impatience and irritation that other people inevitably display on occasion. The deaf person must fight constantly against the temptation to withdraw entirely from human contact, with all its difficulties.

Fortunately, few people are entirely deaf. For the more severely handicapped, there are devices which amplify sounds to the extent that they can be heard easily by the hard-of-hearing. Other devices translate sounds into vibrations which can be perceived through the sense of touch. Here again, however, the deaf person has an emotional problem: he must overcome the false pride which sometimes keeps him from wearing a hearing aid.

Although we usually think of deafness simply as inability to hear, there is in reality more than one kind of deafness.

Intensity deafness. Many people are "hard-of-hearing" in the sense that they cannot detect faint sounds easily heard by normal persons. With such persons it is necessary to shout in order that they hear. This type of partial deafness, known as intensity deafness, is a serious hindrance in many occupations. It is often an occupational disease— that is, a disease produced by the particular working conditions of an occupation. Aviators and boilermakers, for example, often become partially deaf from the loud noises to which they are constantly subjected.

Tone deafness. Some people are unable to tell one note on the piano from another, or at least they are unable to tell which of two tones is higher, and so are known as "tone deaf." Tone-deaf persons can never become good singers or violinists, although it goes without saying that the mere ability to discriminate tones with a high degree of accuracy does not assure a person that he can succeed in a musical career.

Ability to differentiate between musical tones is, of course, not an all-or-none condition. People vary in their sensitiveness to differences in pitch. The average person is unable to make many of the delicate judgments of pitch that the musician can. Many observations reveal that even when a person practices very hard, as does the professional musician, he reaches a final limit in his ability to hear differences in pitch. This limit varies from person to person and is presumably dependent upon the quality of the structure of his ear.

THE SENSES OF TOUCH

ALTHOUGH sight and hearing are man's most important means of contact with the physical world which surrounds him, he learns much about the external world through his sense of touch. There are four types of touch sensation: pressure, pain, cold, and warmth.

Pressure

The sense of pressure is of great use to individuals who do fine manual work of any sort. Engravers at the Bureau of Printing in Washington use their hands to wipe ink from the plates used in printing, and can feel accurately just how much to wipe off. In fact, their sensitivity to pressure is delicate enough to detect a film of grease only one layer of molecules thick.

The blind have in this sense of touch a partial substitute for their lost vision. They read by means of the Braille system (so named after its inventor, a Frenchman), which uses different patterns of raised dots to indicate all the letters and punctuation used in reading. The blind person "reads" his book by feeling these patterns of dots. In some schools, blind children are provided with a kind of punching board by which they can "write" their lessons, using the Braille code. The disadvantage of the Braille over printed material is that the sense of pressure is much coarser than the sense of vision, so that raised characters must occupy more space than printed characters. Moreover, the time required for the fingers to explore and interpret the letters is long as compared with the time for visual perception.

Although the sense of pressure is useful in many special situations, we all use it every day to verify what our eyes tell us. Something may look like wood, but we rub it to make sure it is not plastic. A dress may look like silk, but the best way to tell is to feel it.

The average person is likely to think that every point on the tip of his finger is equally sensitive to pressure. In ordinary life, the finger tips usually encounter pressure from blunt objects (such as rings, clothing, etc.) which stimulate more than one small area at a time, so that it is difficult to determine just what the pressure-sensitive areas are. The truth of the matter is that pressure sensitivity exists in tiny spots that are surrounded by relatively insensitive areas. The richness with which a given portion of skin is endowed with pressure spots will determine the sensitivity of that region.

For example, the sensitive ball of the thumb has about 135 pressure-sensitive spots in each square centimeter of its surface; the back of the hand, 30; and the upper arm, 10. The number of pressure-sensitive spots which can be located by systematic application of a stimulus varies with the strength of the stimulus, since some have a high threshold (Guilford and Lovewell[9]).

The pressure sense is decidedly subject to fatigue and adaptation effects. If a gentle pressure is maintained constantly, we soon become unaware of it. For example, after you have been wearing a ring for some minutes you cannot tell whether you have it on except by looking at your hand or by moving your hand so that the ring will stimulate some new areas of the skin of your hand.

Pain

Pain sensation may be aroused by intense stimulation of most of the sense organs of the body. Any object or substance which will injure the nerve endings located in the skin or other tissue of the body serves as a stimulus to pain. Pain spots are located by pressing the skin with a fine-pointed needle. Pain (like pressure, warmth, and cold) shows a point distribution rather than a continuous or even one. Pain spots are much more numerous than pressure-sensitive points. The number of pain spots per square centimeter of body surface is about 50 on the sole of the foot; 60 on the ball of the thumb; 170 on the eyelid; 230 on the neck. When it is necessary for the physician to draw a few drops of blood, he often pricks the ball of the thumb, for that area is easily accessible and is relatively insensitive to pain.

The tissues of the inside of the body have few pain spots as compared with the surface exposed to the world. The adaptive significance of this fact is easily seen. In primitive life, injuries to the skin served to make the organism avoid situations in which such injuries were encountered. By the time a wound reaches the inside of the body, it is usually too late for a warning of danger to be useful. A sensitive outer skin is a warning and thus a protection.

It is not only stimulation of nerve endings in the skin that arouses pain. Excessively strong stimulation of *any* sense organ will produce pain. The merciless intensity of the light from an electric arc is actually painful to the eyes if continued a few seconds. It is well known that excessively hot or cold objects are painful to the skin. Loud sounds hurt the ear. Certain intense smells are also painful.

One theory explains the pain caused by very strong stimuli by saying that the pain serves as a warning against danger. Each part of the body surface is supplied with pain receptors which come into play only when any stimulus is strong enough to bring about actual injury. Thus the pain receptors are activated by strong stimuli which would not affect them at lower intensities. These receptors serve to protect the organism against danger by giving warning that the stimulus energy is actually destroying the tissues. Usually the pain precedes actual destruction, so that a warning can be useful in avoiding the danger. However, this is not always so, as anyone who has had a bad case of sunburn will testify. We have no sense organs that are sensitive to the ultra-violet light of the burning sun.

Cold, warmth, and heat

Physically, cold and warmth are simply degrees of the same thing—amounts of heat. But psychologically, they are entirely separate. It is possible to map the warmth-sensitive areas of the body's surface by placing a pointed metal object of suitable temperature here and there on the skin, and asking the subject to report when the sensation of warmth is experienced. The cold-sensitive spots may be mapped in a similar fashion. When the same area of the skin is mapped for both warmth and cold sensitiveness, we see that the two sets of spots do not coincide. That is, warmth receptors are separate from cold receptors. The exact physiological structure of these cold and warm spots is not known, although several theories have been advanced.

The number of cold spots varies with the region of the body and the manner in which they are determined. In general, according to the usual method of exploration, there are more cold spots than warm on the same area of the body.

The stimulus to the warmth-sensitive spots is the addition of heat, while the loss of heat from the cold body stimulates the cold spots. Objects which are at the same temperature as the skin itself—usually about 90° F.—stimulate neither type. Hence this temperature is known as the "psychological zero point" or "point of indifference." This indifference point is not constant, however. Dip your left hand for a few minutes into a pail of water at 80° F. and your right hand into a pail at 100° F. After a short time, your hands feel neither warm nor cold. *Sensory adaptation* has taken place in each hand: that is, a new psychological zero point has been reached and the receptors are no longer stimulated. Now plunge both hands into a pail of water at the normal indifference point of 90° F. Water of this temperature will seem warm to the left hand and cool to the right hand.

So far nothing has been said of the quality of *heat*. Heat as a psychological experience is not merely extreme warmth, but is aroused by the simultaneous stimulation of pain, warm, and cold spots.

There is a curious phenomenon of the temperature sense which is called *paradoxical cold*. Cold-sensitive spots are normally stimulated only by temperatures below the psychological zero point. However, they may sometimes be stimulated by temperatures above it. For example, a cold spot on the skin has a psychological zero point of 90° F. and gives no response to temperatures ranging between this point and about 110° F.—but to temperatures above 110° F. it responds with an intense sensation of cold. This is called paradoxical cold because the sensation is actually aroused by a warm object. A similar phenomenon of *paradoxical warmth* is obtained when warmth-sensitive spots are stimulated by cold objects ranging in temperature from about 75° F. to 88° F.—that is, below the psychological zero point. These phenomena leave little doubt that sensations of warmth and cold are brought about by separate mechanisms in the nervous system.

To understand the real stimulus to the sensations of heat, warmth, and cold, suppose you go into a room on a summer day, when the thermometer reads 90° F. There are several objects lying on the table—a water glass, a metal letter-opener, a woolen necktie. You hold each one of these objects against your perspiring cheek and observe that the glass and the metal letter-opener actually seem cold, while the woolen tie feels warm. Of course all these objects are actually at the same temperature since they are all in the same room. The point is that glass and metal, especially glass, absorb your body heat and so "cool off" your skin, while wool prevents body heat from escaping and keeps your skin feeling warm. Thus you see that the effective stimulus to the temperature senses is the *addition or subtraction of heat* from the tissue of the receptor.

OUR SENSES OF MOVEMENT, BODY POSITION, AND BALANCE

IT MAY APPEAR quite a simple thing for a person to stand erect. After all, a statue can do it without having a nervous system at all. But the erect position of a statue and the erect position of a person are dependent on quite different processes. A human being is made up of very flexible material, and when he attempts to stand motionless he absolutely cannot do it. His "standing motionless" actually depends on constantly changing muscular activity and sense-organ activity on his part. As can be demonstrated with the aid of delicate apparatus, when he starts to fall in one direction, he senses that this is happening and changes his muscular contractions to correct this falling tendency, then he starts to fall slightly in another direction and again adjusts his posture—a continual process.

Our common-sense knowledge does not yet include knowledge of the sense organs involved in maintaining a "motionless" position. However, when the person has suffered a destruction of the sense organs required for the *static sense*, as it is called, he cannot stand erect in the dark or with his eyes closed and cannot walk without the aid of vision. In the same way, his command over his muscular movements depends upon another type of sense organ not yet recognized in our everyday knowledge. In this part of the chapter we will deal with these important but unappreciated servants of the body.

Kinesthesis or the "muscle sense"

Close your eyes and relax your body. Have someone place your arm in a certain position and observe that you can report the position of the arm without looking at it. Now let your friend move your arm slowly, bending it at the elbow through an arc of two or three degrees. Notice that such slight bending gives rise to definite sensations of movement, even when your eyes are closed. The receptors which produce these *sensations of movement—or kinesthetic sensations—*are located in the muscles, tendons, and joints of the body. When the parts of the body move, these receptors are stimulated by stretch and pressure, giving rise to kinesthesis.

Much of what we call "touch" involves muscle sense as well as pressure. The so-called "feeling" of velvet or silk as contrasted with oil or glass or again with sandpaper, is composed partly of the muscle sensations produced by different degrees of resistance to the movement of our skin over the surface. Such "feeling" is sometimes called "active touch."

Sense of body position

Imagine yourself lying completely relaxed in some heavy fluid which would support your body in any position without your making any conscious effort or muscular contraction. Even though you did not consciously move your body, every time your head changed position you would know it. The receptors involved in giving you a cue to body position under these circumstances are located in the *labyrinth* or *semicircular canals,* which are a part of the inner ear but have nothing whatever to do with hearing. Their function is to keep you informed as to your position in space—whether you are moving up or down, right or left, backward or forward. They operate, of course, only when there is movement of the head, containing the labyrinthine receptors.

Motion sickness

Ordinarily the labyrinthine sense and the kinesthetic senses cooperate with vision in giving the cues to distance and direction in space. These cues are necessary to maintain the balance of the body or awareness of its position. When these various sensory cues are conflicting in nature, motion sickness frequently results. Ordinarily, we expect the labyrinthine sensations to be accompanied by visual sensations. For example, when we jump, we see our position in space change and we also experience labyrinthine and kinesthetic sensations of movement. But in an airplane during bumpy weather, the visual field (the interior of the plane) remains unchanged while rather sudden changes of position in space cause us to have intense labyrinthine sensations. This conflict between two sets of sensory evidence often produces dizziness. The elevator supplies a similar situation: the walls of the cage remain stationary to our vision, but we have strong sensations of falling and ceasing to fall. This conflict of sensations causes motion sickness.

You will remember that the labyrinthine sense is stimulated only by stopping and starting of the body through space. On a quiet day an airplane, even when flying close to the earth, gives the passenger no labyrinthine or kinesthetic stimulation. The passenger might just as well be sitting in a comfortable chair in a hotel room as far as sense of movement is concerned, and no illness will occur as long as he closes his eyes or confines his visual field to the interior of the plane. But if he looks out of the window at the earth rushing past at 250 miles per hour, he may very well get sick. For he is not in the habit of seeing the earth move past him when he has no sense of movement within him. It is this lack of the expected correlation of sensations which may produce illness.

THE SENSE OF SMELL

Most people would say that human beings do not depend much on the sense of smell. Actually, however, much which we attribute to taste, and which is essential to our enjoyment of food, is a matter of odor instead. It is true, though, that human beings do not use the sense of smell to nearly the degree to which they might use it, for it is an amazingly delicate sense. Perhaps no case has shown this as well as that of Helen Keller, who was both blind and deaf. She had to learn to use the sense of smell to tell her about parts of her environment which she could not touch at the moment. There is no reason to believe that she had any better anatomical equipment for smelling than does the average person, but by her efforts to learn to use her sense of smell, she could get rich perceptions utterly unknown to the ordinary person. For instance, she could recognize by smell a person entering the room. Imagine yourself in her place—unable to hear footsteps or voices, unable to see other persons, and yet possessed of an active, intelligent mind—and you will see why she developed some potentialities which you also have but which you probably will never learn to use.

Among wild animals, of course, it is easier to find instances of the important functioning of the sense of smell. With them it is easy to understand that the sense of smell does not just add to the enjoyment of life but is indispensable to survival. Each of the senses gives a sampling of the possible means of contact with the environment. The eyes give a means of sensitivity to some typical light waves, but not, of course, to all; the ears are sensitive to a good sampling of sound waves. A deer might avoid a cougar either by seeing it or, at night, by hearing it. But if the cougar were lying motionless on a branch overhanging a water hole or other spot, then the sense of smell would be the only means of detecting its presence. Gradually, the animals defective in this sense were eliminated, and the sense of smell attained the sensitivity now found in deer, foxes, and even in man—though in man the sense of smell rarely is used to its full capacity.

One interesting fact about the sense of smell is that certain odors leave long-continued aftereffects. For example, a good whiff of kerosene will cause everything smelled in the next few minutes to smell of it.

> An unscrupulous lawyer once took advantage of this fact to obtain acquittal of a client who was on trial for setting fire to his business establishment in order to collect insurance. The main evidence presented by the state was the testimony of the firemen that they had smelled kerosene upon breaking into the burning shop.

The attorney for the defense suggested that the firemen were obsessed with the notion of arson, that they had hallucinations, and that they were hence unfit to testify. To prove his point, he passed several small bottles to each fireman and asked him to say what they contained. The firemen reported after sniffing each bottle that all contained kerosene.

The "shyster" lawyer then turned in triumph to the jury and asked them to smell the bottles one by one. They reported that only one contained kerosene, the others containing perfumes of subtle fragrance. The explanation is simple. The bottles were passed to the firemen with the one containing kerosene first and to the jury with the overpowering kerosene last. Nobody noticed the difference, and justice was defeated by trickery, since the jury willingly believed after so convincing a demonstration that the firemen really were "smelling things."

THE SENSE OF TASTE

There are four elemental qualities of taste: sweet, sour, bitter, and salt. Sour-sensitive spots are located mainly along the sides of the tongue; the sweet along the tip; the bitter at the base; and salt-sensitive spots on the tip and sides.

When the same substance activates two different sets of receptors, each will give rise to its own characteristic sensation. For instance, saccharine is sweet when tasted on the tip of the tongue and bitter when tasted on the base.

In taste, as in vision, there are contrast effects. Lemonade tastes sour right after you eat sweet cake. Likewise, there are complementary tastes, mixture of which tends to neutralize both. Sugar takes the sourness out of lemonade. Sweet and bitter also tend to neutralize each other. Bitter and sour are complementary to a lesser extent, as are salt and sweet.

What is called "flavor" in food includes far more than mere taste. Added to the taste elements are warmth and cold, cutaneous and kinesthetic impressions, mild pain in some cases, and smell. To prove to yourself the importance of smell, eat a meal with the nostrils plugged tightly. Or just recall how flat and insipid food tastes when you have a cold and cannot smell.

The receptor cells of the sense of taste are activated through some sort of chemical stimulation by the material tasted. These receptors are located in clusters called "taste buds." The newborn baby has his full quota of taste buds, about 245 of them. But as the individual passes middle age, there is a marked tendency for the number of taste buds to decline. Some very old people have no taste buds whatever. This progressive loss of taste buds is accompanied by a corresponding loss of the sense of taste and of the ability to enjoy food. Old people who complain that their meals taste flat are not merely crotchety and hard to please; they are simply unable to taste as well as they once could (Laird and Breen[10]).

Smoking temporarily reduces the taste sensitivity (Sinnot and Rauth[11]). This does not seem to bother many Americans, who insist on smoking before, during, and after meals. But in many European countries where eating is an art, the better restaurants will not permit smoking in the dining room, and good manners prohibit smoking between courses in the private home—practices which are psychologically sound.

Taste adds greatly to the appreciation of good food, and so increases our joy in living. But like smell, it is not absolutely essential to keeping alive. It is just one part of the cooperative system of sense organs that enable us to see, hear, touch, taste, smell, and know our bodily position and movement. It is just one means of receiving stimuli—the first step in knowing the world.

CHAPTER 8

Perception, attention, and report

The Processes of Perception

Factors in Attention

Reporting Our Observations

IN THE LAST CHAPTER we studied the special senses which receive stimuli from the world around us. In this chapter, we shall investigate the complex question of how we observe: of how we apprehend the meaningful relationships that the sensations we receive have to each other and to ourselves. For instance, if you hear someone calling you or see an oncoming truck, you must be able to judge how far away they are. If you are writing an examination, you must be able to judge time correctly in order to cover each question without having to consult your watch every few minutes. If you smell smoke in your hotel room and run to the corridor looking for an exit, you must not see the sign near by as a series of unrelated letters—F-I-R-E E-S-C-A-P-E—and actually, of course, you would not, for you have been trained to see the parts as they make up a whole, and to perceive the phrase FIRE ESCAPE. These important processes of observation occur in all our daily life.

Observation in general is likely to be a complex operation, involving three essential processes which are so interrelated that one can hardly be separated from the others even for the convenience of study. These three processes are called *perception, attention,* and *report.*

The drawing above is from a test of perception: A. F. Street, "A Gestalt Completion Test: A Study of a Cross-section of Intellect," *Columbia University Contributions to Education*, Teachers College Series, 1931, No. 481, p. 63.

THE PROCESSES OF PERCEPTION

ONE OF THE OUTSTANDING things about our psychological processes is that they are *organized* or *patterned*. This organization is mainly something accomplished by the person, for it does not exist among the stimuli that come to him. Consider a very simple example:

When a sound is coming to you from a position to one side of you, each sound wave reaches the nearer eardrum a very short time before it reaches the other eardrum—perhaps one ten-thousandth (1/10,000) of a second earlier (Stevens and Davis[1]). The nearer ear also is stimulated somewhat more vigorously than the farther ear. Nevertheless you do not hear two sounds—a slightly louder and earlier sound coming from the ear closer to the source of sound, and a weaker and later sound from the other ear. Instead, you hear one sound *and you hear it as having a directional quality*. Your central nervous system has taken the nervous impulses from the two ears and, by a quite unconscious process which you cannot observe introspectively, has organized these impulses so that you hear the sound as coming from a given direction.

This process is an example of the kind of work which the nervous system is doing all the time—a very important and indispensable work. The stimuli which reach the sense organs have no organization in and of themselves. There is nothing which keeps some of the light waves together just because they come from the same object. There is nothing which separates different sound waves from one another, and yet a person can listen to a full symphony orchestra and (if he has had some training) can follow the theme played by just one instrument.

The study of this organizing activity of the nervous system is, in part, a study of *perception*. There are three types of vital relationships that you perceive among the impressions you receive from the environment: (1) You perceive different impressions as *wholes*, instead of as series of unconnected parts. (2) You perceive the relation between objects in *space*. And (3) you perceive the relation between events in *time*. We shall consider one by one these three types of sensory perception, and then take up the question of whether there is *extra-sensory perception*.

How we perceive parts as a whole

Sometimes, in psychological studies of perception, use has been made of examples in which the perceptual organization has resulted in some distortion or inaccuracy. For example, much use has been made of what are called *visual illusions,* such as the following:

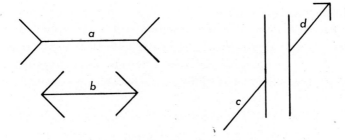

As you may readily prove by using a ruler, the lines *a* and *b* are of equal length, but when they have such surroundings as in this case, they no longer look equally long. Line *c* in the other drawing does not seem to be a continuation of *d,* but it is. In such cases as these, the process of perceptual organization has resulted in a distorting of a *part* because of the larger *whole* in which it is found.

Psychologists often illustrate perception by material in which a number of different organizations may be secured from the same stimuli. For example, if you stare for some time at this figure, it will start to do "tricks"; it will swing back and forth periodically, and you will not be able to keep it from having such reorganization.

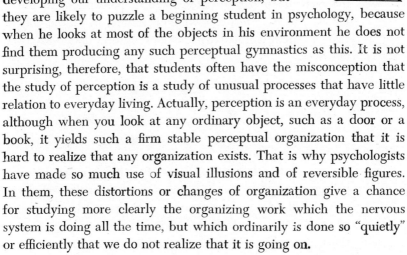

Examples of this sort have been a great help in developing our understanding of perception, but they are likely to puzzle a beginning student in psychology, because when he looks at most of the objects in his environment he does not find them producing any such perceptual gymnastics as this. It is not surprising, therefore, that students often have the misconception that the study of perception is a study of unusual processes that have little relation to everyday living. Actually, perception is an everyday process, although when you look at any ordinary object, such as a door or a book, it yields such a firm stable perceptual organization that it is hard to realize that any organization exists. That is why psychologists have made so much use of visual illusions and of reversible figures. In them, these distortions or changes of organization give a chance for studying more clearly the organizing work which the nervous system is doing all the time, but which ordinarily is done so "quietly" or efficiently that we do not realize that it is going on.

In this section on *How We Perceive Parts as a Whole,* we will be considering the kinds of organizing work done by the nervous system, and we will be considering the factors which determine the kind of organizing that is done.

Factors determining the grouping within perceptual patterns. The first perceptual processes to be examined in more detail are those which involve a grouping of different elements within a larger collection. There are a number of different factors that govern such groupings. They are:

1 *Nearness.* The nearness of the elements to each other makes for their perception as parts of a pattern. Look at the row of dots below. Do you see four groups of dots?

● ● ●   ● ●   ● ● ● ●   ● ●

2 *Likeness.* Elements which are alike tend to be perceived as belonging together. Look at the squares below. You will observe that the squares composed entirely of circles or of X's will be seen more clearly than those made up of both circles and X's.

O   X   X   O   O

O   X   X   O   O

3 *Inclusiveness.* The pattern which "uses up" all the elements is the one which has the advantage in perception. In the figure below, you see a torpedo, which is formed by all the dots, rather than a square formed by the four middle dots with two dots left over.

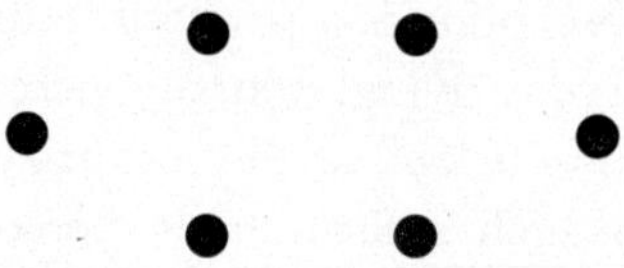

● ●
●   ●
● ●

4 *Part-whole relationship.* Parts of a situation are perceived as belonging to a whole. The manner in which the whole is perceived will influence the meaning of the part. This is another way of saying that what we see depends upon surrounding conditions (Fuchs[2]).

Look at the figure below. The same set of lines may be seen as forming a block of wood or as outlining a recess in a block of wood. The
lines are physically the same, but their meaning depends upon the
whole to which they belong.

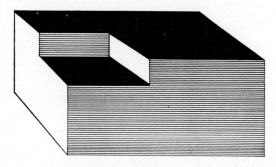

5 *Past experience.* When elements are thrown together in chance
order, we tend to see objects that are already familiar. When you
look at clouds against the sky, you see faces, animal forms, or
even buildings, rather than unfamiliar and meaningless figures.
Past experience also helps you identify the whole to which a few
parts belong. For example, a recent experiment was performed
which showed that past experience is very powerful in conditioning the perception of objects presented to the observer.

One group of subjects was shown an ambiguous picture, which when
examined with one emphasis looked like a young woman's head, but
when seen with another emphasis appeared to be a drawing of an
old woman's head. In this first group 65 per cent of the subjects saw
the young woman and only 35 per cent saw the old woman.

Old woman   *Composite*   *Young woman*

Drawings from W. E. Hill and *Puck.*

Two drawings were then made from the original ambiguous drawing, both resembling the original closely. In one, the original had
been changed so that the face was no longer ambiguous, but was
the face of the old woman exclusively. The other was a similar
alteration except that it represented only the face of the young woman.
The old-woman picture was shown to one group of subjects, and the
young-woman picture to another. Then both groups were shown

the original ambiguous drawing and asked to report what they saw in it. Of the group which had previously seen the old-woman picture, about 97 per cent saw the old woman in the ambiguous picture, while *all* those in the group which had been shown the young-woman drawing saw it in the ambiguous drawing. (Leeper[3])

Obviously what we perceive at one time influences later perceptions.

6 *Interest or set.* We see what we want to see. Any compelling interest to a pattern will cause it to gain over other perceptual factors.

In one recent unpublished study, two hundred college students were shown this drawing and asked: *"Which of these five objects does this drawing most resemble? (1) cooking utensil, (2) electro-magnet, (3) hat, (4) chimney, (5) spool of thread."* The results follow:

Response	Males	Females
Cooking utensil	3	16
Electro-magnet	42	1
Hat	41	53
Chimney	6	3
Spool of thread	8	27
	100	100

Men and women differ in their interest and under the influence of different "sets," they perceive different objects in the same objective stimulus.

The shifting of perception. One of the most interesting things about perception is that the same impressions may be organized into different wholes or patterns. This means that the same objective situation may be observed in several ways. When a situation may be perceived in more than one way, there is a quick, automatic shifting from one to another, as in the figure shown at left.

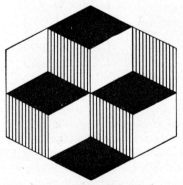

Redrawn from R. H. Wheeler. *The Science of Psychology.* Thomas Y. Crowell Co., 1940, p. 304.

The shifting of perception has a distinct biological advantage. It often happens that the elements of a problem situation may be so perceived that no solution is suggested. Later, the perception of the situation shifts in such a way as to suggest the solution. The whole which will be perceived from an ambiguous group of parts depends upon what we are looking for at the moment.

The organization of parts into a whole is not the only function of perception. One of man's most important adjustments to his physical environment involves the correct perception of how physical objects are related to each other in space. We will now consider *Perceiving Space Through Sight;* in the next section, *Perceiving Movement,* and then, *Perceiving Space Through Hearing.*

Perceiving space through sight

Most occupations and sports depend heavily upon the perception of space through sight. Surveyors use instruments to overcome the physical limitations of man's sense organs. But in golf, baseball, aviation, navigation, and the like, the naked eye, unaided by mechanical devices, must at times be relied upon. How can the human eye, which contains only a curved, two-dimensioned surface sensitive to light, actually perceive a world of three dimensions? How do our perceptions of the third dimension of depth arise? The short answer to this question is that depth is inferred from very simple sense impressions. But the manner in which this is done is, as we shall see, as complicated as it is wonderful.

Cues from joint action of the eyes. The two most fundamental and important cues to depth and distance depend on our having both eyes in working order. They are (1) convergence and (2) difference in retinal pictures.

1 *Convergence of the eyes.* Normally, the two eyes, located at different points in space, converge in looking at a single point or small area. The eye is controlled by three pairs of muscles, which work together to direct it toward any point in the visual field and to hold it there. These muscles contain tiny receptor cells which are stimulated when the muscles contract. For every position of the eyes there is a corresponding pattern of muscle stimuli which tells us how far the eye has moved and where it is at a given moment.

To illustrate convergence, hold the tip of one finger as far away from you as you can;

Eyes and Their Care, Encyclopaedia Britannica Films, Inc.

look at it steadily with both eyes open as you bring it closer and closer to your eyes until it nearly touches your nose. Observe how the sensation of strain of the eye muscles increases as the finger comes closer. This cue of muscle strain is not nearly so strong if you are using only one eye, as you can see by repeating the above exercise with one eye closed.

The perception of space ordinarily involves a complex pattern of eye-muscle stimulation, plus stimulation of the muscles of the body involved in turning the head. Unfortunately, however, the two eyes become for all practical purposes parallel when looking at objects thirty feet or more away, so that convergence has little value beyond that point as a basis for perceiving depth.

2 *Differences in retinal pictures.* Hold your left hand over your left eye and study carefully the view of a book or some other solid object close by. Now, without changing the position of your head or eyes, take your hand off your left eye and shut off the vision in your right eye. Notice the difference in the two retinal pictures. With the right eye you see more of the right side of the object; with the left eye, more of the left side. This is a normal condition of vision. From experience we have learned to interpret distance from an automatic comparison of the two slightly different retinal images.

The stereoscope, which was found in every front parlor a generation ago, is a commercial application of this principle. This apparatus is simply a device whereby the two eyes see two different pictures: the left eye looks through a lens at one picture, and the right eye looks through another lens at another picture. The pictures used are taken by cameras mounted slightly apart from each other, just as our eyes are mounted in our heads a slight distance apart. By increasing the difference between the angles at which the two pictures are taken, it is possible to increase the illusion of depth up to a certain point. But when the two views become too different, they no longer merge in perception but are seen alternately by the person. In some manner or other, the brain tends to act so as to prevent a confusion from the two perceptual processes. The activity aroused by one eye is inhibited for a time, and the impulses from the other eye are able to dominate the main cortical activity. Then the previously inhibited processes dominate, and the perceptual activity which previously was dominant is now inhibited.

A modern application of the stereoscope is used in the study of aerial photographs. Airplanes in flight take a series of photographs which overlap in area covered. Naturally, as a plane travels, the angle at which an object is photographed changes. For instance, the diagrams below show the top of a monument as it might be seen from two different positions—or as a small model of it would look from directly above with first one eye focusing on it and then the other:

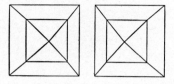

The two diagrams shown above can be used in a simple demonstration of the stereoscopic principle. Procure a piece of light cardboard about ten to fourteen inches in length and of convenient width. Place the cardboard vertical to the surface of the book page so that all the left diagram is on one side and all the right diagram is on the other. Next hold your head in contact with the upper edge of the cardboard in such a way that the left eye sees only the diagram at the left and the right eye sees only the diagram at the right. Notice that the two flat images fuse into a solid which appears to be located at a position between the two flat drawings. This is the stereoscopic phenomenon.

The essential principle in the stereoscopic effect is that images cast by some parts of the object fall on slightly non-corresponding parts of the two retinas. We have learned to interpret these slight retinal differences as depth. Truly flat objects, viewed from different positions in space, result in retinal images in which all parts of the object fall on corresponding points on the two retinas.

There are a variety of instruments known as *stereoscopes* on the market. Some make use of magnifying lenses, some of prisms, to divert the lines of vision of the two eyes, but they all operate on the principle of retinal disparity or differences, and they are all intended to reveal the third dimension—or depth—in photographs which otherwise would look flat. These instruments are invaluable in peacetime as a means of obtaining information for maps without the expense of extensive and lengthy surveying on land, and in wartime as a means of discovering enemy installations. In one instance in World War II, the Japanese placed flat dummy models of airplanes on a flying field to make our forces believe they had greater strength than they actually had, but stereoscopic examination of aerial photographs of the field showed that the planes did not have the normal third dimension of real planes.

The serviceman below is using a simple lens-type stereoscope to see the third dimension or·relief in aerial photos.

Cues to space from one eye only. When you are looking at distant objects and trying to judge their distance from you, it does not matter appreciably whether you use one eye or two eyes. But when you are looking at objects that are relatively close to you, one-eyed vision is much less exact than vision from two eyes. We might consider now the question as to how a person judges distance when the distinctive cues from the two eyes are too slight to be of much help. These cues include: (1) accommodation, (2) distinctness, (3) light and shadow, (4) relative position, (5) relative motion, and (6) relative size.

1 *Accommodation.* The lens of the eye bulges out as we look at close objects and flattens when we look into the distance (Sinclair[4]). The shape of the eyeball probably changes also. As a result of these changes, the image is kept in focus on the retina. This effect is known as "accommodation." Each degree of bulge of lens and eyeball gives rise to its characteristic pattern of stimulation, and hence gives us cues to the distance or depth of an object. We have been using these cues so long that their use has become automatic. We can judge distance without thinking about it.

2 *Distinctness.* Because of dust and smoke in the air, objects which are a long way off appear to be blurred and indistinct in outline, and even details we know to be there are not observable. This phenomenon is sometimes called "atmospheric perspective." The extent of the dimming depends upon the distance, and is one of the cues that help us judge distance.

We learn to interpret distance according to the atmosphere we are used to. The tenderfoot at the dude ranch, deceived by the clear mountain air, frequently amuses the old hands by announcing that he will ride to a certain hill and back before breakfast, only to learn that the "hill" is in reality a mountain forty miles away. The photographs below, taken from the same spot, show how atmospheric conditions influence our perceptions of distance.

3 *Light and shadow.* When light strikes an irregular surface, certain parts are brightly illuminated and others are in shadow. The distribution and direction of shadows are important cues to the relative distances of various objects in view. For instance, the shadows are different in the two photographs of the jet fighter at right because of the difference in the angles and direction from which the plane was photographed. As a result, the wings in the top photograph seem to be tipped downward and the wings in the bottom photograph to be tipped upward—thus giving different impressions of how far the wings are above the ground.

4 *Relative position.* When two objects are in the same field of vision, the nearer one conceals all or part of the farther. Near objects in the outer world usually appear at the bottom of the two-dimensional field of vision, and distant objects at the top. Moreover, the nearer object often obscures part of the view of the farther object. In the picture at left, the farther houses are both above and behind the nearer ones, in the field of vision—one of the cues for judging distance.

5 *Relative rates of apparent motion.* When you look from a rapidly moving train, near objects seem to pass by more rapidly than those at a moderate distance, as is evidenced by the blurred foreground in this picture. When you observe objects very far away, still another effect of relative motion is apparent, since such objects actually seem to be traveling with you.

6 *Relative size.* The farther away an object is, the smaller it appears. When we know the size of an object, we automatically judge its distance by how big it looks. Here again, known standards are an influence. For instance, once we are familiar with the height of a particular man, we can tell about how far away he is by how tall he appears. Naturally, the farther away he is, the smaller will be our retinal image of him. Coordinating judgment of size and distance is automatic in the adult, but it is often lacking in the child. When a small child sees a man in the distance, he often calls him a "boy." Below, you can see that the distance between the lions can be judged by the difference in their apparent sizes.

Perceiving movement visually

The motion picture was at one time hailed as a marvel of modern science. Now we are so accustomed to it that we rarely speculate on how this interesting phenomenon works. The motion-picture film is simply a series of still pictures flashed on a screen one after the other at the rate of fifteen to twenty-five per second. How, then, can we see a series of still pictures as smooth, continuous motion? Why do the movies not jump? Why is the motion we see so perfect and realistic?

Movement is simply change of the position of an object in space. When the object is perceived first in one position, then in another, then in another, it is perceived as in motion—provided that the second position follows quickly enough and is not too far removed from the one preceding. It is not necessary for the object to be perceived in all of the intermediate positions in order that it be seen as moving. In fact, the eyes never follow a moving object with sufficient precision to keep that object in full view at all times.

Normal perception of motion is an act of filling in the blanks between the successive positions that an object takes in space. When the gaps between are not too great and when the successive positions are perceived rapidly enough, the perception of continuous movement takes place. The motion-picture film is no more wonderful than ordinary visual perception. It is merely an application of a fundamental fact about the visual perception of motion.

Perceiving space through hearing

We have just analyzed some of the many cues our eyes give as to how the things we see are arranged in space. Our ears, too, give us cues as to the direction and the distance of the sounds we hear.

How we perceive the direction of a sound. In crossing a busy intersection, our safety depends upon our accuracy in determining the directions from which sounds come. Our ability to localize sounds is almost entirely due to the fact that we have two ears located at different points in space. A given sound affects the two ears differently in three respects. (See the diagram.)

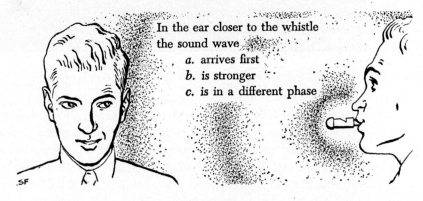

In the ear closer to the whistle the sound wave
a. arrives first
b. is stronger
c. is in a different phase

1 The sound coming from the whistle at the left of the head strikes the left ear before the right. This difference in time can be very short, but it serves to tell us from which side the sound is coming.

2 Notice also that the sound wave coming from the left stimulates the left ear more strongly than it does the right, because the right ear is farther away.

3 As you remember from Chapter 7, sound waves consist of areas of high and low pressure in the air. Since the two ears are at different points in space, the sound wave will be in different parts of its cycle as it stimulates the two ears. That is, a low-pressure area may hit one ear, and a high-pressure area may hit the other. Sounds directly in front of us cannot be distinguished from those directly above or behind us because the two ears are stimulated similarly in these three respects.

A person often locates the direction of a sound by turning his head until his two ears are stimulated identically by the sound waves. Then he knows that the sound must be coming from some point in the mid-plane. This essential principle of hearing has been reproduced in various types of auditory equipment which can accurately determine what direction a sound is coming from, and thus help locate the object making the sound. Equipment of this kind is actually used in listening for approaching airplanes or distant guns. It greatly improves on the accuracy of our unaided perceptions of what direction a sound is coming from.

Photo by U.S. Army Signal Corps

A new type of airplane locator uses three highly sensitive microphones mounted on a movable frame and can determine both horizontal position (direction of approach) or *azimuth,* and elevation position (altitude) at the same time. The microphones are placed as though at the angles of a right-angled triangle, the microphone at the right angle of the triangle being common to the other two. The horizontal, or azimuth, operator uses the common microphone and the "ear" beside it. Both microphones are connected so that the sounds they pick up can be heard by the operator. One is connected with a receiver in the left ear of the operator and transmits to it all sounds picked up, while the other transmits sounds to the right ear of the operator. The direction of any object making a sound is established by turning the frame until the operator can determine that the sound from each microphone is coming in with equal intensity and is therefore at a point at right angles to the line between the two microphones. Thus the operator knows the *direction* of an unseen target. The elevation listener uses the common microphone and the "ear" below it, and he raises and lowers the frame until the sound is centered, thus giving the *elevation* of the unseen target. The azimuth and elevation measurements combined give the *position* of the airplane. A third operator compensates for the time it took the sound to travel from the airplane to the ground and the distance the target traveled in the interim. When this is done, the instrument points directly to the target, and a searchlight synchronized with it spots the airplane.

How we perceive the distance of a sound. There are two ways in which we can tell how far a familiar sound is from us.

1 The farther away a sound is, the weaker it will be. The ear-splitting locomotive whistle heard in the station becomes fainter and fainter as the train moves into the distance.

2 The sound of familiar objects changes in tone quality as their distance from us increases. The farther away the sound is, the purer it is. The tinny jangle of the cheap phonograph gives way to mellow music when heard in the distance, as from across a lake. This increase in the purity of the tones results from the loss of the irregular sound waves, which are noise, and from the loss of the shrill overtones, which lack sufficient energy to carry very far.

How we perceive time

In observing the relationships between himself and the world around him, a person must not only be able to perceive how parts make up wholes and how objects are arranged in space; he must also be skilled in a third process of perception: judging intervals of time. Our daily activities demand that we constantly adjust ourselves to the time dimension of the world. Although we have clocks and watches available to guide us, we cannot depend entirely on their help for judging how rapidly time is passing. Whatever you are doing, you gauge your speed according to how much time you have available and how rapidly you think time is passing. If you have an hour before class to finish reading a book, you cannot judge how fast to go—whether to read every word or skim the contents—unless you know how late it is getting.

Since this ability to judge time thus has some importance, we must consider how it is affected by the length of the interval to be judged, the age of the person doing the judging, and the kind of activity he engages in during the intervals.

How we perceive short intervals. As we have already seen on page 278, the ear is the most accurate instrument for the perception of short intervals. Many lines of evidence point to the fact that when clocks are not available, the mechanisms people use in the perception of short intervals are quite different from those used for longer intervals. The perceived length of short intervals of time is somehow related to the speed with which life activities go on in our tissues.

> This fact has been shown in a careful experiment performed by a French psychologist who tested the ability of normal subjects to tell when a certain amount of time had passed (François[5]). The subjects were tested by their ability to judge accurately the length of gradually increasing intervals.
>
> First, under normal temperature conditions they were instructed to signal when one of the specified intervals had elapsed. They were then put in an electric apparatus which raised their body temperatures by several degrees. They were tested again, and it was found that they thought the time interval was of shorter duration than it actually was. In other words, as a result of the higher temperatures their lives were being "lived faster"—every moment contained more experience. The amount of "living" they had formerly experienced in a given time T they now experienced in less time than that, say L. That is why they would judge that period T had passed when in reality only L had passed.

How we perceive long intervals. Plautus had some understanding of the process of time perception when he wrote:

> When I was young, no timepiece Rome supplied,
> But every fellow had his own—inside;
> A trusty horloge, that—rain or shine—
> Ne'er failed to warn him of the hour—to dine.

When you go to bed, can you "set yourself" to waken at any designated hour, regardless of how sleepy you are or of how soon that hour is to arrive? Some people can do this so accurately that they do not need alarm clocks.

Most of our physiological processes are correlated nicely with time. There is a distinct rhythm in our periods of hunger, which can be taken advantage of in the way described in the verse above. But there are many changes inside us which reveal the passage of long intervals of time, whether we are awake or asleep: among them are the growing tension on the bladder and the growing bodily fatigue.

Ability to perceive time varies with age. Children are quite poor in ability to perceive time. The average three-year-old child can point on command to his nose, eyes, mouth, and hair; can name a key, penny, closed knife, watch, and pencil; can tell whether he is a girl or boy; knows his last name; can repeat after one hearing such a sentence as "I have a little dog." But not until the average child is six years old can he tell you whether it is morning or afternoon. His ability to think in terms of the future is even slower in developing (Terman[6]). However, accuracy in judging intervals of time improves enormously between the tenth and sixteenth years.

> In one experiment, children were asked to estimate intervals of five seconds and of five minutes (Elkine[7]). It was found that, on the average, ten-year-olds were 82 per cent off in judging a short interval of five seconds and 57 per cent off in judging a longer interval of five minutes. But sixteen-year-olds, on the average, were only about 32 per cent off for the shorter interval and 30 per cent off for the longer. (Apparently the longer interval was easier for both age groups to judge accurately.)

Part of the difficulty children have in telling time may be due to their lack of familiarity with the units adults use. They may not be able to translate their sensations of time into seconds or minutes, even though they may feel the passage of time quite strongly and accurately.

The kind of activity affects judgments of time. Everyone has observed that time spent in monotonous work is overestimated *at the time,* while time spent in interesting work is underestimated *at the time.* Psychologists confirm this everyday observation.

> In one experiment two subjects were engaged in the dull task of sorting balls (Wyatt, Fraser, and Stock[8]). At various intervals each subject was asked to estimate the length of time already spent. The record of one subject follows:

Actual Time in Minutes	Estimation When Slightly Bored	Estimation When Greatly Bored
30	25	30
50	50	55
70	75	85
90	100	110
100	110	120

> Obviously, the amount of error in estimating time depended upon the degree of boredom.

It has also been shown that time spent in making easy discriminations is estimated as longer than time spent in making difficult discriminations (Harton[9]). This confirms the above experiment, for easy work soon becomes boring. And successful activity is judged to occupy less time than unsuccessful activity.

> Subjects in one experiment learned mazes (Harton[10]). Some of them were encouraged by being told how well they were doing; others were disparaged. Those who felt successful judged the time as shorter than did those who felt that they were failing.

So, in general, time spent pleasantly is estimated to be shorter than time spent unpleasantly, when it is estimated *at the time*.

Is there extra-sensory perception?

The three processes of perception discussed so far—seeing parts as a whole, determining spatial relations, and judging the passage of time—all involve our special senses, especially sight and hearing. But what about perception which does not involve any of our senses? Is there perception which is "extra-sensory" (outside the senses)?

During the past few years, a great deal of publicity has been given the problems of clairvoyance and mental telepathy. Results of "experiments" were broadcast. As a result, the psychologist often is asked: "What is there in extra-sensory perception?"

There are two kinds of "E.S.P." Extra-sensory perception, or "E.S.P.," as it is often called, is said to comprise two closely related phenomena: *mental telepathy,* or the passage of ideas or knowledge from one mind to another without intervention of the sense organs; and *clairvoyance,* or becoming aware of a physical object without the use of sense organs.

A typical mental telepathy test is conducted as follows: There is a deck of twenty-five cards containing five cards for each of five symbols—star, circle, square, plus sign, and parallel wavy lines. After the cards are shuffled, one subject, the "sender," picks up a card and studies it carefully, while the other subject, the "receiver," tries to tell what card he has picked. After the receiver has called out "square," "circle," or whatever card he thinks the sender has picked up, his judgment is recorded as a hit or a miss.

In clairvoyance experiments the cards are shuffled, and the "receiver" (there is no "sender" other than the cards themselves) attempts to record the order of the symbols in the pile of cards (Pratt *et al.*[11]).

What psychologists think of E.S.P. Numerous critics have pointed to two important sources of error in clairvoyance and mental telepathy experiments: (1) poorly controlled experimental conditions, especially with regard to the operation of cues, such as shadows and changes of voice or expression on the part of the sender; and (2) inadequate statistical procedures.

1 It has been discovered, for example, that the standard E.S.P. cards can be read from the back (Kennedy[12]). The printing process apparently leaves on the back of the card a readable impression of the symbol on the face of the card. The impression is so clear that it even shows in a photograph of the back of the card! It has also been shown that cues can be used by a subject without his being aware that he is using them (Collier[13]). If the receivers and senders in the telepathic experiment are adequately isolated from sensory communication, negative results are usually obtained. (Coover[14])

2 But even with complete control of experimental conditions, there have been errors of a statistical nature in certain E.S.P. experiments (Leuba[15])—errors too complex to go into here.

In fact, psychologists as a whole are not convinced of the reality of extra-sensory phenomena. In a survey, a group of qualified psychologists were asked to check one of five statements to show how they stood on the matter of extra-sensory perceptions (Warner and Clark[16]). They were given several alternative answers to choose from. The number of psychologists expressing each attitude follows:

In your opinion, is extra-sensory perception:

1. An established fact.................... 5
2. A likely possibility.................... 26
3. A remote possibility....................128
4. An impossibility 51
5. Merely an unknown...................142

Total 352

The answers show that psychologists, though not convinced of the reality of the phenomenon of extra-sensory perception, are open-minded on the subject. Notice that "merely an unknown" received the highest vote of the five alternatives. However, "a remote possibility" was a close second.

What about Dunninger? Psychologists who are skeptical about the existence of extra-sensory perception are frequently asked to account for the well-known radio exploits of Dunninger. Sometimes the questioner concludes, from the inability of the psychologist to explain how Dunninger operates, that the showman's feats cannot be explained by ordinary natural laws, and that he is actually reading minds.

In considering the Dunninger question, however, remember the lifework of the great showman Houdini. Houdini did things in his day which were just as spectacular as those accomplished by Dunninger, but they all had perfectly understandable explanations in the laws of physics, chemistry, and psychology. It is well within the realm of probability that Dunninger's feats also have perfectly understandable explanations. But until psychologists are able to study his work under conditions where the possibility of trickery is excluded, the question of whether Dunninger can "read minds" by extra-sensory perception must go unanswered.

FACTORS IN ATTENTION

HUMAN BEINGS exist in the midst of a complex of stimuli to which they may or may not respond. There are notes too high or too low for the human ear to detect; above the blues and below the reds of the spectrum there are colors which the human eye cannot see. From all the energies about us, our sense organs are responsive to only certain ones.

However, the selectivity of the human organism goes far beyond mere sensitivity or insensitivity in the sense organs. There is not only a *sensory* but a *psychological* selectivity—an emphasizing or ignoring of responses to certain stimulus patterns—which varies from time to time and which does not result only from changes in the sense organs. Although several stimulus patterns compete, only those fitting the need of the moment are selected. For example, when you are reading an interesting book, the sounds of the clock ticking are not heard. When a person selects certain stimuli from all those in his environment, and responds mainly to them, he is said to be giving them his *attention*.

Ways of defining attention

Attending can be looked upon in three ways:

    1 As an adjustment of the body and its sense organs.
    2 As clearness and vividness of conscious experience.
    3 As a readiness to respond.

    Attention as a bodily response. In attention, the body and its sense organs are adjusted to receive a stimulus readily. You have seen a garage mechanic "tuning up" a motor: his head is cocked to one side, and he is literally "putting his best ear forward." And you have seen a physician with his stethoscope listening for certain faint sounds in the chest of his patient—wheezes that reveal difficulty in the lungs,

or barely perceptible murmurs which indicate to his trained ear that all is not well with the patient's heart. The physician's postural adjustment is as complete as is humanly possible; he even closes his eyes to shut out distracting visual stimulation. These familiar examples show how the body is adjusted to produce a selection of the significant stimuli from the distracting ones.

Attention as clearness in consciousness. Do you wear glasses? If so, were you noticing the rims just now? Probably not, although they are in your field of vision. Look for them, and there they are. Is there a clock ticking in the room where you are studying? Is a radio playing softly in the next room? If so, were the sounds vivid in your consciousness a few seconds ago? Probably not. Listen for these or other sounds to which you were deaf a moment ago, and you will hear them.

Such apparent changes in the vividness with which a stimulus is received, apart from any change in its physical intensity, are one phenomenon of attention.

Attention as a set toward response. Attention may also be regarded as a *set*, or readiness to respond in a selective way to some stimulus situation which permits a variety of possible responses. For example, when a gym teacher says "Ready, set, BEGIN!" the response of the class will depend upon what set has been established by his prior instructions—whether they have been told to bend over and touch the floor, to stretch their arms upward, or to perform some other particular exercise.

The practical experience of everyday life shows that set is an important variable in determining the speed and accuracy of performance. If a job requires frequent changes of set on the part of the operator, it will not be done so quickly as when few changes are required. This is one of the principles behind the modern assembly line, in which a complex process is broken down into many small tasks, each one performed by a different man.

Many of the stimulus patterns in the world about us do not receive emphasis because we are set to respond to other stimulus patterns. The clouds in the sky go unnoticed unless we want a fine day for a picnic or a football game.

Factors determining the direction of attention

What are the factors which make an object or situation attract attention? This is a question of enormous importance in all spheres of life. Advertising and salesmanship, for example, aim to attract the attention of the prospective buyer. Likewise, the political candidate must make an impression upon the minds of the voters.

Here we will discuss seven factors that influence direction of attention: change, size, repetition, striking quality, motivation, social suggestion, and interests.

Change. Change is the passing from one form or condition to another —from one place to another, from one intensity to another, from absent to present, from red to green, from high to low, from moving to stationary. All these are changes, and all attract attention. Some birds of prey seem able to perceive only moving objects, and animals remaining entirely still are safe from them. White lights flashing on and off draw your attention to a restaurant sign. Change should not be underestimated as a factor in getting attention.

Size. A large advertisement attracts attention better than a small one; a loud sound better than a faint one. A shout makes you "sit up and take notice," while a whispered word is ignored. A visual stimulus can, of course, be so large that we do not notice it. Very large lettering in an advertisement does not attract attention so readily as does small type in the middle of white space.

Repetition. From a distance the crack of a rifle is not so likely to be heard as is the repeated rattle of a machine-gun. A weak stimulus frequently repeated may have as much effect as a strong one presented once. There is, however, a limit to the effectiveness of repetition. If overdone, monotony results.

Experience shows that repetition of a fundamental theme or motif with minor variations is more effective than exact repetition. An effective advertising campaign repeats an essential idea with numerous small variations. Music and architecture offer many examples of how attention can be maintained through repeating the central theme with small modifications.

Striking quality. Some stimuli are more potent in attracting attention than are other physically stronger ones, even in the absence of previous experience and conditioning. For example, high sounds prevail over low sounds; tickling and itching over broad, smooth pressure; saturated colors over pastel shades.

Motivation. The stimulus which will win your attention is the one that relates to the strongest need of the moment. If you are hungry, stimuli related to food will arouse your interest. If you are tired, stimuli related to coziness and sleep will be most effective.

Social suggestion. People usually attend to what is pointed out to them because they have enjoyed many satisfactions and avoided many discomforts or injuries in the past through acting on the suggestions of others.

> The presence of social suggestion explains the effectiveness of the following old prank. When in a crowd, start looking intently toward the sky. Move your head slowly, as your eyes sweep through a wide arc. Notice that many of the people about you will do the same thing. Even when there is nothing of interest to see, people will respond to social suggestion by paying close attention to something which another person is apparently observing closely.

Interest. People vary greatly in their response to attention-seeking stimuli. A person's own interests—like his internal drives—predispose him toward or away from responding to a particular stimulus.

> Let us suppose that a geologist, a farmer, an artist, and a real-estate promoter are looking at the same plot of ground. The geologist's attention might be attracted to the layers of rock exposed when the road cuts through a hillside, for such layers tell much about the physical history of the region. The farmer would probably examine the soil and any plants or weeds growing on it. The artist might walk about until he found the position from which the landscape was a balanced composition to be painted. The real-estate promoter would look the property over carefully to see how it could be subdivided. The objective stimulus is the same for all four of these individuals, but their interests differ. Their attention and consequent behavior vary accordingly.

Thus a person's interests not only determine his reaction to a situation but even determine what aspects of the situation will call forth a reaction. The illustration on page 124 is another good example of this process.

Kinds of attention

So far we have considered the three ways of defining attention, and the factors which determine its direction. Now we come to the three kinds of attention: involuntary, voluntary, and habitual.

Involuntary attention. Certain stimuli seem to possess a natural potency for attracting the attention, the "striking quality" already mentioned. In everyday language people say that they pay attention to these stimuli "against their will." Such prepotent stimuli are so strong that they win the battle when they come in competition with other activities of the moment.

Suppose you are busy reading your assignment in psychology when suddenly a loud report outside draws your attention. You stop reading to investigate. Was it a shot?—you remember the crime wave you have been reading about in the newspapers. Or was it a backfiring motor? Finally, you conclude that the police are the logical ones to investigate, and you return to your book. The characteristic thing about such involuntary attention as this is that it is accompanied by no consciousness of effort. In fact, it requires effort to pay attention to your work when some such prepotent stimulus intrudes on your attention.

Voluntary attention. Self-observation during voluntary attention reveals a mass of strain sensations which ordinarily are not present. The effort may be great or small, depending on the person's motivation. For instance, if a college girl has no real interest in her studies, the effort will be greater than if she were interested. But even with interesting work, prolonged voluntary attention ultimately results in boredom.

Habitual attention. Habitual attention is like involuntary attention in that it requires no conscious effort. The important difference between these two forms of attention is in the length of time they last. Habitual attention is involuntary attention prolonged. We arrive at the comfortable state of habitual attention only when we have practiced and when we have a strong motivation to give continued attention.

When a child first learns to read, he cannot read for long periods at a time. As he grows older, however, two things happen to make habitual attention easier. First, he practices reading for longer and longer periods. But more important, he discovers that through reading he can satisfy his curiosity and, to some extent, his emotional needs. The nine-year-old who will sit for a couple of hours reading about firemen is satisfying his curiosity about fire engines and at the same time is deriving emotional gratification from imagining that he is a big brave fireman. Books and classroom discussions that appeal to the student's interests and needs help bridge the gap between the forced voluntary attention stage and the final, easy, effortless stage where attention becomes habitual. The more a child reads, the more he learns, and—if the material is interesting—the more he wants to read and learn, and the easier he finds it to maintain habitual attention.

The shifting of attention

The individual's attentive adjustment is not stable and fixed. Attention is constantly shifting from one part of the scene to another. For example, notice the eyes of a person who enters a room full of strangers. You will see that they move here and there, pausing but a short time in any one position. This is typical attentive exploration.

There is also *involuntary* fluctuation of the attention which is just as real, though not so easily noticed.

> This phenomenon may be demonstrated in the auditory sense by holding a watch far enough from the ear so that you can barely hear it tick. Now listen to the ticking, and you will observe that it grows in apparent intensity, and then fades away to a point at which it cannot be heard, then grows again, then fades. The period of these fluctuations in hearing varies with the individual and the conditions of the experiment, lasting between a fraction of a second and several seconds. Similar results can be obtained by fixing the gaze on a faint gray smudge on a blank sheet of white paper. Hold it at such a distance that you can barely make out the smudge, and you will observe the same variation in the subjective strength of the sensation aroused.

> It is also possible to fix the eyes on a stimulus and maintain that fixation and yet have fluctuations of attention. Everyone has had the experience in an absent-minded moment of staring at an object without out seeing it. In that case there is adjustment of the sense organs without out attentive adjustment.

These self-experiments demonstrate the important fact that adjustment of the sense organs and attentive adjustment are not entirely the same.

The distraction of attention

Distraction is simply having attention drawn from one thing to another. It can, of course, seriously interfere in many activities, but it

is at its most dramatic when employed by magicians, pickpockets, and crooked gamblers. This photograph was taken during a demonstration to soldiers on how distraction may be employed for dishonest purposes. After the deck has been cut, the gambler slips it back to its original order while reaching for an ashtray.

When the distracting stimulus strives to attract the same sense organ that is concerned with attention, there is extreme interference with attention. The interference has two sources: for one thing, you are drawn to respond to some other stimulus; and for another, the new and stronger stimulus drowns out or masks the weaker original stimulus. For example, a nearby juke box will interfere more with your telephone conversation than will bright, flashing lights.

Not all distractions come from the outside. Mental worries and vague, objectless fears can intrude to interfere with the work at hand. In one investigation it was found that taxicab drivers who had family worries were more prone to accidents than those who were not so hampered.

The bad effects of distraction. The most obvious effect of distraction is an actual reduction in efficiency.

> An experiment was conducted with typists to determine the cost of distraction in terms of energy required per unit of work. On some days the typists worked under conditions of quiet, which the experimenter produced by enclosing them in cubicles of suitable size constructed of a sound-insulating material. On other days they worked in the same places, except that the partitions were removed so that the usual office noises prevailed. Energy cost was measured by having the girls breathe out into a bag specially constructed to capture the expired air. This was analyzed to determine the amount of carbon dioxide, and from this the consumption of oxygen was computed. The more oxygen consumed for a given amount of work, according to physiologists, the more energy consumed. Results were that the amount of typing accomplished was the same under the two conditions, but the energy cost of the typing done (the amount of oxygen used up) under noisy conditions was decidedly greater than that of the same amount of work done under conditions of quiet. (Laird[17]) These results have been confirmed by other experiments (Freeman[18]).

The energy cost of work performed under noisy conditions is greatest immediately after the shift from quiet to noisy surroundings. It is apparently possible for the subject to get used to the noise (Harmon[19]).

The obvious conclusion is that the employer who makes his employees work under noisy conditions at one time and under quiet conditions at another will obtain as much work from them as he would were conditions better, but they may be expected to show more effects of fatigue because they are using up more energy.

Controlling distraction. Because noise has become such an important source of distraction in our large cities, many efforts are now being made to reduce it. The drive against din is on. Horses drawing milk wagons through the city streets wear rubber shoes; the wagons themselves are mounted on pneumatic tires; ash cans are provided with rubber cushions. Efforts are also being made to reduce the noise of elevated trains and streetcars, and in some cities it is against the law to sound an automobile horn except in an emergency. This is only a sample of what is being done to combat the high energy costs of noise.

Many external distractions can obviously be prevented by removing their sources. When you study, for example, turn off the radio, don't let the light shine in your eyes, and try to keep your roommate quiet, if you have one. However, the control of the objective factors in distraction is not nearly so important as the control which must come from within. Inattention usually results from lack of interest in the matter at hand and as such is a personality problem. Explore your own motives and weigh the importance of what you are doing. Make clear to yourself why you must control your attention, and how your task is related to your interests and needs. And do not forget that the longer you stay with a subject, the easier and more interesting it will become.

Distraction implies a conflict between two stimuli or activities. Conflicts are painful and costly. When confronted by uncontrollable distractions, it is sometimes better to give in for the moment and come back with renewed resolve than to seesaw irresolutely. The latter accomplishes nothing and leaves you completely discouraged and tired. After a rest, attention is renewed.

REPORTING OUR OBSERVATIONS

IN THIS CHAPTER on how we observe, we have so far discussed the two processes of *perception* and *attention*. Now we come to the third and final phase of observation: *report*. Since we are living with people and sharing our observations with them, the study of observation would be decidedly incomplete without some reference to the way in which we report our observations to others. Accuracy and speed in reporting is the only way they have of estimating the accuracy and speed of our attention and perception.

The report of an observation does not have to be made to some other person. The observer may merely report to himself. That is to say, he may give some name or label to the things he observes. The person who has a wealth of descriptive terms to apply to the things he experiences will actually see more than the person who lacks an adequate vocabulary, because he will be set to experience more forms or conditions corresponding to those terms. Women are more sensitive to the color of fabrics, because they have a richer supply of exact terms —such as *henna, russet, maroon, crimson, beige, ruby,* and *auburn*—to apply to fabrics which men would simply call *red* or *brown.*

How quickly we observe and report

In the psychological laboratory, reaction time is measured with a high degree of accuracy. The unit in which the psychologist measures and expresses reaction time is equal to one thousandth of a second. This short interval of time is called a millisecond or a sigma (σ). To obtain such accurate measurements, special apparatus is required. The typical setup for a reaction-time experiment is shown below.

Reaction time and the chronoscope. *The experimenter, seated at the left of the table, has before him a chronoscope (also shown on p. 2). He presses the key on top to make the hooded light,* center, *flash red, green, or amber. As he presses the key, he automatically starts the chronoscope. At right, the subject, watching the light, presses one of the three reaction-keys to indicate whether the light is red, green, or amber. As he presses the key, the chronoscope automatically stops. Thus the experimenter determines the total amount of time that has elapsed between his pressing down the stimulus key and the subject's pressing down the reaction-key. This amount of time, which is shown on the dial in hundredths of a second, is the subject's reaction time. The separate parts of the apparatus are shown in the close-up below:*

This apparatus is much more accurate than the stop-watch method, and is also useful in detecting individuals who are color-blind to the red, green, and amber lights used in industry, in railroads, and in traffic systems. (Photographs courtesy C. H. Stoelting Co.)

All this complicated apparatus merely serves to measure the amount of time elapsing between the presentation of a stimulus and the execution of a prescribed response. During this time, a complex process is occurring in the nervous system: a stimulus is received by the receptor cells in the eye, is transmitted through the optic nerve to the brain, which "registers" the nature of the situation and sends out an impulse to the muscle in the hand, which then makes an appropriate response. How long this process takes is dependent on many factors: the particular sense organ involved, the strength of the stimulus, the nature of the fore-period, the amount of practice in responding to the stimulus, the age of the observer, his body temperature, the altitude he is in, and the complexity of the reaction.

Reaction time depends upon the sense organ. Certain sense organs give rise to rapid reaction times; others, to slower ones. The chart shows average reaction times for the different sense organs, as determined by many investigators.

Average reaction times of various senses

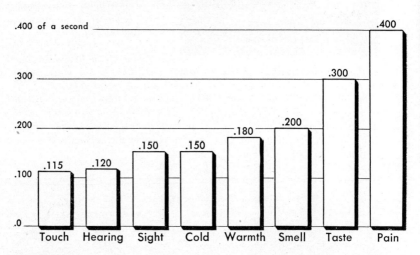

Data from E. G. Boring, H. S. Langfeld, and H. P. Weld, *Introduction to Psychology*, John Wiley and Sons, Inc., 1939.

Notice that the eye is slower to respond than the ear. The reaction time in braking an automobile is slower in response to a red light than in response to a horn (Elliott and Louttit[20]) because of the different ways in which sight and sound stimuli are received. The visual stimulus does not stimulate a nerve-ending directly. When light enters the eye, it sets up a chemical reaction which in turn stimulates the nerve-endings, and which takes a certain amount of time. But for the ear, the stimulation is mechanical rather than chemical; the sound wave is immediately translated into physical pressure by the eardrum and the bones in the middle ear. The reaction times of taste and smell are also long as compared with the others, because these, too, are chemical senses. While the physiological bases of warmth and cold are not known, you will notice that they have a fairly rapid reaction time. Pain has the slowest reaction time of all, as measured by this method.

Reaction time depends upon the strength of the stimulus. In general, the stronger the stimulus, the quicker the reaction time for all sense organs. In the case of light, however, this difference is rather negligible. For instance, in one experiment with light it was found that the reaction to a stimulus of moderate intensity was .191 seconds; but when the stimulus was reduced by 90 per cent, the reaction time was reduced by only .017 seconds, or by only about 9 per cent (Froeberg[21]). Similar effects are obtained when we increase the area of exposure to the stimulus or when we increase the duration of the stimulus.

Reaction time depends upon the nature of the fore-period. At a track meet the starter says to the competing runners, "On your mark —set—" and then comes the "BANG" of the pistol. The pause which elapses between the word "set" and the "BANG" is usually varied by a skillful starter, so that the runner cannot anticipate the exact moment of the pistol shot. Careful experiments have shown that the reaction times are shorter when the subject is warned. Some time is required to build up the state of readiness making for the quickest response. Consequently the period between warning and stimulus should not be shorter than one second. On the other hand, the state of readiness to respond cannot be maintained for more than about four seconds; therefore, the warning should come about one to four seconds before the final stimulus. The experienced starter varies the period of warning within these limits; the runners are thus forced to respond to the sound of the gun itself rather than starting just before they expect the gun in order to get the "jump" on the others.

Measurements have been made of muscular activity during the fore-period of a key-pressing reaction (Davis[22]). It has been found that muscular tension in the forearm increases toward the end of the fore-period and is greater during any part of the fore-period than when at rest. Also, reaction time has been found to be quickest when the muscular tension at the end of the fore-period is greatest.

Reactions become quicker with practice. Although reaction time does become shorter with practice, the improvement is largely limited to the first trials. A person soon reaches his physiological limit of reaction time to a particular stimulus under given experimental conditions. Another effect of practice is that, as the person becomes adjusted to his task, his reaction time varies much less from one trial to the next, tending to stay pretty constantly near his average. One important reason why reaction time becomes shorter and less variable with practice is that the subject learns to ignore distractions and pay close attention to his task of responding as soon as the stimulus is perceived.

Reaction time varies with age. Representatives of the Galton Eugenics Laboratory in England set up apparatus for measuring reaction time at various public places, such as railroad stations and fairs (Pearson[23]). They had thousands of people of different ages serve as subjects, out of curiosity or to kill time while waiting for a train. They found that reaction time decreases from infancy until the age of maturity, and then increases in adulthood and old age. The performance of a seventy-year-old is equal to that of a child of ten. Similar results have been found with large groups of subjects tested on a brake-reaction apparatus (DeSilva[24]).

The effect of high altitude on reaction time. Quick reaction time is an important characteristic of the good airplane pilot. He is often called upon to "do something and do it quickly," and slowness may lead to injury or death. One of the obstacles to altitude flying is that the low oxygen pressure at high altitudes slows the pilot's reaction time. That low oxygen pressure continues to have this effect as long as one stays in it is indicated by the fact that people who live in the Andes have slow reaction time (McFarland[25]).

Body temperature and reaction time. Reactions are quicker when the temperature of the body is high from natural causes than when the temperature is low (Kleitman *et al.*[26]).

The effect of caffein on reaction time. Coffee and certain soft drinks contain a stimulant, caffein. This drug shortens reaction time temporarily (Gilliland and Nelson[27]).

Complex reactions are slow. In the reaction-time experiments considered so far, the subject knew in advance what his response was to be. He also knew what stimulus to expect, and the stimulus in successive trials was always the same. Here the problem was that of discriminating the stimulus from no stimulus. But in other reaction-time experiments the reaction is more complex. Conditions are so arranged that the subject is to react in one way if a particular stimulus is given and in another way if another stimulus is given. For example, he is instructed to press a key with his left hand when a red light flashes, but to press a key with his right hand when a green light flashes. Such experiments are called *discrimination*, or *choice*, reactions. Reaction times under these more complicated (and more lifelike) conditions are considerably longer, especially when the stimuli are very similar and thus hard to discriminate.

Experiment has shown that it takes longer to distinguish between two colors which are near each other on the color wheel (like red and orange) than it does to distinguish between two colors which are far apart (like white and black). Similarly, it takes longer to tell which of two lines is the shorter as the difference between the lengths decreases. (Henmon[28])

One of the reasons why complex reactions are slow is that there can be no preparatory "set." The subject knows that any one of several different reactions may be called for, and does not know which to prepare for—for instance, whether to be set to press the key for the red, green, or amber light. And actually, of course, most of the reactions we are called upon to make in daily life are much more complex than this. The man driving down an icy street must utilize many complex visual and auditory stimuli to judge the slipperiness of the street and the distance and speed of oncoming cars, and must be quick to observe traffic lights or drivers' signals. He must then integrate his responses into the complex behavior patterns of using his hands on the wheel and his feet on the accelerator, brake, or clutch. Often, too, the discrimination is made more difficult by the presence of many other complex stimuli, like the car radio or the conversation of a friend.

Knowledge of individual reaction time is very helpful in sports, in laboratory work, in aviation, and in industry (especially in high-speed precision work like inspecting parts on an assembly line). The emphasis on speedy and accurate perception permeates our everyday lives.

How accurately can we observe and report?

If this is an age of speed, it is also an age of precision. From football to chemistry to machine design to newspaper reporting, people must observe and report accurately the conditions around them.

Causes of faulty observation. Errors of observation and report arise from many causes. Of course, the person who has some defect in sensory equipment, whether temporary or permanent, cannot observe accurately—nor can the person who is not giving his full attention to a situation. But even if a person receives all the necessary stimuli he may not perceive the situation accurately, for his perception is, as you know, influenced by many factors, such as his interest and set. Finally, a person may observe a situation accurately but if he does not have occasion to give a report on it until sometime later, lapses in memory may cause him to give a faulty report.

How false testimony arises. An unusual experiment was once performed to test how well college students can observe and report. In the middle of a no more than usually dull lecture—just as the lecturer was pointing to an exposure apparatus which showed a large card bearing the letters NIZ—an excited man clad in a white laboratory gown burst into the classroom by the east door, shouting, "Did you take my memory apparatus?"

> *Lecturer:* Yes, I need it for a demonstration.
> *Stranger:* You can't have it. I have a subject waiting. I need the apparatus for my research.
> *L (with dignity):* Kindly wait until the end of the hour and then you may have the apparatus.
> *S (loudly):* I want it right now, and I am going to have it.
> *L (angry and shouting):* You'll leave that apparatus alone if you know what is good for you.
> *S (very angry):* You'll give me that apparatus if you know what's good for *you.* I'm going to the Chief.
> *L (through clenched teeth):* Please leave this room.
> *S:* If I do, this goes with me. (*He seizes apparatus and throws it on the floor, scattering cards in many directions. Leaves by the east door.*)

By the time the dispute was well under way, the students were paying close attention. Some showed clearly their feelings of distaste toward such childish behavior in two adults. After order was restored, the lecturer explained that he and the visitor were really good friends, and that the whole episode was prearranged to test the abilities of the class to observe and report with accuracy a simple incident. Mimeographed sheets containing questions as to what had happened were distributed, and the students were asked to answer them to the best of their knowledge.

Under these conditions, you might expect the accuracy of report to be at its highest. In the first place, the students were already looking at the lecturer's platform; second, they were asked to give their reports immediately and before talking with anyone who might influence their reports; third, the printed blanks served to help them organize their memories of the situation; fourth, the situation was not one to provoke strong emotion, which can so easily upset our ability to observe.

In spite of these factors favorable to accurate observation, the answers were extremely inaccurate. A total of seventeen questions was asked, and no student answered all of them correctly. Four of the questions follow:

1. *At what time did the stranger enter the room?* (He had entered the room at 9:30 A.M., just as the clock struck.) Despite this aid, the estimates of the time varied from 9:20 to 9:43. A difference of twenty-three minutes might easily mean an alibi in a criminal trial.

2. *What was the color of the stranger's necktie?* (He wore none.) Out of a group of 97 students 51 refused to answer, 17 said that he wore none, 29 named the color of the nonexistent tie. The colors mentioned were tan, brown, green, gray, red, blue, black, and "dark." Undoubtedly the form of the question was responsible for the great inaccuracy in reporting this fact. Questions so worded as to suggest an incorrect answer are called "leading questions." They are sometimes used by unscrupulous lawyers to obtain false testimony from honest but naïve witnesses.

3. *Did the stranger's companion enter by the east door or by the west door?* (There was no companion.) This is another type of leading question which is effective, because in suggesting two alternatives it has the air of authenticity. The results from this question are shown in the table below:

East door	51
West door	5
No answer	13
No companion	28
Total	97

You will remember that the stranger came in alone by the east door and left the same way. Now, suppose that the observer had no memory of the companion. The form of the question in assuming that there was a companion would probably cause the observer to reason like this: "The companion *must* have come in by the east door if he was with the stranger." Thus inference is substituted for observation.

4. *What nonsense syllable was in the apparatus?* This was a straightforward question with no attempt to lead the answer. The results here were gratifying. Seventy-eight students gave the syllable NIZ correctly. This indicates that meaningless facts can be accurately observed if the attention is directed to them. The students quite naturally thought that the nonsense syllable was to play a role in the demonstration and noted it carefully before their attention was attracted to something else.

Many sources of error combined to account for the faulty observations made by the students. Most of the errors are to be attributed to poor attention, however. The students were poor observers because they "didn't know what they were supposed to see." Observation errors of this type can be greatly reduced by training. An important part of this training consists in knowing what you are expected to observe. Detectives are decidedly better than others in ability to observe, because they practice intensively for their tasks. They know what clues to look for.

We observe what we expect to observe. Advertisers make use of an important psychological principle when they build up in people the expectation that their product has certain desirable qualities. Some of the best illustrations are found in cigarette advertising. The manufacturer of each popular brand of cigarettes makes distinctive claims for his product, and habitual smokers profess to have deep-seated preferences for certain brands of cigarettes. How much of the preference is based on some real difference between the taste or smell of the smoke of the cigarette—and how much is purely the result of expectation built up through clever advertising? To answer this question, a "blindfold test" was conducted on habitual smokers, who were asked to identify the cigarettes which they sampled without knowledge of the trade name.

Each of the subjects in this experiment (fifty-one college students) was blindfolded and given five cigarettes of different brands to smoke in random order. Each was told that one of the five cigarettes would be of the brand that he had previously announced as his favorite, and each was asked to identify each brand. The table shows how well the subjects succeeded in identifying five brands of cigarettes on the basis of taste and smell alone. (Italics indicate correct identifications.)

ACTUAL BRAND	Camel	Lucky Strike	Chester- field	20- Grand	Spud	Misc.
			PERCENTAGE CALLING THE BRAND:			
Camel	*31*	14	38	6	2	10
Lucky Strike ...	19	*41*	21	4	0	14
Chesterfield	27	23	*33*	2	0	15
20-Grand	38	26	3	*17*	0	15
Spud	0	6	6	0	*76*	11

Notice that Camels were more frequently identified as Chesterfields than as Camels. The erroneous identifications of 20-Grands as Camels were over twice as frequent as the correct identifications. Chesterfields and Lucky Strikes, on the other hand, were correctly identified more frequently than they were named as any single other brand. On the average, the accuracy of identification for all subjects and all brands was only slightly better than would be expected by chance in the case of the nonmentholated brands. Even the mentholated Spuds were correctly identified only about three fourths of the time. (Husband and Godfrey[29])

After studying the results of this experiment, you may wonder why people "always buy Chesterfield" or "walk a mile for a Camel." These results seem to indicate that many people cannot tell one brand from another with much accuracy. So why do so many smokers insist that their own particular brand has such special qualities? The answer is that the advertisers have told them that the special qualities are there, so that when they smoke a cigarette they may imagine they observe the qualities described in the advertisements.

When we observe our psychological processes introspectively, the main impression we can get is that, ordinarily, we engage in some rather unified and relatively simple processes. We listen to music as something which is not just a medley of sounds, but which has a definite pattern of sounds. We are conscious of the meaning of the remark which someone has made, perhaps, but we do not bother with noting the exact tone that he used or the exact words he employed. We see that a car is approaching so rapidly that we need to wait before trying to cross the street, but we are not conscious of the process by which we judge the speed of the oncoming car.

Thus there is a great deal of difference between the unorganized nervous impulses which pour into the central nervous system from the sense organs and, on the other hand, the well-organized and meaningful processes of which we are conscious. This organizing occurs through the processes we have been considering in this chapter. As we have said, they are processes that go on so automatically, for the most part, that we do not ordinarily appreciate the fact that there are such processes. But psychological research on these processes can help you to appreciate the fact that they are both complex and important.

An ingenious tri-dimensional maze used with rats to derive principles of learning. Invented by Dr. Walter S. Hunter of Brown University.

CHAPTER 9

Learning: its basic nature

What Is Learning?

Conditions Necessary for Learning

How We Measure Learning

Learning and Age

Learning is the great means of adjustment in human beings. We do not have the wealth of instinctive reactions found in some animals —for example, we cannot instinctively build our houses as the beaver can build its dam. But human beings have an enormous capacity for learning such as is found in no other animal. The use of this learning capacity is what especially distinguishes human life in all its richness, complexity, and potentiality.

For decades psychologists have been formulating theories and conducting experiments on just what learning is, how it can be measured, and under what conditions it occurs. This work is of special interest to the college student, for he is investing time, energy, and money in trying to learn efficiently and effectively the things which will make him more adequate in his vocation and in his social, emotional, and intellectual life. Many of the student's problems in learning and thinking have already been discussed in Chapter 2 on *The Management of Learning*, along with some practical procedures for meeting those problems. This chapter on *Learning: Its Basic Nature* and the next on *Remembering and Thinking* will discuss some of the theoretical principles which explain the efficacy of those practical procedures, and will suggest further applications.

LEARNING: ITS BASIC NATURE 314

Knowledge of the learning process is useful not only to the student but to everyone interested in social and personal problems. We live in a rapidly changing society in which the working out of new materials and methods by industry and by science is creating a host of social problems. We now have the opportunity—as did no previous civilization—of eliminating poverty, economic want, widespread disease, and war. To take advantage of this unique opportunity, we must learn more about "what makes men tick." How do some people *learn* to be Fascists (whether they call themselves that or not)? How do some people *learn* to be strongly prejudiced against other races or religious groups, and how do other people *learn* to resist pressures that would tend to make them intolerant? How do individuals *learn* the emotional patterns that determine their relationships to other people and their attitudes toward themselves?

We do not need to stress exclusively the practical reasons for interest in the problems of learning. From a purely theoretical standpoint this is one of the central topics of psychology. Human nature as we know it is so strongly a product of learning that any person who wants to get a better understanding of human life must center much of his interest in problems of learning.

WHAT IS LEARNING?

IT IS IMPOSSIBLE to give a brief definition of learning. Learning is a broad, diversified field which influences almost every phase of human activity. Thus the definition of learning which holds true for one part of the field of learning may not hold true for some other part. There are several different ways of looking at learning which are accurate enough for parts of the field of learning, but only for parts. Only the last of the ways we shall now list is broad enough to cover the field of learning as a whole.

Ways of looking at learning

Learning as improvement. We often are inclined to define learning in terms of improvement—to say that the way to tell whether a person is learning is to find whether his responses are becoming faster, more accurate, more efficient, or less fatiguing. But while learning can accomplish such desirable changes, it can also produce opposite effects. The person who is studying to be a musician can learn to have stage fright. The bricklayer or the golfer can learn to make some movements which make his performance worse, rather than better. The child who grows up in a harsh and unsympathetic home can learn some emotional habits which will make his life unhappy as an adult. We cannot think of learning merely as a process which leads to improvement.

Learning as a product of rewards. Sometimes learning is said to arise from a frustrating situation in which the learner at first cannot reach his goal and tries out several different ways of responding before one response finally secures him a reward (or a relief from the frustration). By this definition, learning results from conflict, varied response, and reinforcement of one response through reward.

But while it is true that learning occurs in such situations and as a result of such influences, there are other situations in which it occurs *without* such goal-seeking, varied responses, and reward. Psychologists speak of some of such situations as *conditioning* situations. You are already familiar with conditioning experiments in which, for example, infants were taught to make innate toe responses to the sound of a buzzer. For the present, let us consider a more familiar example:

Suppose that a boy is walking past a house when a dog runs toward him from the porch, does a little preliminary growling, and then grabs him by the calf with a businesslike nip. Just then the owner appears on the porch, calls the dog off, listens to the boy's opinions about such dogs and their owners, and then takes the dog inside. The boy then goes on down the street, perhaps a little hurt physically, but much more shaken up emotionally.

In this situation there was not much time for the boy to try varied ways of dealing with such dogs. Nevertheless, learning has occurred. Depending on the boy's temperament and past learning, he is likely to act like a changed person when he goes past that same house the next time. If he has to walk past often on his way to school or work, he may adjust by walking on the other side of the street, by carrying a stick, or in various other ways. This learning, of course, did not occur in that earlier actual situation, but *after* it and by a process of thinking; and that thinking, in a way, would correspond to the picture of learning as resulting from a varied trial-and-error activity. For instance, the boy may consider the possibility of suing the man; he may think of carrying a bone so that he can make friends with the dog (or so that he can at least implement a policy of appeasement); if he is angry enough he may even think of poisoning it or shooting it. In his thinking he "tries out" a greater variety of responses than he tries out in reality.

This situation does show, admittedly, that learning may result partly from a varied response—in thinking. But the boy's thinking takes place only because some learning has already occurred in the previous situation where there was no time for varied response. Thus we see that learning cannot be thought of simply as a change of response in relation to a goal. For learning can occur in situations in which there is no opportunity for trying various means of reaching the goal.

Learning as the result of motivation. Obviously the boy in the example above was frightened and angry, or else he would not have taken the time and energy to think out the best procedure for dealing with the dog. From such examples, we are inclined to draw the conclusion that learning must depend partly on motivational processes. But this conclusion likewise does not prove true as a universal statement.

In the previous chapter, in connection with the discussion of perception, you will remember the drawing which could be seen as portraying the head and face either of a young woman or of a haggard old woman. As you learned there, the person who looks at either one of the single-phase drawings first—even though he merely glances at the drawing and then looks at the composite—will have learned something that will influence his perceptual organization of the composite drawing. Here is a situation in which learning takes place *in the absence of motivation.*

It may be argued, of course, that the subject has to be motivated sufficiently to get him to look at the several drawings, but actually very little motivation is required for that. There are no varied responses —the single-phase drawings are simple enough that when the person looks at either one of them, he sees immediately what it represents. And he feels no reward from this (unless we are to say that the person has an urge to "perceive clearly" and that this urge has been satisfied). Yet in spite of this absence of strong motivation or of varied response or of any very specific reward, learning does occur.

Learning as a change in the nervous system and thus in response. Quite apparently, then, we are not attempting a simple task when we try to answer the question "What is learning?" Perhaps the best we can say is that *learning is a changing of the individual's ways of responding.* It is a changing which comes from his thinking, perceiving, emotional reactions, or other psychological activity. But it is not such changing of his behavior as comes, for instance, when he gets tired because of the work that his muscles have done and because of chemical changes of the blood stream. *Learning involves a changing of the central nervous system* so that it will operate in a different way with the nervous impulses which come in to the central nervous system. We do not know

Learning is a continual process

enough yet about the nervous system to say what kind of changes these are, but we do know with reasonable certainty that learning in the vertebrates is dependent on changes in the brain—changes in the one part of the body in which man is most strikingly different from the lower animals.

When we say that learning is a "changing of the nervous system so that a different response is later made in the same situation," we ought to make clear that we are not using the word *response* merely in the sense of a muscular or glandular reaction—that is, merely in the sense of an *effector response* or *response of the effector organs*. In psychology, the more generalized word *response* means *internal responses* as well. For example, when you learn to understand and enjoy music, you are not concerned with the muscular movements that you make as you listen to music, but with a conscious response process which is much richer than might be suspected by anyone watching your effector reactions, and which can be observed directly only by an introspective approach.

In human society, much learning depends upon the transmission of the results of learning from one generation to the next. It is almost impossible for us to appreciate the degree to which our present human

ability is the product of the intellectual tools (like language, mathematics, and writing) and of the other cultural tools which we have inherited from long ages of human learning. So important is the communication of the products of learning that one of our largest professions is charged with the task of helping the young to learn. But while school activities and books are very important, learning is not limited to formal education—it is part of our leisure activities and recreation. Much learning is acquired through radio, the theater, the movies, athletic activities, advertising, museums, public lectures, and discussions with friends. Because of the continual change and variety in human life, the opportunity and necessity for learning do not cease to exist outside of school. Learning is and must be a continual process, as suggested in the illustration above.

Kinds of habits established by learning

The preceding discussion has shown that learning is not always a matter of improvement of responses, nor is it always a product of reward, of motivation, or of trial and error—but learning must be considered in more inclusive terms. Learning is a matter of producing changes in the person (or, more accurately, in his central nervous system) so that the later presentation of the same situation or similar situations will evoke a different response. These modifications which learning leaves in a person are known to the psychologists as *habits*. Here there is a difference of usage between popular speech and psychological terminology. In everyday speech the word *habit* refers only to extensively practiced and well-established modes of response. In psychology it refers to *all* products of learning, even to impressions which result only from one learning experience or which are so transitory that they rapidly fade away. When psychologists wish to refer to automatic ways of responding, they speak of "well-established habits" rather than just of "habits."

Just as the psychologist might hesitate in trying to establish a general definition of learning, so he might well hesitate in trying to distinguish different *kinds* of habits. Since our present knowledge is incomplete, it may well be that we will list different kinds of habits as separate from one another when they really belong together. Only as we get a more detailed knowledge of the principles of learning in all areas can we say with assurance what habits display different properties or are described by different laws, so that we will know adequately what habits to group together. In the meantime, we must make some tentative classifications and interpretations. Here we shall consider: (1) sensory organization or perceptual habits, (2) motor habits, (3) conditioned responses, (4) emotional and motivational habits, (5) adjustment techniques, (6) interpretive habits, and (7) symbolic habits (which are used especially in thinking).

Sensory-organization or perceptual habits. From the discussion of perception in Chapter 8, you will remember that even when a person sees or hears something new and strange, the central nervous system always operates to organize into some kind of patterned activity the nervous impulses which result from that stimulation. For example, if you are unfamiliar with the following drawings, you will nevertheless see each of them as one unified drawing:

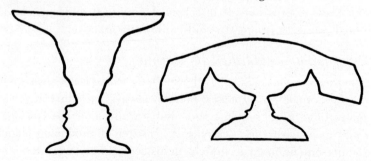

What is more, if you glanced at such drawings only briefly each time, you could see them a great number of times without learning to perceive them in any other way. The figure on the right, for example, might remind you of one type of telephone, and that would be all. The other would look merely like some peculiar urn or perhaps a bird bath. If you stare rather fixedly at each figure, however, you find that your perception finally reorganizes itself. And from that experience, you *learn* to see such drawings in a second way which tends essentially to separate each drawing into two parts. The skill thus acquired is an example of a sensory-organization or perceptual habit.

A considerable amount of human learning is of this sort. An untrained person, for instance, cannot get any adequate perceptual processes from complex music—if you asked him to listen to the melody played by the oboes in a symphony concert, you would be asking him to do the impossible. A person who has not had clinical training would be unable to hear, through the stethoscope, the heart murmurs that the physician can identify. The expert on football can see precisely a large number of details in each play, but to the novice there is only a confusion of arms and legs out there on the field.

When a complex flood of nervous impulses comes into the brain, therefore, the organization or patterning which they will have is a consequence not merely of innate or unlearned organizing properties of the nervous system, but also of one type of habit acquired by the person. In other words, the perceptual habits you have learned in the past (for instance, through hearing a piece of symphony music repeatedly) help determine what you perceive.

Motor habits. When a person is acquiring new muscular coordinations as a mode of response to some situation, we ordinarily say he is acquiring *motor habits*. When a person is just learning to swim, he is likely to complain that he has to remember to do too many things at once—that he cannot get his breathing, arm movements, and leg movements into one smooth pattern of action. But after he has learned to swim, this problem of coordinating his movements offers no difficulties.

Some psychologists have preferred the term *perceptual-motor habits* to the term *motor habits*. There is some advantage in this expression, for any motor habit depends on learning to utilize the stimulations available in the situation. Any complex muscular activity has to be guided not only by some stimulation by external materials but also (and this is very important) by kinesthetic stimulation resulting from previous phases of the activity. For example, when you are swimming, you learn to perceive when you can breathe without getting a mouthful of water, and the timing of one part of the stroke with reference to another is dependent on kinesthetic perceptions. But there is not time, in such rapid movements, for each phase of the movement to wait for the kinesthetic experience or kinesthetic perception from earlier phases, so that they can still be regarded as habits in which there is *an organization of nervous activity for discharge to the muscles.*

Conditioned responses. A very important type of habit, as you already know, is the change of response occurring through conditioning. The classical experiment in conditioning was performed by the Russian physiologist, Pavlov, at the start of this century.

> Meat powder was placed in a dog's mouth, and it was observed that saliva flowed more freely than before. This automatic, inborn behavior was called the *unconditioned reflex.* But when a bell was sounded in the presence of the dog, there was no change in the rate of flow of saliva. When, however, a bell or some other suitable incidental stimulus was presented just before the meat powder was placed in the mouth, and this association was repeated a number of times, the bell alone came to produce the increased flow of saliva. This new connection between bell and salivation was called a *conditioned response,* and the bell or other previously neutral stimulus was called the *conditioned stimulus.*

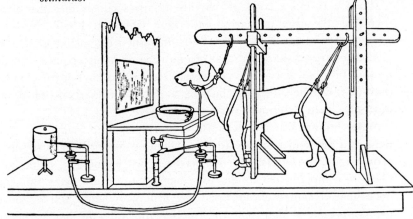

Pavlov's early experiments on conditioning. *The dog is held in place with a harness, and the dish of food is placed before him. The duct of one of his salivary glands has been opened out on to the outer surface of the cheek by a relatively simple and painless operation. Into this opening is inserted a small glass funnel, through which the saliva flows into a small glass tube. As the saliva drops fall out of the tube, they activate a lever* (center) *which in turn, through an airtube, activates a stylus* (far left). *The stylus moves upon a revolving drum, thus recording both the quantity and the rate of salivary secretion—that is, the number of drops that are secreted in a given interval of time.*

(From R. M. Yerkes and S. Morgulis, "The Method of Pavlov in Animal Psychology," *Psychological Bulletin,* 1909, 6: 257. Courtesy of American Psychological Assn.)

In the case of such conditioned responses, it does not at first appear that any very complex process is involved. Especially in earlier years, conditioning was rather commonly interpreted as merely the establishment of a nervous connection between (1) the new stimulus or signal (the bell) and (2) the same effector activity (the glandular secretion) which originally had been called out by (3) the conditioning stimulus (the food).

However, as psychologists have accumulated a richer experimental knowledge about conditioning, they have come to the conclusion that conditioning is not so simple as was originally thought. For it is not always true that the animal will make exactly the same response to the signal, after conditioning, that he made to the stimulus in the original learning situation. Instead, the learner is likely to make a response which is more or less adapted to, or appropriate for, the later situation. For example, a person who has been conditioned to lift his finger from an electric grid at the sound of a buzzer will not necessarily give the same muscular response when he is tested later in a situation which is similar except for the fact that his hand is placed on the grid in such a way that a different muscular movement is required to lift it from the grid.

Psychologists now are more generally inclined to say that in a conditioning situation, the learner to some extent is learning to make some preparatory response to the situation. He is not necessarily learning to make the same reflex reaction which he made in the learning situation. That is one reason why modern psychologists almost always use the term of *conditioned responses,* rather than Pavlov's term of *conditioned reflexes.*

What, then, is learned in a conditioning situation? *Primarily,* the learner in a conditioning situation is learning what to expect from that situation. When he is stimulated by the signal, a process of anticipating the other stimulus is aroused within him. From this anticipatory process and from the learner's perception of his present situation, there is produced, *secondarily,* some effector reaction which is more or less appropriate to the situation. Thus, when the human subjects were tested with their hands placed on the grid in a new way, their reactions were determined by the combined effect of their perception of how their hands were placed, and of their expectation that the signal would be followed by an electric current in the grid.

To say that conditioned learning involves anticipation does not mean that the person or animal needs to be *conscious* of the effector activity which finally is produced. You cannot be conscious of whether the glands in your stomach are producing a gastric secretion, but if you suddenly are put in a situation in which you anticipate that there is going to be a wreck, your gastric secretions will suddenly stop. The situation in conditioning is the same: Pavlov's dogs apparently were anticipating the fact that they were to receive food, so that the natural effector reaction would be a salivary reaction. In this case, it happens that the original response and the conditioned response have a similar element to them, but this superficial similarity does not alter the fact that conditioned responses can be different from the unconditioned responses in many situations.

As psychologists have come to understand the role that anticipation plays in conditioning, they have been helped to relate the experiments on conditioning to the experiments on trial-and-error learning. For, in such trial-and-error learning, as is well proved, the animal becomes modified in such a way that it will now be able to make a rather flexible and adaptable response to the situation.

> Thus it has been demonstrated that, after a rat has learned to go through a maze without entering the blind alleys, the rat can receive rather serious injuries to the spinal cord, so that it may virtually have to roll through the maze to get through, and yet it will still be able to dodge the blind alleys (Lashley and Ball[1]). In the same way, a monkey that has learned to open a puzzle box with one paw will shift to the other paw if he is prevented from using the paw employed in the original learning (Lashley[2]).

Results like these can best be harmonized with the conclusion that *conditioning is a matter of the animal's learning to expect the second stimulus.*

Emotional and motivational habits. In most respects it is probably not necessary to list emotional and motivational habits as distinct from conditioned responses. But our habits of responding emotionally in one way or another are so important that they deserve emphasis. A chief way in which people differ from one another in their personalities is in their emotional habits. In a friendly social gathering, for instance, one person will respond with spontaneous, whole-hearted enjoyment of the situation; another person responds mainly with anxiety or perhaps with an undercurrent of hostility toward the others. As we shall see in Chapter 14, psychotherapy frequently is directed toward changing such emotional habits.

Recent experiments in animal learning have shown the necessity for taking into account both emotional habits and other types of motivational habits.

In one significant experiment, four groups of rats were trained to run down a straight pathway to get some pellets of food in the end-box. In one group, each rat received 4 tiny pellets at the end of its daily run; in another group, 16 pellets were the reward; in another group, 64 pellets; and in another, 256 pellets (about two thirds of the day's diet). The rest of each rat's food supply was carefully controlled so that all the rats were kept equally hungry at the time of each day's run.

It was found, first of all, that the speed of running was somewhat proportional to the size of the reward. That is, the rats that were "paid most" ran fastest. In itself, this finding does not tell us very much —we could not say, for instance, whether the 256-pellet group actually were *expecting* such a large reward on each trip, or whether the large reward had operated merely to establish in them a rather mechanical habit of running more rapidly. However, by a variation in his situation, the experimenter secured the means of finding what had produced the difference of speed. On the twentieth trial, every rat received merely 16 pellets. Starting on the very next trial and lasting for at least half a dozen trials more, there were some remarkable changes in the behavior of the different groups. The rats formerly rewarded with 64 or with 256 pellets now ran more slowly than the group trained with 16 pellets throughout. The rats formerly rewarded with only 4 pellets were now the ones with the best speed record of all. (Crespi[3])

All these changes are shown in the graph below (except for the earlier runs on the 4-pellet group, which originally had been trained with 16 pellets for 21 trials, then had been trained with 4 pellets reward for 14 trials, during which their speed dropped to the point indicated for Trial 20; after which they were returned to the 16-pellet reward with the results shown on the graph).

Performance curves of rats in maze learning, showing influence of expectation of reward

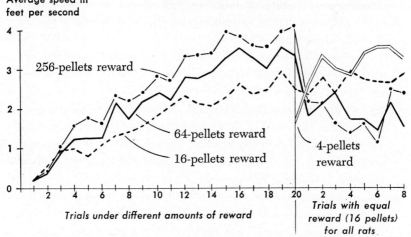

Graph after L. P. Crespi, "Quantitative Variation of Incentive and Performance in the White Rat," *American Journal of Psychology*, 1942, vol. 55, pp. 488 and 508.

In other words, a rat in a maze is not running merely because it is motivated by hunger or by some other bodily drive; it is running also because it has learned to expect a certain amount of reward. Such sets or expectations of amount of reward have motivational significance. And if experiments with animals must make allowance for this factor in motivation, it is obvious that in thinking of human behavior, we must think in terms of such motivational habits.

Adjustment techniques. As we shall see in Chapter 13, people differ widely in the habits which they develop as a means of responding to frustrations and to difficult situations. Thus some persons learn to depend upon boasting, upon "bossing" and dominating, or upon being very submissive and obliging even to the extent of producing serious conflicts within themselves by doing things they do not really want to do.

Such characteristic ways of handling life situations are called *adjustment techniques*. They are not always defective means of adjustment. A person might learn, for example, that the best way in which to get along with other persons is to try always to be honest, unpretentious, and interested in other people's ideas and problems. If he can make habitual such ways of responding, they would be adjustment techniques in just as true a sense as boasting or giving alibis. Sometimes psychological discussions of adjustment techniques have tended to stress faulty adjustments because so much of our knowledge of personality is drawn from clinical work with maladjusted persons, but the term *adjustment technique* refers both to unfavorable and to favorable means of handling life situations.

Interpretive habits. A large amount of our learning leads to the development of habits of understanding, or of knowing the meaning of many objects and situations. Such habits might be called *interpretive habits*. For example, when you see a car try to pass you on a bad curve, you react to that situation in terms of dangers which you know are present, and even though cars pass you on curves repeatedly without causing an accident, you still do not change the meaning that situation has for you. For these interpretive habits contain within themselves some consideration of both probabilities and seriousness. You would not say that every time a car passes another on a curve there will be a bad crash, but you might say, "one time out of fifty, maybe only one time out of five hundred—still, it is too much of a risk to take."

Of course such interpretive habits can be incorrect. In medicine, for example, it formerly was believed that a good way to treat many types of illness was to remove some of the blood from the person.

Farmers used to pull the "suckers" off corn to increase the yield; now we know from experimental studies that this actually reduces their crops by depriving the plants of part of their food-manufacturing facilities. The great aim of scientific research is to test the properties of things so that our interpretive habits can be sound.

Symbolic habits. A great many of the complex mental activities of human beings require the special type of interpretive habits which may be called *symbolic habits*. Essentially, these are habits of using stimuli (such as printed words, maps, or musical scores) or of using response processes (such as your own internal use of words when you are thinking about something). But they are habits of using stimuli and response processes which are only arbitrarily related to the things actually represented. For instance, there is nothing in the symbol 2 which looks any more like two objects than does the symbol 5—in fact, the old Roman *II* was a less arbitrary designation than is the arabic numeral.

Such symbols, or systems of symbols, have had great value in helping us to handle complex problems, and great gains have been made in civilization as better symbols have been developed, even though they might be more arbitrary in some ways. You might compare, for example, the relative ease of making these two additions:

2046	as against	MMXLVI
34		XXXIV
697		DCXCVII

Human beings have a great capacity for learning to use symbols which are entirely arbitrary as designations, and modern culture owes a great deal to the earlier periods which developed most of the basic symbols now in use.

In this section we have surveyed what are now thought to be the main types of habits—sensory-organization habits, motor habits, conditioned responses, motivational habits, adjustment techniques, interpretive habits, and (last but far from least) symbolic habits. It is a long list, but it can help us realize how large and how important an aspect of human life is being considered when we are dealing with the field of learning.

The essential nature of different kinds of habits

Scientific work always tries to summarize its knowledge briefly and concisely. Consequently, when we are talking about the kinds of habits, it is natural and appropriate to ask whether our long list of kinds of habits cannot be reduced to some brief statement of the essential nature of habits of all types. Psychologists have, indeed, made such brief statements in several different forms, one of which has received tentative acceptance in the light of modern research into the basic nature of learning.

Habits as associations. For many years, psychologists generally were inclined to a concept of habits which runs back to the philosopher John Locke (1690)—the concept that habits are essentially "associations." Habits were thought of as linkages between separate things (between several sensations, several ideas, between stimulus and response, or between sense organs and muscles). In a sense this is true, and such terms have some value. But our available knowledge of physiological psychology indicates that we need some term which puts more emphasis on the idea that a habit is something which can produce a relatively elaborate pattern of activity in the *cortex* of the brain (shown on the color plate at the end of this book).

Stimulus-response connections. Psychologists have put a great deal of work into the question of whether habits may be described as "stimulus-response connections." Is this brief description accurate?

From some learning situations, it does appear that the subject's habit causes him to make some particular type of muscular movement or *response* whenever a certain *stimulus* is received. These muscular movements may even be ones which the person does not realize that he makes.

> For example, one experimenter taught his subjects to contract the muscles of the blood vessels in their arms. First, he sounded a buzzer or a bell or had the subject whisper the meaningless word "prochaska," and then immersed one hand of the subject in ice water. Finally, the subjects contracted the blood vessels in their arms in response to the sound of the buzzer, bell, or whispered word. (Menzies[4])

Such a conditioning experiment seems to suggest that the essential character of a habit is a connection or linkage between a stimulus and the muscular response brought out in the learning situation.

The facts, unfortunately, do not correspond with this concept. For example, when you learn to hum a certain piece of music, you produce all the variations of pitch by changes of the muscles in the larynx which govern the vocal cords. But *after* you have acquired this "habit" by your practice with humming, there is essentially no connection between each tone and further movements of the larynx. This is revealed by the fact that you now are able to whistle the same piece of music, and variations in pitch in whistling do not depend at all on the muscles of the larynx, but on the lips and tongue.

The same adaptability of muscular activity has been demonstrated in careful laboratory experiments.

> In the experiment already described on page 324, serious injuries to the spinal cords of rats did not prevent them from running without errors through a maze they had learned to run before the injury. The rats were so seriously injured that their muscular movements had to be most peculiar—one rat virtually had to roll through the maze. But the habit which the rats had acquired was apparently not just a connection that would produce certain movements, but some change in the nervous system which would permit surprising variations of movements to adapt them to serve, still, the same objective. (Lashley and Ball[5])

So even though psychologists would like to have some simple formulation of the essential nature of a habit, most of them are now dissatisfied with the theory that habits essentially are connections between certain stimuli and certain movements. Instead, they have been compelled to accept another conception of habit.

Habits as reintegrative mechanisms. Interestingly enough, it was a British philosopher, William Hamilton, who proposed in 1858 that we should think of learning as resulting in the establishment of *reintegrative mechanisms* (or, as he wrote the word to make it more euphonious, "redintegrative" mechanisms). This term is well suited to our present understanding of habits. It suggests very naturally the idea that the brain activity or perceptual processes in the original learning situation are complex and strongly patterned activities. It suggests, too, that when a habit is established, some change is made in the nervous system which makes it possible for the brain to rearouse or reintegrate, from some slighter stimulation, a brain process that originally could be called out only by much more adequate conditions of stimulation. In other words, a habit is some sort of modification of the nervous system —or more specifically, of the brain. It is a modification which makes it possible for a person or animal to *represent* to itself some properties of the situation which, before the habit was formed, could not be represented except by perceptual processes more heavily dependent on actual sensory stimulations.

From this statement, it might be expected that when we use a habit, we would actually perceive sounds, sights, and movements that do not exist in the present situation. And under certain conditions, this does happen. If you are accustomed to the movement of a second-hand over the face of an electric clock and if you happen to glance at the clock when it is stopped, you are likely to see the second-hand, momentarily, as though it were moving. You are able to get, "redintegratively" or "reintegratively," the same brain process which formerly could be aroused only from the adequate stimulation of the moving hand.

Ordinarily we do not get such "hallucinations" from the operation of habits. As we will see in our discussion of the conditions governing performance, habits are not used in isolation, for almost always we have some strong perceptual processes in operation as well. These processes tend to override the reintegrative representations of the situation where those representations are in conflict with the perception. Thus, even though you see the second-hand as moving momentarily, you cannot continue to get this effect for more than an instant. The perceptual processes get under way in more exact detail and correct the total brain process, although they cannot override some parts of the representational process aroused by the habit. For example, if you have learned to be afraid of riding in an automobile, your perceptual processes can inform you merely that an accident has not occurred up to that point on a particular trip. They cannot contradict or eliminate your habit-given representation of the situation as potentially dangerous.

Thus we may say that a habit is something which may lead to many different actions, depending on the details of the particular situation. It makes you anticipate, or be ready for, certain effects in the situation. And because of this anticipation or representation, all sorts of effects may follow. If a person anticipates that a car ride may be dangerous, he may invent some elaborate reasons why he cannot make the trip. If he anticipates that his hand is going to be immersed in ice water after he has heard a certain signal, the blood will leave the surface of his hand.

In this latter case you cannot demonstrate, just from that situation itself, that the habit is anything more than a connection between the *stimulus* of the buzzer sound and the "vasomotor" *response*. But the purpose of scientific experimentation is to locate the factors responsible for effects even when they cannot be seen directly. So as psychologists take into account all the range of their factual knowledge, they more and more are coming to the conclusion that *habits are changes that make it possible for relatively complex patterns of brain activity— which represent the properties the person or animal has learned to anticipate in that situation—to be aroused by less extensive stimulation than was required before learning occurred.*

As habits are retained and used over long periods, however, they may tend to deteriorate into more and more simple nervous mechanisms, so that eventually they may be virtually "stimulus-response connections." For example, a professional typist often will be unable to tell you, offhand, where the different keys are located on the typewriter keyboard. For many of the letters and characters she may have to stop and imagine that she is typing in order to find where they are placed. And even at that, she may describe their location incorrectly and not realize her error until she actually gets at the typewriter. Early in her career as a typist she would not have had this trouble, but all her original verbal habits regarding the keyboard, and her habits of visually imagining the keyboard, have not been used for years. So they have been forgotten, and the habit has tended to become more and more a *relatively* simple nervous connection between the stimulation she receives and the typewriting movements she makes.

This is true of many other habits as well. Originally you might have been able to give detailed reasons why you like one person and dislike another. After a lapse of some years, you would have forgotten most of the specific incidents which you once had learned to recall with reference to such a person. But the process of forgetting still would have left you with a friendly feeling for the one person and a dislike of the other.

Reintegrative mechanisms are not always used consciously. In fact, as our habits become better developed there is a tendency for them to operate unconsciously. Thus even in the early study of telegraphy it was noted that the experienced telegrapher is no longer conscious of the pattern of dots and dashes which convey the message or of the single words of which it is composed, although he may perhaps be conscious of the general meaning of the message. Reintegrative mechanisms do not always operate to produce conscious meanings and conscious expectations; they sometimes operate merely to govern behavior.

Ways of learning

For clarity and accuracy we need to make a distinction between *kinds of habits* and *ways of learning* because the same kind of habit, essentially, might be established by any of several ways of learning. You might learn to tie a certain knot, for example, by imitating someone else, by working it out through outward trial and error, or by attentive response.

Trial and error. The opportunity to learn by imitation does not eliminate the need for some trial-and-error activity on the part of the learner. Thus, when someone has shown you how to drive a car or how to swim, you still have not completed your learning. You have been helped, and you have learned something, but the whole process takes practice, or trial-and-error activity, on your part. *Trial and error* is a process of trying first one solution, then another, until the best one is found. There is a time in the life of every person when trial and error enters into the solution of even so simple a problem as adding two and three. The young child learns to solve his problem by manipulating small objects, such as beans, gum wads, his fingers, etc. When the problem has been successfully solved often enough by the trial-and-error method, no further trial and error are necessary.

Insight. Of recent years certain psychologists have made much of the fact that some solutions come suddenly and in the absence of observable trial-and-error manipulation of symbols or objects. Often there is a

period in which no progress toward the solution is apparent, followed by a sudden arrival at the solution. This phenomenon has been interpreted as due to the development within the person of *insight*, by means of some sudden reorganization of the perception of the situation. Especially has this suggestion been proposed in connection with several experiments with apes and children, respectively, in which rather sudden solutions were observed.

1 In a famous series of experiments with apes, the animals were placed in problem situations where materials at hand, if properly employed, could be used in reaching a solution. The problems were to get food by the proper use of various materials placed in the cage. In one of these experiments a basket of fruit was suspended from the

The experiments illustrated on this page are two in a series designed by Dr. Harry F. Harlow of the University of Wisconsin to discover, in monkeys, laws of thinking which will ultimately apply to human thinking. The first row of pictures shows a trial-and-error learning situation in which the monkey must learn to obtain a reward hidden under the problem box. In picture 1 at far left, the monkey studies the setup before making any move to take it apart. In picture 2, the puzzled monkey has removed the outside blocks and has tentatively pulled out one of the large pegs. Picture 3 shows him making a further effort to get at the hidden reward. Finally he succeeds in dismantling the box completely and gets the reward.

The second series of pictures shows the monkey faced with the problem of obtaining food placed out of his reach. He tries various methods. In picture 1, he attempts to reach the food by swinging from a rope. This failing, he strikes at the reward with a stick that is too short to reach it. The third picture shows the monkey trying to reach the food by standing on a box, which proves to be not high enough for the purpose. Finally (picture 4) he suddenly seems to gain insight into the fact that the reward can be obtained by climbing the pole instead of handling it in the way he had previously used the short stick. This last solution represents true insight, since the monkey had never before attempted pole-climbing, and such a method of getting the reward was new to him.

wire roof of the cage in such a manner that the basket could be made to swing back and forth by pulling a string. At one point of the arc described by the swinging basket was a scaffolding. The animal could catch the basket as it swung by jumping up on this scaffolding, although he could not reach it from the ground. The problem was to see whether he would be able to grasp this solution.

At the beginning of one set of observations the basket was set swinging and three apes, Chica, Grande, and Tercera, were let into the cage. Grande attempted to reach the basket by jumping—a routine response—but failed. Chica had in the meantime looked over the situation and suddenly jumped to the scaffolding to catch the basket as it swung past. The interpretation put on this behavior is that Chica had "insight," where the other animal was employing trial and error. (Köhler[6])

2 Another psychologist set up similar situations with children of pre-school age. In general, the children did better than the apes. Some of them used trial and error, while others seemed to "size up the situation" and then do the one right thing to get to the goal. For example, a toy would be placed far enough outside the play pen that it could not be reached. Some children would waste a considerable amount of time trying vainly to reach the toy, while others would seize a stick lying in plain sight and rake the toy in. The suddenness of the correct response and the lack of preceding trial and error are taken as signs of insight. (Alpert[7])

The interpretation of these studies is difficult, because it is not known whether the subjects had had previous experiences with the same kind of situation. If the subjects had previously worked out a similar situation by trial and error, it is quite possible that the original solution would be suddenly recalled and used, so that the behavior could not properly be called "insight." The further possibility is that the solution was worked out by trial-and-error use of symbols. The fact that the overt acts of the solution came suddenly would not afford

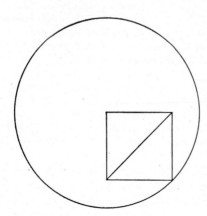

unmistakable evidence of insight, for insight may be nothing more than a suddenly successful trial.

If you wish to observe how you yourself may suddenly get insight into a situation, you should attempt to solve the following problem. (The answer will be found at the end of the chapter, but do not look at it until you are certain that the solution will not come.) Look at the figure. The diameter of this circle is two inches. One corner of the square is at the center of the circle. How long is the diagonal line?

Those of you who get the solution will notice that when it comes it comes very suddenly. Many students report that even here there is a preliminary period of trial-and-error solution which is eventually given up.

Trial and error and insight are not easily separated. Insight may come during an attack which started as trial and error and terminated in a sudden recognition of the adequate solution. But the final solution may also be arrived at by a sort of trial-and-error exploration of a series of hypotheses, each of which comes by insight. Mathematicians frequently employ both insight and trial and error in solving mathematical problems.

Attentive response. A great deal of learning is accomplished in still another way besides those mentioned above—merely by responding attentively to the stimulus-situation. Perhaps we should not stress that word "merely" too strongly, for in situations where the learner is "merely responding attentively to the stimulus-situation," some very complex processes are going on within him. That is, he is perceiving different parts of the situation as having some relationship to each other and is giving meaning to different parts of the situation. Thus, in a conditioning situation, a dog hears a buzzer and then tastes the food placed in his mouth. Partly because of the close time-relations between these two events and partly because other distracting stimuli have been removed, he perceives these two events as related to each other—that is, he learns to expect food when the buzzer is sounded. In the same way, from having reacted attentively to your friends, you will have learned to distinguish the sounds of their voices. And from reading attentively the modern scientific views on human "instincts," you acquire certain factual material and new ways of interpreting other factual material you may encounter.

Of course, as you react attentively to some stimulus-materials, you are likely to engage in an appreciable amount of thinking, in a process which runs on faster than the perception of the particular material you are working with. For example, suppose that you were asked to memorize the following list of numbers: 2, 4, 8, 16, 32, 64, 128, 256. You would find that you could not work on this task merely by trying to remember the numbers as such. You would begin to see a relationship between them almost immediately, and it would be so much easier for you to learn them in terms of that relationship system that your thinking would be the main means of learning. In the experiments on rote memorizing, psychologists found that their subjects constantly looked for some means of organizing the materials to make the learning easier. So when a psychologist says that one of the means of learning is "merely reacting attentively to the stimulus-situation" he is stressing the fact that learning can go on *without any actual trial-and-error activity* but is not neglecting the fact that, as we shall see in the next section, learning cannot go on without some rather complex organizing or relating processes.

CONDITIONS NECESSARY FOR LEARNING

Everyday experience shows that some situations are much more effective than others in producing learning. The conditions productive of learning are not just of theoretical significance but have great practical importance in school, in industry, in athletics, in homemaking—in all the many life situations in which learning is a continual process. In this section we shall examine the factors which determine what is learned and how rapidly it is learned.

The general factor of internal organizing processes

In any learning situation (we might say, "in any life situation"), various parts of the situation are stimulating the person and arousing perceptual, and perhaps also motivational, processes within him. *Learning depends most essentially on some activity of the person whereby he perceives or grasps one part of the situation as being related in some particular way to another part of the situation.* Without this activity—without this relating of different things on the part of the learner—there may exist some of the external conditions which might be favorable to learning, but there can be no learning. A rather significant example can help to make this clear.

In the 1840's a young obstetrician, Ignaz Semmelweiss, became concerned about the problem of puerperal or childbed fever, a fatal disease which occurred with distressing frequency in the best obstetrical wards of his day. In the clinic where he was working, he found that 1989 women had died of puerperal fever in the last six years, and that in some months the mortality rate was as high as thirty per cent of all women who had given birth to children in that clinic. Physicians had been deeply concerned about the problem for more than half a century, and had formulated many hypotheses: perhaps it was a miasma, they said, or a product of too long confinement in the horizontal position, or a wandering of the mother's milk settling in the uncontracted womb. But all these hypotheses were ineffective in preventing the disease.

Now, Semmelweiss knew various facts about puerperal fever. (1) It was rare in women who gave birth to children soon after arriving in the hospital. (2) It was relatively unknown in rural districts. (3) It was less frequent during the vacations of the medical school, when there were few internes around to help with the work. (4) It was rare in cases handled by midwives rather than by the supposedly well-trained obstetricians! But still he did not learn the cause of childbed fever until one of his colleagues, conducting a post-mortem examination, cut his own hand with a scalpel, and within a few short days, died with the typical symptoms of childbed fever.

Pondering on all that he knew, Semmelweiss finally came to think of the fact that it was the practice for the medical workers to perform such post-mortem examinations and then, without sterilizing or even washing their hands, examine well patients. He formed the hypothesis, accordingly, that the disease was caused by the carrying of some trouble-making material from the bodies of infected persons to the bodies of women in labor. The hypothesis made sense of all the rest that he knew—the decrease of cases during vacations, when the curtailed staff could not make so many post-mortem examinations; the absence of it in case of hasty births; the absence of it in rural districts and in the midwife cases, where such examinations were not made at all. So he laid down strict rules that all workers must wash their hands in a disinfectant solution before treating well patients. And finally from March to September 1848 there was not a single death from childbed fever in his wards!

As we look back now, it may be hard to believe that intelligent men could not see the relation between their actions and the results, but today we are just as blind to the cause-and-effect relationships in some of the accepted features of our behavior. Learning does not occur just because the person is stimulated by separate aspects of a situation. The learner, by some internal activity, must perceive the relationships between the various aspects of the situation.

What are the specific conditions of learning—that is, the conditions which tend to facilitate or obstruct this occurrence of complexly organized perceptual processes in the learner? It is not sufficient for us to know merely that this organizing process in the learner is the essential or key feature of the learning process. We must know also what makes such processes more likely or less likely to occur—and the answer will not be simple or brief. Learning can be explained only in terms of a whole series of specific factors.

The specific conditions of learning

Exploration as a factor in learning. In many learning situations the learner has had no basis yet for representing to himself some properties of the situation. For example, when the baby starts to creep around on the floor and gets near the radiator, he has no past learning and no innate means of response that would cause him to represent the radiator as able to yield a painful burn, as being something to avoid. He can learn this only by exploring—either crudely by his own efforts, or with the aid of adult guidance so that he has a chance to touch the radiator without being badly hurt. He can learn efficiently from this situation. Part of what is required for this learning is exploratory activity.

The same thing is true of rats in mazes, cats in puzzle boxes, scientists trying to find a kind of mold more productive of penicillin, criminologists trying to find some way to make reformatories serve as real reformatories rather than crime colleges. The learner often has to get himself stimulated in some ways that will put him in contact with some properties of the situation which have previously been outside his experience.

Motivation as a factor in learning. There are various ways in which motivation contributes to learning, and one of the most important is especially relevant here because of its connection with exploration. *Motivation* is essential to produce the vigorous exploration which is indispensable in many learning situations. The rat in a maze, for instance, needs to have certain motivational conditions. It needs to have been tamed previously, so that it will not have some emotional reactions of fear which might prevent it from exploring or from eating readily when it finally reaches the end-box. And not only must the rat be fairly free from hampering motivational factors, but it must have some motive to induce it to explore actively. For this purpose hunger may suffice, or thirst, or the urge of a mother rat to return to her litter, or still other motives. The vigorous exploratory activity cannot occur, however, unless there is some favorable motivational situation.

One illustration of this same effect in human learning is given by the following study:

> In an elaborate study of how students' interests and attitudes are related to academic success, it was found that those students who had definitely decided upon their lifework received higher marks than those who had made no choice of vocation. The superior scholarship of the vocationally oriented students remained when the factor of intelligence was ruled out by a statistical procedure. According to this same study, students do their best work in elective courses, in which they are presumably more interested than in courses they are required to take. (Crawford[8])

Subject matter need not relate only to vocational plans to be of interest. Certain information is useful to anybody, regardless of how he earns his living. For example, the material in psychology which relates to personality adjustment is far more interesting to most students than material of a less personal nature. But the student who is able to become interested in material which is not directly relevant to himself and his immediate problems is the student who finds learning most rewarding. Other things being equal, the student who has broad interests will probably learn more than the student whose interests are narrowly oriented.

Another important example of the influence of motivation on learning is found in efforts to solve complex social questions. The problems of war, unemployment, housing, and lynching are, of course, far more complex than the problems confronting the rat in a maze or problem-box. Nevertheless, in both types of problem-solving situation, the same basic principles apply: (1) problem-solving learning depends upon persistent attack on the problem, or on persistent exploration; and (2) this in turn will occur only if the learners are strongly motivated to reach some goal. Some of our greatest difficulties in solving some of our social problems come because of this lack of motivation, or strong interest, in the individuals who possess most political influence, most control of policies of newspapers, and most education. An outstanding example is the difference between the way we have handled the problem of kidnapping and the way we have handled the problem of housing. In the early 1930's there was a wave of kidnapping crimes involving members of wealthy families, so that people of great political influence were motivated to help solve the problem, and it was solved. But the people who are strongly motivated to improve housing are generally without such influence, so that there has been no corresponding progress toward solving it. In learning to solve both simple and complex problems, motivation is a vitally important factor.

Close time relations as a factor in learning. One of the reasons why the ten-month-old baby can learn to avoid the radiator—and in merely one trial—is that there is great closeness in time between his seeing the radiator and his feeling the heat of it. Where there is a greater space of time between an action and its effect, learning becomes much more difficult. Several experimental studies recently have shown that learning apparently is made impossible in rats and in chimpanzees when a delay of as much as four or five seconds is introduced in discrimination-learning situations between the choice of one stimulus or the other and the attainment of either the related punishment or the related reward (Spence[9]).

In human beings our considerable use of symbolic habits might help to reduce the disadvantages of such delays; but even in human life it is noteworthy that the introduction of a time separation of cause and effect makes it very difficult for us to learn. Not until the start of this century, for example, was it learned that mosquitoes were the carriers of yellow fever and malaria. People knew that they were bitten by mosquitoes; they knew that they got such diseases; but, partly because of the temporal separation between the two events, they could not learn the relation between them. Here again is an example of how, in our modern world, we are dependent upon scientific research to learn about situations in which the conditions are absent which make for easy learning. Another interesting example is the fact that many primitive tribes are unaware of the relationship between sexual relations and pregnancy.

A laboratory demonstration of the importance of even brief temporal delays with human beings was given by the following study. In this experiment, comparisons were made of learning speed when knowledge of the accuracy of a response was withheld for different periods of time.

> Educated adult subjects tossed balls back over their heads at an unseen target. The results of the throw were announced to the subjects one, two, four, or six seconds after the throw, or not at all. With the longer delays, the rate of improvement in accuracy was slower than when the results were announced to the subject one or two seconds after the throw was completed. (Lorge and Thorndike[10])

The more immediately reward or punishment follows attempts at learning, the faster the progress of learning.

Favorable and unfavorable perceptual conditions as factors in learning. If the learner is to see two aspects of his life situation as related to each other—the essential condition for learning—then the learning situation must be suited to accomplish three things.

1 It must guarantee a clear perceptual response to the stimuli which might serve as cues or signals in the situation.

2 It must guarantee a clear perceptual response of the effect attained.

3 It must favor a perceiving of the signal as something related to the effect attained. (Or, in a case where the subject needs to learn the relation between some act and its consequence, the learner needs to have conditions which will favor the clear perception of that relation.)

Some learning situations present all three factors. For instance, suppose that a person drives his car off the road onto some wet, recently filled-in ground, and that the car soon stops, sunk in up to the hubs. It takes no great effort for the person to learn not to drive onto such ground again, because he can easily perceive the kind of ground onto which he drove, the effect which he secured thereby, and the means whereby the situation produced that effect.

On some other problems, any one or two or even three of these factors may be missing. During the Middle Ages, a common problem was the appearance of maggots on meat. In this case people could clearly perceive the end result; they could also clearly perceive the flies which swarmed around the pieces of meat and which laid the eggs which produced those maggots. But the connecting agents (the eggs) were so inconspicuous, and the perceptual qualities of the maggots were so different from the perceptual qualities of the flies, that centuries passed before people learned the true cause of the appearance of maggots. In other cases, only the end result is clearly perceived. Thus, only at the present time are scientists beginning to understand one of the causes of tooth decay, although they could clearly see the end result. Previously, they could not readily perceive the causal factors (such as low calcium and phosphorus content in food grown on inadequately fertilized ground), nor the means whereby such causal factors could get translated into dental troubles. Much of the work of science is devoted to the task of developing means of perceiving or identifying factors which otherwise would be passed over. For example, research men are trying to discover the means whereby poliomyelitis is transmitted, because, if a means of perceiving the connecting medium could be developed, much faster progress could be made in controlling the spread of the disease.

Even in animal experimentation, perceptual conditions have to be taken into account. Several types of experiment illustrate the importance of factors which facilitate the perception of the essential signals and of their relationship to the end results attained.

> In the type of apparatus originally used to study the capacity of animals for visual discriminations, the animal was placed in an apparatus in which, to reach food, it had to run past a card mounted on the wall of the apparatus and avoid running past a second card placed at another spot on the wall. The positions of the two cards were reversed from trial to trial (as in all discrimination experiments) to guarantee that the animals would not be able to reach food merely by learning which side of the apparatus to go to. When the rat made a wrong choice, it was punished by an electric shock from a grid on the floor in front of the wrong design; when the rat made a correct choice, it was allowed to proceed down a short passageway and reach food. With this type of apparatus it was found that rats apparently had extremely poor vision. They could learn to distinguish black from

white cards, but not one figure from another, even when these were grossly different.

In later experiments, however, it has become apparent that the failures in such earlier experiments were due *not* to the limited learning capacity of the rat, but to the deficiencies of the learning situation. In the later experiments, the rats were required to jump against one card or the other, so that it was sure that they looked at the cards. The punishment, particularly, came directly and immediately from the one card, since, if they jumped against it, they bumped their noses and fell to a net below. Under such conditions the rats were able to learn efficiently. Such experiments have proved that rats have fairly good vision, in fact. But note that the animals were not able to learn to make visual discriminations until the conditions were such as to create a favorable perceptual situation. (Lashley[11] and Lashley[12])

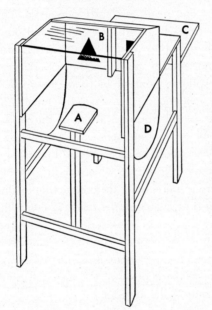

The discrimination apparatus used with rats. *The rat stands on the small jumping platform (A), barely large enough to hold him. Before him he sees two cards (B). Behind them, as he knows from past experience, is the platform with food (C). One of the cards (the "wrong" card) is fixed securely in place, so that if he jumps against it he will fall into the net below (D). The other ("correct") card will give way when he jumps against it and so permit him to reach the food.*
(K. S. Lashley, "The Mechanism of Vision: XV. Preliminary Studies of the Rat's Capacity for Detail Vision," Journal of General Psychology, 1938, 18:126.)

Dealing functionally with the situation. The learner, for best results, must actually work with the real materials he is trying to learn to deal with. For example, typewriting is not taught by the lecture method, and courses in music and home economics and sports have to provide the means whereby the student can actually work with the real materials.

When the learning task becomes less tangible, however, educators still typically neglect the principle that efficient learning requires the opportunity to deal functionally with real materials. It will prove expensive to teach animal psychology, child psychology, sociology, law, and other subjects in this way, and probably we will move toward this technique only rather slowly. But good learning requires it. As long as you still find that your academic courses do not provide opportunities for such learning, you might well keep in mind that you will need to find opportunities to do this same thing for yourself, if at all possible. You need to practice the functions you are trying to learn. If you are trying to learn to think, to plan experiments, or to direct social groups, you must actually be doing such work, not just reading or hearing about how it should be done.

"Set" as a factor in learning. Often we express surprise that a person has failed to learn something which, objectively speaking, he has had a chance to learn. We are sure that he saw or heard certain things, we are sure that he made some response, and we are sure that some reward or some punishment followed soon afterward (as in the case of the obstetricians of Semmelweiss' day). And yet nothing was learned. In such a case, it often may be found that the progress of learning was obstructed by some "mental set" on the part of the learner. This has been illustrated clearly by an experiment with animals.

> Using the jumping apparatus with rats, the experimenter (Lashley[13]) first of all trained each rat to jump to the card bearing a large circle and to avoid the card bearing a small circle. Then, after the rats had mastered that problem, he tested them by presenting them with the same small circle as opposed to a large triangle. All the rats, without error in ten trials apiece, chose the triangle as the card to jump against. They were then given another two hundred trials with this small circle and large triangle—more than twice as many trials as had been required in the original training. When the rats were then tested with a circle and a triangle of *equal area,* however, they showed no preference for either figure.
>
> The crucial feature of this experiment lies in the fact that we can be certain that the rats had looked at the triangle on each trial—in no other way could they tell which was the larger figure as the one to jump to. But the rats had learned originally to look for "relative largeness." As long as that quality still was available to guide their responses, they apparently either did not perceive the new shape which marked the larger figure or else did not perceive it as related to the attaining of the reward. Under other circumstances, rats can easily learn to distinguish a triangle from a circle.

Here is a good example of the fact that even in animal learning, the "set" within the animal is a factor which determines what will be learned.

"Hypothesizing before choosing" as a factor in learning. For efficient learning, the situation must often be arranged so that the learner cannot base his response merely on some easy perceptual guidance, or merely on some easy trial-and-error activity, but must be induced to stop and make up his mind as to which is probably the correct response before he actually makes that response. For example, you repeatedly have walked up a certain flight of stairs, but without learning how many steps there are—in each case you guide your walking perceptually, and you do not learn anything about the number of steps.

If you want to learn something, you must arrange the situation so that you do not have very much help from outside sources. If you want to learn your way through a city, you must make the decisions yourself as to which way you ought to go at each choice point: even a large number of trips in which you passively allow another person to steer your path will not teach you as much as a few trips taken on your own, with "hypothesizing" at each choice point (that is, with some deliberation at each corner as to the best route). This is the more general principle underlying a procedure mentioned in Chapter 2—that efficient studying depends upon reciting the material or recalling it with a minimum of help, rather than upon merely reading and re-reading notes, textbooks, or outlines prepared by someone else. Any device or procedure which induces what has been called "vicarious trial and error" will facilitate learning.

> This principle is well illustrated by experiments in which college students learned to trace with a metal pencil or stylus a maze consisting of a series of passages with numerous turns and blind alleys (similar to the one shown on p. 19). The object was to get through the maze with no lost motion and as quickly as possible. Each entrance into a blind alley was counted as an error. Some subjects received a sizable electric shock when the stylus entered a blind alley, while others did not. The end result was that those subjects who received shocks for errors learned more quickly to avoid the incorrect response than did the others. The reason apparently is that the shock forces the individual to hesitate—and hypothesize—before making a choice. (Bunch[14])

Reward or positive reinforcement as a factor in learning. Most of our perceptual processes disappear almost as soon as they have occurred, leaving behind them no particularly enduring traces or changes in the nervous system. This is necessarily the case, because our perceptions are changing endlessly from one second to another, and marvelous as our brains may be, they still are not equipped to keep enduring records of every perceptual process. For learning to occur, some perceptual processes must be accented or stressed as important. The occurrence of a reward—the satisfaction of a motive—is one of the chief means by which such an accenting or stressing can occur.

For example, a man hiking through the woods comes to a particularly beautiful spot, and his enjoyment causes him to receive a more enduring impression from his perceptual response to that spot than from the thousands of other perceptual responses he has had while moving through the woods, most of which were not accented in any way and so left no strong traces. And not only does the rewarding experience cause him to "learn" that spot now; it also operates to induce further learning. On a later hike, it gives him a goal to work for—it motivates his behavior. If he sets out again to find that same spot, he pauses and "hypothesizes" at many different choice points; he learns the route to that spot. In this indirect way, reward helps him to learn some things which he otherwise would not learn.

Reward does not teach you merely to make the same particular responses that you made in the original situation. Rather, it helps you to learn *what effects you can secure in what situations and by what means*. So only if the situation is repeated in exactly the same way—that is, only if you have the same motivation when you have a chance to use what you have learned—will you tend to make exactly the same response. For example, suppose the hiker walks through the woods with a person whom he does not like, whom he does not want to please, and with whom he does not want to share this location. His earlier rewarded experience will not cause him to go automatically to the spot where the reward was experienced. Instead, his past learning guarantees that they will *not* chance upon that spot on this trip. In this description, substitute a rat for the hiker, a maze for the woods, and food for the aesthetic situation, and the account fits what we now know about the influence of rewards on maze learning. That is, the rat that learns to run the maze is not learning a series of movements but is learning what path to follow to reach a certain spot with certain goal-material in it.

Rewards are important for learning in two ways: (1) by their influence in emphasizing some of the perceptual processes of the goal attained and of the means whereby it was attained; and (2) by their influence in establishing motivating "goal-expectations" which operate all through the course of subsequent trials. They operate in much of our daily learning—whether it is the two-year-old who watches his mother open the refrigerator door and learns to do it himself, or the college student who is helped to grasp and retain difficult material through the experiencing of less tangible rewards.

Punishment as a factor in learning. In our efforts to control the behavior of others in ordinary life, we tend to place great reliance on punishment as a factor in learning. However, experimental findings do not indicate that punishment always works in such a simple and sure way as our everyday thinking assumes. For example:

> The experimenter pronounces to a person a series of words, and after each word asks him to guess which numeral, from one to ten, has been assigned by the experimenter as the number corresponding to that word in the code known to him but not to the subject. In some cases he tells the subject his guess was right; in some cases he tells him his guess was wrong; in other cases he says nothing. Then the experimenter goes through the list of words again, and asks the subject once more to try to give the right number for each word. He is likely to find that the subject will tend, in more than a chance degree, to give the associations that he gave the first time, provided they were followed the first time either by the comment "right" (that is, by *reward*) or by the comment "wrong" (that is, by *punishment*). (Thorndike[15])

Such findings indicate that punishment might have rather unpredictable effects—tending to prevent the repetition of the punished response in some situations, but increasing it in others.

This fact has application in many situations in everyday life—for example, in the training of small children. At mealtime, a sixteen-month-old can start to slap his hand on a plate of tomatoes, laughing at the splattering he creates. The parent naturally wants the child to learn not to do this, but it is safe to say that punishment would operate the way that the comment "wrong" operated in the experiment described above. The wise way to handle the situation is to end the child's activity as inconspicuously as possible (perhaps by distracting his attention to something else while removing the plate from his reach), not laughing or scolding or showing concern about the situation, but letting it pass without either reward or punishment.

To explain this operation of punishment more fully, we would do well to go back to the fact mentioned in discussing reward—that most activities and most perceptual processes leave only rather transitory aftereffects if they are not emphasized in some way. Punishment, by accenting the perception of some activities, can cause learning which otherwise would not have happened. And if the situation is rather hard to organize into any meaningful pattern (as with numbers linked arbitrarily with different words) or where certain unusual motivational conditions may be present (as in the baby), this accenting of some activities may actually enhance the likelihood of their being used again in the same situation.

In some cases, however, it is true that punishing a response tends to make the subject less likely to repeat that response when the same situation recurs later. This fact has been demonstrated in an experiment with rats (Brown[16]), but most people know of convincing evidence without having to look to scientific experiments. Any parent knows that when a baby has been given a spoonful of cereal that is too hot, the baby will tend for some time to refuse his cereal. And anyone who has paid a five-dollar fine for failing to stop at a traffic signal knows that this punishment tends to make him more careful when he comes to stop signs.

In a case where some factor—like punishment in this case—seems to operate sometimes in one direction and sometimes in an opposite direction, it is not scientifically sound procedure to dismiss that factor from further consideration as though it did not operate by any discoverable cause-and-effect relations. Our task, instead, is to try to determine and state the conditions under which punishment tends to prevent the recurrence of a response and the conditions under which it enhances the likelihood of its recurrence.

Even when punishment operates to eliminate some outward response, it does not do so by "eliminating some nervous connection between the situation and that response." Instead, the punishment eliminates the *outward* response as a result of the fact that it helps the learner in a positive sense: it helps to establish some knowledge of what effects are obtained by what actions. Then when the same situation recurs (that is, when the learner is still motivated in the same way in the same environmental setting), he will tend *not* to do what was punished previously. However, if certain changes of motivation have been produced, a "punishment" of some sort will work in an opposite way, to make him repeat the response. Two experiments by two different workers may be compared in this connection.

> In both experiments, rats were trained to take one arm of a two-way maze when they were hungry and the other arm of the maze when they were thirsty. In most respects the two experiments were essentially alike, but there was one major difference:
>
> The maze in the first experiment (Hull[17]) was set up so that if a rat ran to the wrong side on any given day, its run led to a door which blocked its entrance into the *single* end-box provided with that maze. It had to retreat as though out of an empty blind alley and go around the other way. On the next day, with the motives reversed, the rat would meet such a closed door on the side which previously gave access to the end-box, and now had to go the other way to find the desired goal-material. With this situation, the learning task proved exceedingly difficult. About eight *months* of training, five trials a day, were required before the rats achieved an accuracy of about 80 per cent correct choices on their first trials of each day.

Conditions Necessary for Learning 347

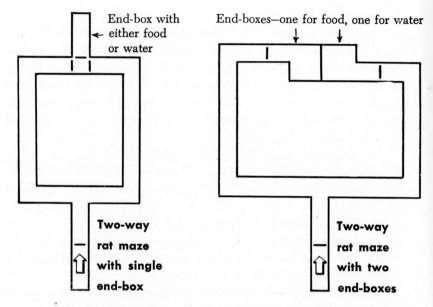

End-box with ← either food or water

End-boxes—one for food, one for water

Two-way rat maze with single end-box

Two-way rat maze with two end-boxes

In the other experiment (Leeper[18]), the situation was comparable except that the maze had *two* end-boxes, both of which were open on all trials, and one of which contained a pan of food and the other of which contained a similar pan filled with water. In this maze, the situation on *correct* trials was much the same as in the maze described above: there was a choice, a run to the correct side, and a quick settling down to eat or drink. But on the *wrong* runs a different situation was met: instead of being turned back by a closed door, the rat had to enter the wrong end-box and see that the pan therein contained the goal-material not desired on that day. With this situation, the rats reached more than 80 per cent correct on first runs after merely eight *days* of training, and achieved about 94 per cent choice accuracy on first runs in their third eight-day period of training. In this case, in other words, it seems as though the "punishment"—e.g., of finding dry food when the rat was thirsty—was not a handicap to the rat the next day, with altered motivation, but in fact seemed to speed up learning.

In other words, punishment basically does not eliminate responses, but establishes some knowledge of what effects are reached by what responses. How the animal will use that knowledge, or that habit, depends upon its motivation at the time of performance.

"Frequency" as a factor in learning. If we are going to talk about "frequency" we must always ask, "frequency of *what?*" The question of the relation between frequency and learning is sometimes put this way: Does frequent repetition of some overt response tend to make the person more likely to repeat that response still further? To that question, the answer is *no*. It has been shown, for example, that one of the most effective means of eliminating some faulty habit is deliberately to make the faulty response, over and over again, while at the same time thinking about the disadvantages of the action (Dunlap[19]). The findings with this "negative practice method" (see p. 535) give ample evidence that a person will not learn to make a response just by repeating it often enough.

But such findings do not disprove the principle that frequency of operation of some other factors is unimportant for learning. In some situations the learning is extremely rapid, once the solution is attained. This may readily be seen in the puzzle in which a person is required to make four equal-sized equilateral triangles out of six matches. The problem proves to be extremely baffling as long as the person continues to work with possible arrangements just in two dimensions. But when he is shown that he can solve the problem by making a three-dimensional figure—a pyramid—he can learn the solution immediately and retain it efficiently for years, even though at first he was not able to discover the solution in several hours of work.

On the other hand, there are many other cases in which the learning materials do not readily yield such well-organized processes. In studying geography, in learning irregular verbs, or in studying the spelling of many English words, the learner may have to go over the materials time after time, trying to introduce into the learning situation all the factors in learning which we have described above. And in such a case, the more frequently he permits these factors to operate, the more will learning occur. Properly understood, the principle can still be accepted that frequency of operation of factors favorable to learning does tend to be an important factor in learning.

The factors favorable to learning are many, and their interaction is complex. In fact, the very definition of learning is not a simple one and involves, as we have seen, a consideration of the many different kinds of habits that learning can produce. If learning is a continual process, it is also a complex one.

HOW WE MEASURE LEARNING

WE CANNOT DIRECTLY SEE or measure "learning." The only thing which we can observe and measure directly is *performance,* or the use of what has been learned. Regardless of whether our method of observation is objective or introspective, we see merely the processes which learning makes possible, and not the learning itself.

Graphic aids in measuring performance

But even when the criterion of learning has been established, and the results of learning have been given in statistical form, the progress of learning is often hard to interpret. See if you can grasp the learning progress in the following experiment:

In this test, the subjects were given a list of words and asked to supply the words of opposite meaning. They were given several trials, each lasting the same amount of time. At each trial, the experimenter counted the number of words for which the subject was able to supply opposites within the set time-period. Thus the test was to see how fast the subject could increase the number of "opposites" supplied within a given time—it used speed as a criterion of learning.

Here is the record of the number of words one subject was able to supply at successive trials. Read them carefully: 165, 238, 260, 299, 335, 334, 341, 373, 390, 396, 412, 415, 448, 436, 448, 476, 498, 477, 502, 507, 526, 545, 522, 546, 557, 554.

The chances are that by reading these figures you do not get a clear mental picture of the rate at which learning progressed. But when plotted as a learning curve, below, these figures are more easily understood (after Thorndike[20]).

**Number of correct word opposites
given after successive learning periods**

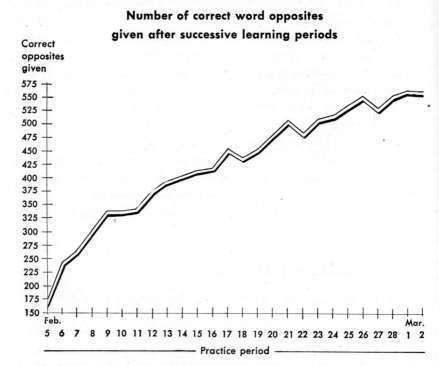

Data from Thorndike, *Adult Learning*, Macmillan, 1928, p. 210.

Learning versus performance

Rather commonly, such curves have been spoken of in psychology as *learning curves*. A more accurate term is *curves of performance*. For example, in the curve illustrated, the score was lower on February 22 than on February 21, but this does not necessarily mean that the person had "unlearned" to some extent between these two trials. Some internal or external distraction, or some other chance factor, might have caused this difference of score—in a curve like this we have a record merely of performance, not of learning. Still more importantly, this point is illustrated by the part of the curve which finally has leveled off. Our common-sense knowledge might say that, by March 2, the subject had completed his learning. But actually, tests made after several weeks prove that even after the subject has seemingly brought his habits to a state of perfect mastery, there still is the possibility of further learning from further trials. Thus, learning is something which can be *inferred* from performance under a variety of conditions; it is not revealed directly in a graph of correct responses or a graph of errors on successive trials.

There is one type of situation in which this distinction between learning and performance is especially important. Sometimes the conditions of motivation are different at different times, or are different for different learners. When this is true, differences of performance are likely to be seen as a result, but these differences of performance do not necessarily reflect differences of learning. This fact has been shown by experiments on animal learning.

One experimenter trained some rats which were both hungry and thirsty. If a rat took one arm of the maze, it came to an end-box in which it could get water. If it took the other arm of the maze, it came to food. In this situation the rats on successive trials showed a great variability of reaction. You could not tell what they had learned. But, when the rats were made thirsty, and not hungry, they ran rather accurately to the water; when they were merely hungry, they ran rather accurately to food. Their *motivation*, in other words, governed their performance, and was not related merely to their learning. (Kendler[21])

In another type of experiment, several workers have shown that when rats are given no reward at any point in the maze, they continue to wander aimlessly on successive trials. Their curve of errors shows practically no change. If performance curves were really learning curves, we could say in such cases that no learning is occurring. But when such rats are given an opportunity to find food in the end-box, their error curve drops with greater speed than was true of the error curve of the rats rewarded from their first trial on. In other words, some learning can occur which will not be manifested in external performance until conditions are such that the learner is motivated to use what he has learned. (Tolman and Honzik[22]; cf. also Haney[23])

Although it is not a simple or easy thing to judge or measure the amount of learning, we still can use performance curves as *indicators* of learning in certain cases. Thus, if the learner is equally motivated throughout and yet if the curve changes in ways that apparently are not due merely to chance fluctuations, a safe conclusion is that the person has learned more at one point than he had learned at some earlier point. Or if two groups are equally motivated, so that they have equal reason to try to use what they have learned, we can say that the group with the more favorable performance curve presumably has learned more than the other group.

We must keep in mind, as still a further point, that learning is not always manifested as a change in performance in the direction of satisfying some motive. For example, a golfer can learn to slice, and in successive games he can slice more and more often, but his change of performance is not directly related to the satisfaction of some motive.

When we are dealing with intellectual materials, we generally are inclined to arrange our learning as though we could assume that once we have learned to the point that permits immediate recall (or, at least, recall within a day or so), we have then sufficiently learned that material. The discussion in the several preceding pages should indicate clearly the incorrectness of that viewpoint. An athletic coach never would assume that skills in sports are learned adequately when they have been practiced only to this point—he always makes sure that the learning can be translated into automatically effective performance. In the field of intellectual skills, adequate learning can be secured only if the learning activity continues far beyond the point at which the curve of "apparent" improvement has leveled off.

The distinction between learning and performance is especially important in accounting for the short-run deterioration in performance caused by shifting to more efficient work habits. When a person tries to learn some improved technique of action to replace a more clumsy technique which he has used previously, it is almost certain that he must go through a temporary period of decreased effectiveness of performance. This effect often tends to deter him from shifting to better methods of work. From the point of view of long-range efficiency, however, the occurrence of such temporary setbacks should not be regarded as serious. For example, after he has learned to typewrite with a one-finger hunt-and-peck method, his speed will decrease when he tries to typewrite by the touch method. When he tries to learn to use a slide rule for multiplication, he cannot achieve, at first, as much speed or accuracy as he can with the method learned in grade school. Or to take a more complex and more important example—when a student first enters some new field of work such as psychology, and tries to deal with familiar subject matter in terms of new concepts, he is certain to find, for the time being, that his thinking will be more difficult than with the rougher, simpler concepts of everyday tradition. In all such cases, it is important to realize that the best level of final effectiveness can come only by learning to use the best technical tools that the cultural environment provides.

Measuring different aspects of performance

You have just seen that performance curves are by no means learning curves. Furthermore, it is worth noting that, to get such performance curves, we may use a variety of aspects of performance. We may take a record of *accuracy of response* (or, conversely speaking, the number of errors); we may take a record of *speed;* we may record introspective reports of *feeling of effort;* we may take a record of *probability of response* (especially as measured by the per cent of a group who make the response on each trial); or we may use still other criteria, such as *strength of the response* (as the number of drops of saliva in Pavlov's experiments). An interesting example of more delicate means of measurement of changes coming from learning is given by some experiments on *reduced energy cost* of different activities:

> In one such experiment, two scientists demonstrated that the effort to learn requires appreciable energy. They had subjects write lists of nonsense syllables under the following two conditions: (1) with intent to learn and (2) passively without trying to memorize.
> When the instructions to the subjects were to copy the syllables passively without trying to learn them, the energy turnover was increased only about 3 per cent as compared with the resting value; but when the subjects tried to learn, their energy turnover was increased as much as 25 per cent. (Becker and Olsen[24])

According to this experiment, writing with intention to learn takes more energy than does "passive" writing. The experimenters also found that with practice the energy cost of learned activity decreased:

> At the beginning of their experiments, one subject learned three lists of sixteen syllables in eighteen readings with a carbon-dioxide cost of 1.48 cubic centimeters per second of learning time. One month later, after much practice, the subject could learn similar lists in only twelve readings and with a carbon-dioxide cost of only 1.38 cubic centimeters per second. (Becker and Olsen[25])

In a similar experiment, a subject added columns of ten three-place numbers while wearing the mask. As practice continued, the amount of energy consumed in a given period decreased. (Rounds, Schubert, and Poffenberger[26])

Energy cost is not often used as an indication of how learning is progressing—first, because of the difficulty of using the apparatus in life-like situations, and second, because there are several other aspects of performance from which psychologists can infer the progress of learning. In interpreting performance curves, it is very important to note which particular aspect of performance is being recorded.

Interpreting performance curves

Since performance can be measured in terms of several criteria, the particular criterion being used is one of the variables determining whether the general shape of the curve will move up or down as learning progresses. Obviously, a person who is successfully acquiring a new habit is likely to have a curve of *decreasing* errors and a curve of *increasing* correct responses. If he is performing more and more poorly, he is likely to have a curve of *increasing* energy cost and decreasing correct responses. However, the curve may move upward or downward in different parts of its course, depending on the progress that is being made during different parts of the learning period. Such reversals of trend are of special interest to the psychologist, who wants to discover the factors behind them.

Besides determining the general trend of the graphs, it is important to determine the *rate* at which performance is changing. The method of analyzing the rate of performance may be illustrated by a simple arithmetical example and then applied to some of the more complex curves to be presented in the next chapter. Suppose that there are three subjects learning some task, and that each one is increasing the number of his correct responses with every practice period. Yet each one may have a different performance curve:

Subject A may have a curve which shows that as the total amount of practice increases, the returns from a given amount of practice increase. Note that after the first unit of practice, the number of correct responses increases from 1 to 2, or by 1; with the second, from 2 to 4, or by 2; with the third, from 4 to 8, or by 4. (This is unusual; in most learning situations people do not continue indefinitely to improve in performance.)

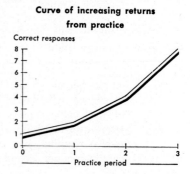

Curve of increasing returns from practice

Subject B may have a curve which shows that the returns from a given amount of practice remain constant as the total amount of practice increases. With the first unit of practice, the number of correct responses increases from 1 to 3, or by 2; with the second, from 3 to 5, or by 2; with the third, from 5 to 7, or by 2. (This also is an unusual performance curve.)

Subject C may have a curve of diminishing returns which shows that as the total amount of practice increases, the returns from a given amount of practice decrease. During the first trial, the number of correct responses increases from 1 to 6, or by 5; then, from 6 to 8, or by only 2; then from 8 to 9, or by only 1. In other words, the curve is "flattening out"—that is, the person seems to be reaching his top level of performance.

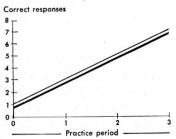

Curve of equal returns from practice

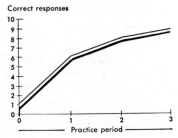

Curve of diminishing returns from practice

All this discussion of *How We Measure Learning* should have helped to emphasize the point that learning is a process which we know only by inference, and not by direct observation. All that we can observe directly in another person is his performance, not his learning. Sometimes we can judge that changes of his performance indicate that learning has taken place, but so many factors help to determine the performance of the person that great care must be used in trying to determine what has been learned.

LEARNING AND AGE

As PEOPLE go through life, there are numerous changes in their ability to learn, which are as fascinating to study as they are important from the social point of view. Teachers, students, and parents obviously must know at what age one should attempt to learn certain things with expectation of maximum returns on the investment of time and effort. And since social statistics show that the proportion of old people in our population is growing larger all the time, it is interesting to know, for example, whether human beings reach an age beyond which no further learning is possible.

How learning ability varies with age

Numerous researches with various types of learning tasks show that, in general, learning ability increases from year to year to find its peak near the age of twenty years (Thorndike[27]), and then declines. It is no accident that the average person receives most of his formal education by the time he reaches the age of twenty-three or twenty-four. Educators long ago discovered that the "golden age" for learning is during youth. The general ability to accomplish highly complex learning which is dependent upon basic skills or knowledge grows until an age well beyond twenty.

The exact course of the rise and fall in learning ability does seem to depend, however, on the nature of the material to be learned. This has been clearly shown by a specially designed series of experiments.

In these experiments, groups of young and of old people learned two motor and three verbal tasks. One of the motor tasks was learning to perform a coordinated movement of the right hand when seen in direct vision. The other motor task was learning to perform the same type of movement when the vision was not direct, the hand being seen through a mirror. Notice that in the first of these tasks the habits of a lifetime were useful—many of the basic elements of the coordinated movement required had been practiced in random fashion through daily manipulation of objects. The second motor task, however, was of such nature that the old visual habits would actually interfere. So before the mirror-vision habit could be set up, the old direct-vision habits had to be torn down. The results showed quite clearly that the aged learners suffered the greater loss of ability in the case of the mirror-vision learning task.

The three verbal tasks showed results which were subject to the same interpretation. These three tasks were the following:
1 Associating meaningful pairs of words, such as *horse-sheep*.
2 Associating nonsense materials, of which $F \times P = V$ is a sample.
3 Associating interference materials, such as $2 \times 4 = 9$.

The subjects learned to give the second member of the pair upon seeing the first. Notice that the meaningful words can be grouped by some logical principle—i.e., both are animals which eat grass. But the nonsense materials are purely arbitrary—$F \times P$ could equal V or it could equal any other amount. The third pair, the interference material, is so labeled because old verbal habits interfere with learning. We are so used to thinking and saying 8 when we see 2×4 that it is very hard to learn to say 9.

The results showed that the young group was superior to the aged in all three tasks. The differences between the young and the aged subjects were least for the meaningful pairs of words and greatest for the interference materials, with the nonsense equations standing in an intermediate position of difficulty. (Ruch[28])

These experiments show that the rise and fall in learning ability depends upon the task. It has also been found that seven is the best age for learning the first ten piano lessons (Brown[29]), and numerous studies show that reading, too, should start at about this age, rather than earlier, as has been the traditional practice (Gray[30]). Ability to exercise sound business judgment continues to grow into middle age and is, in fact, one of the last abilities to be lost in old age. But apparently athletic proficiency, unlike business judgment, reaches a peak in the early prime of life.

> The relation between age and excellence of performance of motor skills has been studied through an analysis made of the data given in the "All Sports Record Book" (Menke[31]). When each sport is listed in the order of the increasing ages of maximum proficiency, it is found that the average age of maximum proficiency ranged from about twenty-six in professional football players to about thirty-six in world-record-breaking billiard players (Lehman[32]).

Learning in later years

Whatever the particular nature of the learning problem, learning ability starts to fall off at an increasingly rapid rate soon after the fiftieth year of life. Of course, there are great individual differences in the loss of learning ability with age. Although everyone loses some of his early ability—thus making the average ability of an older group less than that of a younger one—nevertheless those individuals who were very superior in their youth will remain superior to many younger individuals of less initial ability. But by the time the average person has reached seventy, his ability to learn material unrelated to his past experience is very low indeed.

This fact may explain the increased conservatism of older people. Times change as the years pass, calling for the acquisition of new facts and skills in every walk of life. Old people progressively lose their ability to master new materials and habits and by consequence find themselves reacting to present problems upon the basis of past experience which is no longer applicable. Such persons are conservative or even reactionary, depending upon the degree of loss of learning ability. (Ruch[33])

Popular belief has it that the memory of the older person is decidedly inferior. This conclusion is based upon the unanalyzed results of everyday experience and is not altogether trustworthy. There is no doubt that older people lose some of their ability to recall names of recent acquaintances, but the fault here may well be merely one of original impression. Perhaps they did not learn the name properly in the first place. In that case the ability to memorize is at fault, and not the ability to retain that which has been memorized. There is some evidence that memory of material well learned does not decline nearly so rapidly as ability to learn new material.

In life, useful things that are learned early are usually practiced most. For example, a person learns his own name first, then the names of his parents, then as an adult, the name of wife or husband; later the names of children and grandchildren. In extreme old age, an individual may forget the names of his grandchildren. Cases have been known where the person even forgets the names of his children, but it is extremely unusual for the person's own name to be forgotten. How much of this effect is due to earliness of the original learning and how much is due to amount of practice cannot be said with certainty, but the evidence by and large indicates that primacy of impression is more important than amount of practice in determining differential forgetting.

For the average man or woman in the seventies to take up some entirely new type of activity and achieve a high degree of proficiency is most unusual. We frequently read of some aged person achieving success in an outstanding way in a new field, but close study of the case will usually reveal that the individual had for many years been an amateur in the field. For example, William De Morgan wrote his first novel after he had reached the age of seventy years, but he had always associated with literary people and during his entire business career as a manufacturer of pottery had read widely in anticipation of the time when he would be free to try his hand at writing.

There is no reason why older people should give up trying to learn skills and gain knowledge that are extensions of past learning. Many people look forward to retirement from active business or professional life as an opportunity to pursue interests that have been neglected due to the pressure of work. This is a thoroughly fine practice, provided that the older person chooses interests that are not too new to him or, if he chooses quite new fields of endeavor, provided that he is more lenient in setting standards for himself than he was in his youth. A person who had devoted the first two thirds of his life to accounting or literature would probably have too much difficulty at the age of sixty in learning chemistry to select a hobby in which it is required. But a woman who has always taken an interest in furnishing her home could reasonably expect to profit greatly from the study of interior decoration in later maturity. While youth is the time for learning, maturity is the time when the human being can enjoy the products of all the learning he has been constantly acquiring in the process of living.

It is because learning is such a continual process—and such a vital one —that psychologists have given it intensive study. In this chapter we have studied the different kinds of learning and the necessary conditions for learning. We have examined the progress of learning and ways of recording it, and have seen how learning varies with age. In the next chapter, we shall study the manifestations of learning in *Remembering and Thinking*.

Answer to problem given on page 334: Since the two diagonals of a square are the same, and since one of them is also the radius of the circle, the diagonal line is one inch long.

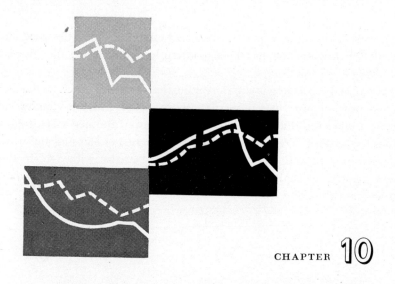

Remembering and thinking

IN THE PREVIOUS CHAPTER we dealt primarily with the questions of what kinds of habits we acquire, our ways of learning such habits, and the conditions governing the learning. But learning needs to be studied from further points of view. When you encounter something important, you do not aim merely to learn it—you also try to *retain* or *remember* what you have learned, and to translate it into *performance*. Often, moreover, the habits remaining from earlier learning are not satisfactory and must be *modified*. (Remember, in this connection, that psychologists use the term "habit" to refer to *all* products of learning, and not just to firmly established ways of responding.)

For practical as well as for theoretical reasons, there is great importance in the problems this chapter will discuss. Three of these main problems are the retention, use, and means of modification of habits, after which we will turn to a more particular discussion of thinking. In a sense, such a distinct or separate discussion of thinking is not required, because thinking is one of the means of acquiring, using, and modifying habits, and will already have been considered, to some extent, in all the preceding discussion of the more inclusive problems of learning. However, thinking is such an important process in human life—such an important means of problem-solving learning in complex situations—that it seems to deserve some special treatment. It is for this reason that our discussion of learning will conclude with a special discussion of those processes which we term *thinking*.

Several problems confront us here. First of all, what methods do psychologists use to measure retention of learning? What do they find about forgetting and retention? Does forgetting proceed rather evenly and steadily from the time of the original learning or does it vary? How long are habits retained? What are the factors governing their retention? What are the factors governing the use of the habits we learn? How can we change the habits we have learned? What is "thinking"? We shall consider each of these problems in turn.

RETENTION AND FORGETTING

THE STUDY OF LEARNING always involves the questions of whether some more or less enduring change has been produced in the person. We cannot conclude that learning occurs in a certain situation merely from observing that the person's behavior changes in that situation. For example, a baby might creep toward a cat and pull its tail, and then cry and creep away when the cat scratched it, but just in itself this change of behavior is not sufficient to indicate that the baby has learned anything. We can conclude that learning has occurred only when we see that when the baby is confronted again with the chance to tease the cat, he acts in a way which shows that some change in his ways of responding was produced *and has been retained* from the previous experience.

For this reason, experiments on learning or acquisition always involve measurements of retention. Nevertheless, our understanding of this whole aspect of human life is helped by keeping clearly in mind the distinction between acquisition and retention. Psychologists, by appropriately designed experiments, have been able to "hold constant" either one of these processes in order to study the factors influencing the other process. By such means, it has been possible to distinguish a number of important principles which hold true for each of these processes separately. In this section, we shall consider some of the factors in retention and its related process, forgetting.

Ways of measuring retention

It might seem on first thought that there is no great difficulty in finding a way to measure retention. All that has to be done, you might say, is to see whether the person still can do what he learned to do, regardless of whether that is spelling, typing, ice-skating, or giving dates in history.

This **method of recall or reinstatement** is, in fact, the most widely used and important method of measuring retention. However, research on learning has demonstrated that for an adequate understanding of retention, psychologists must use more sensitive means of measuring retention. Therefore they have developed and used some additional methods: *recognition, rearrangement,* and *relearning.*

The method of recognition. In working with the method of recognition, the subject of an experiment does not try to recall the items learned. He is given a list containing the previously learned items, interspersed among many that are unfamiliar. He is instructed to label each one recognized as belonging to the original list. His score is the percentage of original items correctly recognized, minus the percentage of added items which he wrongly "recognizes."

This method is frequently used by the police in getting identification of suspected criminals. The suspect is sandwiched in among others known to be innocent, and the witness is instructed to designate the criminal. In this application of the method it is important that the chance element be made very slight by having a large group of people in the lineup who are known to be innocent.

The method of recognition always yields a numerically higher score than the score yielded by tests of recall. We can recognize many items which we cannot recall unaided. Everyone has had the experience of trying to recall a name and failing utterly to do so until somebody suggested several, of which one was immediately recognized as correct.

The method of rearrangement. The method of rearrangement is much like that of recognition. This is a method used specifically to test a person's memory of the order in which a series of items is presented. At the test period, the items are given to the subject in scrambled order, and he is asked to rearrange them. His score is determined by the degree of correctness of the final product.

The method of relearning. The method of relearning is the most sensitive of the four methods. In this method of testing retention, the subject merely relearns the original task under the original conditions. A record is kept of the number of errors made, the number of trials taken, or the time consumed by the subject in relearning to the original degree of mastery. The subject's score is the difference between the amount of effort required for the original learning and that required to relearn. This difference is called the *absolute savings score*. The amount saved is sometimes expressed as a percentage of the original learning score. The method of relearning will often reveal some effects of prior learning when conscious memory is completely absent.

The course of forgetting

In most cases, the findings of experiments on forgetting indicate that, just as we might suspect from everyday experience, forgetting does not proceed at a steady rate after the original learning period. It is most rapid immediately after the end of the learning period, and as time goes on, the remaining knowledge becomes more and more stable. This fundamental fact was first discovered by the German psychologist Ebbinghaus and has been repeatedly verified (Ebbinghaus[1] and Cain and Willey[2]). The figure on page 367 is a curve of retention.

Psychologists find that the height of the curve of retention is quite different in different cases. With some kinds of learning material and with some kinds of methods of learning, forgetting proceeds much more slowly than in other cases. The outstanding problem we need to consider is not just when forgetting is most rapid, but the problem of *what factors* govern retention, which we shall consider shortly.

The curves of retention indicate not merely that forgetting is more rapid at first but that later the curve of forgetting seems to level off. This naturally gives rise to the following question:

Is anything ever completely forgotten? In one of his later experiments, Ebbinghaus gave an interesting demonstration of the fact that the effects of learning may be retained after many years. He has reported that he relearned stanzas of the poem *Don Juan* after a lapse of twenty-two years (Ebbinghaus[3]). At the time the relearning was started, no evidence of memory was apparent upon introspection, and there was no objective recall of the lines of the poem. However, the time required to relearn these stanzas he had once learned was less than that required to learn stanzas not previously studied. The fact that old people frequently recall quite vividly the scenes of their childhood after many years of not thinking about them suggests that the effects of experience are not completely lost but persist in some form throughout the lifetime.

The recurrence of youthful memories was studied by the late Professor Warren, who reported two cases of the spontaneous recurrence of memories of which the subjects had been completely unconscious for long intervals of time (Warren[4]). Professor Warren's father, at the age of ninety years, suddenly recalled a poem he had learned seventy-five years before. He was unable to recall ever rehearsing the poem during the long interval. A similar case was that of an elderly gentleman of eighty-three who recalled an oration which he had learned as a young man and had not recited during the interim.

Youthful memories come back in reverse order. As the person becomes older, earlier memories come back. The writer once observed a typical case of a German-speaking person who had come to the United States as a young man and who had not used his original language for nearly sixty years. He began to complain that he found himself forgetting English words for familiar objects and that the German words kept intruding in their place.

The special phenomenon of reminiscence. In most cases forgetting is rapid at first, immediately after the original learning, and then slower and slower with time. Occasionally, however, it seems that the learner is able to remember or recall a *larger* amount some time after the conclusion of the learning than he was able to recall immediately afterward. This holds true even when it is certain that he has not practiced in the meantime, either by actually going over the materials or by reviewing them mentally. This phenomenon, which psychologists call *reminiscence*, has inspired a number of studies. In these experiments it has been found that reminiscence will occur in a wide variety of subject matter, provided that the original learning was incomplete. The degree of reminiscence seems to depend on the following factors, which have been demonstrated by careful experiment:

1 *The meaningfulness of the material.* Experiment has shown that meaningful material produces a greater degree of reminiscence than does nonsense material, just as it is less affected by retroactive inhibition. (Martin[5])

2 *The determination to recall.* Individuals who try hard to recall show a greater degree of reminiscence than do those who give up more easily. (Martin[6])

3 *The degree of mastery of the task.* In motor learning, at least, the degree of reminiscence increases up to a certain point as degree of mastery of the task increases. Beyond that point of mastery, further mastery of the task reduces the degree of reminiscence. (Buxton[7])

4 *The length of time involved.* Fast learners, as compared with slow ones, show most reminiscence over short periods of time (a

few days to a few weeks). However, slow learners show the most reminiscence over periods of a few months. This is true for both nonsense syllables and motor learning. (Leavitt[8])

Reminiscence indicates that you do not learn something once and for all or forget it once and for all. Thus it serves to confirm the idea that forgetting is not passive decay but an active process involving dynamic forces which continue to change and interact with each other and with new forces later introduced, long after the original learning.

The phenomenon of reminiscence may be thought of in this way: Sometimes it happens that a person is in a situation which he does not completely understand. He learns a number of facts about the situation, and he retains them, but he cannot "make sense" of the situation. Then sometime later, perhaps after he has had some experience with similar situations, he may try to recall the situation again. And this time he will say to himself, "Ah, now I see why they did it, and why the whole situation came out that way." And, when he gets this better organization of his knowledge or memory of the situation, he is able to describe it more adequately than he could before.

When you are working at any learning task, you are doing more than merely learning something—you also are "getting worn out." Your interest in the material diminishes, and you become motivated to shift to some other activity. Accordingly, when you are tested for recall immediately after your learning, your performance at that time is under not too favorable conditions. If you are tested later, the temporary factors of fatigue and of satiation with the task are likely to have been removed. This is probably part of the explanation of the reminiscence phenomenon, along with the more complex factor described above. It indicates that immediately after the original learning, performance may not reveal fully all that has been learned.

The factors governing retention

No single factor can explain the retention of habits, any more than any single factor could explain the acquisition of habits described in the preceding chapter. Of all the factors involved in retention, the following are particularly important: different amounts of practice of different parts of the total habit, retroactive inhibition, meaningfulness or coherent organization in what has been learned, the influence of pleasantness and unpleasantness of the original experiences, and in some cases, the process of repression.

Different amounts of practice of different parts of the habit. Habits sometimes change their character during the period of retention. Some parts of the total habit may fade away much more extensively than other parts. A simple enough explanation for this can be found in some cases. Some parts of the habit which was originally learned are necessary for the use of the habit, and they are developed and strengthened by further use, but other parts of the original habit, which are not thus essential, are given less and less use and are forgotten. For example, if you have tried to teach another person to drive a car after you yourself have driven for years, you may have been surprised to find that you did not really know (in verbal and in visual terms, that is) how to shift gears. It is quite a common event, in a situation like that, that the experienced driver has to say, "Well, now, wait a minute. Let me get over there and see how I do it. I guess I've forgotten." In a way, he *has* forgotten. He has practiced the shifting of gears only as a response guided by tactual, kinesthetic, and auditory stimuli, but not as a response guided visually or verbally. When he himself learned to drive, he could have explained more easily how to shift gears, but the verbal and visual parts of his original habit have been unused, and so they have not been retained.

In a sense, of course, this is not a problem of retention, because there is a difference in the amount of learning activity related to the several aspects of the original habit. But the phenomenon here involved is often tied up with questions which really are matters of retention following learning; so it is well to keep it in mind in this connection. Now let us turn to the problem of what factors operate to determine the fate of a habit (or of those parts of a habit) which do not receive further practice and which are not kept in "good repair."

The phenomenon of retroactive inhibition. Much experimental evidence has been accumulated which indicates that forgetting comes partly because of the influence of the learning of other material after the original material has been learned. This influence of other learning activities (and possibly even just of ordinary psychological processes of some other sorts as well) is called *retroactive inhibition.*

Important evidence of retroactive inhibition is the fact that learning followed by sleep does not yield the same amount of forgetting as that resulting from learning followed by waking activity, even though the total length of time spent is the same.

This evidence was established by experimenters who had some subjects learn tasks just before going to bed; others learned the same tasks upon arising. All subjects mastered their material to the same degree. Tests showed that a given lapse of time spent in the ordinary activities of the waking day brought more forgetting than did the same length of time spent in sleep. (Jenkins and Dallenbach[9])

Another psychologist repeated this experiment, with confirmatory results. Retention was measured by the method of relearning. The graph clearly shows the relation between sleep and forgetting. (Van Ormer[10]) The dotted lines represent the record of one subject, "G"; the solid lines the record of another subject, "V."

Retention after intervals of sleeping and waking

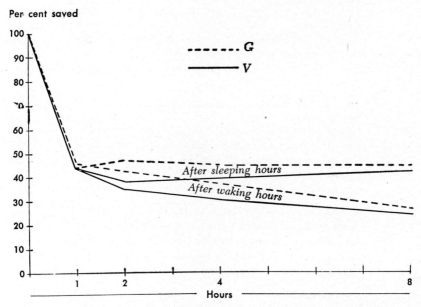

Graph from E. B. Van Ormer, "Retention after Intervals of Sleep and of Waking," *Archives of Psychology*, 1932, 21: Number 137, p. 37.

Both these experiments point to forgetting as brought about by the destructive effect of other activity. Everybody will agree that the human being is much less active in sleep than when awake. However, the sleeping person is not completely inactive, for people do dream and move about in their sleep. The point is that the activity level is lower when one is asleep and that forgetting is also observed to be less.

The obvious next step is to compare the effects that engaging in different kinds of waking activities has on the retention of material you have just learned. The kinds of waking activities studied include nonlearning, learning similar material, and learning dissimilar material. Which one will have most effect in making you forget material you have just learned?

In one experiment, all the subjects in the experiment memorized a list of adjectives. Then, for each subject, a ten-minute period followed, after which the subject first tried to recall all of the adjectives in the

Retention and Forgetting 367

original list, and then secondly tried to relearn the original list. For each subject, then, two scores were secured: first, a score in terms of "per cent recalled," second, a score in terms of "readings to relearn." With different groups of subjects, the ten-minute interval was occupied differently. One group of subjects rested during this period. Another group learned a second group of adjectives composed of synonyms of the adjectives in the first list. Another group learned a list of adjectives that were antonyms of the original words. Another group learned a list of adjectives unrelated to the original list. Another group worked with nonsense syllables. And a last group occupied the ten-minute interval with memorizing a list of three-digit numbers. The results of this experiment were as follows:

Group	Per cent of the original list recalled	Readings required for relearning
Group learning synonyms	12	9.1
Group learning antonyms	18	7.0
Group learning unrelated adjectives	22	6.7
Group learning nonsense syllables	26	7.2
Group learning numbers	37	5.1
Group with interval of rest	45	5.2

In these results, it may be seen that there are a few slight reversals of order in the number of trials required for relearning, but that, in general, there is a striking demonstration of the way in which retroactive inhibition increases with an increase of similarity between the original learning and the interpolated activity. (McGeoch and McDonald[11])

This experiment clearly shows that in retroactive inhibition, learning activity produces more interference than nonlearning activity, and that the greater the similarity between it and the original type of learning activity, the more the forgetting of the first material learned. Subsequent experiments have shown repeatedly that it is the similarity between the two that is the important factor, irrespective of the nature of the material used. Original learning may be of words, numbers, nonsense syllables, geometric designs, or what you will. If what follows is very similar, the interference will be very great; if learning of a different type of material follows, interference will be less. If nonlearning activity follows, the interference will be still less; where sleep follows the original learning, there is little activity of any kind, and forgetting is comparatively slight.

Is forgetting *entirely* a matter of learning something else during the period between the original learning and the relearning? The only way to answer this question would involve putting a subject into a state of suspended animation immediately after the original learning period. He would have to be kept in that condition for a long period of time and then brought back to normal and tested. If he had forgotten nothing at all during the period, we would conclude that forgetting is entirely a matter of reorganization of habits and that it is independent of time. But there is little likelihood that such an experiment can be conducted. Attempts have been made to approximate these conditions by putting subjects under anesthetics during the resting period. The results, however, are difficult to interpret because there is no way of knowing how many new factors are introduced by the anesthetic.

Meaningfulness as a factor in retention. Activity following learning is not the only factor in retention of the learning. Recent experiments have pointed to the factor of organization in the original material learned as lessening the amount of retroactive inhibition.

A study has been made of the forgetting of meaningful material after sleeping and waking periods of equal length. Short stories were constructed to contain twelve items not essential to the plot and twelve essential items. The subjects read each story, at a different time of day, and were asked to recall it approximately eight hours later. The material recalled by each subject was scored by three judges independently, with the following results:

Material	Percentage recalled after waking	Percentage recalled after sleeping
Essential	86	87
Nonessential	23	47

It will readily be seen that retention was markedly different for the two types of material. Apparently nonessential learning, like the learning of nonsense material, is more seriously affected by waking activities than is more meaningful material. (Newman[12])

Thus it appears that material with little or no organization—such as lists of unrelated items (nonsense syllables, dates, names, etc.)—is less well remembered than that in which there is organization—such as material which is meaningful to us. Organized material seems to resist interference from things learned later in a way that unrelated items in a series are unable to do.

All these findings concerning retroactive inhibition have definite applications for the everyday life of all of us, particularly for students. Since forgetting appears to result from the destructive effect of other activity, especially similar learning activity, it is not wise to study French right after Latin. When learning material which is particularly important, follow it with rest or with an entirely different activity. We have seen that meaningful, organized material resists interference from later learning activity; thus, when learning lists, unrelated facts, or verbatim material of any kind, it is important to make it as meaningful as possible—timing and spacing the learning to avoid as much interference as you can.

Even in animal experiments there has been evidence of the value that good organization has for retention.

> One experimenter trained two groups of white rats in two mazes which had exactly the same sequence of turns in each case. With one group of rats, however, the maze was painted black throughout, and the rats had to learn to run the maze by learning the sequence of turns LRRRLLRLLR (L meaning a left turn at the choice point, R meaning a right turn). In the case of the other group, the correct pathway through the maze was painted black, but each blind alley was painted white inside. In this case, in other words, it was possible for the rats to learn to run correctly by learning the simple meaningful fact that they should always pick the dark side. In this study, the rats in the black-white maze learned very quickly and, what is more, they were able to run through the maze, after learning, with a consistently high accuracy which the other group could not rival. Still further, it was found that, following a lapse of several weeks of no training, the rats that had to guide themselves by memory of the sequence of turns gave very poor retention scores; the rats that could guide themselves visually showed high retention. (Snygg[13])

Of course, you might well remark in this instance that the two groups of rats were not having to remember the same thing. One had to remember only the simple rule "take the dark pathways," while the rats of the other group had to remember a nonsensical series of turns. The point is, however, that a student often has to make this same choice. He can try to handle a given learning task by trying to memorize his material without seeing the essential logic involved. When he does this, he is trying to learn something different from what is learned by the student who works out the essential point and who tries to remember it. The student who learns the essential principles can retain these over longer periods of time precisely because of the fact that, to handle the same external materials, he has given himself the task of learning something better suited for quick learning and long retention. Both he and the other type of student finally have to "run through the same exams," somewhat as the two groups of rats had to run through mazes with the same sequence of turns. But the student who has learned a meaningful explanation of the material has something to guide him which can be retained much more efficiently than can rote-memory material.

Pleasantness and unpleasantness of the material. The psychoanalysts have made much of the repression of extremely unpleasant experiences—ones which the person feels it would be painful to remember. The clinical evidence they have found seems adequate to justify their view that the repression of such material can have far-reaching consequences in emotional life. But what happens to the little experiences of daily life which are only *slightly* pleasant or unpleasant? Is there any tendency for unpleasant experiences to be forgotten more quickly than pleasant ones? Many psychologists have investigated this problem with conflicting results.

> Of twenty-six experimental investigations made prior to 1929 on the problem of pleasantness and unpleasantness in relation to forgetting, sixteen showed that pleasant, unpleasant, or both kinds of experiences are remembered better than those which have no feeling of pleasantness or unpleasantness attached to them. (Meltzer[14])
>
> A review has been made of twenty studies of the problem conducted between 1929 and 1938 (Gilbert[15]). Thirteen of these twenty strongly support the principle that pleasant memories tend to persist while unpleasant ones are lost; four deny it; and three give ambiguous results.

A cleverly designed experiment has recently established a definite relationship between pleasantness-unpleasantness and rate of forgetting.

> Twenty-nine college students rated themselves by selecting adjectives from a list of forty-five. All of the adjectives on the list were subjective and ambiguous, such as "wistful," "adaptable," etc. A week later the subjects were shown bogus ratings of themselves, presumed to be genuine estimates by their fellows. Some of the adjectives were favorable and some not. Still another week elapsed and the students were asked to recall the ratings assigned to them and to mark the adjectives as desirable or undesirable. Fewer errors were made by the subjects in recalling those ratings that either were favorable or agreed with their self-ratings. (Shaw[16])

Pleasantness and unpleasantness, like activity, seem to have some effect on forgetting, though the exact relationship is not understood as yet. The evidence, however, adds weight to the hypothesis that forgetting occurs as the result of actively working factors rather than from mere passive decay.

Repression as a factor in forgetting. Work in psychotherapy is involved with habits that are much more important to the person emotionally than are the habits or memories that the experimental psychologists have studied. In working with such cases, the psychotherapists generally have come to the conclusion that, when a person tries to remember something which he has done or felt, or something which has happened in his life, he may be greatly hampered by processes of *repression.* By repression is meant an active but unconscious process within the person whereby he is kept from recalling some disturbing experience or recognizing some disturbing emotional tendency within himself, despite any deliberate efforts he may make. The person does not tend to avoid *all* unpleasant memories; he encounters resistance to remembering and facing only those memories and feelings which he feels it would be dangerous to remember or recognize.

One psychologist has given a clear-cut example of this process.

> It had been found that two girls—children of only about twelve years of age—had been placed by their parents in a house of prostitution under almost unbelievably degrading circumstances. When their situation became known to the authorities and the children were encouraged to tell their story, they were able to give highly detailed information quite adequate to incriminate not only their parents but also a number of others who had been responsible for their situation. But some months later, when the girls were questioned again, it was found that they had lost so much of the factual detail, even regarding some of the more drastic parts of their experiences, that the prosecution of the case would have been greatly handicapped if it had had to depend on their memory at that later time. Even when some of their earlier testimony was summarized for them, they indignantly and apparently quite sincerely denied that any such things could have happened to them, and said that such stories must have been made up maliciously to discredit them. (Erickson[17])

In a case like this, where the original experiences had been so vivid and so emotionally significant, it would seem that the retention of such material should have been easy. But repression often acts like a self-protective device, tending to make the person forget such painful material. Often, however, it is a self-protective device of questionable value, one which does not entirely prevent such repressed tendencies from producing emotional conflicts within the person. We need not consider this process in more detail now because we will be returning to it in Chapter 13 on *Reactions to Frustration.* For the present, it is sufficient to say that repression is a normal process which, to some extent, occurs in everyone as a factor in forgetting.

FACTORS GOVERNING PERFORMANCE

THE BENEFIT OF LEARNING is not realized, of course, unless habits can be used. Consequently, even though psychologists originally did not pay much attention to this question, the more recent workers on learning (cf. Tolman[18] and Hull[19]) are coming to place a great deal of emphasis on the question of what factors govern *performance,* or the use of habits. A number of important factors have been discovered: *Sensory Generalization, Present Perceptual Conditions, Intelligence, Motivation, Active Reconstructions, General Set, Audience,* and *Failure to Complete a Task.*

Sensory generalization in the use of habits

One of the most extensively demonstrated principles of learning is the principle that habits can be evoked, not merely by the exact patterns of stimulation which were involved in the learning situation, but by other patterns of stimulation which have roughly the same characteristics. The usefulness of habits is greatly increased in consequence of this phenomenon of *sensory generalization.* Even from a single learning experience in a situation clearly structured, a small child or an animal can learn to respond to situations which have a great range of specific characteristics. The child needs to be burned by a campfire only once to learn not to creep into campfires of many different sizes and colors and backgrounds.

Sensory generalization occurs particularly often in cases in which the learner has had little or no training that would have developed his capacity to distinguish between different objects or other stimulus materials such as he has learned to respond to. The person who knows nothing about snakes, for instance, and who has been warned, on seeing a rattlesnake, that its bite could be fatal, will then be afraid of all kinds of snakes. The person who already had learned to distinguish between different varieties of snakes would not show as wide a "sensory generalization" in his use of some added caution which he might acquire with reference to rattlers. Thus sensory generalization is not a product of learning, but a reflection of lack of learning. It is a consequence of the fact that the central nervous system acts on the basis of *patterns of stimulation,* apparently, rather than on the basis of specific or absolute qualities in the stimulus object.

A great many examples of such sensory generalization have been found in experiments on conditioned responses, and in experiments on discrimination learning.

Pavlov was much interested in the phenomenon and was able to demonstrate it easily with reference to the conditioned salivary reactions. It has also been clearly demonstrated with reference to the reactions of rats with the jumping apparatus described on page 342. For example, one experimenter (Lashley[20]) used these cards and trained some rats to jump to the triangle and to avoid jumping to the cross. Following this training, he found that

the rats, without special training on these other figures, were able to jump "correctly" (that is, to the side having the triangle-motif in it in some way) with the following sets of cards:

They were apparently unable to discriminate, however, with the following pairs of cards:

From K. S. Lashley, "The Mechanism of Vision: XV. Preliminary Studies of the Rat's Capacity for Detail Vision," *Journal of General Psychology*, 1938, volume 18, pp. 139 and 141.

Of particular interest in this collection is the pair of cards in which the figures were still the same as on the original cards—still a triangle versus a cross—but in which each figure now was a black figure on a white card, instead of a white figure on a black card. To a human adult, who has been extensively trained in symbolic habits, such cards would be highly equivalent to the original-training pair, but they did not appear equivalent to the rats, for some reason. Whenever the brightness relationships of the figure and ground have been reversed, it has always been found that the rats lost the means of discriminating.

Appropriate training can remove this phenomenon of *sensory generalization* or, as it is sometimes called, of *initial generalization* or equivalence of stimuli. What is effective, however, is not a mere prolonging of training with the original stimulus. Thus, suppose that through simultaneous presentation of food and the sound of a tone of middle C, a dog originally is trained to salivate at the sound of the tone. It can receive hundreds of trials with just this one tone; but even so, if it is tested at the end of that training, it will salivate to tones an octave and a half above or below middle C. The dogs can be taught to differentiate, however. This is accomplished by continuing to pair middle C with feeding, but to sound repeatedly some much higher or lower tone without giving any food after such signals. By this means it is found that dogs can be taught to make such fine distinctions that the experimenter cannot trust his own ear and has to refer to his apparatus to tell with certainty what tone he has given. Such fine differentiations are products of much learning; sensory generalization is, instead, a product of factors which exist *before* training in discrimination.

The carry-over of learning sometimes is extended to other materials where the habit is not appropriate. A complex example of generalization is seen in the use of language. The three- or four-year-old child often will use such expressions as "This is the goodest thing," and "Look, it's winding and raining outside." He has no formulated rules which cause him thus to defy the illogical elements of his mother tongue, but he is carrying the benefits of his learning from some materials to others. Some serious emotional maladjustments of personality, too, are partly products of this tendency of habits to be called out in situations only roughly similar to the original learning situations. So, from many different angles, sensory generalization is one of the important factors to recognize in the use of habits.

Present perceptual conditions

The conditions in which a habit is used are usually more or less different from those in which the habit was created. Even in Pavlov's experiment, for instance, the dog in the original situation was stimulated not only by a signal, but also by some meat powder put into his mouth. When the dog is tested to see whether it has learned the conditioned response, however, there is merely the signal, and no meat powder. Since the perceptual conditions are different from what they were in the original situation, the behavior of the animal in such tests is also different. The dog still salivates (still makes a response which has some appropriateness as a preparatory response for the situation which it expects next to meet), but it does not go through the other movements of chewing and swallowing.

This is typical of what occurs in the use of habits. The process in the subject at the time of performance is a product, not merely of its reintegrative mechanisms, but also of its perception of the current situation.

Intelligence

Performance is also a product of the various abilities or capacities of the individual.

> For example, a Cebus monkey first learned to use such an object as a stick to obtain food which was outside its reach. The monkey was then given further tests to see whether, from this learning, it could use some other implements which originally it could not have used for this pur-

pose. What was found was that the monkey quite readily adapted its behavior. It could bring the food within reach with a sack, tossing the sack over the food and then pulling the sack in, etc. It could use a chain, a triangle of cardboard, and other objects. In one test the only possible material for a tool was a newspaper pinned down by a box too heavy for the monkey to move. In this situation, it tore pieces from the paper, worked them together into a more or less rigid "stick" and used this to secure the food. In all of this, certainly, the monkey was show-ing that its use of its habit depended also on some intelligence on its part. But some further work showed just as clearly the *limitations* of the monkey's mental ability. The experimenter hung the food from the ceiling with a string, high enough so that the monkey would have to use a stick to knock the food down. Instead of securing the food within a few seconds, the animal was baffled for a long time. Even when it picked up the stick it tended to poke around aimlessly on the floor underneath the food. It finally solved the problem, but only with con-siderable difficulty. (Klüver[21])

Of course, the degree of adaptability of behavior depends not only on intelligence and on perceptual conditions, but also on what habit was acquired. The teacher who gives purely mechanical rules may help the students to handle one particular type of situation, but since there is usually considerable variety in the situations in which learning is to be applied, the really effective teacher explains *why* the student would do one thing or another.

Motivation as a factor in performance

You already know from the last chapter that in order for a habit to be used in overt behavior, a condition of appropriate motivation usually is required. Even in Pavlov's food-bell experiment, the dogs would not salivate after learning unless they were hungry. It is far from correct to say, however, that motivation is required for *all* use of habits. All day long our life involves the use of sensory-organization habits and interpretive habits. We perpetually are reacting and living in terms of meaningful things around us, and such meaning is not dependent on the simple kind of motivation required for overt behavior. You have to be thirsty to be inspired to use a water fountain, but you do not have to be thirsty to recognize it automatically as you walk past it.

Active reconstructions as a factor in performance

Often we have been inclined to speak as though the use of habits involves an exact reproduction of the behavior originally learned. We have just seen, however, that behavior usually is adapted to the special features of the situation existing at the time the habit is used. There is still another respect in which the use of habits is dependent on active and intelligent processes within the learner.

At the time when the person tries to recall something he has learned previously, it often is true that he can recall only some general schema of the original material. Even in a simple thing as remembering a name, as you probably know from experience, you can remember only that it was a name "something like Harriman or Berriflin or Countryman." But you cannot remember the name—even though, interestingly enough, you can rule out a long string of names as incorrect. When you finally do remember the name, you see the resemblance between it and the general pattern or schema that you had been able to recall—perhaps it was "Sullivan," which also has three syllables and ends with an "n" on its soft last syllable.

The same process goes on with materials of rather complex sorts as well (Crosland[22] and Bartlett[23]). Some general schema is retained, and when the person attempts to recall the original details he does not strictly "recall" but now "reconstructs." That is, he adds details which are consistent with his general impression. He does not realize he is doing this but believes, honestly enough, that everything he is giving is what he originally learned.

Especially when some strong interests or prejudices are involved, this reconstructive activity tends to give such bias an opportunity to operate. Studies of rumor have shown that people add details which are consistent with what they have tended to believe anyway, and, when a series of people pass the story from one person to another, all of them tending to change it in the same direction, some really remarkable transformations can occur.

General set as a factor in performance

A number of lines of evidence give support to the interesting suggestion that the "stimuli" which arouse a habit are not merely external stimuli, even when they are quite clear-cut and distinctive stimuli, but are also certain internal conditions of "set" as well. This fact has come out strikingly in a detailed case study.

> The man observed had suffered a severe blow on the back of his head, and it was almost certain that he was suffering from some appreciable injury to the brain. From superficial observation it did not seem that the behavior or mental ability of the man had been very deeply affected, but when careful note was taken of his reactions, a very profound change was discovered.

This change expressed itself particularly in the man's inability to recognize even familiar objects, unless they were in their natural setting and unless there was some opportunity to deal with them appropriately. When he was placed before a mirror, for example, he stared at his figure in the glass as though he were seeing another man —he even demanded that this man should answer him. But when a comb was handed to him, he took it, his face cleared, and he started to comb his hair before the mirror, obviously understanding now that the mirror was something which reflected his own image. When given a pencil he would handle it awkwardly, as though it were a strange object, until he tentatively tried to make a mark with it and saw that it left a black mark on the paper. Then, without hesitation or uncertainty, he spoke of it as a pencil. (Hanfmann, Rickers-Ovsiankina, and Goldstein[24])

This, of course, is a case of a brain-injured person. You might well ask whether a normal human being has this same dependence on *dynamic* action-qualities or behavior-set, or whether we normal human beings can guide our responses quite adequately by the more *static* visual stimuli which we receive from an object. The answer to this question would seem to be that a good human brain is able to give us the means of using our habits merely from static stimuli. In other words, we do not need a complete and familiar behavior situation in order to know how to deal with various objects, but depend on the automatic internal organizing processes of perception.

It is undoubtedly true, however, that we are not so free from this influence of "set" in using our habits as we might imagine. For example, a very common phenomenon which can be seen within the life of the ordinary family is that the parents often call their children by the wrong names, confusing one child's name with another's. Almost never does one parent call a child by the other parent's name. The confusion grows out of the parent's tendency to assume the same general behavior-set toward all the children. They all have to be looked after, they all have a more restricted vocabulary, they all can be allowed to do only certain things, and so on. This set, which is general from one child to another, must be the factor in evoking the wrong name, because the parent can obviously distinguish visually between one child and another.

The same point is illustrated by the type of definition which children give of objects. "What is a chair?" you ask. "It's to sit on," says the child. The child's thinking is in terms of action; it is directed toward functioning with reference to things. It seems highly probable that our use of habits involves much more cooperation from such sets for activity than we might generally have imagined.

The effect of audience on remembering

An investigation has been made of the influence of reciting learned material for the benefit of an audience as compared with reciting it to a single experimenter. We have already seen that the desire to impress one's social group and to receive their approval is one of the most fundamental human motives. This experiment actually shows that the desire for the social approval of an audience can improve memory.

In the experiment in question, twenty college students were read a story which they later retold twice—once to the experimenter alone and again to an audience of ten or twelve of their classmates. When the subjects retold the story to the group, more words were used, more ideas were correctly recalled, more pains were taken to make the story interesting. There was more explanation and clarification of the basic ideas, and more invention and introduction of materials not in the original account. The audience, by operating as a factor of motivation, had a facilitating effect on recall. (Hanawalt and Ruttiger[25])

The effect of failure to complete a task

It has been well established that tasks which are not completed are more likely to be recalled than are tasks which are completed

In a German experiment, the subjects performed simple tasks, such as writing down a favorite quotation from memory, solving a riddle, or doing mental arithmetic problems. The tasks were simple ones the subjects could accomplish if given enough time. In some of the tasks, subjects were interrupted before they had a chance to carry out the instructions in full. Other tasks they were permitted to finish. Despite the fact that the completed tasks took more time than the interrupted ones, the subjects were more likely to recall the unfinished tasks than the finished tasks when they were questioned a few hours after the testing. But since this superiority for the unfinished tasks disappeared within twenty-four hours, it appears that this short-run advantage of the unfinished tasks was a consequence of short-run motivational factors, rather than being a difference of learning of the two sets of tasks. (Zeigarnik[26])

A similar experiment was conducted in which a series of twenty simple tasks were assigned informally to college students. The subjects recalled the uncompleted tasks about 57 per cent better than they recalled the completed ones. (Marrow[27] and Marrow[28])

A familiar example of the effect of noncompletion upon memory is the college student who studies a difficult problem in algebra just before going to bed. He cannot solve it, and so decides to try in the morning, refreshed by a night's sleep. However, the problem keeps coming into consciousness, sometimes making sleep impossible. Because it is not completed, it remains in his mind. Even more persistent in memory are more complex problems of personal life.

This effect is an instance of "activity in progress." Once we get started toward a goal, we tend to persist. After the goal is reached, our motivating tension is reduced, and the whole effort may be forgotten. You can see examples of this all around you. For instance, you look up a seldom-used telephone number and dial it but find the line busy. After five minutes you try again without having to look up the number. This time the line is free; you complete your conversation and hang up the receiver. The telephone number is immediately forgotten, for it has served its purpose. Items needed for activity in progress are remembered only for the duration of the need; it might be said that this is an "economy" to the organism.

The use of a habit, then, is a much more complex matter than merely "making a learned response to a stimulus." Like the original learning, it is a truly complex activity. And as we have seen, there are many factors which need to be taken into account if we are to have any adequate understanding of how the actual performance of the person is produced.

CHANGING OUR HABITS

OF COURSE IT IS BETTER to learn things right in the beginning than to learn them wrong and to have to change our habits later. But since we often do learn them wrong—even in some very important matters that determine the happiness or unhappiness of our lives—there is great importance in the problem of how habits are changed.

Experimental extinction in conditioning

One of the phenomena discovered originally in Pavlov's laboratory has particular value for this discussion of changing habits. It is the phenomenon of *experimental extinction*. Pavlov found, for example, that after he had trained a dog to salivate at the sound of the bell, he could eliminate this response from the dog by sounding the bell over and over again without giving the *reinforcement* (the food which originally had been used to teach the dog to salivate in this situation). Without such training, the dog might retain its habit for three or four months without much decrease of response, but with this technique of experimental-extinction training, the dog could be taught within a few days not to salivate to the bell. This process is much more rapid than ordinary forgetting.

How is experimental extinction accomplished—what is involved in it? To understand this phenomenon, suppose that, on a given day of training, the bell has been sounded twenty different times, each time without being reinforced (that is, without any food being given after it is sounded). As the bell is thus sounded time after time, the dog salivates less and less in each case, and shows less and less tendency to look toward the bell or toward the food pan while the bell is sounding (cf. Zener[29]). It might happen that, on the last three of such extinction trials, the dog would have no extra salivation at all beyond that which normally occurs under conditions of no special stimulation. Examining the record for these twenty trials, we may conclude that the task of experimental extinction has been accomplished. But when the dog is given a rest for a day, and then is tested in the laboratory once more, we find that the conditioned response has had a *spontaneous recovery*. Once more the dog is ready to salivate when it hears the sound of the bell. But on this second day, it reaches the point of zero salivation in fewer trials; and within a few more days of such work the dog might be brought to the point where the conditioned response has been permanently "extinguished."

In these trials with no reinforcement, the dog is learning or acquiring a *second* habit—a habit of expecting that the signal will *not* be followed by food. This habit, like habits generally, tends to suffer from forgetting (as a product of retroactive inhibition from other activities, or by whatever causes). Thus, even though it is strong enough to dominate the original conditioned-response habit in the first period of extinction training, this second habit will not be strong enough to control the response process on the second day. After all, the original habit was established by quite a protracted training, and only twenty trials have been given in which the dog had the chance to learn that the signal would not be followed by food. So this second habit suffers more from forgetting during the lapse of one day than does the originally established habit. With enough practice, however, the new habit becomes well enough established so that it regularly determines the response to the signal, even after a considerable lapse of time.

Such experiments suggest several conclusions of importance:

1 Forgetting is often not the most efficient means of eliminating a habit.

2 Eliminating a habit depends particularly on building up some other habit with reference to the same situation.

3 Eliminating a habit depends on actually calling out that habit, or using it, under certain appropriate conditions.

If conditioned responses depended on mechanical connections in the nervous system, we might well expect that, the more invariably the signal had been paired with the reinforcement, the more resistant to experimental extinction would be the resulting conditioned response. Curiously enough, the opposite has been found to be the case.

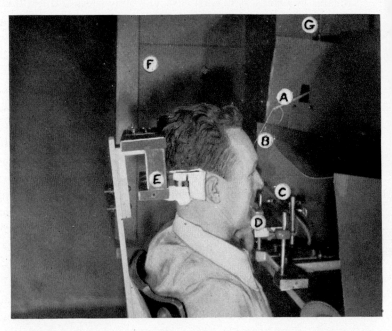

The apparatus for conditioning eyelid reactions in the experiment below. *The eyelid is attached to a light wooden lever (A) by a thread (B). The stimulus is a puff of air blown into the eye through an air-puff jet (C). The subject, in order to hold his head steady, keeps his teeth clamped on a biting board (D) and leans against a head rest (E). Every time the subject blinks his eyelid, the lever moves. A small mirror mounted on the fulcrum of the lever reflects light upon a film. The film is mounted upon a swinging pendulum in such a way as to indicate the time relations between successive reactions shown on the film. At (F) is the partition hiding the pendulum, and at (G) is the lever and mirror support. (Photograph courtesy of Dr. Lloyd G. Humphreys.)*

One psychologist compared human subjects who had had invariable reinforcement with those who had received reinforcement on only half of the same total number of training trials. In the first group, the subjects always felt a puff of air against the eye after the signal had been received. The members of the second group received such a puff irregularly (but with never more than two trials without this reinforcement). In terms of the percentage of subjects who came to make some movement of their eyelids before receiving this puff of air, both groups of subjects seemed to be learning the habit with about equal speed. But when the two groups were subjected to training for experimental extinction, quite a difference was discovered, as can be seen from the graph below:

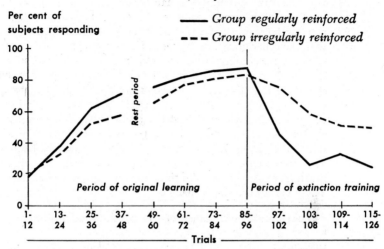

The conditioned eyelid reflex

Adapted from L. Humphreys, "The Effect of Random Alternation of Reinforcement on the Acquisition and Extinction of Conditioned Eyelid Reactions," *Journal of Experimental Psychology*, 1939, volume 25, pp. 146, 148.

The following graph shows the results in the individual trials of the early part of the extinction training with the regularly and irregularly reinforced groups, compared with the average record of the same groups in the last 24 hours of the original training (trials 73-96).

A "close-up" of the first six extinction trials

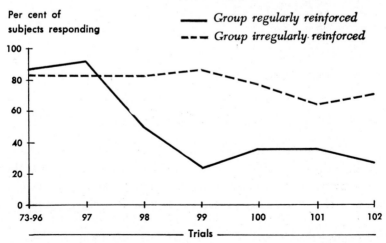

Adapted from L. Humphreys, "The Effect of Random Alternation of Reinforcement on the Acquisition and Extinction of Conditioned Eyelid Reactions," *Journal of Experimental Psychology*, 1939, volume 25, p. 152.

As can be seen from this graph, the group formerly given invariable reinforcement stopped making the response very quickly after they met the first trial without reinforcement. It took little evidence to help them to learn that the situation apparently had been changed, and their behavior reflected this changed understanding of the situation. But with the other group, which had received only half as many reinforcements and an equal number of unreinforced trials, the responses actually increased for a few trials, and then, much more slowly than with the other group, decreased. (Humphreys[30])

The same findings were secured in a second experiment in which the response measured was an involuntary response (measured by a change in the electrical conductivity of the skin). In that experiment, when the irregularly reinforced subjects now were started on the part of the training when the signal no longer was followed by a painful electric shock (as the stimulus producing the reaction which produced the change of skin conductivity), they also had some increase of response-tendency for several trials, and then their curves fell off much more slowly than did those for the control group. (Humphreys[31]) These curves are shown below.

Experimental extinction of the conditioned galvanic response

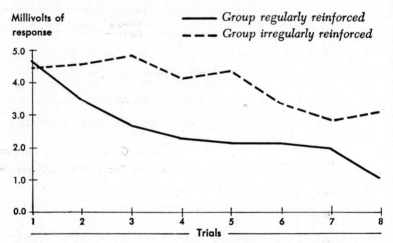

Millivolts of
response

———— Group regularly reinforced
－ － － Group irregularly reinforced

Adapted from L. Humphreys, "Extinction of Conditioned Psychogalvanic Responses Following Two Conditions of Reinforcement," *Journal of Experimental Psychology*, 1940, volume 27, p. 73.

Thus even in the cases where the effector reaction is governed by the autonomic nervous system, it still seems to be true that the effector activity is governed by the subject's *understanding of the nature of the situation and his expectations as to what is likely to happen.* When the original situation has been inconsistent, it is difficult for the person to know later whether what he finds are just additional "exceptions" or some indication that the situation really has been changed.

Negative practice as a means of changing habits

A somewhat different kind of habit-changing has been explored by a method known as the *negative-practice* method; that is, deliberate repetition of an undesirable habit. One psychologist (Dunlap[32]) reports that persistent typing errors (such as typing *hte* for *the*) may be eliminated if the *wrong* habits are practiced for even a short time, but if the error is of a kind that is habitual in more than one situation, a removal in one sphere will not cause its removal in the others. He explored the technique further with reference to some cases of finger-nail biting and a few other responses in students who were anxious to have some help in overcoming such habits, and had considerable success.

This is the same process that is involved in experimental extinction. The habit is eliminated, not by waiting for forgetting to occur, but by actually using the habit under certain conditions which permit the person to realize *at the time that the habit is being used* the inappropriateness or undesirability of the habit. This process will be discussed further on pages 534-536. For now, it is enough to say that the process obviously has its limitations. Some habits (alcoholism, for example) have such undesirable consequences that they cannot be attacked by negative practice.

So far in this chapter on *Remembering and Thinking*, we have been discussing learning of all sorts, regardless of whether it was accomplished by relatively simple means such as trial-and-error or memorizing or conditioning, or whether it was accomplished by relatively more complex processes of thinking. But the problems of thinking are of special interest to us because of the crucial importance of this process in human life. So even though thinking already has been described in part by principles which hold good for many simpler phenomena as well, we shall give attention now to some of the special problems presented by this complex psychological process. The remainder of this chapter will be concerned especially with the two problems of *The Role of Thinking* and *How We Think*.

THE ROLE OF THINKING

THE PRECEDING CHAPTER showed that the most essential factor in learning is the internal organizing activity within the individual—that learning does not result merely from being stimulated, from making a response, or from receiving a reward for the response to that stimulus.

In all learning situations there is an organizing activity suggestive of thinking or of thought processes. This activity yields a perceptual response which is something more than the perception of the several elements of the situation separately.

In some learning situations, this internal organizing activity is much more complex than in others. The learner, instead of bringing together several perceptual processes which depend directly on the immediate situation, utilizes processes, and works out an organization from them, which represent things *not actually present to his senses.* For instance, while an architect is trying to decide what kind of house would be best for a given location, he may actually visit the lot where the house is to be built, and actually walk around and perceive the land and trees and surrounding buildings. But he will also engage in some thought processes which will run far beyond what is actually present to his senses. For example, he may consider the question of how the driveway should be placed and what view would be more interesting from the still nonexistent dining-room window.

Obviously, then, there is no clear dividing line between thinking and other more simple modes of response. The distinction is just one of degree. Thinking appears in proportion as the individual is able to represent different properties of a situation, and is able to manipulate or organize those representations, in ways which go beyond those processes that rest directly on actual manipulation of materials.

In other words, thinking is behavior in which at least some of the objects dealt with are not physically present to the senses but are represented by symbols. These symbols are manipulated in thinking in much the same way that our hands manipulate actual physical objects. Symbols, and the relationships among symbols, are apprehended in thinking much as the relationships among physical objects are apprehended in perception. Symbols are many and varied in nature: words, gestures, and pictures are some of the most widely used.

Kinds of thinking

There are two basic kinds of thinking: *problem solving*, which is directed toward action (whether immediate or deferred) and which arises when we are face to face with a problem; and *autistic* (self-directed) *thinking*, which satisfies our desires often with disregard for objective realities, as in night-dreaming and daydreaming.

A little dreaming by day or night is good for us. In fact, some inventors and artists report that a fundamental idea or suggestion may come in a dream and then may be criticized and elaborated in the waking state. As a rule, however, dreams do not stand the light of day. What seems such a wonderful idea during a doze is found upon critical examination to be poor indeed. A person who is dissatisfied with his everyday life often has daydreams of success and gratification, which can become so satisfying in themselves that real satisfactions are no longer desired.

This self-directed kind of thinking, however, represents only one extreme kind of thinking, with reasoning at the other extreme. In everyday life, our thinking may be at any intermediate point between them. This section will be much more concerned with reasoning and creative imagination than with autistic thinking.

The values of thinking

Thinking prepares for action, gives new meanings to old facts, helps formulate beliefs, and affords enjoyment. It is the ability to reason and invent which brings man far above the lower animals. Controlled thinking, which prepares for the execution of an enterprise or for the invention of instruments and techniques, constitutes man's most important function in carrying out the work of the world.

Thinking prepares for action. By a process of thinking, many false steps are eliminated, much waste avoided, numerous possible disasters averted, and valuable time saved in the stages of behavior which must precede the actual execution of a project. For instance, in preparing for final examinations, the thoughtful student plans and budgets his time according to the amount of material he has to cover in each course and the total amount of time he has available.

Thinking may produce new meanings. By thinking, it is possible to work out new relationships among facts which are already familiar. This process of "putting two and two together" is an important part of the work of both the scholar and the man of science. Certain persons can best discover new meanings through research aimed at discovering new facts; others excel at arriving at new meanings by putting together in new forms the facts which have already been discovered. Within any field of learning there exists a great deal of this division of labor.

Let us take from the field of medicine a case in which thinking ended in new meanings, finally producing a cure for syphilitic insanity. It had long been known that syphilis can attack the nervous system to produce a form of insanity. It was also known that the natives of a certain community in Africa were one hundred per cent infected with syphilis, that they all had malaria fever, but that cases of syphilitic insanity were unknown there. One physician put these facts together. "Could it be," he reasoned, "that there is something in the reaction of the human body to malaria germs which renders the nervous system impervious to the effects of the syphilis germs?" That was one way in which the three facts could be put together. Work based on this hypothesis brought results. Insanity caused by syphilis can be arrested by giving the patient a slight case of malaria.

Not content, the medical researchers asked themselves, "Why? What is it about malaria that kills the disease syphilis? Is it a chemical action, or is it the temperature?" Devices were developed to raise body temperature without giving the patient malaria fever. Cures were accomplished, and this rapidly came to be the standard method of treatment for syphilis and the type of insanity caused by it.

Here you see that a new meaning was arrived at when familiar facts were combined in a new pattern of reasoning.

Thinking may produce belief. When a person has a confident idea of how to solve some problem, this confident interpretation might be called a *belief*. It is significant that, regardless of the degree of confidence, such beliefs may have been evolved rationally or nonrationally. In rational belief, after the facts have been carefully considered and a conclusion reached, we find it worthy of full acceptance. The practical sign of belief is willingness to act according to it. The motorist travels around a curve in the highway at a good clip even when he cannot see what is ahead, because he believes the highway to be clear on his side of the road. Past experience with highways, knowledge of traffic rules, plus observation of the immediate situation, are evaluated to produce this belief. If the belief were not there the motorist would stop, or at least would travel more slowly and cautiously.

Not all beliefs result from rational analysis. In all phases of our lives much is believed wholly or partly on faith, with certain facts or attitudes being accepted without critical reasoning. A belief evolved through nonrational channels has about the same firm grip in a person's mind as one evolved rationally. Once a belief or conviction has been established, it serves as a basis for the classification and evaluation of other facts.

Thinking affords enjoyment. One of the great values of thinking is in the recreation that it affords. A person with a vivid imagination may frequently endure conditions which would be painfully boring to a less imaginative person. Time hangs very heavily on the prisoner-of-war who is not occupied with work. Numerous reports from liberated prisoners leave no doubt about the value of playful thinking as a means of "killing time." A mind well-stocked with things to think about is of great value.

The value of thinking as recreation goes beyond merely passing time away. Mental reviewing of past achievements and experiences, indulged in for its pleasure at first, frequently leads into reflective analysis which in turn contributes new meanings, prepares for new actions, or culminates in new beliefs.

Thinking and perceiving compared. A striking similarity can be noted between thinking and perceiving: both may culminate in action and meaning. How, then, do thinking and perceiving differ? The answer to this question has been suggested already. *Perceiving* is a process of organizing present sensory data and interpreting them on the basis of past experience, whereas *thinking* can utilize exclusively objects not present to the senses.

HOW WE THINK

RESEARCH WORKERS in many fields find that if they want to understand some phenomenon, they must try to understand how it is carried on. For example, research workers on poliomyelitis would like to know *how* the disease is spread, because then they could work much more effectively on the problem of how to prevent it from spreading. In the same way, psychologists investigating the nature of thinking have directed their research and discussion, not merely to the question of the conditions governing thinking, but to the question to which we now turn: What kinds of processes are involved in thinking?

The basic procedures in thinking

Since so much thinking takes the form of problem solving, our main understanding of how thinking proceeds comes by considering the processes in solving problems of differing complexity.

Controlled association. One of the simplest problem situations is that in which some specific idea must be recalled. For instance, if you want to introduce a person whose face is familiar, you must recall his name; another example would be to recall your telephone number when asked. In these simple situations the required idea is recalled and is immediately recognized to be correct. The psychologists call this "controlled" association to differentiate it from "free" association. In *free association* there is no set; the person is permitted to think of anything. But in *controlled association* the response must be related to the stimulus in some predetermined way. For example, the set may be to give synonyms. Thus, to respond with the word "white" to the stimulus word "black" would not be right, but the word "dark" would be acceptable. In such controlled-association situations, the set of the person operates to help the person locate an appropriate response from all the wealth of associations which he might have with some given stimulus-word. The speed of reaction in such cases is even somewhat greater than in situations in which the person is asked merely to give an association of any kind.

The essential steps in productive thinking. A number of workers have tried to discover the steps by which thinking takes place—both in problem-solving thinking (Dewey[33]) and in creative thinking in artists (Patrick[34]). The steps which have been described are so comparable that we can fuse these descriptions into the following account of the steps involved in productive thinking:

1 *Becoming concerned about or interested in a problem.* Thinking must satisfy a need; the person who is completely satisfied will not think. There must be a distinct recognition of some lack —no matter whether it is a lack of some practical device for economizing on labor, or a lack of some aesthetically satisfying piece of music.

2 *Assembling the materials with which to work.* The problem-solving thinker must examine more closely the situations with which he is concerned. Why do the machines now available prove inadequate for the work, and what are the areas in which trouble most often appears? The creative worker has a similar period of preparation. Edwin Markham, for instance, has told the story of how he wrote the poem, "The Man with the Hoe." When he came upon Millet's painting by that title in a museum, he was deeply impressed, and instead of walking on after a few minutes as most museum visitors would have done, he stayed before it, absorbed, for about two hours. There was no thought, so far as he could later remember, that he might try to write a poem about the picture. He not only had the interest (step 1), but also gave time "for the wheels to grind around." And of course his gathering of materials was not confined to that brief period: throughout his life he had been developing the emotional and intellectual interests which had made him responsive to that painting.

3 *Deriving a number of possible solutions* during the period of thinking about the problem, with the aid of the materials which have been assembled. Sometimes these solutions come so suddenly and so dramatically—so adequately—that the thinker is inclined to think of them as "inspirations" or "illuminations." Sometimes it seems that this occurs particularly with artists. Markham

found that when he awoke the morning after having seen this painting and after having pondered on it through the rest of the day (but not trying to compose any poem about it), the first stanza of his poem was in his mind, ready to write. He put it down, thinking of it as completed, but the next morning a second stanza was recorded in the same way. This process is not really different from what has been reported by scientists who have been curious about their own thinking processes. It must be remembered that the technically trained worker (whether he is a mathematician, poet, or musician) has put an enormous amount of time and work into mastering the tools of his trade—into achieving an easy skill in all the subprocesses which could only be performed most laboriously by the novice in that field.

4 *Evaluation of the suggested solutions.* Further data pertinent to the suggested hypothesis are recalled and used as a standard against which the hypothesis is checked. Frequently this procedure will be sufficient to justify the discarding of the first hypothesis. In this case another hypothesis is suggested from past experience with related problems, and it in turn is subjected to evaluation by attempts to square it with the related facts as one knows them.

5 *Objectively testing and revising the solution.* Details often have to be changed in artistic work in order to iron out the rough spots. In scientific work and in practical life, too, the tentative evaluations of the solutions must be subjected to some careful tests before they are used practically. The layman, for instance, often is impatient because new medical discoveries are not adopted immediately in practical medical work; but the physician knows that hasty applications may have unforeseen ill-effects.

Here is an example of the use of these fundamental steps in problem solving. It is the description of an attempt to discover the purpose of the short metal chain which trails behind gasoline trucks.

> *Step 1 (Problem)* What is the use of the short iron chain hanging from the back of a gasoline truck?
> *Step 2 (Data)* It is on all gasoline trucks, very rarely on other trucks. It is short, but long enough to trail on the ground. It is made of metal. Gasoline is highly inflammable. Trucks sometimes get stuck and have to be towed. Trucks sometimes pull trailers. Trucks running on icy pavement often use chains to prevent slipping.
> *Step 3 (Hypothesis)* It may be used to attach a trailer to the truck.
> *Step 4 (Evaluation of the hypothesis)* It is not long or strong enough to hold the trailer back when going downhill. (Hypothesis rejected.)

Step 3′ (Suggestion of another hypothesis) It may be just a spare chain, to use on the tires, or to fix something on the truck.

Step 4′ (Evaluation) Why keep it back there? Why not put it in the tool box? (Hypothesis rejected.)

Step 3″ (Suggestion of still another hypothesis) Maybe it has something to do with preventing the truck from catching fire and exploding.

Step 4″ (Evaluation) There is lots of friction in a truck, especially of the tires against the road. Friction generates electric sparks, and one of the sparks might ignite the gasoline. Something is needed to conduct that electricity to the ground. Metal is a good conductor. And the chain trails on the ground all the time. (Solution judged to be satisfactory.)

Step 5 (Objective test) Questioning of the driver shows the solution to be correct.

Often, of course, some of these steps are condensed or omitted.

The tools with which we think

The process of thinking enables a person to consider and solve problems which are far removed from him in space or time, but which are represented instead by symbols. These symbols mainly take the form of imagery, word symbols, and implicit bodily movements.

Imagery in thinking. A half century ago psychologists were deep in a controversy over the problem of imageless thought. Some of them held that thought required the use of images or mental pictures of actual sensory experiences such as sights, sounds, and smells. Subsequent discoveries force us to abandon the notion that images are the only materials with which we think. Many persons report that they can solve problems or even dream without the use of images. We cannot, of course, deny that recalled facts are necessary to thinking. The point is that people who do not have imagery or who have very little of it recall their facts through words or other symbols.

Sir Francis Galton made a study of the kinds of visual images used by people in thinking (Galton[35]). He questioned many people in various walks of life, including a number of great scientists of his time. His detailed analyses of the descriptions of the imagery experienced by his subjects revealed that those very persons who were engaged in the highest and most complicated type of thinking, such as mathematical analysis, are likely to be deficient in visual imagery. For example, Poincaré, the great French mathematician, was very poor in visual imagery. Children and less gifted persons, on the other hand, often possess clear visual imagery to a much higher degree. This casts doubt upon the proposition that all thinking involves the use of visual imagery.

A British psychologist made a careful study of the conditions under which mental images are aroused in thought. He came to the conclusion that images occur in greatest numbers when the situation does not permit action or when movement is difficult; and that few images occur when action is easy and routine (Fox[36]). Images are typically much stronger in dreams than in the adaptive activity demanded by the needs of the day.

People vary greatly in the strength of their images. Most people seem to be strongest in visual imagery. Some, however, are strongest in their "mind's ear"; a small minority find that images of touch, muscle movement, taste, or smell are strongest. In rare cases, individuals possess powerful imagery which is almost like actual perception in its clarity and accuracy. These strong images, usually visual, are called *eidetic images*. People with eidetic imagery can frequently tell the exact position of a formula or fact on the printed page of the textbook. The R—— boy (see p. 196) had eidetic imagery; he carried around in his "mind's eye" a clear picture of calendars for years back, so that when he was asked what day of the week a certain date fell on, he had only to refer to his mental image to give the answer. People with this ability can even glance for a fraction of a second at an object, such as a comb, and then call up the image and give a complete description of it, such as the number of teeth in the comb as presented in imagery. In examinations they copy from their mental image of the printed page, thus keeping within the rules of the game but performing with an accuracy as great as if the book were actually open before them, as in the following case:

> A law student was once called before a discipline committee on the charge of cheating in an examination. One of the questions called for the details of a law case which was given in the textbook. The student had turned in a description which was word for word that of the textbook. The reader had quite naturally concluded that the student had followed an open copy. Upon being questioned the student defended himself by saying that he had felt that the professor might call for that case and so had looked it over just before class. To test his ability at such exact reproduction of verbal material, the student was given a page of unfamiliar material to study for five minutes. At the end of that period he was able to reproduce some four hundred words without error. Not a single word or punctuation mark differed from the text. He had eidetic imagery.

Eidetic imagery is most often found in children; they lose much of it as they grow older. One psychologist who has made a careful review of the literature on eidetic imagery comes to the conclusion that eidetic imagery is simply very clear visual imagery (Allport[37]). Recent unpublished evidence gathered in connection with training in aircraft identification indicates that the average person can greatly reduce the time required to observe and reproduce a familiar pattern, and thus can closely approach or actually attain eidetic imagery.

The enjoyment of imagery is a potent factor in mental life. Think of someone you know well. Can you get an image of that person's face? Can you hear the sound of his voice? Try to relive in imagery some particularly lovely landscape you have seen on a trip, or try to see again the people and surroundings at a dance or party you went to some time ago. Through the recall of images in our various sense departments we are able to enjoy past experiences, now far removed in space and time. William Wordsworth has expressed his enjoyment of visual imagery in the familiar poem, "Daffodils."

Auditory stimuli may often give rise to visual imagery, the most common example of a condition known as *synesthesia*—that is, the translation of sensory experience from one sense department to another. There are no absolutely fixed relationships between visual imagery and the nature of musical stimuli, but certain tendencies can be observed (Karwoski and Odbert[38]). For instance, a rise in pitch or quickening of tempo usually brings increased brightness of the image. Smooth music brings graceful, flowing lines in the visual images; syncopated music gives rise to jagged lines. Different instruments give rise to lines of different color. Increases of volume bring increased area of the images. About ten per cent of the adult population enjoys some colored hearing when listening to music or other sounds. Some people have colored images even when just recalling music, not hearing it directly. All such images are useful aids in thinking.

Symbols and reintegrative processes. As culture has progressed, a great host of symbols have been developed to supplement the direct representational processes. For instance, if you were asked to judge which of two tables was larger, you would find the length and width of each as expressed in terms of some standardized unit of measurement. Then, drawing on your skills in using such symbolic materials, you would do some multiplying and get your answer to the problem. You could achieve an exactness by this means which you could not secure by some perceptual comparison.

However, it must not be thought that when a person acquires more technical symbolic responses, they eliminate his use of the other representative processes involved in thinking. The verbal symbols we use are valuable as means of manipulating and organizing our more basic tools of thought (our reintegrative processes), but they are not in themselves so rich or detailed as are these underlying processes. This can be seen most clearly in the case of a small child whose vocabulary is still highly restricted. Such a child may call a strange man "daddy," since he has no word "man" as yet, but his equivalence in his application of the word "daddy" to various men does not mean that he fails to distinguish between them—in his behavior he shows quite unmistakably that he knows the distinction. Another interesting example was given by a small child presented with one of the test items of the Stanford-Binet test. The child had been given the card bearing ten geometrical designs. Then he was handed a sample of one of these drawings and asked to find one like it. In the case of three of the ten drawings, his comment was the same—to wit, "There's a ball." But in each case, he matched the drawing correctly—a circle with the circle in one case, an ellipse with the ellipse in another case, and an octagon with the octagon in the third case. In other words, his behavior was showing that it was guided by some process more precise than his verbal reactions.

The same relation exists between language and thought all through our lives. Our words themselves do not have very much in them; it is "what the words mean to us" which is used in our thinking. We think basically in terms of our reintegrative processes, aided and organized by the verbal processes. But while words are only the tools of thought, they are essential tools. Especially valuable in complex adult thought are abstract *concepts*.

The use of concepts. As we have seen, the evoking of a habit does not require exactly the same stimulus-situation or signal which was present during the acquiring of the habit—in fact, the signal can be changed markedly and still call out the same conditioned response. In other words, there is something about the nervous mechanisms which gives a considerable measure of generality to our learned ways of responding.

Such generalization is very important in thinking, and is partially accomplished by the use of concepts. Even when very young, children use each new word with surprising freedom; it almost seems sometimes as though they are never at a loss to name new things, if they have any word at all in the same general area. Sheep seen for the first time are called "doggies"; a threshing machine is a "truck." In all such cases, the child is doing the same thing that is shown in conditioning, as we mentioned earlier in the chapter in discussing sensory generalization. From roughly similar patterns of stimulation, he is using the same habit.

Although such generality in response is important and valuable, it is quite primitive and needs to be supplemented by some more sophisticated bases of generality as the child grows older. On the one hand, he needs to learn that some things are to be grouped together which perceptually have little in the way of superficial similarity: he needs to learn, for instance, that dogs and fish and earthworms and mosquitoes all are animals. On the other hand, he needs to make distinctions in some cases where the superficial perceptual characteristics are highly similar: he needs to learn that bats have more in common with dogs than with birds, or that whales have more in common with bats than with tuna fish. And, in order to have a basis for such "unusual" groupings of materials, he must learn to recognize properties which mark off the members of such groups. He learns, for instance, that some animals like whales and bats and dogs maintain a constant body temperature (are warm-blooded), but that other animals like frogs and tuna fish tend to have the same body temperature as their surroundings (or are cold-blooded). That is, he is learning to group things according to some important properties which are not easily perceived at first but which are common to a wide variety of things. He is developing *abstract concepts*.

Much of the education of an adult consists in his learning to employ such abstractions or concepts in his thinking. "Mass," "velocity," "energy," "time," "distance," and "inertia" are concepts essential to physics. Other organized bodies of knowledge have similar lists of basic concepts. The psychologist, for example, uses the two very important concepts of "maturation" and "learning." Technical terms are employed in science and in every type of accurate thinking, because the concepts they represent are precise. The limits of the concept have been sharply drawn and agreed upon by experts in the field, so that the meaning of the term is clear to everybody.

Man's superiority over the lower animals in ability to think is due in part to his relative ease in forming concepts. It is possible to develop concepts in animals as high as the monkey, but a great deal of time, patience, and ingenuity are required.

> One psychologist was able, for example, to teach a rhesus monkey the concept of *color*. The monkey was first taught to match two objects similar in both color and form. Then he was taught to select all objects of the same color as the one he was matching, regardless of their size and shape, or of variations in the brightness and saturation of the color. In the final step of the training, the animal learned to select all the red objects in response to a stimulus in the form of an uncolored triangle, and to select all the blue objects in response to an

uncolored ellipse. This psychologist hopes some day to teach monkeys to respond to the spoken words "red" and "blue" by selecting objects of appropriate color. (Weinstein[39])

Naturally we may expect that the capacity for forming abstract concepts will be demonstrable in some measure in animals below man, just as all other psychological functions appear, in at least some degree, in animals lower than man. Here it may certainly be said that the most profound psychological difference between man and the lower animals lies in the number, complexity, and subtlety of the abstract concepts which man can acquire and in the complex thinking which these concepts help to make possible.

Is there a muscular basis in thinking?

It has been discovered that thinking is accompanied by highly reduced bodily movements. The lay person is likely to challenge this discovery and offer the argument that the characteristic posture in thinking is one of inaction—that the person in deep thought typically sits "like a stone" with no trace of muscular activity. But this conclusion is another instance where psychology disproves everyday observation. Experimental evidence shows that there are tiny movements accompanying thinking which are too minute to be seen by the unaided human eye. The problem still to be solved is whether they are a necessary basis to thinking.

Implicit body movements. It has long been known that contracting muscles produce tiny electric currents. For a long time, the problem confronting physiologists was how to amplify or magnify these tiny electric currents to such an extent that even the momentary twitch of a tiny bundle of muscle fibers could be recorded. The development of radio tubes solved this problem. Amplifiers are now available which will pick up the tiny electric impulses of a contracting muscle of the wrist and translate them into a sound like that of a group of heavy bombing planes taking off. In fact, apparatus of this sort has been made so sensitive that it is necessary to train subjects in a special technique of relaxation so that their incidental movements will not interfere with the study of the special movements occurring during thinking. Experiments made with this apparatus have established definite correlations in time between the thought of an act and the appearance of tiny muscular movements.

> In one experiment, the subject was told to think of different actions, and then records were made of the action currents of the muscle and skin at the elbow of the right arm.

He was told, "Upon hearing the first signal, imagine lifting a 10-lb. weight in the right forearm. Upon hearing the second signal, relax any muscular tensions, if present." The results are shown in the record below, with the signals indicated by the short bars at the top:

"Upon hearing the first signal, imagine lifting the weight with the left forearm." The results are shown in the record below, which is similar to that obtained from the instructions "Do not bother to imagine," or "Imagine bending the right leg."

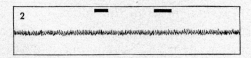

"Imagine hitting a nail twice with a hammer held in your right hand."

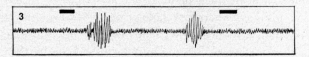

(Graphs courtesy of the experimenter, Dr. Edmund Jacobsen,[40] and of *The American Journal of Psychology*.)

The results of these experiments have been confirmed by many others. It has been shown that when a person is thinking of a geometric design, his eyes actually move to outline the form of it. (Totten[41])

Implicit muscular speech movements. You have often observed people in deep thought whose lips were motionless and silent. What about them? Can they be talking to themselves? Several psychologists have attacked this problem by fitting sensitive recording apparatus to the lips, tongue, and voice box. Subjects were instructed to read poetry or other material to themselves silently (Thorson[42]). Most of the subjects showed movements of the speech apparatus which were too small to be detected by the senses unaided but still large enough to affect the sensitive recording apparatus. These highly reduced speech movements are not observable from without but are contained within the organism. They are usually called *implicit movements*. Although they are possible carriers of meaning in thinking, it is not known whether they are a cause or an effect of thinking.

Further understanding of the role of muscular "speech" movements in abstract thinking is gained from a highly interesting experiment which shows that deafmutes make tiny "speech" movements with their hands during thought just as normal people make tiny movements of their vocal apparatus.

> Such implicit movements were studied in the cases of sixteen persons who had normal hearing and eighteen persons who were deaf. It might logically be expected that deaf persons, who make greater use of gestures in communicating with each other than do persons with normal hearing, would also make greater use of small muscle movements while engaged in abstract thinking. And actually, it turned out that in abstract thinking such as multiplying and dividing mentally, the deaf subjects showed measurable action currents in the arm muscles in 84 per cent of the cases, as against 31 per cent for the normal subjects. However, when normal and deaf subjects were instructed to imagine that they were performing tasks which would require the use of their arm muscles, the percentage of electrically measured small muscle movements of the arms was the same. (Max[43])

Here again are facts consistent with—though not conclusive evidence for—a motor basis of thought.

The presence of implicit muscular movements in thought gives a clue to how the Ouija Board works. The Ouija Board consists of a smooth surface upon which are printed the letters of the alphabet, the numerals, and the words "yes" and "no." There is in addition a small platform mounted on three smooth and short legs or, in a more expensive set, on ballbearings. The platform is shaped in the form of an elongated heart. The fingers of one or two sitters are placed loosely on the platform.

A question is asked and after a period of concentration the platform moves about pointing to letters, numerals, or the two words, supposedly signaling the answer from the spirit world. A more plausible explanation is that the movements of the board, if not the intentional faking of a charlatan, are caused by the muscular accompaniments of thought.

Is muscular movement necessary to thought? There is no doubt that thinking of some act is correlated with action currents appropriate to the muscles that would be brought into play by that act. This is true regardless of whether images are present. However, there is still lacking acceptable evidence of the direction of cause and effect. Logically, it is as possible that the thought caused the implicit movement as that the implicit movement caused the thought. The fact that subjects could not imagine while relaxed is consistent with the interpretation that tiny muscle movements are essential to thinking, but it is not conclusive proof. It might be that thinking always causes tiny muscle movements. The final proof of this relationship would come only if the time sequence of the two things could be established, for a cause must always precede its effect.

The process of human thought involves many highly technical tools, including concepts of experimental method, statistical techniques, rules of evidence in legal work, and other tools which we have not had opportunity to consider in this chapter. So much depends upon the soundness with which these tools are used that psychologists have realized the importance of investigating this particularly important type of human activity. We have had a glimpse at some of the work which has been done and at some of the concepts which have been developed, but the future will see much more research into the nature and processes of thinking.

In this chapter we have also discussed other aspects of the use of learning: retention and forgetting, and performance. Here it has become clear that learning and the use of learning involve many factors, such as attention, perception, motivation, and intelligence, which have been discussed in earlier chapters. Here is still more evidence of the complex nature of learning, as well as the close interrelations between the various fields of psychology—interrelations which arise, essentially, from the fact that man functions as a whole, with his various processes strongly influencing each other.

R

nt

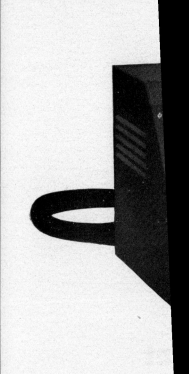

CHAP

At left is the galvanometer, an instrument that measures minute variations in an electric current. In the laboratory study of emotion, it is used to measure variations in the electrical resistance of the skin tissues, changes of this kind being one of the elements in emotional response. Electrodes are attached to straps fastened to the subject's arm, and a current is passed through the skin tissues from one electrode to the other. Variations in the resistance of the skin tissues cause slight current changes that are indicated on the dial of the galvanometer. Another type of galvanometer, with its commercial applications, is pictured on page 417. (Courtesy C. H. Stoelting Co.)

Studying Emotion in Laboratory and Clinic

Objective Description of Emotion

The Conditioning Theory of Emotional Development

Eliminating Conditioned Emotions

New Light on Conditioned Emotions

E MOTIONS PLAY AN EVEN GREATER PART in our lives than most of us realize. From infancy on, our emotions are intimately connected with all our thought and behavior, even with our physiological well-being.

Chapter 5 gave an introductory discussion of *Emotions: Inner Springs of Action.* It explained the various ways of looking at emotion, presented studies demonstrating the importance of emotions in all of daily living, and showed how we detect emotions in others. The four chapters to follow will be concerned with a more detailed account of what psychologists have discovered about emotional adjustment. This chapter and the next present *Emotional Development: Experimental Findings* and *Emotional Development: Clinical Findings*—that is, some of the many causal factors in emotional life that bring people to feel and think and act the way they do. Chapter 13 discusses in some detail the complex *Reactions to Frustration* that are characteristic of emotional behavior. Chapter 14, *Psychotherapy and Readjustment,* describes the techniques that clinical psychologists have discovered for helping people with emotional difficulties.

STUDYING EMOTION IN LABORATORY AND CLINIC

THERE ARE TWO chief ways by which we can study emotional development. One way is by experimental investigation, stressing laboratory techniques and rigorous controls; the other is by clinical investigation, stressing the study of individuals in terms of their troubles and problems.

The experimental psychologists believe that only through objective observation of overt behavior is there any hope of deriving scientific principles of human emotions. They insist that in the study of emotion, as in other fields of psychology, there must be *standardized description and rigorous control of all the variables.* For this reason their work, like the physiologists', takes place in the laboratory.

The clinical psychologists believe that the most valuable information on emotions comes from describing the reactions of persons to significant *real-life situations.* They feel, too, that the person in clinical treatment is much more consciously motivated to cooperate in the study of his emotional reactions than is the person tested in the laboratory. He realizes that he needs to be as honest and complete as possible in the data he gives so that he can enhance his chances of correcting his emotional difficulties (although it often takes considerable time before the person develops enough confidence in the clinical worker to be willing to talk frankly with him). For the clinical worker, the clinical situation is not regarded as a poor substitute for the laboratory situation; he often feels that it is also the one best suited for research purposes.

Why two approaches to emotion?

An interesting analysis has recently been made of the reasons for the lack of coordination between the psychological laboratory and the psychological clinic (Miller[1]):

Different histories. Clinical psychology developed as an outgrowth of medicine. When a patient showed symptoms of mental illness or serious emotional upset, the clinician was faced with the main task of doing something specific for that specific patient. He was more concerned with abnormal than with normal psychological processes, and he was oriented more toward mental disease and poor adjustment than toward mental health and good adjustment.

Laboratory psychology, on the other hand, grew up largely within the shade of universities, relatively well insulated from clinics and hospitals. It has concerned itself with psychological processes in general, independent of the factors influencing the individual case. The child of a marriage between physiology and philosophy, laboratory psychology took "mind" as its subject matter. It adopted the methods of the natural sciences, especially physiology, its parent. As one psychologist puts it: ". . . these circumstances bent the twigs of laboratory and medical psychology far apart so that only a few of their branches have grown into proximity again" (Miller[2]).

Different purposes. A second reason for the split between the two fields has already been indicated and has to do with the purposes of the laboratory and the clinic. The clinical psychologists think first of the welfare of the individual patient, and secondarily of the principles of emotional development which they may discover from analyzing and treating his difficulties. The laboratory psychologists think essentially in terms of psychological processes in general and are constantly seeking to find laws of mental life. Consequently, the two groups seem to have different goals as well as different origins.

Different procedures. A third reason for the difference between the two approaches is to be found in the procedures used by the laboratory investigator and the clinician. The laboratory psychologist attempts (1) to observe a large number of individuals, (2) to isolate for study one factor only, (3) to vary the conditions of his experiment in a highly controlled and systematic fashion, (4) to take careful quantitative measurements of the factor studied, and (5) to generalize his findings into a law.

The clinical psychologist has been unable to do this kind of work. For one thing, he feels that it would be a serious breach of medical ethics to give one group of patients beneficial treatment while withholding treatment from another group to study the effect. For another, he believes that many of the variables operating in the individual's emotional life can best be discovered and studied, not in the laboratory but in the clinic, where he can gain intimate knowledge of the patient and of his particular life history.

The need for a working partnership

Because of these differences in historical development, purpose, and procedure, the laboratory and the clinic have led separate existences, to the disadvantage of each. The laboratory psychologists claim that the clinical approach does not permit the rigorous control and accurate description that they insist are required by true science. The clinical psychologists assert that the experimental method is very appropriate to the natural sciences and to many fields of psychology, but that it does not yield deep understanding of emotion as a conscious and unconscious experience. Thus laboratory psychologists have been deprived of the rich human material gathered by clinicians in the course of their study of troubled people, and the clinical psychologists have been unable to profit from the precision and generality of the findings of laboratory workers.

Part of the controversy arises, of course, from different ways of looking at emotion. The experimental approach to emotion has tended to concentrate on the internal and external changes which accompany emotion and which can, of course, be studied by the method of objective observation. The clinical approach, on the other hand, has always been interested in emotional responses from the standpoint of their *significance in the life of the person.* The clinical worker is interested in the question as to what effect emotions have in the life of the patient, and only secondarily in the problem of analyzing what physiological and subjective components make up the emotion. This study of the cause-and-effect relationships between emotions and other factors has begun to interest the experimental worker as well, but it offers appreciable practical problems. Later in this chapter we will see that Watson and some of the other experimental psychologists have been making some very real beginnings on this work, even though their studies have had some of the limitations or crudities which are inevitable in pioneer investigations.

Actually, there is developing at the present time a useful coordination between laboratory and clinic. Each is discovering that the other has its own special advantages: the clinician is becoming interested in obtaining experimental verification for his theories of emotional life; and the experimentalist is coming to realize that the clinician can investigate cause-and-effect relationships which are not easily available to objective observation. Thus there is real justification for the hope that the coming together of these two disciplines will result in progress for the psychologist's understanding and treatment of emotional experience —just as the coming together of laboratory medicine and clinical medicine has led to progress in both physiological research and physiological treatment.

Eventually the working partnership between laboratory and clinic will undoubtedly lead to a unified system of theories and information about emotional adjustment. For the present, however, it is convenient to separate our discussion of emotions into two chapters. This chapter will discuss *Emotional Development: Experimental Findings,* and the next, *Emotional Development: Clinical Findings.*

OBJECTIVE DESCRIPTION OF EMOTION

THE FIRST experimental data on emotions that we shall consider aim at a refutation of some misconceptions and downright false beliefs which man has accumulated concerning the origin of his emotions. Many strange superstitions have developed as to which emotions are inborn and which are developed in the process of social living. Only within the last half century have psychologists attempted to arrive at a scientific understanding of emotional life. In testing for inborn emotions, the experimentalists have made a unique contribution.

Testing for inborn emotions

J. B. Watson is a foremost member of the behavioristic school of psychology. Believing that emotion can most accurately be understood through careful observation of overt behavior, he and his students undertook, with considerable success, to separate the true from the false in common beliefs about emotional life (Watson[3]).

Their method was simple, direct, and effective. Children whose complete histories since birth were known were shown fire, snakes, rats, dogs, cats, and frogs, to see if they would be afraid even without previous experience of what in adults are commonly objects of fear. And to test for any "innate fear of falling," the experimenter would drop the tiny babies only to catch them without injury after a free fall through space. Their body movements were restrained to test for "instinctive" defense movements. Stimuli were presented unexpectedly and suddenly to test for inborn "startle" behavior. In short, an effort was made to present all imaginable stimulus situations which might be expected to arouse emotion. All this was done to find out whether certain emotional reactions commonly displayed by adults are "inborn" or learned.

The responses of the infants to each of these stimulating situations were carefully recorded by trained observers. The records were later analyzed to see if definite patterns of response stood out. As a result of this type of work—initiated by Watson and carried on by his students and others—far more is known than formerly about the inborn versus the learned nature of emotional patterns of response. For instance, until Watson made his studies on emotion, infants and children were generally thought to have inborn fears of many things, among them furry and feathery objects, fire, dark, and reptiles. Let us examine the evidence.

Fear of furry and feathery objects. Popular belief holds that babies and young children instinctively fear furry objects. Through the centuries this belief has persisted because nobody was sufficiently interested or trained to put the notion to a rigid test. Watson was the first to perform such a test of emotional behavior. His methods here are typical of the behavioristic approach to the problem of determining the elements in our emotional repertoire.

The subjects were hospital-reared babies four to five months of age whose complete histories were known. Nothing had happened to these children in the way of injury or other unusual experience which was not carefully recorded by the specially trained and instructed nurses and experimenters. Thus the criterion of appearance-in-the-absence-of-opportunity-to-learn could be applied in a way that would never be possible with children reared in the rather hit-or-miss atmosphere of the average home. These babies had been reared in virtual isolation from the numerous emotional stimuli normally encountered. These stimuli were thus experienced for the first time under laboratory conditions, with trained observers recording their responses.

> In the first test of this series, a lively black cat was shown to the infant. In tests of this sort given to many infants, the children invariably reached out to touch the animal's fur, eyes, and nose. These results certainly invalidate the old notion that the black cat is a naturally fearsome thing.
>
> A rabbit was presented in similar fashion. The responses were essentially the same except that the child often grasped the ears in one hand and thrust them into his mouth. No evidence of fear of the furry rabbit was obtained in any of the trials with any of the subjects. When friendly Airedale dogs both large and small were presented, the results were similar, except that with the large animals little manipulatory behavior was observed.

Since children with no previous opportunity to learn showed no fear of any of the animals used, the conclusion is that the prevalent beliefs that children instinctively fear furry objects are just "old wives' tales." (Watson[4])

> In other experiments, feathery objects, usually pigeons, were presented in paper bags. The bird would struggle and move the bag about on the couch, and would often make cooing noises. The child rarely would touch the pigeon while it was rustling the paper bag, but when it was held in the experimenter's hand, he would manipulate it in his customary fashion. When the pigeon, its wings flapping violently enough to make an adult flinch, was held near the baby's face, the manipulatory responses did not occur, but no evidence of active fear was observed.

Here the essential conclusion was that feathery objects have no more native potency to elicit fear than do furry objects.

Only the burned child fears the flame. This caption is a necessary revision of the old saying—"The burned child fears the flame." Numerous experiments performed on young babies whose previous emotional life is known show that no fear of the fire is present until the child has been burned or otherwise taught to avoid the flame. The first response the baby makes to a flame is to reach for it.

Do babies fear the dark? Reasoning unsupported by objective observation has convinced many unscientific thinkers that there is a hereditary fear of the dark, dating from that age of man when darkness gave the advantage to his prowling enemies of the jungle. "It seems logical that we fear the dark, for such a fear would make us keep in shelter at night, safe from our enemies," reason these arm-chair philosophers. Controlled observations show this notion to be groundless and the logic to be hollow. When a child cries as the light is turned out at night, it is either because his nurse or parents have not been sufficiently careful in protecting him against acquiring fears or because he is angry at being taken away from the family group.

It is not necessarily true, however, that when the two- or three-year-old child begins to ask to have a light left on at night or to have the door left ajar, he has been conditioned directly against darkness. One very important process occurring in the small child during this period is that his intellectual horizon is broadening—but more rapidly in some respects than in others. From storybooks, newspaper tales read to him, radio broadcasts, and comments of other children and of adults, he is learning about the existence of tigers, bears, wolves, burglars, and tornadoes. He can understand what they are, even with the limited intellectual capacity of his age, but when the parent tries to explain, for example, that tigers can be found only in jungles thousands of miles across the ocean, he is going beyond the child's intellectual depth. Almost every key word—*mile, thousand, ocean*—means nothing to the young child. He listens to what the parent says and yet believes that the woods where tigers live are those he has seen near his house, and he is afraid to be alone at night.

It is very common, therefore, for the preschool child to develop fears which look foolish to the adult. There is a sense here in which children may be expected to "outgrow" their fears, because they are essentially the product of the uneven intellectual development of the small child.

Is there an instinctive fear of snakes? In the symbolism and mythology of many peoples, the snake is an object of fear and loathing. In the Old Testament it is the symbol of the downfall of man. No doubt

Watson's claim that fear of snakes is not inborn is confirmed by the life history of Annette Avers. Since this child was six months old, she has had snakes for pets and has never displayed the slightest fear of them.

our tradition would suggest to an uncritical mind that our fear of the snake is inherited. But what are the facts? Watson and others have shown that the fear of the snake does not manifest itself in babies less than a year old or in children two or three years old who have been reared away from contact with snakes and discussion about snakes.

All these experimental studies indicate that human beings are not born with fully developed emotional reactions to specific situations. How, then, do emotions develop?

Describing early emotional development

The work of Watson and his group in showing the error of some common beliefs regarding the instinct of fear was of great value because it stimulated a series of many similar studies. One of the most significant of these studies consisted of observations on the emotional behavior of sixty-two newly born infants in the Montreal Foundling and Baby Hospital (Bridges[5]). The subjects were carefully studied and accurate records were taken over a period of three to four months. The nature of the response was carefully noted and the conditions of the environment which preceded it were set down with equal precision. This study yields many interesting conclusions, and will be the main concern of this section.

Criteria of emotional development. What are the earliest signs of growing up emotionally? The Montreal studies showed that as a child grows older, there are the following changes in his emotional behavior:

1 Intense emotional responses become less frequent.

2 The reaction to any given stimulus becomes more specific.

3 Emotional responses are transferred from one situation to another which did not originally evoke them.

4 Patterns of emotional response gradually become more complex, as shown in the chart on page 412.

Excitement, the original emotion. The Montreal studies discovered that in infants, certain strong stimuli gave rise to the generalized response of *excitement*. This pattern is regarded as the original emotion and is observable in the second week of postnatal life. Excited children are described as follows:

> ". . . their arms and muscles tensed, their breath quickened, their legs made jerky kicking movements. Their eyes opened, the upper lid arched, and they gazed into the distance."

It is interesting to note the wide variety of stimuli which were capable of bringing about the above-described response of excitement. Some of these would appear, by adult standards, to be pleasant while others would be unpleasant.

> The list includes ". . . bright sun directly in the infant's eyes, sudden picking up and putting down on the bed, pulling the child's arms through his dress sleeves, holding the arms tight to the sides, rapping the baby's knuckles, pressing the bottle nipple into the child's mouth, and the noisy clatter of a small tin basin thrown onto a metal table whence it fell to the radiator and the floor." A sound like the latter was thought by Watson to arouse fear or startle in the newborn infant. But of the ten one- and two-month-old babies tested the noise startled only four, and not one of the ten babies actually cried at such a noise.

The records show that general excitement continues to exist throughout the first two years of life. Other studies have revealed its presence in adults. But at an early age, general excitement becomes differentiated into *distress* and *delight*, each with its derivative emotions.

The emotion of distress and its derivatives. The Montreal studies also show that by the time the baby is three weeks old it is possible to distinguish an emotion in addition to the original one of general excitement, which of course still persists. This new emotion has been called *distress* and can be evoked by the following stimulus situations:

"... on waking suddenly from sleep, struggling tʋ breathe through nostrils blocked with mucous, when the ears were discharging, when lying awake before feeding time, after staying long in the same position, lying on a wet diaper, when the child's buttocks were chafed, when the fingers were rapped."

These situations might be analyzed as consisting of what adults would call discomfort, pain, and hunger.

The response pattern differed from that of general excitement in the following details. In distress there is greater muscle tension, more interference with breathing, and frequent closing of the eyes; crying is louder, more irregular, and higher pitched. In infants over two months of age the eyes become moist and tears may flow in distress, which does not happen in general excitement at any age. The eyes are "screwed up" tight, the face becomes flushed, the fists clench, the arms tense, and the mouth becomes distorted.

According to these studies, distress later becomes differentiated into (1) anger, (2) fear, (3) disgust, and (4) jealousy. By the fifth month the baby shows unmistakable *anger* reactions. By this age the normal baby has formed attachments to small objects such as rattles, stuffed animals, his milk bottle, and others with which he has daily contact. Removal by force of one of these objects may elicit the distress response or it may give rise to anger. The clearest sign of anger is a protesting wail without the closing of the eyes and the accompanying tensions of crying as seen above.

The early development of emotions

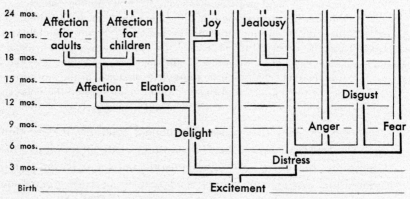

From K. M. B. Bridges, "Emotional Development in Early Infancy," *Child Development*, 1932, volume 3, p. 340.

These Montreal observations essentially agree with those of Watson, who reported that restraining the child's movement could be the cause of what looked like rage reactions. He asserted in rather strong terms that this was the one and only condition productive of anger except as other situations had been altered by conditioning. However, studies following Watson's pioneer work have indicated that he spoke too strongly. Among the Hopi Indians, for example, the practice of binding the infants in cradles (in which, naturally, there is a great restraint of movement) does not appear to alter the emotional reactions manifested by such infants as compared with those now being brought up by their parents in "white man's" ways (Dennis and Dennis[6]). Furthermore, the condition that arouses anger is not necessarily just a restraint of physical movement. The more important feature of the situation is some interference with an interesting activity on the child's part. The wise mother, for instance, does not yank the baby out of the bath water, but gives her child a moment's warning first (and then really takes him out, rather than letting him learn that protests can delay, at least for a while, the end of such an interesting activity).

The Montreal studies show that *disgust* reactions are clearly recognizable during the fifth month of life. These include coughing, sputtering, frowning, and crying while being fed. Cereals, milk, and sweetish foods are always accepted with evident enjoyment, but some babies observed showed disgust at soup that was too thick, as well as at chopped vegetables and at certain rather bitter foods.

Fear reactions are clearly observable at seven months of age. The most frequent stimulus to fear is the presence of a stranger. The behavior pattern in fear includes a general inhibition of all movement, followed by a burst of tears or by steady crying. The body remains rigid and inactive, the eyes close tightly, and the head bends. If the stranger touches the infant, he turns away. These reactions become more marked with the passage of time, until at the twelfth month the fear pattern is easily evoked by sudden withdrawal of support.

Watson had previously found two stimuli which caused fear: loud sounds produced by striking a gong or an iron bar, and the loss of bodily support, produced by allowing the child to fall freely through space to the hands of an assistant. However, later writers have reported other situations inducing fear without previous conditioning (Hunt[7]). It now appears that almost any unexpected, strong stimulus, such as a sudden flash of light, will produce fear in the infant. The important factor in fear here seems to be the suddenness or painfulness.

During the fifteenth to eighteenth months, the Montreal studies show, the emotional reaction of *jealousy* appears. The attention of familiar and interested adults is highly prized at this age. When such attention is withdrawn from a baby, and particularly when it is bestowed upon another, a violent jealousy reaction may occur. Typically, the jealous child stands stiffly, motionless, head bent forward, and bursts into tears. Some children will show definite anger and aggression directed against the rival child who is receiving attention, frequently ending in hitting, hair pulling, or even biting and scratching.

Jealousy, definitely in the broad category of distressful emotion, appears to have elements of fear and anger. It is usually evoked by the actions of adults rather than by those of other children, except as the other child is the recipient of adult attention.

The emotion of delight and its derivatives. The emotion of delight is much later in its appearance than is distress. The baby under a month old is either calm and quiescent or else he is excited. At this age, gentle stroking, swaying, and patting soothe the infant and induce sleep, but there is not yet a positive reaction of delight that can be observed in any distinctive facial reaction or bodily response. However, such physical stimulation from the outside is apparently very important to the infant, especially within the first few months after birth, as a means both of facilitating necessary physiological responses (such as digestion) and of inducing the general emotional condition needed for the infant's best development. Clinical workers (cf. Ribble[8]) have proved rather conclusively that babies cannot thrive, either emotionally or physiologically, if the care they receive is limited to the minimum of physical care required. In hospitals, for instance, it has been found that sometimes the very life of the child depends upon its having someone who picks it up, holds it, and plays with it for a while before each feeding. The baby, after all, is not left motionless in the mother's womb, and a healthy physical development after birth seems to demand a continuation of physical movement and stimulation.

At the second month the baby smiles fleetingly when nursed, warmly wrapped, rocked, tickled gently, fondled, or spoken to by the nurse or mother. By the third month the emotion of delight has become quite clearly differentiated from agitated excitement on the one hand and passivity on the other. This reaction has been described as follows:

> "The child kicks, opens his mouth, breathes faster, and tries to raise his head upon sight of his bottle. He gives little crooning sounds when being fed, nursed, or rocked. He smiles when an adult comes near and talks to him; he will even stop crying momentarily at the sound of a person's voice. He may also show delight in distant moving objects." (Bridges[9])

The outstanding characteristics of the emotion of delight are free as against restrained movements of the body; open rather than closed eyes; smiles instead of frowns; movements of approach rather than withdrawal; vocalizations of lower pitch than in excitement or distress; and more or less rhythmic movements of the arms and legs.

At the seventh month the baby is becoming more and more interested in small objects and in the act of reaching for and grasping them. He will even struggle for some time in an attempt to attain objects outside his reach. When these efforts succeed, there is a typical emotional reaction which has been called *elation*. The baby smiles, takes a deep breath, and appears to express satisfaction in a sort of grunt. After the object has been examined for a while it is discarded and some new one attracts his attention. By the eighth month this sort of activity is all the more frequent. The noise made when he bangs a spoon is especially productive of elation, but throwing things out of the crib runs a close second. Learning to walk sometime around the end of the first year is a never-ending source of elation.

At eleven months of age the average baby shows many signs of love or *affection* for adults. He puts his arms around the neck of the nurse or mother, stroking and patting her face with obvious delight. He will sometimes bring his lips close to the adult's face in incipient kissing movements. At first the affection emotion is evoked only by familiar adults, other babies being ignored. By the fifteenth month, however, babies show definite affection for each other. They hold each other's hands, pat each other and smile, put their arms about each other, and sometimes kiss each other. This sort of behavior continues, and by the eighteenth month there is a great deal of loving jabber of nonsense sounds. The affection reaction to other babies and to adults becomes selective, certain individuals being liked better than others.

At the eighteenth month babies show a great deal of affection for each other, although they continue to hit each other when the situation arouses anger. It is interesting to note that children of this age show no preference for other children on the basis of sex. Nor is there any evidence that older children protect younger ones.

The emotion of shame. The Montreal studies and other careful observations of the emotional patterns of babies show no evidence of the emotion of shame. Evidently it is absent in early life, yet it is an everyday emotion, common to all adults. Why children have no sense of shame during their early months and years is not clear. It is quite possible that shame is a native reaction which must mature; it is equally possible that the feeling and behavior of shame are brought about largely by conditioning. Thus far psychologists have not been able to isolate the two factors of maturation and conditioning.

The cultural anthropologists—social scientists who study and compare the cultures of different societies—say that shame-provoking situations vary widely among the different cultures. People are ashamed of the things of which their particular culture disapproves. In other words, people are afraid of the social consequences of being caught doing something they have learned is "bad." According to this evidence, shame seems to be largely learned and is basically a fear reaction. Here is an indication of the importance of social experiences in the development of emotions—an interesting clue to the question of how emotional behavior becomes complicated.

THE CONDITIONING THEORY OF EMOTIONAL DEVELOPMENT

GRANTING that there are a limited number of fundamental emotional responses in infancy, how can man become the emotionally complex person that he is? What is the origin of his morbid fears, his daily annoyances, his fine sentiments of patriotism and filial piety? Do these all come as the result of the process of conditioned learning? Watson would say "yes." Later you will see that such an answer is a little extreme. You will find that other factors besides conditioning play their role in the development of adult emotional complexity. However, an understanding of the role of conditioning is so important in helping us to guide emotional development that it will be given very careful attention. While there is nothing man can do to speed up the maturational process in the normal human organism, conditioning of emotion results from contact with environmental situations and, as you will see later, can be controlled by parents, teachers, or friends who are interested in eliminating a person's undesirable emotional responses. Here we shall consider some typical studies of emotional conditioning.

Conditioning the galvanic response

One of the changes which takes place in emotion is the *galvanic response*. This is comprised of two electrical phenomena: (1) the tissues actually generate an electromotive force (voltage); (2) the electrical resistance of the skin is changed.

Some experiments were made with infants to determine how this galvanic response could be conditioned and how long the conditioning could be retained. The fact that this one part of emotion can be conditioned is just further evidence for considering emotion as changing partly as a result of environmental conditioning. The type of apparatus used in this experiment is shown on page 402, and opposite.

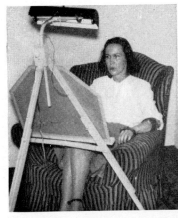

The galvanic response. *One practical application of galvanic response is in testing the effectiveness of advertising. In the picture at left above, the subject is reading an ad while sitting in a quiet room. The electrodes on her hand and arm are connected to the electropsychograph (a complicated mechanism based on the galvanometer principle) which is located in another room (above right). As various advertisements are placed before her, the electrodes pick up the electric force generated by the tissues in her arm as part of her emotional reaction. This force is then amplified in the large instrument operated by the experimenter. The amplified current is recorded on the graph at the experimenter's right. The advertisements which arouse the greatest galvanic responses are judged to be most effective, whether or not the subjective reaction to the advertisement is "favorable" or "unfavorable." The results given by this method correlate well with either sales results or coupon returns on the same advertisements. (Photograph courtesy Gilliland, Ranseen, Wesley, and Ragan, Inc.)*

In the experiments with infants, a galvanometer was used to measure the changes in the skin resistance of the subject. The unconditioned or biologically adequate stimulus was an electric shock, which causes pain and fear. The secondary (originally neutral) stimulus was a low sound produced by the vibrator of an induction coil.

On the first day of the experiment, a conditioned galvanic response to the sound alone was established by presenting the electric shock and the sound together six times. In the course of thirty-five presentations of the stimuli the response to the sound alone became as strong as the galvanic response originally produced by the electric shock. On each of the following four days, marked galvanic responses were at first obtained when the sound (secondary) stimulus was presented alone. Each day, however, after a few presentations of the secondary stimulus alone, the galvanic response would disappear. That is to say, further repetitions of the sound stimulus in the absence of the electric shock would not call forth the conditioned response. This phenomenon

The Conditioning Theory of Emotional Development 417

is known to psychologists as "experimental extinction" (it has already been discussed on pp. 380-384). On each occasion, however, it was found that on the succeeding day the secondary stimulus presented alone was again capable of bringing about the galvanic response: a phenomenon called "spontaneous recovery." (Jones[10])

Possibly the most interesting thing about this experiment is the evidence it gives that painful experiences leave an effect on the organism which is not always observable in its customary outward behavior. A whole month after the end of the original conditioning experiment, tests were made to find out whether the vibrator would elicit a response. There was by this time no evidence of muscular response to the sound of the vibrator. The galvanic response, however, occurred almost as strongly in response to the sound alone as on the first day. Evidently the mechanism responsible for the galvanic response had retained the conditioning, although the outer muscles of the body had lost it. The effects of emotional conditioning are not always immediately apparent on the outside.

How a conditioned fear develops

Watson reports a case of a boy, Albert, a remarkably happy child, who, prior to any experiments, was rarely seen to cry. His reaction to a loud sound was the typical fear pattern described earlier (p. 413) as being characteristic of most children. Repeated tests were conducted to see that nothing but loud sounds and loss of bodily support would evoke this fear response in the child. (Watson[11])

In the first experiment with Albert, an attempt was made to see whether he could be taught to fear a white rat. The adequate stimulus chosen was a loud sound produced by striking a metal bar; the neutral or "conditioned" stimulus was a white rat. The results of this experiment were unmistakably clear. For the sake of accuracy, the actual laboratory notes as taken on the spot by the experimenter will be used to tell the story of how a conditioned fear develops:

"Eleven months, three days old

"(1) White rat which he played with for weeks was suddenly taken from the basket (the usual routine) and presented to Albert. He began to reach for rat with left hand. Just as his hand touched the animal, the bar was struck immediately behind his head. The infant jumped violently and fell forward, burying his face in the mattress. He did not cry, however.

"(2) Just as his right hand touched the rat, the bar was again struck. Again the infant jumped violently, fell forward, and began to whimper.

"Because of the disturbed condition of the subject no tests were made for a week.

"Eleven months, ten days old

"(1) Rat presented suddenly without sound. There was steady fixation but no tendency at first to reach for it. The rat was then placed nearer, whereupon tentative reaching movements began with the right hand. When the rat nosed the infant's left hand, the hand was immediately withdrawn. He started to reach for the head of the animal with the forefinger of his left hand but withdrew it suddenly before contact. It is thus seen that the two joint stimulations given last week were not without effect. He was tested with his blocks immediately afterward to see if they shared in the process of conditioning. He began immediately to pick them up, dropping them and pounding them, etc. In the remainder of the tests the blocks were given frequently to quiet him and to test his general emotional state. They were always removed from sight when the process of conditioning was under way.

"(2) Combined stimulation with rat and sound. Started, then fell over immediately to right side. No crying.

"(3) Combined stimulation. Fell to right side and rested on hands with head turned from rat. No crying.

"(4) Combined stimulation. Same reaction.

"(5) Rat suddenly presented alone. Puckered face, whimpered, and withdrew body sharply to left.

"(6) Combined stimulation. Fell over immediately to right side and began to whimper.

"(7) Combined stimulation. Started violently and cried, but did not fall over.

"(8) Rat alone. The instant the rat was shown the baby began to cry. Almost instantly he turned sharply to the left, fell over, raised himself on all fours, and began to crawl away so rapidly that he was caught with difficulty before he reached the edge of the mattress."

Here is unmistakable evidence of how a fear response becomes attached to a stimulus which was previously neutral. The fact that you may not be able to trace in your memory the conditioning events which make you fear some object or person does not detract from the strength of this finding. Emotional responses, once they are set up, frequently outlast conscious memory of the happening that was originally responsible.

How a conditioned fear spreads

Watson conducted further experiments to find whether a person who has been conditioned to fear one stimulus object will develop fears of similar stimulus objects. Before the conditioning took place, Albert had been playing with fur muffs, false faces, rabbits, pigeons, and other similar objects. He had never shown the slightest fear of any of these. During the five-day period following the conditioning he was not allowed to see any such objects. On the sixth day he was tested again.

"Eleven months, fifteen days old

"(1) Tested first with blocks. He reached readily for them, playing with them as usual. This shows that there has been no general transfer to the room, table, blocks, etc.

"(2) Rat alone. Whimpered immediately, withdrew right hand, and turned head and trunk away.

"(3) Blocks again offered. Played readily with them, smiling and gurgling.

"(4) Rat alone. Leaned over to the left side as far away from the rat as possible, then fell over, getting up on all fours and scurrying away as rapidly as possible.

"(5) Blocks again offered. Reached immediately for them, smiling and laughing as before."

These observations leave no doubt that the conditioned response was carried over the five-day period. The infant was next shown, in order, a rabbit, a dog, a sealskin coat, cotton wool, human hair, and a false face.

"(6) Rabbit alone. A rabbit was suddenly placed on the mattress in front of him. The reaction was pronounced. Negative responses began at once. He leaned as far away from the animal as possible, whimpered, then burst into tears. When the rabbit was placed in contact with him he buried his face in the mattress, then got up on all fours and crawled away, crying as he went. This was a most convincing test.

"(7) The blocks were next given to him, after an interval. He played with them as before. It was observed by four people that he played far more energetically with them than ever before. The blocks were raised high over his head and slammed down with a great deal of force.

"(8) Dog alone. The dog did not produce as violent reaction as the rabbit. The moment fixation of the eyes occurred, the child shrank back, and as the animal came nearer he attempted to get on all fours but did not cry at first. As soon as the dog passed out of his range of vision he became quiet. The dog was then made to approach the infant's head (he was lying down at the moment). Albert straightened up immediately, fell over to the opposite side, and turned his head away. He then began to cry.

"(9) Blocks were again presented. He began immediately to play with them.

"(10) Fur coat (seal). Withdrew immediately to the left side, began to fret. Coat put close to him on the left side, he turned immediately, began to cry, and tried to crawl away on all fours.

"(11) Cotton wool. The wool was presented in a paper package. At the ends the cotton was not covered by the paper. It was placed first on his feet. He kicked it away but did not touch it with his hands. When his hand was laid on the wool he immediately withdrew it but did not show the shock that the animals or fur coat produced in him. He then began to play with the paper, avoiding contact with the wool itself. Before the hour was up, however, he lost some of his negativism to the wool.

"(12) Just in play W., who had made the experiments, put his head down to see if Albert would play with his hair. Albert was completely negative. The other two observers did the same thing. He began immediately to play with their hair. A Santa Claus mask was then brought and presented to Albert. He was again pronouncedly negative, although on all previous occasions he had played with it."

Thus we see that a conditioned fear response spreads to other objects resembling the first conditioned stimulus. This generalization of the emotional behavior gives further possibilities for the complication of emotional response. Notice that the amount of spread is in general proportionate to the amount of similarity between the various objects.

The experiment just described should give you some insight into why you may immediately dislike some person upon first meeting him. A negative emotional reaction attached to one person through some unpleasant contact can transfer to someone else bearing a resemblance to him, even though you are yourself unaware of the resemblance between them and do not even think of the original individual at all.

Such experiments form the basis for the behaviorists' theory that *emotional life becomes complicated as a few basic emotional reactions spread—through conditioning—from one situation to another.* They also form the basis of the behaviorists' method of emotional readjustment: *Eliminating Conditioned Emotions.*

ELIMINATING CONDITIONED EMOTIONS

A THOROUGH knowledge of how emotional responses are set up through conditioning in childhood is extremely valuable, since it makes possible the prevention of many unfortunate emotional acquisitions. Mere prevention is not enough, however. To rely upon prevention of unfortunate associations between innocent secondary stimuli and those which are ordinarily adequate to produce fear would demand such a close supervision of the child's environment as to be impracticable and undesirable.

Obviously, cure must be added to prevention if we are to rear our children with good expectations of a happy and useful life in society.

Watson and his students recognized the important problem of cure and explored the possibilities and limitations of numerous methods of redirecting the emotional life of the individual who has picked up some handicapping emotional responses. Discussion of this problem will be limited to fear responses because they are best understood.

A laboratory situation in emotional conditioning. This child has been partially fear-conditioned to the rabbit through associating it with fear-producing situations or objects, and this fear may spread to objects similar to rabbits if it is not checked through reconditioning. (Photograph courtesy of Dr. Harold E. Jones, whose work on conditioning is discussed in this chapter.)

Any fear response to an object not ordinarily adequate to produce fear is a conditioned response, one that has been learned and is open to further modification. The first step is to determine, if possible, whether the fear response (say, fear of cats) has been established by direct association or by transfer from some similar object. If the latter, it is important to discover what the original conditioned-stimulus object was, and devote efforts to eliminating this fundamental response.

Perhaps, for example, the child was originally conditioned to fear a dog because a dog once barked at him suddenly. In this case, the sight of the dog would have become the conditioned or secondary stimulus to a fear reaction, the native fear-producing stimulus having been provided by the loud noise of the dog's barking. This emotional conditioning could then have transferred to other objects of a similar nature, such as cats, fur coats, and Easter bunnies. The response to the dog, however, will remain strongest and most deeply set; accordingly much time is saved if it is dealt with first. *Elimination of the original conditioned response will go a long way toward doing away with the derived responses.*

Several methods of limited value have been tried in an effort to eradicate conditioned responses: (1) the method of disuse; (2) the method of frequent application of the stimulus; (3) the method of ridicule; (4) the method of social imitation; and (5) the method of verbal appeal. Some of these methods, as you will see, have been found to be either totally without effect or very slow. Some of them are even fraught with the possibilities of dangerous consequences. But there is another method—(6) the method of reconditioning—which yields more satisfactory results. Let us consider each of these in turn.

The method of disuse

In the method of disuse the child is carefully kept away from the conditioned fear object in the hope that the unfortunate reaction will be forgotten through sheer disuse—that is, that the fear will disappear if the original disturbing situation is not repeated. The following case (taken from Jones[12]) illustrates the method of disuse:

> *Rose D. Age 21 months.*
> "General situation: Sitting in play-pen with other children, none of whom showed specific fears. A rabbit was introduced from behind a screen.
> "Jan. 19. At sight of the rabbit, Rose burst into tears, her crying lessened when the experimenter picked up the rabbit, but again increased when the rabbit was put back on the floor. At the removal of the rabbit she quieted down, accepted a cracker, and presently returned to her blocks.
> "Feb. 5. After 2 weeks the situation was repeated. She cried and trembled upon seeing the rabbit. E. (the experimenter) sat on the floor between Rose and the rabbit; she continued to cry for several minutes. E. tried to divert her attention with the peg-board; she finally stopped crying, but continued to watch the rabbit and would not attempt to play."

In the following case, a conditioned emotion lasted over a period of three years:

> An attractive girl, aged 17, came to the attention of a certain clinic as a voluntary case. For several years her parents had been concerned over the abnormal shyness which she exhibited in the presence of young men or boys. In the presence of members of the opposite sex

she would blush violently and lapse into a nervous silence after a few stammered remarks. Her behavior was arrogant when she was with girls of her own age, and at least confident in the presence of adult women.

The medical findings were negative. There was no organic disease apparent. In fact, the girl's physical health was decidedly above average. The social investigation revealed nothing in the home environment at the moment which would seem to be responsible for her mental condition. But social investigation did yield the significant fact that her shyness had developed quite suddenly three years before. The parents had no explanation to offer as to the possible cause of the condition.

The psychologist talked with the girl in a friendly and informal manner. In the course of the conversation it was observed that, while she discussed sports and school activities quite freely, she would invariably become emotional when the subject of boys was mentioned. After several talks the girl had become quite friendly with the woman psychologist and was by then looking upon her as a competent and sympathetic adviser.

Little by little the following story came out: Three years before at a children's party the girl had been playing with some boys. In some manner she caught her fingers in a door when it was slammed shut. This caused the child such extreme pain that she became ill and vomited. The incident was quickly forgotten by everybody but the little girl herself, to whom it remained as a crushing misfortune. Although she tried not to think of it, the bitter memory was always there to be reinstated by the presence of boys.

Tests of various children and numerous case histories lead to the conclusion that the method of disuse is not as adequate as many people have supposed. Do not wait for a child to "outgrow" an undesirable emotional response. The results are certain to be disappointing.

The method of frequent application of the stimulus

We have seen that guarding the child from exposure to a stimulus is not an effective way of removing a fear response. What would be the effect of frequent application of the stimulus? Would it be possible to bring about elimination of the fear response by this method?

This method worked with some children to the extent of eliminating negative responses at least temporarily. In no case did frequent showing of the animal bring about positive responses. In some cases frequent application of the stimulus actually seemed to make the children more afraid, but in general the indications are that this method if used carefully will eventually yield the desired results. You can probably recall some fear, dislike, or annoyance which has been lost in this way. Perhaps its main disadvantage as a technique for training children is its slowness.

The method of ridicule

Traditionally, scorn and ridicule have been relied upon in the elimination of conditioned fear responses, in both children and adults. The following case, reported verbatim, serves to indicate the inadequacy and even the danger of this method as applied to a child:

> *Arthur G. Age 4 years.*
> "Arthur was shown the frogs in an aquarium, no other children being present. He cried, said 'they bite,' and ran out of the play-pen. Later, however, he was brought into the room with four other boys; he swaggered up to the aquarium, pressing ahead of the others who were with him. When one of his companions picked up a frog and turned to him with it, he screamed and fled; at this he was chased and made fun of, but with naturally no lessening of the fear. . . ." (Jones[13])

The danger inherent in the use of the method of social ridicule is that if the fear reaction is strong enough, it is possible that it will become attached to other persons. That is, the conditioning may go in the wrong direction. The conditioned response of fear or dislike may spread to the other people present, instead of being lessened by their ridiculing behavior. In this way the desire to earn approval of others may be frustrated and a dislike of people develop. The result would be the production of an asocial or antisocial individual.

The possibility of ill effects from this method of treatment is even greater in the adult than in the child, for the adult is more socialized and more sensitive to approval and scorn. The further fact that a conditioned fear of sufficiently long standing to last into adulthood must have been well set up originally makes even clearer the dangers in attempting to shame adults out of their fears.

World War I and World War II serve as convenient mileposts to mark progress in applying knowledge of psychology in the prevention and control of fear among adults. During the first war, a great deal of use was made of ridicule and humiliation, not only during the training and indoctrination period but in actual combat. Here is the report from a pilot of World War I on how his flight instructor went about eliminating fear in "green" fliers:

> "Then he lined us up and sounded off something like this:
> "'There's just two kinds of men in this world and the Army don't want the one kind. Some guys have got guts and the other guys haven't got guts. If you haven't got guts, you will never be a flier; I don't care how many college diplomas you got.
> "'Now I'm gonna spend the next few days taking you guys up one at a time and see if I can shake out a few gold bricks we got around here.'

"During the ensuing days each cadet was taken up by a hardboiled and sadistic instructor who executed one stunt after another and obviously felt that his mission was completed only when the inexperienced neophyte vomited—or worse. Upon landing, insult was added to injury by making the sickened beginner clean out the cockpit while the onlookers jeered."

Such methods proved ineffective and were officially frowned upon during the second World War. Contrast these methods of the old-time flying instructor with those of modern instructors as they are revealed in reports from a veteran pilot of the second World War:

"I'll admit to being a little afraid. I had been up before but always in a regularly scheduled passenger plane and never a small one. I knew that small trainers are rougher and the air was choppy. I wasn't as much afraid of anything happening as I was of how I would act, of whether I would get sick or not. The instructor took me over to the trainer and said: 'Have you ever been up?' I told him just what my experience had been. He walked around the plane and explained the action of the controls, then asked me to get in and work them. Pretty soon he said: 'Do you feel like taking a little hop?' I nodded, because I didn't quite feel that I could trust my voice to be natural. He lowered his voice and said, 'Don't worry if you are a little scared this first time. *I* sure was. In fact, I find that some of the fellows that are nervous that first time make the best fliers after they get used to it.' All at once I realized that I wasn't frightened any more because I knew that even if I did act nervous or even get sick, nobody would give me the razzberry."

The method of social imitation

What are the effects of social imitation on conditioned fear responses? The two following cases illustrate two possible outcomes of this method.

Bobby G. Age 30 months.

"Bobby was playing in the pen with Mary and Laurel. The rabbit was introduced in a basket. Bobby cried 'No, no,' and motioned for the experimenter to remove it. The two girls, however, ran up readily enough, looked in at the rabbit, and talked excitedly. Bobby became promptly interested, said 'What? Me see,' and ran forward, his curiosity and assertiveness in the social situation overmastering other impulses."

Vincent W. Age 21 months.

"Jan. 19. Vincent showed no fear of the rabbit, even when it was pushed against his hands or face. His only response was to laugh and reach for the rabbit's fur. On the same day he was taken into the pen with Rosey, who cried at the sight of the rabbit. Vincent immediately developed a fear response; in the ordinary playroom situation he would pay no attention to her crying, but in connection with the rabbit, her distress had a marked suggestion value. The fear transferred in this way persisted for over two weeks."

"Feb. 6. Eli and Herbert were in the play-pen with the rabbit. When Vincent was brought in, he remained cautiously standing at some distance. Eli led Vincent over to the rabbit, and induced him to touch the animal. Vincent laughed." (Jones[14])

The method of social imitation, like that of social pressure, must be used carefully if unfortunate consequences are to be avoided. It is safer than scorn, but it is not foolproof.

The method of verbal appeal

Many mothers and teachers depend on talking children out of their fears. Such verbal appeal quite naturally is of little value in dealing with babies too young to have much of a stock of words. How does it work with older children? The case of Jean E., a girl of five years, will help to answer our question.

Jean exhibited great fear of the rabbit when it was shown to her at the beginning of the experiment. Since previous experiments had shown that many children do not fear the rabbit, we are safe in concluding that Jean's fear of the rabbit had been acquired through learning. For a period of several days she did not see the rabbit again, but she was talked with for ten minutes a day about rabbits. The talk was varied and interesting. It involved looking at pictures in the book *Peter Rabbit*. Brief stories about bunnies were told. She was shown clay models of rabbits. During these chats she pretended great interest in rabbits. Once she said, "I touched your rabbit and stroked it and never cried"— which was not true. At the end of one week of this sort of treatment the rabbit was shown again. Her reaction was practically the same as the first encounter. She jumped up and ran away. When coaxed, she touched the fur of the animal while the experimenter held it safely in his hands, but when the rabbit was placed on the floor, the little girl sobbed, "Put it away—take it." (Jones[15])

Verbal organization, when unrelated to actual motor and visceral readjustment, has little value for removing fear responses.

The method of reconditioning

We have seen that some of the above-mentioned methods are more valuable than others, but none of them is certain to succeed. Fortunately, there is a procedure which is much more effective, in dealing with children. The treatment consists in substituting the desirable emotion of delight for the undesirable one of fear. A very interesting experiment (Jones[16]) has been conducted to determine whether it is possible and safe to recondition undesirable responses.

Peter was an active three-year-old with many acquired fears of white rats, fur coats, feathers, cotton-wool, frogs, fish, and mechanical toys.

"Peter was put in a crib in a playroom and immediately became absorbed in his toys. A white rat was introduced into the crib from behind. (The experimenter was behind a screen.) At sight of the rat, Peter screamed and fell flat on his back in a paroxysm of fear. The stimulus was removed, and Peter was taken out of the crib and put into a chair. Barbara was brought to the crib and the rat introduced as before. She exhibited no fear but picked up the rat in her hand. Peter sat quietly watching Barbara and the rat. A string of beads belonging to Peter had been left in the crib. Whenever the rat touched a part of the string he would say, 'my beads' in a complaining voice, although he made no objections when Barbara touched them. Invited to get down from the chair, he shook his head, fear not yet subsided. Twenty-five minutes elapsed before he was ready to play about freely."

The next day Peter was taken into the laboratory, where the following reactions were noted:

Stimulus Situations	Response
"Playroom and crib	Selected toys, got into crib without protest
White ball rolled in	Picked it up and held it
Fur rug hung over crib	Cried until it was removed
Fur coat hung over crib	Cried until it was removed
Cotton	Whimpered, withdrew, cried
Hat with feathers	Cried
Blue woolly sweater	Looked, turned away, no fear
White toy rabbit of rough cloth	No interest, no fear
Wooden doll	No interest, no fear"

Attempts to eliminate Peter's unnatural fears by use of the method of social pressure had already been made with some evidence of improvement. But before that series of experiments was completed, he fell ill and was placed in a hospital for two months. When he was being brought back from the hospital, a large barking dog attacked him and the nurse just as they entered the taxicab. Both Peter and the nurse were terribly frightened. Peter lay back in the taxicab, weak and exhausted from the encounter. After a few days allowed for recovery, Peter was taken to the laboratory and tested. His fear responses had returned with more than their former vigor.

Here was an extreme case, demanding some sort of effective action. The experimenter determined to try a new method, that of redirection or reconditioning. This method consisted in associating the presence of a furry object with the pleasurable activity of eating. The procedure was simple and direct but required great caution.

At lunch time the child was seated at a low table in a room about forty feet long. Just as he began to eat his lunch, the rabbit was displayed in a wire cage at a distance just far enough away not to disturb his eating. This was a very important point, for were the strong conditioned stimulus allowed to work too actively, it is quite to be expected that the positive reactions to the food would change. That is, the food might in turn become a conditioned stimulus to the fear response. To prevent accidents in this admittedly ticklish matter, the rabbit was kept in his cage during the early phases of the work. Each day the position of the cage was marked. The next day the cage and rabbit were brought somewhat closer. Eventually the rabbit could be placed on the table and even in Peter's lap. We may assume from this that Peter's inner emotional response had been reconditioned even as his outward behavior toward the rabbit had been redirected, for in children of his age the two aspects of the emotional response are not often disassociated.

Once the fear reaction to the rabbit was completely eliminated, observations were made to determine to what degree this elimination of fear had been transferred to other similar furry objects. Fear responses to cotton, the fur coat, and feathers were completely gone. The responses to white rats were greatly improved. The rats were tolerated in silence, although there was no enthusiastic manipulation of them. Peter now picked up and carried around the room tin boxes containing rats and frogs. A new test was now tried. The boy was handed a mouse, which he had never seen before, together with a tangled mass of earthworms. His responses were at first slightly negative to the whole situation, but after awhile they became positive to the earthworms and neutral to the mouse.

The efforts of the experimenter to eliminate the fear responses to furry objects had been somewhat hampered by her lack of knowledge as to the order in which these fears were built up. If the original fears are built up by a dog, then the reconditioning should involve a dog and not some other furry object to which the fear may spread. However, repeated success in reconditioning indicates its efficacy in eliminating any conditioned fear in a child. If the object which was first conditioned to the response is unknown, it is necessary to continue testing until all fears of a similar kind have been eliminated. Knowing where to start is a timesaver, not an essential.

NEW LIGHT ON CONDITIONED EMOTIONS

WATSON AND HIS FOLLOWERS were so keenly aware of the great possibilities of environmental control in training children to be emotionally healthy that they neglected somewhat the important factor of maturation in accounting for the growth of emotional complexity. Gradually, too, other experimenters have discovered that the problem of conditioning of emotional responses is not quite so simple as the results of the Watson group seemed to indicate. The criticisms of Watson's work come down to these two: (1) maturation as well as conditioned learning is involved in the growth of emotional complexity; and (2) the nature of the stimulus seems to determine whether it is adequate to arouse emotion.

Maturation and emotion

Let us look first at the evidence indicating the importance of maturation in emotional growth.

Fear of strange surroundings. A study has been made of the crying behavior of sixty-one infants. The babies were put through a series of standard or test situations every month during the first year of life, and their crying behavior was carefully observed and recorded. Special attention was paid to crying from fear in strange situations.

> This type of fear behavior occurred when the child was brought into strange rooms, or when he was taken from the mother by a stranger. Besides crying, the response usually involved turning to the mother. The fear behavior disappeared when the child became accustomed to the strange person or room. Apparently, strangeness is a stimulus to fear which was overlooked or underemphasized by the Watson group. (Bayley[17])
>
> The graph below shows the amount of crying due to fear of strange surroundings as a percentage of crying due to all causes:

Per cent of all crying due to fear of strange surroundings

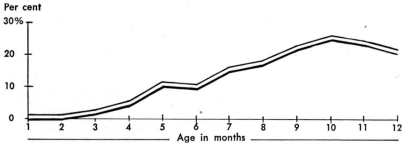

Data from N. Bayley, "A Study of Crying of Infants During Mental and Physical Tests," *Journal of Genetic Psychology,* 1932, volume 40, p. 321.

From this study it is clear that crying from fear of strange surroundings is absent during the first two months but becomes relatively more frequent with increasing age. (Cf. also Washburn.[18]) Now why should this relationship exist? One explanation would seem to be that the babies became conditioned to fear new situations. This is possible but not probable. Care was taken not to harm them or in any way to permit the building up of conditioned fear responses to strange persons and situations. A more probable explanation is that with the increase in age comes an increase in intelligence, and, by consequence, a clearer perception of whether surrounding things and persons are familiar or strange (cf. p. 409). By and large, these results seem to demonstrate the role of maturation and of indirect learning in the growth of emotional behavior.

Reaction to confinement. Additional evidence for the maturation of emotional behavior is given by studies of how fear of confinement increases with age.

> In this experiment, a number of infants of different ages were placed in an enclosed space two by three by four feet in size. The results of the observations are summed up as follows:
>
> ". . . At ten weeks the child may accept the situation with complete complaisance; at twenty weeks he may betray a mild intolerance, a dissatisfaction, persistent head-turning and social seeking, which we may safely characterize as mild apprehension; at thirty weeks his intolerance to the same situation may be so vigorously expressed by crying that we may describe the reaction as fear or fright. . . ." (Gesell[19])

The fact that fear appeared more strongly in the older than in the younger children when confronted with the confining chamber for the first time indicates the operation of the maturation factor.

Children's fear of snakes. You have already encountered the question of whether children "naturally" fear snakes. You know how Watson would answer it, but other experiments give a different answer. One study was made of the emotional behavior of children and adults suddenly confronted with a large and active snake. One experimental situation was described as follows:

> "A pen eight by ten feet by six inches high was built on the nursery floor. Within this a number of blocks and toys were scattered, and two black suitcases were placed flat on the floor near the wall. The suitcases could be opened easily by a child; one contained a familiar mechanical toy, the other contained a snake of a harmless variety (Spilotes corais) about six feet in length and slightly under four inches in girth at the middle of the body. When free in the pen, the snake glided actively about, showing a powerful, agile type of movement, and frequently protruding a black forked tongue about an inch in length. If the child did not open the suitcase containing the snake, an observer was able to do so from a concealed position, behind a screen, by pulling a string attached to the lid of the case." (Jones and Jones[20])

As a result of observations made in this and similar situations on children and adults, the experimenters came to the following conclusions:

"In our group of 51 children and about 90 adults, children up to the age of two years showed no fear of a snake; by three or three and a half, caution reactions were common; children of this age paid closer attention to the snake's movements, and were somewhat tentative in approaching and touching it. Definite fear behavior occurred more often after the age of four years, and was more pronounced in adults than in children. No sex differences were observed. . . ." (Jones and Jones[21])

The experimenters point out that this increase in fear behavior with age has three possible explanations: (1) it is the result of conditioning; or (2) it is the result of maturation of an innate fear of snakes; or (3) it is the result of general maturation of intelligence, which leads to greater sensitiveness and discrimination.

They feel that the first explanation is not to be considered, as the children were carefully reared in isolation from any contact with snakes. These children had never seen snakes or pictures of snakes, nor had they been told stories about snakes. It is hard to select the correct one of the second two hypotheses. The most probable hypothesis is that as the children mature they have built up more definite expectations regarding life situations. To a baby of twelve months there is nothing especially strange about the appearance of a large snake from a black box, nothing stranger than it would be to have the box contain a typewriter. But as the child builds up his background of knowledge of what to expect from given situations, many things, because of their contrast with what is expected, produce fear.

We are completely in the dark about the nature of the fear response as shown by the adults in this experiment, since the adult has had so many opportunities to become conditioned against snakes through actual contact or through stories and conversation about them.

The nature of the stimulus to emotion

As you have seen, Watson's conception of conditioned emotions has to combine with the fact of maturation in emotional development. Still further qualification must be made of the conditioning theory. There have been some notable failures to obtain conditioning of emotional responses. These failures must be taken into account in any attempt to assemble the whole story of emotional growth.

One psychologist attempted to condition a child to fear a pair of opera glasses and a caterpillar. In both instances the native or unconditioned stimulus to fear was the sound of a loud whistle. The fear response was invariably aroused by the loud whistle and through conditioning, by the caterpillar, but—curiously enough—could not be conditioned to the opera glasses. (Valentine[22])

This failure to establish conditioning with the opera glasses raises such a fundamental issue that we must pause to examine still more convincing evidence.

> Another psychologist presented the sound of an electric bell simultaneously with a wide variety of objects which had no known relation to the needs, appetites, or biological aversions of the infants in the experiment. The sound of a bell produced a fear or startle response in the infants, but it was impossible to condition this response to the biologically neutral stimuli, such as a cloth curtain, wooden blocks, and rings, even when a large number of trials were given. (Bregman[23])

Apparently, then, there is a hierarchy in emotional stimuli. At one end are such things as loud sounds and loss of body support, which will bring about a fear response the first time they are presented. Then there are such living objects as rats, rabbits, snakes, dogs, and caterpillars to which children can be conditioned in a few trials. Finally, there are neutral objects, such as opera glasses, which cannot easily be set up as conditioned stimuli to the fear response. The nature of the stimulus seems to have a definite limiting effect on the conditioning theory of emotion.

You will remember from Chapter 9 that the one really essential condition of learning is some activity within the learner which will result in an organizing of the person's reaction so that several features of the situation are perceived as related to one another. This concept may now be used to help us to understand why "conditioning" was accomplished in some of the cases just discussed, and not in others. Even a rather small child has enough understanding of the properties of inanimate objects (like wooden blocks, cloth, and opera glasses) that he can perceive, when a loud sound is produced, that it comes from some source other than these objects. The habits and mental set of the child, in other words, make it difficult for it to grasp the relation between these stimuli and the fear-producing loud noise. The relation, after all, is an arbitrary or artificial one, imposed merely by the experimenter. In the case of such an object as the caterpillar, however, there is a strangeness about it which gives the child no means of knowing what might be related to it. Especially if it moves, too, the child has the basis for representing it as an "active" element in its environment, rather than as the motionless things it can see that the wooden blocks or opera glasses are. Hence it is much easier for the child to respond to the caterpillar as something significantly related to the loud noise. There is a very good illustration here, in other words, of the active factors in learning which we considered in Chapter 9.

New Light on Conditioned Emotions 433

Emotional conditioning below the level of consciousness

In the early work with conditioned emotional responses, the emotions studied were always conscious—that is, the subject was always aware of whatever fear or other emotion he was experiencing. A more recent experiment has shown that emotional responses can be transferred from one stimulus to another even when the subject is not conscious of the relationship between the stimulus and the emotion it produces.

In this experiment with 52 college students, a list of words was read aloud by the investigator. The word *barn* appeared several times, and each time it was pronounced, the subject was given a painful but not dangerous electric shock. The word *barn* was known as the "critical" word and was always preceded by the word *red*.

Immediately after the presentation of the list of stimulus words, the subjects were asked to recall as many of the words as they could. Critical words were recalled by fewer of the subjects than were the noncritical words. In other words, the painful emotion connected with these words had made the subject become unconscious of them.

Five minutes after its first presentation, the list of stimulus words was repeated, this time without shock. The students' emotional reactions to these words were measured according to their galvanic responses (see p. 416). It was found that noncritical words produced no emotional responses as measured by the galvanometer, whereas the critical words did. *Even the subjects who could not consciously recall the critical words still responded emotionally to them. In fact, those subjects responded even more violently to the critical words than did subjects who could recall them. Obviously, then, emotional conditioning can exist without the person's being able to verbalize the basis of his reaction.* Reintegrative mechanisms have been developed which can operate to control the emotional responses but which are not able to govern a conscious, verbally formulated memory of the relationship between particular stimuli and the effects which went with them.

Emotional responses occurred also in response to the word immediately preceding a critical word, for example, to *red*. In fact, words not in the original list but having to do with things rural, such as *farm*, produced emotional responses. This finding was clearest in the case of those subjects who could not recall the critical words. Thus *an emotional response can spread from one stimulus to another, even on the unconscious level.*

After the deconditioning series (hearing list of words without shocks), all subjects became less reactive to all critical words, but the subjects who could not recall the critical words did not lose as much emotional reaction as those who could recall them. Apparently, *unconscious emotions are stronger than conscious ones.* (Diven[24])

This experiment shows clearly the possibility of fears of unrecognized origin developing in us and transferring to innocent objects and situations further to complicate our emotional life. Moreover, it indicates how a person may be entirely unaware of certain emotional reactions. Adult emotional life is made complex and mystifying by virtue of the fact that many of our responses are acquired through some experience which escapes introspective analysis. We simply cannot remember what has caused certain of our fundamental emotional reactions. In the next chapter on *Emotional Development: Clinical Findings*, we shall discuss some of the childhood experiences which, although they may be forgotten by the time adulthood is reached, are extremely important in shaping our emotional patterns.

Clinical psychologists derive principles of emotional development by studying the adjustment problems of all ages. Here Dr. W. E. Blatz of the St. George School for Child Study in Toronto discusses with a mother which of her own emotional problems may be affecting the emotional adjustment of her child. (From the film What's On Your Mind, *courtesy National Film Board of Canada.)*

CHAPTER 12

Emotional development: clinical findings

Emotional Life During Infancy

The Socialization Process of Childhood

Frustration and Aggression

Problems in Sexual Development

THE CLINICAL PSYCHOLOGISTS gather their data on emotional development from observations made on maladjusted individuals whom they interview in their offices and in mental institutions, and from studies of children in nursery schools and special study situations. Their method differs from that of the experimental psychologists in that they do not try to vary one emotional factor while holding others constant. They study each individual as a whole, and then from many case histories draw general principles about emotional processes and emotional development.

Most of us at one time or another are troubled with difficulties in our relations with other people, with doubts, fears, or feelings of depression. Clinical findings on emotional development, like the experimental findings, may give us insight into our own emotional problems. And clinical findings can help us understand others as well as ourselves. For instance, they shed a great deal of light on the importance of childhood in the development of emotional health; a study of the vital, formative factors in the child's experience will help make better parents. Clinical findings also indicate that what we regard as the "peculiarities" or "lack of character" shown by many of the people we know are the result of their particular emotional histories. Knowledge of certain principles of emotional development will help us to understand and be more tolerant of our fellows.

MEETING EMOTIONAL NEEDS IN CHILDHOOD: THE GROUNDWORK OF DEMOCRACY

(Stills from the film produced by the Department of Child Study, Vassar College. Synopsis courtesy Dr. L. Joseph Stone.)

A democracy can function only if its citizens are responsible individuals who have self-respect and respect for the rights of others. It is the experiences

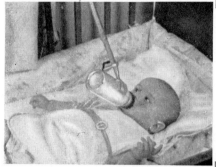

of childhood—of the "loose-tooth" era and before—which underlie the attitudes and behavior of the adult citizen. For example, the child who lacks the warmth of human contact, the security of being loved, is likely to carry all through life the feeling that people are not to be trusted, that "if you don't look after yourself, nobody else will."

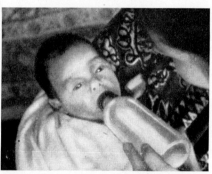

The child who knows that he is loved, and feels secure that his individual needs are respected, will be able in later years to feel interest in the problems of others. The search for love and approval is universal and must be guided toward constructive ends. The wise teacher encourages the anti-social "show-off" (below, left) to share his rock-collection with his classmates (right).

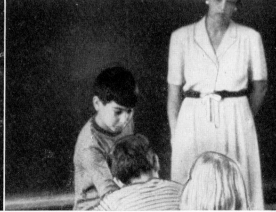

Another fundamental requirement for the democratic citizen is independence: the ability to make decisions and take action without continual support from authority. The beginnings of independence are in the young child's first explorations and exploits in the world around him. Even in infancy, his fundamental attitudes toward people and toward himself are being formed. Independence and self-confidence begin when the child freely explores the world around him—and is allowed to assert himself within the limits of safety and the reasonable convenience of others.

Later—in learning to walk, talk, dress himself, build with blocks, swim—in all the activities and skills which are enjoyed and mastered in the process of growing up—the child enjoys a sense of competence and self-respect. Parents should encourage his budding self-confidence, but at the same time should not push him too fast. Children should have help when they need it, and should always feel that they have a secure "home base" to which they can return temporarily when they are frightened. Thus they can achieve a true independence which will enable them, as adult citizens, to resist encroachments on their liberty, and not give in to unreasonable authority because their emotional needs for security and self-respect were unsatisfied in childhood and persist through later life.

School-age children often dramatize the need for independence and competence with their secret societies and clubs. Here they shut out parents and learn the real meaning of a "society of equals" who decide together.

The feeling of independence rests on real responsibility, not just shutting doors on the family. Children thrive on the knowledge that they can contribute something to family life. They find that helping others can be fun, and they take an interest in the needs and problems of others. From such experiences civic responsibility naturally follows.

Family life can be a democracy in miniature. The members hold "councils" to decide where to hold a picnic—or who is to have the family car. Each contributes; each acts his age; no one rushes him to act older or artificially prolongs his infancy. A happy sense of belonging, or enjoying group living, is fostered when each individual shares in community decisions and feels the others respect him.

Life in modern society is not all picnics, but children with a firm emotional groundwork can go forward confidently to meet the problems which confront them as individuals and as members of their community. They have security and self-respect, independence and responsibility, and a respect and concern for the needs of others. They are ready for democratic living.

439

To appreciate better the kind of problem that clinical psychologists meet in the course of their work, let us look at a representative case, the case of Alfred:

". . . because [of] his father's vocation as a Protestant minister, [it was] necessary for [Alfred's] family to reside in the slum section of a large city. Because she was afraid that her boy's conduct would suffer from too intimate contact with the ragamuffins of the neighborhood, his mother did not often permit him to venture beyond the confines of a small back yard. She explained to him that he was not like the children whom he saw on the streets but that he was different from them in a highly desirable way. Furthermore, she succeeded in causing him to develop an interest in artistic pursuits; and he took great pride in the fact that visitors in the home complimented him on his remarkable accomplishments. . . .

"When Alfred was twelve he was sent to a public school for the first time. By reason of the fact that his contact with boys of his age had been so restricted he was poorly qualified to make a social adjustment to his fellows of the classroom and playground. His speech was over-nice, his manner was too much that of an adult, and he had an attitude of self-appreciation. In short, he was irritating and he was immediately met with such intense persecution and badgering that he developed a typical inferiority complex. . . .

"Alfred first attracted special attention when he was a sophomore undergraduate by expounding, and putting into use, a curious theory of the way in which the hands should be held in walking. He insisted that the common practice of permitting the arms to swing is undignified and unesthetic; that a more impressive effect is got from holding the hands rigid and slightly in front of the body. Having developed this habit thoroughly he undertook to mark himself off from his fellows in many different ways. He began to memorize portions of the writings of Mencken and Wilde and became very adept at expressing the notions of these two men in ordinary conversations, securing thereby notable effects. He also ventured into the field of literature on his own account, though he neglected the regular university courses in that subject. He wrote *vers libre*, only his verse was considerably more *libre* than most free verse is. All of his poems were painstakingly copied on very expensive Japanese vellum and visitors to his room were given the manifest privilege of listening to his reading of his own compositions. . . .

". . . after he had received his [college] diploma and had been commissioned in the United States Army, he achieved with his new associates a reputation for being peculiar. He constantly did the unexpected and showed an intense interest in breaking military regulations which he required his subordinates to observe with the utmost strictness. Moreover, after the signing of the Armistice, Alfred married a young Spanish woman before returning to America. This was not strange in itself but, although his wife has lived in this country for seven or eight years, she has never been permitted to learn the English language. In fact, she is not even able to order the family groceries and is otherwise inconvenienced. Conversations in the home are carried on in any one of a number of different tongues: French, German, Italian, Spanish, Polish, and Russian. Furthermore, if a guest is fluent in any one of these, he will be forced to listen to a discourse in the others. . . .

"[Alfred] often expresses openly the idea that his peculiarities are evidences of superiority, and he charges that the persons who withhold credit are animated by jealousy. 'Most people are fools,' he says. . . ."
(Bagby[1])

There are a number of points which Alfred's case illustrates. For one thing, it must be recognized that Alfred's peculiarities serve an important function for him in that they permit him to feel superior; consequently, when he meets disapproval and hostility in others, he is able to interpret them as signs of envy of his own superiority. Likewise, his peculiarities permit him to avoid any competition in which he might be unsuccessful. This constant dodging permits him to avoid his share of the defeats one ordinarily must face, contributes to his rationalized feeling of superiority, and lends credence to his insistence that "most people are fools."

Alfred, while undoubtedly an unattractive social companion, emerges as a rather pathetic figure, forced to spend an enormous amount of energy to combat feelings of inferiority and to sacrifice the approval and affection of his fellows to build up a false sense of personal worth. The whole case seems particularly tragic when it is remembered that Alfred is an extremely competent linguist and that no one of merely average ability could gain command of such a variety of languages. Intelligence alone is no protection against emotional maladjustment.

When we ask how Alfred got that way, two crucial points emerge: (1) the difficulties which characterize Alfred as an adult have their roots in experiences of his childhood; and (2) his difficulties focus in his relationships with people. It seems that something went wrong with Alfred during the process of *socialization*. In other words, he ran into trouble while developing from a babbling infant, unaware of his social surroundings, to a mature individual accepting his rights and responsibilities in a social group.

In Alfred's case the importance of the socialization process is all too evident. But while most of us have not had such unfortunate experiences, our emotional lives have been shaped by much the same kind of socialization process. To understand both the Alfreds of this world and the less unhappy people we see around us every day, we must

441

study *Emotional Life During Infancy* and *The Socialization Process of Childhood.* We shall then be ready to consider the two areas of emotional life which give the most difficulty to children, adolescents, and adults alike: *Frustration and Aggression* and *Sexual Development.*

EMOTIONAL LIFE DURING INFANCY

❙T IS STILL somewhat of a surprise to many people that small children —under a year old—have active emotional reactions, and that emotional life during infancy has a profound effect on emotional life during later years. In fact, our ideas about human infants have changed radically in the last century.

Outmoded views of human infancy

There are two fundamental misconceptions about human infancy which have had great popularity in the past and which still continue to influence many people today.

The baby as a "little man." People used to think of babies as miniature adults, differing in no way from older human beings except in size, appearance, and the possession of language. Parents subscribing to the idea felt quite justified in subjecting their children to cruel punishments if they failed to live up to the standards of grown-ups. Little allowance was made for their psychological and physiological immaturity. If the baby did not obey or act in a thoroughly adult manner, it was considered a sign of willfulness, moral depravity, or "lack of character."

The "pretty baby" and "big nuisance" philosophies. As knowledge of children increased, the belief that infants are miniature adults disappeared, to be replaced with the idea that infants are hardly human at all. Many people still seem to believe that children are just cute

One expression of the idea of the baby as a "little man" was the old belief that the child was fully formed, in miniature, in the sperm, as shown in the drawings above. (From You and Heredity, © 1939 by Amram Scheinfeld, pub. by J. B. Lippincott Co.)

little ornaments or tremendous nuisances until they are five or six years old, when they mysteriously acquire "reason" and become amenable to training. As a result of this belief many parents feel justified in any kind of punishment or reward that serves to maximize the baby's ornamental value and minimize its nuisance value. Since they think it is impossible to train the child until he reaches the "age of reason," they do not see how the way they act toward the small child can have any great effect on his personality and emotional development.

Both these points of view have died out of scientific thinking, but both still have repercussions in the thinking of many parents whose ignorance of child development frequently defeats their good intentions. Some parents still feel that the baby is capable of behaving like an adult, and they expose him to the process of socialization immediately, driving him along by threats, cajoling, and punishment. These are the people who point with pride to the fact that their children are successfully weaned at five months, toilet-trained at one year, broken of thumb-sucking by two weeks after the behavior is first noticed, and at three show only the most elegant of manners to company. Other parents alternate between periods of extreme indulgence and extreme rejection—claiming that the baby is too young to understand anyway. Modern clinical psychologists have discovered, however, that babies are not adults, but immature organisms with special emotional needs, and that the satisfaction of these special needs is vital to healthy emotional development.

Babies have special emotional needs

A fundamental principle of clinical psychology is that infancy and early childhood are of vital importance in the development of personality, and that the first few years after birth are of special significance in the establishment of emotional tendencies (Erickson[2]). The process of birth itself, while it is only one milestone on the developmental road, is highly important because it severs quite finally the physical relation between mother and child. For the entire period of pregnancy, all the baby's needs have been automatically satisfied without his ever having to take responsibility for his own adjustment. As one psychologist has put it, the infant at birth "has to bear the loss of intrauterine happiness; he learns what it means to desire something without receiving it" (Roheim[3]).

Ordinarily, the desires experienced by the newborn baby are thought of as needs for sleep, nutrition, elimination, activity, and general physical comfort. Modern clinical findings indicate that infantile needs are much more inclusive, subtle, and complex. The importance of the small infant's emotional needs is dramatically illustrated by the story of the medical conquest of *marasmus*, a disease which is particularly virulent during the first year of life. A child who suffers from marasmus just "wastes away" for no apparent organic reason.

Emotional Life During Infancy 443

GRIEF: A PERIL IN INFANCY

Synopsis of film by Dr. René A. Spitz. (Stills and synopsis courtesy of Dr. Spitz.)

Before separation from mother

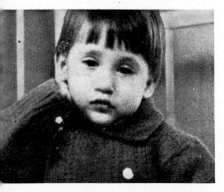

Depression after separation

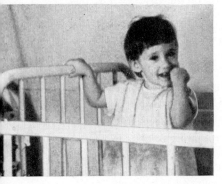

After reunion with mother

During most of its first year of life, the sum total of the baby's human relations, as well as nearly all its sensory perceptions, take place through its mother or her substitute. Losing the mother during the first year of life without adequate substitution severely limits the child's emotional and neuro-muscular development. Even if a later attempt is made to correct the loss, lasting damage can be avoided only if the emotional deprivation is held within narrow time limits.

The film shows the consequences of medium and of severe emotional deprivation during the first year of life, in an investigation conducted on 259 infants. In one institution studied, the infants were reared from birth by their own mothers or mother substitutes who had one other child to care for. In some cases, for unavoidable reasons like sickness, the mother had to be separated from her child for prolonged periods. The substitute mother available was not always appropriate. In children who had had a good relationship with the mother, such substitution resulted in a progressive condition resembling depression in adults. At first these infants become weepy, showing a conflict between disappointment at the approach of a stranger and the craving for human contact. Later they become withdrawn and reject any approach. Toward the end of the third month the facial expression becomes rigid; screaming subsides, weeping also; and the child often presents eating and sleep disturbances, lies mostly prone in its cot. With the return of the mother, facial expression and general behavior return to normal.

In another part of the film, children from the second institution (situated outside of this country) are shown who have been deprived of their mothers beginning with the end of the third month. The hygienic, environmental, and nutritional conditions in the two institutions were comparable, with the second having a slight advantage over the first one in regard to hygiene. But in the second, unlike the first, each child was entrusted to a nurse who had eight to twelve children to care for, thus depriving it of all emotional interchange. The periods of separation varied from five to twelve months and the children showed progressive degrees of physical and mental deterioration.

At the close of the first World War, marasmus was accounting for about half the deaths of babies under a year old. To cope with the problem of marasmus, a special study was undertaken by both physicians and social workers, with some astonishing results. Babies who were cared for in hospitals or in the homes of economically well-off people and who received the best of physical care frequently slipped into the marasmic condition of slow, wasting death—whereas babies who lived in economically poor homes but who were favored by an attentive, affectionate mother frequently surmounted the obstacles of poverty and slipshod hygiene to become husky youngsters and adults (Ribble[4]). The difference was apparently due to the factor of what has been called "adequate psychological mothering" (Ribble[5]). Doctors of that time did not fully understand the nature of this intense need in babies for mothering experiences, but they recognized the vital importance of meeting it adequately if the battle against marasmus was to be won. As a consequence, hospital authorities began to look for suitable foster parents for unloved children who fell into their hands. The medical care of children or *pediatrics* underwent drastic changes. One story, popular among medical students, gives us a leading child specialist who is supposed to have written on the hospital charts of babies under his care: "This baby is to be loved every two hours."

Marasmus is now a rather rare illness, but its defeat at the hands of medical clinicians has served to point up the urgent need for psychological as well as physical care. A baby must have love during its first year of life if it is to achieve optimum development both physiologically and psychologically. Some of the vital points in this connection are to be seen in the case of little Bob:

"Little Bob was born in the maternity hospital where the writer was making studies of infants at the time. He was a full-term child and weighed six pounds three ounces at birth. During the two weeks' stay in the hospital the baby was breast fed and there was no apparent difficulty with his body functions. The mother, a professional woman, had been reluctant about breast feeding because she wished to take up her work as soon as possible after the baby was born, but she yielded to the kindly encouragement of the hospital nurses, and the feeding was successful. Both mother and child were thriving when they left the hospital.

"On returning home the mother found that her husband had suddenly deserted her—the climax of an unhappy and maladjusted marriage relationship. She discovered soon after that her milk did not agree with the baby. As is frequently the case, the deep emotional reaction had affected her milk secretion. The infant refused the breast and began to vomit. Later he was taken to the hospital and the mother did not call to see him. At the end of a month she wrote that she had been seriously ill and asked the hospital to keep the child until further notice.

"In spite of careful medical attention and skillful feeding, this baby remained for two months at practically the same weight. He was in a crowded ward and received very little personal attention. The baby nurses had no time to take him up and work with him as a mother would, by changing his position and making him comfortable at frequent intervals. The habit of finger sucking developed, and gradually the child became what is known as a ruminator, his food coming up and going down with equal ease. At the age of two months he weighed five pounds. The baby at this time was transferred to a small children's hospital, with the idea that this institution might be able to give him more individual care. It became apparent that the mother had abandoned the child altogether.

"When seen by the writer, this baby actually looked like a seven months' foetus, yet he had also a strange appearance of oldness. His arms and legs were wrinkled and wasted, his head large in proportion to the rest of the body, his chest round and flaring widely at the base over an enormous liver. His breathing was shallow, he was generally inactive, and his skin was cold and flabby. He took large quantities of milk but did not gain weight since most of it went through him with very little assimilation and with copious discharges of mucus from his intestines. The baby showed at this time the pallor which in our study we found typical of infants who are not mothered, although careful examination of his blood did not indicate a serious degree of anemia. He was subject to severe sweating, particularly during sleep. A thorough study showed no indication of tuberculosis. The child's abdomen was large and protruding, but this proved to be due to lax intestinal muscles and consequent distention with gas and to a greatly enlarged and distended liver, which was actually in proportion to that of the foetus. There was no evidence of organic disease, but growth and development were definitely at a standstill, and it appeared that the child was gradually slipping backward to lower and lower levels of body economy and function.

"The routine treatment of this hospital for babies who are not gaining weight is to give them concentrated nursing care. They are held in the nurses' laps for feeding and allowed at least half an hour to take the bottle. From time to time their position in the crib is changed and when possible the nurse carries them about the ward for a few minutes before or after each feeding. This is the closest possible approach to mothering in a busy infants' ward. Medical treatment consists of frequent injections of salt solution under the skin to support the weakened circulation in the surface of the body.

"With this treatment the child began to improve slowly. As his physical condition became better, it was possible for our research group to introduce the services of a volunteer 'mother' who came to the hospital twice daily in order to give him some of the attention he so greatly needed. What she actually did was to hold him in her lap for a short period before his 10 A.M. and 6 P.M. feedings. She was told that he needed love more than he needed medicine, and she was instructed to stroke the child's head gently and speak or sing softly to him and walk him about. Her daily visits were gradually prolonged until she was spending an hour twice a day, giving the baby this artificial mothering. The result was good. The child remained in the hospital until he was five months of age, at which time he weighed nine pounds. All rumination and diarrhea had stopped, and he had become an alert baby with vigorous muscular activity. His motor coordinations were of course retarded. Although he held up his head well and looked about, focusing his eyes and smiling in response to his familiar nurses, he could not yet grasp his own bottle or turn himself over, as is customary at this age. The finger sucking continued, as is usually the case with babies who have suffered early privation.

"In accordance with the new hospital procedure, as soon as the child's life was no longer in danger, he was transferred to a good, supervised foster home in order that he might have still more individual attention. Under this regime, his development proceeded well and gradually he mastered such functions as sitting, creeping, and standing. His speech was slow in developing, however, and he did not walk until after the second year. The general health of this child is now excellent at the end of his third year; also his 'I.Q.' is high on standard tests, but his emotional life is deeply damaged. With any change in his routine or with a prolonged absence of the foster mother, he goes into a state which is quite similar to a depression. He becomes inactive, eats very little, becomes constipated and extremely pale. When his foster mother goes away, he usually reacts with a loss of body tone and alertness, rather than with a definite protest. His emotional relationship to the foster mother is receptive, like that of a young infant, but he makes little response to her mothering activities except to function better when she is there. He has little capacity to express affection, displays no initiative in seeking it, yet fails to thrive without it. (Ribble[6])

It seems safe to predict that as little Bob grows into adulthood, he will have hard sledding in his relationships with people, owing to the insecurities he has acquired during this crucial period of infancy.

The infant's needs must be continuously satisfied

Such clinical evidence as the case of little Bob has led to the modern doctrine that for the first year of life the baby should be as continuously satisfied as possible. Of course such treatment is in direct contradiction to the idea, so popular a few years ago, that a baby should not be picked up and fondled too much, for fear of "spoiling" him. Many a young mother, filled with the currently fashionable theories and anxious to do the best for her baby, would listen to him crying and would force herself not to pick him up. "He's not hungry or wet," she would say, "and there's nothing wrong with him except that he just wants attention." Other conscientious mothers would stick to the child's schedule to the minute: if the chart said a ten o'clock feeding, then he must not be fed until exactly ten, no matter how hard he started crying at nine-thirty. Other mothers have deliberately let their six-months-old babies cry for a while before feeding them, on the theory that "he's got to learn sometime that he can't have everything exactly when he wants it."

Today clinicians agree that babies must be babied. Mothers are told that a small baby is harmed, not helped, by efforts to teach him "self-control." The schedule, too, has been deposed from its once-powerful dominion over mother and baby. Schedules are now set by "self-demand": that is, the infant is allowed to set his own rhythm of life activity. If he is hungry he is fed, for babies, like adults, do not always get hungry at exactly the same minute every day. Mothers are also told not to be afraid of cuddling and rocking their children, for cases like that of little Bob have dramatically shown that infants need affection. All these modern "discoveries" are, of course, what every old-fashioned mother knew. Cuddling and the lullaby were once part of every infant's experience, and the rigid feeding schedule is a modern invention.

The general import is that mothers should perform the motherly function of keeping the child from unnecessary frustration of both his psychological and his physiological needs. What are some of the specific reasons for this advice on the part of the psychologists and physicians who have been most intimately connected with the problems of child development?

Physiological reasons for continuous satisfaction. It is obvious that the newborn human child, unlike the offspring of lower animals, is born in a state of almost complete helplessness and is completely dependent upon his social and physical environment for his very existence. His brain and nervous system are incomplete; circulation of blood is not yet well established; and such vital functions as breathing and gastro-intestinal functions are poorly organized, as is demonstrated by shallow, irregular breathing and the frequency of regurgitating, hiccups, and diarrhea.

During the crucial first year, the maturation process must bring these basic bodily systems into a condition of sufficient integration to insure adequate functioning throughout life. Obviously, then, the care of the child must take into due account the usual factors mentioned in the manuals of child care: diet, sleep, fresh air and sunshine, adequate elimination, a fairly constant temperature, and freedom from pain. Even in the first few months after birth, the care given the infant is deciding, in a very fundamental way, what kind of emotional attitudes he will have in later life. If the child does not have enough of being played with, held, and fondled—in other words, if he receives only impersonal attention to his physical necessities—he seems to undergo tautness and unpleasantness. But with adequate "mothering," an opposite type of emotional life is developed—a life of cheerfulness, enjoyment, and good humor. This kind of emotional life is essential to the best physical health.

The popular point of view is that catering to the needs of the baby results in a "spoiled brat." Here it must be replied that the "spoiled" child is usually the one who has had inconsistent attention rather than too much. He has sporadically been smothered with attention and affection and then neglected, instead of receiving continual satisfaction of his needs.

One important physiological advantage of adequate psychological mothering has been surrounded by many widespread misconceptions. It is not generally recognized that sucking is a real need quite independent of the need for food.

> One series of interesting observations has shown that thumb- or finger-sucking generally occurs in babies who have inadequate opportunity to suck during feeding. If the breast or bottle is withdrawn too soon, or if the hole in the nipple is too large so that the infant receives his nutriment too rapidly, there is a strong tendency for the child to indulge in finger-sucking (Levy[7]).
>
> These same findings have been confirmed in an experiment with a litter of six newborn puppies. One pair, the long-feeders, was fed with a bottle which had a small hole in the nipple. After each meal, they were permitted to suck on a nipple-covered finger until they voluntarily stopped. Another pair, the short-feeders, were fed with a large-holed nipple and were not given a finger to suck after meals. The third pair, the breast-feeders, were left with the mother. The short-feeders gave evidence of sucking deprivation by chewing and sucking on each other's bodies between meals and by a high degree of responsiveness to a nipple-covered finger whenever it was offered between meals. But interestingly enough neither the long-feeders nor the breast-feeders ever engaged in body-sucking or were ever responsive to a finger (Levy[8]).

It seems logical to conclude from this study that sucking constitutes an independent drive. When sucking occurs independent of the eating process, it is at least partially a function of lack of opportunity to suck for a sufficient period of time while eating. Consequently, interference with sucking behavior represents a frustration which can produce considerable emotion and so may have serious effects on the child's development.

The baby should be allowed to suck as long as he wants on the bottle or breast, and if this does not satisfy the need, then thumb-sucking or even the old-fashioned "pacifier" is in order. The usual objection people make to infantile finger-sucking is that it tends to deform the dental arches and cause crooked teeth in later childhood and adulthood. Finger-sucking is generally looked upon as undesirable because it is supposed to necessitate costly teeth-straightening in later life. Studies have shown, however, that this disapproval of infantile finger-sucking is unwarranted.

> In a careful investigation of this idea, casts of children's mouths were taken as they grew. It was found that children who sucked their fingers tended to have a greater frequency of "baby" teeth pushed out of alignment than did those who did not suck their fingers. But it was also found that this condition corrected itself when the habit was given up—especially during the "baby"-teeth period (though occasionally as late as ten or eleven years). (Lewis[9] and Lewis[10])

The important thing, then, is to see that the child stops sucking his fingers before his second teeth come in. But since finger-sucking in children of this older age is rarely a problem, there seems little justification for the widespread concern over finger-sucking.

A fact perhaps still more fundamental to realize is that the main means of preventing the small child from thumb-sucking is to provide an abundant and enjoyable opportunity for performance of this sucking function. The child who is in danger of having an enduring problem of thumb-sucking is the child who has been required at too early an age to start drinking from a cup or a glass rather than being allowed to continue nursing at the breast or bottle. Or the baby with persistent thumb-sucking problems is the child who was fed on some rigid schedule which did not meet his individual needs.

Psychological reasons for continuous satisfaction. When parents are continually alert to prevent the small baby from suffering unnecessary frustration of any of his needs, they are safeguarding his psychological as well as his physiological well-being. For by keeping him from frustration they are keeping him from feelings of *anxiety:* that is, the psychological distress with respect to some anticipated frustration. Anxiety is a common characteristic of emotionally maladjusted individuals, and will be discussed further on pages 504-505.

The important fact for us here is that anxiety has its roots in infancy, particularly in the helplessness of the baby and its complete dependence upon its parents for the satisfaction of its needs (Symonds[11]). The first stage in bringing up a child who will be free of the tormenting feelings of anxiety is to see that he suffers as little frustration as possible in his infancy. But just how does anxiety develop?

Anxiety very often results when a baby is separated from his parents, even for the briefest intervals. For as he matures, he comes to regard the presence of his mother or father as a sign of security and potential need-fulfillment, and to regard their absence as a sign of potential need-denial. When he is hungry and cries for his mother, he is too young to know that she will probably come "in a minute"—for all he knows, she may never come. For the small baby, any frustration of his needs creates the most distressing feelings of anxiety. And since he is frustrated only when his mother is not there to care for him, he associates her absence with frustration and discomfort. Thus by the simple process of conditioning, the infant comes to react with anxiety to separation.

It is now clear why close attention and prompt response to the infant's expression of need is psychologically so important. It insures that he will be relatively free from anxiety and will help to build his sense of security—both of which are essential to a good start on the road to psychological health.

Social reasons for continuous satisfaction. A child's love for his parents is not native, but acquired. The baby learns to love his mother and father because they are the central agents by which his needs are met. They keep him fed and physically comfortable and they protect him from the onslaughts of emotion and feelings of anxiety and insecurity. Consequently, the infant's first experience in trusting and loving other people lies in this process of learning to trust and love his parents. Moreover, the pattern of the youngster's later relationships has its roots in this first important social experience. The child who experiences anxiety and distrust in this first crucial relationship will tend to have difficulty in meeting social situations, making friends, or forming a satisfying marital relationship later (Bergler[12]). But the child who learns to love and trust his parents and to feel secure with them will be more able to form warm affectional bonds with a widening circle of acquaintances as he grows up.

The relationship of the child to its parents has an important bearing on the problem of how easily and how effectively he can be trained to conform to the expectations of his society. It is common knowledge that a child will much more readily make sacrifices for an adult whom he loves than he will for one whom he does not love. An adult who is loved and trusted and who symbolizes satisfaction and protection is able to help his child learn to behave in a socially desirable way, and to learn without undue emotional stress. In the next section, we shall see just what are the demands society makes of the growing child.

THE SOCIALIZATION PROCESS OF CHILDHOOD

DURING INFANCY, the child's self-centered demands for complete and immediate satisfaction must be met. But when he is about a year old, he begins to reach the level of physical and psychological development where he must learn to bear frustration. Toward the end of the first year, children in all societies must begin to give up the complete satisfaction of their needs and must learn to meet the demands of the culture in which they live (Frank[13]). They must learn bowel and bladder control; they must learn to talk; they must learn the accepted ways of eating, dressing, and grooming; they must learn to avoid dangerous situations. In short, they must acquire the ways of doing things that are approved by the culture.

Most adults have forgotten how difficult it is to learn these things. This important period of life is almost entirely forgotten by the time one is grown up. Yet observations of small children show that they often resent having to use the toilet, to be quiet in the presence of adults, to share their toys with other children, to keep off the streets, and to refrain from jumping on the furniture. These unavoidable demands which society makes of the child are often difficult for him to accept. He tends to regard them as an intolerable infringement of his independence, and he naturally does not want to give up the complete attention and satisfaction which his parents have hitherto given him. If the parents do not follow certain guiding principles of socialization, they are likely to run into difficulty in helping their child to self-sufficient, contented maturity. However unimportant the early childhood experiences may seem on the surface, they have a powerful effect on the individual's fundamental emotional patterns.

Guiding principles of socialization

There are two essential principles with reference to the socialization process.

First, no behavior can be successfully demanded of a child that he is not able to perform. For example, we cannot require a youngster to feed himself before his physical coordination permits his handling a spoon accurately. As the child matures, he becomes progressively more ready to conform to the demands for social behavior. Careful observations on many children have shown the average ages when the child can be expected to sit up, walk, feed himself, play cooperatively with other children, dress himself, and so forth (see the illustration on pp. 454-455). Such observations are just one more evidence of the power of maturation to shape human thought, feeling, and behavior.

In recent years, more and more parents have come to realize that their children can do certain things when they are ready and not before. Many young parents now rely for guidance on the developmental schedules which most children seem to follow in the socialization process (Gesell and Ilg[14]). Of course any such schedules always carry with them the proviso that every child follows his own individual course of development. Parents need to understand that they should not base their demands on any records of what the "average" child attains at different ages. There is actually a great deal of variation from one child to another in the ages at which they start to walk, begin to talk, learn bowel and bladder control, learn to climb stairs, and to do all the other things easily recorded regarding infant behavior. But these variations are not important in influencing the long-range development of the child and should not worry the parent. The child will develop at his natural rate, and if he is healthy physically and emotionally, there need be no fear that he will not develop fast enough. There is a strong exploratory drive in the healthy child, and he will undertake more difficult activities as fast as he is ready for them. He will go through all necessary stages—at his own rate.

Second, the parents must take care not to arouse anxiety in the child by making him feel that they do not love him or that he is a failure if he does not learn social behavior quickly and easily. They must take the process slowly and calmly, without undue excitement or disapproval of failures and setbacks. They must be matter-of-fact and reassuring, so that the child will not become emotionally distressed. Rewards for successful behavior are often useful in helping the child feel that social compliance is worth while, but most important to him is the secure feeling that he will not lose his parents' love if he does not measure up completely to their expectations.

An example of socialization: toilet training

A good example of these principles is in bowel and bladder training in our society. Parents rather frequently feel that their baby must be clean and dry just as early as their friends' babies—earlier, if possible. If their youngster wets and soils himself for a period that they consider too long, they feel it as a reflection on their ability as parents to "control" their child. On the other hand, if the baby is trained early, they are inordinately proud and probably bore their friends by boasting of their offspring's—and their own—achievement.

The essential point here is that parents put a tremendous emotional emphasis on this phase of socialization, so that naturally the child puts a great deal of emphasis on it too. The result is that the youngster's learning becomes shot through with emotion. Sometimes he is unable to gain control and continues wetting and soiling long past the time when he would achieve regular cleanliness and dryness if his control of elimination were treated as an incidental process, instead of as a major problem and a source of concern and pride to his parents. Sometimes he develops a functional constipation, not defecating at all for a period of days. An even more undesirable outcome may be the development of strong attitudes of resignation or revolt toward his parents if they punish him for urinary or bowel incontinence before he is able to recognize and make known his need, walk to the toilet, and manipulate his clothing (Aldrich and Aldrich[15]).

Maturation and socialization. *The wise parent recognizes and respects the child's level of development. For instance, he does not expect him to feed himself skillfully until he has the necessary coordination. In recent years, psychologists have made detailed studies of the developmental stages that all children go through—though at different ages, depending on the individual. The photographs above were taken in the testing rooms of the Yale Clinic of Child Development. They show the increase in coordination which permits a gradual improvement in relatively complex behavior such as self-feeding. Such studies of the course of maturation, intelligently followed, are very helpful to parents and teachers.*

At four weeks (left), the child has little physical control, or interest in the world around him. He can hold a straight rod only if it is put directly into his fist, and then it is only by the reflex grasp (see p. 101).

At four months (center), he can move his head sideways to follow a moving object and is acquiring a measure of muscular coordination that enables him to bring his hands together as he grasps different objects.

At six months (right) he can grasp directly on sight with either hand.

Socialization with respect to eliminative functions is by no means a simple process, but is fraught with difficulties and dangers. A study of 213 cases of "problem" children referred to a psychiatric clinic showed that over half had experienced coercive bowel training. Among the undesirable reactions developed were constipation, fear, negativism, and other undesirable types of behavior (Huschka[16]). Investigation showed that the emotional experiences associated with toilet training were very important in the development of the behavior problems which caused these children to be referred to the clinic.

Learning to avoid dangerous situations

What has been said in detail for the problems connected with toilet training applies equally well to problems connected with feeding, dressing, and learning to avoid dangerous situations. But it is in connection with dangerous situations that it is frequently argued, even by people who do not generally believe in using force with children, that the use of punishment and fear is justified. They put the question this way: if a baby's hands are not slapped as he reaches up toward a

At six months (left), tests show that the child's manual dexterity and eye-hand coordination have increased to the point where he can reach for a small pellet with assuredness, though he cannot pick it up with ease.
At a year (left center), his coordination is remarkably improved over only a few months earlier, but his sense of physical self is still so poor that he reaches into a mirror for a ball held behind him. At this age, or at about 15 months, he can pick up a spoon but cannot use it easily. Now his coordination improves until at 18 months he can fill the spoon effectively.
At two years (right center), fitting blocks into a form board is no problem, and the child can insert a spoon into his mouth with only moderate spilling. Self-feeding can now be encouraged with hopes of reasonable success.
At three, mental and muscular coordination have progressed so far that the child can build a pyramid of blocks (right), and he can use a spoon with very little spilling. Only when the child has progressed through all the earlier stages at his own individual rate can parents expect self-feeding. (Photographs from Life with Baby, March of Time film on the Yale Clinic of Child Development.)

pot of boiling coffee, or if he is not spanked for running into the street, how can he be expected to learn to avoid these situations without experiencing damaging or even fatal consequences?

The answer seems to be that until it is possible to communicate rationally with the youngster, it is much more practical to keep him away from dangerous situations than to try to teach him to discriminate between those aspects of his environment that are dangerous and those that are safe. For instance, he can be kept in a fenced-in yard until he is old enough to recognize the dangers of automobiles, and the coffee pot can be kept out of his reach.

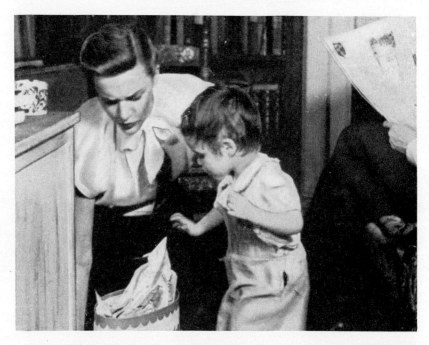

Understanding of developmental stages is important not only in helping the child avoid dangerous situations but also in helping the parent acquire tolerance of "naughtiness." Here a mother scolds the child for pulling the wastebasket contents all over the floor. She fails to realize that typically at this age the child loves to pull things out of boxes and containers. Only at a somewhat later stage will he come to take pleasure in putting them back. (Photograph from Life with Baby, *the March of Time film on the Yale Clinic of Child Development.)*

On the other hand, it is often well to give the child minor "object lessons" in the unpleasant effects of disregarding his parents' warnings. When the child wants to do something moderately unsafe, warn him of the consequences and then let him go ahead and experience the natural consequences of going against parental warnings. If he insists on touching a hot light-bulb, for instance, let him get a little burnt. This procedure not only permits a stronger negative reinforcement of the undesired act, but causes the child to regard the parent as someone who interprets the dangers of the world for his benefit, thus further cementing the bonds between parent and child which are of such vital importance when discipline must be more strongly enforced at a later date. Before the child is ready to obey prohibitions, he must be protected from danger and from too exacting demands which are likely to make him feel either rebellious or inadequate.

Protection and prohibition in socialization

The protectiveness and indulgence which the younger child needs are in no way inconsistent with the idea that the final goal of socialization is an independent, relatively self-sufficient adult who is capable of fulfilling his responsibilities and accepting his rights in a social group. Clinical findings indicate that the best way to reach this final goal is to permit the child to be as dependent as he wants until he has the strength to achieve independence and individuality. As one group of psychologists put it:

> "To the child the adult represents society in both its protective and prohibitive aspects, and the main problem of the child is to accept the protection without becoming too dependent upon it, and to accept the prohibitions without being too cramped or limited by them." (Murphy, Murphy, and Newcomb[17])

Clinicians, then, are obviously not advocating that parents, teachers, camp counselors, and older brothers and sisters adopt a laissez-faire policy toward small children. They are not saying that for optimum emotional development one must never thwart or frustrate children. Since adults generally and parents especially are the agents through whom the child is socialized, they must impose limits on his needs and behavior. In short, every child must be frustrated in certain needs and activities. What clinical investigations do indicate is that these unavoidable frustrations and thwartings must be minimized until the child reaches the developmental stage where social rules and regulations can be imposed on him without damaging him or making him an asocial or antisocial being.

Withdrawing protection and support too soon—attempting to force independence upon the child before he can possibly handle it—can seriously warp a child's social and emotional development. This has been dramatically demonstrated by the fact that lack of family protection is an important factor in juvenile delinquency and crime (see pp. 595-596).

A far more common phenomenon than *lack* of protection, however, is *over*protection—especially in middle- and upper-class families.

Definition of maternal overprotection. An excessive prolongation of childhood dependency can usually be traced to the mother rather than to the father in our society. Parental overprotection has become almost synonymous in clinical thinking with maternal overprotection. The condition can be recognized by four chief signs (Levy[18]):

1 *Excessive contact between mother and child.* The mother has the child sleep with her well beyond the usual age for that sort of thing; there is a great deal of physical demonstrativeness between the two; and the mother puts great emphasis on having the child in sight.

2 *Excessive extension of infantile care.* The mother refuses to wean the child until much later than is usual. She maintains an infantile style of dressing him. She insists on bathing him, dressing him, feeding him, and otherwise ministering to his physical needs long after the majority of children have taken responsibility for themselves on these scores.

3 *Prevention of independent development by trial and error.* The mother constantly does things for the child rather than letting the child do them for himself. The result is that the youngster never fights a battle, chooses for himself, experiences his own achievement, or builds up immunity through experience to the petty defeats involved in growing up.

4 *Inconsistency in maternal control.* The mother is highly changeable in discipline, first indulging the child overwhelmingly and then dominating him strictly. Domination tends to be more frequent than indulgence in the overprotective mother.

The effects of maternal overprotection. When a parent is overprotective, the effects on the child depend on whether the overprotection involves excessive indulgence or excessive domination. When the control is indulgent, the child is likely to be somewhat as follows: He is highly selfish, demanding what he wants when he wants it without regard for the comfort of others. He is unable to bear even the usual frustrations of life; the slightest delay in gratification is unbearable. He is unable to adjust easily to authority; he must have his own way and "run his own show." He usually has little regard for social amenities, displaying bad manners and lack of social insight. He has a good deal of difficulty in adjusting to routine work or tolerating monotonous tasks; he tends to be restless, and even with adequate capacity, he turns out sloppy work. (Cf. the case of Alfred.)

An overprotective mother usually exercises control over her child by dominance rather than by indulgence, and then the effects are quite different. Children who have grown up under a dominant parent are generally submissive, obedient, and ridden by anxiety and apprehension. They are highly dependent upon the dominant persons in their social environment and try to maintain favor by sweetness and submission rather than by achievement and equality of status. (Cf. the case illustrated on pp. 586-587.) The boys in this group tend to marry maternal women who baby them and run their affairs.

Causes of maternal overprotection. The causes of maternal overprotection are threefold, and while they can be isolated for purposes of study, in real-life situations they operate together in the determination of the parent-child relationship just described.

1 One important cause of maternal overprotection is prolonged frustration of the desire for a child. Long periods of sterility, the death of previous children, spontaneous abortions, and economic privation leading to delay of childbearing seem to contribute to the development of overprotectiveness in mothers. When the woman finally gets a child, she feels a need to keep him all to herself, not allowing him to become independent or to have relations with other people.

2 A second factor, marital incompatibility, is at the bottom of other cases of maternal overprotection. One important reason why a mother often puts excessive emphasis on her role as mother is lack of satisfaction in her role as wife. The incompatibility may be due to sexual maladjustment or to disparity in the interests and social lives of wife and husband. But whatever the cause, a wife who finds little happiness with her husband may well turn to her child as the only available outlet for her affections and interests. Conversely, a woman who is happy with her husband will not turn all her emotional energy on the child.

3 But the mother's personal history is perhaps the most important factor. Overprotecting mothers generally have a history of (1) childhood deprivation of affection and (2) childhood responsibility. They are women who lack the comfortable and security-building experience of being loved and protected in childhood. Early in their lives they may either have gone to work to support themselves or their families, or they may have accepted a good deal of responsibility for the home care of the family. Because of

this early shouldering of responsibility, they show clear evidence of blocked ambitions and frustrated desires. As a result, they "take out" on their children their own feelings of disappointment and frustration. *Such "taking out" represents a form of aggression against the children, and actually such mothers are generally quite aggressive women who have shown aggressive tendencies for some time in their life histories.* Overprotection may superficially resemble love, but is actually a form of rejection.

It would seem, then, that what clinicians would call poor parenthood tends to repeat itself through the mechanism of a vicious circle: poor parents tend to develop children with personality traits that predispose *them* to become poor parents, and so on and on until chance occurrences or clinical help break the sequence. Nowhere, perhaps, is the significance of the parent-child relationship so well demonstrated as in this self-perpetuating aspect. Ineffective parents do not make just one generation of unhappy and poorly socialized people; they may begin a chain of demoralizing parent-child relationships that will work to the detriment of many generations.

FRUSTRATION AND AGGRESSION

THE RELATIONSHIP between frustration and aggression in the case of overprotective mothers calls attention to the whole matter of aggressiveness. Aggressiveness (or hostility) is one of the three problems seen most often in clinical cases. We have already seen that the problems of anxiety or cravings for protection are also frequent, and later in the chapter, we will see that the handling of sex urges is another common difficulty. But in recent years there has been increasing recognition of still another major type of personality problem—one which we may have underestimated in our culture partly because of the tradition in Christian religion that we should "love even our enemies." Clinical workers have come to realize that the social environment of the child teaches repression of hostility as truly as it teaches repression of sexual interests. They are learning that many problems of personality rest upon this basically emotional motive, and they are now giving it a new prominence in their thinking.

In most of the situations to which a person must learn to adapt in the course of socialization, his *goals* of behavior remain essentially the same, but he must find *means* of satisfying them that conform to social expectations. In toilet training, for example, the essential goal of relief from specific visceral tensions is not altered; the means for achieving that end, however, undergoes considerable modification in the direction of greater social acceptability. Instead of the immediate release utilized by the baby, there develops a regard for the proprieties of time and place. And in the case of eating, the simple sucking activity of the infant gives way to the adult's dexterity in handling his knife and fork according to the manners prescribed for grown-ups in the culture.

But with aggression and sexuality, it is not true that goals remain constant while only the means of satisfying them change. Society requires the complete inhibition—under certain conditions or for certain periods of time—of all behavior associated with the fundamental impulses of sex and aggression. It is this complete blocking of behavior that gives rise to some important clinical considerations.

The necessity for curbing aggression

Aggression is produced by emotion which has its roots in the thwarting or blocking of drives or motives (Dollard[19]). The basic process is this: frustration provokes anger, which tends to arouse aggressive tendencies, which serve the purpose of eliminating or overcoming the barriers causing the original frustration. (Other reactions to frustration are of course possible and will be discussed in Chapter 13.)

Aggressiveness would be highly adaptive in overcoming barriers were it not necessary to man's very existence that he live as a member of social groups. But life and property must be safeguarded if society is not to disintegrate into a mob of lawless individuals plundering and killing as their emotions dictate. Thus it is obvious that aggressiveness must be carefully curbed. Individuals simply cannot be allowed to give full vent to their aggressive tendencies. The social outlawing of murder is merely the outlawing of aggressiveness expressed at the level of deadliness. And if men are not to destroy each other—that is, if society is to continue—the restraint of aggressions must include not only direct aggressions like murder and assault, and symbolic aggressions like libel and slander, but also noncriminal forms of aggression like overstrict child discipline, nagging, and violent displays of temper. Every day in psychological clinics, aggressive feelings are found to be at the root of many human difficulties in parent-child, husband-wife, and subordinate-superior relationships.

Ways of dealing with aggressive behavior

Aggressive behavior may be handled in two ways: by punishment, or by allowing controlled expression of the aggressive feelings in some manner which does not violate the rights of others.

Punishment. The most familiar way of dealing with aggressive behavior is to squash it by means of taboos on aggressive behavior, with counteraggressions when the taboos are violated. This is the method of punishment as it is used in law enforcement and much home discipline. When the child violates the "laws" of his household or when the criminal commits an aggressive, illegal act, he is subjected to punishment. For his aggression, he suffers an aggression of greater intensity than the one he has just inflicted on his parents or on his society. This method means that aggression, which stems from frustration, is to be controlled by means of frustration. Yet if the frustration-aggression hypothesis is as useful as it appears to be, it would seem that such a policy should result in an increase rather than a decrease in aggressive behavior. There is some evidence on criminal behavior that bears out this possibility.

> Two separate studies have indicated that when juvenile delinquents are institutionalized for punishment, their behavior when they are released does not indicate that they have been "cured" of aggressiveness (Healy and Bronner[20] and Bowler and Bloodgood[21]). Actually, the evidence seems to indicate that as a result of commitment to a reform school there is an increase in delinquent behavior and an intensification of the personal problems in which it is rooted. This evidence is in line with still another study demonstrating that severe punishments tend to increase rather than decrease the crime rate—a finding which is certainly in accordance with what we would expect from the frustration-aggression hypothesis (Wilson[22]).

It is not *always* true, however, that meeting aggressiveness with more aggressiveness will cause the person to become more overtly aggressive. Severe repressive training can produce a very fearful person as well as a very hostile one. The fearful person can try to bottle up within himself the hostile reactions which tend to be created by the attacks of others, but the hostility will still exist as an unconscious emotional undercurrent of his life. This fact is especially clear in clinical work with small children who have been very shut-in and inhibited; they often display some startling aggressiveness during treatment. They apparently have learned in their ordinary life that they do not dare to explore these hostile tendencies within themselves, but the therapy gives them a chance to explore some tendencies within themselves which their parents or teachers would not expect them to have.

Controlled expression. The second way of dealing with aggression is to give it relatively free but harmless expression, directing as much of it as possible into socially acceptable and constructive channels. Mortimer's case is revealing in this respect:

"Mortimer is an interesting lad whose behavior from the age of six has been a source of increasing difficulty to many community agencies. At the present time, aged 17, he is an inmate of a reformatory because of persistent automobile stealing. His last capture by the police was made after an exciting high-speed chase with police bullets whizzing about his ears. His future looks dark indeed. Intelligent efforts to treat his difficulties were blocked all the way through childhood by neurotic and rejecting parents, who resisted all attempted therapy. His turbulent and unsatisfying home environment was without doubt one of the major causes of his problem and delinquent behavior, and it seemed impossible to reach these parents. Yet when one looks back over Mortimer's behavior record, bristling with truancies, school expulsions, non-promotions, runaway trips, delinquencies, and the like, there is one year which is singularly free from trouble. While he was in the seventh grade there were no complaints to school authorities, the visiting teacher, or to social agencies. And if we inquire further as to the reason for the temporary cessation of problems, we find it in the school. A gifted teacher, observing the boy's aggressive drive for notice and attention, gave some thought to the matter of satisfying this need. She interested Mortimer in drama. The interest 'took,' and she encouraged him to write a play, with the understanding that if it was of good quality it could be acted by the class. For months, along with the normal amount of regular school work, Mortimer worked on the writing of the play, then on the selection and direction of the cast, for by that time he had earned by his labors and efforts the right to direct the production. It was successfully staged for the school. Mortimer was much in the public eye, he received approbation from his own class group, and problems were practically non-existent. . . .". (Rogers[23])

The central idea in this method of dealing with aggressive behavior is to give the individual some place or some time for working off his aggressions, either verbally or in violent work or play. He must be without fear of retribution or blame for these aggressions, so that he does not have to store up his frustrations and bury his aggressive tendencies until they spill out of him in a cascade of delinquent or asocial acts. By the use of this kind of emotional safety valve, one builds up what the clinicians call *frustration tolerance:* the capacity to bear thwartings without the need for strong aggressions. This method has been looked upon as a kind of immunizing procedure. By repeated exposure to small amounts of frustration, one builds up a capacity to withstand greater amounts—in much the same way as one builds up immunity to certain diseases by experiencing mild cases of them through vaccination (Rosenzweig[24]).

But whatever the means parents and teachers may work out for allowing the child some controlled expression of the aggressive feelings that every normal person experiences at times, there is still the problem that aggressiveness cannot be allowed full expression if society is to survive. Learning to curb aggression is one of the fundamental processes of emotional development, and one which often gives rise to difficulties in later life. However, the problem in this connection is more than a matter of *curbing* aggressiveness. After all, aggressiveness is not an inborn motive, undetermined in amount by the life experiences and habits of the individual. The amount of hostility in a child's or adult's life can be changed very greatly by his learning experiences in the environment. It is true, of course, that a certain amount of hostility will develop in the life of every person and every child, more than the traditional or popular ideas of human nature have ever realized. But the task of the parent is a double one—first of preventing, as much as possible, the development of unnecessary hostile and resentful feelings; and second, of helping the child to find constructive means of dealing with those that inevitably develop.

PROBLEMS IN SEXUAL DEVELOPMENT

SEXUALITY, like hostility or aggression, develops under the process of socialization not so much by changes in the means of its expression but in its socially enforced inhibition. What this amounts to is frustration of the sex drive. Thus it is not surprising to find aggressive behavior sometimes linked rather closely with sexual frustration. In childhood and into adolescence and even adulthood, sexuality does not involve the learning of new habits to replace earlier ones that were less approved socially. The formal demands of society are that the unmarried person inhibit all behavior directed toward the relief of sexual tensions.

One reason for the forbidding of early sexual expression has to do with the relationship of parents and children. Most parents in their own childhood experienced great pain, guilt, and social disapproval in their desire for sexual gratification. Therefore they are disturbed when they see other children, particularly their own, striving for sexual expression. How much sexuality they will tolerate in their children and how much emotional upset they themselves will experience in connection with it depends largely on the kind of socialization process which they themselves underwent. Very important factors in their attitudes toward their children's sexual behavior are the sexual attitudes which they themselves acquired as children, and the balance between freedom and affectionate dependence which they were able to maintain with their own parents.

In addition to the pleasure of satisfying the sexual appetite, sex activity in both children and adults affords a welcome escape from anxiety and disturbing emotions (Klein[25]). It is well known that while strong emotion can destroy sexual drive, sexuality can counteract the effects of anxiety and more mildly unpleasant emotional states. While the orgasm of adults is certainly tension-reducing, the period of sexual excitement that precedes orgasm is also generally found to be a rewarding experience. This fact seems explicable partly by the tension-reducing value of sexuality. This function of sexuality explains the experiences of children, with whom sexuality seems rewarding almost entirely on the basis of the excitement of fore-play, since orgasm is not experienced in the usual sense until puberty. It also explains the early genital manipulation of infants, which tends to occur most frequently when they are charged with anxiety or loneliness.

Sexual activity in children

What are some of the essential problems that clinicians find to be associated with sexual development as it undergoes socialization? Perhaps the greatest sexual problem is that of infantile auto-erotic behavior in both boys and girls. In boys, the erectile tissue of the genitalia is responsive from the earliest days of life. Here is what appears to be an inborn response.

> One study reported "spontaneous" erections at birth (Blanton[26]). A more elaborate study of nine male infants (Halverson[27]) revealed frequent instances of tumescence, varying from an average of 4 to 35 per day from baby to baby. Erections were accompanied by behavior usually indicative of discomfort—fretting, crying, and restlessness. This contrasted with the behavior associated with detumescence, which seemed to represent playful activity and relaxation.

It is not at all surprising that even a young infant readily learns auto-erotic responses, since he can thus reduce the tensions underlying crying and restlessness. By trial and error and through random movements, the child finds that he can relieve disturbing sensations through manipulating his genitals, which are a source of pleasure. Studies show that auto-erotic responses are by no means "abnormal" but occur frequently even in very young children.

> Since coordination and grasping are at first quite poorly integrated, actual manual masturbation is not often seen during the first three months. But even at this early age a few instances have been noted of infants grasping at the penis. (Halverson[27])
> One psychologist interviewed the mothers of 49 boys and 26 girls and obtained somewhat differing findings from the two groups. Among

the 49 boys, auto-erotic activity had been noted in 26 cases during the first three years, with 19 of the 26 manifesting the activity during the first 18 months. Among the 26 girls, only 4 cases of genital touching were reported, but as the investigator points out, female children often employ thigh rubbing or squeezing, which is difficult to notice and so probably occurs much more frequently than is reported by parents. These findings are very likely conservative, since parents usually make no systematic observations and have varying degrees of resistance either to the recall or the reporting of facts about their children's sex activities. (Levy[28])

It seems safe to conclude, then, that auto-eroticism is quite common among male infants and somewhat less common among female infants. From about one to six years it is frequently indulged in by children of both sexes. From about the age of six until adolescence, there tends to be less of it than before, but at adolescence it reappears together with a more direct interest in sexual expression generally (Wolf[29]). The fact that auto-erotic activity is found among most normal children certainly indicates that it is not an abnormal and harmful practice, but probably no aspect of normal human development has been more surrounded by old wives' tales than has this common practice.

The happy, active child engages in auto-erotic activity, but not to excess. It occurs as the child becomes aware of his physical self, and he will pass on to other interests and to more mature levels of sexual development. But when a person engages in auto-erotic activity with increasing frequency and decreasing pleasure as he grows up, then a serious problem is indicated. The excessive and prolonged genital manipulation is merely a symptom which has possibly arisen as a means of escape from his fundamental conflicts. The basic question for those concerned with guidance problems is not "How can his habit be broken?" but "Why is this person troubled and unhappy?" Here again sexual activity is significant of the individual's total emotional patterns.

Actually, then, the treatment of masturbation should be simply a matter of seeing that the youngster leads an active life, with friendly social relations and play activities to keep his interests turned outward rather than inward, and of minimizing the tension-producing factors that prompt him to rely on masturbation as a comfort. Occasionally professional aid may be needed (see pp. 522-523).

Some new light on homosexual behavior

Another serious problem in the course of growing up sexually is homosexuality. The popular idea is that homosexuality and heterosexuality are entirely separate from each other. This idea is essentially false. It has been found, for instance, that one half of all adult males have had one or more homosexual contacts at some time in their lives (Kinsey[30]). Far from being unusual, homosexuality is at one end of a continuum ranging from complete homosexuality to complete heterosexuality, with the great majority of the population falling near the heterosexual pole.

When the homosexual component tends to be dominant in a person's life, and when the preference for like-sex sexual partners outweighs heterosexual preference, a host of problems arise. Only a few of these problems have to do with sex itself. In the first place, how does homosexual orientation affect the social life of an individual? Secondly, what is the relationship between homosexuality and general personality traits? Third, what are some of the causes of homosexuality?

Homosexuality and social adjustment. Homosexuals are often people who appear to be quite normal in all respects except their choice of love partner. There is no relationship between homosexuality and defective mentality, and homosexuality is in itself no indication of mental disease. Homosexuals are frequently capable people who have made good adjustments to their work and to a society that looks upon them with a good deal of animosity. It is more this social rejection than their sexual difference from the majority of people that results in the troubles that homosexuals experience. It is possible for homosexuals to be fairly well satisfied with their lives, and they are rarely seen in clinics unless they are arrested for attempted seductions, especially with children, or unless they have developed anxiety because of the scoffing and hatred they encounter from people who have a predominantly heterosexual orientation. Because of social disapproval, homosexuals are frequently socially maladjusted individuals, but the signs of maladjustment may result from the extreme social disapproval they receive and not necessarily from the homosexuality itself.

Sexual interests and personality traits. The best known type of homosexual is the *invert*, the mannish woman and the womanly man. There are appreciable differences in the interests and personality traits of the average man and woman, and inverts tend to be characterized by the reactions of the opposite sex (Terman and Cox[31]). For instance, the female invert tends to have the interests and personality traits more generally associated with men. She rejects cultural interests, the sentimentality characteristic of women in our society, and a taste for pretty clothes, whereas she shows the "hard-boiled" point of view, the practicality, and the aggressiveness which are more common to men in our society.

It must be pointed out, however, that measurements of "masculinity" and "femininity" do not yield clear-cut differentiations. Masculinity-femininity seems to distribute itself along a continuum, with all people showing some masculine and some feminine components in their personalities. Frequently a rather sizable degree of inversion with respect to interests and personality traits appears without the presence of homosexual preference in love relationships.

Of course, the very definition of "masculinity" and "femininity" varies from country to country. In America, there is a tradition that men are aggressive, physically strong, logical, and uninterested in—or at least not strongly affected by—appeals to emotion or the sense of beauty. There is also the tradition that women are gentler than men, physically helpless, and so easily swayed by emotion and beauty that they lack the logical hardheadedness of the male. Now of course very few people fit into these arbitrary categories. There are many women who have logical scientific minds, others who are efficient, others who are strong and athletic, others who are not interested in the traditional feminine areas of home-making, clothes, and child-raising. There are also men who are unaggressive or highly "emotional" or fond of art and colorful clothing. Many times such men and women are said to be "unfeminine" or "not very masculine"; sometimes there is even the whispered accusation that they are homosexual. It is important to bear in mind that our definitions of masculinity and femininity are so general that they cannot possibly apply to everyone.

It seems safe to say that the greater the similarity of training and experience, the smaller the differences between the sexes, indicating that the differences in personalities and interests of men and women result more from social conditioning than from inborn constitutional factors. This is just further indication that no person is exclusively either homosexual or heterosexual.

Causes of homosexuality. What are the factors that determine the so-called "masculinity" or "femininity" of a person's behavior and interests? What determines whether a person who is latently homosexual will become overtly homosexual? The causes of homosexuality are complex and varied, and little is definitely known about them. Occasionally there are structural factors that underlie the inversion, with the genital organs of the opposite sex coexisting with those of the individual's dominant sex. At other times there may be a predominance of estrogens in the endocrine balance of a homosexual man or of androgens in a homosexual woman. That the glandular factor probably is not a significant factor in homosexuality is shown by the failures to cure it through changing the hormone balance by injections (Glass and Johnson[32]). In some cases, the hormone injections actually intensify the sex drive of the homosexual without changing its object; in other words, they strengthen the desire for homosexual contact.

Apparently learning as well as biology is involved. Boys and girls are encouraged from toddling age to develop certain habits and interests and ways of behaving. Girls play with dolls, boys with tinker-toys; girls are cuddled and comforted when they hurt themselves, but boys are told not to be "crybabies." In the same way, experience in the environment may cause a person who is latently homosexual to develop certain social or psychological characteristics which influence him to become overtly homosexual. For instance, in some cases a slightly effeminate man, or a masculine woman, may be rejected by members of the opposite sex and thus encouraged into homosexual companionship. Or a little girl who has a cruel or domineering father may come to hate all men.

More importance is attached to the psychological factors in homosexuality than to the organic ones (Seward[33]). Often homosexuality is a function of limited opportunity for heterosexual contacts. Sex segregation, as in military life, often gives rise to homosexual episodes which are usually of a transient character. Lack of opportunity for wide acquaintance between boys and girls as they are growing up, however, may more permanently tip the balance to the homosexual side. And the child whose early family life is unhappy and who, hating his like-sex parent, tries to model himself after his parent of the opposite sex may also develop into a predominantly homosexually oriented adult (Henry[34]). Another possible cause of homosexuality is to be found in the difficulties experienced by adolescents in adjusting to the hetero-sexual interests which society demands that they cultivate. Homosexual relationships are often sought out as refuge from the difficulties encountered in adjusting to the opposite sex (Willoughby[35]).

Adult sexual difficulties

Two other sexual disturbances of clinical importance should be mentioned: impotence and frigidity. *Impotence* is the term given to a male's inability to achieve adequate erection for sexual performance. *Frigidity* means the female's inability to achieve the normal reduction of sexual tension through orgasm. Statistics show that these sexual difficulties are quite common.

The importance of sexual adjustment. It is not commonly realized that impotence and frigidity are not *absences* but *blockings* of sexual desire. Women who are orgasm inadequate are far from indifferent to sex, for they spend more time in daydreaming about sex than do women whose sex adjustment is satisfactory (Ferguson[36]). It is probable that a quite comparable situation exists with regard to males. What this means, of course, is that frigid wives and impotent husbands are experiencing a severe frustration in one of the most important spheres of married life. Sexual activity not only has a direct biological basis (as you learned in Chapter 4) but satisfies the individual's emotional needs for affectionate, trusting human relationships.

While sexual satisfaction is very important to the well-being of the husband and wife as individuals, it is also important to the well-being of their marriage and family relationships. Sexual adjustment is a vital factor in the happiness of marriages, and if inadequate frequently leads to divorce (Hamilton[37]). And without a stable, happy family, children cannot grow into psychologically healthy adults.

Sexual maladjustment is thus a crucial problem for both the individual and society. What are its causes?

Causes of sexual difficulties. Neither impotence nor frigidity is commonly based on organic factors, the overwhelming predominance of causes being psychological. Moreover, the dynamic factors underlying sexual inadequacies in both sexes tend to be highly similar. Some of the common factors in frigidity and impotence are fatigue, anxiety, false fears about physical normality, and feelings of inadequacy or of conflict concerning the marriage. Other factors are illustrated in the following case, taken from a study of one hundred frigid women:

> "Case 975. A frail and delicate woman of forty-six comes about marital problems. She is pallid, sad, has always been cold. She had excessive Puritan training. She and her husband were engaged for years—seeing each other only rarely. 'Father told me not to kiss him—mother said she never kissed her husband until after marriage.'
>
> "No one told her there was any pleasure for a woman until 3 or 4 years after marriage. Relatives told her repressive things about coitus. Her mother said, 'No good woman ever has pleasure; passion is for the vile . . . I'd be ashamed if I enjoyed it.'" (Dickinson and Beam[38])

One basic factor in this woman's frigidity is a highly repressive sex education, based on the false idea that frigidity is ladylike. But another factor probably present is the unsatisfactory nature of her childhood experiences with her own parents, who were maladjusted sexually. Because they were not happily married, they could not guide her smoothly through the process of socialization. Her resulting attitudes and personality traits probably had as much influence on her sexual capacity as did the specific sex information she received.

Here again we see the importance of parent-child relationships in determining healthy patterns of emotional development. There is an old saying to the effect that "you can choose your friends but not your relatives." The clinician would say that many unfortunate cases arise because the infant and growing child cannot choose his parents. For it is his view that the foundations of a happy emotional life are laid down in childhood.

Parents who make a real effort to give their child continuous satisfaction of his infantile needs and who guide him wisely through the socialization process of childhood—avoiding the dangers of overprotection on one side and overstrict prohibition on the other—are not likely to see him turn to the clinics for aid in making his life adjustments. He will be able to express his individuality in socially constructive ways, and he will be relatively free of anxiety and emotional difficulty in two chief problems which confront every person in our society: expressing aggression and expressing sexuality. And he will be able to handle the inevitable frustrations which every one of us encounters and to which every one of us reacts in his own way.

The student must not conclude that the only major problems a person must handle are just these relatively tangible problems of dealing with his anxieties, his hostilities, and his sexual motivation. These are three very important problems, and clinical workers have been especially attentive to them, but the individual has other important emotional needs as well. For example, he craves the approval, acceptance, and companionship of others; he wants the feeling of being appreciated and respected; he is driven by a need for achieving a feeling of self-respect; he has a need for interesting experiences. All such motives can be subjected to more or less severe frustrations, and frustrations in any of these areas can lead to difficulties. The well-adjusted person is the one who has learned to guard against unreasonable and unnecessary frustrations, partly through ways of learning how to handle situations he meets in life, and partly through learning how to endure frustrations which cannot be avoided. The next chapter will go into this problem of some of the *Reactions to Frustrations* which distinguish different personalities.

One of the common reactions to frustration to be discussed in this chapter is nomadism— that is, aimless wandering to escape an emotional frustration which cannot be left behind by a change in locale. Some trailer families, for example, are engaged in a realistic search for improved economic conditions, but others move just to be moving.

CHAPTER **13**

Reactions to frustration

Sources of Frustration
Healthy Modes of Adjustment
Unhealthy Modes of Adjustment

Adjustment is a never-ending process of overcoming obstacles to the satisfaction of our biological drives, our appetites, and our derived motives. These obstacles are of many different kinds: they range from a broken shoelace, to physical defects, to the lack of affection, to poverty and war, to the sexual tabus imposed by the moral code of society. Frustration is and always has been an inevitable part of human living, for only in the womb are the individual's needs continuously and automatically satisfied.

The particular reaction any given person will make to a frustrating situation depends first of all upon the nature of that situation; obviously, for example, the loss of a job would usually involve action in the economic sphere. It also depends upon many factors in the individual's life history: important among these factors are, of course, the emotional experiences he has had as an infant, child, and adolescent, especially in the expression of sexuality and aggression.

There can be no easy answer to the problem of why one person reacts one way and another person reacts another way. Every one of us has a complex emotional life and complex emotional history. Only thorough clinical examination can determine for certain why any given person behaves as he does. In this chapter we shall examine some of the many different ways of adjusting to the frustrating situations—major and minor—that are inevitable in every person's life.

SOURCES OF FRUSTRATION

THERE ARE three main kinds of obstacles to the satisfaction of our motives. Correspondingly, there are three types of frustration: environmental, personal, and conflict.

Often a person encounters an obstacle in the environment which blocks the satisfaction of some need, so that he suffers what is known as *environmental frustration.* Examples of environmental frustration are

not hard to find. There is the young college graduate who cannot find a job during an economic depression, the orphaned child whose need for maternal affection goes unsatisfied in an institution, and the driver who gets a flat tire "in the middle of nowhere." All these individuals have some drive or motive which is frustrated by some circumstance outside themselves.

The second type of frustration arises when a person has some characteristic of body, personality, or intelligence which prevents him from satisfying his drives or ambitions. It is known as *personal frustration.* For instance, there is the boy who wants to play football on the college team but is thwarted by his lack of skill. Another boy wants to be highly popular with girls but is hindered by superficial unattractiveness.

The *conflict frustration* arises when an individual has opposing drives and must choose whether to satisfy one drive or the other—for example, between studying and playing baseball. Or a businessman confronted by an opportunity to make some money dishonestly is blocked by his fear of punishment, by his desire for self-approval, or by his desire for social approval. A young girl is tempted to marry a middle-aged man for his money, but she is restrained by the feeling that she would be unfair to him because she loves someone else. In each case, the individual is faced by a situation in which he may make either one of two responses—each satisfying one of his drives but preventing another drive from being satisfied.

The adequate reduction of frustration occurs when the individual develops a satisfactory pattern of response which overcomes the obstacle.

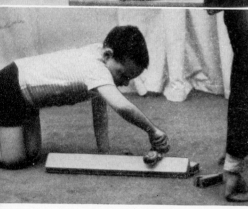

EGO-BLOCKING GAMES

(Synopsis by Lawrence Joseph Stone, Associate Professor of Child Study, Vassar College. Stills from the film, Frustration Play Techniques: Part 1. Blocking Games, produced by the Department of Child Study, Vassar College, in cooperation with the Sarah Lawrence College Nursery School, under grants from the General Education Board and the Joseah Macy, Jr. Foundation.)

Some of the many different reactions an individual may make in a frustrating situation have been demonstrated in a film on frustration play techniques. In this film, several children in succession play with an adult in a game which is actually a projective technique—that is, a means of discovering the individual's feelings by analyzing how he projects them on some play object in an experimental situation (see p. 555).

In this particular game, developed by the late Eugene Lerner at Sarah Lawrence College, the child meets a series of playful obstacles. He is confronted first by a situation in which the child's and the experimenter's ("E"'s) "cars" are on a narrow track. E says, "Let's meet in the middle— how can my car pass?" RALPH answers very coyly, "It can't," then slowly pushes E's car back (top left). In the next situation (center) E's doll "stops" the child's car. "What happens?" RALPH decides the doll "gets run over."

RALPH refuses to let E's doll ride on his train. "He can't cross the street. He'll get run over." He becomes more and more assertive and confident: his car always "gets there first"; E's car "crashes" because "mine came so fast"; "my doll comes in and touches everything and knocks the whole house down" (lower left).

The process of arriving at a solution is a combination of trial-and-error, rational analysis of the situation, and emotional insight. Since mental well-being depends on your success in handling the frustrations you are bound to have, and not on whether you have any, it is extremely important for you to examine your reactions, without deceiving yourself, so that you can modify them if they are ineffective in reducing frustration.

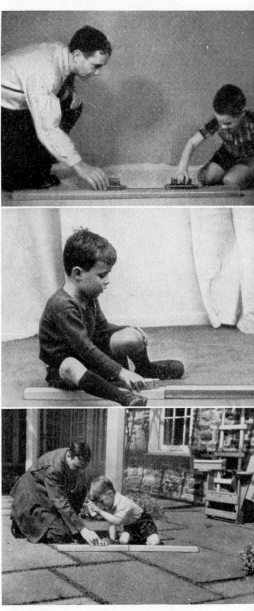

The games reveal that reactions to frustration differ from time to time in one person as well as among persons. For example, a year earlier (top right), we see how RALPH turns his car around and goes back so that E's car may proceed. He cannot be even coyly assertive to the adult. SAM (right center) shows a different way of responding to the situation. When E says, "How can my car pass?" SAM replies, "How can mine?" He is very uneasy even in a playful challenge of adult authority but still eager to hold his own. The result is a standstill. SAM looks a little worried and seems to want to change the subject. He says, "Are these all the toys you got here?" Then he points to a bruise on his knee and says, "Oh, look here. That's what I did outside. It's got a little mud in it. It's all right." But his fundamental respect for authority is shown in his quickly returning to the game the experimenter insists on playing and in his anxiety to please. ROBERT (lower right) immediately pokes at E's car and flails at E's hand and arm. Such violence suggests a displaced aggression which is pent up and finds an outlet here.

As Dr. Lerner points out at the conclusion of the film, "In the hands of trained persons, these play techniques can be useful for research and educational guidance, for they can reveal characteristics which may not be seen as readily in school or at home. In a world beset by manifold frustrations, it is important to learn something about each growing young citizen's picture of himself in relation to other people. This can help us plan for a more balanced and rational management of the emotional energies of human beings. Such psychological planning is sorely needed in the present period of crisis in human relationships."

Sources of Frustration   475

HEALTHY MODES OF ADJUSTMENT

IN A FRUSTRATING SITUATION you will do one of two things: either you attempt to escape, physically or mentally, or you attempt to reduce the frustration in some way. Sometimes the situation is just too much for you, so that your best course of action may be to leave the frustrating circumstances in order to find a situation where a satisfactory adjustment is possible. This is essentially a flight reaction, but at times flight is a realistic solution. For instance, the boy who simply does not have and never will have the motor skills necessary for top-flight football would be wise to stop trying out for the college team—that is, to withdraw from a situation in which frustration is inevitable. In most cases, however, frustration should be faced and resolved.

Of course, sometimes an individual is not skilled enough in self-analysis to select his best line of action. Sometimes he is so upset emotionally that he is unable to solve any sort of problem. In such cases, the problem can be solved or the frustration reduced if some experienced person is available to point out the way. In recent years, psychiatry and clinical psychology have been developed in order to help the perplexed person with his problems. Diagnosis and cure of the underlying causes of frustration may take a long time, but adjustment can be greatly helped by a trained therapist, and early consultation can avoid serious results.

Most discussions of reactions to frustration have been descriptions of ineffective reactions, since clinical workers have been primarily concerned with persons suffering from poor adjustments. It is true, of course, that the various faulty means of adjustment can be used in such extreme ways that they very seriously cripple the person's life. In milder forms, however, such faulty adjustment techniques are found in the general population, and the insight which comes from the more pronounced cases seen in clinical work can help us to understand a much wider range of human life as well.

Some of the types of adjustment recognized by clinical workers can operate in rather healthy ways in the person's life. For example, while daydreaming or fantasy can occur in such extreme forms that the person will have lost all important contacts with reality, it may also occur in much milder degree and even serve some valuable purposes in the person's life (by giving some relief from temporary disappointments, by helping to revivify his goals, and so on).

Thus, any one of the various reactions to frustration may be either healthy or unhealthy—depending on the degree to which it is used, its usefulness in reducing frustration, and (to some extent) its acceptability to society. These three criteria are helpful to us in distinguishing, first, a group of predominantly healthy means of reaction to frustration, and then a group of predominantly unhealthy means of reaction. The healthy ways of dealing with frustrations include *Realistic Hard Work, Development of New Skills, Reinterpretation of the Situation, Cooperation and Sharing as Techniques of Social Relations,* and *Detour Behavior* (including sublimation and substitution, and compensation).

Realistic hard work

It is certainly possible for a person, when he meets frustrations, merely to work blindly, using some technique poorly adapted for reaching his goals. Obviously, however, the most worth-while results call for a realistic investment of hard work. No star football team ever made its record without strenuous training; no musician ever achieved mastery of his instrument without years of patient practice; no student or scientist can get the necessary mastery of intellectual tools without hard work. In fact, some psychologists have said that the chief mark of a well-adjusted person is his ability to recognize the demands of reality and to meet them willingly.

For the development of this readiness to do hard work, it is necessary that the individual, as a child, have had tasks which were adapted to his ability, so that he could succeed with them and thus gain some confidence in his capacity for reaching worth-while goals by his own efforts. One of the fundamental lessons of the small child is that he can get worth-while things by real effort.

Development of new skills

Often, of course, the frustrated individual needs more than just hard work; he also needs new attitudes and new skills in adjustment. For example, a person may have been using ineffective methods of winning love and admiration; he may have been trying to impress people with his ability and past accomplishments, or he may have been trying to bully them into accepting him. Obviously what he needs is not renewed vigor in such efforts but new skills in personal relations. If a man is failing in business, he may need to study the methods of efficient business management. If a mother is getting poor results as a parent, she may need some scientific information on parent-child relations.

In general, the development of new adjustment skills is a complex process, involving a change in the emotional patterns built up over a lifetime. In some cases, psychotherapy may be of value in helping the individual accomplish this process (see Chapter 14).

Reinterpretation of the situation

Sometimes the frustrations which the person suffers are a product of his own judgment of his life situation, rather than a product of any defects in the situation itself. It sometimes happens, therefore, that the main thing which the person needs—but often not an easy thing—is to get a more sound interpretation of the situation. For example, the parents of a child may (deliberately or unintentionally) have given him the impression that a really fine person would not experience sexual desires except in marriage. When he comes to adolescence and finds that he does experience a sex motive much more insistent and powerful than his parents' comments led him to expect, he may feel intense guilt and shame. Then he needs a more accurate picture of the realities of human life before he can resolve his emotional conflict.

The same thing is seen in many other areas of life. A parent, for example, may be greatly perturbed at the behavior of his adolescent children—behavior which seems to him ungrateful and rebellious. The truth may be, however, that the children are going through a difficult but very important process of asserting their independence from the home. The wise parent is tolerant of the rather extreme demands for independence that adolescents sometimes make as they experiment with the new role of adulthood and does not interpret them as signs that the children no longer respect his opinions or value his companionship.

Today many life situations are interpreted quite differently than they were ten or fifty or a hundred years ago. As just one example, scientific findings on the developmental stages of children are gradually leading parents to more realistic expectations of what their children can and cannot do at different ages. As psychology and the various social sciences develop, we will find increasingly that we will need to rest our interpretations of many things on their technical findings. Such reinterpretations can give us much more effective ways of handling some of the tasks which face us.

Cooperation and sharing as techniques of social relations

Most writers describing personality have apparently found difficulty in making some brief characterization of the kind of technique which marks the well-adjusted person's relations with other people. It has been relatively easy to describe poor ways of dealing with others, such as withdrawing and isolating oneself from others, becoming unduly submissive to others, and becoming overaggressive and overdominating. In fact, some writers (like Karen Horney) have said that healthy adjustment consists just in using these three different types of social relationships in the places where they are appropriate—withdrawing some times, submitting at other times, dominating at still other times.

A healthy type of social relationship—one which we ought to define so clearly that we can work for it deliberately—is found in cooperation or sharing. This type of social relationship is made more enjoyable and satisfying for each person because of the element of joint participation. There are a great many human activities, after all, which the individual cannot engage in most satisfactorily by himself—activities like those of an orchestra, in which the joint activity is much more satisfying to the participants than their individual performances can be. But this does not mean that the main emphasis of activity is "submissiveness" or "domination." The chief thing is working together, cooperating for the attainment of more interesting results than can come individually. Personal friendships are particularly good examples. We become more rounded persons, more adequate persons, as we share our lives openly and frankly with others. Once again it is not submission or dominance that is the keynote, but the participation of equals—getting a richer meaning out of life.

Detour behavior

Sometimes the person has to face the fact that a frustration is insurmountable. For example, a girl may want to be beautiful and "glamorous"—but even though she can make some improvements in her appearance, she knows that she will never look like a Hollywood actress. Then the healthy reaction is essentially the same as the reaction you make when you meet a sign on the highway: "Road closed for repairs." Instead of just coming to a standstill, or turning back, you make a detour.

There is one main difference between this example and many life situations. In your experience in driving, it is easy for you to recognize your fundamental objective, and it is easy to see that alternative "means" might be used to reach it. In the case of personality situations, however, it often is hard for a person to tell what he has been trying to achieve, so that a main part of the readjustment which is needed is a careful reinterpretation of one's own real wants or motives. For example, the man who has suffered a severe physical handicap may feel that it is an insurmountable obstacle to marriage, that no woman would ever fall in love with him except out of pity. But actually, if he examines the situation realistically, he may come to realize that perhaps he would not want a woman who could be so easily repelled by a handicap in a man. He may come to see that while a mature woman would naturally prefer her husband not to have such a handicap, the most important things a woman looks for in a marriage are love, companionship, and mutual respect. Of course, it is not easy then for the man to decide exactly which qualities he should develop to become a desirable husband, but at least he sees that all roads to a normal happy life are not closed to him.

Among the most important "detour routes" around inevitable frustration are sublimation and substitution, and compensation.

Sublimation and substitution. An emotion or drive may be satisfied by more than one activity, so that if there is some obstacle to the most direct means of satisfaction, the individual may resort to indirect means for obtaining satisfaction. The indirect behavior chosen may involve either sublimation or substitution.

Sublimation is an indirect way of satisfying drives which changes the goal of the emotion and thus its conscious quality. It results in activity which is not only socially acceptable but is often of the greatest social or artistic value. (The word itself comes from the Latin and literally means "making sublime.") To choose but one example of sublimation, our society surrounds the exercise of the sexual function with many restrictions. When direct satisfaction of the sexual need is not possible, many people express their sexual emotion in behavior which does not have sexual activity as its direct goal. This indirect expression may take the form of interest in romantic literature, writing love poetry, or even composing sentimental love letters. These are all interests and activities which society approves even though their sexual element is thinly disguised. Or people may express sexual emotions in activities which do not seem to have any sexual element, such as art, music, and aesthetic dancing. According to some psychologists, all forms of work—science and business as well as the fine arts—result from the sublimation of sexual energy, very broadly defined.

Substitution is also an indirect means of satisfying emotions or drives. It is unlike sublimation in that the quality of the drive is unchanged because its goal is unchanged, in that it involves activity which is not socially acceptable, so that it is often (but not necessarily) accompanied by feelings of self-disapproval, guilt, and inferiority. Common forms of substitution involve language behavior: telling risqué stories, writing obscene poetry, singing smutty songs.

Compensation. When a person is frustrated by failure in one activity, he may earn social approval or self-approval by entering an activity in which he can succeed. Such an effort to counterbalance failure is known as *compensation*. Compensation, like sublimation, can be socially acceptable. For instance, a person with features that are not pleasing when in repose can compensate for his physical unattractiveness by developing a charming manner and by learning how to converse interestingly with others. Such a person is welcomed as a friend, and his physical unattractiveness is no longer an obstacle to social success. He has reduced his frustration by compensating in a socially acceptable way.

The compensatory reaction to inferiority in one sphere can cause a person to strive hard to achieve real success in some other sphere. Compensation is wholesome if the new activity can bring social approval. For example, some of our greatest scholars were driven to intensive study because they felt themselves inferior in social grace and compensated through scholarship for their failure to get along with people.

The person with inferiority feelings must realize that what he wants most deeply is not superiority or competitive success but the respect and affection of other people. His shortcoming bothers him because he feels that it frustrates his deep human craving for acceptance, appreciation, and companionship. His friends are likely to advise him to find some area in which he can demonstrate his ability, and thereby get free from his feeling of inferiority. This is risky advice. It may even cause him to become embittered with social relations, because other people, also, are trying to prove that they are successes, competitively, and he will merely be intensifying their frustrations. Instead, he needs to use the more adequate "detour reactions" which we mentioned earlier. He needs to see that his fundamental goal, of affection and acceptance, is not to be reached by proving that he is better than others, but by making his life pleasant and helpful to others. He needs to see that the whole keynote can be shifted from the question of "Who's better?" to the keynote of "What activities can I find which will take advantage of the opportunities which life affords me?"

UNHEALTHY MODES OF ADJUSTMENT

THE REACTIONS USUALLY CHARACTERIZED as "unhealthy" may, as has already been pointed out, be found in mild forms in all normal persons. This important fact is dramatically illustrated by the transition of compensation into overcompensation. Accordingly, the first of the "unhealthy" reactions to frustration we shall consider will be *Overcompensation*, to be followed by discussions of *Aggression as a Reaction to Frustration, Repression, Logic-tight Compartments, Rationalization, The Flight into Fantasy, Identification, Nomadism, Regression, Alcohol and Drugs, Psychogenic Illness as a Reaction to Frustration,* and *Anxiety, Phobias, Compulsions,* and *Obsessions.*

Overcompensation

Sometimes attempts to counterbalance failure have undesirable results. Suppose the unattractive person described on page 481 were to develop differently. As a child he may be teased by his schoolmates and generally "left out of things." Then he may feel so very inferior that his desperate attempts to assert himself lead him into activity which is either antisocial or so extreme that it does not effectively reduce his frustration. For instance, he may alienate his classmates—and thus defeat his purpose—by talking too loudly and too much or by "showing off" whatever assets he does possess. He may even resort to stealing or dishonesty if they will bring him prestige—prestige that comes either directly through the admiration of his less daring companions, or indirectly through the money he can spend. Or he may concentrate all his energies in one or two activities, to the neglect of others. The unattractive person may devote all his energy to winning social success and may neglect other sources of satisfaction like studies and athletics. Such extreme or antisocial attempts to counterbalance inferiority are the main characteristics of *overcompensation.*

Aggression as a reaction to frustration

Often a person reacts aggressively in frustrating situations—that is, he attempts to injure either the obstacle blocking him, or some substitute for the obstacle. It may happen that aggression does reduce frustration, as when a man kills the burglar who has entered his home and is about to deprive him of money and possessions. Usually, however, aggression does not reduce frustration. First of all, it does not eliminate the obstacle to satisfaction—it simply reduces temporarily the mental or physical tension which accompanies frustration. Moreover, aggressive behavior is usually not acceptable to society.

Aggressiveness may be expressed either directly or indirectly against whatever obstacle is causing frustration. You have all seen a child kick at a door he cannot get open, not because he hopes to get it open that way but because he wants to relieve his irritation at being frustrated.

His aggression is being expressed directly. However, the aggressiveness may also be *displaced*—that is, expressed indirectly against some person or object other than the one causing the frustration.

There are two main reasons for displacement—or indirect expression—of aggression. First, the frustrated person is often afraid of being punished if he acts directly. For instance, a branch manager asks his superior in the central office for a pay raise and is refused. He is afraid that he will lose his job if he tells his superior how angry he is at what he feels to be a serious injustice. He may then "blow off steam" by firing one of his own subordinates, or by snapping irritably at his children at the dinner table. Or—another common reaction—he may be afraid to express his anger outwardly at all, and will turn it on himself by blaming himself and feeling that he does not deserve a raise.

Second, the frustrated person may not know whom or what to blame for his lack of satisfaction. Certain phases of history and certain kinds of social statistics furnish good examples of this reason for indirect aggression as a reaction to frustration.

> Aggressive acts are more numerous during periods of economic depression, when many human needs are unsatisfied, than during periods of prosperity and well-being. A significant relation has been discovered between lynchings and hard times. During depressions, lynchings are frequent; during prosperity, their frequency declines. Apparently, the whites turn against the Negroes to relieve the frustration caused by their fallen incomes or unemployment. They do not know who is to blame for their frustration, so they use the Negro as a "scapegoat"— as a substitute object of aggression. (Hovland and Sears[1] and Minz[2])

The "scapegoat" mechanism. It is easy to understand how displacement of aggression is an important mechanism in such social phenomena as race prejudice. The stronger group, when frustrated for some reason, turns its aggressions on a weaker minority group rather than on the actual sources of the frustrations (Wechsler[3]).

> Anti-Semitism in Nazi Germany affords a tragic application of this principle. The Germans between the two wars were frustrated in many ways: for instance, their national self-esteem was injured by their defeat in the war; and their need for material security was frustrated by the inflation and severe economic dislocation which the nation was suffering. The Germans already had a long tradition of prejudice against the Jews, and they could easily turn their aggressions on them when their emotional frustrations mounted up. The persecuted Jews were the "scapegoats"—that is, they were blamed for all the frustrations which the Germans were suffering, and suffered accordingly.

Self-aggression or suicide. At times the process of displacement has the extreme result of causing aggression to be turned against the self, instead of against substitutes in the environment. This is particularly evident in suicide, a psychological problem that is extremely complex but that illustrates clearly the process of internalized aggressions and the widespread applicability of the displacement mechanism.

Here is a passage from the diary of a suicidally depressed patient, who during the time she kept the diary had to be constantly watched by hospital attendants to prevent her from committing suicide.

> "Do not ask me why I should like to die. In a more energetic mood I would defy you to tell me why I should live, but now I only wonder, and even wonder is difficult when one has a preconceived conviction in favor of death.
>
> "Objectively speaking . . . I am deluded but I am much distressed by the delusions I have and I am at a loss to know where my delusion ends and reality begins. I live in a world where delusion leers in my face under a horrid mask which seems to me to hide reality.
>
> "I find no encouraging successes in recognition to lead me on to more strenuous effort. Far rather would I turn my back on such a world and mingle with the earth's insentient elements, to share no whit of responsibility for its ghoulish monstrosities.
>
> "The ego which once satisfied me seems now so paltry that I despise myself for being duped. An ego so useless as mine, without value to myself or others, might better drop from the world and make its last graceful gesture in a series of dimpling ripples in the surface of a river into which it might sink with a delicious finality." (Menninger[4])

Here it can be seen that the woman has very low self-esteem, considering herself "useless." She obviously feels some aggression against the world and its "ghoulish monstrosities" but has turned most of it into a powerful hatred of herself rather than of the outside world, where she suffered severe frustration.

Repression

One way of handling the feelings resulting from frustration is to repress them. Repression is putting away from consciousness a thought, feeling, or memory that causes pain, shame, or guilt.

> An extreme case of repression was the woman suffering from an incurable cancer, who on learning of her condition was at first deeply depressed and worried about the future of her husband and children. Later she became so abnormally joyous and elated that she was taken to a mental hospital. She maintained that she was now perfectly well, that her disease had been completely cured.
>
> The explanation is obvious. The tragic frustration resulting when her desire to live had to meet the fact of her hopeless condition was resolved by a process of *repression*. The painful reality was pushed completely out of consciousness. (Hart[5])

Comparing repression and forgetting. A certain amount of repression is part of daily life. All of you have suddenly realized after it is too late that you have completely "forgotten" to make a telephone call you did not want to make. A psychologist would say that you had not forgotten but repressed it. Just how are repression and forgetting alike and different?

1 Repression and forgetting are basically similar in inhibiting the memory of material formerly within consciousness.

2 As you learned in Chapter 10, ordinary forgetting occurs through "retroactive inhibition." That is, the learning of new material actively interferes with or inhibits the recall of the old. Repression, like forgetting, is accomplished by inhibition of recall. Recall is a response to stimuli like any motor response. The person simply learns not to respond to stimuli which remind him of the painful subject, just as he might learn not to walk into a new piece of furniture after he has bumped his shins a few times. Both become automatic and unconscious inhibitions of response. In one case he inhibits the response of remembering, and in the other case he inhibits the response of walking in a direction where formerly there was no obstacle.

3 One important difference between forgetting and repression lies in the cause of the loss of memory. The rate and amount of forgetting are determined not only by the pleasantness or unpleasantness of the material but by many other factors as well. However, the rate and amount of repression seem to depend mainly on the unpleasantness of the material.

4 Another important difference between them is that ordinary forgetting, unlike repression, is usually not complete. Even if the person cannot directly recall forgotten material, he at least can recognize it, or can relearn it more rapidly than he can learn unfamiliar material. But repression is often so complete that the person can neither recognize nor rapidly relearn the repressed material. That is, he actively keeps himself from responding to any of the stimuli which formerly caused him to "remember" certain painful things. However, if the repressed material is ever brought to consciousness (through psychotherapy or some unusual circumstance which breaks down the inhibition against recall), the recall is likely to be complete. Then the person will express genuine wonder: "How could I ever have forgotten that?"

5 While both repression and forgetting occur all the time in all of us, each has a different function. Forgetting is essentially a way of eliminating useless material from our minds. It would be impossible for us to remember the innumerable impressions, situations, people, ideas, and objects that we encounter during a single day. Some of them are soon forgotten. They are neither pleasant nor unpleasant; they simply are of no interest to us, do not register strongly in our consciousness, and are genuinely forgotten, not repressed. Can you recall the color of the tie your psychology professor wore at your last class meeting? Do you remember the name of the publisher of this book?—it is printed on the back binding where you probably see it every time you pick up the book. You probably do not remember either of these things, simply because you were not interested enough to notice them in the first place.

Repression, however, is not just a means of eliminating from mind the trivial or uninteresting experiences of daily life. It serves to save people the pain of certain thoughts and memories. You have all repressed the memory of some social *faux pas*, some embarrassing incident, something you did though you knew it was wrong.

The ill effects of extreme repression. Repression in moderation is quite normal. When it is extensive, however, it can prevent effective adjustment. Let us consider from a new angle the case already familiar to us from Chapter 11.

Suppose that the young girl who was so abnormally shy with boys had repressed the memory of the birthday-party incident which originally caused her to avoid boys. The incident may be so humiliating for her to remember that she does not allow it to enter her mind. At first, this repression is difficult. Every time she sees one of the boys who were at the party (or perhaps any boy), she remembers her shame over vomiting in public. Many other stimuli—the mention of birthday parties, the sight of the dress she was wearing that day or even of a large cake or streamers—call up the response of remembering the humiliating experience. Because this recall response is so painful, she inhibits it every time she meets one of these stimuli. She also inhibits the recall response to such inner verbal stimuli as the *thought* of the incident or of anything connected with it. Finally, she avoids boys altogether because it is they who most strongly remind her of her shame.

However, this extensive repression does not help her at all to overcome her shyness. The constant necessity to be on her guard against remembering keeps her under a nervous strain which makes social contacts, especially with boys, very painful. And she is unable to solve the problem of her shyness because she no longer remembers how it began, even though it is influencing her feelings and behavior every day.

Extensive repression is a poor reaction to frustration. Part of its in-
effectiveness is due to the constant tension of striving to keep unpleasant thoughts away from consciousness. If the person inhibits the
recall response to many objects, people, ideas, or situations, then he
suffers continually from the tension accompanying an inhibited response. When under this emotional tension, he is not calm or rational
enough to set about solving the frustrating situation in any effective
way. And—more important—he is incapable of reaching a solution because he has no recollection of the origin of his frustration. Often, he
is actually unaware that he is frustrated.

Interestingly enough, repression is one of the adjustments most approved by society. The repressed person usually checks even mild
and healthy antisocial impulses. Then he is known as "that nice quiet
boy," and he is held up by the harassed schoolteacher as a model
for better-adjusted children, whose sometimes noisy way of expressing
themselves gets on grown-ups' nerves.

Dissociation is repression at its extreme. Occasionally the amount
of repression becomes so great that it leads to a very abnormal condition known as dissociation. In dissociation, whole areas of the personality are removed or "split off" from consciousness because they cause
an unbearable amount of fear, guilt, shame, frustration, or other strong
and painful emotion. The following case shows the abnormal reaction of an unstable girl to a frustrating and painful situation.

> "Miss B. Q., aged seventeen years, was brought to the clinic in a
> complete state of amnesia. She was found at a church, in a disheveled
> state, and could not tell who she was. She spoke coherently, but did
> not know her name, her address, who her relatives were, how old she
> was, where she went to school, or any other fact about her past
> life. Her mental processes were otherwise intact, and she could read,
> write, and discuss specific problems intelligently.
>
> "Under hypnosis, the essential history of her past was brought to
> light. She and her sister lived with their widowed father. He was a
> domineering, sadistic person who demanded implicit obedience and
> exact accounting of the household budget. On the day the amnesia
> developed, the patient was given the money for rent, and when she
> arrived at the agency discovered the money had been lost. The fear
> and panic that seized her was so great that rather than go back
> and face certain and severe punishment—she 'forgot' all about herself."
> (Kraines[6])

Dissociation is a form of repression in that it permits an escape from
the consciousness of painful reality. It causes violent changes in the
way the personality is divided between the conscious and unconscious
parts, and so it causes violent changes in feeling and behavior. There

Unhealthy Modes of Adjustment 487

are several different kinds of dissociation, varying in (1) the extent of the part of personality "split off" from consciousness, and in (2) the length of time that the "split" lasts. A very brief escape is called *somnambulism* or "sleepwalking"; longer episodes are called *fugues* or "flights."

"Split personality" is one form of dissociation. One of the most dramatic forms of dissociation is the so-called "split personality." This occurs when two different parts of the personality alternate frequently in consciousness, each taking over conscious control of the person for relatively equal periods of time. Each part of the dual personality contains drives which are in conflict with drives of the other part. These two sets of conflicting drives originally existed simultaneously in the individual, but since he could not choose which set to satisfy, he unconsciously adopted the device of repressing consciousness of one set while temporarily satisfying the other set. The reason why dual personalities are often "Dr. Jekyll and Mr. Hyde" is that they represent conflicting drives or motives. If one of the two "personalities" is selfish, the other is generous to a fault; if one is quiet and obedient, the other is violently aggressive. Often, one side of a dual personality does not know what the other side is doing, or else he feels a lack of connection with it. The "split" is then complete.

In the following case, the split was not complete. The woman was consciously aware of the two parts in her personality, although she did not feel any emotional identity between them. Obviously, she was expressing in the second, "B," part of her personality the aggressiveness and vanity which the first, "A," part would not allow to be expressed.

"A is a woman twenty-nine years of age, the fifth of a family of six children, all living. The father was fifty-six at the time of his death. The mother is still living. The mother's side is negative. The father, an habitual drinker, committed suicide. One brother has reputed 'psychic powers.' A, while not robust, has no organic trouble. As a child she was very emotional, high-tempered, and much older in manner than her years. She has never had any serious illness. Her height is five feet, and she weighs eighty-one pounds. This is seventeen pounds under her maximum weight. At present she is a saleswoman, and is considered a good one.

"B's appearance as an alternating self began about three years ago. The change was, at first, accompanied by brief trauma. This has now disappeared, and the change is generally made without disturbance. The transformation produces a marked change in the face and bearing. Respiration is deeper, and goes from eighteen to twenty. The body is slightly flushed, and the eyes are brighter. The expression of the whole face is altered. Her manner is vivacious and aggressive. The timidity of A is replaced by the utmost confidence and self-assurance. Although A may have been fatigued, no trace of it will be seen in B. Indeed, I have never known B to show any signs of weariness. After A has come home utterly exhausted, too tired to eat, B has come, eaten a hearty dinner, and enjoyed the evening. . . .

"The cause of the dissociation was, undoubtedly, a shock which A received from the tragic death of her father. A loss of coordination followed this event, and for a while she was hardly able to walk. It was, as she says, 'Like learning to walk again.' At this time hallucinations began to appear. Further, according to B's statement, it was at this time that she secured partial control of the body. The behavior of A, from that time, shows noticeable signs of instability. She was subject to moods of extreme vanity, and occasional bits of conduct which were to her, at the time, inexplicable, such as, without intention, getting out of bed and going through weird dances. Many things occurred during the years that followed that now clearly show that a well-organized subconscious complex was formed, and that, at the time, it exerted a dominating influence. It was not, however, until A was twenty-six that she learned of B's existence and then what little she knew was shrouded in mystery. I give A's own account of the incident. 'One evening while alone in the house I was seated at the piano, and it seemed like something said to me, "take a deep breath," and a sound of singing came from me that I had never heard before, and it frightened me. Just before the song I shuddered as if something had possession of me. I went to the kitchen to get a drink then, and I asked mentally who that was that sang, and I got the name ————.' It was several weeks, however, before B learned, to use her expression, 'to get completely out,' or to submerge A, and take full possession of the body. Since that time they live as alternating selves. If A is abstracted B may appear. Generally A's consent is required, but sometimes B will catch her off guard and be 'out' before she knows it. Much as she desires to come she has a dread of meeting awkward situations, and as a result of this fear she leads a very restricted life. In the immediate household A's mother is the only one that has seen her. For a year A was completely mystified by the strange appearance. B had announced herself as the reincarnation of the soul of a Spanish woman, and this claim was, in a way, accepted by A. After hearing a voice that was not her own, and singing in a tongue that, as we shall see more fully later, she could not understand, what else was there for her to believe? Thus neither A nor B thought of themselves as completely separate personalities, A assuming that B on occasion took possession of her body. In this she was confirmed by some spiritualistic friends who became greatly interested in her. B's own idea of herself, that is, her belief that she was a returned spirit, was also, of course, encouraged by this atmosphere. Over this coterie of believers, B exerted a tyrannical influence and in every whim she was indulged.

Unhealthy Modes of Adjustment 489

"Each, if interested, is conscious of, and remembers what the other does. When subconscious A plays the role of an onlooker, but is powerless to determine B's conduct. Frequently conversations are carried on between them. In this case an inner voice expresses the thought of the self that, at the time, happens to be subconscious. B, when subconscious, may, if she chooses, profoundly influence A, whereas A as subconscious leaves B comparatively free.

"A is a bright, cultivated woman, of a good family, and when young had all the advantages that money could give her. B is older in manner, more dignified and serious. She has read Sally Beauchamp, Prince's Volume on the Unconscious, and several works in the field of abnormal psychology. These she reads with ease and understanding. She also expresses herself with great clearness. She is acquainted with my own analysis of her case, and has helped in every way she could. Yet notwithstanding her ability to follow a psychological analysis, after a full statement of the case she retains unmodified her conviction that she is a reincarnated spirit, and that she lived and died long ago. What seem to her to be memories impose themselves upon her, and prevent her from *feeling* that any other explanation can be true. A, however, now understands enough of the case to know that B is a dissociated self, and much of her past life, hitherto strange to her, has become clear." (Cory[7])

Both frustration and reactions to frustration may be repressed. So far you have seen the bad results of extensive repression. A moderate amount of repression, however, is entirely normal. Everyone is sometimes influenced by thoughts, memories, or wishes that are no longer conscious. As you study the various reactions to frustration, you may be thinking: "This is all very interesting, but it certainly doesn't apply to me. *I'm* not frustrated about anything. And *I* certainly never do any of these things—like regressing or overcompensating or daydreaming."

It is important to keep in mind that often a person is entirely unaware that he is frustrated. The pain of thinking about the frustrating situation is so great that he will not let himself be conscious of it. Moreover, it is not only the frustration itself that may be unconscious. The reaction to frustration may also be unconscious. A boy who finds satisfaction in fantasy does not deliberately choose this reaction. He does not think to himself, "Well, if I can't be popular with girls, I guess I'll just have to daydream about them." People are often entirely unaware that they are being aggressive or are rationalizing or are regressing. In fact, they may deny it indignantly when their behavior is pointed out to them by a psychologist. Frustration and the reactions to frustration are normal and are found in everyone, whether or not they are consciously recognized.

Logic-tight compartments

People often avoid a conflict between two opposed drives by keeping them apart in consciousness. A certain system of drives and ideas is sealed off, as it were, and allowed to function in isolation from conflicting ones. The conflicting ideas are never allowed to come into contact with each other, so that the person never has to choose between them. He simply refuses to see the logical relationship between the two sets of ideas or drives. These mental compartments are closed off from logic in the same way that a thermos bottle is closed off from air. The thermos bottle is said to be "airtight" and these mental compartments are said to be "logic-tight."

People with logic-tight compartments think and act inconsistently. In one situation they do or say one thing. In another situation, they may do or say quite the opposite and never recognize their logical inconsistency. Examine the following statement:

> "Those radicals are ruining the country. They have no respect for law and order. They're always causing violence with their strikes and demonstrations. If I had my way we'd organize the vigilantes and we'd tar and feather every Red in the country."

The close juxtaposition of these contradictory ideas makes it obvious that the speaker thinks in logic-tight compartments. In one breath he holds out for law and order; in the next, he advocates illegal violence. Obviously, there is a conflict between his love of law and order, and his desire to attack illegally those people who he firmly believes are disturbing law and order.

Here is an example of logic-tight thinking which differs from present-day examples only in its picturesque language (Phillips[8]).

> In the year of Our Lord, 1682
>
> To ye aged and beloved, Mr. John Higginson:
>
> There be now at sea a ship called *Welcome*, which has on board 100 or more of the heretics and malignants called Quakers, with W. Penn, who is the chief scamp, at the head of them. The General Court has accordingly given sacred orders to Master Malachi Huscott, of the brig *Porpoise*, to waylay the said *Welcome* slyly as near the Cape of Cod as may be, and make captive the said Penn and his ungodly crew, so that the Lord may be glorified and not mocked on the soil of this new country with the heathen worship of these people. Much spoil can be made of selling the whole lot to Barbadoes, where slaves fetch good prices in rum and sugar, and we shall not only do the Lord great good by punishing the wicked, but we shall make great good for His Minister and people.
>
> Yours in the bowels of Christ,
> COTTON MATHER

Rationalization

Rationalization is giving false reasons for one's behavior in order to preserve self-esteem. It is another way of avoiding conflict: such as the conflict between what we actually want and what we think we should want, or the conflict between our actual accomplishments and our high aspirations.

Rationalizing takes many forms. There is the "sour grapes" attitude, so well told in the old fable of the fox who tried in vain to reach a bunch of grapes hanging over his head, and then decided they were too sour anyway. There is the jilted lover who suddenly realizes that his former girl friend had certain flaws. And there is the "sweet lemon" philosophy of J. M. Barrie: "Not in doing what you like, but in liking. what you do is the secret of happiness." A little "sweet lemon" is fine, but like garlic, a little goes a long way. Most familiar of the rationalizers is Alibi Ike and his classic words: "The sun was in my eyes," or "I would have passed, but the teacher had a grudge against me."

Many everyday rationalizations are inconsequential, but others may hinder logical thinking in important ways.

For example, there is a certain physician who refuses to admit the value of giving vaccines to prevent diseases caused by germs. He stoutly maintains that this well-accepted medical practice is both ineffective and dishonest. There is an interesting history behind his belief, which persists in the face of what most medical experts consider to be overwhelming evidence in favor of vaccines.

As a young man, this physician was a ship's surgeon. During an epidemic among the passengers of his ship, he resolved to protect every child by injecting him with the serum used against the disease. At that time he obviously believed in using vaccines. But while he was vaccinating the children, one of them involuntarily coughed in his face. Since that particular disease is communicated mainly by contact with the sloughed-off linings of the throat, the doctor became frightened for his own safety. He then injected all the remaining supply of vaccine into his own blood stream, and several of the untreated children died.

The danger to his own life had obviously aroused a profound conflict in the young man between his devotion to others and his impulse toward self-preservation. Physicians take an oath to put the consideration of their patients above all else, even their own lives and safety. By injecting the life-saving vaccine into his own body, the doctor committed an unethical act which he could not bear to admit, even to himself. He then reasoned that if vaccines are ineffective in preventing disease, he was certainly not a coward in injecting himself rather than the children, and he could not possibly have been responsible for any of their deaths. Thus his belief that vaccines are of no value represents a rationalization which protects him from conscious recognition of his selfish and unethical conduct.

Flight into fantasy

The person in whom a drive is thwarted frequently finds satisfaction in imagining it has been satisfied—that is, in creating fantasies or daydreams. This is a perfectly normal and natural activity, provided it is not carried on to such excess that the individual gives up striving for satisfaction in the real world. Fantasy or daydreaming is frequent among college students, as is shown by a study in which a psychologist (Shaffer[9]) had 195 college students report the frequency and type of their daydreams. His findings are shown in the bar-chart below:

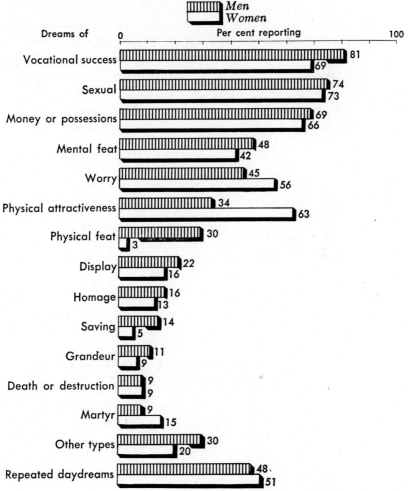

Per cent of normal college students reporting various types of daydreams

Men
Women

Data from L. F. Shaffer, *Psychology of Adjustment*, Houghton Mifflin Co., 1936, p. 194.

Unhealthy Modes of Adjustment 493

This study shows that daydreaming is a well-nigh universal activity among normal young people. The frequency of daydreams seems to be determined by the strength of the motives underlying them in relation to the degree of frustration these motives suffer. Obviously a rather weak motive which is occasionally frustrated does not give rise to so many daydreams as a very strong motive suffering serious frustration.

Satisfaction may come from night-dreaming as well as daydreaming —both express unsatisfied drives. For example, take the dream of a crippled boy of nine (Kimmins[10]):

> "Last night I dreamed that I was a brave knight. A great big monster came running after the most beautiful lady I ever saw. I drew my sword and hit the monster on the back. He roared so loud that the lady screamed. I said, 'I will soon slay this monster,' and I hit him again and then I cut off his head, and he fell dead on the ground. The lady said 'You are a hero.' Then I awoke."

Young children daydream of food more often than do those who are in their teens, because food (especially sweets) is one of their greatest satisfactions. The adolescents, in turn, daydream about love more frequently than do the young children because they are far more ready for and interested in adult sexual activity.

The flight into fantasy can take many forms, depending on the particular frustration the daydreamer is trying to escape from.

> The Army private may see himself as the "conquering hero," badly wounded and slowly bleeding to death but with supreme courage leading his small handful of men against the superior forces of the enemy. Victory is his: he returns home, makes a miraculous recovery, and the crowning moment of his life comes when the President pins the Congressional medal upon his manly chest.
>
> The pre-medical student may imagine that he is a great surgeon who has been called from a distant city to perform an operation for which he alone has the skill and daring. World-famous physicians and scientists crowd the amphitheater and look on in reverent awe as he saves the life of a great senator.
>
> A young girl preparing to go away to college for the first time may see herself in a whirl of popularity. She is voted Beauty Queen during Freshman Week, she is pledged to the most exclusive sorority, and she dances around with the football star while envious senior girls look on and other men try unsuccessfully to "cut in."
>
> Another common reaction to frustration is the "suffering hero" fantasy. A boy whose parents have punished him for staying out late may brood in the solitude of his room: "They don't appreciate me now, but they will! I feel terrible. Maybe I'll die and then they'll be sorry for the way they've treated me!"

A famous fictional example of extreme dependence on fantasy for emotional satisfaction is the "case" of Walter Mitty. But the flight into fantasy for temporary relief from frustration is characteristic of everyone. Daydreaming is abnormal and dangerous only when it is too frequent or too absorbing, and when it leads to no constructive action to make the daydream come true. The daydream can be of great inspiration to the individual who actually tries to create in real life the situations he has created in fancy; but when fantasy becomes more satisfying than the real thing, we quit working for the real thing.

Identification

Often the person who flees reality does not create his own daydreams. He buys them ready-made in the form of radio programs, movies, adventure stories, and love stories. The essential mechanism here is that of *identification*, by which the frustrated person regards as his own the achievements or qualities of others. Identifying himself with the hero of a pulp magazine story, he rides the purple sage with his two six-shooters roaring; or with the handsome movie actor, he crushes the voluptuous blonde heroine in his arms.

Perhaps the unhappy person feels that society has not given him a chance, and, turned against his fellow man but lacking the means to act, he identifies himself with the gangster of real life. That is, he admires the gangster for his violence and acts it out with him. When the notorious gangster, Dillinger, was shot and killed by Federal officers while resisting arrest, an onlooker was heard to remark bitterly: "They shot him down in cold blood. The dirty rats didn't even give him a chance to draw his gun." And there is a well-known American folk song written in sympathy with the bandit Jesse James.

Nomadism

When someone continually shifts from place to place even when the moves bring no economic gain, he is often called a *nomad*. This nomadic reaction represents an attempt to get away from a frustrating situation, but does not work because the frustration comes along.

The tendency toward nomadism is often evidenced by frequent moving from town to town, by frequent changing of residence within a community, by frequent divorce, or by excessive changing of occupation. Hundreds of thousands of people move about "just to be going." They beat their way on trains, "hitchhike," stow away on ships, or even walk. The great interest in automobile trailers indicates the wanderlust or nomadism in the United States. It is more than coincidence that this interest grew rapidly during the depression when so many essential needs and ambitions were being frustrated.

Regression

In regression the frustrated individual unconsciously seeks to return to an earlier period of his life. He flees from the painful realities and responsibilities of his present life to the protected existence of the child. He reverts to old habits of adjustment that were satisfactory in the past but are inadequate for solving his present problems.

Regression can occur at any age. Parents must be skillful in their treatment of children to provide the proper balance between independence and regressive tendencies. A common problem in households where a new baby has just arrived is that the three- or four-year-old often forsakes his toilet-training habits and reverts to bedwetting. He is afraid his parents will no longer love him as much as they did when he was "the baby," and so he tries to become one again.

Regression, like any other reaction to frustration, occurs in varying degrees of completeness. When present life becomes very painful, even a grown-up individual may regress very far back into his past life. The following is a case of an adolescent girl whose early emotional environment prevented her from passing onward from the early attachment to the father which is characteristic of many children, and who later tried to re-establish her early infantile position of being completely protected and loved.

"A seventeen-year-old girl was brought to a psychiatric clinic by her mother with the complaint that for the preceding five months her behavior had become increasingly destructive and irrational. The history revealed that after the patient was about four years old her parents had begun to quarrel violently, making her early environment extremely contentious and unstable. At about this age she first developed various neurotic traits: nail-biting, temper-tantrums, enuresis and numerous phobias." She was excessively attached to her father, but when she was seven the mother "obtained legal custody of the girl and moved away with her to a separate home. The patient resented this, quarreled frequently with her mother, became a disciplinary problem at home and at school and acquired a police record for various delinquencies. Three years later" . . . a brief visit to the father brought on a violent scene between the parents, after which the mother . . . "again contrary to the patient's wishes, took her home. There the patient refused to attend school and rapidly became sullen, withdrawn, and noncommunicative. During her mother's absence at work she would throw the house into disorder, destroy clothes her mother had made for her, and throw her mother's effects out of the window. During one of these forays she discovered a photograph of herself at the age of five, which, incidentally, was so poorly lighted and faded that, for one detail, it did not show her eyebrows. Using this as a pattern, she shaved off her own eyebrows, cut her hair to the same baby bob, and began to affect the facial expression and sitting posture of the pictured child. When brought to the hospital her general behavior was correspondingly childish: she was untidy and enuretic, giggled incessantly or spoke in simple monosyllabic sentences, spent most of her time on the floor playing with blocks, or paper dolls, and had to be fed, cleaned, and supervised as though she were an infant. In effect, she appeared to have regressed to a relatively desirable period in life antedating disruptive jealousies and other conflicts; moreover, she acted out this regression in unconsciously determined but strikingly symbolic patterns of eliminating the mother as a rival and regaining the father she had lost in her childhood." (Masserman,[11] case of Dr. John Romano)

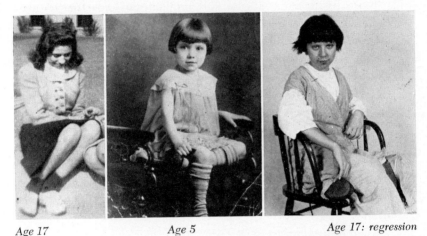

Age 17   Age 5   Age 17: regression

Courtesy Dr. Romano, Dr. Masserman, and W. B. Saunders Co.

The "Old Oaken Bucket" philosophy expresses the regressive mechanism in its milder form: "Things are different from the old days," and "They don't build cars like they used to." Another familiar form of mild regression is homesickness, which results when a person has to face new problems in a new environment. Finding adjustment difficult, he falls back upon the thought of home, where he was used to everyone and could always rely on his family's interest and understanding when any problem arose.

Alcohol and drugs

People use alcohol, not because their body tissues demand it, but because alcohol provides a temporary escape from the frustrations of life. Alcoholism is all too common in modern society (see p. 510).

The line between social drinking and alcoholism is a fine one, indeed. The chronic alcoholic usually denies that he has crossed the line. The true alcoholic is one who feels such an uncontrollable need to drink that his economic, social, and family life is being injured. Solitary drinking is usually a mark of the alcoholic, but solitary drinking is hard to define. The person who frequently buys a bottle of whiskey and retires to his room to drink alone is certainly a solitary drinker. But how about the stranger who sits by himself at the end of a hotel bar and gets quietly drunk without saying more than "Another one of the same"? Is this solitary drinking? And is it a sign of chronic alcoholism? The passage from social drinking to solitary drinking is purposely made easy in bars, in order to stimulate the sale of liquor.

Excessive drinking is a serious problem not only for the alcoholic individual but for society as a whole. Every community has habitual drinkers whose families are neglected or are cared for at public expense. The experiment illustrated on page 500 shows a very clear relationship between frustration and alcoholism: Emotionally frustrated cats will turn to alcoholic beverages, when available. This experiment has interesting implications for treating alcoholism in humans.

One long-tried cure for alcoholism has been court punishment of alcoholics through fines and imprisonment. The experience with this legal cure has been most unsatisfactory. The courts and jails have become clogged with drunkenness cases, but the unfortunate offenders are not in the least helped to overcome their psychological need of liquor.

Another legal measure for curing the liquor evil—national prohibition —produced only mediocre results. Many people object to prohibition on the grounds that the few abusers of liquor should not be restrained at the expense of those who use it moderately without ill effects to themselves, their families, or society. However that may be, the evidence makes it appear very doubtful that prohibition in the United States succeeded in reducing the amount of harmful drinking.

> A reliable index of the frequency and intensity of drinking in a community is the incidence of alcoholic psychoses—that is, severe mental illness of which excessive drinking is the principal cause or symptom. Figures on admissions to state hospitals are a good barometer of alcoholic psychoses in that state. Such statistics from New York were studied for the years 1889 to 1943, a time which contained a middle period of prohibition which could be compared with the earlier and later periods of unrestricted drinking. No relationship was found between the prohibition of drinking and the incidence of alcoholism. (Landis and Cushman[12])

The fact that repeal is still in effect in the United States is ample evidence that most Americans now realize that drunkenness is not a legal but a psychological problem. Numerous other cures for alcoholism have been suggested. One of these is of particular interest, more because of its interesting use of the conditioned-response theory than because of its success.

> One highly advertised treatment of the drinking habit is aimed at disgusting the patient with alcohol so that he will let it entirely alone. The patient is taken into an institution and given alcohol to drink. However, the liquor is mixed with emetics and is served at such intervals that, as one patient put it, "the second one on the way down meets the first one on the way up." The soiled bedding is not changed right away, in order to make the patient thoroughly disgusted with liquor because he associates it with his disgust at smelling his vomit. Most authorities agree this "conditioned-response" cure has little or no merit, even when electric shocks are administered along with the alcohol. The desire to escape frustration through alcoholic intoxication is so strong in the true drunkard that the pain- or disgust-response to alcohol is never established strongly enough to prevent his drinking, or else it rapidly becomes extinct.

The only effective cure of alcoholism comes through personal and social therapy (treatment). The therapist helps the patient to understand what frustration he is trying to escape, and then to work out a solution which will give him the satisfactions he is lacking. Only then will the craving for alcohol subside. Such treatment requires profound reorganization of the individual's ways of reacting to life situations. Often it must be carried on in an institution, where the patient can reorganize his emotional patterns without the continual temptation of alcohol as an escape. Experience shows, however, that therapy works best on the person who has only recently begun to drink excessively. The alcoholic of long standing is rehabilitated with great difficulty or not at all, partly because his body has become accustomed to the effects of alcohol, but also—far more important—because he has come to depend on the extreme escape of alcohol and cannot make the painful psychological transition to ways of facing and solving his problems. Chronic alcoholism is not a sign of "moral weakness" any more than is any other form of severe emotional illness.

Psychologically the cause of drug addiction is quite similar to that of alcoholism, being based on a desire to escape frustration. Fortunately, the use of most habit-forming drugs, such as opium and its derivatives, is very rare in the United States because of effective enforcement of the antinarcotic laws. However, the use of barbiturates is not adequately controlled at the present time.

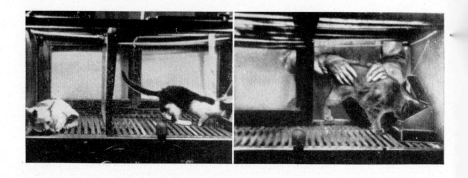

FRUSTRATION AND ALCOHOLISM

In this experiment (Masserman[13]), cats were taught to fear their food boxes, because every time they tried to open them they were subjected to sudden blasts of air. Thus they were made extremely timid and agitated, not only in the food-frustration situation but in many others. At left above, the white cat, which has been made fearful by air blasts, crouches rigid in a corner of the cage. However, her litter mate has been taught to respond to the air blast as part of the feeding signal, and feeds avidly.

The fear-conditioned cats were then forcibly fed with a sizable amount of alcohol, which relieved their fear behavior. At right above, a cat which has displayed severe conflict frustration in the experimental feeding situation has been fed 3 cc. of alcohol in 27 cc. of milk. Twenty minutes later it responds to the signal and feeds spontaneously.

However, alcohol disorganizes not only the fear behavior caused by conflict frustration, but also the patterns of learned, goal-directed behavior. The cat at left below, which has been brought to fear the food situation, has been given one dose of alcohol. It now operates the switch which will allow it access to the food box, but not in the direct and skillful way it did before fear-conditioning. As illustrated, it often remains poised for several seconds between the switch and the food box, without carrying through the learned behavior of reaching the food and feeding.

As soon as the "jag" worked itself off, the animals became fearful and upset again. At mealtime the cats were offered a choice between plain milk and a mixture of 95% milk and 5% alcohol. After a few weeks about half the cats chose the milk-punch in preference to plain milk, as at right, below. But when they lost their fear-reactions through retraining, they rejected the alcoholic mixture in favor of the pure milk. (Stills from the film, Neurosis and Alcohol, *by Dr. Jules Masserman, assisted by K. S. Yum.)*

Psychogenic illness as a reaction to frustration

Another common reaction to frustration is psychogenic illness (*psychogenic* means "originating in the psyche"). The illness may be real or largely imaginary. If real, it may have a physiological as well as psychological basis. The three common types of "frustration illnesses" are hysteria, neurasthenia, and hypochondria.

Hysteria. Frustration sometimes leads to the development of a physical ailment that seems to be of organic origin, but whose symptoms rest on the emotional adjustment of the person and come from his present psychological processes. Such a reaction is known as *hysteria*. Sometimes a physician may have a great deal of difficulty in telling whether the person is suffering from deafness of organic origin or from hysterical deafness—from a pain of organic origin or from a hysterical pain. But these difficulties of diagnosis do not alter the fact that the cases of hysteria are basically different in nature from cases of organic physical ailments.

One investigation of failure among college students showed that those who did the least studying were most likely to get eye trouble just before the final examination, when only physical ill health could keep the mark of failure off the record. Many people have noticed that their headache or cold is always worse when there is a disagreeable task to be done or an unpleasant situation to be faced. Such reactions are common to everyone and are well within the realm of normality. But these same reactions in extreme form can become seriously maladaptive.

The dangers of combat and training for combat are frequent sources of hysteria. We are not referring to deliberate faking of illness, or "malingering," as it was called by the military surgeons. The psychological defense is usually more subtle and is completely without conscious intention. Let us study the classic case of hysteria which developed in a British soldier of World War I. This man found in his symptoms an honorable escape from the conflict between his fear of injury and his fear of social disapproval.

> One psychologist reports his experience with this soldier who had been "sent home from the Mediterranean with lower limbs paralyzed and anaesthetic; a diagnosis of post-diphtheritic paralysis had been made. However, the signs were all in favour of a functional paralysis; and it appeared that, though he had suffered from a sore throat, the paralysis had set in just about the time that the transport . . . had come within sound of the guns. . . . I tried hypnotic suggestion; but, though he passed into hypnosis, I could not fully control him; when he was forced to move his legs, he fell into weeping and moaning. I there-

fore decided to proceed more slowly by waking suggestion. Following an explanation that the anaesthesia would recede day by day and that, when it was gone, he would have full use of his legs, I ostentatiously mapped the upper limit of the anaesthesia on both limbs each morning, and in this way drew off the anaesthesia like a pair of stockings, drawing it two or three inches lower each day." (McDougall[14])

Do not conclude that the soldier was deliberately choosing illness as a way out of his difficulty. Had his choice been deliberate and well-planned, it would have involved some less disagreeable mode of reaction, something which would not have interfered so greatly with the pattern of his whole life.

Neurasthenia. The patient suffering from neurasthenia feels tired all the time and suffers from unpleasant physical sensations which have no organic basis but result from emotional strain. Among these sensations may be mysterious "shooting pains," ringing in the ears, and palpitations of the heart. These physical symptoms result from continued emotional frustration of some sort. The frustration may be caused by some unresolved conflict, or by personal or physical obstacles to satisfaction. But whatever the source of the frustration, it puts the patient under a severe emotional strain which drains his energy and causes him to feel tired and vaguely unwell. The patient does not realize why he has these symptoms and he seizes them as the reason why he fails to get satisfaction from life, although his lack of satisfaction is in reality due to his emotional frustration. The "nervous housewife" is frequently a neurasthenic type.

Neurasthenia is difficult to diagnose because symptoms similar to those of neurasthenia can develop from purely physical causes. It is important to determine whether a given case is neurasthenia or a physical ailment. If the latter, rest or medical treatment may be required. The neurasthenic, however, should be encouraged not to rest but to try to achieve real satisfaction in his emotional life and social activity. In many cases, psychiatric treatment will help the sufferer to discover what frustration is causing his physical distress.

Hypochondria. Overconcern for health and bodily condition is given the name of hypochondria. The hypochondriac usually seems self-centered and aloof, since his interest centers in his physical condition. The following case of hypochondria may very well remind you of some friend or acquaintance who uses ill health to escape his frustrations.

"A college student complained of extensive gastric disturbances, indigestion, 'weak' stomach, belching, aches, and many other symptoms. Questioning showed that he had made a full-time job of studying his eating, his digestion, and his eliminative processes. For instance, he had menus made up for a month in advance in which everything was weighed to the ounce. He always cooked his own meals, because he did not trust this important task to his mother. After each meal he would watch himself carefully for an hour to see if it agreed with him. If it did not—and this happened often—he would change his eating plans and make new menus. In this way, he had slowly eliminated one food after another because it was not good for him; as a result, his diet was extremely restricted. He had kept charts of his bowel movements for over a year.

"He spent several hours each day using muscle exercisers, breathing according to a special system, and reading medical books.

"The problem that brought him to the psychologist was his relation to his fiancée. Questioning revealed that she loved him intensely but had angered him by disparaging his symptoms. He apparently did not love her at all, but intended to marry her because 'everybody gets married.' He had broken off with her without any feeling of loss, even with relief. He now wanted to know if marriage was necessary to health.

"It took some time to convince him that he needed psychological treatment, and this was possible only after a very detailed examination by a medical specialist showed negative results. He never really made contact with the therapist and no results were being obtained by interviews; therefore, he was sent to another therapist with whom he got along a bit better. However, when he was instructed to give up his pills and laxatives, he never returned." (Maslow and Mittelmann[15])

Some hypochondriacs are anxious and depressed. They frequent clinics and the physicians' offices, seeking examinations for suspected cancers and other diseases. They are greedy readers of popular medical literature and engage in orgies of self-pity, self-diagnosis, and medication. The patent-medicine business would suffer a serious slump if all hypochondriacs were to disappear suddenly.

Other hypochondriacs are not worried or depressed, but take an exaggerated interest in their bodily functions, love to talk about their operations, hold forth at great length to anyone who will listen on how their symptoms today compare with those of yesterday, with possibly a few well-thought-out predictions about the probable changes that tomorrow will bring. Such persons are said to be "enjoying poor health."

These illnesses which develop as a reaction to frustration must not be confused with the psychosomatic disorders referred to in Chapter 5 even though the physical symptoms may actually be the same in both cases. Hysteria, neurasthenia, and hypochondria are essentially efforts on an unconscious level to *escape* emotional pressures; the psychosomatic disorders are the actual bodily *effects* of emotional pressures. In the case of hysteria described above, the psychological stresses the soldier felt in connection with combat were *converted* into physical signs for which no organic basis could be found, but in the man whose stomach changes in emotion were recorded (p. 174), there were actual bodily changes. This close connection between body and mind is dramatic evidence of the psychological principle that man functions as a whole. In whatever situation he finds himself, his reaction will involve the whole organism.

Anxiety, phobias, compulsions, and obsessions

The anxiety neurosis has been aptly described as a "feeling of impending doom." Anxiety differs from ordinary fear in that there is no objective danger or threat in the environment. The patient is afraid but he does not know what he fears. The true source of his fear causes him so much pain or guilt that he cannot permit it to have conscious expression. It is repressed but, like all repressed tendencies to act, it remains active at an unconscious level.

The anxious person may remain in this state of objectless fear and become extremely depressed and dissatisfied with life without being able to point to the source of his dissatisfaction or to do anything about it. Frequently, however, the unplaced fear becomes attached to some object in the environment other than the one that was originally responsible for it. For example, a young girl falls in love with her older sister's fiancé, but is so fearful and guilty about her attraction to him that she represses it from consciousness. However, she develops at this time a strong irrational fear of crossing streets alone, and insists that someone always accompany her when she leaves the house. The fear that her love will be discovered becomes fastened on this simple, everyday act.

Such irrational, displaced fears are called *phobias*. The list of phobias has no end because any object or idea can serve as the stimulus to the abnormal fear response. In fact, psychologists have given up trying to name these phobias.

A repressed tendency may also lead to *compulsions*—to bizarre and incomprehensible actions which have no observable value to the individual, but which press for expression in a most uncomfortable and compelling way. The person may carry out the compulsive acts if there is no great damage from them; he may even carry them out when the injury to himself or others is serious and unmistakable. But in a great host of other cases the compulsion is just a tendency—a tendency which the person recognizes, fights, and masters, but one which is very costly to him in terms of the emotional turmoil it produces.

Compulsions are usually symbolic. That is, the action represents a way of solving some inner conflict or anxiety. The person himself is not aware of why he performs the action, but by psychotherapy he often becomes conscious of its real meaning to him and is helped to give it up. The following case history illustrates this type of behavior:

"When first seen by the writer, Mrs. X was busily engaged hanging up an apron, preparatory to answering the call to lunch. This process required about twenty minutes on this particular day, although as a rule five minutes was sufficient. Her problem appeared to be that of getting the folds in the apron to break right. She moved and adjusted the apron, patted it, creased it with her fingers, stepped back to view the result and then repeated her adjustments for more than a quarter of an hour.

"Her case history contained a complaint from the husband that his wife frequently insisted that they drive to the country, stop the car on a dusty side road, get out and grovel through the dust as though searching for something. The object of the search could not be stated by the patient, and, of course, the whole procedure seemed entirely senseless to the husband.

"Subsequent analysis of this case revealed that the 'putting things right' as demonstrated by the apron routine and the 'searching for something that is lost' were symbolic acts by which the patient was attempting to solve a problem that she no longer consciously recognized.

"Prior to her marriage the patient had had a sexual affair. All knowledge of this had been concealed from the husband but had remained a source of much painful worry and guilt-feeling on the part of the patient until it was finally 'forgotten.' The strange behavior of the patient symbolized attempts to find the virtue that she had lost."[16]

The compulsive act may or may not be accompanied by an *obsession*. An obsession is a persistent and irrational idea that comes into consciousness inappropriately and cannot be banished by an effort of will. It is familiar to almost everyone through the experience of having a tune "run through his head" regardless of his attempts to dismiss it. Frequently, the obsessive idea is unpleasant in nature. Another common kind of obsession is seen in the mental intrusion of some minor worry: "Did I turn off the iron?" or "Did I lock the door?" You are reasonably sure that you did in fact turn off the iron or lock the door but the question keeps annoying you. Another obsessive symptom grows out of the attempt to repress some unpleasant experience. Have you ever tried to drive away the thought of some humiliation, some embarrassment at a social gathering, only to have it come to mind time after time? These familiar patterns are all obsessive in nature, but they become abnormal only when they are so strong and come so frequently that they interfere with more useful actions.

The development of compulsive symptoms is, of course, determined by the individual's emotional development, particularly in childhood. An unusual film has been made of the early history of a child who at the age of ten displayed recognizable compulsive symptoms, including "(1) a compulsive need to wipe and wash her hands frequently, with corresponding restriction in play; (2) utilization of the play situation for carrying out compulsive and systematic acts (i.e., placing dolls in rows, straightening blocks, etc.) rather than as a medium for creative fantasy; (3) inhibition of touching, preventing fulfillment of task." (Fries[17])

The child's background and history were as follows:

Mary was an only child. Her parents came from a foreign background in which boys were much more valued than girls. Mrs. B's rejection of Mary began at the child's birth, when she was so distressed at Mary's sex that her own mother had to come to the hospital and literally forgive her for having borne a girl. From birth on, she handled the child awkwardly and at times callously. She was very resistant to nursing the child, and "enraged at being awakened for night feedings, she occasionally slapped the baby, then, overcome with guilt, tried to make amends by caressing her." She herself had compulsive traits, "was inordinately neat, developed anxiety when interrupted before completing scheduled tasks, and rigidly observed time schedules." She punished the child for infantile auto-eroticism, thus adding to Mary's already developing anxiety. In her general attitude to the child, she alternated between a narcissistic pride over Mary's superior accomplishment, and an extreme repression of the child's developing personality and behavior. She unconsciously encouraged the child to become deeply dependent on her, especially during the time that the father was away in service.

The father had a much more genuinely tender feeling toward the child, but was unable to be as effective as desirable in his relation with her because he permitted his wife and her family to dominate him and treat him like an "outsider." Moreover, his suppression of Mary's early curiosity about sex undoubtedly inhibited her emotional and intellectual development.

Mary was tested and filmed from birth onward. Her case is particularly tragic because she started life with "an apparently fine capacity for healthy physical, intellectual, and emotional development." At birth, her neuromuscular development was good and her Congenital Activity Type was active; and later tests revealed her to have an excellent I.Q. Yet because of the interaction of her particular make-up with the people in her environment, she experienced continual frustration of some of her basic needs in development and could not fulfill her potentialities.

"Evidence that Mary was repressed greatly could be found in her daily activity. Whereas she had formerly mastered the physical environment and responded to frustration with overt aggression, by her fourth year she began to turn this activity against herself. She became overtly quiet, compliant, compulsive, and inhibited." At seven she showed "increasingly poor posture, dependence on the mother, and lack of initiative. Her schoolwork was undistinguished (despite her superior I.Q.) and her social behavior inhibited. Controlled play test findings of the period indicated that: (a) Mary no longer solved her problems, but relied increasingly on others; (b) she released the hostility felt toward members of her family onto persons outside the family group."

Mary's life history clearly shows some of the fundamental emotional patterns that an individual may develop in a situation where his needs are continually frustrated. In the next chapter we shall examine some of the clinical methods which can produce information about a person's emotional reactions and can help him change those reactions which are ineffective or antisocial.

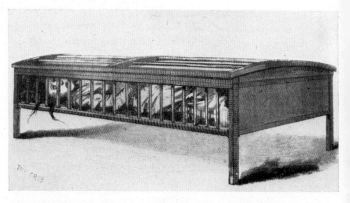

As recently as 1882, mental patients were cruelly confined (above), and little attempt was made to understand or cure their disorders. Today, psychological knowledge has increased and actual cruelty toward mental patients has decreased, but because of inadequate funds and overworked staffs, many patients receive little of the benefit of recent advances in psychotherapy. The patients below sit all day in a dark hallway, "waiting for nothing."

CHAPTER 14 **Psychotherapy and readjustment**

In institutions which have adequate facilities, patients are kept occupied with many kinds of activities, depending on their particular needs. At left, a depressed patient in a British hospital is being taught to weave, a task which combines stimulation and automatic activity in the right proportions. Patients are also given some of the various kinds of psychotherapy we shall consider in this chapter. (Photograph from the film Psychiatry in Action, *courtesy British Information Services.)*

The Practitioners of Psychotherapy

Counselor-Centered Therapy

Client-Centered Therapy

Eclectic Methods in Psychotherapy

Facts and Figures on Psychotherapy

PSYCHOTHERAPY is a term which literally means "mental healing." Like the physician who cures the body, the psychotherapist may employ a variety of techniques. But all psychotherapy, no matter what its particular nature, is aimed at helping the mentally ill person to reduce emotional tension and develop better means of handling those life situations which previously have brought serious conflicts and frustrations. To accomplish these ends, psychotherapy does not aim primarily at giving the client intellectual insight into his personality problems. This is only a helpful means to the fundamental objective of improving the individual's modes of response to his real-life situations—improving his emotional reactions, his ways of handling difficulties, and his ability to serve his fundamental needs.

Psychotherapy is as old as recorded history, having been referred to in the Old Testament, in the writings of the ancient Greek philosophers, and in many other sources. But though mental healing is no innovation of twentieth-century psychotherapists, they do know more about the strengths and limitations of these methods than was known a few centuries ago or even a few generations ago.

The clinical investigations with which we will be concerned here indicate that people who suffer from emotional ills can be helped by specially trained personnel just as people suffering from physical ills can be helped by specialists in medicine. It is as foolish to look down upon someone who seeks the help of a psychiatrist or clinical psychologist as to look down upon someone who seeks the help of a surgeon or an ear-nose-and-throat specialist.

The importance of understanding the materials of this chapter is brought out by the following conservative estimates of the annual incidence of mental abnormality and illness in the United States (Coleman[1]).

Psychoneurotics or "neurotics" (mild personality disorders which usually do not require institutionalization)	9,000,000
Psychotics (individuals who lose adequate contact with reality and must be institutionalized)	1,000,000
Psychopathic personalities (a group of personality disorders characterized by emotional immaturity, impulsiveness, lack of responsibility, and an inability to make moral and social adjustments)	1,500,000
Epileptics	500,000
Alcoholics	2,000,000
Drug addicts	150,000
Juvenile delinquents	300,000
Criminals	1,000,000
Prostitutes	300,000
Attempted suicides	100,000
Suicides	25,000
Feeble-minded	1,500,000

Every one of these persons is a logical object of study and treatment by clinical psychologists and psychiatrists.

THE PRACTITIONERS OF PSYCHOTHERAPY

THE GENERAL PUBLIC is still somewhat confused as to the legal status and academic training of the various kinds of practitioners in the field of psychotherapy. Here we will describe the psychologist, the psychiatrist, the neurologist, and the psychoanalyst.

A *psychologist* is anyone who cares to call himself such, for the law does not define psychology nor give it legal status and protection. Ethics, however, demand that the nonmedical psychologist who practices psychotherapy for a fee must have training and supervised experience equivalent to that required of the medical practitioner. This usually involves a Ph.D. degree from an accredited university.

The *psychiatrist* practices the branch of medicine that treats mental ills, whether it is of psychological or organic origin. The law provides penalties for the non-M.D. who calls himself a psychiatrist. The psychiatrist may legally give medicines, prescribe diets, use surgery, and administer electric-shock therapy. He may also practice psychoanalysis or any method of therapy.

The *psychoanalyst* is anyone who chooses to call himself such, because the law does not define his status and training. Psychoanalysts have a special system of theory and practice which distinguishes them from other clinical psychologists and psychiatrists. The organized psychoanalysts in this country now require the practitioner to possess an M.D. degree, even though Sigmund Freud, the acknowledged leader of the psychoanalytic movement, urged that some of the most valuable contributions to the development of psychoanalysis had come from psychoanalysts who had not been medically trained, and that the work should not be restricted to medical doctors. Today non-medical workers are making quite extensive use of the concepts and techniques of psychoanalytic work.

The *neurologist* is an M.D. who specializes in treatment of mental abnormalities which have their basic origin in unhealthy body tissue, most often involving the brain and nervous system. He uses surgery, diet, drugs, exercises, electric shock, and other physical treatments.

Practice of psychotherapy is complicated by the fact that the patient may reveal his guilt in connection with some punishable crime. It is the duty of all to report such information to the authorities unless one enjoys "privileged communication." This privilege is granted only to lawyers, physicians, and clergymen who are duly registered and licensed to practice. Clinical psychologists are working toward a legal status which will give them this same privilege.

Not all mental disturbances are produced by unhealthy patterns of emotional development. Some are produced by certain bodily diseases (such as syphilis of the brain and nervous system, and brain tumors). These require straightforward medical and surgical treatments, usually in a hospital. Outside the institution or hospital, however, there are many methods of psychotherapy. There is nothing static or cut-and-dried about these methods, which are adapted to particular circumstances—to the training, education, and personality of the counselor, and to the particular problem of the client. Each method has something in common with one or more of the others, but each has its own peculiar emphasis, and one method may blend into another without either the counselor or the client realizing it.

Any attempt to label methods or to place them in categories can be only tentative, but for convenience the methods of psychotherapy may be described as *Counselor-Centered Therapy, Client-Centered Therapy,* and *Eclectic Methods in Psychotherapy.*

COUNSELOR-CENTERED THERAPY

In some forms of therapy, the counselor directs and guides the client along certain lines. Much advantage is taken of the therapist's prestige and authority; he is the doctor and the patient does not forget it. *Information-Giving, Reassurance,* and *Suggestion and Hypnosis* are the three chief examples of counselor-centered therapy.

Information-giving

The simplest type of psychotherapy or counseling consists of merely supplying accurate and authoritative answers to problems which are consciously worrying the client. For example, a young widow is forced to work to support herself and her child. She is a stranger in the community and does not know how to solve the problem of having her child cared for during her absence at work. The counselor gives her a list of day nurseries known to be competently run, along with the cost and location of each. From this information, the young mother is able to make the proper arrangements for her child, and her problem is solved.

During the recent war, many industrial organizations were obliged to employ married women with children and other family obligations. Since these people had never worked outside their homes before, they quite naturally experienced a number of worries, fears, and irritations growing out of their ignorance of factory life. It was found worth while by management to employ counselors who worked, largely through simple information-giving, to dispel these emotional tensions. This is the simplest, fastest, and safest type of counseling; it requires less training and experience than the other kinds and has proved itself to be worth while in a variety of situations. Naturally, information-giving carries with it a certain degree of reassurance, particularly when the information shows the client that the problem is not very serious. Information-giving, even in its simplest form, is not entirely counselor-centered, since the client must be encouraged to "open up" and tell all of his problem. Any skillful employment interviewer, social worker, or emotionally mature adult can practice this form of therapy safely and effectively, if supervised by a trained psychologist.

Information-giving, as a form of psychotherapy, can be accomplished in group talks as well as in interviews between one patient and psychotherapist. These men in a wartime British hospital are all suffering from physiological disorders of psychological origin. The psychiatrist is explaining, with charts and model brain, the structure of the nervous system which permits emotional frustration to take the form of physiological disturbances. Through listening to this talk, and through group discussion and question periods, the patients gain insight into the nature of their difficulties—the first step toward recovery.
(From the film Psychiatry in Action, *courtesy British Information Services.)*

Reassurance

The method of reassurance is best adapted for use with clients whose problems are not so serious as they are inclined to believe. In these cases it is quite effective for the counselor to listen carefully to the client's complaint or statement of the problem. When the client is reasonably convinced that the therapist understands it, he is told not to worry and is assured that he will get well in time, outgrow the difficulty, or learn to get along in spite of it. Although this method is of some value, it is not sufficient in serious cases. It is not so fool-proof as the method of information-giving and can be downright dangerous when unjustifiable reassurance causes the client to delay in obtaining more effective methods of psychotherapy. Therefore its use requires training, judgment, and competence in the diagnosis of the problem.

In children's behavior problems, for example, it is frequently the parents and teachers—as well as the child—who fail to interpret correctly the real significance of his conduct. Often, the first step in dealing with many problems is to give new information which can reassure the patient, his parents, and his teachers that the "problem" behavior does not really mean what they think it means.

The methods of simple information-giving and reassurance are frequently used with clients who are worried over sexual practices which they consider abnormal or injurious, and in other areas of human conduct where conventional morality and actual practice have become widely separated. Since in such instances it is the feeling of guilt, rather than the act itself, which is responsible for the patient's emotional upset, these methods are quite effective.

The writer has had occasion to use the method of reassurance with several student-veterans who had been discharged out of the service as "psychoneurotic." They are told that a person can be well-adjusted to civilian life and be a useful member of society but can become truly neurotic through exposure to the frustrations of military life and to the dangers and privations of combat. They are assured that they need not necessarily fear the recurrence of the distressing symptoms they suffered in the service. It might also be pointed out, in all fairness to the military psychiatrists, that diagnosis and treatment of minor mental and emotional difficulties cannot be carried on with the same care and effectiveness that are possible in civilian life and that they do not always use the label "psychoneurotic" to mean true neurosis. Also, military psychiatry had unfortunate disciplinary connotations.

Suggestion and hypnosis

Suggestion means establishing some idea or attitude or feeling in a person by relatively noncritical processes rather than by some rational or realistic thinking. The history of man reveals too many forms of direct and indirect suggestion to permit description of them all. Among them are Couéism and the "Four-Square" Gospel of the late Aimee Semple McPherson. The most common types of suggestion used today are faith healing, hypnosis, and the *placebo,* or indirect suggestion.

Faith healing. In general, faith healing is based on denial either of the existence of the symptoms or of their seriousness. For example,

Emile Coué, a French faith-healer who achieved international popularity around the time of World War I, relied on the self-suggestion formula: "Every day, and in every way, I am getting better and better." There can be little doubt that faith healing has frequently removed the symptoms of hysteria (pp. 501-502) and other conditions. One serious limitation is that it does not get at the fundamental cause of the conflict or other frustration. That is why a patient who has one symptom removed by suggestion often develops another.

Hypnosis. In the year 1778 an interesting individual by the name of Franz Mesmer set up offices in Paris to practice a new kind of healing known as *mesmerism*. Mesmer taught that there is a magnetic fluid flowing through all the universe, including the human body, and that illness results from a disequilibrium of the magnetic fluid within the body. A sick person was supposed to be cured by having a "magnetizer" (such as Mesmer) make magnetic fluid flow in or out of him to restore the necessary balance. Mesmer passed steel magnets and rods over the bodies of patients who complained of a variety of symptoms and frequently secured alleviation and sometimes outright "cures." We know now that these symptoms must have been hysterical ones which were cured by suggestion.

Mesmer was bitterly attacked by some medical men and hotly defended by others. Finally he was repudiated by the French Academy of Sciences, which claimed that his cure could not be useful because it depended upon the imagination, upon "the machine of incitement." It is now apparent that Mesmer had made a great discovery which he had misinterpreted and that the French Academy was wrong in its conclusion that the cure was not real because it was a product of the imagination rather than of some physical force or chemical entity. Mesmer's work led directly to the development of hypnosis, which has a real, though limited, value in psychotherapy today.

There is nothing mysterious about hypnosis; it is simply a highly suggestible state into which the willing subject is induced by a skilled operator. The methods of inducing hypnosis are numerous beyond description here, but they all follow similar principles. First, the subject places himself without mental reservation under the direction of the trusted operator, who should for best results be a well-trained person of considerable prestige—a physician or psychologist. The operator starts by asking the subject to execute some simple act such as lying down on a couch. Then the subject is told something which is obviously true, for example, that the room is quiet, the lights are low. His confidence won, the subject is told a partial truth and is asked to execute acts which are only slightly out of the ordinary. For instance, he is told that his eyes burn and that his eyelids feel heavy. In a greater state of suggestibility, the subject may be led to believe the obviously untrue, and to perform acts which he would not ordinarily think of doing and which he might even consider impossible. All this time the operator is speaking in a monotonous tone of voice which lulls the patient into a completely relaxed state.

Once the subject is well hypnotized, he can be given a wide variety of suggestions which he will readily accept. A hypnotized person cannot perform some physically impossible feat (such as floating through the air or lifting a thousand-pound weight) although one can create in him the belief that he is doing so. But interestingly enough, the hypnotist can produce and banish at will many of the symptoms and phenomena seen in hysteria, neurasthenia, anxiety neurosis, and related conditions. If the subject is told that he no longer feels pain in a particular member of the body, he will make no response if this member is pricked with a needle or burned with a hot iron. He can be made temporarily blind or deaf or he can be made to see and hear things that are not there. Moreover, the phenomena of hypnosis are not limited to things that occur only during the hypnotic trance; post-hypnotic suggestions will also be acted upon, as you saw in the case described on page 17. Also, pain and symptoms growing out of organic (rather than psychological) disturbances can be temporarily suppressed. Hypnotic suggestion is sometimes dangerous because it seems to make direct treatment unnecessary. It removes the danger signal of pain without curing the organic disease.

Hypnosis not only produces and banishes physical symptoms, but also displays another phenomenon which makes it valuable to the therapist in diagnosing emotional difficulties. Under hypnosis it is possible to establish *regression*. The hypnotized subject is told that he is himself at a younger age and is asked to tell what he has been doing, how he feels, what his ambitions are. Under hypnosis, a subject will vividly recall experiences that he has repressed for years. Objective evidence that the regression is real is seen in the fact that subjects who have been taken back to a particular age and asked to write their names use the same handwriting that they actually used at that age (as shown by comparison with specimens which have been preserved). Obviously, hypnosis is valuable in recapturing repressed experiences and thus giving the clinician insight into the patient's problems. Then when the patient is in a waking state, the therapist can guide him along lines suggested by the hypnotic revelations.

At the University of Chicago, Drs. Theodore R. Sarbin and Julian H. Lewis conducted extensive research on age regression under hypnosis. The handwriting on the blackboard represents different age levels of regression. At top is the subject's normal handwriting when she is not hypnotized, and progressing downward her handwriting becomes more childlike. Such "returns" to childhood enable the psychologists to gain information which they can then use in diagnosing and treating a patient's adult emotional difficulties.

The following case illustrates the use of hypnosis for diagnosis and treatment of severe depression in a young woman. This procedure has been termed *hypnoanalysis* and represents a technique which is gaining favor but is still in the experimental stage.

"The patient was a capable young woman who was employed in a mental hospital. The depression was precipitated by a proposal of marriage. Several psychiatrists had given a diagnosis of the depressive phase of manic-depressive psychosis. Psychoanalysis was attempted but was unsuccessful. For various reasons, Erickson decided to attempt to hypnotize the patient without her knowledge, while she was ostensibly chaperoning another patient who was supposed to be receiving hypnotic therapy. The attempt was successful and the patient was gradually directed under hypnosis to regress to a vaguely defined period of her life between the ages of ten and thirteen. She recounted serious misconceptions of sex which were given her at that time by her mother, who had died when the patient was thirteen. During a series of interviews in the hypnotic and waking states, the childhood misunderstandings were corrected and the inhibitions and repressions were removed by means of a technique which seemed to allow the patient to withhold anything she did not wish to mention, but which actually aided her in organizing her ideas before presenting them to the therapist. Even though many aspects of the case were unexplored, the patient developed a satisfactory insight into the situation and made an excellent recovery. Shortly afterward she married the man whose proposal had precipitated the depression. Two years later she was reported to be enjoying a happy life with her husband and infant daughter." (Erickson and Kubie,[2] as reported by Jenness[3*])

Thus you can see that in the hands of the competently trained operator, hypnosis has therapeutic value. But it should be left to the

*From Arthur Jenness, "Hypnotism," in J. McV. Hunt (editor), *Personality and the Behavior Disorders,* The Ronald Press Company, 1944, Volume 1, page 490.

expert; it should be practiced in the research laboratory and clinic, not in the home or dormitory. For there are certain precautions to be taken in hypnosis which the amateur might not fully understand. Amateurs will have little difficulty in learning the technique of inducing the trance state, but they are not to be trusted to recognize and cope successfully with some of the possible aftereffects. For instance, there is always the danger that the patient will become dependent upon hypnotic treatment to remove some of his superficial symptoms and will not persist in solving his problem at the source. Then, too, there is the possibility that the operator will suggest ideas to the patient which were not there before and thus even further distort his unconscious emotional patterns.

The placebo. The medical dictionaries contain a term, *placebo,* which comes from the Latin, meaning "I shall please." A placebo is any substance or practice which lacks medicinal value but is administered to the maladjusted patient whose illness is a reaction to frustration (p. 501 ff.) and who will not get relief unless he receives attention and "treatment." Thus administration of a placebo is *indirect suggestion.* A placebo can take any form, from the old-fashioned sugar pill to drastic surgery to electrical shock treatment.

The use of placebos, though common, is very often unfortunate. The physician who relies on them is merely reinforcing the patient's adjustment through illness by treating it seriously—by placing on it, as it were, the stamp of approval of the medical profession. The patient who has received the placebo over a sufficient period of time has been encouraged in his poor reaction to frustration, and the therapist who later attempts to help him change it finds his task difficult. But as a temporary relief, the placebo has its place.

The following case illustrates the characteristics and weaknesses of a placebo in the form of the electric-shock treatment of hysterical symptoms.

"A patient who was suffering from a paralyzed right arm without any neurological basis for it came into the neurological clinic where he was examined and the nature of his disorder discovered. He was not told the facts (that there was no organic basis for his illness) but was simply assured that the physician knew what was wrong with him, that the nerves to his arm were blocked in some way and that it would be necessary to force an impulse through the nerves to the muscles in order to remove the block from the nerves. He was then taken over to the electrical apparatus and given a series of severe and painful electric shocks over the nerves of the arm and hand. These electric stimuli, of course, produced violent and rigid contraction of the muscles involved, which the patient could see. He was then assured that the electric impulse had removed the block from the nerves and that he could now use the muscles, which he proceeded to do. He was further told that if there was any sign of returning paralysis, he should come back immediately to the clinic for further treatment of the same kind, but that if the muscles continued to function well, this would probably not be necessary. While ostensibly done in a kindly way, the treatment was made as painful and as unpleasant as possible, so that the patient would have no desire to return for further treatment. Thus the cure was made more painful and disturbing than the illness itself. This particular patient has had no return of this symptom over a period of several years, but has from time to time developed other symptoms of hysteria, such as blindness, fainting spells and loss of voice. All of these were treated along similar lines, sometimes with success and sometimes without. It was the opinion of the physician in charge that this particular case never merited any more intensive treatment than was administered." (Dorcus and Shaffer[4])

Here it is obvious that curing one symptom by indirect suggestion did not cure the underlying maladjustment, which just caused another symptom to appear in place of the first one. These painful physical symptoms were not "faked." They were unconscious reactions to what must have been an enormously painful frustration of some sort. What the nature of this frustration was, or why it aroused reactions which obviously must have caused extreme physical discomfort to the patient, is not known, because in this particular case the therapy was aimed at removing symptoms rather than causes.

CLIENT-CENTERED THERAPY

IN SOME CASES of psychotherapy, the client is permitted to occupy the major role in the client-counselor relationship. The counselor plays, or appears to play, a secondary and behind-the-scenes part. The major types of therapy falling within this general category are *Catharsis, Psychoanalysis,* and *Nondirective Therapy.*

Catharsis

Catharsis is one of the oldest forms of mental healing and belongs in the category of client-centered methods. It consists basically of "talking out" one's troubles. This does not come all at once. Most of the problems that worry people involve ideas and experiences of which they are ashamed. Experience shows that the early sessions with the therapist are not very productive. The patient who is instructed to lie quietly and talk about anything that comes into his mind usually sticks to the superficial aspects of his problem. In succeeding sessions the patient becomes more and more frank in his report, searches more and more deeply, and eventually tells of experiences and emotions that he has for years been concealing from himself as well as from others.

Sometimes catharsis is accomplished by having the patient write about the problem at moments when it is exceptionally disturbing. Because he is writing at the time he is disturbed, the emotion is apt to be adequately expressed, thus aiding the therapist in analyzing the problem.

The basic rule in the use of catharsis is that "easy does it." The therapist cannot force the process. In fact, attempts to speed up the outpouring, or even to direct the flow, may lead to a resistive attitude on the part of the patient. Within limits, hypnosis can be used to hasten catharsis.

Frequently the effects of failing to face a problem squarely are more destructive to mental health than is the problem itself. Through catharsis the patient comes to face the problem, which is the first step in solving it. Obviously, part of the value of catharsis lies in locating the real problem, and part of the value lies in the consequent reduction in mental tension. Often this is sufficient to bring about the cure of the adjustment difficulty. Most often, however, catharsis merely serves to set the stage for an effective program of active psychotherapy.

In recent years, several interesting techniques of catharsis have been developed. These are finger-painting, play-therapy, psychodrama, and narco-analysis. They are all alike in that they give the subject a chance to express his emotions in a situation in which he is not on his guard because it seems "unclinical." These methods not only help the patient relieve his mind but also help the therapist in diagnosing the underlying difficulty.

Finger-painting. Finger-painting merely means painting with the fingers instead of with a brush. It was started in a private school in Rome, where it was used merely for its decorative value. On this basis it was introduced during World War II as part of the recreational program of Red Cross units, USO Centers, and other services in the hospitals of the Armed Forces. Clinicians soon discovered its value in diagnosis and catharsis.

The following case shows how finger-painting can release the patient's emotions and reveal the problems that are disturbing him.

"A Navy man, aged 28, was referred for being 'disobedient' and for refusing to sleep with others in the room because he was afraid of talking in his sleep. It was impossible to elicit reasons from the subject which would give some basis for his behavior.

"He painted his picture in a few minutes but verbalized for a long time. . . . He was very much absorbed in the procedure, followed directions correctly and used fingers, hands, and arms with assurance. He used green throughout because he 'loves green.' After he completed his painting he added a minute dab of brown in about the center of the picture. He cleaned up neatly while telling how much fun he had. He did not repeat the performance.

"He was right-handed and used only the right hand in the painting. Motion in general was good and free. Rhythm and balance were good. The order of the picture as a whole is the shutting in of contents of the picture. In his verbalization he asks for criticism of his painting and then titled it 'In a Cave.'

"Referring to the three figures in the cave he stated to the administrator, 'You think it's mother and father and child but it isn't—it's the same person three times. The first one is fourteen years old, the third one is sixteen years old, and the middle one is eighteen years old.' When the administrator showed interest he explained that when he was 14 years old he 'got in trouble with a girl who taught him things.'

" 'Then she told the teacher and that was a helluva mess—but my father fixed it up for me and the girl's family moved away—she was a bad girl. Then when I was 16 a woman who lived upstairs over a store invited me and another boy up to her room where she had a friend. My father who is the mayor got me out of this trouble and he and the preacher cleaned up the town and these women left. When I was 18 I visited a friend in his town and I fell in love with a friend of his—a nice girl—but we loved too hard and I got into trouble again. As my friend was going to join the Services I went with him and joined the Navy. Then I went home and told my father and he was so disappointed that I didn't tell him about the girl. I was afraid to. I left home in a few days and couldn't make up my mind to tell him and now it's been nearly a year and I want to know what's happened to the girl. I don't care what my father would say 'cause I love that girl. The fellows say I talk in my sleep and I'm afraid I'll talk about her and tell her name. It's a helluva mess—what must I do?' . . ." (Napoli[5])

Unfortunately, the psychologist reporting this case does not indicate the specific details of its outcome but, presumably, finger-painting was valuable in reducing tensions at the moment and in setting the stage for further attempts at psychotherapy.

Play-therapy. It has long been recognized that play can release tensions which mount through conflict and frustration, and modern therapists use play in treating preschool children. They use these techniques to permit their young clients to work off their aggressions and develop new attitudes. In playing with clay, dolls, and other toys in the permissive, acceptant climate of the therapist's office, the children express deep emotional tendencies lying at the heart of their troubles and arrive at new solutions through this working out of their difficulties. Here is a representative instance of this *release therapy,* so called because it is aimed at the releasing of pent-up emotionality in children:

> "Girl, an only child, aged 8 years, 1 month, referred because she was 'terribly nervous and jumpy,' i.e., actually jumping when excited, general choreoid movements and restless behavior. Onset in infancy. Complaints also of stubbornness and lack of concentration.
>
> "It became apparent in the first session that the child was hostile to her step-father, the mother's second husband, married when the patient was 2½ years old. Play of mother, stepfather and child was her own choice and was encouraged throughout the nine sessions. Otherwise her play had to do with material related frankly with masturbation and urination, in which she displayed destructive behavior with dolls, cutting them up, pulling them apart, sticking an awl in the eyes.
>
> "After the fifth session the governess reported the patient was less jumpy. Though I had recommended that treatment continue, the grandmother and parents thought the child greatly improved and stopped after the ninth session. A telephone follow-up 19 months after the latest session indicated good adjustment in school and at home, without evidence of 'jumpiness.' " (Levy[6])

The content of this girl's play dramatically illustrates the importance of sexuality and aggression, discussed in Chapter 12, as central problems in emotional life. Obviously the therapeutic play activity allowed a healthy release for feelings and desires which the child could not express in her home life, and which she needed to "work out of her system."

In one form of play therapy, as explained by Dr. George Bach, the child is given a "family" of dolls made up of the same "members" as his own real family. The child is simply encouraged to "make up a story about these people. Show me what they do in their home. You can make them do anything they want, anything at all." Thus the child can act out repressed and suppressed feelings, wishes, and frustrations. The clinical psychologist may simply accept these expressions, or he may go further and interpret them with the child—depending on the individual case. Children benefit from working with this material because it affords an opportunity to "experiment" with solutions to problems of social adjustment which the child has difficulty with in reality, and because it also affords an outlet for pent-up emotion.

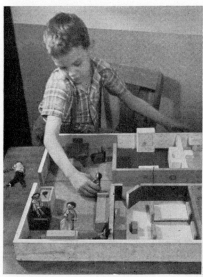

This picture of a play-therapy situation, directed by Dr. George Bach,
shows how a boy can get deeply involved in his fantasy productions. Here
he has just acted out his hostility toward the "father," who is thrown out
of the house on the left, and is continuing the family scene, saying, "Oh,
goody, goody! Now the boy can have a lot of fun with mother." He manipulates
the little boy puppet and is moving him toward the mother and sister. The
mother is playing the piano and the scene of happy family life is wishfully
developed. In this way a boy who is confused about his place in the family
can "try out" various solutions to his problem. In experimenting with
these scenes he will find new solutions which the psychologist
helps him later to apply in real situations.

Other children will create a scene of happy family life that includes the father.
The girl is seating a puppet (which she has chosen to represent herself) at
the family table on the occasion of a Sunday dinner. She says, "The girl will show
the family how well she can eat and she will help her mother serving."

Psychodrama. The most elaborate variant of the modern methods
of catharsis is the psychodrama. Patients are encouraged to act out
plays in which they can express their problems and thus face them
symbolically with less emotional tension (Moreno[7]). The following
case illustrates this method in action:

> "Bob is a 17 year old youth who came to Elgin State Hospital after
> having been diagnosed as schizophrenia at a well-known neuro-
> psychiatric institute. He had been given a course of electric shock
> treatments but was discharged as unimproved with the recommenda-
> tion that he be committed to a state hospital. During the first six
> weeks here he appeared listless, withdrawn, diffident, and autistic.
> He could not be drawn into any group activities.

"The diagnostic staff recommended that he be given psychodramatic treatment. From preliminary interviews and personality tests it was inferred that he fantasied himself as a well-adjusted, popular high school boy. The social skills necessary to transform such a fantasy into reality, however, were lacking.

"He was invited to participate as a spectator during a psychodramatic session when other patients were presenting their own spontaneous plays. At the close of the period, he was asked to have a short scene prepared for the next session.

"At the next session he appeared and reported that he wanted to do a scene in which he was a radio commentator. This turned out to be a very simple action, requiring no supporting characters even though the scenes that he had observed previously had been cast with two to five characters.

"During the second psychodramatic session he was asked to appear as an auxiliary ego to another patient, a young man of 23 who had been discharged from the army. In this scene Bob and the other patient were the joint objects of the wrath of a hard boiled sergeant whose orders they had not followed. During this scene Bob imitated many of the actions of the ex-soldier with whom he was sharing an experience. Then he incorporated such actions into his own repertory of behavior equipments. For the third session, Bob prepared an original play in which he was going off to the navy, and which called for several supporting characters. . . . While in previous sessions he had shown signs of consciousness of the audience, in this session (in which members of his family were depicted on the stage) he acted spontaneously and appeared to be absorbed in the action.

"During the fourth session he acted as an auxiliary ego taking the role of another boy's father. Here he portrayed, unwittingly, his own father's attitude towards him. As a matter of fact, Bob 'stole the show' during this scene. During all these sessions Bob was showing an increasing sociability as evidenced by his coming into the center of the group instead of sitting alone as he had done at first. During periods between scenes, he would now interact with the other patients. This he had not done at first.

"During the fifth session Bob was told to take the role of an American high school boy, and act out, with whatever auxiliary characters were necessary, a day in the life of a typical high school boy. During the scenes which followed Bob revealed many of the difficulties of his home but most important was his conversational ability with the director and with others who were taking the roles of other high school boys. It was during these scenes that he showed the greatest animation and very little signs of his withdrawn, autistic self. A number of other similar sessions were subsequently held but these are not reported here.

"During his improvement, which was associated in time with the psychodramatic sessions, he became more sociable on the ward, he was more alert, and he put on some weight. Each Sunday, he was taken home for the day by his parents. They reported that prior to the psychodramatic sessions he was no different during his visits from what he had been in the hospital; that is, withdrawn, quiet, unapproachable. Following several weeks of psychodramatic treatment he surprised his parents with his interest in people and events. Without prodding, he would go out and talk with neighbors and acquaintances.

"In this psychodramatic treatment, the aim was to build a role for this patient in keeping with his concept of the self. In this case the concept of the self was to a degree capable of fulfillment in reality. The scenes that were selected were designed to give him the opportunity of playing such a role. That the acting was *more* than play-acting is proved by its extrapolation into the social reality of the patient's home community and by his continued improvement in the institution." (Sarbin[8])

Above is a psychodrama scene taking place in the therapeutic theater at Beacon, New York, the first theater for psychodrama, built in the United States in 1936. It has, besides the warming-up levels, a balcony level for the super egos, the messiahs, or heroes. The patients, through acting out their mental conflicts with psychologically trained "supporting casts," achieve a needed catharsis which is supplemented by the guidance and interpretation of the director. Such psychodrama sessions are widely used in mental hospitals throughout the country.

Client-centered Therapy 525

Narco-analysis. In recent years there has been developed a new form of catharsis which makes use of sleep-producing drugs (including sodium amytal, sodium pentothal, and scopolamine, the so-called "truth serum"). It is known as *narco-analysis;* "narco" is from a Greek word meaning "stupor." Considerable success with it has been reported, particularly in treating the emotional tensions produced by combat and the fears and frustrations of military life in general (Horsley[9] and Grinker and Spiegel[10]). Drugs such as sodium pentothal are given in amount sufficient to cause "grogginess" but not deep unconsciousness. This point is easily detected by having the patient count backwards from a hundred; when he begins to stumble around but can still talk the dose is right.

By direct suggestion, the patient is encouraged and even prompted to talk about or act out his painful experiences. Once exposed by this method, repressed emotions are better understood and are accepted by the patient for what they really are. Narco-analysis is usually followed with physical rest, elaborate reassurance, and a program of

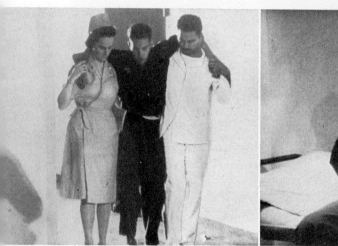

Estimates show that more than 40 per cent of Army medical discharges were for neuropsychiatric disorders. (The vast majority of these men are capable of adjustment in civilian life.) Many men suffered the effects of combat in the form of hysterical symptoms, severe anxiety states, and acute depressions. During the recent war, many of these cases were treated by narco-analysis, which is illustrated above in an unusually dramatic case. At left, a GI suffering from an hysterical lameness enters the psychiatrist's office. He is then injected with a barbiturate drug which, before it puts him to sleep, allows him to pour out the painful experiences and emotions which arose in his combat activity and which, because hitherto repressed, have been expressed in his lameness . . .

recreation as the patient "gets hold of himself." It is most effective when employed immediately after symptoms of repressed emotional tensions appear. One of its wartime uses is illustrated below.

Psychoanalysis

Psychoanalysis is a method of therapy developed by Sigmund Freud and others. It aims at giving the patient a complete understanding of his deep unconscious fears, impulses, and attitudes, especially those related to his early childhood experiences.

Basic concepts of psychoanalysis. The psychoanalysts believe that childhood experiences, especially those related to sexual activities and to the child's relationship with his parents, are the foundation of later emotional experiences. As a result, when adjustment difficulties arise, it is because certain painful conflicts of childhood are repressed ("forgotten") without having been adequately resolved. These conflicts, though unconscious, continue to influence the individual's thought, feeling, and behavior, and are the cause of his emotional tension and

After the effects of the narcotic drug have worn off, the psychiatrist reviews the interview with the patient and encourages him to try walking. A few days later he is recovered and able to play in a baseball game. It must be pointed out that narcosynthesis does not effect a cure of the basic causes of an emotional disturbance, but simply removes a few of the symptoms, which may be replaced by others. However, the drug is very useful in providing the psychiatrist with information which the patient cannot supply in a normal waking state. The psychiatrist can then diagnose the case and in later interviews can accurately guide the patient to a conscious solution of his problems. (Photos from the film Let There Be Light, *courtesy U. S. Signal Corps.)*

inability to adjust. The aim of psychoanalysis is to enable the patient to bring into consciousness whatever painful memories and conflicts are causing his difficulties, and to help him resolve these conflicts in the light of adult reality. As two non-Freudian psychologists have put it: "It is a process of learning that one set of emotional habits has been unsatisfactory and futile and that another set of habits can be acquired which will cause less difficulty in everyday life" (Landis and Bolles[11]).

Techniques of psychoanalysis. There are several techniques the psychoanalysts use for bringing repressed conflicts to consciousness and helping the patient solve them. They include free association, analysis of resistance, analysis of transference, and dream analysis.

In *free association* the individual lies quietly and lets his mind wander freely, giving a running account of his thoughts, wishes, physical sensations, and mental images as they spontaneously occur. Dominant personality trends and unconscious emotional attitudes may be revealed by this stream of association. The therapist explains to the subject the meaning of these thoughts, wishes, and attitudes and their significance in terms of his present difficulties.

During the process of free association, the patient often shows *resistances:* that is, inability or unwillingness to discuss certain ideas, desires, or experiences about which he feels pain or shame, usually because they are connected with his infantile sexual life or with hostile and resentful feelings called out in reference to his parents. Recently psychoanalysts have come more and more to believe that emotional problems come not only from conflicts over sexual feelings but also from difficulties in handling resentful feelings and from conflicts related to the craving for protection or dependence. The psychoanalyst attaches particular importance to the subjects the patient does not wish to discuss, believing that they are most closely related to the childhood experiences causing his present difficulties. The aim of psychoanalysis is to break down resistance and bring the patient to face these painful ideas, desires, and experiences. The theory is that if the patient is not consciously aware of certain problems, he obviously cannot solve them.

During the course of psychoanalytic treatment, the patient develops what is known as a *transference* to the psychoanalyst: that is, he attaches to the analyst the feelings which he originally experienced in his childhood, usually the feelings he had toward his parents. This transfer is called *positive transfer* when the feelings consist of love or admiration and *negative transfer* when they consist of hostility or envy. The psychoanalyst interprets these feelings to the patient, making clear how they originally arose in his childhood life and thus helping him bring his childhood experience to consciousness. The psychoanalysts believe that this is a basic technique in bringing the patient to face his conflicts and keep them from disturbing his present life.

Still another technique of psychoanalysis, *dream analysis*, we shall consider in more detail.

Dream analysis. The Freudian school of psychologists believes that in dreams people very frequently satisfy unfulfilled drives or wishes. When some motive cannot be expressed in waking life, it may find expression in a dream. And if the motive is unacceptable enough, it cannot be revealed openly even in a dream. However, it can be expressed in disguise.

Thus a dream has two parts, or contents. There is the *manifest* (openly visible) content which we remember and report upon awakening because it usually is not painful—and which, in fact, often appears quite amusing to us when awake. Beneath this is the *latent* (hidden) content, the actual motives which are so painful that we repress them when we are awake. An expert can often uncover these hidden motives by studying the symbols and forms appearing in the manifest content of the dream and by finding out what particular meaning they have for the dreamer. The unconscious process which transforms the emotionally painful latent content of the dream into the less painful manifest content is called the *dream work*.

Dream work involves five kinds of distortion. All of them are unconscious methods of making the motives in the dream less obvious to the dreamer, who does not wish to recognize their existence even when he is asleep. They keep unconscious wishes and feelings away from consciousness. The five kinds of distortion are condensation, displacement, dramatization, symbolism, and secondary elaboration.

1 In *condensation*, the unacceptable, latent motives connected with several ideas, words, or persons are disguised in the manifest content of the dream by combining the several ideas, words, or persons into one.

For example, a person who has a great fear of authority may experience so much anxiety that he will repress this fear in his waking life. And even in dreams, this fear will be expressed only in a disguised form. That is, he may dream that he is standing at the edge of a cliff, struggling with a person who is dressed like a very severe teacher who disciplined him in childhood, has the face of his present employer, and yet who he knows all the time is really his father. The common element in all these persons is that they are figures of authority, who he feels can destroy him. Through this common element the fear is expressed, and yet because of the disguise he is kept from directly recognizing his fear.

2 In *displacement,* the emotion a person feels when awake toward one idea, person, or object is removed from its true context and attached to some irrelevant item in the manifest content of the dream. Thus the dreamer is kept from recognizing the actual object of his feeling, though the feeling is expressed as it could not be at all in waking life.

For example, a woman dreams of seeing a man in a coffin. Later in the dream she reads an item in the society page completely unrelated to death and becomes extremely perturbed and fearful. A possible interpretation of this dream would be that it expresses a hidden fear that her soldier fiancé has been killed—a fear which is unbearable when felt in relation to her fiancé and is displaced to the insignificant item in the society column.

3 In *dramatization,* the manifest content of the dream is a series of visual images. These images are seen much as in a motion picture and as though they were related to some other person. Hence they do not arouse the full emotion that is attached to them in the latent content of the dream.

4 *Symbolism.* Objects and situations which are emotionally painful for the person are likely to appear in the dream not in a direct and undisguised form, but in a figurative or symbolic form instead. Thus, a student who is full of anxiety about failing in an examination and being expelled from school may dream that he is pushing his way through a heavy snowstorm, with some wild animals pursuing him. If a person feels very aggressive toward someone, he may dream that the hated person is in great danger and the dreamer tries to save him, but is unable to, even though he tries his very best. Or with rather less disguise, a woman who feels hostility toward her husband might dream of killing a rat—the significance of this symbol being revealed by the fact that she often refers to her husband as "the little rat."

5 The fifth kind of dream work is *secondary elaboration.* The dream work leaves the manifest content rather illogical, disjointed, and lacking in proper time relations—partly because we "forget" some of it (repress it) when we awake. In recalling or telling the dream, we dress it up a little to make it sound more plausible. This process is called secondary elaboration.

Experts who are familiar with the various ways in which the latent content of the dream becomes changed into manifest content are frequently able to locate a conflict of which the patient is not conscious.

Criticisms of psychoanalysis. Some more recent workers in the field of psychoanalysis have felt that the emphasis Freud placed on the periods of infancy and childhood is a mistake. They feel that it is more important to concentrate on the patient's present situation and pattern of emotional responses. They also feel that understanding of one's unconscious feelings and the lifting of repression on childhood experiences are not enough to effect a cure—that the patient must be directed along the path of changing himself and overcoming his inadequate methods of adjustment.

Karen Horney, an American psychoanalyst, has led the revolt against Freud so far that there is some doubt that she could be fairly classed as a Freudian, although she protests that she is modifying an old system, not creating a new one (Horney[12]). The cornerstones of her system have been aptly summarized as follows:

"... Once more, writing more forcefully than ever, Dr. Horney repeats her major premises: (1) that the basic human needs, of which sex is but one, and the various distortions of personality are conditioned by life forces in their entirety; (2) that adult neuroses are not solely a product of childhood experiences within the bosom of the family; (3) that, along with his debits, the disturbed individual has within him certain positive forces or a certain will-to-health that make for growth and development; and (4) that there is no necessary conflict between the individual and society, inasmuch as neuroses are a product of the individual's effort to cope with a difficult environment." (Sward[13])

Psychoanalysis has also been criticized because it is an intensive method of therapy that requires a great deal of time and money. Daily contacts over a two- or even three-year period are not at all uncommon. The objection to psychoanalysis most frequently brought forth by clinical psychologists and medical psychiatrists is that it requires so much time and costs so much, that it is overspecialized in its approach, and that it helps only a small number of cases. Later in this chapter we shall examine the statistical evidence relevant to these charges.

Nondirective therapy

Nondirective therapy, like psychoanalysis, attempts to go beyond the present emotional disturbance which is causing the patient discomfort and to bring about an improvement in his general adjustive capacity. Great reliance is placed upon the individual's own drives and tendencies in the direction of growth and increased maturity. The attempt is made to help him develop the strength to handle by himself the difficult problems of adjustment.

The individual is urged to talk freely about his problem and to "release" his emotional feelings to an understanding and sympathetic therapist who neither praises nor blames him for his feelings and attitudes. It is felt that by this "talking out" process in a noncritical environment, the individual will come to see and understand certain relationships existing between feelings, attitudes, and behavior. In other words, the subject acquires insight into his actions and their bases in his emotional life.

Stress is laid upon the patient's present situation and problems rather than upon childhood memories. Emphasis is also placed upon the therapeutic treatment itself as a growth process. It is looked upon as a miniature life situation and is considered as providing the individual with an opportunity to learn and practice new ways of adjusting to life.

As the term "nondirective" implies, the therapist refrains from giving advice or suggestions. Rather, he provides a situation in which the individual can learn to think more intelligently about himself and to make his own decisions on a wiser basis. The patient is left free to establish his own goals and is urged to accept the responsibility for guiding his actions toward these goals. There is a strong *disbelief* by workers in this type of treatment that "the doctor knows best."

The nondirective method has many well-known practitioners in the United States. Prominent among these is Carl R. Rogers, who was in charge of the training and indoctrination of USO counselors during the recent war (cf. Rogers[14]). His method is well illustrated in an interesting case presented to a psychological counselor:

> Mrs. L., who has been having disturbing problems with her ten-year-old son, tells the counselor of a very upsetting experience she and the boy had concerning a bottle of ink. He wanted to take it to school, and she, feeling there was no reason for his doing so, forbade him to. He became insolent and hid the bottle, whereupon she whipped him severely. Here is her account of the incident:
>
> L. "Then I told him to get the ink, and he said he wouldn't do it. So I said, 'Well, are you going to get the ink, or will I give you another whipping?' And he wouldn't get it, so . . . I gave him another whipping. And he just got so upset—he was almost hysterical. But I couldn't —I don't know. It didn't seem to me that I should let him get away with that. On the other hand, a bottle of ink seems a very trivial thing to cause such an upheaval in the house. Now I wonder . . . what is the answer?"

C. "Well, I doubt that there is any one set, particular answer . . . that would fit all cases like that. You . . . were probably pretty much upset by the time it was over, too."

L. "I was extremely upset and . . ."

C. "Both felt all up in the air and, as you say, probably felt it was a trivial beginning, at least."

L. "Well, I said to my husband afterwards—I—he—he was—the boy was very upset and——oh, he got to the point where he was sobbing, you know—he couldn't get his breath or anything, so I took him upstairs and put him in the tub and let him play in the tub—that almost always calms him down. Then I gave him a boat or something and washed him and let him play while I did the dishes. And I said to my husband when it was over, it was probably all my fault and I was sorry I had refused him the ink in the first place, but having refused it once, I felt I had to . . . carry it through."

C. "M-hm. That's often the case, isn't it—the feeling that you must go on with what you've done?" (Rogers[15])

The clinical psychologist puts into practice this idea of allowing some free expression of aggression. The woman relives the episode before the counselor, who neither approves nor condemns but accepts and understands. Thus she is able to arrive at a new and much less aggressive interpretation of the whole situation: ". . . it was probably all my fault. . . ." Moreover, the new and less aggressive interpretation (1) is focused on a new problem: the things in her own personality responsible for her strictness and authoritarian relationship to her son, and (2) is generalized to the whole parent-child situation. In short, the woman has made considerable progress in working out for herself a new understanding of herself and her boy, which tends to raise her frustration tolerance and to decrease her tendency toward aggressiveness as a mother.

Note that the counselor did not force the issue nor did he introduce any new ideas. It is true that he rephrased the remarks of the client but nothing new was added. Notice particularly that the worker did not employ reassurance or moral exhortation. These are the cardinal rules for the nondirective counselor.

ECLECTIC METHODS IN PSYCHOTHERAPY

As we have seen, the basic procedures which have become traditional in client- and counselor-centered psychotherapy are information-giving, reassurance, suggestion and hypnosis, catharsis, some of the psychoanalytic techniques, and nondirective counseling. In eclectic methods of psychotherapy, no particular procedure is stressed. The method used depends upon and is dictated by the particular individual and his situation. Many therapists, including psychiatrists as well as psychologists, have developed their own systems by drawing on the methods described above, in varying proportions and with new variations.

None of these systems has yet come to be regarded as a separate method; they are often referred to as *general* or *eclectic* psychotherapy (*eclectic* is from a Greek word meaning choosing what is thought best from several sources or systems). The ideal of the eclectic method was first advanced by Dr. Adolph Meyer, the famed Johns Hopkins psychiatrist. His emphasis on the inseparability of the *psycho*logical and the *bio*logical processes in the whole organism is known as the *psychobiological approach*. Most eclectic methods recognize the importance of desensitization and redirection in bringing about effective readjustment.

Desensitization and redirection

Once the true nature of the emotion-provoking situation has been established—by whatever method—the psychotherapist must help the patient to face the situation without extreme emotion, so that he can equip himself with a set of responses which will successfully cope with it. In this regard, the clinical psychologist is deeply indebted to the experimental psychologists who have developed the principles of conditioning and deconditioning. Certain of these studies suggest that there are methods by which a person can hope to make some progress in trying to work on his own problems—by himself, without some technically trained worker to help him.

According to our everyday thinking, when a person has any emotional problem, he should try to keep from thinking about it. If a person feels moody and sad, his friends will try to divert him, and will tell him to "try to cheer up." If the person feels inferior, he is told to try to think about the things in which he is reasonably successful; if he has a hot temper, he is told to practice holding it in check. The assumption which lies back of this everyday conception is that the most efficient way to eliminate a habit is to forget it. It is assumed that the repetition of a response would strengthen the habit of making the response, and that the avoidance of a response would be the best means of weakening the habit that produces it. But as we have seen in preceding chapters, the experimental and clinical work on problems of changing habits has not come to the same conclusion. Instead, it seems probable that one way of eliminating a habit is to use it deliberately and repeatedly *under proper conditions*. This was demonstrated, you will remember, in the experimental studies of extinction in conditioning, of negative practice, and of deconditioning methods.

What would this same basic suggestion mean, if it were applied to the problem of self-therapy? The suggestion would mean that if a young person is trying to fight off some feelings of guilt or inferiority or some fear of social contacts, he should not depend solely on forcing himself to make the kinds of responses he thinks he ought to make. Instead, he should try to accomplish some basic relearning, and one promising approach seems to be by some adaptation of the negative-practice method. For instance, he can deliberately do, at least in imagination, the things he wants to learn *not* to do. This may seem impossible, but actually it is not so difficult or impracticable as it might seem. For example, when the person finds that he is tending to feel guilty and miserable, he can stop trying to fight off this feeling and try to intensify his reaction instead, so that eventually he will be able to rid himself of it.

It might seem, of course, that the only consequence of such a procedure would be to rivet more tightly on the person the habit of feeling guilty, but the psychological processes of the person apparently just do not work that way. There is the same problem in all therapy, even with a trained counselor. The counselor has learned that, generally, his work cannot depend on his giving advice and reassurance except, as we have seen, in the simplest and most superficial problems. At first the therapist is inclined to think that he needs, occasionally, to argue with the client and to straighten him out on the facts. For instance, a student says: "I don't know what to do. I've made a mess out of my school work and disgraced my family. Maybe I should just admit that I'm a failure and leave school." The counselor may know that the student actually has made a rather fair record, one which many other students would be happy to have equaled, but he soon learns that he cannot make progress by arguing. The effective therapist knows that he must encourage the client to explore more fully his feelings of defeat and failure, and thus get to the root of them.

In the same way, the student who tends to feel guilty or inferior and socially disapproved will almost certainly have some knowledge that there are more acceptable aspects to his life as well. But these more recently acquired habits, with all their perspective and sense, have not had the opportunity to interact with his earlier and more childish emotional habits. What he needs is a situation in which his two types of habits will be actively aroused and will interact—just as in the case of the psychologist who deliberately typed "hte" at the same time that he knew explicitly that it was an error. When a person pushes and intensifies his faulty emotional reactions and related imaginal activity, he is doing, in the realm of emotional or personality habits, the same basic thing that the negative-practice method assumes.

Of course, there are many problems in emotional life which are not open to this kind of self-therapy. It is just one of the many varieties of psychotherapy, which must be fitted to the needs of the particular person.

Institutional care

General psychotherapy and institutional care are frequently used in conjunction with each other, just as they are used separately depending on the nature of the illness or problem.

There is a certain benefit in living in an institution under close observation by physicians, nurses, and other personnel. Under these conditions the patient is relieved of making difficult decisions; his life, to a certain extent, is "lived for him." Guilt feelings tend to be reduced in the presence of others who are having similar difficulties. Moreover, the patient is kept from endangering the safety—both physical and financial—of himself and those around him.

The patient in an institution has at his disposal various facilities, aside from pure medical treatment, which are conducive to regaining mental health. Occupational therapy is employed in all good hospitals. This term means simply "healing through keeping busy." The overactive patient is quieted by engaging in such simple, rhythmic activities as knitting, weaving, sewing, polishing metal or furniture. The sad and depressed patient may be helped by activities of a stimulating nature where there is a minimum of routine or stereotyped behavior. Such activities as music, dramatics, and athletic contests requiring close attention and rapid decisions tend to keep the patient from thinking morbidly about himself. The withdrawn patient is frequently helped by some occupation in which the unexpected is always happening. A good many years ago it was noticed that one such patient, assigned as helper to a clumsy plumber, was shocked out of his withdrawn state when a pipe broke and he was drenched with cold water (Morgan[16]).

Life in a well-run institution is kept as close to normal as the condition of each patient permits. Church services, motion pictures, dances attended by patients, doctors, and nurses, all contribute to the cure. It is quite obvious that these numerous activities provide information, reassurance, suggestion, catharsis, desensitization, and re-education, quite apart from the regular therapeutic sessions with the psychiatrists and psychologists.

Since all these methods have some value, and since each is somewhat limited, it is to be expected that the eclectic practitioners—i.e., those who depend upon general psychotherapy—will get the best results. Evidence of this has been lacking until recently, although many enthusiastic claims have been made by various practitioners. We shall now examine the statistical evidence on the outcome of various types of mental therapy.

FACTS AND FIGURES ON PSYCHOTHERAPY

IN VIEW of the number of persons engaged in some form of psychotherapy, the cost in time and money to the patient, and the frustration that the ethical practitioner suffers because of his inability to help all the patients he would like to, it is rather amazing that so few data are available to indicate the relative merits of various types of therapy.

One extensive analysis (Knight[17]) has consolidated and critically summarized the results of psychoanalysis on 952 cases, including those treated at the Berlin Institute between 1920 and 1930; at the London Clinic, 1926 to 1936; the Chicago Institute for Psychoanalysis, 1932 to 1937; and at the Menninger Clinic, where psychoanalysis was used in conjunction with institutional care. The results show that about 60 per cent are discharged as apparently cured or very much improved, and about 40 per cent as no better or as worse. These figures are suggestive but of course it must be remembered that an unknown proportion of cases might have recovered "spontaneously." Since no control group was included, we do not know how large this correction would be.

In estimating the efficacy of psychoanalysis, it is valuable to compare it with other methods used on the same emotional difficulties (although it must be remembered that different schools of psychotherapy may have different conceptions of what constitutes a "cure"). In this regard it has been found that 40 per cent of psychotic patients are discharged from all mental hospitals in the United States as cured, without specific psychotherapy (Landis[18]). However, 32 per cent of similar cases are discharged as cured by the Menninger Clinic, where psychoanalytic treatment is combined with modern institutional regime (Knight[19]).

This comparison, therefore, indicates that psychoanalysis adds nothing to institutional care. It does not indicate how valuable either type of treatment is, since there is no untreated control group on which the rate of spontaneous recovery can be established. Nor do the above figures tell us the most important fact of all—namely, how long the patients, discharged as cured or improved, remain in that condition.

One leading psychiatrist has attempted to answer the important question of the relative permanence of cures effected by various types of psychotherapy (Wilder[20]). His results indicate that, judged on the basis of permanence of results, general psychotherapy is most effective, having shown permanent improvement in 83% of 77 cases; psychoanalysis was second, having shown permanent improvement in 70% of 159 cases; clinics were third, having shown permanent improvement in 54% of 818 cases; and hospitals were worst, having shown permanent improvement in only 50% of 620 cases. The poor showing of hospitals and clinics can probably be explained on the basis of the small amount of time received by each patient. The apparent superiority of general psychotherapy over psychoanalysis, however, cannot be explained on this basis, since the psychoanalyzed patients had many more hours of treatment, on the average, than did the patients who received general psychotherapy. We are thus forced to conclude that psychoanalysis in the treatment of the less severe emotional disorders is more costly, slower, and less effective than is general psychotherapy. In the treatment of the more serious mental conditions (the *psychoses*), the comparison is even less favorable to psychoanalytic treatment; a follow-up study made on patients one to five years after discharge found that only 44% of the patients treated through psychoanalysis were still well, as compared with 50% of the patients who received hospital care (Wilder[21]).

The variety of procedures which have been developed and utilized by clinical psychology in the treatment of emotional disorders is one of the most interesting developments in modern psychology. Although psychotherapy has a long history, it is only recently that the theory and cure of emotional disorders have been systematically worked out. But despite the comparative youth of modern psychotherapy, it has already made notable contributions to our understanding of emotional life. Moreover, it has led many individuals to more satisfactory emotional adjustments—the treatment of psychological war casualties has been especially striking. It is to be hoped that in the future, cooperation between clinical and experimental psychology will bring further progress in the study and treatment of problems of emotional adjustment.

PART FIVE

The individual and the group

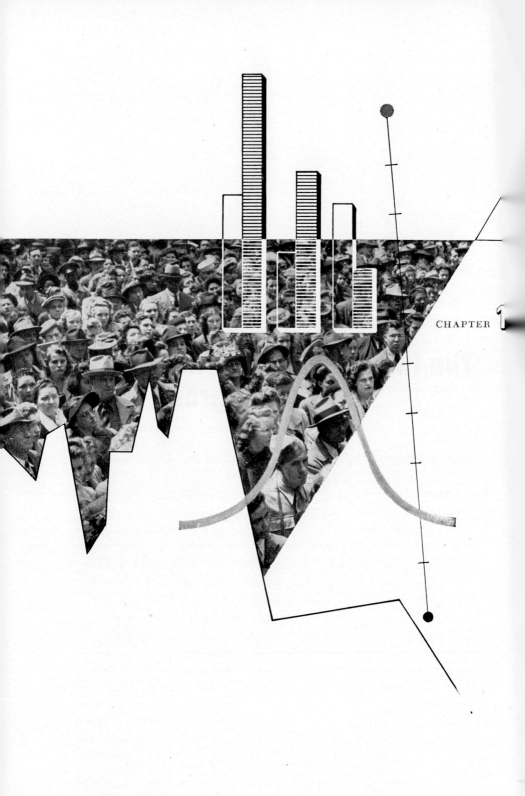

Individual differences and their measurement

Ways of Measuring Individual Differences

Statistics: Aids in Comparing Performances

Patterns in Psychological Characteristics

$\mathbb{A}$LL MEN ARE CREATED EQUAL." These famous words are often taken to imply that people are equally endowed with certain traits and abilities. Of course the real meaning of the statement is that in a democracy, all men are created equal in their rights before the law, whatever their differences in economic, political, or social standing. We can see around us every day the great differences among people that give each individual what we call his "personality." The study of these individual differences is one of the main fields of modern psychology and has been given the name of "differential psychology."

The usual overlapping between the fields of psychology is particularly marked in the case of differential psychology, for to answer the question of why individuals differ in their characteristics, it is necessary to investigate the problem of why and how they come to have certain characteristics. As psychologists have studied all the many differences among people—in aptitudes, interests, intelligence, social and ethical beliefs, and emotional patterns—they have been confronted again and again with the old problem of the relative influences of heredity and environment in determining an individual's characteristics. This problem has already been discussed in great detail in Chap-

541

ter 3 on *Nature and Nurture,* Chapter 4 on *Motivation,* and Chapter 6 on *Intelligence.* This chapter will not ask the *why* of individual differences. It will summarize *what* individual differences can be found as a result of the environmental-maturational interaction discussed in preceding chapters. Also, it will show *how* these differences can be measured in an objective way. Although it is obvious that people do differ markedly, it is by no means easy to discover exactly what these differences are and how large or small they are.

WAYS OF MEASURING INDIVIDUAL DIFFERENCES

To FIND the basic psychological characteristics, we must first measure each of their components, or traits. There are six fundamental methods of measuring individual differences: (1) tests; (2) rating scales; (3) interviews; (4) self-inventories; (5) behavior sampling; and (6) projective techniques. Each type has its advantages and disadvantages, and later each will be discussed in turn. But first, let us look at some of the characteristics of all good measurement, and at some of the special pitfalls to be avoided in the measurement of psychological characteristics.

Characteristics of good measuring instruments

To be of any value, a measuring instrument must have the two essential characteristics of *validity* and *reliability.*

Validity. The validity of a measuring instrument is the extent to which it actually measures what it is intended to measure. In measuring physical things, people are rarely in doubt as to the validity of the measuring devices they employ—for instance, no sane man would attempt to measure length with a thermometer. In measuring psychological characteristics, however, the suitable measuring devices are more difficult to find.

Thus the true index of validity is the extent to which the instrument accomplishes the purpose for which it was intended. For example: if industrial psychologists are trying to develop a test for use in selecting salesmen and if they find that those persons who get high scores on their tests are almost without exception successful as salesmen and that the persons who get low scores are almost without exception unsuccessful, then they can be satisfied that their test is valid. The validity of a test can be known only after certain applicants tested have been hired and have worked for a period of time, so that their actual performance can be compared with their test performance.

Reliability. The reliability of a measuring instrument is the degree to which people earn the same relative rank on it in subsequent tests. Whereas validity means testing the qualities really meant to be tested, reliability means *continuing* to test something with the *same results* each time. If it is a matter of chance whether people do well or poorly on a test, then their scores will not represent what they really know about the subject or what skill they really have, and the test is said to be unreliable. A ruler would be unreliable if it were made of a material which expanded and contracted with slight changes in temperature.

In most practical applications of measuring devices, validity is the important characteristic. Reliability is merely a means to the end of validity. A test may be reliable without being valid, but its validity is limited by its reliability. Another way of saying this is that a test which keeps on giving the same results with the same individuals may or may not be testing what it is supposed to test—but if it does not give the same results each time with the same individuals, it certainly is not testing anything at all, not even what it is supposed to test.

Sources of error in measuring personality

Subjectivity. One of the most common causes of error in a psychological measurement or in a test of school achievement is the inclusion of items which must be scored on the basis of subjective judgment. If a test is to be reliable, the items must be set up in such a way that two or more persons can score it and get the same result.

The measurements that one person makes of another person's personality are always likely to be colored by his own feelings and attitudes. Physical characteristics (like height and weight) can be measured accurately and objectively with precision instruments that cannot easily be influenced by the bias of the person using them. But where we are ourselves the measuring stick, such an accurate, objective measurement is seldom obtained.

The effects of prejudice upon the results of a personal interview are brought out in an interesting study.

> This study was an analysis of the interview records of twelve social workers who had interviewed a total of 2000 homeless men applying for free lodging. Although the interview was scheduled and standardized, the interviewers had unconsciously influenced the applicants to give desired answers.
>
> One of the interviewers was an ardent prohibitionist. He found that the downfall of 62 per cent of the applicants was due to the excessive use of alcoholic drink, while but 7 per cent of the cases of social failure were to be attributed to industrial conditions. An-

other interviewer, a Socialist, found that a mere 22 per cent of the unfortunate men owed their plight to the demon rum, whereas 39 per cent had been reduced to destitution by unfortunate industrial and economic conditions.

It is even more interesting to note that the prohibitionist, although giving the figures cited above as correct for "actual" cause, admitted that only 34 per cent of the *applicants themselves* mentioned liquor as the cause while 42.5 per cent attributed their condition to industrial conditions; whereas the Socialist reported that 11 per cent blamed alcohol and that 60 per cent named industrial conditions. (Rice[1])

Since the groups of men observed by the two workers were comparable, it is obvious that one or both of the interviewers were not only giving distorted interpretations of the items as noted on the interview blanks but were actually suggesting the desired answers to the men interviewed. This does not imply that the interviewers were deliberately attempting to build up propaganda for prohibition or against capitalism. It merely illustrates the influence of prejudice in affecting observations.

The "halo effect." How we see a detail in a complex situation is greatly influenced by how we perceive the total situation (see p. 280). One of the great weaknesses of the rating technique is that human beings cannot completely isolate the trait to be rated from the influence of other knowledge they have about the individual. This type of error has a special name: the "halo effect." For example, people who are likable or who are respected, say, for their intelligence, will be rated as better than they really are in other desirable traits. Let us examine a case in which error in observing human nature results from failure to isolate the trait to be observed.

During World War I a certain captain was rated as to intelligence by many of his associates as "the poorest man I ever knew." Yet this very officer stood first on three different intelligence tests given to 151 officers. He had been a Rhodes Scholar and had made an excellent record at Oxford. Comments of eight of the thirteen officers who placed this man at the very bottom of the scale described him as "impossible to live with," "a rotter," "yellow," "conceited," "a knocker," etc. It seems quite clear that these officers were unable to isolate such a quality as intelligence from the other and objectionable personality traits—that they did not allow for halo effect. (Rugg[2])

The best way to guard against the halo effect is to judge but one trait at a time. If a judge tries to rate more than one trait at a sitting, his earlier ratings of an individual are bound to influence his later ones.

Stereotypes. Closely related to prejudices and other causes of halo effects as sources of error in our estimates of human beings are the effects of "stereotypes." *Stereotypes* are preconceived notions as to how people of a given race or occupational or social group ought to appear or behave (for example, the Frenchman is supposed to be witty and dapper with a pointed mustache). Although many of these popular ideas are misconceptions based on little or no evidence, they constantly influence our observations of people's behavior or appearance. This tendency to classify people according to preconceived notions or stereotypes is illustrated by a striking series of experiments.

> College students were asked to look at newspaper pictures of nine outstanding men. The pictures were pasted on a sheet of paper and numbered from 1 to 9 with no further information or means of identification. The students were then shown this sheet and told (truthfully) that it contained the pictures of an alleged bootlegger, a European premier, a labor leader, a Communist, a United States senator, an editor-politician, two manufacturers, and a financier. They were asked to identify these individuals by number. It should be borne in mind that certain of these pictures must have been rather familiar to the students, as many of the men shown were frequently featured in the daily news. But surprisingly enough, numerous evidences of stereotypes were found. For instance, the senator received the designation of labor leader, Bolshevik, financier, editor-politician, and manufacturer as often as, or more often than, that of senator—he obviously did not fit the senatorial stereotype. (Rice[3])

Reducing error in personality measurement

Fortunately, ability to judge human nature can be improved. Through training we can overcome some of our stereotypes and some of our susceptibility to the "halo effect." A striking example of how we can increase the accuracy of our observations of human behavior through practice is found in the following experiment conducted by a personnel director.

> A class of thirty beginners was being trained for the work of interviewing applicants. The interviewers-in-training witnessed examinations conducted orally by a trained examiner. At the end of each examination of an applicant, the student-interviewers were required to assign one of four possible ratings to the applicant interviewed. On the very first day of the experiment and before any instruction whatever had been given, the thirty students showed large variations in the ratings assigned to each of the applicants. At the end of two weeks of training, however, the degree of agreement among the class had increased enormously. Assuming that agreement was on the correct side, the conclusion is that training had improved the ability of the subjects to observe personality. The interviewer, like the scientist, must strive constantly to increase the accuracy of his observation through intensive study and practice. (O'Rourke[4])

Ways of Measuring Individual Differences 545

The familiar saying that "two heads are better than one" holds true in measuring human personality by means of rating scales or personal interviews. The more judges there are, the more dependable will be their pooled opinions. Increasing the number of judges or interviewers will not, of course, completely eliminate the halo effect, for some persons will be likable or offensive to all judges or raters. Many prejudices, however, are matters of personal whim, and those of one judge may be balanced out by those of another judge.

The great difficulty in measuring personality in terms of the pooled opinions of many judges and raters is that we frequently wish to measure people who are not known to a sufficiently large number of judges or raters. Then, too, such ratings require a great deal of time and arrangement. Moreover, it frequently happens that the individual carefully conceals some traits. Such traits cannot be adequately rated or judged, even in an interview, except by specially trained clinical psychologists or psychiatrists. Those very traits concealed behind the mask are often of extreme importance in determining the quality of a person's adjustments to life.

Psychological tests

A *psychological test* is a carefully planned situation in which the individual's characteristics can be described by a numerical value or score. For example, in a test of reasoning ability the subject is given certain problems to solve. His performance is scored according to the time required to solve the problems or according to the number of problems solved in a given length of time.

Psychological tests may be classified in several different ways:

1 They may be grouped according to the *aspect of the individual's behavior and experience they measure*. Thus there are tests of keenness of the senses, of school achievement, of vocational interests, of emotional stability, of general intelligence, of character traits, of personality, of reasoning ability, of word-association, and so on.

2 Tests are labeled as *verbal* or *nonverbal*, depending on whether or not language is employed either in giving the directions or in "taking" the test.

3 Tests may be designated as *group* or *individual*, to show whether an examiner can administer the test to several subjects at a time or must test them individually.

4 Many tests of ability to perform are classified as *speed* or as *power* tests. In a speed test, the score is the amount of work done in a constant period of time, or the amount of time required to complete a constant amount of work. In a power test, unlimited time is allowed, and the score expresses the degree of difficulty of the tasks in which the individual can succeed.

5 Tests may be further classified as *work-sample, analytic,* or *miniature.* As the term *work-sample* tests suggests, these involve the measurement of a small period of performance of a particular task under standardized conditions. A good example is the procedure used in licensing motor-vehicle drivers in which the applicant drives over a designated course while the examiner rides at his side and marks a check list to show errors of operation and infractions of law. The *analytic test* measures any one of a number of specific and restricted abilities that enter into the performance of a complex task. The use of such tests presupposes that the task in question can be broken down into a number of basic abilities. For example, reaction-time, color-vision, auditory acuity, and other tests are used in licensing automobile drivers. *Miniature tests* present the life situation in miniature; they simulate the real task without reproducing it. The illustration shows a miniature electric-winch test and trainer developed by the author for the United States Navy.

This classification of tests is by no means hard and fast. A particular test as it is actually used will fall within several of these categories.

It will be a group or individual test, and also either a verbal or non-verbal test, and so on. Moreover, even finer distinctions between types of tests could be made, leading to still further classification.

Rating scales

There are certain traits or characteristics of the human being's mental make-up which cannot, as yet at least, be accurately measured by means of standardized tests such as those described above. In fact, such traits as friendliness, generosity, and physical attractiveness exist mainly in the minds of our associates. Obviously, the easiest way to measure such personality traits is to ask a person's acquaintances what they think about him. The rating scale is a device for grading individuals on such traits.

The merit of a rating scale, like that of all instruments for measurement, depends on the degree of validity and reliability it possesses. Reliability of a rating scale is usually determined by finding out how well two sets of judges, using the scale, agree on the traits of the same individuals. The validity of a rating scale depends upon how well the judges understand the definition of the trait to be appraised; for the validity of a rating scale, as of any test, is the extent to which it does the task it was designed to accomplish.

There are at least three fundamental kinds of rating techniques, to be used when characteristics cannot be accurately tested by objective measures. Each of these has its advantages and limitations, and each will be discussed in turn: (1) the method of paired comparisons, (2) the order-of-merit method, and (3) absolute rating scales.

The method of paired comparisons. In the method of paired comparisons, the judge successively compares each individual with every other in the group of subjects to be rated. In each pair, he rates one as superior to the other in the trait under consideration. The subject who takes the largest number of "firsts" in the comparisons is the one who has the highest score.

To make the comparisons in an orderly manner, the following type of chart is usually drawn up. The five subjects to be rated will be known as A, B, C, D, and E.

	A	B	C	D	E	Total
A		+	+	+	+	4
B	−		+	+	−	2
C	−	−		+	−	1
D	−	−	−		−	0
E	−	+	+	+		3

The judge usually starts with individual A and asks himself whether A is more cheerful (or whatever the trait in question may be) than B. If the answer is *yes*, a plus mark is put in the row marked A and in the column B, and, correspondingly, a minus sign is entered at row B, column A. If the judge decides that A is *less* cheerful than B, a minus sign is put in the space where the A row and the B column intersect, and the plus sign in the reverse position. Next the judge asks himself, "Is A more cheerful than C?" The answer is entered in the C column and, of course, in the A row.

This procedure is continued until every subject has been compared with every other subject. When the table is completely filled in on the basis of the judge's decisions, all the plusses in each row are totaled and entered in the column headed *Total*. These totals represent the scores of each of the subjects for the quality being rated.

Notice that in this method the subject is given a position *relative* to the others in his group, not an absolute score. Notice also that the number of judgments grows much more rapidly than the number of cases. In the sample just shown, with five cases, the total number of judgments required is 20. With six cases, 30 judgments would be required; with a hundred cases, 9900. Obviously, the use of this test with large groups is impossible or impracticable.

Order-of-merit method. The order-of-merit method consists in lining up the subjects in a 1, 2, 3 . . . order by picking out the best and then the next best and so on until all the cases have been ranked for the trait under consideration. The objection to this method is the difficulty of considering the whole field and keeping each individual in mind until the best single one is picked out. This method, like the method of paired comparisons, gives relative positions and not absolute ratings.

Absolute rating scales. In absolute rating scales, the judge assigns an absolute value to the trait being rated. With scales of this sort, only one judgment is made for each case involved. Consequently, this method is much speedier than the two preceding ones. It is subject to error in that the standards of the judge might fluctuate during the series. Also, there is a "personal equation" for each judge—that is, some judges assign too many high marks; others give too many low ones.

Below is part of an absolute rating scale which has been used successfully in a large university to determine the causes of student failures. Only two of seven factors are shown.

PERSONALITY RATING SHEET FOR FRESHMEN

Name of student..................................Date.............

Aiding individual students is based on scholastic records of achievement, health, and other factual records. Personality, difficult to evaluate, is of great

importance. You will greatly assist the student named if you will rate him
with respect to each question by placing a check mark on the appropriate
horizontal line *at any position* which represents your evaluation of the student. It is not necessary to locate it at any of the division points or above a
descriptive phrase.

Your rating will be considered confidential and suggestive only. You need
not sign your name to this sheet unless you wish to do so. Fill in as completely as possible.

1. *Scholastic Zeal* Does he display enthusiasm for schoolwork?	Unresponsive	Usually indifferent	Studious	An energetic student	Craves scholarly work
2. *Initiative* Is he a resourceful and original thinker?	Needs constant supervision	Needs occasional prodding	Prepares assignments	Completes suggested supplementary work	Seeks and sets for himself additional tasks

The interview as a means of diagnosing personality

The personal interview is routinely used by employers for selecting
new workers, and by clinical psychologists and psychiatrists in their
attempts to investigate personality disorders and to bring about cures.
In the latter case, the investigatory and the curative phases of the interviewer's work usually run side by side.

The two forms of the interview. Interviews may be standardized or
informal. In the highly standardized interview, predetermined questions are asked in a certain set order. This type of interview is probably
not very much better than having the literate subject write his answers
directly on the interview form without the intermediary action of the
interviewer. At the other extreme, the interview can be so informal that
it appears to be a casual conversation. Each of these methods has its
advantages and limitations, its uses and abuses.

The standardized interview. The standardized interview is to be
employed when the interviewers have little training and cannot be
relied upon to avoid the common sources of inaccuracy and error in
the interview (like stereotypes and the "halo effect"). The outstanding advantage of this form of interview is that no time is wasted—every
word counts. There is little likelihood of the interviewer's being side-
tracked and failing to cover all the significant points.

One disadvantage of the completely standardized interview is that it has the same artificiality that the printed questionnaire possesses. With this type of approach the interviewee is not very likely to "open up" to the interviewer. Simple, routine facts of behavior can, however, be obtained in this manner. Another disadvantage of the standardized interview is that the procedure cannot be varied to meet individual cases. The interviewer must adhere to his plan and get as much of the standard information as he can.

The informal interview. The informal interview takes the form of a conversation. While the interviewer and the person interviewed talk about this and that, the interviewer is alert to guide the conversation into the desired channels. As the various bits of information are supplied, they are jotted down, but in an unostentatious fashion since the very act of writing down what the interviewee says makes the conversation artificial and stilted. The experienced interviewer is sometimes able to defer his note-taking until after the interview. The practice of taking the conversation down on a dictaphone concealed from the interviewee is an excellent—though expensive—way of combating the self-consciousness caused by the paper and pencil. Some of the advantages of the standardized interview can be retained without incurring most of the disadvantages if the interviewer prepares a formal list of the points to be covered and checks off each item as it is supplied by the interviewee.

How reliable is the interview? The reliability of the interview will depend upon who is doing the interviewing, what he is trying to find out, the degree of standardization, and how much time he can spend.

> One study was made of the ability of six experienced sales managers to interview prospective salesmen. Thirty-six applicants were interviewed by each of the six sales managers by any method that they cared to use, and were then arranged in rank order according to their estimated ability. The results showed an amazing lack of agreement among the interviewers as to the rank that should be assigned any particular candidate. One candidate, for instance, was rated as 3rd in ability by one manager and as 30th in ability by another. (Scott[5])

Results of experiments of this sort would seem to indicate that the judgments made through personal interviews depend almost as much on who the interviewer is as upon the personality of the person being interviewed. A greater degree of reliability can be achieved by increasing the number of interviewers—that is, of course, if the applicant is not worn out by being so frequently interviewed.

Interviewing often gives unreliable results when undertaken by unskilled personnel. However, in the proper hands and carefully worked out, the interview can be a very satisfactory means of diagnosing human personality. A standardized interview has been developed which works extremely well in choosing potentially successful applicants for office jobs in a large company (Hovland and Wonderlic[6]). This method has worked equally well in selecting applicants for factory jobs (McMurry and Johnson[7]). The results of this work will be reviewed in detail on pages 648-649.

The self-inventory as a means of measuring personality

To remove the disadvantages of rating scales and interviews, psychologists have developed standardized self-rating scales or personal inventories. The personal inventories differ from the measuring instruments already discussed in that they require the subject to give the needed information about *himself*. In the self-inventory, the subject is asked to answer questions concerning his subjective experience and personal life; he is asked to tell what he likes and dislikes, to indicate his admiration or contempt for various persons in public life, to explain what he does and does not do. Here is a sample (Strong[8]):

"Part I. Occupations. Indicate after each occupation listed below whether you would like that kind of work or not. Disregard considerations of salary, social standing, future advancement, etc. Consider only whether or not you would like to do what is involved in the occupation. You are not asked if you would take up the occupation permanently, but merely whether or not you would enjoy that kind of work, regardless of any necessary skills, abilities, or training which you may or may not possess.

Draw a circle around L if you like that kind of work.
Draw a circle around I if you are indifferent to that kind of work.
Draw a circle around D if you dislike that kind of work.

Work rapidly. Your first impressions are desired here. Answer all the items. Many of the seemingly trivial and irrelevant items are very useful in diagnosing your real attitude.

Actor (not movie)	L	I	D
Advertiser	L	I	D
Architect	L	I	D
Army Officer	L	I	D"

Items in a self-inventory may be regarded as valid only after they have been checked against some outside measure of the trait they are intended to appraise. You can never be certain of the significance of a series of items or questions by merely looking at them. You might guess, for example, that newspaper editors like playing poker and dislike playing tennis—but could you decide on the basis of common sense that life insurance salesmen dislike museums and like educational movies? These are typical reactions, based on responses of men in these professions to a self-inventory blank (Strong[9]).

The first self-inventory was constructed during World War I (Woodworth[10]). Obviously, one of the greatest problems in selecting soldiers and officers for training is to get emotionally stable men who will not break down under the emotional hazards of war. The Personal Data Sheet was devised to reveal the bad risks before their training started. Some typical items from a self-inventory of emotional stability follow (the words *yes* or *no* in the parentheses following the questions indicate the answers that, if typically found, are characteristic of unwholesome emotional organization):

> Do you usually feel well and strong? (*No*)
> Do you often feel that people are laughing at you? (*Yes*)
> Can you stand the sight of blood? (*No*)
> Do you have bad dreams at night? (*Yes*)
> Have you ever walked in your sleep? (*Yes*)

A long series of questions like these is valuable in rating oneself with standards taken from groups of people. Some individuals feel that they are emotionally abnormal when in reality they are fairly sound. In such cases they are relieved to know their true status. There is also the added advantage that honest answers to such questions can conveniently be studied by a trained psychologist, who can use them to diagnose and treat emotional or personality difficulty.

The self-inventory is convenient because it does not require assembling a group of raters or interviewers. It is especially valuable in that it gets below the surface to tap the individual's own personal experience and feelings. The self-inventory has the important disadvantage that a person does not altogether understand himself and hence cannot always give an accurate report. Moreover, it is defective in that the subject can, if he wishes, lie about himself, as the following experiment shows:

> The writer administered a widely known self-inventory to a group of 245 men students of elementary psychology at the University of Southern California. The self-inventory was administered in advance of any discussion of personality or the significance of the items the test contained. The standard instructions were given plus the further information that: "This test does not count toward your grade, but if you follow the printed directions (on the blanks) carefully, this test will give you some interesting information concerning your personality."
>
> After the tests had been filled out according to the standard directions, the subjects were given another blank with the following instruc-

tions: "Imagine that you are applying for a position as a salesman. Your showing on this test will decide whether you get the job. You know the characteristics of a good salesman. See if you can answer these questions as a good salesman would, regardless of whether you really feel that way."

All subjects entered into the experiment with enthusiasm. Both sets of blanks were scored. The average score of the subjects taking the test under the standard or "honest" condition was exactly at the standard for college students established by the author of the test on a nation-wide basis. When, however, the "influenced" blanks were scored, it was found that the average score was superior to 98 per cent of the scores obtained under the standard condition. In other words, the average student could swing himself far over the scale in the direction of a desirable score. (Ruch[11])

This finding is typical of those obtained in several other previously reported studies (Ellis[12]).

You will see in Chapter 17 that the self-inventory method has been very disappointing as an instrument for selecting personnel in business, industry, and the military services. However, it has some value in the clinical guidance situation where the client is seeking self-understanding.

The method of behavior sampling

The method of behavior sampling does not depend upon what a person says about himself or upon what others say about him. Fundamentally, it is more likely to be valid than any of the measuring instruments so far discussed. This is because it deals with actual behavior: the subject's typical behavior in a familiar situation is carefully observed, without his realizing that his behavior is being observed and evaluated. Instead of answering certain definite questions or solving particular problems, he is put in an ordinary situation, and a record is made of whatever happens. It is frequently possible to standardize the situation so carefully that many individuals can be compared at the same time under the same conditions.

For instance, one college teacher made it a practice to introduce slight errors in the totaling of points earned in quizzes. Sometimes the error would favor the student; sometimes not. (In all instances the true grade was recorded.) The object of the experiment was to see how many undergraded as compared with overgraded students would report the discrepancy. Observations over a period of two years showed that 97 per cent of the undergraded asked for corrections as against 9.5 per cent of those who were favored by the supposed error.

The practical limitation of the method of behavior sampling is that an elaborate setup is required. Human adults lead complicated lives and there is consequently great difficulty in getting a behavior situation which will be comparable for all kinds of persons.

A workable simplification and modification of the method of sampling behavior makes use of a standardized questionnaire. The answers on this questionnaire, which can be objectively verified as true or false, reveal the elements of stability and responsibility in the person's pattern of living. There is no end to the number of life facts that can be collected from the individual and later verified—facts concerning which the subject knows the answer. Typical examples are:

> What is your civil status? (single, married, separated, divorced, widowed)
> Do you own life insurance?
> Do you have a banking account?
> Are you a registered voter?

This type of information about a person's life is useful for prediction because people as a rule will continue to behave in the future in much the same way they have behaved in the past.

Projective techniques

In recent years, psychologists have been experimenting with certain methods of personality measurement called *projective* or *depth* techniques. This name has been given them because they are thought to bring out a deeper expression of the personality than that revealed by the more or less conventionalized verbalizations and performances tapped by the methods discussed above. Here is one especially clear definition of the projective methods:

> "[A] projection method for [the] study of personality involves the presentation of a stimulus-situation designed or chosen because it will mean to the subject, not what the experimenter has arbitrarily decided it should mean (as in most psychological experiments using standardized stimuli in order to be 'objective'), but rather whatever it must mean to the personality who gives it, or imposes upon it, his private, idiosyncratic meaning and organization." (Frank[13])

Numerous suitable materials for the projective study of personality are available. Of these, free association (*word-association tests*), ink-blot interpretation (*Rorschach tests*), and picture interpretation (*Thematic-Apperception Tests*) have been most adequately studied to date.

Word-association tests. An early type of projective technique is the word-association test, which consists of having a person listen to, or read, a series of stimulus words to each of which he responds as quickly as he can by giving the first word that comes into his mind. Analysis of such responses can reveal much about the emotional life and personality of the subject. Let us consider some of the ways our responses in word-association tests express emotion.

1 *Variation in reaction time.* If the word arouses emotion, especially an unpleasant one, the subject tends to hesitate before responding, as in the following experiment:

One word-association test measured the reaction times of 100 children in the sixth and seventh grades. Pleasant, unpleasant, and indifferent words were present in the lists. Reaction times were significantly longer for unpleasant words than for pleasant or neutral words; but there were no significant differences between the times for pleasant and neutral words. (Carter[14])

2 *Perseveration.* In the word-association test, it is common for a subject to respond to a stimulus word with the same word he has given as his emotional response to previous words on the test. This phenomenon is called *perseveration,* which means continued repetition of a response.

3 *Failure to respond.* In some ways, failure to respond is simply an exaggeration of slowed response. Especially potent stimulus words may cause complete blocking of a line of thought. The subject sometimes tries to cover up his slow response by pretending that he did not hear the stimulus word, by coughing, by pretending that he thought the word was something else, or by asking a question. Such irrelevant behavior has the same significance as either complete failure to respond or delayed reaction.

4 *Overt behavior.* Sometimes the emotionally significant stimulus word will evoke the overt behavior of blushing, lowering the eyes, or stuttering.

5 *Revealing responses.* Sometimes the subject is caught off guard. His unedited response shows us something about his emotional life. Suppose that in response to the stimulus word *love* one boy says "mother," another says "Jean," while still another says "hate." We should have here strong evidence that these boys differed markedly in their emotional organization.

6 *Unusual response.* An unusual response is one which will be given by very few persons of the same cultural background. A significant stimulus word evokes an unspeakable response; so the subject protects himself by saying anything that comes into his head. For example, he might suppress his original response, name some object in the room, at random, and say to himself,

"Aha, I fooled him that time." But he has deceived no one. Such unique response words, selected for their irrelevance or through some arbitrary association process not common to the group, reveal the suppression of the true response.

The word-association test has other uses besides study of emotion at a given moment. It can be used to detect guilt with a fair degree of success (Crosland[15]). When the word-association test is combined with the galvanic skin-reflex technique, the results in the detection of guilt are even better.

Rorschach Test. One of the oldest of the projective methods is the Rorschach technique, making use of a series of ink blots similar to the sample shown on the color plate at the beginning of the book. The series includes several such ink blots, some being colored and all varying greatly in form, shading, and complexity. The subject observes the cards in order and describes what he "sees" in the blots. The test is thus a semi-controlled association test, where the stimulus material has no objective meaning.

The test gives information about the personality structure which cannot be brought out by clinical interviews. For example, subjects react to the color in the blots in a manner similar to their emotional response to their environments. When presented with a colored blot such as the one at the beginning of the book, a well-adjusted, outgoing subject will probably respond to the color in a well-controlled fashion, perhaps calling the lower red area a brightly colored tropical fish. On the other hand, subjects who respond to their emotional environments in an explosive, uncontrolled way frequently give associations such as blood, or smoke and fire. But the content of the association is not the only variable to be considered. It is important to note whether the responses are determined by movement (as is true of introverts) or by color (as is true of extroverts). The amount of detail is also important: intelligent, normal subjects usually see the pattern as a whole; schizophrenics see it as a series of details.

One obvious limitation of the technique is that its reliability depends upon the skill of the administrator, who must be highly trained, for the scoring is complex and requires precise judgments. Separate scores are made of what the subject sees on the card, where he sees it, and what quality of the blot caused him to see it. The interpretation of a Rorschach record is always based on many variables, never on one or two responses alone.

A great many studies have been made to test the validity of the Rorschach technique, but with differing results.

1 One of the more successful of these was the experiment conducted at Sarah Lawrence College, where a group of girls was given the individual Rorschach. The testing was done at the beginning of the term; the tests were scored and then put away until spring, when a check-up on the predictions could be made. A group of problem students (selected by independent criteria such as academic failure, referral to the psychiatrist, and problem behavior observed by teachers) were shown by the Rorschach to have an average of 7.9 personality deviations per person—that is, indications of emotional maladjustment. Another group of 15 students, selected as unusually well adjusted by teachers, had an average of only 2.6 deviations. But a self-inventory administered to this same group completely missed some of the most seriously maladjusted students. (Munroe[16] and Munroe[17]).

2 On the less favorable side of the picture is an experiment which attempted to validate the findings of the Rorschach on the factor of insecurity in a group of small children. This was done by comparing the Rorschach findings on the children with the ratings of teachers and parents. The subjects were 50 children enrolled in the Pre-School Laboratory at the State University of Iowa. These children were selected without regard to insecurity feelings; they were selected merely by school enrollment. They were given the Rorschach tests, which were scored and rated by an experienced Rorschach interpreter.

Their Rorschach scores were then compared with other data on the children's behavior. Part of these data were collected from their teachers by means of a rating scale covering 15 items of school behavior, and part from their parents in an interview covering 9 items of home behavior. The degree of insecurity in the children was rated by two psychologists from these data. Several studies were made of the data to determine whether there was any agreement between the Rorschach ratings and the home behavior, the "dependency" factor, the school behavior, etc. None of these studies established any strong agreement between the Rorschach results and other data.

There is a possibility that this lack of relationship may result from the fact that the ratings secured from teachers and parents did not really measure insecurity, so that the two tests might not have been comparable. (Swift[18])

The Rorschach technique for determining fundamental personality patterns has awakened keen interest in clinical workers. Its great disadvantage is that the procedure for administration and scoring is not easily reduced to objective rules, so that it must be used only by workers who have had a very specialized and prolonged training.

Thematic-Apperception Test. Another interesting projective technique is the Thematic-Apperception Test (Morgan and Murray[19]). The test consists of three series, each series containing ten photographs representing different situations. The subject is requested to make up a story around each picture, describing the situation, the events that led up to it, the probable outcome, and the feelings and thoughts of the characters. The clinical interpreter's objective is to discover the thought content of the subject through evaluating (1) the formal characteristics of the stories, and (2) the content of the stories (Rapaport[20]). An item from this test is shown below.

Item 12-F from the Thematic-Apperception Test. (Courtesy Dr. Henry A. Murray and the Harvard University Press.) An interpretation of one patient's reactions to this item is presented on page 560.

In evaluating the formal characteristics of the stories, the interpreter may look for *inter-individual consistency* and for *intra-individual consistency*. An example of the former is this: if a prostrate figure whose face is not shown in the picture is usually seen by men as a woman, and if a certain male subject sees the figure as a man, then his perception of the picture deviates from the perceptions of other men and so must be considered significant. And here is an example of intraindividual consistency: if a subject who has given a full background of events in nearly all his stories avoids doing so for one particular story, then this omission must be considered significant and the reason for the omission found.

Let us look at one interesting example of how the content of the stories may be evaluated. Here the principle is that the more frequently a striving (or desire), an obstacle, or an identification figure occurs in the different stories, the more surely it may be assumed that it plays a more or less intense role in the subject's thoughts. For example, when a ten-year-old girl was shown the item on the preceding page, her reaction was as follows:

> "Ooh! Ooh! That could be an old witch, and that's her daughter that was trying to kill every child in the village. One child was the easiest to kill. His name was Joe. Well, his parents had went to New England - - - - pause - - - -. That woman was found killing her mother and she was killed by her own people and that saved 5000 children. That's all of the two witches."

Here are the comments of the interpreter:

> "This is an unusual story for a young girl in the number of references to killing. It is further unusual in that the ideational content strongly suggests some slipping contact with reality (kill 5000 children, confusion over the woman killing the child and then the woman killing her mother). The story evidences strong resentment and hostility toward her own mother. However, I rather suspect that the child is strongly attached to and dependent upon her mother, in spite of what the child sees as rejection of her by the mother.
>
> "The reference to the killing of the mother (fourth line of story) and the previous reference to this woman as killing a child (line 2) suggests a third generation present in the home—presumably a grandmother to whom the girl feels drawn. Note that here the girl refers to the mother as being 'killed by her own people.' This may suggest the girl's underlying resentment of the mother.
>
> "These are the negative aspects of this record, but it should be pointed out that the organization is fairly good, that the high amount of activity words suggests a real interest in things around her (rather than a complete retreat into herself), and that the story of witches, which is a fairly popular one, suggests a still remaining contact with reality.
>
> "In general the story is that of a quite disturbed adolescent who should receive treatment immediately, but suggests further that there are real chances for success in treatment." (Henry[21])

The analysis made of the Thematic-Apperception Test was supported by several other lines of evidence (Sargent[22]):

1 *Report of home situation at time of testing:* "This girl's mother was an unstable person who left her first husband, to whom the child was attached, because of non-support. When first seen at the Clinic, the mother was living with S. and the younger child . . . and was working. For a time after the separation S. lived with her grandmother, of whom she was very fond."

2 *School report:* "Distractable, uninterested in work, lacks persistence, is dependent on teacher. . . . Withdrawn, daydreams, apathetic, shy, feels inferior."

3 *Analytic play session:* "The older girl-doll was always running to her mother for advice—always having the mother say something and disregarding her father entirely."

4 *Rorschach examination:* "The record provides unmistakable evidence of a developing schizophrenia. The reduction in form regard shows a tendency to misconstrue reality. Incongruities in response were not recognized, nor were they corrected in the inquiry. The phantasy activity includes autistic thinking, confused sequence (showing breakdown in logical functions), and irregular tempo. Low conformity indicates that intellectual rapport is barely within the normal range. These findings, combined with scarcely any evidence of neurotic shock, leave little doubt that a schizophrenic process is active. Treatment is not only indicated but imperative if complete breakdown is to be avoided."

5 *Follow-up report on the child:* Two years after testing she spent a period in a private sanitarium where electric shock was given. Latest reports revealed that she had again been placed with her grandmother and had shown considerable improvement. This last is interesting in view of the favorable elements noted by the projective examinations.

The Thematic-Apperception Test, like the other projective techniques, has many interesting possibilities, but much research is needed to refine and standardize it, thus ruling out some of the subjectivity of the interpreter in scoring.

STATISTICS: AIDS IN COMPARING PERFORMANCES

IN THE STUDY of individual differences, it is often interesting to compare the individual's performance on one test with his performance on another test, and to compare the performances of different individuals on the same test. However, such comparisons are often difficult because (1) the scores of many people who take tests on many characteristics necessarily make up a complex and unwieldy body of data; (2) there are several different ways in which test scores can be compared; and (3) even the best psychological test yields only limited data, because it must isolate one characteristic of an individual and test it in an artificially simple situation, whereas actually every individual is a complex organism whose characteristics are continually interacting with each other in a continually changing and complex life situation. To facilitate the comparison of individual performances, psychologists have adopted certain procedures called *statistics*. Statistics are standard methods for collecting, organizing, and interpreting numerical information. Statistical procedures simplify complex data and permit rapid comparisons to be made. It is not possible to derive a satisfactory estimate of a psychological characteristic from limited data, and statistical procedures are a way of examining a series of measurements and analyzing the general picture.

Statistical concepts are a more common part of everyday thinking than is generally realized. From grade school, we are all familiar with one of the most typical statistical measures: the *average*, or, as it is called more technically, the *arithmetic mean*. Everyone readily understands the statement, for instance, that to answer the question as to whether men are taller than women, it is necessary to compare their average heights, rather than comparing the height of one or a few women with the height of one or a few men. Most other statistical devices have essentially the same value: getting away from single measurements which might be misleading, to a more general, universally true picture.

The difficulties of comparing quantitative data have given rise to the statistical concepts and procedures discussed in this chapter. Among them are *The Psychograph, Units of Measurement, The Point of Origin, Measures of Central Tendency, Centile Scores, Measuring Variations Around a Central Tendency*, and *The Correlation Coefficient*.

The psychograph

One simplifying device used by psychologists is the psychograph or "psychological profile." This is a chart drawn up from the results of objective measurements or ratings of an individual's personality traits. By use of the psychograph, the instructor or employer can get a good picture of the strengths or weaknesses of a student or employee, as he is compared with other individuals.

Below is a typical psychograph. At the side of this psychograph, you will see that a number of psychological traits are listed. To the right of each of these trait names, you will see a point which describes the position of the person *as compared with college students in general.* Study this figure carefully and notice the traits in which he excels, those in which he is deficient. Could you predict from this information that the person in question might fail as a salesman and succeed as a statistical worker?

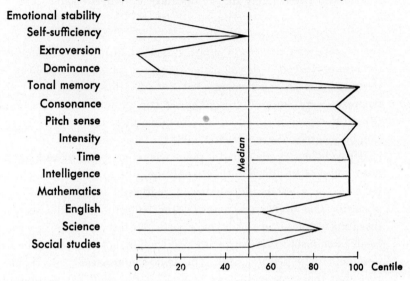

Psychograph, showing the pattern of personality

Units of measurement in psychology

You will notice from your study of the psychograph that all the performances are expressed in the same units. This may seem rather odd if you remember that the examinations with which you are familiar are scored in various units. Sometimes the grades will run from 1 to 10, sometimes from 0 per cent to 100 per cent; and at other times they will be given as A, B, C, D, and F.

One fundamental problem in giving quantitative statements of test results is to standardize the unit of measurement so that comparisons may be made of the test results of different individuals taking the same test or of the same individual taking different tests.

Let us choose a specific example. Suppose that you earned a score of 17 on a spelling test and one of 170 on an intelligence test. Although 170 is much greater than 17 *numerically,* you could not conclude that your intelligence is *higher* than your spelling ability. These arbitrary

Statistics: Aids in Comparing Performances 563

scores (raw scores) must be translated into common terms before comparisons of this type can be made. A universal language of measurement always involves choosing a *point of origin* for the scale of measurement. In this case, for example, you would obviously have to know what the system of measurement was: whether the possible scores ranged from 0 to 50 or from 0 to 200. Moreover, you would be interested to know just how this range of scores was established—just what degree of ability was represented by 0 (the point of origin) on that test, so that you could judge the significance of your particular score.

The point of origin

In measurement devices, a number is used to represent a *degree* of something. Just as a thermometer measures the degrees of heat, so a person's score on a personality test measures the degree to which he possesses a certain ability or characteristic. Now, whenever a number is used to represent a degree of something, there is always the implication of "degrees *above* or *below* what?"

If psychologists could find a point where an ability or characteristic does not exist at all, then they would be able to state a person's performance on a test as the number of degrees he stands above the zero point for that ability or characteristic. Unfortunately, the score representing absolute zero ability in a particular test cannot be determined easily. For instance, a backward child might fail every item in a test designed for superior adults. The child's numerical score would be zero, but that zero would not mean that the child has absolutely no ability. On an easier test, the child might make a score better than zero. In fact, if you wanted to find a performance of zero ability—with which you could compare other performances—you would have to devise something like "the easiest test possible" and then say that complete failure on that test meant zero ability.

Practically, there are all kinds of difficulties in the way of finding such a point of zero ability. Consequently, the psychologist is compelled to give it up as a possible basis of comparison and to use another base for his scores. The most convenient base for comparison in psychological work is some measure of central tendency or average.

Measures of central tendency

Exact statements about the abilities of an individual in relation to the group can be made by placing the individual in relation to a *measure of the central tendency* of the group. The most familiar measure is the one popularly known as the average, or technically known as the arithmetic mean. To obtain the *arithmetic mean,* you add all the scores of a group of individuals and divide by the number of scores. There are two other measures of central tendency with which the student should be familiar: the median and the mode. The *mode* is simply the score which is most often earned by the individuals in the group. The *median* is easily defined as the middle score of the group—in other words, the score which separates the lower half of the scores from the upper half.

Students should study the following tabulation with great care, to make certain they fully understand the three most common measures of central tendency.

This table represents the scores earned by fifteen boys on a vocabulary test. The scores are arranged in descending order, to simplify working with them.

Name of Subject	Score	Name of Subject	Score
John Brown	35	Leonard Larson	23
William Peters	29	George Waters	23
Peter Smith	26	Robert Gray	22
Francis Kelly	24	Lowell Davis	22
Frank Wright	24	Charles Webster	20
Ernest Jones	23	Wilbur Harvey	17
Walter Evans	23	Richard Adams	11
Harry Hughes	23	Total	345

Dividing 345 (the total of all of the scores) by 15 (the number of scores) gives 23, the *arithmetic mean* of this distribution.

A glance at the distribution will show that the score of 23 was earned by five subjects. The *mode* of the distribution is, accordingly, also 23, for no other score was earned so often.

There are fifteen scores in all. The middle one, therefore, is the eighth, that of Harry Hughes. His score, 23, constitutes the *median,* since that score falls at the point in the distribution which separates the upper half from the lower.

Perhaps you are wondering why we should bother with three measures of central tendency instead of using only the familiar arithmetic mean. A full explanation would take us further into statistics than we can go in an elementary course. But you should know—briefly—that the median and the mode are often used when there are a few extremely large or extremely small values which cause the mean to be different from the median. For the sake of simplicity, we illustrated these averages in the discussion above with a distribution of numbers in which the mean, median, and mode were all the same. And in fact, it usually happens that distributions made up of many scores yield close to the same value for all three measures of central tendency. However, this does not always happen. For example:

Suppose that the distribution of test scores shown on page 565 had been as follows:

Name of Subject	Score	Name of Subject	Score
John Brown	210	Leonard Larson	23
William Peters	199	George Waters	23
Peter Smith	84	Robert Gray	22
Francis Kelly	26	Lowell Davis	22
Frank Wright	24	Charles Webster	20
Ernest Jones	23	Wilbur Harvey	17
Walter Evans	23	Richard Adams	11
Harry Hughes	23	Total	750

In this case, the arithmetic mean would be 50, which is less typical of the scores of these boys than the median or the mode of 23. The few very high scores have pulled the mean up.

Our conclusion is that when distributions are greatly *skewed*—that is, when there are a few extreme values—we use the median or the mode rather than the mean as a measure of central tendency.

There is still another situation in which the median may be employed. This is the situation where the mean cannot be calculated because the performance of all the subjects is not known.

Suppose that we are conducting an experiment on learning in which the learning-ability score is the number of trials required to master a problem. Suppose that some of our subjects *never* learn it to the point of mastery. It will be impossible to calculate a mean in these circumstances, since to do so would require that the exact magnitude of each score be known. (Look again at the calculation of the mean on p. 565.) The median number of trials employed, however, can be calculated if more than half of the subjects have completed the task and so have established a final score. Now a frequency distribution can be drawn up showing the score of each of the persons in the first half of the groups—those who have a final score. From this distribution the *median* score of the whole group can be determined.

To take a hypothetical group of eleven persons:

Subject 1 took	2	trials
2	4	
3	7	
4	9	
5	12	
6	17	(the median score)
7	?	
8	?	
9	?	
10	?	
11	?	

Obviously, even if we do not know the final scores of the rest of the group who did not complete the task at all, we can still tell that they are poorer than those of the group that did. And we can still tell something about the general tendency of the whole group from knowing the median score. Then we can compare any individual in the group with this median score.

Centile scores: exact comparisons with the others

Placing an individual above or below the average of his fellows does not tell us all we want to know about him. We usually want to know *how far* the person is above or below average. There are several ways in which this can be done, but the simplest method makes use of *centiles* (or, to use a term which means the same thing but is passing out of use, *percentiles*). The 99th centile is the point below which 99 per cent and above which 1 per cent of the cases are found. The median is the 50th centile—50 per cent of the cases are below this point and 50 per cent above it. By converting an individual's score on a test into a centile score, we know at a glance how many persons in the group fall below and how many above him in performance. That is to say, the individual earning the score is placed with regard to his group.

Thus when we look at the psychograph shown on page 563, we know at once that the young man's intelligence and mathematical ability are superior to his emotional stability. In fact, he surpasses 98 per cent of the population in intelligence and mathematical ability and is far below average in emotional stability—so far below that about 90 per cent of the population show more emotional stability than he.

Measuring variation around a central tendency

The mean score of a group does not tell us all we want to know about the performance of the group. We also want to know how closely the scores cluster around the mean. For instance, if you knew that two spelling classes each had a mean grade of 65, it would be important to know that in one of these classes most of the students had scores around 65, while in the other class there was a sizable number of very high scores, balanced out by a sizable number of near-failures.

There are several measures of variability around an average. You must already be acquainted with the very simplest of these, the *range*. This is the difference between the lowest and highest scores in a distribution. For example, one class of spelling grades may range from 55 to 75, and another from 35 to 95, and yet both have an average grade of 65.

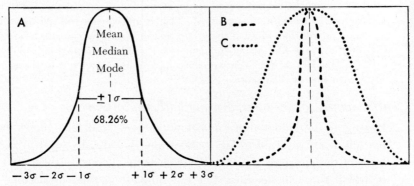

The *standard deviation* (σ) of a distribution represents a distance along the base of a distribution curve. It tells us the per cent of cases that fall within a certain distance from the mean. In a normal distribution curve (A above), 68 per cent of the cases fall within plus or minus ($\pm$) 1 σ of the mean; 95 per cent within ± 2 σ; and almost 100 per cent within ± 3 σ. From the size of the standard deviation, it is possible to tell how closely cases are concentrated around the mean. The smaller the σ, the less is the dispersion of cases from the mean. Of the three curves above, which has the largest σ, which the smallest?

Another simple measure of variability around an average is the *interquartile range*. It is the difference between the score at which the 75th centile falls and the one at which the 25th centile falls. In other words, these score limits contain the middle 50 per cent of the cases. The *interquartile range* is the range or difference between the scores that cut off the highest quarter and the lowest quarter of a distribution (that is, the range covered by the middle 50 per cent of the cases).

The correlation coefficient

In order to study the problem of the relationships among various traits, it is necessary to understand what is meant by *correlation*.

The meaning of correlation. The *correlation coefficient* is a number which expresses the relationship between two sets of measures. In the present connection it is used to express the degree to which standing in one trait is (in general) associated with standing in another trait in a group of individuals.

To compute a correlation coefficient, you need *two* sets of measures on a *group* of individuals. For example, if you wished to determine the degree of correlation between age and intelligence, you would have to know both the age and the intelligence score for each individual in the group. A correlation cannot be determined by studying measurements made on only one individual, because only from a series of pairs of scores may it be determined whether there is a tendency for certain scores in one series to be matched with certain other scores in the other series—whether the scores represent intelligence and degree of biological relationship, or child's I.Q. and parents' vocabulary.

The correlation is the general, *average* relationship found between two traits (say A and B) in the group *as a whole*. If it is very close, we say that the correlation is "high." Then we can predict that in any individual chosen at random the two traits A and B will *probably* be in close agreement. If the general relationship between traits A and B observed in a group is not so close, we cannot predict with so much certainty the standing of any given individual in trait B, knowing only his standing in trait A, or vice versa. If we study a group and find no general relationship between people's standing in the two traits, then there is no correlation at all, and no prediction is possible of what the relationship will be in any particular individual.

The size of the correlation coefficient. When two traits of the persons in a group correlate *perfectly* and *positively*, we could line up all the individuals on the basis of one trait and find them to be properly lined up for the other trait as well. If the correlation were *perfect* and *negative*, their orders would be exactly the reverse—that is, anyone scoring extremely high on the first trait would be perfectly certain to score extremely low on the other.

The formula for determining the coefficient of correlation is too complex to be of much value in a general psychology course. Suffice it to say here that it is written in such a way that when its solution gives a +1.00 it means perfect positive correlation; 0 means no correlation whatever; and —1.00 shows perfect negative correlation. In actual practice, correlations of +1.00 and —1.00 are rarely found. Either +1.00 or —1.00 would mean that if we knew a person's score on one trait we could predict his score on the correlated trait with perfect accuracy. A coefficient of zero means that there is no relationship between the two traits, that there is no systematic condition between them, so that knowing one will not help you predict the other. (A coefficient between 0 and .3 is usually attributed to chance.)

By now you must see the advantages of high degrees of correlation in working with groups of individuals. Suppose that you found that the correlation between high-school record and college scholarship was perfect—whether perfect negative or perfect positive. You could then say to a student, "You made the highest grades in high school; you will make the highest grades in college." Or, "You failed in high school; you will fail in college." Unfortunately, the correlation between high-school and college scholarship, though high, is not perfect.

Predicting from correlation coefficients. Correlation coefficients are *not* read as percentages. Suppose that test A and test B correlate .50. This does *not* mean that scores from test A are 50 per cent dependent on scores from test B. When correctly used, correlation coefficients may be interpreted in either of two ways. Both of these are related to the task of *predicting* a second score from knowing a first score (and from knowing other data such as the central tendencies of both series of scores and their distribution around that central point).

First of all, we might have the task of trying to predict what grades a student will make in high school, knowing the ones he made in grade school. If we have no knowledge of the correlation in such a case, and if we have to make a prediction as to what grades a student will make in high school, we are wise to guess that he will make average grades. But, of course, we do have *some* knowledge of the correlation, for even if we never heard of the word *statistics* we still know that there is a tendency for students to continue the same quality of work. So for the student who was very good in grade school, we predict an above-average high-school record; for the very poor student in grade school we predict a below-average high-school record; etc. When we know the actual correlation in such cases, we can make these guesses or predictions more precise by saying that if the correlation is .50, the likelihood is that, in high school, a student will make a score which will be about .50 times as far from the average of high-school grades (and in the same direction, above or below) as he deviated from the average of grade-school grades. In making this sort of prediction we have to take into account the relative degree of variation around one average in the two sets of scores we are talking about, and we need to emphasize, too, that we are talking only about the *most probable* score. A given individual, of course, may be even more outstanding than he was in grade school, or he may even fall below his former level. But if the correlation is .7, the students who scored at a certain point in one series will, on the average, makes scores .7 times as far from the average on the other set of measurements.

The other main way of interpreting a correlation coefficient is in terms of the degree to which we can reduce our errors of predictions, as a consequence of using the process just described. We must take into account that with students who were *average* in the first set of measurements, the knowledge of the correlation coefficient does not help us at all in increasing our accuracy of prediction. Even if the correlation were zero, we would predict that the average student in grade school will probably be an average student in high school. No matter how high the correlation coefficient, we would still make the same prediction for the average student from grade school; it is only as the first score deviates from the average that we change our predictions as a consequence of knowing the correlation. Even so, the majority of students are close to the average, and the knowledge of the correlation coefficient does not lead to any great change in our predictions, at least in one sense.

But in another sense, there is a change in our predictions as a result of knowing the correlation coefficient. When the correlation is very high, we can say not merely that the average student in grade school will probably be average in his high-school work, but also that there is *very little likelihood* that he will be either far above average or far below average. The extent to which he is likely to deviate from the predicted score will be narrowed down. This extent can be expressed mathematically, as in the following table:

Correlation Coefficient	Percentage of Accuracy of Prediction
.00	00
.50	14
.86	50
.99	86
1.00	100

This table shows that when the correlation is .50, there is only a 14 per cent narrowing down in the extent to which he will be likely to deviate from the score we predict for him; if the correlation is .86, there will be a 50 per cent narrowing down in the extent to which he is likely to deviate in this way; etc. (The procedure used in drawing up this table is too complex to be described here.) You can see that small differences between large coefficients are as significant for accuracy of prediction as much larger differences between small coefficients of correlation. For example, the difference between a coefficient of 1.00 and one of .86 is only .14, but it is as significant as the difference between a coefficient of .86 and one of .00 since each represents half the total possible error. In other words, the percentage of accuracy in prediction increases faster than the size of the correlation coefficient.

The best way for the beginner to visualize the meaning of correlation is to study the following table. This shows what percentage of persons who are above average on one measure will be above average in the other trait as well.

Correlation Coefficient	Percentage of Group Falling in Better Half on Test A Falling in Better Half on Test B
.00	50
.50	66
.60	71
.80	80
1.00	100

The correlation coefficient is constantly used by psychologists to show the relationship between various psychological characteristics—relationships that often show definite *patterns in personality characteristics.*

PATTERNS IN PSYCHOLOGICAL CHARACTERISTICS

Both psychological tests and everyday observation show that the individual differences between people are very great and very difficult to define and measure, whether those differences are due to hereditary or environmental factors. Perhaps because of this very complexity of individual differences, psychologists and laymen alike have been seeking to find certain basic patterns in psychological characteristics which will simplify the problem of analyzing and understanding why people are alike and different. Here we shall discuss some of the popular beliefs about patterns in psychological characteristics and then see what patterns have been discovered through objective measurement.

The outmoded bi-modal theory of types

Most common in popular thought is the *bi-modal* theory of types, which divides all people into two separate and distinct groups when classified on the basis of any particular trait. A person can be *either* a "regular fellow" *or* a "grind," *either* an "introvert" *or* an "extrovert" —with rarely any intermediate degrees between these extremes. For example, the degree of introversion-extroversion (see p. 576), as popularly conceived, would require a curve of two or more modes:

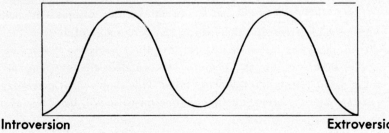

Introversion   **Extroversion**

A mode, you will remember, is a point where individuals' scores "pile up." Thus a curve with two modes is one in which all the cases fall toward *either* one end *or* the other, rather than in a continuous distribution. Actually, very few people are extreme introverts or extroverts; most people have qualities of both types, as in this curve:

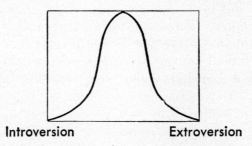

Introversion　　　　　　　　**Extroversion**

Hundreds of studies on individual differences have shown uni-modal curves like these—curves having but one mode—to be the rule.

The distribution of traits within an individual

Individuals when compared with each other do not fall into sharply marked groups or "types." The next question has to do with the manner in which traits or characteristics are distributed within a given individual. Will a particular individual possess all abilities to the same degree? Is an average person average in all his traits?

Already you have seen one example in which this was not the case. Turn back to the psychograph shown on page 563. That young man was average in some characteristics, very superior in others, and very inferior in still others.

Another study made a composite plot of the scores made by six "average" high-school students on 35 different tests. In most of the tests, these "average" students made average scores—scores falling around 75 to 85. A few scores of each individual, however, fell considerably above average and a few others considerably below. (Hull[23])

We are probably safe in concluding that the human individual is not equally superior in all traits, is not average in all traits, and is not equally inferior in all traits. The great majority of his traits fall close to his own average, but in a few traits he will be exceptionally high and in a few others correspondingly low as compared with his own average. Within each individual there is some variation of capacities and abilities. This can mean that a person who is highly successful in one occupation might be only partially successful in another, or that a person who is moderately successful in an ill-chosen line of work might succeed exceptionally well in another occupation.

How traits are associated, i.e., "cluster"

We have seen that an individual is not altogether good, bad, or indifferent in all traits. Next we are interested in knowing the extent to which particular traits tend to be associated with each other.

Numerous studies of correlations of various abilities and characteristics show that the human individual is made up of traits which seem to form *clusters*. Traits are said to form a cluster when they correlate highly with each other and are independent of the traits in other clusters. It is not yet known exactly how many of these clusters exist.

All-round intellectual ability. Very frequently you hear such statements as: "He's a genius in every field," or "He's so stupid he can't catch on to anything." Are such statements at all accurate? Is intellectual ability in one field correlated with intellectual ability in other fields? In other words, is there an "all-round" intellectual ability?

One distinguished British statistician and psychologist (Spearman[24]) points out that a careful study of the correlations between all kinds of intelligence tests would show whether there are general factors running through different abilities. The work of Thurstone (p. 211) indicates that the correlations between the particular abilities he measures, while not very high, are positive enough to warrant the assumption of some general intellective factor, and his work is corroborated by the following study:

> The table below shows the correlations among the scores on four tests in the Navy Basic Test Battery, Form 1. These tests were given to 224 recruits at the Bainbridge Naval Training Station (*American Psychologist*[25]).

| | [CORRELATION WITH] | | | |
Test	General Classification	Mechanical Aptitude	Reading	Arithmetical Reasoning
General Classification	—	.57	.76	.72
Mechanical Aptitude ...	.57	—	.54	.63
Reading	.76	.54	—	.69
Arithmetical Reasoning ..	.72	.63	.69	—

Here all the correlation coefficients are positive and fairly high. This consistency of positive correlation indicates that some common factor is running through all the tests. The nature of this factor cannot be easily determined. It might be high motivation; that is, those individuals who consistently work as hard as they can would do well on all the tests, while those who work less hard would tend to do poorly on all. But whatever the causal factor underlying the correlation, there is no doubt that it does exist. Much research is still necessary, however, to determine what the common factor is.

All-round mechanical ability. We have seen that scores earned on intelligence-test batteries show a high degree of correlation with each other. Is there a similar cluster of mechanical abilities?

> Perhaps the best information on this important subject can be drawn from the results of the Minnesota Mechanical Ability Investigation. In this extensive investigation, a large number of tests were given to groups of subjects and the results were analyzed by statistical methods.
>
> Some six tests of mechanical ability were discovered which showed high correlations with success in such work as electrical wiring, manual training, and shop practice. These six tests were all correlated positively with each other. (Paterson *et al.*[26])

In other words, the evidence indicates that there is a cluster of mechanical abilities as well as of certain intellectual abilities.

But how does the cluster of mechanical abilities relate to the cluster of abilities known as "intelligence"? Can we assume that a man or woman will have mechanical ability if he or she is a person of high intelligence? If we could, the task of selecting people for skilled work would be easy. All we should have to do in that event would be to administer a good intelligence test and pick out those individuals who scored highest. However, the Minnesota Mechanical Ability Investigation found no such correlation. General intelligence and mechanical ability are fairly independent of each other.

The fact that those people who are high in the cluster of mechanical abilities may as often have low as high general intelligence provides a reasonable justification for the practice which is growing in our public schools of allowing those students who do poorly in academic subjects to try their hands at vocational training. Of course, we cannot argue that a student will succeed in vocational work simply because he is below average in a certain cluster of intellectual abilities, but we can expect that many students will do so just as a matter of chance, since mechanical ability and general intelligence (as ordinarily defined) are not closely correlated.

All-round athletic ability. Is there such a thing as an "all-round athlete"? We know that certain individuals excel in a large number of sports, while others fail in all. We cannot assume merely on the basis of this fact, however, that there is a general factor of athletic ability that makes for excellence in all sports. Even if the correlations between the various athletic abilities were zero, it would be possible for a few individuals to excel in all of them by virtue of the chance association of the desirable ones.

We must not attempt to answer this question by thinking of an exceptional person who may or may not follow the rule, but we can answer it by studying careful scientific investigations.

> For instance, a report has been made on the intercorrelations of tests of athletic ability given to 100 junior high school boys. The battery of tests included tests on running the hundred-yard dash, strength of the back, strength of the right and left hands, broad jump, and the twenty-five-yard hop. The correlations between the pairs of these tests were all positive, and some of them were fairly high. Moreover, correlations were low between general intelligence and each of the traits in the cluster constituting athletic ability, or motor agility—a fact further indicating the reality of this cluster. (Paterson et al.[27])
>
> A more recent study suggests the existence of at least three more primary abilities in this motor agility cluster: strength, quickness, and steadiness. (Seashore, Buxton, and McCollom[28])

These findings give support to the idea that there is a cluster of abilities which go to make up an athlete, that there is all-round athletic ability.

Is there all-round musicality? Measurements have been made of the various factors in musical ability—such as pitch discrimination, sense of time, tonal memory, and many others, and then the various factors have been correlated with each other (Seashore and Mount[29]). These elements represent essential abilities in learning to play musical instruments. Their intercorrelations are so low that there is no evidence of a cluster representing general musicality, such as is found clearly in the case of intelligence and less clearly in mechanical ability and motor agility. All in all, the evidence from this early investigation and from more recent ones indicates that there is no all-round musical ability.

The good musician is the one who happens to possess enough of the basic abilities. The fact that one musician is high in a few of these elementary abilities does not mean that he will be high in the others. Certain musical abilities, however, are apt to go with certain others. People who are good in discriminating pitch are likely to excel in memory for combinations of tones, and, of course, in ability to sing a particular note at will. Rhythm, however, is not correlated with pitch discrimination. And all these musical abilities—the senses of pitch, intensity, time, consonance, rhythm, and memory for tones—are unrelated to general intelligence (Tracker and Howard[30]).

Introversion-extroversion. We all know individuals whom we would call *introverts.* The introvert lives within himself. He is interested in ideas, values, and general principles; he is given to daydreaming and reverie; and he is not especially interested in people unless they have ideas. Artists, musicians, scholars, and scientists are usually more or less introverted. At the other extreme are the individuals we call *extroverts*. The extrovert reacts mainly to the external world. He is interested in people and things rather than in ideas and values; he likes people, and he wants to be liked; he would rather make the world go round than understand why it goes round; he is the practical sort of person and is bored with, or even annoyed by, theory.

No one is either completely introverted or completely extroverted. As with other traits we do not find types but a continuous distribution with most of the cases near the average or center. The normal person becomes more introverted or extroverted as the situation demands.

Morality. To behave morally is to behave in the way that society approves. When a person obeys the rules and laws of his society, we say he is *moral* or good; when he deliberately disobeys, we say that he is *immoral*, or bad. There is also the *amoral* person who violates the code because of unfamiliarity with it or because of low intelligence; he is not classed as either good or bad. Since the very beginning of recorded history, people have been much interested in problems of moral philosophy and practical ethics, but only recently has moral behavior been studied by scientific methods.

> In the most noteworthy series of attempts to study moral behavior, observations were made on the actual behavior of children in life situations which had been carefully arranged to permit of acceptable and unacceptable behavior. Children were given an opportunity to *lie, steal,* or *cheat* in a game or examination.
>
> These studies showed that there is no high degree of consistency in the moral behavior of children. Children who cheat in one situation might be honest in another. Children who cheat in a school examination are not much more given to stealing than are children who do not cheat. Older children are more inclined to be deceitful than are younger children. Children of higher intelligence are more honest than children of lower intelligence. Children from the better and wealthier homes cheat less than those from less favored homes. This is true even when the intelligence level of the two groups is held constant. Children from good homes placed on their honor cheat more at school than at home, while children from poor homes cheat less at school than at home. Deception tends to run in families and in classes at school. (Hartshorne and May,[31] and Hartshorne, May, and Shuttleworth.[32])

Thus it appears that while "morality" is definitely related to such factors as socio-economic status and intelligence, it is not easily defined as a single trait or cluster of traits which remains constant for a given individual in all situations whether at home or school, and whatever the opportunities for dishonesty. Apparently it is not nearly so strong a pattern as others already defined and measured.

In this chapter we have studied in some detail the various ways of measuring the individual differences which we see around us every day and which are the result of the complex interaction between all the inherited traits and capacities, all the factors in maturation over the lifetime, and all the learning opportunities the individual has experienced in his environment.

CHAPTER 16

Problems in human relations

Factors in Successful Marriage

Problems of Parenthood

The Individual and Illegal Behavior

Problems of the Group

From the time an individual is born, he must live with other people —in the role of child and later of parent, in selecting a wife or husband and later in making the marriage succeed, and in participating with others in school and in the life of the community.

This chapter will present some of the known facts about human relationships. What are the factors which go into successful marriage? into successful parenthood? What conditions can cause an individual to adopt illegal behavior? What can the psychologist tell us about the individual's relationships with the group, especially with regard to the important problems of leadership, competition, and cooperation? The answers to these questions are obviously vital in everyday living.

FACTORS IN SUCCESSFUL MARRIAGE

The development and social orientation of love constitutes a highly complex phase of growth. It is subject to deviations from the course of normality, often causing unrest, inefficiency, and unhappiness. Our society imposes many restrictions upon the expression of the sexual

Factors in Successful Marriage 579

drive. The social institution of marriage guides the expression of the biological motive of sex and its related emotional motives of affection and the craving for companionship. On its success or failure depends the satisfaction of these basic human needs.

Why marriages fail or succeed

Marriage and family life, like any other career, involve the close cooperation of two or more persons. In marital adjustment, as in vocational adjustment, both selection and training are required. Two persons who are poorly suited to each other, and who are consequently unhappy together, might each find happiness in some other union. On the other hand, two seemingly incompatible persons can often learn to get along with each other. Marriage is partly finding the right person and partly *being* the right person. Many of the factors in marital adjustment have not yet been identified, but some of them are sufficiently well understood to merit a discussion of their tentative importance.

Does marriage in haste mean divorce at leisure? Courtship has long been regarded as of great importance in successful marriage. During this period men and women become acquainted and may learn to be unselfish in the interests of lasting harmony. What happens when this important period of getting acquainted is cut short? Several investigations have been made of this problem:

1 A psychiatric study was made of 100 married men and 100 married women, employing a standardized personal interview. It was found that marriages hastily contracted during the hectic war period of 1916 to 1920 were less happy for both the men and the women than those contracted before and after this period. The cycle is now repeating itself as a consequence of the second World War. (Hamilton and Macgowan[1])

2 The results of this study are in keeping with other statistics on marriage and divorce for the period following World War I, when courtship was curtailed. An analysis has been made of the United States census records on marriage and divorce for the years following the first World War (Hall[2]). This analysis showed that the marriages in the period immediately following the war were less stable than those of later periods.

The situation in the United States following World War II is the same as that following the first great war, only the trend is even more exaggerated. The chart opposite indicates divorce rates in the United States for the years immediately preceding and following the war.

Two hypotheses explain the early postwar marital instability. The first is that the spirit of the times was responsible, that the general unrest and uncertainty existing in wartime was conducive to mismatings and hence to divorce. The second hypothesis is that the shortness of the engagement period was responsible for the instability of the marriages. The balance of evidence is that both factors operate, although the former is definitely more important. (Terman et al.[3] and Burgess and Cottrell[4])

Number of divorces granted in 27 states—1940-1946

Number of divorces

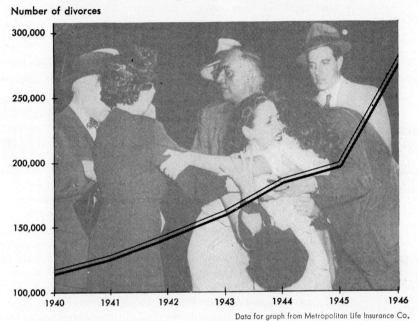

Data for graph from Metropolitan Life Insurance Co.

The importance of a cooperative attitude. Marriages sometimes appear to be wrecked by mere trivialities such as different preferences of room temperature, disagreement as to whether bridge is more important than a basketball game, failure to agree on who shall keep the household books, different views on credit buying, differences regarding the place of pets in the household. Most often, however, these disputes merely indicate a lack of a cooperative attitude between the two life-partners. Marriage, like friendship, is a give-and-take situation in which each participant must be willing to do part of the giving.

1 One study has found, for example, that marriages are happiest when the two partners are about equal in desire to dominate, or when the husband is slightly more dominant than the wife. When the wife is definitely dominant over the husband, trouble is almost inevitable in the spheres of social and sexual adjustment. This is also true to a lesser extent when the husband is extremely dominant over the wife. (Maslow[5])

Factors in Successful Marriage 581

2 Study has shown also that marital compatibility is accompanied by belief on the part of both the husband and wife that the other spouse is superior (Kelly[6]). Each party to a successful marriage tends to assume an attitude of humbleness in relation to the partner. This factor is more important for wives than for husbands. The wife in a successful marriage tends to look to the husband for leadership more often than the husband looks to the wife.

Early marriages vs. late ones. One factor commonly believed to affect the success of marriage is the age of the couple at marriage. Very young people are supposed to be too irresponsible and older people to be "too set in their ways." Is there any basis for this belief?

1 A comprehensive study was made of the personality factors influencing marital happiness in 100 happily married, 100 unhappily married, and 100 divorced couples. With regard to the time of life at which marriage is contracted, it was found that the degree of happiness in marriage showed *no correlation* with age of either party, provided the husband had reached his majority. Marriages contracted before the husband has reached the age of twenty-one are less likely to be successful. (Terman and Buttenweiser[7])

2 Investigators working with a group of 526 married couples roughly equivalent to the 792 couples in the study above came to the same conclusion—namely, that marriages contracted before the age of twenty are comparatively risky, but that age at marriage becomes less and less significant as a correlate of marital happiness beyond that point. (Burgess and Cottrell[8])

3 Another study came to somewhat different conclusions. It disclosed that men and women married before the age of twenty-four were happy in their marriages at the time of the investigation in about 30 per cent of the cases. However, men and women who married between the ages of thirty and thirty-four years were happy in nearly 65 per cent of the cases. (Hamilton and Macgowan[9])

Obviously, the problem of marrying age is a complex one requiring further study. It may be that the discrepancy between the findings of the studies above is due to differences in the selection of cases. The groups in the first study, for instance, were closer to the cross section of all people in the United States than were those of the third. The subjects in the third were, as a group, decidedly superior in socio-economic status, so that the greater unhappiness in early marriages might be the result of thwarted professional ambitions or economic difficulties arising from lower earning capacity at the younger age.

Age discrepancies. Popular opinion has it that marriages between persons divergent in age are destined to turn out badly, and that the groom should be just three years older than the bride. Study shows, however, that even if age differences between husband and wife are considerably greater than this, they bear no relationship to the degree of happiness. (Terman and Buttenweiser[10])

The desire for children. The desire for children by either spouse taken alone seems to have no relationship to happiness in marriage, but *agreement* between husband and wife in either wanting or not wanting children bears a positive relationship to marital happiness. (Terman and Buttenweiser[11])

Happily married parents. Happy marriages seem to run in families (Terman and Buttenweiser[12]). In selecting a mate it is well to inquire into the marital happiness of the prospective mother- and father-in-law. This relation between the emotional adjustment of different generations is already known to you. Happily married parents are most likely to give their child the kind of upbringing which will ensure his capacity to get along in the marriage relation when he becomes adult.

Parental attachments. Investigation has shown that members of the happily married group were *more* given to parental attachments than were members of the less happy group. Here is an important demonstration of the fact that a child must have an affectionate relationship with his parents in order to have a successful marital relationship later on. Otherwise, he will not be able to give and receive love in a normal way, and his whole attitude toward the opposite sex will be full of conflict. (It must be remembered, however, that this conclusion was based upon study of married people and did not take into account any individuals in the general population whose abnormally strong attachments to their parents prevented them from marrying at all.)

Emotional stability. As you might expect from your study of emotional development, a person's emotional stability is very important to the success of his marriage. The emotional stability of one marriage partner has been shown to have a significant correlation with the happiness of the other partner (Terman[13]). Another study of 1000 engaged couples found that freedom from neurotic tendency goes with happiness in engagement; most of the personality traits associated with happiness or unhappiness in marriage had the same relationship in engagement (Winch[14]). The mere act of marriage does not alter established personality patterns.

Agreement and disagreement. One promising development in the scientific analysis of marital problems was the discovery (Terman and Buttenweiser[15]) of certain questions in the study of marital relations on which agreement between the husband and wife was predictive of happiness and others on which disagreement was predictive of happiness. (These questions were taken from Bernreuter.[16]) Here are some questions on which *agreement* is predictive of happiness:

> Are you easily discouraged when the opinions of others differ from your own?
> Do you like to bear responsibilities alone?
> Do you usually try to avoid arguments?
> Are you willing to take a chance alone in a situation of doubtful outcome?
> Do you prefer a play to a dance?
> Do you prefer to be alone at times of emotional stress?
> Do you like to be with people a great deal?

Disagreement on the following questions is predictive of happiness:

> Have you ever crossed the street to avoid meeting some person?
> Do you usually prefer to do your own planning alone rather than with others?
> Do you find that telling others of your own personal good news is the greatest part of the enjoyment of it?
> Are you thrifty and careful about making loans?
> Do you ever rewrite your letters before mailing them?
> Can you usually understand a problem better by studying it out alone than by discussing it with others?

This pioneer study has served to open up a new and stimulating field of research. Why should disagreement sometimes make for happiness in marriage and sometimes for unhappiness? More work is needed before we can understand this relationship.

Education. While it is true that most men marry girls with less education than they, the more educated a man is, the greater his tendency to select a wife of above average education. The more educated a girl is, the more likely she is to marry a man of superior education.

> A study has been made of 330 students who were in the freshman class at the State College of Washington during the year 1936 and who have subsequently married. Of these college students, 71.5 per cent picked a bride or groom with training beyond high school; 27 per cent married persons with high-school training; and only 1.5 per cent chose a spouse who did not reach high school. (Landis and Day[17])

Here is a social pattern so sharply defined that to deviate from it by marrying a person greatly different in degree of education would appear to be jeopardizing the chances of happiness in marriage.

Effect of premarital sex relations on marital happiness. One study (Terman[18]) has indicated that in the case of both men and women, there seems to be a low correlation between nonvirginity at time of marriage and the happiness of the marriage. But since correlation is a general, average relationship found between two traits in a group as a whole (see p. 569), the study does not suggest that in individual cases there will be no direct relationship between any premarital sex relations of the partners and the success of the marriage.

Predicting compatibility in marriage

The investigations described above suggest that eventually tests of marital adjustment can be built to predict success in the career of marriage in much the same way that success in other activities is predicted. In fact, several studies have been made which indicate that it is now possible to predict happiness in marriage about as well as we can predict college grades from high-school grades.

1 A study of 300 newly engaged couples employed personal interviews and a variety of psychological tests, including the same items of personality, biographical, and social background. Of particular interest is the follow-up study made on 82 couples two years after marriage. It was found that marital happiness as predicted from test items answered before marriage correlated with marital happiness, as measured two years later, at .50 for husbands and .56 for wives. (Kelly[19])

2 A scale has been constructed from which marital adjustment can be predicted from adjustment during the period of engagement. An engagement-adjustment questionnaire was given to 505 couples who had known each other an average of 45 months; and they had an average engagement period of 13.2 months. They all lived in the Chicago metropolitan area and were practically all between the ages of 20 and 30. About three fourths of the men and two thirds of the women had reached the college level in education. After three years of marriage the couples were again asked to answer the questions. It was found that the correlation between the adjustment score received before marriage and the adjustment score received after three years of marriage was .43 for the men and .41 for the women. (Burgess and Wallin[20])

These studies all agree that some measure of prediction of adjustment in marriage is possible on the basis of information available on the individual prior to marriage. They also agree that happiness during the engagement period goes with happiness in marriage and therefore that couples who are unhappy in engagement should not look upon marriage as something to rush into as a cure for their conflicts; couples who are unhappy together before marriage are likely to be unhappy together after marriage.

In other words, the success of a marriage depends upon no single factor; it results from the interaction of the total personalities of the partners. It is interwoven with their success in other areas of life—in work, in community life, and especially in parenthood.

PROBLEMS OF PARENTHOOD

THE SOCIAL IMPORTANCE of family life can hardly be exaggerated. It is in the home that the basic attitudes and emotional patterns of future citizens are formed. This section will discuss some of the *Factors in Successful Parenthood* and some of the common *Patterns of Parent Behavior*. But first, as an illustration of the long-lasting effects that

THE FEELING OF REJECTION
(Stills from the film produced by the National Film Board of Canada; based on an actual case history.)

1. When Margaret was a child, her parents showered all their attention on her until another child was born. Then they transferred their love to the baby, ignoring Margaret and her attempts to regain their affection, or telling her not to "show off" when she tried to win their attention.

2. Margaret's mother discouraged her attempts at independent action and exploration. She was overprotective in keeping Margaret from dirt or imagined danger. Such overprotective-ness is often disguised as love: "Mummy doesn't want her darling to be hurt." Actually, it often covers up a deep hostility to the child which arises from the mother's personal history. (Some of the causes and effects of maternal overprotection were discussed on pp. 458-460.)

3. Because Margaret was not allowed to become self-reliant, she was too dependent on her parents for approval. A normal rebuff was felt as a crushing rejection. Here Margaret's efforts at self-expression, a painting, were met with discouragement instead of interest on the part of her father. And when she showed her mother the painting, she was again rebuffed, with "Don't bother me now. I'm too busy.' Already insecure, she withdrew.

parental handling can have on a child, stills from an outstanding film on parent-child relations are presented below. This film, *The Feeling of Rejection,* was produced by the National Film Board of Canada, for the Mental Health Division of the Department of National Health and Welfare. It is based on a real-life case of a girl, aged 23, who was referred to a psychiatrist because of headaches and fatigue for which thorough physical examination revealed no apparent cause.

4. Margaret early learned that if she expressed her own interests and impulses, she would be rejected by her parents, on whose approval she naturally depended. So she became a "model child" of obedience and submission. But underlying her "model child" demeanor and her continual self-effacement was a deep feeling of rejection. Accompanying it was an unconscious feeling of hostility against a world which she felt was repressing her.

5. As she grew up, the "lesson" of her childhood persisted. She lacked self-confidence and was unable to express herself before others. At the age of twelve, she tried out for a part in the school play which her best friend also wanted. For Margaret, competing for attention still meant losing love and approval, and she was unable to do her best. This conflict hampered all her school and social life.

6. As an adult, she was still painfully shy, and her need for affection and approval forced her to sacrifice her own needs. Here, she agrees to do some extra typing for a co-worker. But her underlying hostility ultimately manifested itself in physical symptoms for which she was referred to a psychiatrist. With his aid, she was able to discover the origin of her emotional patterns and thus put herself in a position to change them.

Problems of Parenthood 587

Factors in successful parenthood

To understand the prerequisites of successful parenthood, we must consider three basic motivating factors: (1) the emotional attitudes of the parents toward each other; (2) the emotional attitude of the parent toward the child; and (3) the parents' philosophy of child rearing.

The parents' emotional attitude toward each other. In the home of a happily married couple who have no children as yet, one typically finds two persons drawn together by a variety of shared satisfactions; yet they enjoy a certain degree of freedom and independence in areas where they find no common interest. When the first baby comes, the parents are thrust into a completely new situation which is frustrating in some respects to both parties. The household schedule is upset by the introduction of a completely dependent member. Marriage may have been one long honeymoon until the baby came, but now much must be sacrificed by both parents in favor of new responsibilities.

This frustrating situation may lead to rejection of the child by either or both parents. This rejection may be expressed by physical neglect of the infant—carelessness in feeding or preparation of diet, or lack of promptness in changing diapers—or it may be entirely in the social and emotional spheres.

Not infrequently the husband feels frustrated by the wife who spends too much time and energy in caring for the infant. The husband feels "left out" and may behave like a jilted lover, eventually feeling quite hostile to the wife. Another common reaction of husbands is to transfer the hostility to the child, causing the infant to be over-accepted by the mother. Still a third reaction consists of both parents' attempting to win the child by lavishing special attentions and gifts upon him.

In homes where the child comes after love between the parents has waned and the relationship is one of mutual boredom, one or both parents may attempt to enter into a courtship relationship with the child. The mother, for example, who cooingly calls her son "mother's little lover" may be compensating for her own starved love life. The father who jokingly refers to his daughter as "my girl friend" may be making a corresponding compensation.

Emotional attitudes of the parents toward the child. Family life is a complex of interactions among the members. The attitude of one member influences the attitudes of another, which may at times react upon a third. It is well known by social workers that children from homes broken by death or divorce are more likely to become delinquent than are children of parents living in harmony. Many other dynamic social relationships are known and will be described shortly.

Effect of parental philosophy of child care. Philosophies of child rearing vary in different cultures, just as individuals within the cultures vary. The numerous attitudes parents may take toward children have been described in Chapter 12. They range from the overprohibitive to overindulgent, and have, as you know, important effects on the child's emotional development.

Patterns of parent behavior

A recent report indicates that the complex interactions among children, parents, and social factors in the community can be analyzed into definite patterns (Baldwin, Kalhorn, and Breese[21]). This work deserves detailed review, and will be the subject of this section.

In this study, a trained investigator studied 125 children, visiting their homes and talking to the parents. She made summary reports of the home conditions in general and also filled in a quantitative rating scale of thirty items designed to cover the variables of parent behavior which are the most important aspects of the parent-child relationship. Following are samples of the items on the rating scale:

> "*Child-centeredness of the home:* The degree to which the organization of the household is built around the child's needs and welfare."
> "*Duration of contact with mother:* Hours per day of contact."
> "*Intensity of contact with mother:* The reactivity of the parent in contacts."
> "*Restrictiveness of regulations:* The restrictiveness and severity of the standards to which the child is expected to conform."
> "*Justification of disciplinary policy as presented to child:* The parent's tendency to explain reasons for requirements and penalties. The logic of the policy from the child's point of view."
> "*Democracy of regulation and enforcement policy:* The extent to which the child shares in the formulation of regulations."
> "*Clarity of policy of regulations and enforcement:* The clearness with which the standards of child conduct are manifested to the child."
> "*Effectiveness of policy:* The degree to which the child's behavior meets the standards set by the parent. In the eyes of parent, how well behaved is the child."
> "*Disciplinary friction:* The amount of overt parent-child conflict over questions of policy."
> "*General babying:* The parent's tendency to help child over difficulties even when the child is perfectly capable."
> "*General protectiveness:* The parent's tendency to keep the child sheltered from threats and hazards of all sorts."

"*Direction of criticism:* The extent to which the criticism is approving or disapproving. A high rating indicates approval."

"*Readiness of explanation:* The parent's tendency to satisfy the child's intellectual curiosity. His response to 'why?' and 'how?'"

"*Solicitousness for child's welfare:* Tendency to be overconcerned and anxious for the child's well-being."

"*Acceptance of the child:* Acceptance of the child as an intimate and inseparable partner, sharing in all areas of parent's life."

"*Understanding:* The extent of the parent's insight into the child's wishes, needs, point of view, level of development, etc."

"*Affectionateness:* The parent's expression of affection to the child."

"*Rapport:* The closeness of the psychological relationship between parent and child."

These rating scales were then subjected to a statistical analysis which revealed three main qualities or traits of parent behavior, plus some others of lesser importance. The three main qualities or patterns are:

Degree to which the home is democratic or autocratic:
"Justification of policy
Democracy of policy
Noncoerciveness of suggestions
Readiness of explanation
Direction of criticism (approval)
Clarity of policy
Understanding of the child
Nonrestrictiveness of regulations"

Degree of acceptance or rejectance of the child:
"Acceptance of the child
Rapport with the child
Affectionateness toward child
Direction of criticism (approval)
Effectiveness of policy
Child-centeredness of the home
Nondisciplinary friction"

Degree of indulgence or nonchalance in care of the child:
"General protectiveness
General babying
Child-centeredness of home
Acceptance of child
Solicitousness for welfare
Duration of contact with mother
Intensity of contact with mother"

In this study it was found that the majority of homes might be classified in the following groupings:

1 Homes that were autocratic, rejectant, and nonchalant.

2 Homes that were autocratic and rejectant, and not nonchalant.

3 Homes that were autocratic, not rejectant, not nonchalant.

4 Homes that were acceptant and democratic, not indulgent.

5 Homes that were acceptant and indulgent, but neither markedly democratic nor autocratic.

6 Homes that were acceptant, indulgent, and democratic.

7 Homes that were indulgent, but not otherwise distinctive.

From this listing, it may be seen that the first three different types of home could be recognized as autocratic. Such homes tended also to be rejectant and sometimes also nonchalant (i.e., careless or casual) in their treatment of the children, although the third type of home was distinctive only in its autocratic tendencies. The next three common types of home could be recognized as acceptant in some clear-cut degree, whether or not also characterized by acceptant and/or indulgent tendencies. The seventh type of home was especially distinctive for its strong tendency to treat the children indulgently. The following case histories illustrate three of these patterns of parent behavior, and the effect on the child.

1 Betty McKane's home is classified as *rejectant, autocratic,* and *not nonchalant,* or actively rejective. Her mother is "fundamentally a selfish, ego-centric woman who evaluates events and people in terms of the extent to which they contribute to her own satisfaction . . . She suffers no pangs of conscience in modifying her home, her children's behavior or her husband's mode of life to suit her own convenience and tastes. . . . For Mrs. McKane the model child is the quiet, unobtrusive one. She attains this goal in two ways—by imposing on the child rigid standards of behavior which become habitual, and by meeting immediate situations with arbitrary commands. . . . She seems to feel an active resentment and hostility toward the child. Second only to the severity of the atmosphere is the inconsistency of policy. 'Nonsense' that may draw down severe punishment one time may on another occasion be laughed off. . . .

"Betty has steadily become withdrawn, shy, and stubbornly resistant, in a passive fashion, to adult authority. At school . . . in any situation which demands a response she retreats into an almost inaudible, 'I don't know.' "

2 Diana Mitchell's home is *autocratic, not rejectant,* and not *nonchalant,* and is fairly representative of the "autocratic" farm families. Mr. Mitchell believes "that today's children think they can 'tell their parents off' and that no child of his is ever going to tell *him* what to do . . .

"The Mitchells accept their children and to some degree enjoy them as personalities. When they are exerting themselves as parents . . . , nagging criticism is used exclusively to express parental opinion, for the Mitchells feel that praise for conformity is unwarranted and unnecessary . . . [W]hen no issue is at stake Mrs. Mitchell abandons her parental pedestal and is genuinely friendly with the children, companionable and interested in their activities . . . Though the children recognize and enjoy these periods of intimacy, they are necessarily more keenly aware of the caustic disapproval they so often encounter.

"Mrs. Mitchell's lack of insight and perception, combined with her insistence on parental domination, often leads to a highly emotional reaction . . . [T]he home is rather chaotic, with the children usually testing the limits of the parents' endurance before giving in and obeying . . . [The] blindly emotional reaction, on the parents' part, to the children's behavior and the lack of clarity or consistency, make the children in turn uncertain as to just what they must do to secure approval, frustrates them, and contributes to their rebellion."

3 Leonard Rampion's home is classified as *democratic, acceptant,* and *not indulgent.* It "represents a rather happy combination of those factors judged by the authors to be productive of a good environment for a child . . . The maturity Mrs. Rampion exhibits in her personal life and in her general attitudes is also displayed . . . in her behavior toward the children. Respecting them as individuals, she makes a conscious and conscientious effort to maintain an emotional distance, a detachment giving objectivity to her appraisal of them . . .

"Family council is traditional . . . In spite of the formality of democratic government and in spite of the emotional distance which the Rampions maintain, the home atmosphere is not bleak or forbidding. The warm tone so evident in all the family's relationships characterizes their attitudes toward one another. Without a great deal of fondling or other overt symbols of affection the parents convey to the children their deep devotion."

Another author, after reviewing the literature, thinks that two main factors are at work in parent-behavior: *acceptance-rejection,* and *dominance-submission* (Symonds[22]). These factors may be illustrated as in the figure following, where the X'—X line denotes the acceptance-rejection continuum and the Y'—Y line denotes the dominance-submis-

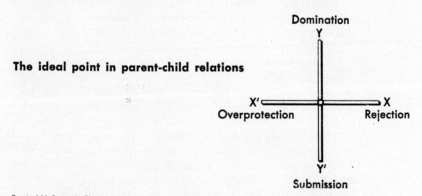

The ideal point in parent-child relations

Percival M. Symonds, *The Psychology of Parent-Child Relationships,* © D. Appleton-Century Company, 1939, p. 20.

sion continuum. "The point of . . . [intersection] represents the ideal parent-child relationship. Such a parent neither overaccepts nor rejects his children—he gives affection moderately. He provides the necessary environment and care for a child's growth and protection, but does not so care for and coddle him as to prevent his maturing emotionally and gaining independence."

THE INDIVIDUAL AND ILLEGAL BEHAVIOR

FAILURE IN HUMAN RELATIONS can occur in purely personal situations —with friends, marriage partner, children—or it can involve a conflict with society and the law. This section will analyze some of the factors in crime and delinquency.

Crime is defined as behavior on the part of an adult which is specifically prohibited by the criminal code. *Delinquency* is defined as behavior of minors which, were it found in an adult, would be criminal. Criminal behavior is usually a departure from the standard of behavior which is accepted by the majority of the group in which the individual is living. Sometimes, however, criminal behavior does not involve departure from social standards, as in communities where violation of the Prohibition Act was socially accepted, or in big cities where gambling, though illegal, is commonly engaged in.

Why an individual becomes a delinquent or a criminal

People behave in ways that give them the greatest apparent rewards. If the conditions surrounding the growing child reward delinquent behavior and frustrate legally acceptable behavior, delinquency will result. The child who has once become delinquent gradually loses the possibility of earning the rewards open to the well-behaved child. He associates with other delinquents, he accepts their heroes and values, and as time goes on, it becomes increasingly difficult to inspire him to seek the approval of honest people. He now belongs to a small group within society whose ideals and laws are different from those of society as a whole. His loyalty is to this smaller group, and his first interest is in its approval of him. A well-known gangster once remarked that he would rather hire grown-up men to do his illegal errands than employ boys in their teens. The boys were too bloodthirsty, for they were out to make reputations for themselves and would not hesitate to use rough tactics, even murder, if the occasion seemed to demand it.

What are some of the many factors that cause individuals to adopt criminal behavior?

The factor of poverty. It is probable that much delinquency has its roots in the frustrations that occur in the lower and middle income-groups. Youth may be driven to illegal behavior in the search for the necessities of life, as well as some of the comforts and enjoyments.

1 Over twenty years ago a British psychologist made an elaborate and rigorously scientific study of the factors associated with, and presumably responsible for, delinquency of the children of England. He compared the economic background of a group of delinquents with the economic background of a group of nondelinquents and found that 19 per cent of his delinquent group came from poverty-stricken homes as against 8 per cent of nondelinquents (Burt[23]).

2 These findings in England have been verified many times since for various communities. More recently, for example, a comparison was made between the occupational distribution of parents of 761 delinquents in Passaic, New Jersey, and the distribution of all male and female workers in the community in 1940. This comparison is shown in the chart below:

Occupations of parents of delinquents, compared with occupations of total male population: Passaic, N. J.

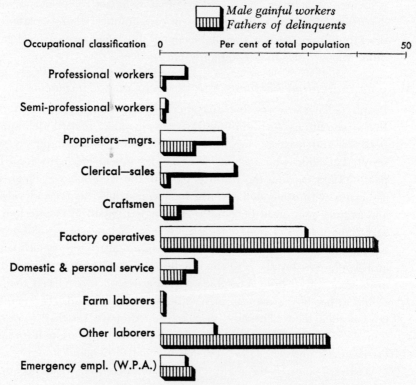

Data taken from W. C. Kvaraceus, *Juvenile Delinquency in the School,* World Book Co., 1945, p. 89.

In the delinquent sample, significantly fewer parents were in the professions or working as proprietors, clerks, sales personnel, craftsmen, and in nondomestic service. Significantly larger proportions were factory operatives, laborers, and domestic servants. (Kvaraceus[24])

The influence of transitional areas. A sociological study has clearly shown that delinquency is highest in areas which are in a process of transition from residence to business and industry.

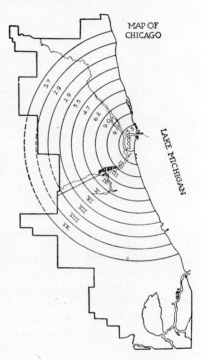

This map of Chicago clearly shows how the rate of delinquency varies with the section of the city. Note that central Zones I, II, and III, which are transitional areas, have the highest delinquency rates, and that the rates grow progressively less toward the residential suburbs. The data on this map was obtained from a study of 8141 male juvenile delinquents making court appearances in Chicago, 1919-1923. The delinquency rate is the ratio of the number of delinquents appearing in the Juvenile Court during the seven-year period to the total population aged ten to sixteen for 1920. (From Clifford R. Shaw, Delinquency Areas, University of Chicago Press, 1929, p. 92.)

The high-delinquency transitional areas are characterized by physical deterioration and poverty. The population is decreasing, and there is a breaking up of neighborhood culture and organization. Consequently, the group code of behavior is not well established and there is less social pressure on the individual to conform to legal standards. This study (Shaw[25]) has been summarized as follows:

"In a careful survey of juvenile delinquency in Chicago among boys from 11 to 17 years of age, it was found that the city could be divided into a number of zones or delinquency areas, starting with the central or Loop district and progressing to the residential suburbs. In all, seven such zones were mapped at one-mile intervals from the center. It was found that there was a progressive decrease in the proportion of delinquency from the center to the periphery of the city. The study extended over a considerable period of years during which the population of the central area changed completely without affecting this relationship. There were, for example, successive waves of migration from various European countries, as well as of Mexicans and Negroes, but the delinquency rate remained substantially the same. This has usually been interpreted as meaning that the social and economic setting, rather than the nature of the people concerned, has a definitive influence upon the delinquency rate." (Klineberg[26])

The factor of family breakdown. A thorough study of factors making for delinquency in the state of Connecticut revealed that delinquency is essentially a symptom of family breakdown. When the family disintegrates, the child is deprived of (1) affection, (2) feelings of security, (3) social opportunities, and (4) physical necessities (Robinson[27]). As a result, he is not emotionally able to accept the social prohibitions on theft and sexual behavior. The case of Terry is illustrative:

"Terry was the youngest in that city jail, not yet seventeen. He was about to be released . . . he stood in the corridor, dressed in blue denim uniform and heavy black shoes. His eyes were sullen, his manner defensively arrogant. Jail was no bad place to be, he said. He had been given unusual privileges, and what the hell! Then his voice broke. He didn't know about going home now that he was to be released; maybe he'd better go off across country some place. His father had never come to see him, had not spoken to him in court the day he had been convicted. What would the neighbors say when he did go back? His family was already ashamed of him. Maybe, after all, he'd come back here; 'lots of them do.' The worker asked why. 'Because no one cares about them; no one really gives a darn; that's why they get in here in the first place.'

"Nine months had elapsed since Terry's conviction. He and Vic had gone out one night during the summer vacation and held up a man. It was only a toy pistol that they used, but the man had been frightened and turned over all his money and a gold watch. Vic had given the watch to Terry, who had put it into the bureau drawer, where the police found it when they arrived.

"His mother had been shocked and heartbroken. He was her baby and had always been such a good boy, had gone to church every Sunday and done exactly as he was told. His father was a chronic drunkard, a good-for-nothing. Neither the wife nor the daughters talked with the father; aside from placing his food upon the table, when they had eaten, they disregarded his presence. The girls, all of whom were much older than Terry, managed the house and in such a way that he, the youngest and the only boy, felt he too had no real place in it. But he obeyed them as he did his mother.

"His sisters and his mother as well despised and scorned the father and were always afraid that Terry, like him, 'would turn out to be good for nothing.' His mother had not welcomed his birth. In order to overcome his 'weakness' during infancy she had placed him on the porch even in zero weather. Later, she worried constantly about his poor health, and prevented his taking part in activities with the other boys, because she 'just knew Terry was delicate,' although the doctor said he was not.

"Dubbed a sissy throughout childhood, Terry was unable to make satisfactory contacts with the other fellows in his group. But a gang of boys from the other side of the tracks, most of them with reform-school records, found that Terry was very amenable, afraid not to follow instructions on peril of being thrown out of the gang. . . ." (Zachry[28])

In the case of this boy we can see the effects of a disorganized family with its consequent atmosphere of emotional tension. Unwanted and unprotected, Terry was quite literally thrust out in the cold as a baby as well as being made to conform too rigorously and at too early a time to the "Thou shalt's" and the "Thou shalt not's" of his mother and sisters. Insecure and looking for the shelter of some group that wanted him, he found a more permissive social environment in a delinquent gang. Here, the factor of social approval of a small group operated in the formation of attitudes, as described in Chapter 4.

Although lack of family protection was found in the Connecticut study to be at the root of most juvenile delinquency, in a very few cases the children were being overprotected in their upbringing. These psychological processes of deprivation and overprotection "become the connecting links between the pathological conditions in the family and the resulting behavior of the children. Through them, the unhealthy family environment is making its destructive impact on the children and impelling them toward antisocial behavior." (Robinson[29])

Homes may be "broken" not only through emotional tensions between the parents and through poor parent-child relations but also by divorce, separation, or death. These latter conditions are objective and can be rendered into statistics.

A British study found that defective marital relations of parents were twice as frequent among the delinquents as among nondelinquent groups of children (Burt[30]). This result was strikingly confirmed for a group of American children: in comparing 1649 delinquent boys with a much larger group of public-school children, it was found that "broken homes" were over twice as frequent among the delinquents as among the nondelinquents (Slawson[31]).

The psychological effects that "broken homes" have on children—whether the homes are broken through emotional tension, death, or divorce—are all too apparent in many case studies of juvenile delinquents.

The factor of emotional maladjustment. Numerous studies indicate that much delinquency has its roots in emotional factors unrelated to poverty or physical surroundings. For example:

> One clinical study was made of 105 delinquent children brought into the child-guidance clinics of Boston, New Haven, and Detroit during a four-year period. Each delinquent child was compared with one of his own nondelinquent siblings, so that socio-economic environment could be held fairly constant. The results showed that serious emotional difficulties were experienced by about 91 per cent of the delinquents but by only 13 per cent of the nondelinquents; and that within this category lay the greatest differences between the scores of the two groups. The psychological stresses most clearly evidenced by the delinquents were rejection, insecurity, guilt, inferiority, jealousy, and internal mental conflict. (Healy and Bronner[32])

Such statistical findings serve to generalize the principles that can be discovered in such single tragic cases as that of Terry, and to emphasize even further the importance of healthy parent-child relations.

Do the "movies" encourage delinquency? The results of studies aimed at discovering the relationship between motion-picture attendance and delinquency in children are conflicting. One study has concluded that movies are a factor in initiating 25 per cent of the girls studied into their careers of delinquency and crime and 10 per cent of the boys (Blumer and Hauser[33]). Another study has concluded that motion pictures are a factor in only 1 per cent of the cases of delinquency (Healy and Bronner[34]). The reason for this apparent discrepancy is that these two studies are discussing two different kinds of causal factors. The first study says that delinquent children have certain deep emotional needs which they can satisfy by identifying themselves with movie characters and acting out in reality the actions they have seen on the screen, and that since movies provide "ideals" for children to follow, they do—in 25 per cent of the cases studied—act as a factor precipitating the child toward illegal behavior. The second study is seeking to explain the basic emotional needs that drive the child to adopt illegal behavior, and therefore considers the movies as much less important than many other emotional experiences in the environment, and as operating strongly in only 1 per cent of the cases. This problem requires careful definition and research.

Intelligence as a factor in crime and delinquency. There is a widespread belief among laymen that crime and low intelligence go together. Has this belief any support from psychologists? Let us examine the evidence with regard to both juvenile delinquents and adult criminals.

One psychologist has brought together the estimates of a number of authorities as to the proportion of delinquent children who are feeble-minded (Pintner[35]). The figures run from 7 to 93 per cent. This lack of agreement among experts has two major explanations. First, in certain communities the children of the better families never get before the juvenile court, no matter what their crime. The parents are well-known and influential men and are trusted to handle their delinquent children in their own way. Under such circumstances only the children of poor and uninfluential families, who tend to score lower on intelligence tests, would get before the court. The second factor accounting for the varying estimates of the proportion of delinquents found to be feeble-minded is efficiency of law enforcement. Where enforcement is strict and fair, the bright and the dull alike will be apprehended. Where enforcement is lax, the brighter children will "get away with it" more often.

In looking over the literature, one comes to the conclusion that low intelligence is just one factor in delinquency and by no means the most important one. This conclusion is based on several studies, a few of which are reported here:

1 Data have been gathered on delinquent soldiers during World War I who were confined in army guardhouses or in Fort Leavenworth, a federal prison. The Leavenworth prisoners were men convicted of serious crimes, which supposedly require high intelligence, whereas the minor delinquents were placed in the guardhouse. The Fort Leavenworth prisoners were slightly superior to the average of the army draft, and the men sentenced to the guardhouse were slightly inferior. (Yerkes[36])

This study may imply that intelligence plays an important role in escaping apprehension and conviction. The men of lower intelligence are probably more frequently caught than those who are brighter, when apprehension depends on routine methods. In the case of the more serious crimes, where greater effort is expended in detecting the guilty persons, the brighter men as well as the duller are brought to justice. There is the alternative, of course, that brighter men commit more serious offenses than do the duller ones, who might be unable to carry out some of the serious crimes which require careful, intelligent planning.

2 A very comprehensive study has been made of the intelligence of convicted criminals in civilian life. The average intelligence of convicts of five states was compared with that of the white draft of World War I for the same states. The results indicate that there is essentially no difference in intelligence between the convicts and the draft groups. The average convict was found to be no less intelligent than the average man. (Murchison[37])

3 A later study based on a group of nearly 1000 Minnesota state prison convicts found them to be much lower than the average of the state in intelligence level (Kuhlmann[38]).

Obviously the question of the relationship between intelligence and criminality is influenced by selective factors which operate differently in the various convict populations. At the most, intelligence can be considered as only one of a large number of factors influencing criminality. Such factors as poverty, broken homes, bad companions, and frustration seem far more important than low intelligence. This is a fortunate fact from the social point of view, for these factors can be counteracted within the life of the individual by measures aimed at improving the environment, such as better schools, supervised play, or improved economic conditions in the home. Were native intelligence the fundamental factor in delinquency, the outlook would be much less hopeful. Some of the measures for improving the environment will be discussed in the following section.

The psychological basis of crime prevention

Criminologists are coming more and more to the belief that a habitual criminal adult is almost hopeless of rehabilitation. Students of delinquency and crime are agreed that prevention should start early if it is to be effective. The determination of the causes of delinquent and nonconforming behavior is merely the first step. The next step consists in manipulating the conditions of the lives of the delinquent children in such a way as to steer their development into socially acceptable channels. The two most important means of crime prevention lie in community action and judicial action.

BAD LIVING CONDITIONS . . .

Community action. Many social institutions can be used to check delinquency in its early stages. Such organizations as the Girl Scouts, the Boy Scouts, the Y.M.C.A., and various church organizations can direct the gang spirit into useful activities. They do much to prevent children from becoming delinquent, and juvenile delinquency from developing into outright criminality. The

◥UNWHOLESOME PLAY ENVIRONMENT . . .

ADULT INDIFFERENCE TO JUVENILE PROBLEMS

. . . are all important factors in the development of juvenile delinquency. In crowded poverty-stricken areas of the city where these conditions are marked, the all-too-common effects on the youth of the neighborhood are scenes of active delinquency . . .

tendency of teen-age boys and girls to form gangs results in evil consequences only when that gang activity is not intelligently directed.

Slum-clearance projects typically provide for playgrounds with adequate equipment and competent supervision. Children who find interesting play in the open are not likely to resort to hideaways in vacant tenement buildings and abandoned stores or factories, as the slum-dwelling children are forced to do.

Organized social work is doing a great deal to prevent delinquency by providing experts who can call at homes to determine the causes of the first symptomatic outbreak. Frequently study of the home situation leads to recommendations and adjustments which will save a child from the reformatory.

An outstanding example of how social-psychological studies may be translated into effective action is the Chicago Area Project. This Project was organized years ago by social scientists at the Illinois State Department of Public Welfare (including Clifford R. Shaw, some of whose research work was described on page 595). It operates on the basic assumption that the local neighborhood can be organized to deal effectively with its own problems. The social scientists who founded the Project did not simply send in social workers and group leaders foreign to the community. They stimulated the local residents to become aware of the problem of delinquency and to take collective action. They guided the local leaders and local organizations in establishing such activities as camping, baseball, football, basketball, boxing, movies, pingpong, pool and billiards, small table games, music, dramatics, handicrafts, printing, newspaper work, and club discussions.

The activities of the Chicago Area Project have been concentrated in those areas where delinquency rates have been very high. The results have been most gratifying. Juvenile delinquency rates have shown a marked decline in at least one area. But most important is the example set by the Project—to attack delinquency as a community problem.

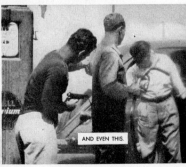

ADEQUATE HOUSING...   RECREATIONAL FACILITIES...   AND COMMUNITY ACTION..

...all these are necessary to counteract juvenile delinquency. Although outside financial aid is necessary for housing and recreation, much can be accomplished through the determined efforts of parents and community leaders to provide new aims and new facilities for youth activity. The picture at right above was taken at a Parent-Teacher Association meeting called by parents of a Chicago school for discussion of a delinquency problem. Community interest in combating delinquency is strong in the lower-income areas which establish community programs in connection with the Chicago Area Project. An indication of the parents' deep concern is that members of one community program allowed their children to appear in the photographs on pages 600-601, which were specially posed to increase public awareness of the causes—and cures—of juvenile delinquency.

Judicial action. In all too many cases, the treatment of juvenile delinquency is delayed until judicial action is necessary. But even then, the hope of rehabilitation is not lost, for the attitude of the juvenile courts toward delinquency is changing. The modern judge of the juvenile court tries to become an expert in human adjustment. He attempts to give guidance to the erring youth and looks upon punishment as the last resort, and he charges society with a failure each time a child is sent to the reformatory.

In the execution of his duties, a juvenile court authority tries to judge the criminal as well as the crime. He tries to impose, within the limits of the law, such treatment of the individual as will, in his opinion, be most effective in preventing a recurrence of the delinquent behavior. In doing so, he is frequently handicapped by the essentially archaic nature of our laws. Compared with the technology of this country, the law is bogged down by precedent and antiquated concepts which cannot meet the many new problems that changing times have brought to the courts.

Some advances have been made and others are in the offing. The practice of probation and parole, the differentiation between juvenile delinquents and adult criminals, the emphasis on rehabilitation rather

PROBLEMS IN HUMAN RELATIONS   602

than punishment are all to the good. However, many serious obstacles still exist in the form of outworn laws and inadequate facilities.

Some recent recommendations for dealing with delinquents have been made by a committee of the New York School of Social Work. These recommendations are based on modern knowledge of the social and psychological roots of delinquency (cf. pp. 593-600). They have been summarized (Klein[39]) in the form of nine specific proposals:

Proposal 1. Separate the judicial and the penal functions. The power of the courts should be limited to the determination of guilt or innocence. Then the delinquent should be handed over to psychologists and social-welfare workers who are trained to handle his custody, education, rehabilitation, and eventual release.

Proposal 2. Provide adequate personnel. Social workers, psychologists, psychiatrists, vocational-guidance experts are needed to change the lawbreaker into a law-abider.

Proposal 3. Refrain from treating delinquent children as lawbreakers. The indications are that rehabilitation is much more effective than punishment in curing delinquent children.

Two separate studies have indicated that when juvenile delinquents are institutionalized for punishment, their behavior when they are released does not indicate that they have been "cured" of aggressiveness (Healy and Bronner[40] and Bowler and Bloodgood[41]). Actually, the evidence seems to indicate that as a result of commitment to a reform school there is an increase in delinquent behavior and an intensification of the personal problems in which it is rooted. This evidence is in line with still another study demonstrating that severe punishments tend to increase rather than decrease the crime rate (Wilson[42]).

Proposal 4. Give public authority exclusive control. This proposal urges that the practice of assigning adjudged delinquents to private associations or denominational bodies through court commitment should cease.

Proposal 5. Let the system set up embrace all parts of the country and all kinds of people. Delinquency is not limited by place, color, or creed nor can its treatment be thus restricted.

Proposal 6. Reform practices within correctional institutions. Prisons and reformatories are still too often places where adults and children are broken in mind and body by cruelty, neglect, and plain ignorance on the part of inadequately trained and underpaid personnel.

Proposal 7. Improve the caliber of judicial practice. Most juvenile delinquents first appear in the lower courts and are handled there. Wisdom and experience in human relations are greatly needed by the judges of the lower courts, but are frequently lacking because of poor pay, low prestige, and generally poor organization.

Proposal 8. Improve police practice. A police officer, if properly selected, trained, and assigned, can become respected by the parents and children of the community. He will detect and prevent some crime and delinquency in the incubation stage.

Proposal 9. Dissolve artificial classifications of criminals. They should be replaced by a legally established concept of "persons having demonstrated behavior injurious to the social order" and needing psychological and social rehabilitation.

All these proposals are based on a recognition of the social and emotional foundations of illegal behavior. Juvenile delinquents and adult criminals are not born but made—"made" by their childhood experiences in the home and in the community.

PROBLEMS OF THE GROUP

H UMAN RELATIONSHIPS are not confined to roles as friend, marriage partner, parent, and member of a legally ruled society. People live and work in groups of all kinds—in politics, business, and education. The analysis of group relations is one of modern psychology's most important tasks. In this final section of the chapter, we shall consider two important problems of group living: *Leadership* and *Competition vs. Cooperation.*

Leadership

The importance of wise leadership in harmonious human relations is apparent in any kind of group activity, since leaders are needed in any group and inevitably emerge therefrom. Possibly the most striking example of the psychology of leadership is in politics, although in business, in academic life, and in sports the same principles hold true.

Psychological effects of different systems of leadership. There are certain fundamental differences between democratic and authoritarian leadership, although many leadership qualities are common to both types. Briefly stated, the most important differences are that the democratic leader uses persuasion rather than force, education rather than propaganda, and conference rather than command. Each type of leadership has important psychological effects on the members of the group. For instance, one striking study has shown that patterns of aggressive behavior differ under different "social climates" (Lewin, Lippitt, and White[43]). This study has been summarized as follows:

"One of the most striking investigations . . . studied the patterns of aggressive behavior in experimentally created 'social climates.' These climates were of three main types, authoritarian, democratic, and laissez-faire. Clubs were formed of boys who, to begin with, were carefully equated, and who were then placed in one of the three experimental groups. In the authoritarian group, for example, all policies were determined by the leader, techniques and activities being indicated by him one at a time so that future steps were always uncertain, and the 'dictator' remained aloof from active group participation except when demonstrating to the others what they were to do. In the democratic group all policies were determined by group discussion, the members were free to work with whomever they chose, and the division of tasks was determined by the group. In the third situation there was complete freedom for group or individual decision, and the leader supplied the information, but took no other part in group discussions. The factor of personality differences in the boys was controlled by having each group pass through autocracy and then democracy, or vice versa. The factor of the leader's personality was controlled by having each of four leaders play the role of autocrat and the role of democratic leader at least once.

"In one experiment hostility was thirty times as frequent in the autocratic as in the democratic group. Much of the aggression was directed toward two successive scapegoats within the group; none was directed against the autocrat. In a second experiment, the boys in the autocratic groups showed less aggressiveness, but their behavior was of an apathetic type . . . due to the repressive influence of the autocrat. Among the boys in these groups there were outbursts of aggression on the days of transition to a freer atmosphere, and a sharp rise of aggression when the autocrat left the room. Nineteen out of twenty boys liked their democratic leader better than their autocratic leader, and seven out of ten also preferred their laissez-faire leader.

"This study is of great interest because it submits to experimentally controlled procedures many of the hypotheses which have been suggested as to the effect of various political structures on individual personality. Students of politics, for example, have observed that fascist dictatorships are frequently characterized by the appearance of a scapegoat upon whom all ills may be blamed. . . . This study has revealed that even in an artificial dictatorship of this type such a scapegoat mechanism may easily be elicited. Although value judgments are not usually regarded as within the province of a social psychologist, the apparent superiority of the democratic over the autocratic form of society may be mentioned as one of the important findings of this study." (Summarized by Klineberg[44])

The experimental situation for this study of leadership in three different "societies" is pictured on pages 606-607.

Policy formation in the three experimental social climates describe on page 605.

In the authoritarian climate, the plans and decisions are made by the leader, who directs the activities of the group along the lines of his policy. The group is relegated to the role of carrying out the policies, and does not formulate or correct them.

In the democratic climate, the leader initiates informal planning discussions and helps the group reach a satisfactory conclusion by leading a process of orderly thinking and decision.

In the laissez-faire climate, the leader stands by inactively. He does not participate in information giving and decision processes except when asked by the group.

Leaders can be trained. One interesting study has shown the efficiency of certain methods for rapid retraining of leaders in a particular field.

Six mediocre leaders on a WPA project for children were chosen and equated on the basis of age, sex, length of time on WPA, length of time on present WPA project, rating of technical skill, rating of leadership ability, and on relevant facts in their life history. These six subjects were divided into two groups: the experimental group, which was trained, and the control group, which was not trained. The training was in the form of group discussions in which the experimenter was the group leader whose conduct was illustrative of the type of leadership the trainees were learning to use. In the training meetings the following points may be noted:

1 The underlying attitudes and general principles of recreational group work were discussed in preference to mere consideration of what to do in a particular situation. As a result the technique which the leaders actually used later in working with groups

Productive activity in the three social climates described on page 605. *In the authoritarian situation, the leader supervision is detailed and continuous. The leader maintains a separate status as a critic and demonstrator, instituting activities of the group rather than participating in them.*

In the democratic situation, the leader is "one of the group," working along as an interdependent member, although with special guidance responsibilities at certain times.

In the laissez-faire situation, the leader is purely an available resource person and exerts no influence toward coordinating successful production. Group interest lags and individual lines of action develop. The psychological effects of these different leadership situations were described on page 605.
(Courtesy Dr. R. Lippitt, Dr. R. White.)

never became a "set of tricks" but remained flexible and easily modifiable to meet each new and specific situation.

2 The qualities of a leader were listed and were defined in relation to how a particular leader in the group stood up under the check list. Along with the clarification of concepts, there was an elaboration of the leader's possibilities for action.

3 The group made a concrete formulation of the objectives of their work. This restructuring of goals led to a re-evaluation of the techniques by which various objectives of group work could be attained.

4 Various procedures contributed toward the building of suitable techniques—observing the trainer leading a group, observing and evaluating each other, film records of experiments in various kinds of leadership, and being children themselves while the trainer used various methods.

The results of the experiment are useful from two points of view in discussing morale. The first of these is the effect of the training on the morale of the retrained leaders. At the start, the leaders did n͏e feel personally very deeply involved in the work and they worked onl͏y as well as necessary to keep the job. Toward the end of the experimen͏t these same leaders showed absorbing interest in their work, went t͏o considerable effort and expense to help their groups get materials, an͏d willingly committed themselves to long-range plans with their clubs͏.

The second result of the training was to increase the morale o͏f the children's groups. The children's groups took on a constant mem͏bership, whereas before the groups were ever-changing. Also, the͏ groups led by the trainees showed great initiative in reaching new͏ levels of productivity. Some of the changes in methods of leadershi͏p in the trained leaders are shown in the following table.

TRAINED LEADER	BEFORE TRAINING Use of authoritarian methods	AFTER TRAINING Use of authoritarian methods	Use of democratic, initiative, stimulating methods
A	77%	4%	73%
C	77%	7%	73%
E	51%	11%	89%

The untrained leaders continued using methods like those of leaders A, C, and E before training. (Bavelas[45])

This experiment clearly shows that the so-called "born leader" is probably *not* born but made. This fact is of course encouraging, for it indicates that education can produce the leaders a democracy needs.

Competition vs. cooperation

In the long history of people's trying to get along with each other, two theories have been evolved. One holds that individuals in a group will naturally compete and should be encouraged to do so—that, spurred on by competition, children will learn more, business will thrive, and nations will become great. The other theory holds that competition is too often destructive, that only as we cooperate can we build permanently. Clearly, two problems are involved here: (1) Is there an instinct of competition? and (2) What are the effects of competition and cooperation? Only as we answer these questions can we help settle the controversy and advise how best to plan conditions so that the most and best work will be done with the best results for the character and personality of the individuals involved.

Is there an instinct of competition? The question as to whether there is a competitive instinct has a profound social significance because it has a direct bearing on our tradition of individualism. People who have been conditioned in an essentially competitive society such as ours in the United States, and for that matter in most of the world today, do respond to the challenge of beating the other fellow. It is an unfortunate fact that in the United States children are often "pushed" by parents or teachers who make them feel that they must excel other children. The competitive race continues all through life; it is deeply ingrained in the American psychological way. Success is king. The American is often made to feel that he must succeed above all others: must be first in school, captain of the baseball team, a member of the "best" fraternity, the boy friend of the most popular girl on campus, the owner of the biggest house and newest car on the block. These goals are of course impossible for everyone to reach. Most people are "average" people, though they are better in some things than others.

Is such competitiveness a necessary characteristic of human nature? There are human societies—that of the Samoan Islands, for example— where life is largely noncompetitive. People work and store the products of their labor in a common warehouse from which all can draw according to their needs (Mead[46]). Anthropologists report that such people are fully as happy as their more individualistic fellow men in other parts of the world. Psychologists today feel that all-out competitiveness is not an inescapable psychological trait—that we can teach children to compete or to cooperate or to achieve a balance between the two (Vaughn and Diserens[47]). The prevailing opinion is that competition is *not* instinctive. And in fact, there are many areas of American life where a spirit of cooperation is mixed with the competitive spirit: for example, in business and industry where people must pull together to accomplish the work of the enterprise, and in social, political, and religious groups whose members share a common goal.

In studying the *effects* of competition and cooperation we must answer three questions:

1 How do they function as motivating incentives?

2 How does the quality of work done under the two conditions compare, and does better quality result from the same conditions that induce greater quantity?

3 What is the effect on character and personality?

Competition and cooperation as incentives to learn. Several experiments have been performed to compare different competitive situations as motivations in learning.

1 One experimenter worked with groups of college students to investigate the effects of the two types of competition on learning to use a code and speed of reading. His results clearly indicate that in our present social pattern, individual competition is superior to group competition among adults as a condition motivating learning. (Sims[48])

2 Another psychologist studied individual and group competition as factors motivating school work, with simple addition as the task. It was found that working for oneself and working for the group are both more effective than work which is not so specifically motivated. Boys persisted longer than girls in working for the group, but girls persisted longer than boys in working for self.

From the experiments just described and from others, the investigator (Maller[49]) discovered that the motivating conditions among school children can be arranged in the following order of strength:

Boys working against girls as individuals.
Working for self.
Working for the team.
Working in partnership.
Working for classroom as a whole.
Working for a group picked arbitrarily by an outsider.

Bear in mind that these are *average* results; there are great individual differences among children in the nature of the motivation which is most effective. For example, in the study just described, 65 per cent of the children showed greater speed in doing the problems when working for self, while 35 per cent showed greater speed when working for the group. As with older people, some thrive in a highly competitive atmosphere; others are motivated more by the ideals of service.

Schoolteachers make particular use of individual competition in stimulating their pupils to greater effort: for example, in this country there is the practice of preparing an "Honor Roll" which includes the names of the members of the class who have never been absent or tardy or who stand at the head of the class in their studies. Children take such honors very seriously and strive hard to be included in the select list. (Salesmen are often grouped by a similar system.)

The practice of grading according to the normal-probability curve is essentially a competitive method of grading. There is room at the top for only a certain percentage of the class; another percentage is certain to fail. By this method the grade earned by a particular student depends upon his rank in the class, as based on his performance in examinations and other measures of his ability.

Competition and performance. Since competition is so prevalent in American life, and serves as a powerful incentive in education and business, it is important to examine the effects of competition on performance. Experiment has shown (Whittemore[50]) that with simple tasks, individuals produce a *greater quantity* of work under conditions of competition than under noncompetitive conditions, but that it is of *poorer quality.*

Another experiment indicates that when the task is complex and novel, the combined experience of a group is superior to that of its average member (Watson[51]). We have long recognized the truth of the old saying that "two heads are better than one" where judgment, factual information, and previous experience with related problems are concerned.

Moreover, the presence of the group exerts a facilitating or energizing influence on the performance of its members, even though the situation is not essentially one calling for competitive effort (Elkine[52]). The individual appears to compete with the group consciously or unconsciously even in the absence of directions to do so.

Effects of competition on individuals. Is it good for people to compete? What does competition do to them? Is there such a thing as too much competitiveness? What are the effects? These are questions which deserve careful answers.

First of all, it is apparent that competition can bring out some of the best efforts of an individual. In business, engineering, and many kinds of intellectual activity, it has been enormously productive. When carried to extremes, however, it can have some unfortunate effects.

One important thing to consider is the effect that competition may have on morals. There is danger that too much emphasis on competition will make children or adults want to win at any price—even through cheating. There is an even greater danger that preoccupation with the competitive aspects of the school situation will blind the student to the less tangible but more fundamental products of education. He should learn because learning makes him a better member of society and because he values knowledge for its own sake.

Another important consideration is the effect of discouragement on the loser. We must not lose sight of the fact that there must be a loser if there is to be a winner. What happens to the fellow who never wins? Does he continue to work hard even though he knows that somebody else will get the prize? Several experiments have shown that the discouragement of failure greatly reduces the person's efforts the next time (Gates and Rissland[53] and Sears[54]). "You can't win; so what's the use of trying?" is his attitude.

Even the winner in competition may suffer thereby, for success comes to mean hurting his competitors as well as reaching his goals. He wants to succeed, but he is afraid that by succeeding he will lose popularity. This is an example of the "conflict frustration" we discussed earlier. Like many other conflicts, it is often entirely unconscious. The development of such a conflict is illustrated on pages 586-587, in the case of the girl whose early experience with her parents taught her that competition for attention would bring disapproval.

Such a conflict between the need for success and the need for love may cause an individual to experience acute anxiety before taking an exam or making a speech; he may find himself unable to concentrate on his work or to "speak up" before his superiors or his classmates. He may then withdraw from competition, either by "losing interest" or by some of the extreme forms of withdrawal like regression, the escape into illness, or the use of alcohol or drugs. Often, however, the individual develops a disinterest in the very activities in which he has the most desire to succeed: that is, he represses this desire. He rationalizes by saying to himself or others that he is "not interested in girls," that he despises "grinds" and would hate to be one, that he'd "rather enjoy life than rush around after money and success." Sometimes he successfully compensates for failure in the activity in which he has conflict by working very hard in another field—but often he feels such a desperate need for success that he overdoes it, "overcompensates." What success he does win he may "belittle" in order to avert what he thinks is the envious hatred of others, or to reassure himself that he is not in danger from their envy. He does all this because he cannot face the possibility of succeeding and thus (as he believes) alienating others, or because he may have thoroughly convinced himself that he is inferior. (Cf. Horney[55])

Individual adjustment to competition. How can this evil of excessive competition be overcome? The first step is to appraise oneself to discover one's special abilities and talents. However discouraged a person may be about himself, there are always some activities in which he can win at least some degree of success and respect. The important thing is to choose goals, whether personal, athletic, or vocational, which are actually attainable. In Chapters 6 and 15, we have seen how psychology can help, by the testing of intelligence, skill, and personality, to indicate to the individual those areas in which he is most likely to achieve success. The problem of dealing effectively with inferiority feelings has been discussed on page 481.

Individuals tend to protect themselves from the bad effects of repeated failure in competitive situations by lowering their "level of aspiration" to some point within reach. This fact has been experimentally demonstrated:

> Each member of a large class of students was asked to state the grade he expected to receive on an important test to be held the next day. Exactly half of the students reached or surpassed their level of aspiration. When the second important test came along, the students were again asked to state the grade they expected to receive. Of those who

failed to reach their expected grade on the first test, 34 per cent lowered their second aspiration to the grade actually received the first time; 66 per cent restated their original aspiration. Of those who had succeeded in reaching the expected grade in the first test, 62 per cent restated their levels of aspiration for the second test; 36 per cent raised them; and 2 per cent lowered them. (Pennington[56])

We change our goals to make them square with our abilities. Once attainable goals are set up, the person does not feel so unsure of himself that he comes to feel "cutthroat" toward his competitors. The conflict between success and love is lessened, and so is the possibility of developing some of the undesirable reactions just described.

Another effective way of lessening the emotional tension caused by competition is through seeking and earning love and respect by virtue of fairness and good sportsmanship in competition. Following the rules of the game will not cause so much guilt over winning, or inferiority over losing, as will "cutthroat" competition at any cost.

Setting the stage for effective competition. There are several formal means that groups can adopt to retain the efficiency of competition and yet avert its evil effects. One plan for awarding prizes takes advantage of competitive drives but also permits the poorer subjects to enjoy the thrill of winning. At the end of the first contest the members of the group are ranked from best to poorest. The announcement is made that in the second contest the prizes will go to the persons who show the most improvement in rank, i.e., who pass the largest number of individuals in performance. This scheme affords ample opportunity for the poorer performers to enjoy the pleasures and benefits of success, and stimulates the better performers to improve their performance rather than "rest on their laurels." In many competitive situations— whether in business, school, or social life—emphasis can be placed on how far an individual is improving *relative to his abilities and to his original achievement.*

A variant of this plan is to reward the person who improves his ranking by the largest number of points. Under these conditions, the members of the group are competing against their own records as much as they are competing against each other. This plan, too, retains much of the effectiveness of the competitive situation in which there can be but one winner but gives an opportunity also for the poorer individuals to enjoy the pride of winning—something which they badly need.

A similar plan avoids the evils of excessive competition and is strongly recommended for use with groups that are becoming too much imbued with the philosophy of the "superman." At the end of a pre-test, the members of the group are instructed to compete against their own scores without regard to the performances of others. The prize or the honors go to the person who improves his previous record by a set number of points. The teacher or director of the contest must be careful to set the standards in such a way that success is fairly easy.

Another practical suggestion involves the utilization of teamwork within the framework of a competitive situation, as is done, for example, in team sports and in the formation of sales teams. This "distributes the risk," i.e., gives company to share the misery of failure and provides the delight of mutual sharing of the rewards of victory.

Unfortunately, these suggestions apply only to relatively simple work, study, and play situations in which the goal is readily discernible and in which progress is objectively measurable. Most informal relations between people depend on the individual's ability to adjust to competition, rather than on any formal arrangements and rules.

Conclusions from experiments on competition and cooperation. The experiments which we have been considering are typical of many which have been conducted in this field. Their results, taken as a whole, show clearly that human beings who have developed in a competitive society work harder in groups than when alone. The individuals in the group work harder when competing as individuals than as members of a team. This fact can be taken advantage of in business, in the classroom, on the playground, or in any situation where we wish people to exert a greater effort. But in our efforts to control behavior we must be careful not to overdo the emphasis on competition. Competitive situations which consistently deny certain members of the group the possibility of success should be avoided. Moreover, competitive situations frequently encourage emphasis on quantity rather than increased efficiency.

Actually, there are many indications that the American culture pattern is swinging away from the extreme competitiveness which characterized the young, expanding, individualistic economy. Psychologists generally feel that a reduction in "cutthroat" competition is emotionally and intellectually beneficial—whatever the relative moral values of competition and cooperation in group living. But the problem is very complex, involving our whole social tradition and its effects on individuals as they participate in many kinds of groups, in marriage, in business, in school, and in informal social life. Here is a problem on which much research has yet to be done, and which is one of the most important of all the problems in human relations we have studied in this chapter.

Recent research has revealed certain psychological needs which are vital to industrial welfare but which are too often unsatisfied in modern life: for example, the need for community living. At right is union-built Unity House, where garment workers relax and participate in group activities. (Courtesy Fons Ianelli and Fortune.)

CHAPTER **17**

Psychology in industry

Human Understanding in Industry

The Employee's Search for the Right Job

The Employer's Search for the Right Employee

THE NOTION THAT POOR PAY and long hours are the only causes of industrial unrest is psychologically unsound. Wages-and-hours disputes have been given undue prominence both in newspaper reports of industrial conflict and in the thinking of labor and management. Of course, much labor unrest is directly traceable to dissatisfaction over the way that certain basic economic problems are being solved in our modern industrial democracy. Today there is constant discussion about the role that labor unions and government should play in deciding on wages, prices, and profit distribution; about labor's right to strike; and about the government's right to control working conditions and take action against depressions. But however we resolve our economic and political problems, there are always certain psychological problems in industry that must be met. Specialists in industrial psychology have discovered that these problems, while interrelated, fall into three fairly distinct areas: *Human Understanding in Industry, The Employee's Search for the Right Job,* and *The Employer's Search for the Right Employee.*

HUMAN UNDERSTANDING IN INDUSTRY

OBVIOUSLY MAN LIVES ON BREAD, but the mistake of many modern businessmen is to assume that he lives on bread alone. This view is no longer accepted by students of psychology, who know that every human being—at work as well as in his family and social life—has strong social and emotional needs.

> "A major part of the administrator's task is to provide satisfactions for those contributing their services to the organization as well as to promote the purposes of the enterprise itself." (Mayo[1])

The modern executive must be able to solve not only the scientific and technical problems of production but also the administrative problems of organizing work-operations. He must have the human understanding which will bring about high morale and friendly cooperation among the workers as well as between workers and management. He must realize that psychological as well as economic dissatisfaction is often at the bottom of industrial disputes.

Employers with the best of intentions sometimes have labor trouble even though the wages they pay are fair and the hours not excessive. Dissatisfaction of the employees in cases like this is frequently traceable to the employer's failure to understand the employees as human beings. This lack of understanding is brought out very clearly in a special study:

> Several hundred employers and 3000 employees scattered throughout the United States were asked to rate the importance of eight morale factors. Here are the results:

Morale Item	Employee Ranking	Employer Ranking	Difference Between Employee and Employer Ranking
Credit for all work done.........	1	7	—6
Interesting work	2	3	—1
Fair play	3	1	+2
Understanding and appreciation...	4	5	—1
Counsel on personal problems.....	5	8	—3
Promotion on merit	6	4	+2
Good physical working conditions.	7	6	+1
Job security	8	2	+6

It is obvious from the table that the employers underestimated the employees' needs for certain noneconomic satisfactions. Notice that the employees as a group considered credit for work done to be of paramount importance, whereas the employers ranked it as seventh in the group of eight items. On the other hand, the employers assigned the next-to-the-top rank to job security, while the employees put it eighth in the order of importance. (Hartmann and Newcomb[2])

The notion that money (whether in the form of salaries, wages, profits, or commissions) is the common denominator of all human aspiration is definitely outmoded. Man has other needs besides a sense of economic security, and these must be satisfied if he is to feel self-respecting and happy. Modern managers are coming to realize more and more that employees have important psychological needs which deserve constant consideration, not only because respect for the individual is part of the democratic tradition but also because efficiency is directly affected by the worker's attitudes and feelings. During times of prosperity and manpower shortage, the manager must consider the human factor if he wishes to ensure an adequate and stable labor supply. During harder times, the manager wants to increase efficiency in order to lower costs, and so again he will have to consider psychological needs as vital factors of production. Among these needs are *The Need for Satisfying Work, The Social Need to Belong, The Need for Physical Safety,* and *The Need for a "Square Hole."*

The need for satisfying work

Modern factory work has, in some instances, developed in such a way as to deny men some of the satisfactions that work gave them in an earlier day. Before the time of huge factories, for example, the shoemaker and cabinetmaker took real interest in craftsmanship. Their work required skill, patience, and often considerable artistic ability. They enjoyed admiration and respect for their work, as well as a sense of performing a useful function in the community. Their work was satisfying both artistically and socially.

Contrast the hand-craftsman with the worker in the modern factory. Industry today is highly specialized, so that the work on a product is broken down into many stages, each performed by a different person. One man performs a few simple operations hour after hour, day in and day out, weeks and months upon end. Many workers enjoy the experience of working with powerful and effective machinery, but even so, they usually do not see the completed product unless they make a special effort to do so after working hours. For the worker on the production line, the materials come to him on an endless nonstopping belt that moves just fast enough for him to perform his simple task and be ready to perform the same operation on the next unit that comes along. And even if the modern worker is not on a factory production line, his work is often of the most routine sort: punching tickets, run-

Before the development of complex machine industry, most manufacturing was done by hand or with the assistance of simple tools. Workers accomplished their tasks in their own homes or as members of small guilds. In either case there was little division of labor, and the craftsman needed a good deal of skill and versatility. The engraving at left shows a jeweler's workshop of 1576, in which the entire process of making jewelry is carried on in one place and with only a few workmen. There was close personal contact among the workers and between worker and customer, and the work of each man was recognized as his own. Under these conditions, work brought both social and aesthetic satisfaction.

ning an addressograph machine, or typing letters from one stranger to another stranger.

Work under such conditions has little intrinsic interest. People who are mentally active soon become stifled because the pleasure of creation is denied them. Doing the same simple piece of work over and over again usually results in monotony, in an unpleasant feeling of boredom and restlessness. As the hours pass, this feeling of restlessness develops into one of frustration and the worker searches for someone or something to blame for his feelings of frustration. He reviews grievances large and small; the small ones become large, and the large ones become gigantic. If monotony becomes excessive, the slightest excuse for stopping work will be seized upon.

But the modern factory worker finds other escapes from boredom besides complaining and work stoppage. His work may be so simple that he can daydream while at work. One psychologist observed the case of a girl who actually resented being given a better-paying job because it demanded a more varied type of movement than did her old job, which was so simple that she could perform it without conscious attention and so have her whole day free for daydreaming. Often, too, the worker looks to sources other than his own imagination to find make-believe satisfactions. After hours he forgets his dull existence through lurid films, burlesque, and pulp-paper magazines, which help him escape to a thrilling world of fantasy. Here he can identify himself with people whose lives are full of excitement and success. Such escapes from reality are not healthful.

Is there any brighter side to the picture?—any relief from the psychological disturbance caused by monotonous routine work? Actually the picture is not completely dark; correctives for industrial monotony are many:

Due to the efficiency of machine production and specialized division of labor, the machine-age worker is better fed, clothed, and housed, and has an infinitely more comfortable and healthy life than the old-time hand workers. But the machine age has entailed certain psychological disadvantages. Some types of industrial work, like the process of examining parts (right), are very routine, are only remotely connected with the finished product, and  *permit little contact with people. Modern management and unions alike are taking action to counteract the unfortunate psychological effects of such work, where it occurs.*

1 *Rest periods.* Industrial psychologists have found that rest periods during the day serve to break the monotony and, if well-planned, actually increase production for the day as a whole.

2 *Allowing social contacts.* Workers often do not mind performing simple tasks if they are allowed to work in social groups where they can engage in friendly conversation. When the task is very simple, conversation does not interfere with efficiency and in fact may even increase it.

3 *Selecting the right workers.* If these measures are impractical or are not completely successful in reducing monotony, care should be exercised to select people who do not object to the monotony of routine work. Someone must be found to perform the highly repetitive work of specialized mass-production, for there is no return to the days of slow, inefficient, small-scale craftsmanship.

4 *After-work activities.* The lack of intrinsic interest in modern factory work can be counteracted to a large extent by the interest of *extrinsic activities*—that is, activities which are not necessary to actual work performance but which are essential to the physical and psychological well-being of the worker. The machine age, which has added to the monotony of work, has also made it possible to shorten the working day from twelve or even sixteen hours to only seven or eight. The new leisure time can counteract some of the monotony of the machine if it is used for recreation and self-improvement. Obviously management cannot supply a complete and satisfactory social life for the employees, but it can sponsor certain social activities which will add variety and fun to the worker's life after work, and so help compensate him to some degree for the dullness of his working hours.

Human Understanding in Industry 619

5 *Showing how the job is important.* Monotonous work can also be made much more interesting by giving it a social meaning. For instance, it is possible to show an assembly-line worker how his simple repetitive operation is related to the whole exciting process of manufacturing the finished product. To meet a common grievance among modern factory workers—that "all of us work on parts of things and never see the complete product put together"—the management of one large company decided to hold an "open house." Every day for two weeks, after the regular working day was over, the employees were invited to pass through the factory—to explore corners they had not previously known existed, to witness operations they had never seen before. Thus they could see that they were working together on a common product, not working in isolation on something that had no meaning or purpose. In fact, their pride and interest in the plant grew to the point where they brought their wives and families with them to tour the plant.

6 Another indispensable basis for emotional satisfaction in work is a *feeling that the work is honestly productive.* It is hard on the morale of workers to feel that they are working on a product which is shoddy and second-rate, and naturally some companies face a much more difficult task than others in getting favorable reactions from their employees. This difficulty, however, is not inevitable because there is no inherent reason in modern technology why products should not be of high quality. A worker identifies himself with the company with which he works and with the products which he knows it brings forth, and turnover tends to be much lower when the workers have this feeling of real pride in the quality of their product.

All these sources of emotional gratification can help counteract the all-too-frequent monotony of modern industrial and office jobs.

The social "need to belong"

You have just seen that giving work a social meaning can compensate to a large degree for the worker's lack of any aesthetic or intellectual interest in the work itself. The reason is that part of the satisfaction of work consists in a feeling that what you are doing has real value to a community of which you are a secure member. Before the days of big cities and big industry, every worker saw his efforts as part of a whole community life. The shoemaker or boatbuilder or farmer often followed his father's trade in an intimate community where his family had lived and worked for generations. He worked either for himself or for people whom he knew well. But in the modern industrial world, the worker makes part of a product he never sees for people he never sees. Even if he is in some line of work where he has contacts with people, they are usually of a very impersonal kind, and he does not feel that he is working as part of a community.

The "need to belong" is especially strong in modern society, because the traditional institutions are losing their power to give the individual a secure feeling of being an accepted part of an established social and moral order. Sociologists have shown that in urban areas especially, the family and the neighborhood are breaking up. Big-city society has no established order of which the individual feels an integral part. People move from place to place, never feeling that they belong anywhere and ultimately becoming disillusioned with a society that seems incapable of giving meaning to their lives or providing satisfaction for their social need to belong.

The modern industrial worker experiences social frustration in his work surroundings as well as in his home, church, and neighborhood life. He works with people who are usually strangers to him, who come from widely different religious, racial, social, and geographical backgrounds. He sees them only during the working day, and then they all scatter to their homes, often widely distant. Moreover, the people he works with are constantly changing because of the way modern workers move from one job or city to another. Unlike the worker in a small-scale society, he neither sees directly how his work has any social function nor feels that he shares any kind of established community life with his fellow workers.

> "For all of us the feeling of security and certainty derives always from assured membership in a group. If this is lost, no monetary gain, no job guarantee, can be sufficient compensation. Where groups change ceaselessly as jobs and mechanical processes change, the individual inevitably experiences a sense of void, of emptiness, where his fathers knew the joy of comradeship and security. And in such a situation, his anxieties—many, no doubt, irrational and ill-founded—increase and he becomes more difficult both to fellow-workers and to supervisor." (Mayo[3])

The social disintegration of the modern world is a problem of the utmost complexity. The industrial manager cannot remedy the social deficiencies of other institutions, but he can see that his plant or office operates as a team. As you will see, teamwork satisfies the worker's need to belong, improves morale, and so increases productive efficiency.

Teamwork, production, and absenteeism. Some years ago industrial psychologists made a discovery that some enthusiasts have called "the social basis for industrial peace." It is the discovery that psychology must work with economics in diagnosing and curing industrial unrest. Interestingly enough, it grew out of a mistaken assumption in an industrial experiment—an assumption that employees' attitudes do not have marked effects on their productivity.

In the late 1920's a series of experiments was sponsored by the management of the Hawthorne plant of the Western Electric Company in Chicago. The investigators set out to measure the effect that changes in environmental conditions had on the production of a group of women who were engaged in assembling a piece of electrical apparatus. In order to make the experiment truly scientific, they placed the group in a special shop where all factors could be controlled and observed. For a period of about two months, the workers, all of them old and experienced hands, operated under the usual conditions and at their accustomed rate. This period was used as a base or control period for subsequent comparisons.

As soon as the group had settled down, it was explained to them that they would be used as subjects in experiments to test the effects of rest periods and various environmental changes, and that their pay would not suffer regardless of what happened to their production. The investigators were anxious to avoid introducing any extraneous, psychological factors (such as resentment at a particular change) which might influence the workers' production after the change was made, and so not allow the true effect of the change itself to be observed in production records. In other words, they wanted to hold the workers' attitudes "constant." So each time an innovation was made in the work schedule or in working conditions, a consultation was held with the workers, and the investigators even asked for suggestions about what changes it would be useful to try. At the same time, supervision was lessened. Certain disciplinary rules were also relaxed: the girls were now permitted to talk while they worked, and since they were rather isolated from other workers in the plant, they became a close-knit, friendly group during the several years the investigation was conducted.

Each time a change was made, the production of the group went up slowly but surely. It did not seem to matter whether the change was in the form of introducing a rest period, changing the work method, or what—each change was followed by improvement. This uniformity of cause and effect eventually aroused the suspicions of the experimenters.

They decided to conduct a control experiment by restoring the original conditions. If the increases in production were actually due to the changes deliberately introduced, then production should fall back to where it was in the base or control period. To the amazement of some, the restoration of the old conditions brought still more increase in production. When the workers were interviewed to discover the reason for such an unexpected result, there was general agreement that they liked being consulted about their working conditions, that they liked the lessened supervision and discipline, that they now felt themselves to be a team participating with management in a cooperative enterprise. Moreover, the closer social relationships within the group made each worker feel part of a solid group of friends. Here cooperation and companionship—extraneous psychological factors the investigators had not known they were introducing—made these workers happier and so more productive. The workers had not even realized that they were producing more with each change. In fact, they actually thought the work was getting lighter because they felt less tired at night. (Roethlisberger and Dickson[4])

This famous experiment disclosed how effective a feeling of belonging can be in increasing productive efficiency. Subsequent studies have confirmed this early finding.

1 During the war, a study was made of absenteeism in three war plants in an Eastern industrial city. The investigators analyzed the attendance records of workers continuously employed for an eighteen-month period. It was found that of the three companies, Company C had the lowest absentee rate, below 2 per cent for every month but one. Company B had an absentee rate which rose to an approximate 5 per cent or 6 per cent. Company A had a rate which at its height was over 10 per cent. On careful investigation, it was found that the reason for Company C's superior attendance record was that it encouraged teamwork much more than the other two companies did. (Fox and Scott[5])

2 Similar results were found in an experiment at the Lockheed Aircraft Corporation which was aimed at investigating the effect of vitamins on production, termination, and absenteeism. Three groups of subjects were selected as follows: One group served as a control group, i.e., they did not even know they were serving as controls. A second group received vitamins, supplied by the company free of charge, and knew that they were receiving the health-giving substances. The third group were told that they were getting vitamins but in reality received capsules that looked just like vitamin pills but contained medically inert ingredients.

Both the true-vitamin group and the false-vitamin group showed reduced absenteeism, but there was little difference between the true and the fake group. The real conclusion (although not that of the author of the study) is that belief on the part of the employees that the employer is sufficiently interested in their health and welfare to supply them with vitamins had effect even when vitamins were not given. (Borsook[6])

These studies and others like them clearly show a fact of vital importance to any firm that wants to increase its productive efficiency.

The need to belong—the desire for association—is a deep-seated social motivation that is sure to find expression in every employee, at work as well as in the home, the lodge, the church. If this need is not satisfied—if a man works in a plant where he does not feel that he is part of some group—his morale is low.

One of the mistakes of modern management is its failure to consider the worker's need to belong and to turn it to good use in encouraging the teamwork necessary to high, efficient production. Teamwork can be of great value in increasing the quantity of production; lowering the cost of production; reducing absenteeism and labor turnover; and preventing open hostility between management and labor in the form of strikes, walkouts, and sabotage.

It is up to management to encourage teamwork among the workers and between workers and management. It can do so by three major measures: encouraging social groupings; keeping clear the channels of communication; and helping the individual worker keep adjusted to his co-workers and to his work (Roethlisberger and Dickson[7]).

Encouraging social groupings. There are many ways in which management can foster the social groups that benefit both the employee and management.

> **1** In large industrial plants, where the background and interests of the workers are likely to be very different, management can make an effort to place together employees who have similar backgrounds, who are friends outside the plant, or who seem to have a natural liking for each other. The importance to workers of friendly associates is shown by a report of a girl who resisted being given a better-paying job because she would have to leave the group of friends in the department in which she was working (Mayo[8]). Of course such groups must be encouraged to have more than a narrowly personal orientation, to work together as a team for the interests of the whole company.
>
> **2** When workers have to be loaned or transferred from one department to another, management should try in so far as possible to keep working teams intact.
>
> **3** When technical innovations are necessary, such as introducing new machines or changing the work routines, management should remember to take into consideration the social patterns that have been established around technological arrangements. For instance, moving a machine may separate its operator from his fellow-workers, or cutting out one step in production may necessitate switching a worker from his accustomed job.

4 Whenever possible, payments should be made according to *group* output rather than *individual* output, in order to encourage teamwork.

Clearing the channels of communication. The Hawthorne experiment showed how morale improves when the investigators discuss with the workers the various changes in working conditions that might improve morale and ask the workers for suggestions. There are many ways of achieving the two-way communication essential to good teamwork.

1 Management should contact the employees through the natural leaders of their social groups. They should realize that the authority of management rests on its acceptance by these social groups.

2 Supervisors and other middle-men between employees and management must be sympathetic toward the workers' psychological needs; must understand their social relations; and must be familiar with their attitudes on such matters as how much they can produce without excessive fatigue and who deserves promotions.

3 Since cooperation means mutual criticism, there must be free communication on matters that are bothering either the management or the employees. Frank discussion is essential. Many well-managed offices and plants provide opportunities for communication in the form of question boxes and suggestion boxes, and secret polls on important issues that affect the employees' welfare. It is also important, however, for management to develop channels for more direct expression of grievances. The employee must know that he has a perfect right to express his grievance, and to expect that it will be considered seriously, without prejudice, and without endangering his job.

When criticism goes the other way—when an employee is to be reprimanded or penalized—it should be criticism that is fairly based, carefully weighed, calmly expressed, and clearly understandable to the employee. And of course, the employee should have a chance to give his side. In most cases, a sympathetic foreman or supervisor who works every day to help the employee overcome his work and personal difficulties can prevent the worker from reaching the stage where formal discipline is necessary.

4 Since cooperation is based on common information, management should give the employee honestly and accurately as much nonconfidential information about his company's history, personnel policy, economic position, and wage policy as the nonspecialist can understand.

5 Since cooperation is possible only when the two parties in the enterprise are in full communication, each employee should know exactly where he stands and what progress he is making. There is nothing more demoralizing for an employee than working in the dark, with no clear idea of what he is supposed to be doing, how he is supposed to be doing it, how long it is supposed to take, or whether it is satisfactory when he has done it.

Helping the worker with his adjustment problems. Free communication between the worker and some member of management serves not only for exchange of information but as a simple form of psychotherapy. The foremen in "Company C," for example, were accustomed to listening attentively to all the workers' complaints and worries (p. 623). Catharsis, which is so effective in the clinic, proves its worth in the office and the factory. It is valuable for the worker to unburden himself not only of difficulties in his work but also of difficulties in his home and social life. No one can work effectively under emotional strain, and management finds it worth while to provide means of relief from such strain, whatever its origin. Man functions as a whole, and his home life affects his working life.

Not every foreman or supervisor is skilled enough in human understanding to help the employee achieve relief and self-understanding through catharsis. For this reason, many firms maintain one or more psychological counselors whose function is to help the dissatisfied worker evaluate his difficulties with his work and his work situation, as well as his difficulties in his home or social life.

Thus psychological understanding—both on the job and in the expert's office—can keep the individual adjusted to his work with the team. In this way, the worker feels a secure member of a group; his need to belong is satisfied. And as his morale is improved, his usefulness to management is also improved.

The need for physical safety

Industrial accidents are not only costly to management but damaging to morale. No one can work at top effectiveness when under the influence of fear. Fortunately, industrial psychologists have been able to locate many of the causes for industrial accidents, so that steps can be taken to control them far more easily than in the past. The specific causes of accidents are varied. Among the more important are:

1 Accident proneness.

2 Improper atmospheric conditions.

3 Poor illumination.

4 Too fast a rate of production.

5 Personal worries and problems.

6 Lack of environmental safeguards.

7 Workers' disregard of safety measures.

Proneness to accident. Industrial accidents are not distributed according to chance. That is to say, in any group of workers engaged at the same task, certain individuals will be involved in far more accidents than others. Numerous psychological studies in the laboratory and in the factory leave no doubt that certain individuals are *prone,* or susceptible, to accidents. Accordingly, one of the most effective ways of screening out accident-prone workers is the application of adequately designed psychological tests before employment. These tests must be exhaustive in nature and must cover all the human abilities involved in the work under consideration—including eyesight, hearing, motor coordination, and emotional stability.

Atmospheric conditions. Numerous studies have shown that when working places are properly ventilated and air-conditioned, there are lower accident rates and greater production per man. There are three atmospheric conditions—temperature, humidity, and air motion—that must be correctly adjusted to maintain health and prevent accidents.

> One of the most thorough studies of the relation between temperature and accident frequency was made in the British coal mines. An analysis was made of the accidents occurring to 18,000 underground coal miners and 4500 surface men working in some ten collieries. A later study, based on groups of approximately half the size, gave the same results. In both studies the number and severity of the accidents showed a marked increase as the temperature rose or fell above or below a certain optimum point. A rise of 18 degrees F. brought an increase of 80 per cent in the accidents to the surface workers. In the case of the underground miners, a temperature rise of 16 degrees F. brought a 73 per cent increase in the accident rate. (Vernon, Bedford, and Warner[9])

Illumination and accidents. Many proofs of the beneficial effects of proper lighting are given by the increased production per man and by the decreased errors and accidents per unit of work. One study found that key-punch operators increased their production rate by 58 per cent and at the same time reduced their errors by 69 per cent when adequate illumination was provided (Luckiesh and Moss[10]).

Safety and the rate of production. The effects of increased production rate upon accuracy of work and accident frequency have been studied by many psychologists in a number of experimental situations and actual factory operations. Although the quick worker tends to be the most accurate when working at his natural pace, he becomes more susceptible to accidents if pushed beyond his natural rate of work.

A study was made during the first World War of the effects of increased production rate on the frequency of accidents among the workers in a fuse factory. Because of the war pressure, the workers in the munitions factory were pushed up until they had achieved a 25 per cent increase in hourly output of fuses. This 25 per cent increase in production rate was accompanied, however, by a 60 per cent increase in frequency of accidents treated at the hospital or dressing station. (Vernon[11])

To some extent, of course, this rate varies with the individual.

One of the industrial pioneers in developing favorable employee-employer relations is the Western Electric Company, manufacturing unit of the Bell System. This company has long realized that it is good business, as well as good industrial psychology, to provide good working conditions. One of the outstanding examples of the "pleasant working conditions" technique is Western Electric's toolroom (above) at its Hawthorne Works in Chicago. In all cases where such improvements have been installed at Western Electric, diligent research and careful study have been made of the needs of each individual situation, with special attention to natural and artificial lighting, color combination on machines, walls, and ceilings to relieve eyestrain, and physical layouts that offer safety and convenience for the workers.

Personal worries and problems are another important cause of accidents on the job.

> One personnel psychologist reports an observation based on seven years of study of industrial accidents in Germany and America. In the course of his study he made a careful clinical investigation of four hundred cases. His conclusion: ". . . more than half took place when the worker was in a worried, apprehensive, or some other 'low' emotional state." (Hersey[12])

This finding only makes more urgent the need for human understanding in industry, and the need for some kind of catharsis and reorientation for the worker who is having adjustment difficulties either in his home and social life or at work.

Lack of environmental safeguards. Even today there are serious accidents in industry which could be prevented by the safety devices the management would have to supply. For example, many coal mines should be provided with platforms balanced in such a way that in case of an explosion, they would tip over and spill into the air a fine rock dust that would prevent the spread of the explosion to other parts of the mine. But some employers have been careless in the provision of such safety devices, with the result that employee-compensation laws now impose high rates on plants with a history of many accidents.

Workers' attitudes toward safety devices. Even where safety devices are provided, there often is an additional problem in the attitudes the working group has about using them. Sometimes workers do not like to use safety devices either because they reduce the speed or ease with which the work can be done, or else because the workers feel that only "sissies" use them. Here again is the group-morale factor—just another example of the fact that accident prevention involves psychological as well as technological problems. The intelligent supervisor recognizes its importance and works with the group as a whole to change employee attitudes.

The need for a "square hole"

The dissatisfaction which a poorly placed worker suffers is a powerful factor in disrupting morale.

> In one industrial study, an absentee group of employees was matched with a nonabsentee group on the basis of job classification, sex, department, shift, and period of employment. Comparison of these two groups showed that the proportion of individuals placed on jobs which they disliked and which were unrelated to their previous experience was significantly higher in the absentee group than in the nonabsentee group. (Stockford[13])

Obviously these people stayed away from work because they were "square pegs in a round hole." The importance of job placement has been shown in still another study:

> The American Institute of Public Opinion[14] sounded the ideas of war workers themselves on the question of plant efficiency by having their interviewers talk to workers in industrial areas all over the country. Workers were asked the following question: "What do you think is the greatest mistake that your company makes?" As many respondents mentioned poor job placement as mentioned unfair wages and lack of proper pay scale for different types of work. No more conclusive evidence of the value of job adjustment to the individual can be demanded.

Unfortunately, management does not yet universally realize the value of adjusting the abilities and aptitudes of the worker to the requirements of his job, of "fitting a square peg into a square hole." Job placement is more than a responsibility of management, however. It is up to the individual to exercise mature judgment in choosing the line of work he wishes to enter. Employment, whether it be a job or a profession, is a contract between the employer and the worker, or between the doctor, lawyer, or engineer and the client who employs him.

Psychology can help both employee and employer fit the peg to the hole. The rest of this chapter will discuss both vocational psychology, which is concerned with *The Employee's Search for the Right Job,* and employment psychology, which is concerned with *The Employer's Search for the Right Employee.*

THE EMPLOYEE'S SEARCH FOR THE RIGHT JOB

THE AVERAGE PERSON spends about as much time at work as he does in sleeping, and more time than he does in play. If properly chosen, his job gives him, as you have seen, the opportunity for satisfying several fundamental needs. There has always been, and probably always will be, a great need for vocational guidance. Placing members of society in occupations that will bring them happiness and success is an essential part of social planning at any time. But only in the past few years have adequate methods of scientific vocational guidance become available, and only very recently has the general public become aware of them.

The average college student is not capable of making the choice of a vocation unaided. All too often he knows next to nothing about the various jobs and occupations that are open to him. He has no accurate conception of the special abilities and other psychological characteristics required for success in a particular vocation. When at all possible, he should seek the services of a vocational counselor who has accurate knowledge of the requirements for numerous occupations that would give him the greatest chances for successful, happy adjustment of his abilities.

In the choice of a vocation, certain important questions must be considered: *What does the job require,* in the way of education, intelligence, special abilities, physical strength and endurance, and temperament and personality? *What satisfactions does the work give?* Do they coincide with the satisfactions required by one's particular interests? *What opportunities exist* in this occupational field?

What does the job require?

Educational standards. For any job there are certain educational requirements. For some, a high-school education is sufficient, while others demand a college degree—some a Bachelor's, some a Master's, and some a Doctor's degree. Others require specialized courses, lasting sometimes a few weeks, sometimes several months or even longer. Especially for certain branches of law, medicine, architecture, and scientific research, it is important to discover exactly how many years of training (including apprenticeship and internship) are required before well-paying work will be available. Such information can avoid wasted effort in a career that might eventually have to be given up as impracticable.

Intelligence needed for the work. Numerous psychological surveys have shown a direct relationship between level of intelligence and success in a particular occupational activity. These studies show that a person may fail to make good in a particular occupation if he is either too low or too high in intelligence. The individual whose intelligence is too low for his job soon becomes unhappy and frustrated because he has to make judgments far too complex for his understanding, while the person whose intelligence is too high for his job soon becomes bored with the job's monotony.

> Figures have been collected to show the relationship between the intelligence level of cashiers in a chain of restaurants and the length of their service in that capacity. It was found that girls with the lowest test scores lasted only a few days, obviously not having sufficient mental alertness to do the work well. Nor did girls of high intelligence stay long on the job; obviously they became restless because they needed more complex work to occupy their full abilities. It was the girls of middle intelligence, significantly enough, who stayed longest on this job requiring middle intelligence. (Viteles[15])

How can a person tell whether his intelligence is suited to the line of work he is considering? The table below may be of help:

Occupation	Mean Army G.C.T. Score	S.D.	Mean Equivalent I.Q.	S.D.
Accountants	128	12	125	11
Lawyers	128	11	125	10
Engineers	127	12	124	11
Teachers	123	13	121	12
Stenographers	121	13	119	12
Bookkeepers	120	13	118	12
Clerk-Typists	117	12	115	11
Radio Repairmen	115	15	113	13
Receiving and Shipping Clerks	111	16	111	14
Sales Clerks	109	16	108	14
Auto Mechanics	101	17	101	15
Painters (General)	98	19	98	16
Barbers	95	21	95	18
Farm Hands	91	21	91	18
Teamsters	88	20	89	17

This table gives the intelligence standards for certain representative occupations expressed in terms of Army General Classification Test Scores and I.Q.'s (Harrell and Harrell[16]). These figures are based on the testing of Army Air Force personnel drawn from various civilian occupations during World War II. (Similar results were indicated in a study of ten thousand British Army recruits by Hemmelweit and Whitfield.[17])

This table not only shows what the mean intelligence is for each of these occupations, but also shows how far a person's intelligence can deviate from this mean and still enable him to succeed in this occupation. Notice that for each occupation is given the "S.D." or *Standard Deviation from the mean.* The S.D. indicates the range of I.Q. or A.G.C.T. points on either side of the mean within which 68 per cent of all the cases fall. For instance, the mean I.Q. of the accountant is 125, and the S.D. is 11. Since 68 per cent of all cases are included within plus or minus one S.D. from the mean, you know that 68 per cent of all accountants have I.Q.'s between 112 and 136. If a person wants to be an accountant, his I.Q. should fall within that range to ensure reasonable chance of success. For if he is as intelligent as most (68 per cent of) accountants, he can expect to do as well as they in so far as intelligence is concerned.

The chances are that a person could hardly do acceptable work in any such occupations if his intelligence falls more than one S.D. below the mean for that occupation. In many fields he is likely to be restless if his intelligence is much higher than is typically found in that field. But in this latter connection it must be recognized that some fields offer opportunities for work of almost unlimited complexity and interest if the person has the intellectual ability to do it. Law, for example, has no upper ceiling with regard to the possibilities of difficult intellectual activity. Persons vastly superior to the average may expect to receive nothing but help from any unusual excess of intellectual ability they may have, if they choose a suitable occupation.

The best way to determine your intelligence, of course, is to take one of several standardized intelligence tests. The practice of testing students in high schools and colleges is growing so rapidly that before long any student in a progressive community can reasonably expect to be tested and informed of his standing by the time he needs such information.

Physical requirements. Each occupation makes its own peculiar demands on the physique and health. For example, civil engineers, meteorologists, and geologists often work in extreme climates and bad weather. In choosing a vocation it is important to bear in mind the physical requirements, selecting something in keeping with your actual physical strength and endurance.

Temperament and personality required. In many types of work, the right personality and temperament are as important as intelligence. Inspectors, bookkeepers, and research men are usually introverted, since the process of natural selection and the exercise of voluntary choice have eliminated the extroverts, who are ill-adapted to detailed work performed without close human contact. On the other hand, successful salesmen, supervisors, and other people who have to get results through human contact are typically extroverted, because only extroverts can be consistently aggressive in face-to-face relationships with people. In fact, most business and industrial executives tend to be extroverted, although there are certain executives specializing in organizing and planning who may be somewhat introverted.

There has been considerable research into the problem of what personality traits are associated with various occupational groups.

In one typical study in this field, nurses were compared with college girls on the basis of emotional stability and introversion-extroversion. The nurses as a group showed far fewer emotional troubles than did the college girls and were decidedly more extroverted. (Elwood[18])

Chapter 15 described some of the personality tests that the vocational counselor can use in helping the individual choose an occupation for which he is temperamentally fitted.

"Social intelligence," or the ability to get along with people, is an important determiner of successful vocational adjustment. In one study, some four hundred occupations were rated as to the degree of five basic qualities each required of the people engaged in them. One of these qualities was social intelligence. It was defined as follows in terms of six levels:

"*Persuasive—face-to-face*—direct contact with the public in attempting to convince or in some way directly influence the people in question. Examples: Politician, life-insurance salesman, bond salesman.

"*Managerial*—requires ability to understand and control people either as workers or as clients; must be able to inspire confidence and cooperation. Examples: Executive, factory manager, foreman, lawyer, physician, secretary.

"*Persuasive—indirect*—seeks to convince or influence the public in other than direct, face-to-face situations; usually through mediums of communication such as the newspaper, radio, etc. Examples: Advertising-copy writer, publicity writer, radio speaker, actor.

"*Business contact and service*—direct contact with the public in retail sales work involving a small degree of salesmanship, or contact with the public for the purpose of giving information or assistance. Examples: Sales clerk, information clerk, hotel clerk, theater usher.

"*Rank-and-file workers*—require only ability to get along with supervisors and fellow workers. Examples: Day laborer, factory worker, office clerk.

"*A-social occupations*—no public contact; individual work usually requiring specialized skills and knowledge. Examples: Watchmaker, bookkeeper, night watchman, mathematician, technical laboratory research worker." (Bingham[19])

In general, extroversion, emotional stability, self-confidence, and social intelligence as defined above, all go together.

Special abilities for different occupations. Most occupations require certain special abilities. An engineer's work demands the use of complicated mathematics, for which he must have special ability. The surgeon needs good vision and good motor coordination. The architect must be able to visualize spatial relationships. Standardized tests are available for many such special abilities. Among these are the Meier Art Judgment Test (items from which are reproduced opposite); the Seashore, or Kwalwasser, Test of Musical Talent; the Ishihara Test for Color Blindness (p. 259); the Minnesota Test of Mechanical Aptitude; the Minnesota Manual Dexterity Test (p. 3); and the Minnesota Paper Form Board, which measures the special ability involved in visualizing relationship of objects in space. Testing for many complex occupations (such as law and medicine) is still in its infancy, but as the abilities required are subjected to more precise definition, they can be tested by refined measures of special ability such as those developed by Thurstone (p. 211) and others.

(*Courtesy*
Dr. Norman C. Meier.)

One successful test of special abilities, as needed in different occupations, is
the Meier Art Judgment Test, from which two items are reproduced here. The
test is designed to measure aesthetic judgment by having the subject choose
between two pictures which differ in some specified way. Actually one of the
pictures is a work by a well-known artist, and the other is a redrawing with
certain elements changed. After the subject has named one of the pictures as
superior, he is asked to state why. The position of the girl is different
in the two pictures above, the one on the right being artistically superior in
balance and composition. In the pictures of herons, the background has been
varied, and the left-hand picture possesses the setting most appropriate to the
technique and mood of the work. This test has been subjected to extensive checking
to ascertain its validity and reliability, which have both turned out to be high.

What satisfactions does the work give?

The successful person is the one whose work brings him the satisfactions he wants. Explore and appraise your motives critically and carefully, then find the work offering the rewards you consider important.
Ask yourself what satisfactions you require. What do you regard as
success? Is the man who makes the most money the most successful?
Or is it the man who works the fewest hours? Is direct service to humanity an important goal of yours? Do you require the respect, even
the envy, of your fellows, or are you capable of being happy in doing
what you like regardless of what prestige it brings?

The Employee's Search for the Right Job 635

The person who likes to have social approval of his work will be interested in a study originally conducted in 1929 (Counts[20]) and repeated in 1946 (Deeg and Paterson[21]). College students rated the prestige of various occupations in rank order, with the results shown in the table below.

COMPARISON OF SOCIAL STATUS RANKS OF TWENTY-FIVE
OCCUPATIONS OBTAINED IN 1925 AND IN 1946

Occupations	Rank Order 1925	Rank Order 1946	Difference in Rank Order
Banker	1	2.5	+1.5
Physician	2	1	−1
Lawyer	3	2.5	− .5
Superintendent of Schools	4	4	0
Civil Engineer	5	5	0
Army Captain	6	6	0
Foreign Missionary	7	7	0
Elementary School Teacher	8	8	0
Farmer	9	12	+3
Machinist	10	9	−1
Traveling Salesman	11	16	+5
Grocer	12	13	+1
Electrician	13	11	−2
Insurance Agent	14	10	−4
Mail Carrier	15	14	−1
Carpenter	16	15	−1
Soldier	17	19	+2
Plumber	18	17	−1
Motorman	19	18	−1
Barber	20	20	0
Truck Driver	21	21.5	+ .5
Coal Miner	22	21.5	+ .5
Janitor	23	23	0
Hod Carrier	24	24	0
Ditch Digger	25	25	0

In 1927 a comparative study (Davis[22]) was conducted in Russia using categories of occupations similar to those above. The test was administered to a group of Russian youth whose average age was 17.9 years, and the results were later compared with those of the 1929 study above. High-school teachers received about the same rating in both groups, and so did many other occupations: for instance, carpenter, barber, and house porter. Other occupations were ranked very differently by the two groups; mechanic and common laborer rated higher in the Russian survey than in the American, while physician was ranked lower in Russia than in America.

Many lines of evidence show that success in a given occupation depends upon the individual's pattern of interests as well as upon his abilities and other qualifications. However, students sometimes think they want to enter a certain profession but find that they do not have the fundamental interests required by it. The motives leading young people to choose their vocations are frequently quite superficial, or at least unreliable. For example, a young man wants to enter law, thinking of the thrill and drama of a court trial and not knowing that most of the lawyer's work is done at his desk outside of court hours.

If a person has interests largely the same as people already successful in a certain occupation, he has a good chance of a happy, successful career in that occupation. However, there is not a high correlation between interests, intelligence, and special aptitudes. Even if a man's I.Q. and mathematical ability are suitable for his being an accountant, his pattern of interests may be quite unsuitable. Measurement of a person's pattern of interests is an important factor to be considered in the prediction of vocational adjustment. The Strong Vocational Interest Blank, if honestly filled out, is of great value in predicting the degree of satisfaction that you would actually receive from engaging in the various occupations for which standards are available.

Its value is clearly shown in the chart below, which is based on a study of 588 men attending a training school conducted by Aetna Casualty and Surety Company (Bills[23]). These men filled out the Strong Vocational Interest Blank while in training, and then a year later were rated by their managers on their actual selling success.

Score Received on Strong Interest Test	Per Cent Rated by Manager as		
	Outstanding	Fair	Failure
+6	25	53	22
+4 to +5	16	56	28
+3 to −2	11	47	42
−3 to −5	8	39	53
−6	4	20	76

Strong himself reports the results of a survey of 210 life-insurance salesmen which shows the accuracy of his device in predicting which men will succeed vocationally. Men who received an "A" rating on his Vocational Interest Blank sold annually $169,000 worth of paid-up insurance—and men who received a "C" rating, only $62,000 (Strong[24]).

One procedure in psychology, still in the developmental stage, may some day simplify the practical problem of determining for what occupation a person's interest patterns fit him. An intricate method of statistical analysis has been employed to determine the number and nature of the factors accounting for similarities and dissimilarities among the interests of members of eighteen professions and occupations (Thurstone[25]). Four fundamental clusters (combinations) of interests have been found, which are represented in varying degrees in

The Employee's Search for the Right Job   637

the members of various callings. These clusters are interest in *science*, interest in *language*, interest in *people*, and interest in *business*. For example, it has been found that psychologists, chemists, and medical men are typically more interested in science than they are in people.

Such procedures indicate that eventually all professions and occupations may be grouped according to the few basic interests involved. Someday perhaps a person can be tested to see how much of each basic interest he possesses and whether his combination of interests fits the vocation he wants to enter. But until these interest clusters have been more thoroughly investigated, and until they have been incorporated into workable tests, we must treat interest in each profession as separate and distinct, and administer a different battery of interest tests for each occupation.

What opportunities exist?

Whether or not a job of the kind you want is available is not a psychological problem, but it is a very important economic one. One way of determining the likelihood of finding an opening in the occupation you are considering is to note whether such employment is expanding or contracting and at what rate.

The table below shows the employment trends for men and women engaged in various professions and occupations according to the United States Census. It shows how much (by what per cent) employment increased or decreased from 1930 to 1940 in occupations often chosen by college students.

MEN	Per Cent Change from 1930 to 1940
Social Welfare Workers	+274
Stenographers	+ 92
Teachers (Academic Subjects)	+ 27
Chemists	+ 21
Reporters and Authors	+ 11
Lawyers	+ 11
Engineers	+ 9
Physicians	+ 8
Clergymen	+ 8
Architects	+ 8
Art Teachers	+ 5
Bookkeepers and Accountants	+ 1
Draftsmen	+ 1
Dentists	0
Insurance Agents	− 16
Music Teachers	− 17
Real Estate Agents	− 50

WOMEN	*Per Cent Change from 1930 to 1940*
Welfare Workers	+84
Saleswomen	+25
Stenographers	+23
Librarians	+18
Nurses	+16
Physicians	+10
Reporters	+ 8
Bookkeepers and Accountants	—11
Teachers	—14
Insurance Agents	—17
Art Teachers	—22
Music Teachers	—30
Actresses	—80

Opportunities in psychology will interest many students. A continued upward trend in employment has been predicted for psychology (Marquis[26]). The largest numbers will be employed as college teachers; next come clinical psychologists, then school psychologists, followed by those in business and government.

In choosing an occupation, such information is very helpful in determining what job opportunities exist. In general, an increase in employment means expanding job opportunities and a decrease means the reverse—this is especially true when the pay and working conditions are desirable. But in the case of women teachers, the declining trend means that teachers are leaving the profession for better-paying work and are therefore leaving job opportunities for those who are still willing to enter the teaching profession in spite of its low salary level.

THE EMPLOYER'S SEARCH FOR THE RIGHT EMPLOYEE

THE PSYCHOLOGY of choosing a career (vocational guidance) and the psychology of selecting employees (employment psychology) are very much alike. Both are concerned with the adjustment of the individual to his work. Both make use of the same tests, interviews, and rating-scale techniques in appraising the psychological make-up of the individual. The only difference between employment psychology and vocational guidance is one of emphasis. The discussion so far has shown that vocational guidance is oriented primarily toward the job-seeker, but employment psychology works from the employer's point of view. In vocational guidance the attempt is to find the best job for the man; in employment psychology the emphasis is on finding the best man available for the job. Fortunately, the best man for the job is usually a man for whom that job is best.

Reasons for efficient personnel selection

The cost of improper selection of workers is borne by both employer and worker. If a man is hired for a type of work that does not arouse his interest and enthusiasm, he will ultimately be dissatisfied. Or if the employer is careless enough to hire a man likely to be inefficient on the job, the worker himself will eventually discover that he is a misfit and will become discouraged. If the employee does not eventually seek transfer or quit outright, his employer will probably discharge him. Either way, the employer and employee are likely to terminate their working relationship.

Preventing excessive turnover. The *termination rate* of a company means the number of individuals in each hundred employed who are discharged, are laid off, or quit voluntarily. If the termination rate is high, new workers must be hired to replace those who have left, and the company is said to have a high rate of labor turnover.

Excessive labor turnover is costly. One employment manager gives the following figures to suggest the relative costs of hiring and training employees who have had different experience for the job:

Experienced worker (skilled job)	$500.00
Semi-experienced worker	$190.00
Old employee rehired for same job	$ 24.00

The cost of hiring and training a new worker in industry is, of course, much greater than the cost of just the training procedure, for he is likely to damage equipment, to waste material, or to suffer serious and costly accidents. His production record at the outset will be poorer than that of the worker with a long period of employment behind him. If termination rate and labor turnover are high in a particular plant as compared with similar plants in the same community and industry, something is wrong. The trouble may be either faulty selection procedure or management's failure to see that the workers' psychological needs are satisfied.

Preventing excessive absenteeism. *Absenteeism*—failing to come to work—might be defined as "partial termination." While illness and other personal causes will require that an employee stay away from work on rare occasions, most experts agree that 3 per cent absenteeism (or missing one day in every thirty-three working days) is a reasonable standard. When the absentee rate is higher than that, something is wrong. As was shown in the study described on page 629, an important cause of absenteeism is management's failure to fit together the right worker and the right job.

Termination and absenteeism are the most obvious indications of inefficient adjustment of the employees to their jobs. However, there are many other ways of measuring this lack of adjustment. If many employees ask to be transferred to other departments, inefficient hiring methods may well be to blame, although other important psychological dissatisfactions may also be at work. Wherever workers are maladjusted and dissatisfied, part of the trouble is probably due to inefficient selection methods.

Selecting employees without using tests

Despite the rapid advances in the field of psychological testing as applied to the selection of employees in business and industry, the most frequently used method of employing still remains the personal interview, frequently supplemented by letters of application and letters of recommendation. It is not necessary to repeat the advantages and limitations of the personal interview (which were discussed on pp. 550-552).

Letters of application. The letter of application has practically no value as a means of judging the fitness of an individual for a particular job. Perhaps its most serious limitation is that the prospective employer has no assurance that it was actually written by the applicant. Moreover, such a letter is often very general with regard to the applicant's capacity to do the work required, although a complete and accurate record of the applicant's past employment is usually enclosed. But despite the inherent weakness of the letter of application as a means of predicting performance on the job, many employers still want one, and the serious applicant learns to write a good one.

Letters of recommendation. According to a recent survey, about 82 per cent of employment offices still require a list of references from nonrelatives of the applicant (usually including past employers) who know something of his past life or work history.

Letters of recommendation have certain limitations which greatly impair their value as a means of hiring. For one thing, the past employer is not an unprejudiced source of information concerning an employee. It sometimes happens that the employer of a worker whose record is not altogether satisfactory will jump at the chance of getting rid of him and so will write a falsely enthusiastic letter. Conversely, an employer who wants to retain an able employee against his will may write a rather unfavorable letter.

Another weakness of the letter of recommendation is that it is usually written by an influential person who is often too busy to dig out the record necessary to an accurate report of the applicant's performance on the job. In addition, he may almost have forgotten about some individual who worked for him several years ago. At any rate, he usually loses interest once an employee has left the firm. And even in the universities, in these days of mass education and large classes, the professor sometimes does not have the time or facilities to follow the development of each of his many students. For instance, a professor may have as many as one thousand students in his elementary-psychology lecture section in one year's time, so that although he is frequently asked to write letters of recommendation, he must often refuse on the grounds that he does not have adequate information available.

The photograph. Many employers still insist that applicants supply their photographs. However, it is impossible to judge character, personality, or intelligence from a photograph.

> Two psychologists went through the autobiographical sketches of the graduates of a large university, published in connection with a class reunion (Landis and Phelps[27]). The alumni publication contained, in addition to the biographical material, two photographs of each individual, one taken at the time of graduation and the other at the time of the class reunion twenty-five years later. From the autobiographies, which set forth in minute detail the various accomplishments of each alumnus, it was possible to select five successful and five unsuccessful men in each of the professions of law, medicine, education, and engineering. Then these photographs were projected on a screen before judges, who were asked to pick out the successful and the unsuccessful. In the original study, college students were used as judges, and in a later study (Viteles and Smith[28]), trained personnel workers. By chance the judges would be right in their choices about one half of the time, and the results showed their judgments were no more accurate than chance.

Even trained personnel workers, despite their daily contacts with applicants for employment, cannot accurately judge successfulness and unsuccessfulness on the basis of a photograph.

The value of psychological tests

During the past twenty years, a growing number of organizations have discovered that psychological tests used in hiring, if conducted by experts, can contribute enormously to efficient hiring. The evidence is impressive, both in private industry and in the armed services. (The necessary steps in job testing are shown on the opposite page.)

Psychological tests in industry and government. The United States Civil Service found in one study that 93 per cent of the appointees selected by psychological tests were more efficient than average employees selected by other means. The Philadelphia Electric Company

JOB-TESTING IN MODERN INDUSTRY

A careful analysis and description of the psychological and physical demands of specific jobs is essential in order to match men and jobs. At right, a job analyst is discussing with a supervisor the particular skills required for certain jobs. From such information, he groups together certain jobs into "job families" which require certain abilities and aptitudes. The problem then is to find individuals who have these particular combinations of abilities and aptitudes.

First: the men at right are taking "screening" tests (some are group tests, some individual) to determine the general type of work for which they are qualified.

Below left: on the aptitude assembly line, the men move from one test to another where their different abilities and reactions are observed by trained examiners. In industry, these tests often include, for example, the Minnesota Tests for manual dexterity, mechanical aptitude, and spatial visualization. Other types of work require tests specially designed to measure the abilities involved (see p. 634).

After the tests are completed, a trained counselor (below right) analyzes the applicant's pattern of abilities in the form of a psychograph, to see how it compares with the pattern of requirements which have been drawn up for different jobs. He then discusses with the applicant the kind of job for which he is best fitted. (Photographs courtesy Dr. Orlo L. Crissey, AC Spark Plug Division, General Motors Corporation.)

The Employer's Search for the Right Employee 643

reports a 90 per cent decrease in operating mistakes since it started using psychological tests in the selection of substation operators. Not only were mistakes reduced, but there was a noticeable improvement of morale among employees who were hired on the basis of their performance on psychological tests. The Scoville Manufacturing Company developed a test for selecting apprentices which required only thirty minutes per person but accomplished a "weeding out" that had previously required a year of observation on the job.

Let us examine some more detailed evidence of the effectiveness of psychological tests for hiring in industry.

1 One evaluation of selection tests studied the relationship between the aptitude-test scores and actual sales performances of a large group of young life-insurance salesmen. It was discovered that the salesmen who had received an *A* rating on the aptitude test sold over twice as much insurance in their first year as did the average of the group, whereas those individuals receiving an *E* rating sold less than half as much as the average. The individuals rating *A* sold five times as much insurance as *E* raters did. (Kurtz[29])

2 Even more impressive results are reported in the selection of life-insurance salesmen by a recently developed system (Steward[30]). The following table, which shows the average earnings of groups of salesmen rated by this system, speaks for itself.

Scientific Rating	Average Earnings	Number of Cases
Very superior	$6176	13
Superior	4549	33
Good	2685	32
Fair	2278	17
Borderline	1308	18
Poor	733	5
Very poor	229	2

3 A study was made of the work performance of 394 drafting trainees at Lockheed Aircraft Corporation, who were tested and hired prior to training. The study showed that termination rate was lowest with those who scored highest on the tests, as you can see from the table:

Test Standard Met	Rate of Termination
A	7.7%
B	14.9
C	16.4
D	26.6
E	30.6
F	61.3

Notice that those applicants who scored *F* had a termination rate eight times greater than that of the *A* applicants.

In another group of 165 trainees who had been hired, the A-scoring trainees not only stayed on the job longer but their work was rated as superior by the instructors in charge of the training program:

Test Standard Met	Per Cent of Group Meeting Standard Who Were Rated above Average of Total Group
A	100
B	89
C	74
D	58
E	43
F	30

In other words, high-scoring trainees stay longer on the job and do better work as well. (Grimsley[31])

Psychological tests in the armed services. The United States Army Air Forces made history during World War II by the speed, economy, and efficiency with which their selection and training program was able to put a vast body of trained men into action. The graph below (*Psychological Bulletin*[32]) demonstrates how valuable pilot aptitude scores, as determined by careful psychological tests, can be in ascertaining which men will make good pilots.

Relation between elimination rate and pilot aptitude score

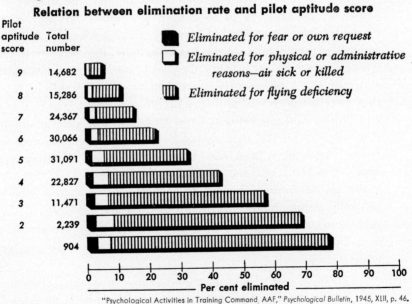

Pilot aptitude score	Total number			
		■ Eliminated for fear or own request		
		□ Eliminated for physical or administrative reasons—air sick or killed		
9	14,682			
8	15,286	▥ Eliminated for flying deficiency		
7	24,367			
6	30,066			
5	31,091			
4	22,827			
3	11,471			
2	2,239			
	904			

Per cent eliminated

"Psychological Activities in Training Command, AAF," *Psychological Bulletin*, 1945, XLII, p. 46.

Note that as the pilot aptitude score decreases from 9 to 1, there is an increase in the per cent of men quitting through fear and in the per cent of men eliminated for flying deficiency.

The Employer's Search for the Right Employee 645

In studying this impressive evidence of the value which psychological testing can have in predicting occupational fitness, bear in mind that the results represent what the tests accomplish over and above the medical examination, which had already eliminated the physically unsuited. Other branches of the service used scientific testing procedures with comparable results.

In the Army Air Forces alone, over a period of four years, the Psychological Units which ran the testing programs for the selection of pilots, navigators, and bombardiers tested approximately 1,500,000 cadets at an average cost per man of only five dollars. Apart from the contribution this program made toward winning the war—a contribution which can never be measured in money—it saved billions of dollars in training costs, through eliminating the unfit.

All this evidence leaves no doubt that desirable results can be accomplished through the use of psychological tests in selecting men for certain jobs.

Can personality be tested for a job?

During the past ten years much emphasis has been put on personality, temperament, and interest as factors determining the success of the employee. As progress in measuring job knowledge and aptitude reached a satisfactory level of accuracy, these subjective factors have assumed greater significance. It has been found that many well-trained workers with high aptitude for their jobs failed or became dissatisfied and quit either because they were emotionally unstable or because they were not interested in their jobs. Since personality tests, temperament scales, and interest tests have worked well in clinical situations, it is only natural that they should be tried out in employment work. Several types have been tried: the *self-inventory*, the *standardized application blank*, and the *standardized interview*.

The self-inventory. The results with the self-inventory have been generally disappointing. Apparently it does not work well when the subject has a strong incentive to create a good impression by consciously distorting his answers, or when he unconsciously engages in wishful thinking.

> The most widely publicized self-inventory is the Humm-Wadsworth Temperament Scale. This test was administered to 59 appliance salesmen after they had been selected by the usual procedure. When the tests were scored and interpreted, the results were very disappointing. The candidates with poor scores on the self-rating test succeeded on the job as often as those with good scores. (Viteles[33])

The National Research Council Committee on Selection and Training of Aircraft Pilots made validation studies of a wide variety of self-inventories. These included not only the Humm-Wadsworth Temperament Scale but also the Maslow Dominance Test and the Guilford STDCR Test, which are widely used in clinical work. These studies were pursued over a period of five years and were conducted by well-trained experts at a number of universities. It is therefore of considerable significance that such devices were not recommended for the selection of aircraft pilots. (Viteles[34])

The standardized application blank. One way of measuring the stability factor has proved workable time after time. It is known as the *standardized application blank* or the *biographical inventory*, and in recent years has been widely used.

Many application blanks, unfortunately, are limited in their usefulness because the items they contain are a result of slow growth in which hunch and inspiration have been more important than careful analytical study. All too often the questions in the application form reflect some misconception of bygone management. It is possible, however, to subject each item in the application blank to rigid analysis to determine whether a particular item actually differentiates the successful worker from the unsuccessful one. Let us take a typical study of the predictive value of items in an application blank.

A comparison was made between the application blanks and work records of five hundred life-insurance salesmen (Russell and Cope,[35] and the Phoenix Mutual Life Insurance Company[36]). When a certain answer to a particular question was given more frequently by the successful than by the unsuccessful salesmen, that question was given a positive weight. When an item was answered in a certain way more often by the unsuccessful than by the successful salesmen, that answer was given a negative weight. It was thus possible to assign weights to each answer for each item in the application blank—weights which would indicate the probability of success.

A total score for each salesman was arrived at by combining the various items in the blank, by adding the positive and negative weights. There was such a high correlation between a salesman's total score and the amount of insurance he actually sold that further research was done to improve the value of this application blank as a means of hiring. Success was defined in two ways: as the amount of insurance sold during a beginner's first year, and as the persistence of each man in his work, measured by the number of years he stayed with the company.

The following items, which are frequently included in application blanks, had high value in selecting successful insurance salesmen: (a) Marital status. It was found that married men make better life-insurance salesmen than unmarried men of the same age, and that the married man with a few children is a better salesman of insurance than the married man with no children. (b) Education was found to be an important factor. (c) The higher the applicant's previous income, the more likely he was to become a successful insurance salesman. (d) The more insurance the individual carried himself, the more likely he was to be successful as a life-insurance salesman. (e) Previous occupation bore an important relationship to success as a salesman. As might be expected, men with previous selling experience were more successful than men with other kinds of previous experience. (f) The longer the man's residence in the community, the greater his success in selling insurance. (g) Membership in organizations such as lodges, fraternities, and so on, goes with success in selling insurance.

Alert management today has an efficiently organized personnel or employment office which is geared to use psychological tests and weighted application blanks, along with the personal interview. Where this is done, the desirable procedure is to use the psychological test and the application blank first to make a preliminary selection. The survivors of the preliminary selection may then be more adequately interviewed by a well-trained personnel interviewer.

The writer installed a procedure like this in a plastics company in Los Angeles with the result that 23 per cent fewer persons needed to be hired to maintain the working force when only persons ranking above average in application-blank scores were employed.

The personal-history inventory has proved of value in the selection of aircraft pilots and other air-crew personnel (Guilford and Lacey[37]). This type of information has recently been useful in predicting absenteeism and termination at Lockheed Aircraft Corporation (Stockford[38] and Palmer, Purpus, and Stockford[39]).

By and large, the standardized application blank has been as valuable in predicting stability on the job as the self-inventory method has been disappointing. The reason for this superiority is that the questions are objective and the answers can easily be verified for accuracy by the prospective employer, which is not true of the self-inventory used for selection or promotion.

The standardized interview. The strengths and weaknesses of the personal-interview method in diagnosing human personality were reviewed in an earlier chapter. Experience in industry is showing that a carefully standardized personal interview can be extremely effective as a selection device.

One procedure of this sort has already demonstrated results in a variety of situations (McMurry[40]). It may be briefly described as closely resembling the standardized application blank, except that the information is taken in a personal interview. The interview is conducted so as to bring out the data relevant to the following points: the applicant's work record, schooling, early home environment, present domestic and home situation, and health. A skillful interviewer, following an established pattern, is able to draw from the applicant personal facts that would be refused in filling out a printed application form.

> One study made of this interview procedure found a high validity coefficient (.68) between a person's standardized-interview score at the time of hiring and his success-on-the-job rating made after the employee's supervisor became familiar with the quality of his work. The interview procedure obtained just as good results in predicting stability on the job, as measured by length of employment before termination, as in predicting work quality. (McMurry and Johnson[41])

These psychological procedures used for selecting employees are just part of the contribution that modern psychology has made to the problem of dealing with the human factor in industry. In recent years there has developed an ever wider realization of the fact that the employee's relation to his job is not purely economic, that it involves his intelligence, his special aptitudes, and his deepest emotional needs. This realization has brought extensive research into the psychological problems in industry—research which has been translated into action as modern business executives and vocational counselors have come to realize the importance of giving employer-employee relations a sound psychological basis. Here is an area where modern psychology is making a vital contribution to a critical social problem: the relation between man and his work.

Psychology and social issues

As YOU SAW IN CHAPTER 1, one of the fundamental aims of psychology is to make the world a better place in which to live. Although this task is far too large for any one science or discipline, the psychologist does have certain worth-while insights and suggestions to offer.

EUGENICS AND EUTHENICS

EXPERTS IN THE APPLIED SOCIAL SCIENCES have presented two broad lines of approach to the problems of increasing the quality of the human race and advancing its welfare. These are *eugenics* and *euthenics*. The basic difference between them is that eugenic programs would work through control of heredity, euthenic programs through control of environment. Which is more effective in curing some of the social problems that now confront us?

Advocates of eugenic programs point to forces which are now acting to lower the quality of the human race. The foremost of these is war, which eliminates the strongest and most healthy young men (later in the chapter we shall analyze some of the psychological causes of war). More significant, however, is the fact that families of lower intelligence level and economic status are producing more children per family than are the superior families because the less fortunately situated parents have more children and have them earlier in life. This differential is found both in the United States and in England (Lentz,[1] Sewell,[2] Conrad and Jones,[3] Dawson[4]). To reverse this trend through eugenics, several programs have been suggested: the elimination of war, bonuses to parents of superior ability, dissemination of birth-control knowledge to all classes of society, and sterilization of the unfit.

The only one of these programs which has made any real headway is that of sterilization of the unfit. By 1945 thirty states had passed some sort of sterilization law, but the total number of operations performed by that date fell short of 44,000 (most of which were cases of feeble-mindedness). But since the first sterilization law was passed in the United States, approximately 150,000,000 feeble-minded and insane persons have been born, indicating that sterilization of the unfit has made little progress toward solving the problem. Sterilization has never been seriously advocated as a program for the reduction of neuroses or crime and delinquency, which do not depend primarily on hereditary factors.

Even if we assumed that feeble-mindedness and insanity were produced largely by heredity and even if it were feasible to sterilize every person *showing* these characteristics, we still would not expect any appreciable results from such a program. The reason lies in the mixed nature of the genes we all possess. As you will recall, many traits can be inherited by a child even though his parents do not show those traits. This is because the parents are carrying *recessive* genes for that trait (see p. 90). So even if all the obviously feeble-minded people were sterilized, there would still remain the "carriers," people who were not feeble-minded but carried the genes and passed them on to their children. An estimate has been made (Scheinfeld[5]) that there are ten times as many "carriers" of feeble-mindedness as feeble-minded in our population, so that even if all mental defectives were sterilized, the number of feeble-minded in the next generation would be cut down by only around 10 per cent. For in each generation, sterilization would catch all the feeble-minded children of carriers but would be unable to detect the carrier children of carriers. Even after a thousand years, the recessive genes for feeble-mindedness could never be completely eliminated. And the same is true for many important hereditary defects: they may be "carried" by normal people and so may not be eliminated by sterilizing defectives. (Curiously enough, the best justification of sterilization is as a *euthenic* measure: while defective parents will not necessarily produce children with inherited defects, they will obviously provide a far from adequate environment for their children.)

Thus the possibilities of eliminating hereditary defects through eugenics are seriously limited by the mechanics of heredity. But there is a more serious limitation to eugenic programs as curatives for social problems. This is the fact that most of the human traits that give rise to social problems (as distinguished from purely medical problems, like cancer) are not inherited but are mainly learned from the social environment (see pp. 82 and 149). Greed, prejudice, cruelty, ignorance, indifference to community welfare—all these traits, and many others, are amenable to different forms of learning in the home, school, and community.

All in all, then, we are forced to look to the euthenic programs as the chief means of meeting the problems that confront us as members of a complex and changing society. The present chapter will concern itself with what psychology has discovered about the origins and possible euthenic cures of a few of the more urgent social problems.

The most important euthenic program is public education.

PSYCHOLOGY AND EDUCATION

THE SOCIAL RESPONSIBILITY for educating the children and adults of this country and of the world is a staggering one. If all educational activities are grouped together, they form one of the biggest industries in the United States. America is justly proud of her widespread school system. In no other country can an education be acquired so easily—a fact which explains the important part that public education has played in raising the standard of living in the United States above that found in any other country. We have not gone all the way, however. There are still too many persons of high ability who, because of economic factors, are denied opportunity for an education which is commensurate with their ability. A thoroughgoing system of education conceived as a euthenic program must eliminate such cases, for an educated citizenry is essential to an effective democracy.

The selection of students

Certain interpretations of the democratic principle hold that all persons are created equal and hence that all persons are equally entitled to a free education provided at public expense. But, as we have already seen, there are individual differences in the ability of human beings to learn, just as there are individual differences in any other human trait.

To attempt to educate a person beyond the point where he can profit from instruction is obviously futile; the limiting factor of intelligence cannot be ignored. One of the most significant problems facing higher education at the present time is that of selecting the most promising students. Many of our great private universities have long exercised their right to pick and choose, although the state-supported institutions have been slower in adopting such measures.

Numerous studies on the relationship between intelligence (as measured by standardized tests) and educability (as measured by subject-matter tests and school marks) show that intelligence plays an important role in determining students' grades in elementary school, high school, and college (Harris[6]). However, there is a decided tendency for the correlation between marks and intelligence to be highest in the elementary school and lowest in college, with high school intermediate. There are many reasons for this difference in correlation:

1 The pupils in the lower grades represent practically the entire range of individual differences in intelligence. As they grow older, they are subjected to more and more selection as the less intelligent either drop behind or leave school to go to work. The variation in intelligence grows less, and there is consequently less opportunity for grades and intelligence to "vary together"—that is, to be "correlated." Thus the coefficient of correlation is lower.

2 As education advances, it becomes more and more specialized, so that scholastic success comes to depend more upon special abilities and less upon general intelligence.

3 Then, too, in the lower grades the hours of working are held rather constant for all children. At the high-school level this is less true. The college student has still more freedom to regulate the amount of work he does, so that the student can compensate for poor ability by working hard.

Nevertheless, we may safely conclude that variations in intelligence are accompanied by variations in ability to learn, especially in the lower grades; and that selection of students must be made accordingly.

Allowing for individual differences

Since individuals vary in ability to learn, our schools are confronted with a real problem. Slow learners retard the progress of the group. If they are allowed to set the pace, the brighter pupils become bored and troublesome. If the fast learners are allowed to set the pace, the slow ones, humiliated by their inability to keep up, soon become so lost that they quit trying (i.e., they lower their level of aspiration).

Two attempts to meet the problem of individual differences among the children in the lower grades have been made. These are grouping on the basis of ability, and the project method.

Grouping on the basis of ability. In many schools there is the practice of sectioning learners on the basis of mental age. The children are tested to determine their mental ages, and those of about the same mental age are put together in classes for instruction. Such a procedure enables the teacher to adjust the methods of presenting the subject matter to the intellectual abilities of the pupils. Thus the brighter students do not become bored by too simple a course of study, and the duller ones do not become discouraged by failure to master material beyond their comprehension.

This practice of selecting and sectioning on the basis of intelligence is carried all the way up to and through college. Because of the excessive cost of higher education, the problem of weeding out the unfit and selecting the most promising becomes crucial at that level. That intelligence as measured by tests is an important factor in scholarship is shown by a study the writer has made of students at the University of Illinois. The table below compares the scholastic fortunes of 113 students who were in the *lowest* 10 per cent on the basis of an intelligence test, with the fortunes of those in the *upper* 10 per cent.

Record	Per cent of poorest tenth	Per cent of best tenth
Withdrew before the end of the semester....	12	4
Were dropped by the university..........	24	0
Were placed on probation...............	37	2
Made average grades or better...........	10	84

As we have seen in Chapter 15, there are certain special aptitudes, such as mechanical ability, which bear no strong relationship to the kind of intelligence required in the mastery of academic subjects. Modern educational practice is providing opportunity for an individual with such abilities to take special courses in vocational work which prepare him for some skilled trade which lies within his abilities. There are, of course, a few individuals who are poor in both general intelligence and special aptitudes. For these the school can do little beyond teaching reading, writing, and simple arithmetic useful in daily living.

The necessity of recognizing differences in learning ability in children of the same chronological age is brought out by a carefully controlled experiment which showed that likeness in learning ability is related to likeness in mental age.

A group of average nine-year-old children were compared with a group of children of the same mental age but ranging in chronological age from ten to sixteen years. In other words, a group of children of average I.Q. were paired with a group of older children of the same mental age and consequently lower I.Q. The two groups were put through a learning experiment under carefully standardized conditions.

This experimental setup is adequate to reveal whether learning of the particular subject matter used—sorting geometrical forms—depends upon mental age or upon I.Q. It was found that the results were identical for the two groups. Consequently we must conclude that learning ability depends upon mental age and not upon I.Q., and thus that sectioning of young children in schools must be done on the basis of mental age rather than intelligence quotient. (Woodrow[7])

An adequate program of sectioning school children on the basis of mental age must provide for frequent regroupings. A group of children who have the same mental age but differ in chronological age will gradually become a group dissimilar in learning ability, because, as you know (p. 204), children who are mentally retarded at a given chronological age tend to become more and more retarded (as measured in years of mental age) as time goes on, while the brighter children increase their margin of superiority.

There are certain defects in the practice of sectioning students on the basis of ability. Since individual differences are great, certain very bright students will be much younger than other duller ones of the same mental age. Putting such individuals together results in a group which is quite mixed in degree of physical, social, and emotional maturity. Recent experience in education indicates that if such differences in a group are too great, they are just as harmful as too great intellectual differences. Certain plans attempt to get around this difficulty by treating the classroom situation in one way and the playground situation in another way. Children of equal mental age learn together; children of equal emotional age play together. This compromise has not proved satisfactory, for effective learning, as recent research in education has revealed, is based on social and emotional as well as intellectual experience in the classroom.

The project method. The considerations outlined above led to the development of a still newer practice in education: grouping children of the same chronological age together in the classroom but at the same time providing for individual intellectual differences by a several-track course of study. The subject matter is set up in units or projects which individuals complete as rapidly as their interest and ability permit. The brighter pupils are permitted to go more deeply into the subjects by executing additional projects, while the other students are expected to learn merely the fundamentals. Brighter students, in some instances, help the teacher by coaching one or more of the slower learners.

The technique of teaching

Psychology has made so many contributions to the technique of teaching that it is difficult to give anything but a rough outline in a book of this sort.

Recognizing the role of motivation. One of the outstanding contributions of modern psychology to education has been a greater emphasis on motivation in learning. In the old days the teacher was a drill master who felt obliged to make the pupil learn "or else." The content was presented in arbitrary outlines in the textbooks or in the classroom. Key sentences were designated by the teacher or the author to be

In schools around the turn of the century, pupil and teacher were poles apart. The teacher was a director who gave assignments and examinations, but who was seldom concerned with the process of assimilation that occurred between these two points, or with the relation between learning and personality. A successful repetition of specific facts was all that was considered necessary, regardless of whether this repetition was based on rote memory or a genuine understanding.

committed to memory. Examinations required that the learner give back those words of wisdom in a letter-perfect fashion. The pupil was not held responsible for the understanding of the materials learned and was not encouraged to see new relationships between the ideas; neither was he encouraged to apply his learning to life situations. The research of modern psychology has shown clearly the futility of such educational practices—has shown that meaningful material is retained much longer than is material learned verbatim.

In more and more schools throughout the country today, the learner is being given great freedom of movement. He is permitted to study in his own way problems which interest him. Of course, the teacher does some unobtrusive directing and stimulating of interest, but is not heavy-handed and dictatorial as formerly. Modern education, both private and public, provides interest by bringing real, true-to-life problems into the classroom. The philosophy of modern education is rep-

In modern schools, the teacher is a human being who leads through suggestion rather than command. She realizes that learning is part of the child's total personality development, and she relates what she teaches to the child's developing interests and needs. The ideal is that the child will learn not just specific facts, memorized today and gone by adulthood, but principles and skills which he can use in all areas of living. (Madison, Wisconsin, Public Schools.)

Psychology and Education 657

resented by the slogans *learning by doing* and *learning by living*. The interesting thing is that the children who are permitted to learn by studying problems of everyday life usually learn more of the solid subject matter than those who are forced to study that same subject matter when it is presented with less attention to the students' interests.

A very revealing study has been made on the value of the progressive principles of education which are gaining strength through the modern educational systems. It was conducted by the Commission on the Relation of School and College of the Progressive Education Association (Aikin[8]).

> The first step was to secure the cooperation of the colleges of the country in accepting students from thirty progressive secondary schools without the customary formal transcript of "college preparatory" units. With this accomplished, the thirty schools, distributed throughout the country, were free to reorganize their curriculums. Each school made its own plans with the aid and cooperation of the Commission. Once a year from 1933 through eight years, the principals and teachers of the schools met with the Commission to discuss their problems, findings, and new ideas. In general, they all followed two major principles: (1) The general life of the school and methods of teaching should conform to what is now known about the ways in which human beings learn and grow. (2) The high school in the United States should rediscover its chief reason for existence, i.e., it should give the youth an understanding and appreciation of the way of life we call democracy through living that kind of life every day at school.
>
> An example of the type of curriculum found in the thirty schools is taken from a Denver high school in which the students took a "Core Curriculum" for two hours every day throughout the high-school period, and then chose their other subjects, which were all oriented to what they desired to do after they graduated. The "Core Curriculum" took up such problems as the following: (1) understanding ourselves through discovering our interests, aptitudes, and powers; (2) developing interests and appreciations which we already have and exploring others in such fields as reading, painting, singing, etc.; (3) exploring the problems of living in a modern family; (4) studying the problems of human relationships (boy-and-girl relationships, for example); (5) studying the community, its history, its government and taxation, etc.; (6) discovering the unique characteristics of American democracy and comparing them with the other methods of political and social organization of the world; (7) studying economic problems such as consumer problems, living conditions under a machine civilization, vocational opportunities, and employment problems.
>
> Beginning in 1936 for four years, the members of the College Follow-up Staff studied 1475 matched pairs of students, one student in each pair coming from a traditional high school and the other from

one of the thirty progressive high schools. The students were carefully matched on the basis of intelligence, sex, race, age, church affiliation; size and type of secondary school; public or private education; size, type, and geographic location of home community; the socioeconomic status of family; extra-curricular activities in secondary school; and vocational objectives.

This study included reports of the college on school and student-activity achievements, as well as conferences with the students themselves. It was found that the graduates of the thirty schools—

"(1) earned a slightly higher total grade average;

(2) earned higher grade averages in all subject fields except foreign language;

(3) specialized in the same academic fields as did the comparison students;

(4) did not differ from the comparison group in the number of times they were placed on probation;

(5) received slightly more academic honors in each year;

(6) were more often judged to possess a high degree of intellectual curiosity and drive;

(7) were more often judged to be precise, systematic, and objective in their thinking;

(8) were more often judged to have developed clear or well-formulated ideas concerning the meaning of education—especially in the first two years of college;

(9) more often demonstrated a high degree of resourcefulness in meeting new situations;

(10) did not differ from the comparison group in ability to plan their time effectively;

(11) had about the same problems of adjustment as the comparison group, but approached their solution with greater effectiveness;

(12) participated somewhat more frequently, and more often enjoyed, appreciative experiences in the arts;

(13) participated more in all organized student groups except religious and "service" activities;

(14) earned in each college year a higher percentage of nonacademic honors (officership in organizations, election to managerial societies, athletic insignia, leading roles in dramatic and musical presentations);

(15) did not differ from the comparison group in the quality of adjustment to their contemporaries;

(16) differed only slightly from the comparison group in the kinds of judgments about their schooling;

(17) had a somewhat better orientation toward the choice of a vocation;

(18) demonstrated a more active concern for what was going on in the world."

It is quite obvious that these progressively run high schools did not leave students with a poor background for college work—a false charge often made by ultraconservatives. In fact their graduates were a little more frequently the recipients of academic honors, such as Phi Beta Kappa and the Dean's List, than were the graduates of more traditional schools. Nor did they turn out a group of pampered weaklings incapable of leadership, to take one more false charge. In fact 45 per cent of them won nonacademic honors, such as class and student-body offices, debate and athletic managerships, as compared with 40 per cent of the graduates of traditional high schools.

At one time the results of this study would have been used as ammunition in the fierce controversy between "progressive" and "traditional" educators. As is frequently true when a new ideology appears on the scene, the two forms of education were once represented as being poles apart. But with time, the extreme progressivists have come to recognize their own defects, at the same time that the more traditional educators have come to accept the sound principles emphasized by the progressive group. Today more and more schools throughout the country—both private and public—are moving toward a working integration of the two forms of education. It is true, of course, that in the modern schools operated on progressive principles, greater demands are made upon the personality of the teacher. Real leadership and understanding of children's motivation are required of the teacher if she is to stimulate and direct the interests of students into productive fields of inquiry. In addition, she must be skilled at employing the various types of diagnostic tests which are used to reveal the weaknesses of the learner to both himself and his teacher. Such tests are frequently followed by special discussion and drill sessions which enable the student to iron out his difficulties.

Psychology and the curriculum. Educational psychology has contributed greatly to the efficient preparation of textbooks and of courses of study. Careful analyses have been made of children's learning abilities and interests at various stages of their development. Such analyses have shown that certain concepts within a subject ought to be delayed a year or two to permit the student to achieve greater intellectual maturity; others can be moved up a year or two. The modern writer of textbooks tries to present material in a way which has interest or utility for the student, and to present it in the order in which it will be easiest to learn. As you know (p. 64), the old notion that certain subjects which lack interest or utility can "strengthen the mind" is no longer accepted by modern educators.

An important contribution to the education of the human being in groups—and one that is especially adapted to the needs of the slow learner in our schools—is the motion-picture film and other audio-visual aids. Numerous experiments in the schools and in the military services have shown the superiority, in certain areas, of visual methods (whether motion pictures or slide films) over the more traditional reading and lecture methods, although they are not the ideal medium for all types of material.

> In one experiment conducted with Army Air Force personnel it was discovered that seeing an animated cartoon on the subject of flexible gunnery taught 50 per cent "more facts per person per minute" than did studying a well-written manual with numerous carefully drawn diagrams and illustrations. The superiority of the sound film over the printed presentation was much greater in the case of the slower learners. (Gibson[9])

Such research and experimentation in techniques of teaching are among the most useful contributions that psychology can make to the solution of social problems. For an educated citizenry is essential to effective democracy, and yet a study conducted by the National Opinion Research Center has indicated that only 21 per cent of American adults have a reasonably accurate knowledge about the Bill of Rights, which is one of the cornerstones of American liberty (*Opinion News*[10]). Obviously our educational system needs reform, and psychology is providing some of the information and procedures necessary to achieve it.

PUBLIC OPINION IN A DEMOCRACY

IN AMERICA, PUBLIC OPINION FUNCTIONS as the "voice of democracy," choosing leaders and deciding questions of public policy. In a democracy, public opinion both influences and is influenced by leaders; in a totalitarian state it is controlled through fear and force when persuasion fails. In all areas of society, public opinion is powerful. It sets codes of behavior, formulates standards of morality, establishes rights and principles under which people must live. It is the supreme court of society. Ten years ago, for example, certain diseases could not be mentioned in polite society, in motion pictures, or over the radio. Today, thanks to a change in public opinion, the word *syphilis*, for example, can be used by the newspaper reporter or the radio commentator without fear of popular protest. Public opinion is the principal power which governs our social and economic life.

How public opinion is formed

Public opinion changes but changes gradually. What is "wrong" at one time becomes "right" at another; this is illustrated by the gradual change in public opinion with regard to cigarette smoking by women.

Countless surveys over the past few years show that public opinion is not "left" today and "right" tomorrow; it does not say "yes" this week and "no" the next. What are some of the forces responsible for this slow, gradual change?

Public opinion and the social structure. One important fact about public opinion is that it is not the same in all parts of the society. An expert on public opinion (Lasswell[11]) has stated that there are the following sources of division in public opinion:

1 *Differences in income.* "Chicago's poor wards are by tradition Democratic; in Philadelphia, poor wards usually support one faction within the Republican party."

2 *Social class lines.* "We expect to find differences in outlook between semi-skilled factory workers, skilled factory workers, clerical workers, small shopkeepers, foremen and sub-managers, small farmers, and low-income professional groups . . ."

3 *Specific occupational experience.* It is well known that big business, small business, farmers, the professionals, factory workers, the unemployed, the consumer all have special interests—and special legislative demands which they are interested in satisfying.

To this analysis we may add:

4 *Differences in region, race, religion, and nationality.* These affect opinion on many issues in domestic legislation and foreign policy.

5 *Differences in age and sex.* It has been demonstrated that young people are more likely than are their elders to adopt new ways of thinking and acting. There is also "the woman's side" to many an issue.

Public opinion changes when the social structure changes. For example, during a depression the growing number of unemployed and the general shift toward lower incomes cause marked changes in attitudes toward direct governmental participation in the economy, tax measures, foreign-trade policy, and other issues.

Majority and expert opinion. People tend to believe what they think other people believe. They are influenced both by what "the majority" believes and by what "experts" believe, although an interesting experiment has indicated that they are influenced more by majority opinion than by expert opinion (Marple[12]). In other words, people's opinions change when they are shown that other people think differently about the subject; it is well known by salesmen that popularity of a product is a strong talking-point. The reason is that people hope to win the approval of other people by thinking the way they do.

Admiration or dislike for authority plays an important role in shaping people's opinions.

1 In a nation-wide study two logically equivalent questions were asked of strictly comparable groups.

Do you like the idea of having Thanksgiving a week
earlier this year? Yes: 16.7%
Do you like President Roosevelt's idea of having
Thanksgiving a week earlier this year? Yes: 21.4%

It is quite apparent that the admiration for the late President influenced the responses of the second group in the direction of greater acceptance of the changed date of Thanksgiving day. (Raslaw, Wulfeck, and Corby[13])

2 Coupling an idea with the name of a disliked person has the effect of lowering the acceptance of that idea. The present writer surveyed the opinion of the American public on the issue of propaganda in motion pictures. The following two questions were asked in this nation-wide study with the results indicated:

Do you think there is too much propaganda in the news-
reels and shorts you have seen recently? Yes: 36% No: 64%

The logically equivalent question, asked of a similar but not identical cross-section of the public, was:

Do you agree with Senators Wheeler and Nye that there is too much
propaganda in the newsreels and shorts you have seen recently?
Yes: 32% No: 68%

This poll was conducted in the summer of 1941 just after the isolationist Senator Wheeler had attacked the motion-picture industry from the floor of the Senate, accusing it of war-mongering. By that time most Americans felt that war was inevitable and disliked Senator Wheeler for his opposition to our defense program. (Ruch[14])

This fundamental fact of psychology has many practical applications. Advertisers have long used endorsements by celebrities to sell their products. If you want to move people to action or conviction, tell them of liked persons who hold the views you are fostering. However, not all people are equally influenced by the opinions of individuals or of their group as a whole, as the following study shows:

A group of over two hundred college students participated in what was called a "word-usage questionnaire" but was actually a test of social suggestibility. They were given a list of words, with a choice of equivalents following. One of the possible equivalents was italicized, and the subjects were told that the italicized word was the one which most people voted to be the most frequently heard equivalent. They were then told to circle the word they thought was the most frequently heard equivalent.

The words were italicized purely at random, so that the indicated answer would vary from the correct to the incorrect. The evidence of group pressure would be clearest when the word italicized in the test form as that given by most people is really the one with the least frequent usage. Some of the subjects agreed with every word; a few never agreed. That these individual differences in suggestibility are real was shown by the fair degree of reliability of the test. One half of the test agreed with the other to the extent shown by a correlation coefficient of .86. Had the response of the subject been due to chance, this correlation coefficient would have been zero.

In a second experiment with this test, a group of college fraternity men and a group of sorority members rated each other on the basis of contrariness in social relations, after which the "word-usage test" was given to all of them. In general, the students who refused to accept the suggestion on the word test were the ones rated by their fellows as contrary or negativistic. Evidently individuals do differ in the extent to which they are inclined to hold out against social pressure. It is interesting that women, who are traditionally supposed to be more suggestible than men, earned the same average score as the men in this test.

The subjects seemed to be more disposed to accept suggestions than to resist them. Since the marked answers were assigned by chance to one of four possible responses, the person who was neither suggestible nor negativistic would agree with the suggestions exactly 25 per cent of the time. Actually, the average person in the group studied agreed 40 per cent of the time. In other words, the average college man or woman is decidedly willing to follow the crowd in his or her judgments as to the frequency of word usage. Similar tests have been devised using other objects of judgment, such as size of irregular areas, resemblance of ink-blots to known objects, and the like. The results are in agreement with those for the word-usage test judgments. (Ruch[15])

Stereotypes in thinking also play an important role in public opinion, in judgments of both political personalities and political issues.

One investigation indicates that voters at the polls vote for party names rather than for the actual issues represented. House-to-house interviews were made in an agricultural county in Pennsylvania in which voters were asked to indicate their party preference and also to reveal their attitudes toward a number of political issues such as government ownership of railroads, reduction of huge fortunes, government old-age insurance, worker-ownership of industry, and many others. There were twenty statements in the questionnaire, the acceptance of ten of which would indicate thoroughgoing radicalism and ten of which, if accepted, would indicate conservatism. The majority of the group of 168 representative citizens in the small community studied—farmers, miners, laborers, small shopkeepers, housewives, and clerks—accepted more radical statements than conservative ones. Yet this group of voters whose attitudes were fundamentally liberal or radical put the Republican party first and the Socialist party much lower in their preference. Apparently the name "Socialist" has for some people an emotional connotation which makes it unpleasant to them even when their political views are more or less in agreement with the platform of that party. (Hartmann[16])

One of the aims of education is to build up habits of independent thought which will enable the individual to consider whether political, moral, and social stereotypes actually conform with his values and opinions.

Propaganda and public opinion

Any attempt of any individual or group to change ideas and attitudes or to induce a desired action is *propaganda*. The aim of propaganda is to change people in some way, to make them accept a certain condition or vote a certain way. To change people is also the aim of education, but there is an important difference. Propaganda is aimed solely at getting action or conviction, so that it calls on emotion and prejudice as often as it appeals through logical analysis. But education in America strives to equip the individual with the techniques for getting the right answer himself, so that once these techniques are mastered—once the person learns to think—he will be able to decide on his values and choose the means appropriate for realizing them.

Many people believe that propaganda is essentially a force for evil. In fact, there is some reason to believe that fear of propaganda is actually tending to undermine public confidence:

> "At the moment the American public has symptoms of a light anxiety neurosis on the subject of propaganda. General suspiciousness is directed against all sources of information. Citizens may convince themselves that it is hopeless to get the truth about public affairs. If magazines, newspapers, radio reports and news reels are believed to be manipulated by powerful influences for selfish ends, the effect on attitudes may be this: 'If you can't believe anything you read in papers, or hear over the radio, or see on the screen, what's the use of trying to use your mind at all?' " (Lasswell[17])

Such fear can be counteracted, first, by recognizing that propaganda can be directed toward *different goals* and that these goals can be good or bad; for instance, much-needed social reform is often accomplished not only by education but also by propaganda. The second step toward overcoming excessive distrust of propaganda is to increase public skill in detecting, analyzing, and overcoming the influence of prejudiced propaganda. Here we shall examine the techniques of propaganda.

The techniques of propaganda. Propaganda, or the deliberate attempt to influence the thought and actions of others, is a potent force in our life today. Most striking, of course, is the high-powered propaganda of wartime. The following is an analysis of the Nazi short-wave propaganda given to different parts of the world concerning the Anglo-American Bases-Destroyers deal of August 1940:

"1. The home front was told that the deal was a sign of British weakness; 'they are selling out the Empire for scrap iron' (i.e., the old destroyers).

"2. The French Canadians were advised that now that the West Indies had been sold to the United States, they should be prepared to exchange their British masters for Yankee domination.

"3. The United States listeners were assured that, while the deal seemed favorable, it was really a first step toward [the United States] becoming once more a British colony.

"4. The Latin-American nations were shown that Yankee imperialism was encircling their continent; it was predicted that the Faulkland Islands would come next. It was said that the essence of Mr. Roosevelt's policy was to prolong the war in order to 'grab' the British Empire. Germany, a land power, and Britain, a seafaring nation, might well have come to an agreement without this well-planned Jewish scheme.

"5. The British listener was naturally given the second part of this version: The interest of the United States was to prolong the war by half-hearted help in order finally to inherit the Commonwealth. Here for the first time the theme of 'Washington is fighting to the last Tommy' was struck—a theme which, in its application to the disintegration of Anglo-French collaboration, had just proved its power, a theme which German propaganda to Britain continues to emphasize." (Kris[18])

Such propaganda had certain characteristics which have been analyzed as follows:

"1. If you have an idea to put over, keep presenting it incessantly. Keep talking (or printing) systematically and persistently.

"2. Avoid argument as a general thing. Do not admit there is any 'other side'; and in all statements scrupulously avoid arousing reflection or associated ideas, except those which are favorable. Reserve argument for the small class of people who depend on logical processes or as a means of attracting the attention of those with whom you are not arguing.

"3. In every possible way, connect the idea you wish to put over with the known desires of your audience. Remember that wishes are the basis of the acceptance of ideas in more cases than logic is.

"4. Make your statements clear and in such language that your audience can repeat them, in thought, without the need of transforming them.

"5. Use direct statements only when you are sure that a basis for acceptance has already been laid. Otherwise, use indirect statement, innuendo, and implication. Use direct statement in such a way that the attention of the audience shall be drawn to it sufficiently to take it in but not sufficiently to reflect upon it.

"6. For the most permanent eventual results, aim your propaganda at the children; mix it in your pedagogy. Follow the example, in this respect, of the successful propagandists of the past." (Dunlap[19])

The power of propaganda. In this day and age the media for the dissemination of propaganda are legion. Propaganda may be launched by the person-to-person technique known as the "whispering campaign," which has a certain effectiveness because its content is passed in such an informal way that the hearer never thinks of questioning the source. During the second World War our enemies made use of this device for spreading propaganda. They also made use of the short-wave radio, with rather effective results:

> It is interesting to note that during the war, 22.8 per cent of a sample of the general public in New York and Boston had heard one or more of the following rumors broadcast from Berlin and that 23.4 per cent believed one or more of them, whether or not they had previously heard them. This circulation had to come through word of mouth, since none of these items was carried by standard wave-length programs, newspapers, or magazines, and since direct listening to short wave was negligible at that time. The Nazi agents listened secretly to German short-wave programs and then went out to circulate such rumors as these:
>
> "More than 300 draftees recently deserted from Fort Dix in New Jersey."
>
> "Hawaii was so effectively attacked by Japanese forces that American authorities now consider that its further defense is not possible and are withdrawing forces to use in the defense of the west coast, which is in serious danger."
>
> "During the night of December 6th, a formation of American bombers appeared over Formosa from the Philippines and were driven off by Japanese reconnaissance planes before they could launch their attack."
>
> "Labor union pickets will be excluded from air raid shelters according to a recently issued order from Washington."
>
> "Young men with religious convictions against war who choose non-military service instead are being black-listed so that they cannot get their jobs back after their service is over." (Ruch and Young[20])

Of recent years the radio has assumed an ever more important position among the media of communication—and of propaganda. The presidential campaigns of 1932, 1936, 1940, and 1944 were of considerable interest to social psychologists, because they were to some extent tests of radio versus newspapers as agencies for effective political campaigning. (For elections prior to 1932, the radio was not important as a means of mass communication.) Most of the important newspapers of the United States were frankly unfriendly toward President Roosevelt in their editorials and, in some instances, even in their news. His strongest publicity weapon was the radio, by which his talks reached millions of voters. Of course, there were many other issues determining the final outcome, but the landslide to Roosevelt in the election of 1936—and the elections of 1940 and 1944—showed that the newspapers do not have the overwhelming and all-powerful influence that they are often believed to have.

The daily newspaper and the magazine, in addition to having constructive functions, are the traditional media for propaganda of all types. While in real life it is difficult to eliminate all the factors operating to influence people's attitudes, in the laboratory these variables can be brought under control. An experiment by two social psychologists shows what can be accomplished in the way of scientific study of the power of the press.

In this experiment, one large group of college students were given editorials to read which were favorable to Hughes, the Prime Minister of Australia during the first World War; other students were given editorials unfavorable to him. A preliminary test revealed that the subjects of this experiment had never heard of Mr. Hughes prior to the experiment. The favorable and unfavorable editorials were printed in the *Daily Iowan* and were in the same style and of the same length of its usual editorials.

The students in the experimental groups were given their copies of the *Daily Iowan* at the beginning of a class hour and asked to read only the editorials. They were requested not to look at the paper again. Fifteen favorable and a like number of unfavorable editorials were "planted" in the *Iowan* and given to the subjects throughout the course of the experiment. The favorable editorials pointed to Mr. Hughes as a strong advocate of those things which students hold to be desirable; the unfavorable editorials showed that Mr. Hughes was against such things.

At the end of the experiment an attitude scale was given to the subjects to determine how favorable their opinions were toward Mr. Hughes. Of the students who had read the favorable editorials, 98 per cent were biased in favor of Mr. Hughes. Of the group who had read the unfavorable editorials, 86 per cent were biased against him. When the attitude scale was given after an interval of four months, the bias of each group was almost as strong as it had been at the end of the experiment. (Annis and Meier[21])

The conclusion should not be drawn from the foregoing discussion that newspapers are simply means of creating bias and prejudice in the minds of their readers. Newspapers are also important means of educating people, and the ethics of journalism demand that the facts be given, even though they hurt some party or person. It sometimes happens, however, that news is suppressed or altered to give a propaganda value favorable to some special interest. Such practices are undesirable, for the success of a democracy depends upon an educated and intelligent electorate in full possession of the facts. Our best protection is a free press, and along with it we need a variety of publishers and editorial policies so that no one special interest will prevail.

Overcoming the influence of propaganda. Can people be taught to disregard or see through propaganda? There have been a number of studies in this field with conflicting results.

> **1** One psychologist, for example, tested students to determine what effect the critical study of propaganda methods would have on their attitudes toward Nazi Germany. (The tests were conducted in April and again in May of 1941.) One group was carefully instructed in principles and practices of the propagandist and was also' exposed as a part of the instruction to a quantity of pro-German material. A control group neither received instruction nor came in contact with the German propaganda. Comparison of the two tests of the control group showed a reliable shift toward the anti-Nazi side, coming probably as a reflection of the current popular shift occurring at that time. The experimental group, on the other hand, became more tolerant of the Nazis. These results indicate that even those who are aware of the nature of propaganda devices may be positively influenced by it, which leads us to conclude that the protective power of such insight as these subjects possessed has apparently been overrated. (Collier[22])
>
> In evaluating this experiment we must not lose sight of the fact that insights gained into propaganda in general might cause the subjects to discount British propaganda of the period, which was swinging American opinion farther and farther away from the Nazis.
>
> **2** Other investigators report some benefit from reading a newspaper Rumor Clinic column in which current rumors were scotched. (Allport and Lepkin[23])

Propaganda and rumors are most likely to be believed when they fit in with the previously existing hopes and fears of the persons to whom they are addressed. Successful studies of propaganda take into account the emotional predispositions of the receiving groups.

Measuring public opinion

Leaders of all kinds have long recognized that successful leadership consists in part in giving people what they want. In a democracy, the leader cannot be independent of public opinion, whether he is in politics, business, education, or any other social activity. Thus it becomes of critical importance that we devise ways to determine what public opinion is on any given subject. The familiar polls of election years conducted by magazines or large newspapers are attempts to measure public opinion in advance of public action, on the assumption that the one will predict the other. Such material is high in reader interest, and agencies have sprung up which measure public opinion on all manner of issues and topics and at all times rather than only before election. The demands for accurate measurement of public opinion and mass behavior have been so great that many psychologists and others have worked hard to develop adequate methods in this important field. In this section we shall review some of their problems and accomplishments.

Getting a fair sample. The problem of obtaining a sample of people who will represent all the people in the country is one of the most important in the whole field of measuring popular reactions. The correct sample in an opinion survey must reflect every kind and condition of individual in the total population. Each age, sex, income, and racial or religious group must be represented in accurate proportion. A straw ballot cannot go out to the many millions of voters of the United States, for the cost would be prohibitive. Suppose, however, that a list is made up and a straw ballot is sent by mail to some of the voters. Even then only a small portion of them will return the ballot, and several studies have shown that the voters who answer and mail back questionnaires are not typical of the total population (Cahalan and Meier[24] and Shuttleworth[25]).

The mere accumulation of numbers of cases will not compensate for bias in the sample. A straw vote of one million unrepresentative people will come no closer to representing the vote of the nation as a whole than would a straw vote based on one hundred equally unrepresentative people. The practical problem of getting a fair sample is a highly technical one, requiring the use of numerous techniques too complex to discuss here.

The American Institute of Public Opinion, known as the "Gallup Poll," and the magazine *Fortune* were successful in predicting the outcome of the presidential election of 1936, while the *Literary Digest* poll was unsuccessful. The explanation lies in the different samples used. First, the Gallup and *Fortune* polls used sampling methods more representative than those employed by the *Literary Digest*, which built its list from telephone and automobile owners, who are a relatively prosperous class and so are not representative of the total population. Second, the *Literary Digest* used mailed questionnaires, which, as explained above, are not returned by a representative sample of the population, while the Gallup and *Fortune* polls employed trained interviewers who talked personally with men and women of all social and economic classes.

Asking the question. The second problem in opinion polling is how to ask the question. The technique of asking questions is a subtle combination of art and science, but there are certain basic rules which have been tested and retested and found to be valid. Knowledge of these will be helpful not only to the person conducting a poll but to the general reader of magazines and newspapers, which are coming more and more to feature the results of public-opinion polls. An analysis has been made (Jenkins[26]) of the known facts and principles of phrasing questions, showing four basic defects to avoid:

1 *Biasing or predetermining the answer.* Questions may be so worded as to suggest some answer other than the truth. Leading questions such as "You are a Republican, aren't you?" are obviously defective. Answers may be predetermined through the use of emotionally worded questions such as one which was reported in an anti-organized-labor newspaper: "Do you approve the use of force, intimidation, and violence in coercing employees to join a labor union?" The fact that 99 per cent of the respondents said "No" probably means that they do not approve force, intimidation, and violence but tells us very little about their regard for labor unions.

2 *Failing to determine sufficiently the direction of response.* Questions which are ambiguous, vague, or indefinite may elicit misleading answers or answers that resist analysis and understanding. For example, "Do you think that the most deserving people should have a cut in taxes?" would be a question to which almost everyone would answer affirmatively. However, the definition of "deserving" would vary greatly from one person to another, so that the answers to this question would not cast much light on public opinion on how taxes should be levied.

3 *Exceeding the ability of the respondent to answer.* It is also possible to formulate questions which are too difficult and technical for the respondent to answer. The question "How do you think depressions could be avoided?" needs a considerable knowledge of economics and sociology to be answered plausibly, and a great part of the population does not possess such knowledge.

4 *Exceeding the willingness of the respondent to answer.* Questions which will embarrass the respondent or incriminate him will not be answered honestly. Sometimes the respondent escapes

embarrassment by lying; other times he simply refuses to answer. In the Gallup and *Fortune* polls of the 1940 presidential election, the Democratic vote in the South was appreciably overestimated, as was the Republican vote in the North. These errors probably reflect the influence of social pressure and the unwillingness of the respondent to express *publicly* his private opinion.

Is there a "band-wagon" vote? We have seen that group opinion often exerts considerable influence upon the individual's opinion. Among the serious criticisms of polls is the suggestion that voters may be influenced by the knowledge that a particular candidate or issue is winning. If this is true, close governmental supervision of polls might well be justified to see that unscrupulous pollers do not deliberately publish false results to influence an important election. This problem of the band-wagon effect is a special aspect of the influence of the group opinion on the opinion of the individual, an aspect which must be considered in detail. The evidence is interesting but not conclusive.

In the period from 1920 to 1932 the *Literary Digest* poll was widely read. It enjoyed an enormous prestige, due to the size of the sample used, running as it did into millions of the more prosperous and influential members of society. Its accuracy was taken for granted. It successfully predicted the presidential elections of 1920, 1924, 1928, and 1932. In 1936, however, its sweeping, confident, and much publicized prediction, "Landon by a landslide," was followed not by a Republican victory but by a Democratic one. "As Maine goes, so goes the nation" became "As Maine goes, so goes Vermont." The enormous prestige of the *Literary Digest* poll did not create enough of a "band-wagon" effect to swing the election.

In 1936 two psychologists measured the effect of knowledge of the *Literary Digest* poll results on a group of 349 students. The following explanation and instructions were given:

"Polls of this kind are being conducted all over the country. The largest of these polls is the *Literary Digest* poll with a total of over two million votes. As you probably know, Landon is leading in the *Literary Digest* poll with a total of 54 per cent of the votes cast. Roosevelt is second with a total of 40 per cent.

"You simply fill in your choice for President, your school, and your class on these ballots. Do not write your name. Indicate your sex by printing *M* or *F* for male or female."

The control group received the same instructions except that the paragraph telling about the *Literary Digest* poll was omitted. The results showed that there was a slightly higher Landon vote in the experimental than in the control group, but it did not meet the conventional test of statistical significance. The band-wagon effect was not demonstrated but, of course, it was not disproved, either. (Cook and Welch[27])

A weakness of the above experiment is that many of the subjects had *already* been influenced by knowledge of the *Literary Digest* polls in their outside contacts and that repeating this information to the experimental group was "throwing salt in the sea." To avoid this source of error, another experiment was conducted by the same workers. Subjects indicated whether or not they were familiar with the results of the *Literary Digest* poll. Sixty subjects who did not know of the poll and fifty-seven who did, all of whom voted for Roosevelt in the experimental straw votes, were then told of the *Digest* results. The percentage of unacquainted who subsequently shifted to Landon was not significantly greater than that of the acquainted group.

Although the question is still an open one, we are safe in concluding that the band-wagon effect is only one determiner of voting behavior in real elections and in straw votes.

How accurate is the public-opinion survey? It is difficult to discuss the accuracy of public-opinion surveys with regard to particular commercial products, for such information must be kept confidential to protect the interests of the firm for which the survey is made (in one case, however, a sampling survey on brands of automobile tires in use agreed to within one tenth of 1 per cent with actual sales figures). It is easier to investigate the accuracy of political polls. In 1936 the Gallup poll missed the actual major party vote by 6.6 per cent; in 1940, by 2.6 per cent; and by 1.9 per cent in 1944. The *Fortune* poll, slightly better, missed only by .6 per cent in 1940 and .2 per cent in 1944.

The public-opinion survey has proved itself so valuable in business and journalism that we may reasonably expect that it will be employed by governmental administrators of the future in determining public policy and in deciding at what time to launch projects that depend for their success upon receptive public opinion. One of the serious objections to the democratic form of government has been that the election system is slow and cumbersome. The duly constituted representatives of the people have often been obliged to cast their votes in real ignorance of the wishes of their constituents. It is not difficult to visualize a plan whereby a government agency could conduct unofficial surveys based on house-to-house interviews at critical times during the periods that representative bodies are in session. Such a plan would enable the legislator to represent his constituents much more effectively and would go far to increase the efficiency of the democratic form of government. It would be extremely important, however, for the legislator or administrator not to follow this "voice of the people" too literally. The public is notoriously excitable about many issues, and moreover, may lack some information available to the legislator, who presumably makes careful studies of public problems. The function of the representative in a democracy is to act in what he believes to be the long-run best interests of one people, and he must be ready to act contrary to public opinion if he thinks it wise. Too frequent a flaunting of public opinion, though, is obviously a breakdown in the democratic process.

THE PSYCHOLOGY OF RACIAL CONFLICT

THE UNITED STATES TODAY is made up of people from nearly all the nations of the world, with all the races of the world represented. Although it has been extolled as a "melting pot" in which peoples of disparate backgrounds become fused into a harmonious unity, there are many situations in which this harmonious unity is lacking. Some of the most serious instances are discrimination in job opportunities; restrictive covenants forbidding Negroes, Jews, or citizens of various foreign extractions to live in certain housing sections; exclusion of various racial elements from many restaurants, hotels, and resorts; and general mistrust and dislike in race relations. All these are in direct conflict with the ideals of democracy, and often result in race riots and other violence. In examining this problem, it is first necessary to see what social scientists have to say about the concept of race.

What is a race?

There are two facts about man which almost all scientists accept: *first,* that all men are different from each other, and *second,* that all men belong to a single species—that there are no divisions between any varieties of mankind like those which separate the different species of lower animals. Horses and cattle, swine and sheep are of different species that cannot mate, but all types of human beings can mate and have children, regardless of skin color, blood type, hair texture, or any other biological characteristic. In other words, human groups constitute an intra-fertile group, or species.

How different "races" developed from the single ancestral group. Geneticists have shown that the probability is great that mankind was at one time a homogeneous group, which had common genetic materials and common physical characters. Then migrations from an original ancestral group led to the geographic isolation of various migrating groups. Among these isolated groups, two main processes tended to produce characteristics differentiating group from group:

1 *The inherent variability of genetic materials.* This simply means that random variations in genes occur spontaneously, so that originally homogeneous groups come to exhibit differences.

2 *Gene mutation.* Very frequently in all forms of life a particular gene undergoes a change of some sort, expressing its change in the appearance of a new form of an old trait. Thus variations in eye color or hair texture may arise spontaneously through mutation.

Once these primary biological differences appeared, they were accentuated by generations of inbreeding, which was encouraged over the centuries by geographic boundaries between groups, social restrictions on marriages between members of different groups, and learned individual preferences in mating.

The essential point is that human variability is a natural process and one that is going on all the time. Human differences are continually being produced through random variation among genes and the action of mutant genes. This dynamic character of hereditary differences means that *any scheme for classifying races can have whatever validity it may have only for a brief length of time.* The natural process of biological change does not slow up because some man-made system for naming races has just been devised. Each system is a little outdated as soon as it is published, owing to the steady process of genetic variation and natural selection. Nevertheless, classifications of race continue to be made.

What are some of the physical and psychological characteristics commonly used to distinguish races?

The physical differences among races have been the basis of a classification which divides the human group into three subdivisions, called "races": the Mongoloid or "yellow race," the Negroid or "black race," and the Caucasoid or "white race." These differences include the following: skin color, cephalic index (the ratio of skull breadth to skull length), eye form and color, hair color and texture, stature, nose shape, and "blood." Let us examine each of these in turn to see whether it varies enough from people to people to serve as a reliable index of racial "differences."

1 *Skin color.* The layman usually thinks of "races" as being distinguished by skin color, but this is by no means an adequately differentiating trait. Biologists have found that the color of one's skin is determined by two chemicals, carotene and melanin. The former imparts a yellow tinge to the skin and the latter determines how dark the skin will be. These colors, together with the pinkish cast that is given to one's skin when the blood vessels show through, give all the various shades of human skin color. Research has also revealed that these pigments are not unique to any one race but that every human being (except the albino) has some of both pigments in his skin. His complexion is a function of the relative amounts of both elements present. Thus skin color is a quantitative rather than a qualitative matter—a matter of *degree* rather than of *kind*. As a matter of fact, variations in skin color are probably the least reliable measure of racial difference. The spread of shades is world-wide. Students of the problem have had to use as many as thirty-four colors to describe the human complexion.

2 *The cephalic index* is the ratio of skull breadth to skull length. It was once considered one of the most stable and permanent characteristics of human races, and has from time to time been regarded as an indicator of superiority—that is, "long-headed" peoples were supposed to be superior to "broad-headed" peoples. Modern anthropology, however, has raised several serious objections to the usefulness of the cephalic index in differentiating races.

One objection is that this measurement, when used alone, fails to distinguish Negroid, Caucasoid, and Mongoloid groups— some Indians, for example, have the narrowest heads ever measured, while others have the longest. Another objection is that the stability of the index is highly questionable within any group —for example, in groups of Europeans migrating to America, the characteristic head shape underwent far-reaching changes after the first generation, possibly as a result of dietary or climatic changes (Boas[28], Guthe[29]). Another important objection is that the same skull characteristics can originate among widely separated groups which are not in contact with each other; this parallelism in development casts considerable doubt upon skull measurements as a basis of race classifications (Boas[30]).

3 *Eye form and color.* The oblique or slant eye is produced by a fold of skin (the epicanthic fold) which covers the inside corner of the eye. It appears frequently among white infants but does not usually persist into adulthood. It also occurs among some American Indians and appears in several Ethiopian strains. Thus it is not confined to the Mongoloid peoples, although it is frequently considered the sign that sets them off from other groups. As for hair and eye pigmentation, they are highly uncertain indicators of race, since blue eyes and blond hair are not the property of any single ethnic group, and dark eyes and dark hair are common to all peoples.

4 *Hair texture.* Hair texture is classified as woolly, wavy, or straight and is a helpful classificatory trait when used with other measurements. It cannot be used alone because the various kinds of hair texture tend to cut across racial subdivisions. The Australian Bushman, for example, has wavy hair (like many Caucasoids), but is usually classified as a member of the Negroid group, which typically has woolly hair.

5 *Stature.* Height fails to discriminate among races. Tallness, rather than being a hereditary racial characteristic, is often a function of diet and physical environment. For example, Japanese born in this country are on the average taller than their forebears born in Japan (Spier[31]). If group averages are considered, the majority of averages in height of population do not differ more than two inches from the general human average of 5 feet 5 inches (Kroeber[32]). Stature, therefore, must be understood as a modifiable trait that is so distributed in the total population of the world that there is much overlapping among groups.

6 *Nose shape.* Noses are classified according to nostril shape or the contour of the bridge, and all variants of these characteristics are found in all races. The straight "Roman" nose is reported by anthropologists as occurring in some individuals among all groups of people, from the Ethiopian to the American. And the hooked nose usually thought to be characteristically Jewish is in reality common throughout the entire Near East, although it also occurs in other parts of the world.

7 *Blood.* There are four blood types, A, B, AB, and O. None of the types will mix with each other without fatal clumping—with the exception of type O, which will mix with all types. All types are found in each variety of mankind. Moreover, in making blood transfusions, it makes absolutely no difference whether the racial backgrounds of the donor and the recipient are the same so long as the types are compatible. Contrary to popular belief, a type-A Caucasian can receive blood from a type-A Negro just as effectively as from a type-A Caucasian.

One other point needs to be made clear before leaving the subject of the biology of races. *There are no "pure" races in the world.* The evidence for this statement lies in the fact that all the principal characteristics just discussed can be found in all the "races" of mankind.

The Psychology of Racial Conflict 677

The circle of sculptures above illustrates the difficulty of setting up hard-and-fast classifications of races. In these individuals the so-called "distinguishing" features of the different groups of mankind are shown to merge into each other almost imperceptibly. For example, head (1) is a Javanese boy whose features are primarily what would usually be known as "Mongoloid." Yet these features exist only in degrees, as is shown by the adjacent head (2) of an African Bushman woman whose features are so mixed that it is almost impossible to tell whether she is Mongoloid or Negroid. Similarly, head (3) would ordinarily be classified as Negroid, but next on the circle (4) is a West African who possesses both Negro and Caucasian (5) characteristics. The Ainu man at upper right (6) belongs to a group which has baffled physical anthropologists for years, since Mongoloid and Caucasian traits are so intermingled that classification in either group would be purely arbitrary. Perhaps the most striking example of the continuity of races is the center head of a Samoan man (7), who is a mixture of all three of the "main stocks" (1, 3, and 5). He is found to possess features from all three, and to such a degree as to make it virtually impossible to categorize him as a member of any one "race."

(Sculptures by Malvina Hoffman, courtesy of Chicago Natural History Museum.)

PSYCHOLOGY AND SOCIAL ISSUES 678

It might be a good idea to drop the term *race* entirely. Through the widespread use of this illogical term, a great variety of people of differing biological backgrounds are lumped together and treated in essentially the same way. A more accurate term is *ethnic group*, which refers to those people who are treated socially as though they belong to some special group on the basis of one or two identifying characteristics. In the United States, for example, it is customary to call all people Negroes if they have even a single known Negro ancestor, but it would be just as logical to call anyone white if he had a single white ancestor. Actually, there has been so much intermingling of whites and Negroes that the Negroes are not a pure "race" but an ethnic group —that is, they are set off from whites more by social than by biological characteristics.

Psychological differences among races. Some racial theorists believe that the physical characteristics which are supposed to differentiate races are simply external signs of internal "psychological" traits. Regarding this belief, it has been shown (Hogben[33]) that there is no connection between bodily traits and psychological traits. But this fact in itself does not prove that there are no inherited psychological differences among ethnic groups, and we must examine the evidence in more detail:

1 *Sensory differences.* It has long been a popular notion that primitive men have keener senses than their civilized relatives. However, in 1904 a psychologist (Woodworth[34]) examined a group of three hundred persons, representing such diverse peoples as the Negritos, Eskimos, Ainus, Filipinos, Patagonians, and American Indians, who had been conveniently brought together at the St. Louis World's Fair. After extensive testing, he concluded that sensory acuity differs in degree from individual to individual but is about the same from one group to another.

2 *Behavioral development.* There is no valid evidence for the belief in a biological "white superiority," since heredity and environment both may have varied to favor one ethnic group over another in studies which report certain races as superior.

This vital point is further borne out by a study of the development of Negro and white infants, conducted in New Haven, Connecticut. Among other things, this investigation demonstrated that the average Negro infant born and raised in New Haven is equal in behavioral development to the average white infant. In the third half-year a retardation of developmental rate sets in among Negro children that can be explained best in terms of cumulative effects of the substandard

The Psychology of Racial Conflict 679

environments in which many New England Negroes live. (Pasa-manick[35])

3 *Intelligence differences* among races have already been discussed (pp. 229-231).

It seems quite safe to conclude, then, that the characteristics usually regarded as a basis for dividing mankind into different "races" are dubious foundations for racial theory. They are products of genes common to all men; they occur in some degree in all human groups; and they are largely quantitative rather than qualitative differences in human structures and functions. Moreover, the personality and character differences among races seem to result from environmental rather than hereditary influences.

Sources of race prejudice

If there is, then, no scientific basis for a belief in the innate superiority and inferiority of races, what are the origins of racial conflict? The analysis of this problem will suggest a practical program for action.

Race prejudice is not "instinctive." It has been pointed out that "the impression prevails widely that the child is born with instinctive responses of different kinds, one of which is an extreme dislike of and shrinking from persons of markedly different race" (Lasker[36]). Enough has been said throughout this book on the way that social attitudes are acquired through learning to indicate the falsity of the "instinct" hypothesis of race prejudice. If race prejudice were an *inborn* human characteristic, it would be found in all human groups, but in China and Soviet Russia there is no anti-Semitism, while in South America and parts of Europe there is no widespread feeling against Negroes. Nor can this difference in attitude the world over be explained on a "racial" basis—for children of Spanish parentage born and raised in the American South tend to be prejudiced against Negroes, while children of Spanish parentage born and raised in Brazil do not.

Scapegoating. Many psychologists feel that the primary mechanism at work in racial conflict is that of *scapegoating*. All peoples from the earliest times have unconsciously assumed that feelings of guilt and suffering can be transferred to some other individual or group. The discussion on page 483 indicated that in the Nazi persecution of the Jews and in the lynching of Negroes in the South, feelings of aggression arising from frustration were displaced from the true source of frustration to other groups of people. This does not imply, of course, that the victim group or "scapegoat" is always innocent of aggression. It often happens that the victim has been guilty of some provocative act or has at least been aggressive himself in his own defense or in retaliation. But, regardless of the amount of provocation, there always is in scapegoating an excessive amount of unmerited and projected blame. Thus, scapegoating can be formally defined as "a phenomenon wherein some of the aggressive energies of a person or group are focused upon another individual, group, or object; the amount of aggression and blame being either partly or wholly unwarranted" (Allport and Murray[37]).

The term "scapegoating" arose from a ritual sacrifice common to many ancient peoples. The most famous of these ceremonies is the ritual of the Hebrews described in the Book of Leviticus. On the Day of Atonement a live goat was selected, and the high priest, garbed in full regalia, laid his hands upon the goat's head and confessed over it the iniquities of the Children of Israel. By this procedure the sins of the people were supposed to be symbolically transferred to the animal, which was then driven into the wilderness. Believing their feelings of guilt, shame, and remorse to have gone with it, the people felt psychologically cleansed and free from anxiety.

Throughout history, there has been a tendency to transfer guilt and blame from person to person or group to group, rather than from group to ritual animal as in the ancient Jewish rite. The victims have always been minority groups who are highly distinguishable either because of some physical characteristic or because some traditional practice sets them apart from the great majority. If the identification of the group is based on physical characteristics of some kind, the hue and cry of racial inferiority is usually raised. If the identification is based on some special tradition, the charge is usually made on the basis of religious differences—for example, the persecution of the early Christians by the Romans, the persecution of nonconforming religious sects in medieval and Renaissance Europe, and the persecution of Catholics by nineteenth-century American Protestants (shown on pp. 682-683).

To view scapegoating as an aspect of the frustration-aggression hypothesis is to gain insight into the causes of scapegoating, many of which have already been mentioned but which may be summarized here. The prime causes are frustration, guilt, fear, and the need for self-glorification. The first and foremost cause of scapegoating is *frustration* or, as it is sometimes called, thwarting and deprivation. When unable to get what they want, people often behave aggressively, the aggression being directed not necessarily against the source of the frustration but against any person or group who happens to be convenient and visible. In times of great stress, deprivations or frustrations are multiplied. Since there is no direct way in which to relieve these thwartings, scapegoating tends to occur with heightened frequency. In depressions, for example, lynchings increase (see p. 483).

Guilt is a second source of scapegoating. Feelings of guilt arise from the performance or lack of performance of certain acts or from the

Scapegoating is as old as recorded history. Frustration, guilt, or anxiety (of whatever origin) take the form of aggression against some racial, political, or religious minority. For centuries, the victims were religious groups, like the early Christians, whose martyrdom under Nero is shown above.

As the Christians grew to be the dominant group in Europe, deviants from the accepted order were often relentlessly stamped out. Above is a contemporary painting of the famous Saint Bartholomew massacre of 1573, in which hundreds of Protestants were killed and wounded.

harboring of the wish to do certain forbidden things. In modern America, as you have seen, sexual activity is a frequent source of guilt in individuals and "cutthroat" competition is another, although such guilt may be entirely unconscious. But whatever the source of guilt, the important thing is that if it exists in many individuals in a

The memory of their own persecution and flight did not keep the New England Protestants from opposing the propagation of religions other than their own. Here Quakers are being whipped through the streets of seventeenth-century Boston. The victims of scapegoating often vent their frustration on other groups.

Above is a contemporary drawing of an anti-Catholic riot in Philadelphia, 1844. Twenty-four persons were killed and two famous old Catholic churches burned. Although the victims of scapegoating change from period to period, the underlying relation between aggression and emotional frustration is the same.

The Psychology of Racial Conflict 683

society, scapegoating will probably be widespread. For one of the most common reactions to guilt is to project it on to someone else—that is to blame others for one's own real or fancied sins of omission or commission. Rumors run high during wartime, charging high officials with failure to adhere to the rationing programs they enforce on the rest of the population; often these rumors are rooted in guilt feelings about one's own purchases of black-market gasoline or butter. Guilty persons often project their guilt on to members of other races: for example, one of the reasons for the frequent rumors about Negroes assaulting white women may be unconscious guilt over sexual activity. The reports of Gentile businessmen that Jewish businessmen are dishonest and unscrupulous may arise partially from their guilt feelings about certain of their own business dealings.

Fear or *anxiety* is a third causal factor in scapegoating. The anticipation of danger and threat stems from feelings of insecurity that can be alleviated by aggressive behavior which does not necessarily discriminate between real and false dangers. This is particularly true in wartime. During World War II, for instance, fears of spies and saboteurs and anxiety about the possibility of subversive activity within the United States resulted in widespread suspicion of all foreigners and most minority groups. The internment of *all* Pacific Coast Japanese-Americans for many months, rather than the arrest of only those who could not stand scrutiny of the Federal Bureau of Investigation, is one example of fear-motivated scapegoating. Another is blaming hypothetical Japanese-American fifth columnists for the fate of Pearl Harbor.

The need for self-glorification is still another basic motive in scapegoating. Here again the factor of insecurity is at work, driving the individual members of groups to prove to themselves and others that they are all right, that they are as good as anyone else, or that they really count. This urge operates to cause people to become closely identified with movements and causes which have, as part of the program, the scapegoating of others in order to enhance themselves. For example, a German psychologist who was imprisoned by the Nazis (Bettelheim[38]) tells how a number of individuals in the concentration camps—themselves the victims of scapegoating—accepted as their own the values and attitudes of the Gestapo, in order to protect themselves from breaking down under the dreadful psychological conditions of Dachau and Buchenwald. These people, taking over camp duties under Gestapo supervision, scapegoated other prisoners, and imitated guards in an effort to salvage their self-esteem and make themselves feel important. Here is scapegoating arising from intense personal need.

Conditioning from isolated experiences is another important source of race prejudice. Just as conditioning can operate to give a child a fear of dogs, it can sometimes operate to form prejudiced attitudes in people with regard to certain ethnic groups. A few frightening or irritating contacts with Mexicans, for example, if they produce a sufficiently strong emotional response, may result in aggressive feelings toward Mexicans *as a group* that may persist throughout life.

The contact does not have to be of a particularly dramatic kind. Contact maintained over a period of time with a Mexican who is not liked *as an individual* may build up a powerful prejudice against Mexicans *as a group* that will manifest itself in scapegoating.

Exposure to prejudiced attitudes in others. Contact with prejudiced people and the stereotypes of prejudice are the chief ways by which prejudiced attitudes are acquired as foundations for scapegoating. Parents are the first source of racial biases. The mother or father who forbids his child to play with children of other ethnic groups sows the seeds of prejudice. Likewise, parents who, while not actively inculcating aggressive attitudes in their children, give apparently approving acceptance to scapegoating, lay the groundwork for future scapegoating by their own children. Thus, the boy who learns that Jews are rejected from many medical schools and then hears his father comment that "there are too many Jewish doctors anyhow" will probably assume the same attitude.

Teachers are also potential sources of prejudice. Actions of the teacher will often influence the choice of a scapegoat on the playground, because children frequently vent their aggressions on someone who has previously been subjected to aggressions by an adult in authority. The teacher who tends to be a little firmer than necessary with pupils of some minority group is unwittingly building a group of scapegoaters among her pupils. Further, any open expression of personal biases by a teacher will influence the attitudes of children in a prejudiced way.

Age-mates, too, are highly influential. Conforming to the ways of a gang means that one will be accepted and not made an object of scorn or rejection. Consequently, children tend to develop race prejudice if they associate with a group which is characterized by aggressive behavior patterns toward various ethnic groups, which excludes the members of minority groups from membership in the gang, or which relegates minority group members to menial positions.

Movies, comic strips, books, and occasionally schools and churches contribute to the development of prejudice through the purveying of stereotypes. For example, Negroes are generally portrayed on the screen as servants or laborers and are definitely stereotyped:

> One careful study shows that anti-Negro prejudice is almost non-existent in white children of kindergarten age but grows steadily with age and is still increasing at the eighth-grade level. Prejudice depends not so much upon the degree of blackness as upon the fact of appearing Negroid to any extent—a finding which is in keeping with the white adult stereotype. (Horowitz[39])

In like manner, the French are thought of as highly immoral, the Italians as excitable and shiftless, the Japanese as treacherous. These false stereotypes are perpetuated in jokes, the words of popular songs, and the columns of daily newspapers.

Through early contacts with biased racial attitudes in people, children build up the prejudices that are the foundations for scapegoating and socially costly violence.

What can be done about race prejudice?

The foregoing discussion of scapegoating has revealed it as a highly complex process, involving dynamic motivational forces within individuals in much the same way as do the problems of emotional development discussed in Chapters 11 and 12. Furthermore, an understanding of scapegoating reveals the rather startling fact that *race prejudice has little to do with races.* We have discovered three main lines of evidence for this statement:

1 There seem to be no significant differences yet discovered among the major ethnic groups that would justify aggressive action on the basis of inherited racial inferiority.

2 The selection of scapegoats is a matter of convenience and visibility, not a matter of carefully defining a threatening group.

3 The phenomenon of scapegoating has its roots in the aggression-producing frustrations of people who for some reason do not act out their aggressions on the agents of the original deprivations.

What, then, should a program involve which is aimed at reducing the amount of scapegoating?

Education is the most fundamental cure for scapegoating. It must take several directions:

1 The reduction of prejudice and scapegoating must begin by the elimination of the bias-breeding instruction of children by the home, school, comic strips, and movies.

2 People must be brought to understand scapegoating, to understand their own motives and the irrationality of their own preju-

dices. They must understand that scapegoating represents a wide-spread human tendency to shift psychological burdens onto other people. Likewise, they must understand that scapegoating solves no problems—that beating Jews did not help the Germans solve their problem of national humiliation, although it may have brought momentary relief from feelings of frustration and inse-curity.

3 There is no longer any serious doubt about the potential equal-ity or near-equality of the so-called races, nor is there any doubt whatever that variability among people is greater within groups than it is between groups—this fact must be made known.

4 People must learn that prejudice and resultant scapegoating are not inevitable correlates of human community life. There must be widespread information about the variation in prejudices from culture to culture.

5 Another activity that would tend to increase the understanding of other groups is the promotion of contact between groups par-ticipating in common projects. It has been shown that actual experience with members of a discriminated group is quite effective in changing attitudes in the direction of greater under-standing and greater appreciation of the members of minority groups as individuals (Smith[40]). Children whose parents allow them to play with children of different ethnic backgrounds—with no fuss or special comment—accept them just as people, and are not so likely to grow up feeling that there are unbridgeable gaps between different groups of mankind.

Treating the causes of scapegoating. The attainment of understand-ing and self-knowledge cannot do much to reduce the amount of scapegoating without a change in some of the factors in the environ-ment that lead to prejudice and aggressive behavior.

For example, many of the cases cited to illustrate the relationship between scapegoating and the frustration-aggression hypothesis had to do with the effects of economic deprivation. It is certainly true that economic insecurity tends to increase frustration, anxiety, and a feeling of failure, which in turn cause scapegoating to grow with speed and vitality. The research of social psychologists indicates that this economic factor must be given due attention if scapegoating and its unfortunate consequences are to be eliminated. A minimum program, it is argued, would involve a general raising of the standard of living, the development of adequate programs of social security to guarantee economic essentials, and the insuring of an adequate, carefully guided education so that every individual can be trained to the highest level of which he is capable, thereby avoiding one serious area of maladjustment.

The victims of scapegoating can take steps, too, to eliminate some of the causes of this malignant social phenomenon. By relaxing their rigid traditions and adapting to a reasonable degree to the larger groups while in direct contact with them, minorities can decrease their own vulnerability. Secondly, they can train highly skilled representatives to act as their "public relations experts," their "diplomats," among the scapegoaters or potential scapegoaters. Marian Anderson and Paul Robeson, for instance, have done much for Negroes, as have Joe Louis and Jackie Robinson in another sphere.

Finally, many social psychologists believe that there are various legal steps which could go far toward establishing favorable psychological conditions. It must be remembered that attitudes cannot be legislated, but law can set certain norms which, when enforcedly practiced for a time, may prove successful and eventually come to be accepted even by former scapegoaters.

WAR AND NATIONALISM

"THE SUPREME ISSUE before all the people of the world today is the elimination of war." This statement was made by President Du Bridge[41] of the California Institute of Technology. As a physical scientist, he is aware of the complete destructiveness that science has made possible through atomic bombs, guided missiles, the conquest of the stratosphere, and techniques of bacterial warfare. Another outstanding scientist, Harlow Shapley[42] of Harvard, has pointed out that "Given time enough, and good intentions, the psychologists, the psychiatrists, and anthropologists should be able to explain our social and mental quirks ... and teach us how to understand ... others." The question now is whether social scientists will be able to discover *in time* the psychological forces underlying war and peace, and whether these discoveries will be put to work *in time* to save civilization from destruction.

Theories of why war occurs

To clarify this matter of the causes of war, it is helpful to review some of the theories as to why wars occur.

War as an expression of unchangeable "human nature." It has sometimes been argued that since there has been war throughout man's history, it must be understood as an expression of a human urge which is unmodifiable, and that wars are inevitable because "you can't change human nature." The outstanding psychologist to champion this theory wrote a book during World War I in which he said:

> ". . . the same instinct of pugnacity makes of Europe an armed camp occupied by twelve million soldiers . . . we see how, more instantly than ever before, a whole nation may be moved by the combative instinct. . . . The most serious task of modern statesmanship is, perhaps, to discount and to control these outbursts of collective pugnacity." (McDougall[43])

As has been demonstrated repeatedly in this book, the theory of instincts is a shaky one indeed and one that is no longer accepted in scientific psychology. The modern view is that while all behavior, including that involved in war, has a broad base in human biology, it is primarily determined by learning. *War is not the result of man's "aggressive instinct" but of the habits, attitudes, and beliefs that he has acquired as a result of social conditioning.*

War as a means of social growth. Two theories of war based on analogies from biological science have been shown to exist (May[44]). One is the idea of war as a method of social evolution, while the other is the theory of war as a social "vitamin."

1 Some students of war regard it as a means toward "selection of the fittest"—a means of spurring the ability to adapt to rough conditions, to invent new machines and equipment, and to develop individual talents, and as a means of weeding out the weak and the unfit. This point of view may be objected to on the ground that instead of promoting the survival of the fit, war tends to eliminate the best human stock available—it is the healthiest and the strongest who are killed in modern warfare, not those whose capacity for contributing to social welfare is the lowest.

2 Allied to the erroneous theory of war as an instrument of social evolution is the theory of war as an essential for social health and vigor.

Actually, it does seem to be true that war affords a stimulating excitement which promotes invention, develops leaders, and calls out the hardier virtues in a population. It seems highly doubtful, however, that such a social ferment is worth the cost in money and life or in the anxiety and feelings of insecurity that arise on a wholesale scale during wartime. There would certainly be a high degree of agreement among people who have lived through a war that the virtues made manifest by the war situation do not compensate for the psychological strain people must suffer, not to mention the heavy toll of human life. This is particularly true of modern warfare, in which no one, including the members of civilian populations, can be sure that he will come through unscathed.

War as a result of nationalistic power politics. History has made it tragically clear that war in the main is a natural outgrowth of power politics among nationalistic states. The sovereign nations maintain a balance of power among themselves through the techniques of international diplomacy. When the methods of diplomacy fail, war is resorted to as the means of re-establishing international equilibrium. The shifts in balance even cause recent allies to become present enemies. From a psychological standpoint, this means that the populations of the nationalist states must take on the typical attitudes of aggressiveness that have been discussed in this chapter; people must believe completely in the superiority of their own national group, their right as superior individuals to subjugate "inferior" peoples, the efficacy of force, and the worthwhileness of war. In short, to survive, nationalistic states must teach their populations attitudes of aggression and supreme loyalty to the nation. The tragedy of the modern world is that man has not yet been able to develop any other effective means by which peoples can guard against attack, and guard they must, as recent years in particular have shown.

Nationalism as a state of mind

It has been pointed out (Bernard[45]) that nationalism is linked to war in two special ways. In the first place, intense and uncompromising feelings of nationalism tend to express themselves in an effort to bring all the members of the real or imagined political unit under the same political administration. This point is illustrated clearly by the Third Reich's successful effort to incorporate Germans in surrounding nations —and by the peaceful incorporation of the Thirteen Colonies into the United States of America.

The second step in the Nazi undertaking exemplifies the second way in which nationalism may be related to war. When a national group becomes strongly self-conscious and strongly assertive of its own superiority, it moves to extend its culture and its sphere of domination. This extension—although almost always accomplished by force—is justified on the grounds of bringing "enlightenment" to the inferior. Thus, Germany was to unite Europe under the great and glorious leadership of the superior Aryan race. Much of nineteenth-century European imperialism was said to be in the interest of bringing civilization to the "naked savages"—many of whom were already enjoying a happy and peaceful, though nonindustrial, culture.

Since intolerance of ways other than those of one's own nation is often a function of ignorance, it would be expected that greater knowledge of "foreign" countries might result in less prejudice.

> In one study, college students were asked to rate ten national groups with respect to a number of traits and characteristics. The subjects were then classified according to the amount of travel they had done in foreign countries. A consistent lessening of prejudice was found according to the amount of time that a student had spent in the nation which he was asked to rate. In other words, the better acquainted a student was with a country, the more favorable was his attitude toward it. Furthermore, the greater his first-hand experience with any foreign nation, the less was his prejudice toward all foreign countries. (Diggins[46])

This study would seem to indicate that knowledge of a foreign people, particularly if it is knowledge derived from direct experience, tends to lessen prejudice and the nationalistic point of view that is a concomitant of prejudice. It must not be inferred, however, that nationalism results only from the lack of correct information. Nationalism in its extreme, irrational forms is a kind of prejudice and as such is based on dynamic psychological motivational factors, just as is scapegoating in the area of racial antagonisms.

What has been said about racial conflict and its analysis in terms of scapegoating is applicable also to international conflict, the most extreme form of which is war. People identify themselves with the states of which they are citizens and act as if they possess more virtues and should possess more supremacy than any other nation in the world. Each nation tends to exaggerate the differences between itself and other nations in the direction of its own superiority. This emphasis on differences tends to promote conflict because of a widespread tendency among people to distrust and fear the unfamiliar and the strange. The absurdity of the extreme nationalist attitude is seen in the fact that, just as there are no "pure" races, so there are no "pure" nations in the cultural sense. The culture of the United States itself is an amalgamation of the culture traits of many different nations and peoples. Nevertheless, many misguided patriots insist on the proposition that "the United States is unquestionably the best country in the world" even though such an assertion often involves winking at inequalities and playing down the obvious rents in the warp and woof of the social fabric—racial difficulties of the kind mentioned earlier in this chapter, inadequate housing, maldistribution of wealth, and high crime rates. The same attitude is cultivated in all the great modern nationalist states; "my country, right or wrong," is the approved sentiment anywhere. In fact, the nationalist psychology has many of the characteristics of a religion (cf. Britt[47]).

The essential point is that the ways of other nations are merely different from, not invariably better or worse than, those of one's own country. While people must always seek and stand for what—on a basis of real thought—they believe to be right, a tolerance for legitimate differences must be achieved if conflicts between nations are to be avoided. Fortunately, man is not committed by biological nature to make war. Psychologists believe that he can learn to make peace.

PART SIX

The brain and nervous system

Illustrated reference manual of the brain and nervous system

An Overall View of the Nervous System
The Components of Neural Functioning
The Brain
What Goes On in the Brain During Thought?
How the Nervous System Functions in Emotion

As a STUDENT about to complete your first course in psychology, you are in possession of many facts about human thought, emotion, and behavior, and you are now in a position to demand some of the why's and how's behind the facts. As you learned in Chapter 1, both our maintenance and adjustment processes begin when our *receptors*—in the special sense organs, the skin, and internal organs—respond to stimuli. The chief *connecting mechanism*, the nervous system, serves to connect the receptors with the *organs of response*—the glands and muscles. In man, the most important system of connections between receptors and effectors is the nervous system.

This chapter will explain the form and functioning of the brain and the other parts of the nervous system, and will outline what is known about the neurological basis of thinking, emotion, and muscular movement. Let us look now into some of the more interesting and well-explored mechanisms underlying human responses.

AN OVERALL VIEW OF THE NERVOUS SYSTEM

The FOLLOWING FACTS having to do with the form and function of the nervous system include so much and require such elaborate explanation that they are listed here only to give the thread of the subsequent discussion and to prevent the reader's getting lost in the maze of detail which is necessary for an adequate treatment of the subject.

The neuron

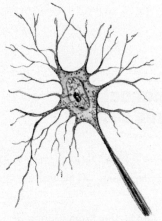

1 The neuron is the structural unit of the nervous system. The neuron or single *nerve cell* has all the characteristics of living cells in general, and is in addition specialized for irritability and conductivity. The neurons correspond roughly to the single wires of a telephone system. The expanded part of the neuron is situated in the central nervous system or ganglia. The elongated part runs either in the central nervous system or in nerve trunks.

Cross section of nerve

2 *Nerves* or *nerve trunks* are larger structural units in the nervous system. They consist of the long extensions or fibers of numerous neurons, joined into one bundle. Sensory and motor fibers are found in the same nerve.

The course of nerve impulses

3 The receptor-connector-effector process operates through the passage of *nerve impulses* (electrochemical excitations) along the neurons.

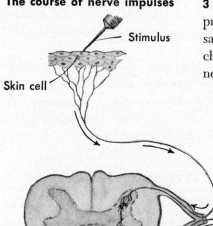

Stimulus

Skin cell

Muscle cell

Correlating neuron

4 The *sensory-motor* arc is the functional unit of the nervous system. Nerve cells are linked in chains of two or more to connect receptor cells with cells in some organ of response. A typical chain consists of an effector neuron, a correlation neuron within the spinal cord or brain, and an effector neuron.

5 Nerve impulses travel along *nerve pathways,* made up of many sensory-motor arcs. In the central nervous system, though not in the peripheral nervous system, there are many alternative pathways by which nerve impulses travel. Moreover, the connections between the elements of the nervous system are not fixed for all time. We are born with certain connections functional; some become functional through a process of maturation independent of learning; others become functional only after learning has taken place. Thus neural patterns in man are not rigid: new ones are constantly being established.

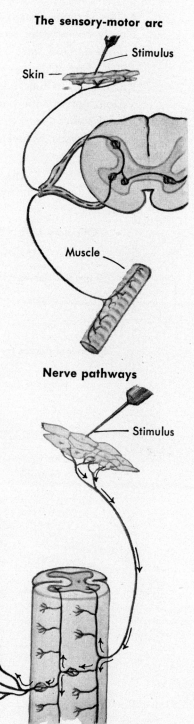

The sensory-motor arc

Stimulus

Skin

Muscle

Nerve pathways

Stimulus

Response

6 The nervous system as a whole has two partially distinct and closely cooperating parts: the central, and the peripheral. The *central nervous system,* as it is called (or, strictly speaking, the central *part* of the nervous system), is made up of the brain and spinal cord. Its function is to correlate and integrate—to make the various parts of the body work together as a good team should. The *peripheral nervous system* (or, strictly, the peripheral *part* of the nervous system) consists of nerve fibers passing from the

The central nervous system

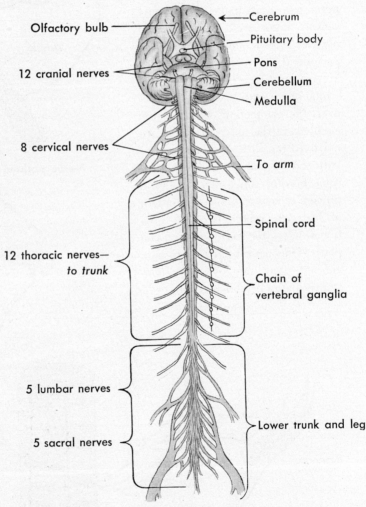

Olfactory bulb

12 cranial nerves

8 cervical nerves

12 thoracic nerves—
to trunk

5 lumbar nerves

5 sacral nerves

Cerebrum

Pituitary body

Pons

Cerebellum

Medulla

To arm

Spinal cord

Chain of
vertebral ganglia

Lower trunk and leg

(After W. Langdon Brown)

receptors to the central nervous system, and of fibers passing from the central nervous system to muscles and glands.

The central nervous system is shown on page 698. The peripheral nervous system is easily visualized as connecting the central nervous system with the various glands and muscles shown. One important division of the peripheral system—the autonomic system—is shown below. (Its functions in the body will be discussed more fully on pp. 733 ff.)

The autonomic nervous system

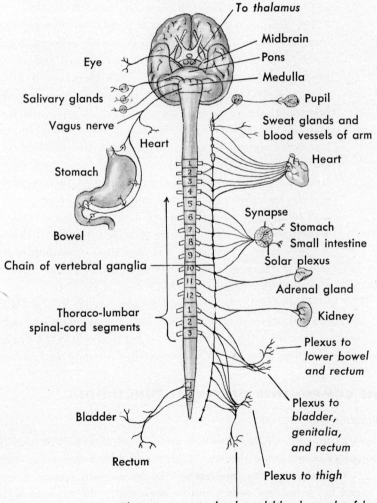

Both the central and peripheral nervous systems have parts which control two types of functions. Both contain *somatic* components—i.e., those concerned with control of skeletal muscles—and *visceral* components—i.e., those controlling glands and the special kind of muscle found in the viscera (internal organs) and in the blood vessels, eye, etc. In general, the somatic musculature can be consciously controlled whereas the visceral cannot.

In the central nervous system the visceral and somatic components are largely intermingled, but in the peripheral nervous system the visceral portion is partly distinct from the somatic portion and is called the *autonomic nervous system.* The drawings on pages 698 and 699 illustrate these structures.

7 The nervous system functions at three levels of complexity: (1) Simple unconscious processes, such as the reflexes, are possible through connections located in the spinal cord and an extension of it known as the *brain stem,* which gives rise to the cranial nerves (p.698). (2) More complex processes, such as walking and breathing, are made possible by the brain stem and by special coordinating structures in the brain. The *cerebellum* and *pons* (p. 698) control equilibrium and aid the cerebral cortex in carrying out smooth, well coordinated, voluntary movements; the *thalamus* transmits sensory impulses to the cerebral cortex; and the *hypothalamus* plays an important role in emotion (p. 738) and temperature regulation (p. 132). This part of the brain is sometimes called the *old-brain* because it was the first to develop in the course of evolution. (3) Sensation, voluntary movements, learning, thinking, and other complex behavior are carried out by the *cerebral cortex* or *new-brain* (see color plate).

This chapter will discuss *The Components of Neural Functioning* (neuron and nerve, neural impulses, the sensory-motor arc, nerve pathways, and reflex action), *The Brain, What Goes On in the Brain During Thought?* and *How the Nervous System Functions in Emotion.*

THE COMPONENTS OF NEURAL FUNCTIONING

Neuron and nerve

A *neuron* is a single nerve cell, and like all other cells it is made up of protoplasm (living substance) surrounded by a thin living membrane.

The neuron is the smallest unit in the nervous system. Every living cell has a *nucleus,* which can be seen under the microscope in a cell which has been properly stained for purposes of laboratory examination. In the neuron, as in other types of cells, the nucleus is necessary to the nutrition of the whole cell; any part of a neuron which becomes separated from its nucleus will die and disintegrate or degenerate. Anatomists have been able to map the pathways of the nervous system by destroying the part of the neuron containing the nucleus and then, with the aid of a microscope, tracing the degenerating parts of the neuron wherever it goes throughout the nervous system. The degeneration stops at the end of the neuron, indicating the validity of considering it as the structural unit of the nervous system.

The anatomy of the single neuron. Every neuron consists partly of the *cell body*, a thickened portion containing the nucleus. At each end of the cell body are slender extensions or *nerve fibers*. The fibers at one end are the *dendrites* and at the other end are the *axons*.

Dendrites are highly branched, usually quite short, fibers at one end of the neuron. They are the receiving mechanisms of the nerve cell, taking in impulses from other neurons or from receptor cells. The *axon* is a fiber on the opposite side of the cell body, terminating in *end brushes* which transmit impulses to the next neurons or directly to the muscle or gland. Certain axons in adults are several feet long; for example, those passing from the lower end of the spinal cord to the tip of the toe. Some axons branch off, providing duplicate pathways; these branches are called *collaterals*.

Anatomy of the neuron

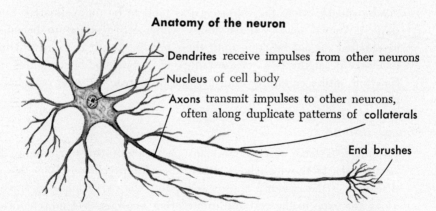

Dendrites receive impulses from other neurons

Nucleus of cell body

Axons transmit impulses to other neurons, often along duplicate patterns of collaterals

End brushes

Neurons vary widely in size and shape, depending upon the function they perform and the length of the distance they run. On the basis of function, neurons are divided into two classes. There are the long, conducting neurons which have single, long axons or long dendrites. All the sensory and motor fibers are of this type, which is shown in the diagram on page 702.

Then there are the *correlating neurons* having many short axons and dendrites to provide many connections or alternate pathways. The central nervous system contains both types; the peripheral system has only long conductors.

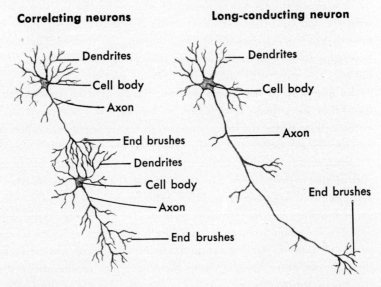

Correlating neurons   **Long-conducting neuron**

Dendrites

Cell body

Axon

End brushes

Dendrites

Cell body

Axon

End brushes

Dendrites

Cell body

Axon

End brushes

Nerves are bundles of axons. The axons and collaterals of large diameter are surrounded by a fatty white covering known as the *myelin sheath,* while the thinner axons tend to be unmyelinated. For some unknown reason, nerve fibers which are destined to become myelinated do not function until their myelin sheath is formed. This fact may be at the basis of the failure of certain bodily structures to function until a certain level of maturation is reached where myelination is complete.

Neural impulses

Physiologists have discovered many facts about the functioning of nerve cells, facts which have significance for psychology. One basic discovery is that when a neuron is excited, the nerve impulses travel along the axon to the end and excite other neurons, or a muscle, or a gland.

Comparison with the fire in a fuse. The nerve impulse may be likened to the chain of fire which sweeps along the fuse of a firecracker. Like the fire traveling along a fuse, the nerve impulse requires comparatively little energy to start it but releases a great deal of energy in the muscles and glands.

The nerve impulse is not conducted in the same way that a wire conducts electricity. Electrical current is conducted passively like sound waves or ripples in a pool of water, and if an obstruction is met, the wave passes on but is reduced in size. However, experiment has shown that the situation in the nerve fiber is quite different: when the impulse at one point in a nerve fiber is experimentally weakened by some drug such as alcohol fumes, the original intensity will be regained as soon as the impulse reaches an untreated, normal stretch of nerve. In this way the nerve current resembles the fire in a firecracker fuse or in a chain of gunpowder which has been dampened at one point; as soon as the fire passes that point, it burns as strongly as ever. The reason is the same in both cases—the size of the nerve impulse or the fire in the fuse depends not on the energy of the original stimulus but on the energy available *in each section* of the nerve fiber or fuse.

Magnitude and speed. At one point, however, the analogy with the fuse breaks down. The amount of energy consumed by nervous tissue is very much smaller. Using the amount of heat liberated as a measure of energy turnover, we find that under the same conditions of stimulation it takes a gram of nerve tissue *two hours* to liberate as much heat as a gram of muscle gives off in *one second.*

The nerve impulse travels very rapidly. In the fastest nerve fibers the speed of the nerve impulse is about 100 yards a second—about ten times as fast as a good sprinter; in others it travels about 1 yard per second.

The nerve impulse is alike in all sorts of nerves, except for differences in magnitude and speed. Different impulses produce different effects only because they pass over particular neurons whose connections are different, not because the impulses are themselves different. For example, impulses in the optic nerve cause visual sensations because they go to the visual center of the brain, not because they are different from impulses in the auditory or other nerves.

Ways of studying the nerve impulse. Although the nerve impulse is not a simple electric current, its passage along a fiber gives rise to electric currents. In fact, physiologists now rely heavily upon the measurement of these tiny electric currents in their study of the conditions influencing the passage of the nerve impulse. The general procedure consists of attaching to a nerve the two electrodes of a system of amplification similar to those used in modern radios. The tiny electric currents which are set up by the impulse are recorded by means of instruments like the electroencephalograph. The patient sits in a relaxed position with the electrodes from the machine placed on his head.

The Components of Neural Functioning 703

(See the photograph on page 2.) The electric currents set up by nerve impulses in the brain are magnified and recorded automatically on a strip of paper. (See page 730 for examples of such records.) In this way physiologists have discovered the following important facts about the way nerve impulses operate in nerve fibers.

The nerve fiber has a threshold of stimulation. Nerve cells vary as to the strength of the stimulus required to set them into action. The amount of energy just capable of setting off the impulse through the fiber is called the *threshold stimulus*. The threshold stimulus varies from time to time, depending upon the condition of the tissue. Fibers of large diameter are more easily stimulated than thin ones.

The nerve fiber has a refractory phase. Following the transmission of an impulse, there is a period of from one to three thousandths of a second during which the nerve cell is *absolutely refractory* (here *refractory* means "unresponsive to stimuli"). No stimulus is sufficiently strong to set up an impulse, and no impulse can pass. For about a hundredth of a second following the absolutely refractory phase, the nerve is *partially refractory:* that is, only a stimulus above the threshold strength can set it off. The next stage is one of *supernormal irritability*, in which a stimulus weaker than the normal one can serve to set it off. Following this is a more prolonged period of *subnormal irritability*.

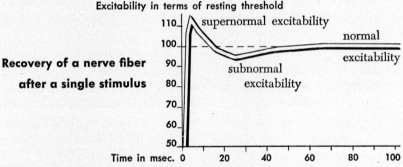

Recovery of a nerve fiber after a single stimulus

Excitability in terms of resting threshold

From H. S. Gasser and H. Grundfest, "Action and Excitability in Mammalian A Fibers," *American Journal of Physiology*, 1936, Volume 117, p. 129.

The nerve fiber is self-charging. A neuron, unlike the train of gunpowder, will restore itself in the small fraction of a second after it has discharged. This restoration after a refractory state is automatic.

Nerve fibers respond "all-or-nothing." The intensity of the impulse in a neuron is independent of the intensity of the exciting stimulus once the threshold value has been attained. Thus, as has already been suggested, the strength of the response of each individual neuron depends on the *condition* of that neuron (its available energy), not on the strength of stimulus. If the neuron responds at all, it responds with all its available energy. This is fuller evidence that nerves conduct actively and not passively.

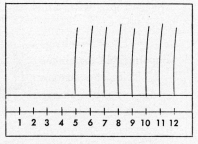

The all-or-nothing response to stimuli is illustrated by this kymograph record of contractions of the ventricle of a turtle's heart. The contractions shown were induced by electrical stimuli of increasing intensity. Stimuli 1 through 4 were too weak to elicit any contraction. Note that the response to stimulus 12 was no greater than to stimulus 5, although the intensity of stimulus 12 was about 20 times greater than stimulus 5.

By permission from A. J. Carlson and V. Johnson, The Machinery of the Body, © 1941, University of Chicago Press, p. 138.

The "all-or-nothing" response raises puzzling problems. We all know from general experience that the strength of the *sensation* does vary (though not proportionately) with the strength of the stimulus when other things are constant. What is the neural mechanism underlying this relationship? How can we reconcile the apparent conflict between the facts that (1) nerve fibers always respond to stimuli with the same intensity and (2) our sensations from stimuli vary in intensity?

Since individual nerve fibers respond in an all-or-nothing fashion, we cannot explain the greater sensation accompanying a stronger stimulus as resulting from a larger discharge of each of the nerve fibers involved. However, studies of the refractory phase of nerve fibers do show that a fiber will respond sooner if the stimulus is stronger. The stronger the stimulus, the sooner will each impulse follow the preceding one and the more often will each fiber send in an impulse. And we also know that fibers differ in their thresholds of excitation. A faint stimulus applied to a sensitive region will be sufficient to excite some of the sensory fibers having their origin in that area; a stronger stimulus will excite *more* fibers than will the weaker stimulus and will, of course, cause those which are excited at a lower level to discharge at a greater rate than they did before. Thus the strength of the sensation accompanying stimuli of various strengths varies with (1) the numbers of fibers contributing and (2) the rate at which they contribute— *even though the response of each fiber involved remains constant.*

The membrane theory of nerve impulses. The most widely accepted theory of the nerve impulse is known as the membrane theory and places emphasis on the molecular structure of the nerve fiber. According to this theory the electrical phenomena are regarded as mere indicators of molecular reactions within the nerve fiber. The membrane of the fiber is surrounded on the outside by a layer of positively charged ions (small, electrically charged particles) because the negatively charged ions with which they are linked cannot pass through.

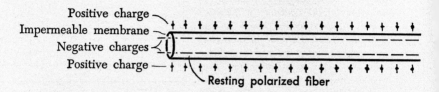

When the nerve fiber is activated, this orderly arrangement of molecules or polarization of the membrane is destroyed, allowing the positive and negative charges to move freely. The membrane is then said to be *permeable*. Once the membrane is permeable at one point, it in turn renders the adjacent area permeable. Thus the nerve impulse "rolls" down the nerve fiber in the direction of the straight arrows:

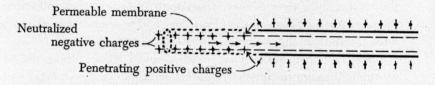

The membrane in the area through which an impulse has recently passed remains open or permeable for some time, thus preventing the building up of positive charges on the outside of the membrane and negative charges on the inside. This is during the absolutely refractory period when, as you have seen, the nerve fiber cannot be stimulated no matter what the strength of the stimulus.

As the nerve fiber regains its impermeability it becomes repolarized, positive ions again coming to lie on the outside and negative ions on the inside. This is the partially refractory period during which an unusually strong stimulus can activate the nerve fiber. As soon as the membrane is completely reorganized, the fiber again becomes normally excitable.

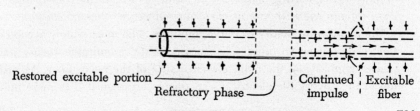

The sensory-motor arc

Neuron units in the sensory-motor arc. The sensory-motor arc in its
simplest form is made up of two neurons. One of them possesses at one
end endings which are sensitive to stimulation from the outer world
(or which connect with a receptor cell). This cell is called a sensory,
or *afferent*, neuron because it carries the nerve message *toward* the
center (*afferent* is from two Latin words: *ad*, meaning "toward," and
fero, meaning "carry"). The other neuron connects with the first and
terminates in some organ of response. It is called the motor or *efferent*
neuron because it leads the nerve message *away* from the center or
point of connection (*efferent* is from *ex* and *fero*, meaning "away from"
and "carry"). The drawing below shows a typical sensory-motor arc:

A typical sensory-motor arc

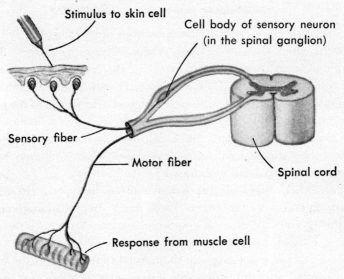

Stimulus to skin cell

Cell body of sensory neuron
(in the spinal ganglion)

Sensory fiber

Motor fiber

Spinal cord

Response from muscle cell

In most sensory-motor arcs there are not only sensory and motor
neurons but also several connecting neurons which serve to correlate
the functioning of the various parts of the nervous system. Such cells
are called *correlation* neurons. They make it possible for a nerve message which originates in a single afferent fiber to diverge into numerous
outgoing or *efferent* fibers.

For example, the correlation neuron receives several impulses and
directs them into one channel, so that there is a single response to
a diffuse stimulus; in other words, connections are provided for the
convergence of impulses from many afferent fibers to excite a single

The Components of Neural Functioning 707

outgoing nerve fiber. Also, the correlation neuron can receive an impulse and direct it along several nerve paths, so that there is a diffuse reaction to a single stimulus, as below:

Correlation neurons

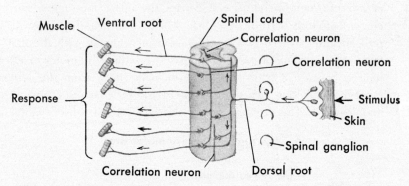

Still other chains of correlation neurons are arranged in self-exciting circuits which work as follows: When a neuron discharges, the nerve impulse passes down the main axon and also into a collateral branching off from it. The side-branch may connect with a second neuron, causing it to be excited. The axon of the second neuron will in turn transmit the impulse to the original cell and excite it a second time. This will be repeated many times. Such self-exciting circuits explain why a momentary stimulus will cause a response which continues long after the stimulus has been withdrawn.

Still other chains of correlation neurons form long circuits which carry impulses to the brain. These keep the "headquarters" in the brain informed of what is going on, and the brain may then modify the activity of the simple reflex arcs.

Neurons never act singly in the normal functioning of the organism. An external stimulus will excite many sensory fibers, and the motor neuron must be excited by more than one correlation neuron before an impulse will be produced.

The synapse. Nerve cells do not join each other physically as do lengths of pipe. The axon branches which make up the end brush of one neuron terminate in rounded expansions applied against the dendrites of the following neuron, but there is no protoplasmic bridge between the two cell walls. This type of association without direct contact is called the *synapse*. As the nerve impulses pass across a synapse between two neurons, there is a lag in their rate of travel. Some impulses never cross the synapse at all.

The way a nerve impulse "jumps" from one cell to another across the synapse has been in dispute for many years. But as noted on page 703, it has been observed that an electrical stimulus from a battery will excite a nerve fiber, and it is believed by most experts that the electrical activity connected with nerve impulses excites the next neuron in the chain in the same way. One fact that is generally accepted is that the synapse serves as a one-way valve. Although the impulse will travel in both directions within a neuron, nerve impulses cross the synapse from end brush to dendrites but never in the opposite direction.

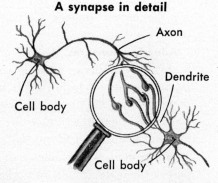

A synapse in detail

Axon

Dendrite

Cell body

Cell body

Nerve pathways

Hundreds of nerve fibers are involved in the simplest stimulus-response act. Each sensory-motor arc is duplicated many times. Frequently the duplicate connections lie side by side, but there are numerous instances in which the duplicates take quite a different course from the receptors of the sense organs to the effectors. This is because the dendrites of most neurons form synapse connections with the axons of many other neurons.

The great number of potential pathways makes possible a variability of response to identical stimuli. The brain is especially rich in such alternatives. The responses of the spinal cord are fairly stereotyped while those of the brain are variable and capable of almost infinite modification.

Experiments which will be described presently show that injuries to certain parts of the brain need not bring permanent disability, for other areas are capable of taking over the lost function. This fact makes possible the re-education of individuals who have become partially paralyzed or insensitive through the impairment of a particular portion of the brain.

The simplest level of neural functioning: reflex action

Spinal reflex action—that is, stimulus-response behavior which can be studied by separating the spinal cord from centers of correlation in the old-brain—is better understood than the more complex reaction involving the higher centers, but there is no reason to suppose that most of the principles of reflex action do not hold for responses involving the higher centers. Certain phenomena of spinal reflex action deserve our attention.

Adaptive character. Reflexes usually perform some movement which is obviously of service to the organism. Withdrawal of a limb when it is injured protects it from further injury, and is therefore termed a *protective reflex.* Other reflexes, such as swallowing, are necessary for vital functions of nutrition; others are involved in walking, blinking, sneezing, and many other of our daily activities.

Localization. If a stimulus is to elicit a reflex response from any given part of the body, it must be applied to a fairly well circumscribed area of the body. Many of the simple protective reflexes involve action at the same part of the body as that which is stimulated. For example, when one leg is pinched, it is that leg which is withdrawn. In the struggle for existence those organisms survived which were equipped with specific reflexes adequate to protect the body from injury.

Reaction time. Even the simplest reflexes do not occur instantaneously. The delay between the presentation of the stimulus and the execution of the response is made up of the time required for the sensory nerve ending to be aroused and for the nerves to conduct, plus time lost at the synapse and time required for the responding muscles to contract or glands to secrete. The more synapses involved in a stimulus-response act, the greater the reaction time for that act. But reflex actions as a whole are very quick, much quicker than voluntary actions controlled by the brain. In fact, protective reflexes are frequently performed so quickly that the adaptive withdrawal is complete before one becomes aware of the stimulus and its danger. When a dust particle lodges in the eye, we blink very quickly to get it out —and without thinking.

Duration of response. A stimulus lasting a fraction of a second often causes the motor neurons to discharge for several seconds or even minutes. This happens because impulses traveling in circular chains of neurons or through long-circuit chains continue to reach the motor neurons long after those which took the shortest path. (See page 708.)

Irradiation. If the strength of the reflex stimulus is increased, the number of muscles coming into play is increased. The area in which fibers respond is also widened. Lightly scratch the sole of a baby's foot, and the toes alone will move; pinch the foot, and the whole leg will be sharply retracted; a stronger pinch may produce a response of the entire body. As more sensory fibers are activated, more correlation neurons come into play, leading to stimulation of more motor neurons.

Facilitation. Certain stimulus-response acts serve to reinforce each other. When the tendon just below the kneecap is struck, the loosely hanging leg will jerk upward. If the subject is asked to clench his fist just before the kneecap tendon is struck, the amplitude of the knee jerk will be increased.

Summation. If a very weak stimulus is repeated, the reflex response will eventually take place even though a single presentation of the same stimulus might fail to be effective. The few afferent fibers excited by a weak stimulus are unable to excite even one spinal neuron, and no reflex results, but when the stimulus is repeated, there is a summation (addition) of effects which causes a reflex response. Such *temporal summation* is represented diagrammatically below:

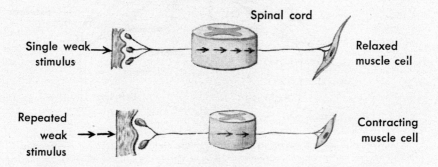

Temporal summation is easily shown on a pet dog. If one lightly scratches the dog's side, no scratch reflex results. But if the same scratch is repeated several times in rapid succession, the hind foot of the dog will start to scratch. The weak stimuli have summated.

Summation also occurs when two different but adjacent points on the skin are stimulated. Each stimulus alone may cause no reflex response, but when the two points are stimulated at the same time, a reflex results. This is called *spatial summation* because different points, and hence different afferent nerve fibers, are involved. Spatial summation is further proof of what the microscope shows (p. 708): that correlating neurons collect the impulses from many afferent fibers to excite a single outgoing fiber. Summation is possible because of synapses. If reflex arcs were isolated from one another, one could not affect the other. But since they do come together (converge), they have the opportunity to work together.

Inhibition and reciprocal innervation. In general the muscles of the body are arranged opposite one another in antagonistic pairs, one extending and one bending a given joint. When one muscle contracts, its antagonist relaxes, for the reflex excitation of one muscle is accompanied by the *inhibition* of the motor neurons supplying the antagonist. Without this mechanism, antagonist muscles would, as it were, be "trying" to do different things at the same time, which might result in no movement being accomplished. Because of this mechanism an arm or a leg can do "one main thing at a time." This is known as the *law of reciprocal innervation,* illustrated below in antagonistic muscles:

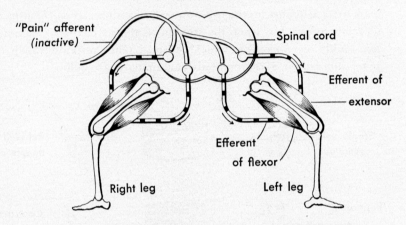

Above: *Flexors and extensors of both legs are shown in a state of contraction, produced by a constant stream of efferent nerve impulses (indicated by shaded segments). Below: When a "pain" afferent from the right leg is stimulated, a reflex occurs which stimulates the right flexor and the left extensor by increasing the nerve impulses to these muscles. The same "pain" afferent produces a decrease in nerve impulses in the efferents to the right extensor and the left flexor. Arrows indicate direction of transmission of nerve impulses. Plus signs indicate stimulating action; minus signs indicate inhibiting action.* (By permission from A. J. Carlson and V. Johnson, Machinery of the Body, © 1941, University of Chicago Press, p. 408.)

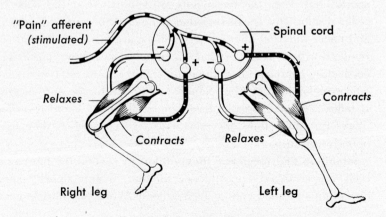

The best example of inhibition is found when we stimulate the sole of the foot with a painful stimulus and at the same time with pressure. Painful stimulation alone will cause the leg to withdraw in protection; pressure will elicit the so-called "extensor thrust" or pushing-out movement used in walking or in catching one's balance. If the two stimuli are presented simultaneously, the withdrawal reflex alone is elicited, for the thrust response is inhibited with the result that it does not impede the withdrawal. Thus, effective reactions inhibit or block other competing reactions. This principle has been extended (Wendt[1]) to cover conditioned, or learned, responses. According to this view, inhibition never occurs alone. That is to say, when a response is lost, it is because some response system takes its place.

How is this selection accomplished in the nervous system? There are three characteristics of the stimulus which give advantage in the competition for dominance in the organism's activity.

1 Painful stimuli usually have the right of way. The organism is innately organized to permit the important business of self-protection to come first.

2 Strong stimuli or weak stimuli repeated have the right of way.

3 Too frequent repetition of a response will give the right of way to a rival response through fatigue and adaptation.

The brain can inhibit up to a certain point the protective reflex actions of the spinal cord. This is seen in the voluntary suppression of pain responses or the blink reflex. Strong drives can take precedence over pain reflexes. These and other functions of the brain will next be considered.

THE BRAIN

IN THE LAST ANALYSIS the superiority of man over the lower forms derives from his superior ability to think and plan, utilizing objects both present and absent in overcoming his problems. This ability is the result of a larger, more complex brain, which operates with intricate division of labor and with more control over the rest of the nervous system than we find in any of the lower forms. Perception, thought, consciousness itself depend on the brain for their occurrence. Clearly, then, if we are to fulfill the aim set forth in Chapter 1, to study all the behavior, motives, and emotions growing out of the interaction between man and his environment, our picture must include a working understanding of the brain. The color diagram of the brain at the front of this book will be helpful for reference throughout this section.

The topography of the brain

The drawings on this page and the next show two views of the human brain. Study them carefully, for an understanding of them will be necessary to an intelligent reading of the discussion. The main part of the brain—the cerebrum—is divided into two halves called the right and left *hemispheres*. Each hemisphere is essentially a mirror image of the other. That is to say, a sketch of one side would look like one of the other side seen in a mirror. It is interesting to note that in general the *left* hemisphere controls the *right* side of the body; and the right hemisphere, the left side of the body.

Each hemisphere of the cerebrum has four parts, or lobes, divided by two fissures or grooves—the fissure of Rolando and the fissure of Sylvius. The figure below shows these parts:

1 The frontal lobe, located in front of the nearly vertical fissure of Rolando and above the fissure of Sylvius.

2 The parietal lobe, still above the fissure of Sylvius but back of the fissure of Rolando.

3 The temporal lobe, separated from the frontal and parietal lobes by the fissure of Sylvius and so named because it lies just beneath the temples, and

4 The occipital lobe, located at the back of the brain.

Study these main divisions of the cerebrum until you are thoroughly familiar with the location of each of the different parts.

A longitudinal cross section of the brain

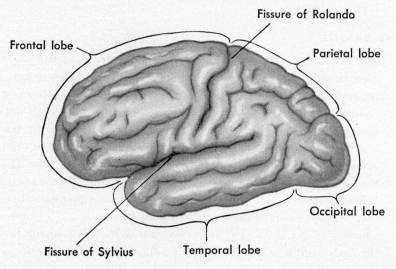

Fissure of Rolando

Frontal lobe

Parietal lobe

Fissure of Sylvius

Temporal lobe

Occipital lobe

The brain viewed from above

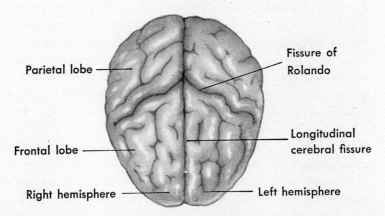

Parietal lobe

Fissure of Rolando

Frontal lobe

Longitudinal cerebral fissure

Right hemisphere

Left hemisphere

If we examine sections of the brain with the naked eye, we see that there is a narrow, grayish rind of tissue covering the cerebrum. This is the *cortex* (which means "bark"). It is made up largely of the dendrites and neuron bodies of nerve cells whose axons extend into the interior section.

Cutting down to the interior section, we find that it comprises by far the larger portion of the brain. It is almost white in color, the whiteness resulting from the presence of the white myelin sheaths of the nerve fibers (see p. 702). Studies have shown that these fibers are of several different sorts. Some are sensory fibers coming up from the spinal cord by way of relay centers in the old-brain; some are motor fibers going down through the cord; others connect one area of the cortex with another area of the same hemisphere; and still others connect with areas on the opposite side. The drawing on page 723 shows the location of the association fibers in the interior of the brain.

What are the roles of the various parts of the brain described above? How is the work divided among them? The brain performs the function of a central control tower. Impulses from incoming neurons are shunted back and forth in the brain and eventually out to organs of response. In any attempt to study division of labor in the brain, our first task is to survey the methods employed in finding out which parts of the brain and which nerves are involved in a particular type of behavior.

How neurologists study the work of the brain

There are several recognized methods of studying the functioning of the various parts of the brain. The most important ones will be reviewed briefly here.

The method of extirpation. To *extirpate* means to cut out or destroy. The neurophysiologist uses the method of destruction systematically. The behavior of an animal is carefully observed and catalogued until the scientist knows just what is normal behavior under given conditions. Next he cuts away part of the brain of the same or of a similar animal and observes how the behavior is changed. Such experiments are performed freely with animals, but with man we have to wait for disease, accidents, or war wounds to destroy parts of the nervous system before such observations can be made. In such cases, of course, the parts destroyed are seldom sharply localized, and in general their observation leads to less clear results than can be derived from the deliberately placed injuries to the animal's brain. Such injuries, whether induced by experiment or accident, are referred to as *lesions*.

When a certain bit of behavior disappears or becomes exaggerated or modified after the loss of a portion of the nervous system, the neurologist concludes that that portion is essential to the normal performance. Such observations do not imply that the area destroyed has the sole responsibility for the behavior in question.

Action-current methods. We know that neurons produce electric currents when they conduct. By studying the action currents of the brain during different kinds of behavior and by correlating the areas of greatest activity with the nature of the stimulus-response behavior going on at a given moment, we can make considerable progress in determining which areas are involved in various types of behavior. This method was explained in connection with the study of tiny muscle movements in the thinking process (see p. 397).

The method of stimulation has been used with great success. Some part of the brain is stimulated, usually with a weak electric current. The experimenter then observes what response takes place. He changes the point of application of the stimulus and notices how the behavior changes. In this manner it has been possible to map the so-called motor areas of the brain.

The use of drugs of specific action. When certain drugs are painted on the brain tissue directly, the effect is the exaggeration or destruction of certain types of response. The points of application of the drug can then be correlated with the changes in behavior which are observed, and the function of the various parts can be inferred.

Localization of function in the new-brain or cerebrum

Thinking back over the material given in Chapter 7 on *The Sensory Processes,* you will readily see that every sensory experience can be classified according to two fundamental dimensions: *kind* and *intensity*. Our visual sensations differ from one another in hue; our cutaneous sensations are labeled warm, cold, pressure, or pain; our auditory sensations are variable in pitch; our taste sensations are salt, sweet, bitter, or sour; our olfactory sensations appear to differ from each other in quality. Moreover, any sensation can differ in intensity from another sensation of the same kind. What are the neural correlates of these conscious experiences? This field is still rich in opportunity for new knowledge despite a century of productive labor in it. Much is known; more remains to be learned.

One hundred years ago Johannes Muller put forth the doctrine of "specific nerve energies." According to this doctrine a sensory nerve will produce a certain type of experience no matter how it is stimulated. Close your eyes and press upon the lids. In a moment you will *see* a wealth of color and design, *yet the stimulus is not light but pressure*. When the cut ends of the nerves are stretched on the healing stump of an amputated leg, the patient sometimes reports sensations of pain, pressure, or itch in the toes that are no longer a part of his body. If a person is struck on the back of the head, over the visual area of the brain, he "sees stars"—that is, the sensations produced (visual ones) are appropriate to the nerve cells brought into action and not to the stimulus itself (which is sudden mechanical pressure).

The *kind* of sensation we experience seems to depend upon the *kind* of brain cell involved. One must not be misled by the phrase "specific nerve energies" to believe that the *electrical impulses* in different kinds of sensory neurons are different, for as you know, nerve impulses differ only in amplitude and rate of propagation. The specificity seems to lie in the *kind of brain neurons* located in the part of the brain where a particular sensory track ends.

Here we come to one of the oldest problems of neurology and psychology: whether or not there is localization of function in the brain. For a long time a controversy raged between one group of workers who held that each part of the cerebrum had a definite function which it alone could perform, and others who held that the parts were more or less interchangeable functionally. As is so often the case, a compromise position is the most tenable one. But for particular motor and sensory functions, special areas in the brain have been located. (See p. 718 and the color diagram at the beginning of the book.)

The motor area. The cortex immediately in front of the fissure of Rolando has to do with motor functions. When this area is stimulated, some voluntary-muscle group responds. It will be remembered that long motor neurons lead down from this area through the spinal cord to the motor neurons, which supply the muscles of the body and of the extremities. When areas in this region are destroyed, movement is impaired in some part of the body. The paralysis following a "stroke" is due either to interruption of the conduction of nerve impulses along these fibers because of their loss of blood supply, or to destruction by hemorrhage of the parts of the motor cortex from which such motor impulses are sent out.

The feet are represented at the upper part of the motor area of the brain, the trunk farther down, and the hands still farther down; the face and tongue are localized at the very bottom.

Localization of function in the cerebral cortex

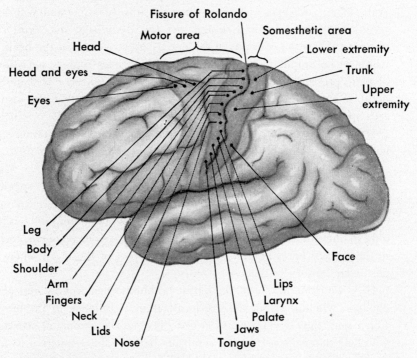

Fissure of Rolando

Motor area

Head

Head and eyes

Eyes

Somesthetic area

Lower extremity

Trunk

Upper extremity

Leg
Body
Shoulder
Arm
Fingers
Neck
Lids
Nose

Lips
Larynx
Palate
Jaws
Tongue

Face

The somesthetic area. Just back of the fissure of Rolando is the *somesthetic* or body-sensitivity area. When this area is destroyed, the human individual suffers some important losses of sensory ability. Such a person cannot tell where an object is touching him; he will be aware merely of an unlocalized pressure. He is able to note the difference between stimuli which are very hot and very cold, and he retains the sense of pain, but he cannot distinguish warm and cool objects. With his eyes closed, he cannot tell what position his arms or legs are in or

THE BRAIN AND NERVOUS SYSTEM 718

how they are being moved by the neurologist. When the somesthetic area of one side of the brain is destroyed, the subject reports that the opposite side of his body does not feel natural. When the skin is touched, he must look to see where the stimulus is, for he has lost the ability to localize the origin of sensations. He is able to handle objects, for he retains the power of movement, but he cannot tell you whether it is a key or a match that he is handling unless he looks at it. He cannot tell sandpaper from silk, although he may report that one is pleasant and the other unpleasant.

If only one side of the area is destroyed, his sensory ability is lost only on the opposite side of the body. If only a part of the somesthetic area is destroyed, the impairment is limited to a part of the body. In general, sensory and motor representation of the same part of the body lie just across the central fissure from each other. Thus the body surface is "projected" onto the somesthetic area by neural connections as a lantern slide is projected onto a screen.

Even when the cerebral cortex is entirely destroyed—so that both sides of the somesthetic area are of course destroyed—not all body sensitivity is lost. The *thalamus,* a part of the old-brain, also plays a part in such sensitivity. In lower animals, having a small cerebral cortex, this old part of the brain is responsible for nearly all sensation. Although in man most of the sensory function has been taken over by the cerebral cortex, pain and a diffuse, poorly localized sense of pleasure or discomfort are still carried out by the old-brain.

The sensations experienced through the activity of the thalamic centers are fairly strong but are vague and diffuse. Without the help of the cerebral cortex, localization of stimuli and perception of space through the body sensations are not possible. The localization of bodily sensitivity has been studied by means of the cortical-extirpation technique as used on animals, particularly monkeys.

> First the animals were trained to discriminate small differences in the magnitude of lifted weights. Then after the animals were well trained, various lesions of the cerebral cortex were produced surgically. Postoperative tests showed that lesions to the motor area, the somesthetic area, and other parts of the parietal lobes produced no great or permanent decline in the ability to make the discriminations. With the whole of the parietal lobe destroyed, the performance of the animals was very poor but not completely abolished. This experimenter suggests that in monkeys, wide areas of the cerebral cortex, including a part of the frontal lobe, cooperate in the performance of the discrimination function; the thalamus, too, seems to play a part. (T. C. Ruch[2])
>
> However, corresponding lesions of the brain of man—produced by accident rather than extirpation—were shown to produce greater im-

pairment of discrimination (T. C. Ruch, Fulton, and German[3]), for apparently man is much more dependent upon the cerebral cortex than is the monkey.

The visual area. More is known about the visual area of the brain than about the other sensory areas. As shown in the colored frontispiece, this area lies directly at the back of the brain. Just as the various parts of the skin of the body are projected upon the somesthetic area of the cortex by means of neural connections, so is the retina of the eye similarly projected on the cortex of the occipital lobe. A huge bundle of nerve fibers constituting the optic nerve leads back from each retina, forming a cross at a point well back from the eyes themselves and located at the base of the brain. Half of the fibers from the left eye then go to the right side of the cerebral cortex, and half from the right eye go to the left side of the cerebral cortex, the others from each eye going on to the same side. (See the figure below.)

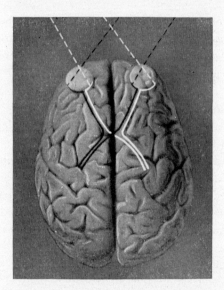

The brain from above, showing location of optic nerves. (From Eyes and Their Care, *Encyclopaedia Britannica Films, Inc.)*

The point of crossing is called the *optic chiasm*. If we cut the optic nerve (between the eye and the point of crossing), the individual would be blind in that one eye. But suppose that we cut the *optic tract* (between the chiasm and the brain itself); the person would suffer from a peculiar sort of blindness. Such destruction would affect the ability of both eyes to function but would affect each in part only. The person would be blind in the left half of each retina if the tract were cut on the left side or in the right halves of his two retinas if the right optic tract were cut. This type of blindness would be noticed with both eyes open or with either one open alone. It must be remembered that when a person is blind in one half of the retina he cannot see objects on the opposite side of the visual field, since the lens of the eye reverses objects from left to right. Because only one half of each retina is blind, this condition is called *hemianopia,* or "half-inability-to-see."

When some fraction of the tract or of the visual cortex on one side is destroyed, there results a blindness in the corresponding parts of the two retinas which is less extensive in area than blindness brought on by complete destruction. All this is further evidence that, when we are looking at anything, there is a fairly close point-to-point correspondence between the visual area and the retina, and hence with the external visual world. This arrangement is believed to provide a basis for visual space perception and for seeing complex visual patterns. The retinal "picture" of the outside world is translated into a pattern of nerve activity on the cerebral cortex.

Beyond the facts just presented, little is known of the brain mechanisms in seeing. How the brain represents depth and hue is still a mystery. There is no space in an elementary book of this sort to discuss the conflicting and unproved theories in this field. But we shall make one exception:

Although certain theories of the mechanism of color vision hold that color mixing is a retinal phenomenon, there is one type of experiment that several psychologists have performed which indicates that such fusion can also be accomplished in the cortex.

> One experimenter, for instance, arranged an apparatus whereby light of one hue can be shone on one retina while light of another hue illuminates the other retina (Hecht[4]). There is no possible criss-crossing of light. If the two hues yellow and blue are used, the subject sees white light; if red and green lights are used, the subject sees yellow light. This is exactly what happens in the color-mixing experiment in which the mixed lights shine on both retinas at a time. These results show that color mixing *can* take place at some point in the nervous mechanism beyond the retinas, although they do not disprove that mixing also takes place in the retinas.

When the visual tract is severed before it has gone very far into the brain, blindness is accompanied by loss of visual reflexes to light. The iris will not close when light is flashed in the eye. If the optic tract is cut farther back, however, or if the visual cortex itself is destroyed, reflex contractions of the pupil to light still take place. The explanation is that the nerve fibers which give rise to this reflex branch off from the optic tract soon after the tract joins the brain.

Clinical studies reveal an important difference between the organiza
tion and functions of the visual and the somesthetic areas of the cortex

1 Destruction of the visual cortex in man is followed by complete blindness. Similar destruction of the somesthetic area, as we
have seen, merely destroys ability to differentiate finely between
stimuli.

2 Destruction of the visual cortex in monkeys, cats, and dogs is
not followed by complete blindness, as it is in man. Seeing of
colors and patterns is almost entirely abolished but light can be
distinguished from darkness by the use of subcortical centers.

These differences are explained by the fact that as we ascend the
evolutionary series, there is more and more *encephalization*—that is, a
progressively increasing dominance of the higher parts of the brain
over the activities of the rest of the nervous system. As we pass from
the lower to the higher animals, we find that the cortex assumes more
and more importance. This encephalization of function is most noticeable in the case of vision, while the somesthetic functions have under-
gone considerably less (Marquis[5]).

The auditory area. From the receptor cells for hearing, located in the
inner ear, nerve fibers lead into the brain to relay stations through
which reflexes to sounds are
made possible. From connections
in these relay stations, other
neurons continue upward to the
auditory area of the cortex,
which is located in the wall of
the fissure of Sylvius that belongs to the temporal lobe. Approximately as many fibers go
from each ear to the cortical area
on the same side of the brain as
go to the cortical area on the
opposite side. Clinical accounts

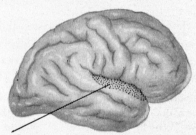

Auditory area (located in superior
temporal gyrus of temporal lobe)

*Profile of the brain, showing location
of auditory area. The fissure of Sylvius
has been opened up to show this area.*

show that the destruction of the cortical auditory area on one side
reduces hearing ability very slightly.

We now have some idea of the manner in which the brain functions
in producing the conscious qualities of auditory sensation, especially
pitch. Different nerve fibers in the auditory nerve and different areas
within the auditory cortex respond to high, low, and intermediate
pitches. Thus the doctrine of "specific nerve energies" (p. 717) seems
to apply even within a single sense department.

The gustatory and olfactory areas. Nerve fibers come from the olfactory patches of the nostrils to connect eventually with a part of the cerebral cortex known as the *hippocampus,* which is located directly beneath the temporal lobe. Fibers from the olfactory patches also lead to the old-brain area, where they set up connections making possible reflex movements to smell stimuli. The centers for taste are usually said to be in a region close to the olfactory area, but some research (Börnstein[6]) suggests that taste is a highly developed touch sensation and is localized near the somesthetic area for the tongue.

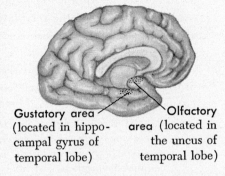

Gustatory area (located in hippocampal gyrus of temporal lobe)   Olfactory area (located in the uncus of temporal lobe)

Profile of the brain, showing location of gustatory and olfactory areas.

The association areas. Attempts to localize the more complex mental processes were carried out at first by physiologists, without the help of psychologists. By the beginning of the twentieth century, however, the psychologists were engaging in active work in the field. Working together, physiologists and psychologists have discovered the value of cooperative research.

We will find, if we make a drawing of the cerebral cortex and then mark off the areas now known to be essential to motor and sensory functions, that by far the larger portion is not touched by our pencil. These parts are not unused, however. They are the *association areas.*

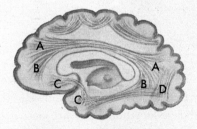

Profile of cerebral hemisphere, showing bundles of association fibers: A-A between frontal and occipital areas; B-B and C-C between frontal and temporal areas; D between occipital and temporal areas.

The association areas of each side of the cerebral cortex are richly connected to each other, to motor and sensory areas, and to similar areas on the opposite side, and, as well, receive numerous fibers from the thalamus. They serve to correlate and integrate the simpler sensory and motor functions. In fact, the sensory areas are the gateway into the cortex and the motor area is the exit, the real work of the brain being done by the association areas. For example, injuries to the cortex just outside the visual area, though not causing blindness, destroy awareness of depth and recognition of visual objects.

Much is known of the relationship between damage to association areas and defects in speech and understanding of words, although there is still much to be learned before speculation is eliminated and clear understanding reconciles theories which are at times discordant. Study of the speech functions of the association areas began in the last century.

> In 1861 Broca reported the classic case of a patient who showed an almost complete loss of speech ability. Careful examination of the patient's brain showed that an area in the frontal lobe of the left cerebral hemisphere just above the fissure of Sylvius and extending to it was destroyed. This area has come to be known as *Broca's area*, and is shown in the diagram below.
>
> About ten years later Wernicke discovered that destruction of the cortex of the left temporal lobe below the auditory area, extending backward and curving up around the end of the fissure of Sylvius, was associated with inability to understand spoken language. This area, known as *Wernicke's center*, is shown in the diagram.

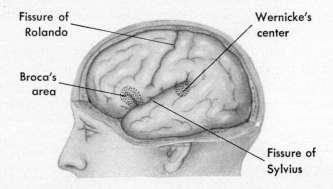

Subsequent investigations have upheld the validity of these early observations and have extended their significance by showing that similar phenomena occur when other association areas are destroyed. As you know, aged people tend to lose their ability to learn new facts, to see new relationships, to solve new problems; and in extreme cases these behavioral losses have been found to be correlated with degenerative changes in the cells of the cortical association areas.

These first observations on the association areas laid the foundation for many detailed researches from which numerous important conclusions have been drawn. In a general way the *association centers* have been found to be the parts which are essential to abstract learning and to the use of symbols to represent absent objects and events in thought and speech.

1 One new approach to the problem of locating the higher centers utilized the extirpation method (Lashley[7]). Monkeys and other animals were trained to perform certain tasks, such as opening a puzzle box or running a maze. After the habit was well learned, portions of the brain would be surgically removed and the animals retested to see how much the habit had been impaired.

Such experiments showed that in the case of some (but not all) habits, the removal of certain parts of the cortex will abolish the habit, which can then be relearned. If the habits had been permanently abolished—i.e., if relearning had not taken place—we would have been forced to conclude that localization of such functions is hard and fast.

However, complete localization did not seem to exist, especially in the rat. Loss of cortical tissue did slow up the original learning of a maze habit by the rat, but the loss in learning ability seemed to be dependent upon the *amount* rather than the location of the cortical tissue removed. It is not hard to find a probable explanation for this. Ordinarily many sensory cues are available to guide the rat through the maze—more, indeed, than the rat needs. Removal of a part of the brain may destroy certain sensory elements but not others.

2 The first work with rats has been followed by many recent studies of great importance on other and higher animals. A dog from which the entire cerebrum has been removed—a very difficult operation— shows some signs of becoming conditioned to an auditory stimulus, but the behavior never becomes as specific and neat as in normal dogs. The response used was the lifting of the foot at the sounding of a tone to avoid an electric shock on the paw. The dog, after many trials, showed a sluggish and generalized reaction to the tone, involving the whole body as well as the foot receiving the shock. (Culler[8])

3 Still another psychologist (Jacobsen[9]) has contributed a number of interesting experiments on the effect of destruction of the most forward part of the frontal lobes, which is a purely association area. Making lesions of varying size and location within the frontal lobes, he analyzed the effects of such lesions on two types of behavior situations: (1) situations in which the essential cues were present in the animal's environment at the time of the response (problem boxes, discrimination habits, etc.); and (2) situations in which certain essential cues had to be *recalled* from recent experience (delayed responses).

In the first series of experiments, involving the problem boxes and the discrimination tests, sensory cues are always present, although symbols are not necessarily involved. In one type of problem situation, the food was obtained by solving a simple puzzle—such as turning a crank through an arc of 270 degrees in a clockwise direction, pulling a rope projecting from the box, opening a latch, or performing in proper sequence five such movements to release the lid of the box containing food. In the visual-discrimination experiments, the food was found behind a stimulus card which differed in brightness from another stimulus card behind which there was no food. The correct card is placed to the left or to the right in random order so that the animal must react to the brightness of the card in making the correct choice, and the monkeys eventually learn to choose the proper stimulus card without false moves.

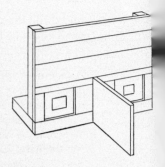

In the second type of experiment—the delayed-response experiments —the monkey is placed in compartment *A* with door *C* raised so that response chamber *B* can be seen through the grill *D*. The monkey's

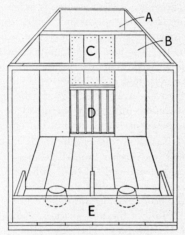

Drawings from C. F. Jacobsen, "Studies of Cerebral Function in Primates," *Comparative Psychology Monographs*, 1936, Volume 13, No. 3.

attention is attracted by the experimenter, who places a piece of food under one of the inverted cups shown at section *E*. The door *C* is then lowered for a period of time, after which the door and the grill are raised so that the animal can walk into the forward compartment and get the hidden bit of food. The object of the experiment is to see how long the animal can delay with the food out of sight and still go directly to the correct cup, which is changed from side to side in random order. The important psychological feature of this situation is that the animal must react partly on the basis of memory. Obviously the position of the food must be represented by some symbol during the period of delay and that symbol must function as a stimulus in guiding the final response after the period of delay has terminated.

The experimenter's results are summarized in his own words as follows:

"1. Unilateral lesions [i.e., on only one side of the cerebral cortex] caused no impairment of performance on any tests. . . .

"2. Bilateral lesions [i.e., on both sides] of the frontal association areas, either partial or complete, resulted in different effects on the two types of tests.

"(a) Memory for simple problem-box habits and for visual discrimination habits was not impaired, nor was ability to learn new tasks of a similar nature reduced.

"(b) The ability to perform delayed response was abolished by complete lesions of the frontal areas. The subjects failed in this test with delays as short as one or two seconds.

"(c) Subtotal [i.e., incomplete] lesions caused a shortening of the time through which memory was effective but did not entirely abolish this ability.

"3. The deficit associated with frontal lesions cannot be attributed merely to an extensive injury of the cortex since lesions in other cortical areas (motor and premotor, postcentral and the parietal and temporal lobes) produced slight, if any, changes; on the contrary, the peculiar importance of the frontal areas in mediating the behavior in question is indicated."

These results confirm for the monkeys the same sort of thing observed in the case of human speech difficulties due to lesions in the speech centers. The association areas are essential to the performance of behavior which involves the use of symbols.

The method of extirpation is possible only with animals. In man, localization of function must be deduced from the study of pathological conditions.

For instance, disease in or injury to certain association areas will bring about an interesting condition in which the person is unable to recognize objects by their "feel." Some familiar thing such as a door key, a bottle opener, or a pencil can be handled indefinitely and still not be recognized. Patients who show this type of disorder are still capable of experiencing normal elementary sensations. Their difficulty is in grouping these elements into normal perceptions: objects are *felt* but not *known*.

Similar disorders of perception are found in other sensory fields. These disorders are called *agnosias* or "inabilities to know," and are classified on the basis of the nature of the function which is impaired. Related disorders affecting language are called *aphasias*. The following list defines the more frequently encountered agnosias and aphasias:

Astereognosis. Loss of ability to recognize solid objects through the sense of touch (cutaneous and kinesthetic senses).

Alexia. Inability to recognize printed words. This is commonly called "word-blindness."

Sensory aphasia. Inability to recognize spoken words. This condition is sometimes called "word-deafness," and it can occur in persons who can hear simple sounds.

These particular conditions seem to be associated with lesions in the association regions close to sensory areas of the cortex.

Similar impairments of the association region near the motor areas will give rise to motor disturbances, especially of the apparatus used in speech. Some of the more common of these are:

Apraxia. Defective ability to perform common manipulation (for example, lighting a cigarette) in the absence of real paralysis.

Agraphia and *paragraphia.* Loss of the ability to write or the employing of the wrong word or some meaningless symbol.

Motor Aphasia. Loss of ability to use spoken language though the larynx is not paralyzed. The use of the wrong spoken word is called *paraphasia.* For example, an elderly lady says in quite a matter-of-fact tone: "I staved the stafflings gage."

Amimia and *paramimia.* The inability to use gestures, and the incorrect use of them, respectively.

In some cases the sensory and motor aspects of speech are little affected, yet there are subtle disturbances of speech which are difficult to describe. Aphasia at this level merges over into intellectual functions, just as it merges into sensory loss and motor paralysis at the other end of the scale.

Early neurologists ascribed quite specific disturbances to specific cortical areas. Such cases are rare, but so are cortical lesions confined to restricted regions. Physiologists now agree, however, that lesions in front of the motor areas have most effect on motor speech functions, and that those in the parietal and temporal regions have most effect on sensory functions. Intellectual speech defects, indicative of faulty intellectual processes, are often caused by mild but widespread damage to the cerebral cortex, rather than to specific lesions of the "prefrontal area" as was once believed.

The student must not forget that these conditions can be encountered in hysteria (see p. 501) as well as in cases of organic lesion. Often the layman is not able to tell the hysterical case from the organic. Once the history and the cause of the condition are known, it can be spoken of more descriptively as *hysterical* or *organic astereognosis* or as *hysterical* or *organic aphasia.*

All this evidence from laboratory and clinic indicates that the association areas do control and integrate speech and complex symbolic activities.

The problem of cerebral dominance and handedness

As you have already seen, there is almost complete crossing over of the sensory and motor fibers from one side of the body to the *opposite* side of the brain. The left side of the brain "sees" the right half of the world, feels with the right half of the body, and, logically, controls the muscles of the right half of the body. Thus we are not surprised to find that human beings who are mainly right-handed have slightly larger left cerebral hemispheres, or even that the left side of the brain (supplying the right side of the body) has a richer blood supply. Here one side of the brain seemingly controls just one side of the body, but there is much evidence to suggest that in certain functions the one side of the cerebrum controls both sides of the body and is therefore said to be *dominant.* In normal right-handed persons, the so-called *mid-line functions* (those located in the mid-line of the body, like speech) are apparently controlled by the left side of the brain.

Whether dominance comes about through heredity or through use is not altogether clear, but there is evidence to suggest that cerebral dominance is at least in part a matter of use. Regardless of how it arises, any disturbance of it seems to be a condition of great significance, as some interesting clinical cases demonstrate:

1 On October 14, 1931, a right-handed woman came to the New Haven Hospital. She was unable to write her name completely, showed a pronounced defect of memory, and was totally blind to objects appearing on her right side. She had difficulty in reading printed matter held in the unimpaired field of vision and in recognizing pictures of familiar objects and scenes.

These symptoms suggested that something was amiss in the *left* half of her brain. A surgical operation was accordingly performed, and a large tumor was found on the left side (of the brain) at the very back of her brain in the posterior aspect of the occipital lobe. (German and Fox[10])

2 Another significant case for our discussion is that of a *left-handed* young man who had his left frontal lobe, including Broca's area, removed because of a tumor but *failed* to develop aphasia or speech disorder (Association for Research in Nervous and Mental Disease[11]). Had he been *right-handed,* he most certainly would have become aphasic because the motor speech centers of the *right-handed* person are in the *left* frontal lobe. Apparently left-handedness goes with the dominance of the motor-speech centers in the right frontal lobe.

3 Another case of a patient suffering from aphasia has a bearing on this discussion. The patient was naturally right-handed and learned to write with the right hand. At the age of ten the right hand was amputated, and the patient relearned writing with the left. Several years later an injury to the right hemisphere produced motor and sensory aphasia. After surgical removal of a cyst, marked improvement in the symptoms of aphasia was noted. (Lovell, Waggoner, and Kahn[12]) Apparently cerebral dominance had become established in the right hemisphere, suggesting that cerebral dominance is produced to a certain extent by usage.

4 Innumerable cases have been reported in which attempts to train the left-handed child to use his right hand have been followed by disorders of speech (Travis[13]). The interpretation is that changing the naturally left-handed child disturbs the dominance of the *right* cerebral cortex, which is normal for him. In the transition stage from left- to right-handedness we would expect a period of rivalry if cerebral dominance is a matter of relative amount of use. This period of conflict or uncertain dominance would cause conflicting impulses from the two hemispheres to reach the speech organs at the same instant. The result would be the spasms and deadlocks which are typical of the stutterer. Moreover, a significant number of such cases have been improved or cured following a deliberate switching back to the left hand. In corresponding manner, there is evidence that forcing a right-handed

person to use the left hand will produce stuttering. If cerebral dominance is at all determined by the native constitution of the individual, we could well expect that attempts to switch to the "unnatural" hand would lead to permanent conflict between the two cerebral hemispheres with consequent persistence of the stuttering. This whole matter is still somewhat unsettled, for the facts are not entirely consistent.

Certainly stuttering can be caused by conditions other than switching from one hand to the other. Emotional conflict, for instance, is one important source of stuttering. It is possible that at least part of the effect of switching grows out of the emotional upset engendered by the nagging of the child by parents and teachers who are trying to "correct" his left-handedness.

WHAT GOES ON IN THE BRAIN DURING THOUGHT?

THERE IS ONE IMPORTANT LINE of evidence concerning the activity of the brain in thinking which remains to be considered. You have already learned that both nervous tissue and muscle tissue have the characteristic of generating minute electric currents when active, and that this fact has been put to good use in studying the functioning of the human brain during mental activity. In recent years many physiologists and psychologists have been attracted to this very promising field. Let us review some of their outstanding discoveries.

It has been discovered that the cerebral cortex gives out rhythmical waves of minute electrical potentials which can be studied by means of amplifying devices connected with electrodes placed on the scalp over the cortex (Berger[14]). These waves are analyzed for frequency and amplitude. Some patterns of "brain waves" are shown below:

Three types of cerebral electrical potentials

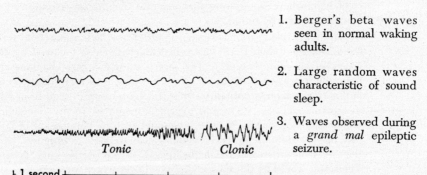

1. Berger's beta waves seen in normal waking adults.

2. Large random waves characteristic of sound sleep.

3. Waves observed during a *grand mal* epileptic seizure.

Tonic   *Clonic*

⊢ 1 second ⊦

1 and 2. From A. L. Loomis, E. N. Harvey, C. Hobart, "Electrical Potentials of the Human Brain," *Journal of Experimental Psychology*, 1936, Volume 19, p. 250. (By permission of the American Psychological Association.) 3. From Association for Research in Nervous and Mental Disease, *The Inter-Relationship of Mind and Body*, Williams and Wilkins Company, 1939, p. 74.

The pattern of these "brain waves" is highly consistent for a given individual and quite similar in identical twins. It differs somewhat for different regions of the cerebral cortex. It is significant that the brain never rests, even in the absence of special sensory stimuli. In fact, visual stimuli demanding attention stop rather than start the characteristic rhythms of the occipital lobe. Sleep and anesthesia produce large but slow activity, whereas alertness or excitement is accompanied by small, rapidly repeated waves. Some interesting studies have been made of brain waves occurring in various situations:

1 One psychologist recorded the waves from the scalp over the visual area of 132 children ranging in age from a few weeks to sixteen years (Lindsley[15]). A certain pattern of electrical discharge is established at about three months of age, and once established, it is never lost. Its frequency increases rapidly during the first year, then more slowly until the adult level is reached at about 12 years of age. Amplitude increases during the first two years, dropping sharply during the third year and more slowly thereafter, to reach the adult level at about 15 years of age. The time at which the brain waves are first observed in infants corresponds closely with the appearance of the first evidences of visual perception. This coincidence in time suggests a functional relationship.

2 In another study, the technique of brain-current registration was applied to the problem of stuttering (Travis and Knott[16]). Records of normal and stuttering subjects were taken during silence and during simple propositional speech. The electrodes were inserted in the scalp over the visual cortex of the brain. The normal subjects gave waves of a duration of one-tenth second while silent. During speaking the waves of the normal subjects were faster, each one lasting .09 seconds. The comparisons between the stutterers and the normal subjects showed such small differences that no definite conclusions can yet be drawn from them.

3 In still another experiment, subjects were asked to sit in an apparatus for measuring brain waves and were given instructions to relax and "let their minds wander" (Travis[17]). Without warning the experimenter would say "Now" and ask the subject what state of consciousness had been interrupted. By comparing the pattern of brain waves with the nature of the conscious state accompanying them, it was found that abstract thought and blankness went with large waves, and that concrete experience, such as sensation and vivid imagery, was accompanied by small waves.

4 It has also been found (Gibbs, Gibbs, and Lennox[18]) that epileptic seizures are accompanied by characteristic brain-wave patterns. Between attacks, characteristic patterns occur and these can be used in diagnosing epilepsy.

5 Perhaps more striking than any of the studies cited so far is one which found identifiable differences in the brain-wave patterns of extroverts and introverts (Gottlober[19]).

What Goes On in the Brain During Thought? 731

Studies of this sort are promising, but it should be noted that they are concerned with quite a different sort of problem from any attempt to hook up the apparatus to the scalp of the subject and read the complete story of his thinking—that is, "read his mind."

HOW THE NERVOUS SYSTEM FUNCTIONS IN EMOTION

ONE OF THE LONG-ACCEPTED FACTS about the nervous system has been the distinction between the autonomic and voluntary nervous systems. It has long been thought that the nervous control of emotional behavior and of voluntary behavior is carried out by different parts of the central and peripheral nervous system—that speech, postural responses, and the movements of arms and legs are integrated through the somatic components of the cranial and spinal nerves, while emotional behavior is brought about by the visceral or autonomic division of the nervous system.

The modern psychologist thinks of will or *volition* as a descriptive category, not as some mysterious mental or moral force capable of exerting a controlling influence on our behavior. Responses which the individual can make or refrain from making at will are called voluntary responses. Muscles acting on the skeleton are sometimes called *voluntary*, and those of the viscera are called the *involuntary* muscles. (Glands are always involuntary in that their activity cannot be controlled directly in response to instruction.) Skeletal muscles differ in their microscopic anatomy from visceral muscles. From the introductory discussion on page 700, you learned that the nervous system has one part (the somatic) which controls the skeletal muscles and another part (the visceral) which controls the visceral muscles.

In recent years, physiologists have come to realize that this division is not hard and fast, however. For instance, the many reflexes which occur in the body are responses of voluntary muscles which take place in the absence of conscious willing. Moreover, *certain involuntary responses can be brought under voluntary control*, as has been demonstrated in an important experiment:

> The natural, or inborn, response to a loud auditory stimulus includes the dilation of the pupil of the eye. A strong beam of light flashed into the eye leads, as we have seen elsewhere, to the constriction of the pupil. Both of these responses are involuntary.
>
> In this study it was found that if a bell is sounded at the moment a beam of light is flashed in the eye of the human subject, the subject will after many repetitions respond to the sound of the bell alone by

a constriction of the pupil. This is a conditioned response involving smooth muscles and is much harder to establish than conditioned responses involving striped or voluntary muscles.

By a clever experimental procedure, it was discovered that the constriction of the pupil could also be conditioned to the following kinds of stimuli: (1) a nonsense syllable spoken by the experimenter; (2) the experimenter's command, "relax"; (3) the gripping of an object by the subject; (4) the subject's saying aloud, "contract," "relax"; (5) the subject's whispering these words; and (6) the subject's *thinking* these words (repeating them in subvocal speech).

When the bell was sounded without the light, the well-conditioned subject would eventually lose his conditioning. This is known as *experimental extinction* of the response: it occurs when the secondary stimulus is presented frequently with the reward or punishment removed. However, the conditioned response to the verbal stimuli spoken by the experimenter or by the subject himself would *not* undergo experimental extinction. (Hudgins[20])

Evidently this problem is more complex than it at first appears, and we have much to learn. But while the division between the autonomic and voluntary nervous systems is not so hard and fast as was formerly thought, it still is useful as a guide to the understanding of how the nervous system functions in emotion.

The autonomic or visceral nervous system

The visceral organs of the chest and abdomen, and the other structures containing smooth muscles or glandular tissue, are controlled by a system of nerves different from those which control the muscles of the skeleton, the organs of speech, etc. The part of the nervous system which sends fibers to smooth muscles and glands is usually called the *autonomic* or *visceral nervous system*. While we still use the former term, the latter is a better word since we now know that this system is neither autonomous (self-regulating) nor automatic. It is made up of a set of reflex arcs which are subject to the control of higher centers of the brain just as the *somatic* parts of the nervous system that activate the skeletal muscles are subject to control from the brain.

There are two striking differences between the visceral and somatic components of the nervous system:

1 Activities of the autonomic nervous system are largely reflex actions; little voluntary control of visceral functions is possible. Control of the skeletal muscles can, of course, be entirely voluntary.

2 Another difference is that the autonomic nervous system has synapses outside the central nervous system. The synapses of

the somatic components are located entirely in the brain and spinal cord. (See the drawing below.)

Arrangement of neurons in spinal cord and ganglia

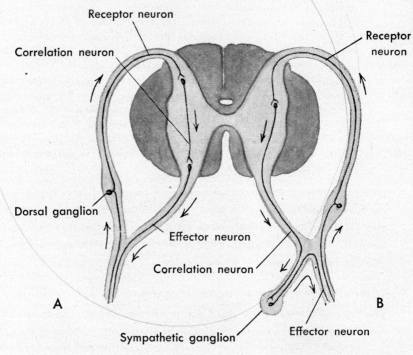

Voluntary system   Involuntary system

Anatomists have discovered that it is necessary to distinguish between two parts of the autonomic nervous system, the so-called sympathetic and parasympathetic divisions.

The sympathetic division. Branching off from certain of the spinal nerves are smaller nerves made up of fibers which run to a chain of *ganglia* (nerve centers) lying on either side of the spinal cord. The fibers run up or down in this chain and then synapse with fibers that run to smooth muscles and glands of the skin, via nerves which rejoin the spinal nerves. At certain points nerves leave this chain and pass to more distant ganglia where their fibers synapse with others that run to the visceral organs. Since these fibers come from only a dozen or so of the spinal segments in the middle of the back (thoraco-lumbar) but ultimately reach structures from the head to the toes, it is clear that the sympathetic chain constitutes a distributing mechanism. This part of the autonomic is called the *sympathetic* nervous system, because the older anatomists believed that its function was to make the visceral organs work in "sympathy."

The parasympathetic division. From the lower segments of the spinal cord and from the brain stem originate certain nerves which look like ordinary cranial and spinal nerves. But when traced, they, like the sympathetic nerves, are found to pass to visceral structures and not to the skeletal muscles. And, like the sympathetic nerves, they are interrupted by a synapse outside the central nervous system. For these reasons such nerves must be counted a part of the autonomic nervous system. Since they branch off from the central nervous system above and below the sympathetic nerve fibers, they are known as the *parasympathetic* or the cranio-sacral division of the autonomic. Most of the organs of the chest and abdomen receive fibers from both systems, and where this happens, the action of the two systems is always antagonistic: one excites the organ to increased activity, the other inhibits or decreases its activity. Thus the autonomic nervous system could be likened to the accelerator and the brake of an automobile and makes for a very effective control of the visceral organs. It must be pointed out, however, that one system is not the accelerator of *all* organs and the other the brake of *all* organs. Whether or not the parasympathetic inhibits a particular organ depends on what that organ does in the body.

Division of labor in the autonomic system. It is important to know under what conditions the parasympathetic system is dominant and under what conditions the sympathetic gets the upper hand.

All the ordinary vital functions of life are carried out by the parasympathetic system. To allow this, the sympathetic takes a back seat; in fact, the whole sympathetic nervous system has been removed from animals without greatly disturbing the ordinary processes of life. The parasympathetic protects the eye from bright light by constricting the pupil, and it adjusts the lens of the eye for near vision. Digestion of food, its passage along the alimentary canal, and finally the elimination of waste products are all actions depending on the parasympathetic nervous system. During sexual excitement, the sexual organs become suffused with a richer supply of blood by the action of this system.

If the parasympathetic is the drudge that carries on the everyday tasks of life and meets the minor exigencies, the sympathetic system is the "trouble shooter" which steps in and takes charge in the case of a real emergency. It operates when the very life of the organism is threatened, and it calls upon all the reserves of energy which para-

How the Nervous System Functions in Emotion 735

sympathetic activity has built up and held in abeyance for just such emergencies. The sympathetic is known to take over under three conditions: (1) when life is threatened by extreme cold, (2) during violent effort or exercise, and (3) during states of fear and rage.

The action of the sympathetic system in an emergency emotion is of special interest to the student of psychology. It includes: dilating the pupil of the eye; lifting the lid over-wide and protruding the eyeball; increasing the rate of the heartbeat; raising the blood pressure; and taking from the organs of sex their supply of blood with the result that they tend to become flabby. In extreme emotion, it enables the liver to pour out sugar to be used by the muscles; the spleen to pour out more blood cells to carry oxygen; and the bronchioles to dilate so that more air reaches the lungs. There is a cessation of the digestive movements of the stomach, the peristaltic contractions of the stomach, and the secretion of the digestive juices. In short, the digestive organs "close up shop" in extreme emotion, due to inhibition by the sympathetic system. The blood is then diverted to the muscles, for in an emergency it is more important to be able to run from danger than to digest food. In hairy animals the hair stands on end, and this is seen as a vestigial response in our bodies in the form of "goose-flesh." Finally, the adrenal glands are spurred to great activity and the adrenin secreted duplicates the actions of the sympathetic system and hence reinforces all of the above processes.

Visceral sensation. In the same nerves with the motor fibers to the viscera are also found numerous sensory fibers coming from the visceral organs. Those found in the sympathetic nerves are chiefly concerned with conducting pain impulses; those found in parasympathetic nerves are not concerned with pain but conduct impulses giving rise to organic sensations such as hunger, nausea, and sensations from the bladder and colon. The latter are necessary for the reflex control of the viscera in such functions as vomiting and micturition (urination). The modern surgeon takes advantage of this double pathway of sensation from the viscera by severing appropriate sympathetic nerves and thus relieving his patients of excruciating pain from diseased visceral organs.

Ordinarily we are quite unaware of any movement going on in our viscera. The pupil of our eye will dilate in pain. We feel the pain but are unaware of the fact that the pupil has become larger unless we see it in the mirror. In other instances, when we think we are aware of our viscera, as in thinking we feel the heartbeat, we are really receiving the sensation from the chest wall, not over the sympathetic nerves to the heart. It is observed by surgeons that if the abdominal cavity is opened under local anesthesia, the viscera can be cut, pinched, or even burned without arousing pain. Yet we know that severe, unbearable pain can arise in the viscera in the form of cramps, stomach aches, etc., and we are all familiar with strong sensations of hunger and nausea. The explanation is that because of the protected position of the viscera there has been no occasion for sensitivity to cutting and burning to be developed. Distentions and contractions, on the other hand, have come to be adequate stimuli.

It may be wondered why, if contraction is an adequate stimulus, we are unaware of the normal peristalsis of the intestines. This is a matter of *threshold*. When the contractions are normal in extent, as in the ordinary processes of digestion and excretion, they do not reach sufficient intensity to stimulate the sensory fibers; hence no sensation reaches consciousness. However, if they are strong, spasmlike contractions, as in diseased states or in extreme physiological states, such as a greatly overdistended bladder or colon, we may become very conscious of our viscera. Visceral sensations are really "danger signals" and bring us to the physician or compel us to some action which corrects the emergency physiological condition. The connection between visceral sensations and "drives" should thus be apparent.

Visceral sensations differ from those arising in skin in that they are diffuse and poorly localized despite their intensity. In fact, they are often wrongly localized and seem to come not from the viscera but from the skin. Thus, when severe pain originates in a diseased heart, it seems to come from the chest wall or sometimes even from a band running down the back of the arm.

Centers of emotion in the brain

The autonomic nervous system is not the only part of the nervous system that functions in emotion. Higher centers in the brain are involved as well as the reflex arcs. Clinical and physiological evidence has been of great value in helping to determine how the brain functions in emotion.

How does the cortex function in emotion? Observations on animals would seem to indicate that the new-brain serves as a check on unrestrained emotional response. With the cerebrum intact the intensity of emotional response is proportional to the seriousness of the situation. But the cat or dog without its cerebral cortex shows no such gradations in intensity, and the emotions it exhibits are only the most primitive emotional behavior responses to pain, rage, and fear, plus certain basic sexual responses.

A dog in which the cerebrum had been surgically removed showed intense emotional responses to stimuli which were ignored by normal dogs and by the same dog before the operation (Culler[21]). A playful pat on the side would cause the dog to whirl with fangs bared—so-called "sham rage." Similar observations have been made on cats deprived of the services of their new-brains (Bard[22]).

Recent studies show that the cerebral cortex has a control over the visceral responses (Fulton[23]). This suggests that the cerebral cortex may be directly responsible for the less primitive emotional responses which are lacking in the decorticate animals. The association centers of the cortex are undoubtedly important too in adjusting the emotional response to the situation since conditioned emotional responses involve symbols.

We have seen that the presence of the functioning cortex serves to check the elemental expression of emotion. What does the cortex have to do with the subjective experience in emotion? This question is difficult to answer from experiments with animals, for animals are incapable of introspection. And unfortunately, most clinical patients suffering from lesions of the cortex are not skilled introspectionists. Up to the present, no skilled introspectionist has suffered a lesion in the right place to make possible this type of report. However, there is reason to believe that the higher emotions or sentiments involve the cerebral cortex. Apparently the "head" *does* rule the "heart."

How do the thalamus and hypothalamus function in emotion? We have seen that there is exaggeration of emotion after removal of the cerebral cortex. Physiologists working with animals have discovered that cutting away the cerebrum, including the midbrain, ends all display of emotion, even though the animal continues to live. The region between the midbrain and the cerebral cortex (the *tweenbrain* or *diencephalon*) must, therefore, contain centers for emotional expression. Below is a closeup of this region; its general location may be de-

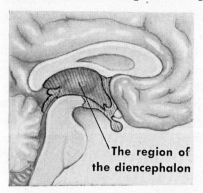

The region of the diencephalon

rived from study of the color plate. The important structures found here are the *thalamus*, which receives impulses from the whole body, including the viscera; the *subthalamus*, just beneath it, which exerts control over the muscles of emotional expression; and the *hypothalamus*, which is an important center controlling both the sympathetic and parasympathetic systems.

Numerous clinical observations have shown that disease or tumor of this important region changes the whole emotional life of the patient. A lesion in one position may bring about a condition of emotional apathy, somnolence, or even narcolepsy. In others, the patients may burst into uncontrollable laughter or tears while experiencing no emotion or even a contrary one. Other patients may experience emotion while giving little outward sign, their masklike faces concealing their true feelings. Still others experience pain and emotion to an exaggerated degree, though the visceral responses are not increased. It seems safe to conclude that outward and inward behavior and the experienced emotion are not one and the same thing (Harlow and Stagner[24]). Experiments on animals tell the same story:

> By means of wires buried in the motor center for emotion (hypothalamus) a cat can be thrown into terrifying rage behavior. The moment stimulation has ended, the cat returns to its peaceful pursuits, even licking the hand that closed the switch. This part of the brain merely executes emotion; the response cannot be attached by conditioning to the situation. On the other hand, stimulation of pain tracts or the thalamus leaves the animal stirred up and emotionally conditioned to the situation. (Masserman[25])

We must conclude that the "tweenbrain" or diencephalon is concerned both with (1) the production of emotional expression, as shown both in the face and in visceral changes, and with (2) the subjective sensations accompanying emotion. In fact, some psychologists believe that disarrangement of this region may be the cause of some of the common forms of psychopathological behavior. It may be hoped that with the fuller exploration of this tiny region will come greater understanding of some of the many factors controlling emotional life.

The prefrontal lobe in emotion. Although the whole cerebral cortex probably acts in linking emotions to sensory stimuli, the prefrontal lobe is particularly concerned with the inhibition of certain kinds of emotion and the expression of others, for it receives fibers from the thalamus and sends fibers to the hypothalamus. Damage to this region on both sides changes the personality of the patient, that is, the kind and violence of drives and emotions, and their appropriateness to the situation. Strangely enough, however, a new form of operation in this region (the prefrontal lobotomy) seems to benefit patients who are suffering from excessive anxieties and emotional reactivity, without seriously reducing intelligence. (This kind of operation is still in the early experimental stages, however.)

Thus we see that the cortex is concerned with the emotional life as well as with the intellect. The cortex is certainly involved in the maturation and learning which bring about a gradation of emotional response. The all-or-nothing character of the infant's emotions and the unrestrained outbursts of the child are somewhat like the sham rage of the decorticate animal. Then through the maturation of the cortex comes the gradual emergence of adult emotional life. And in the learning which the child undergoes, we can see that conditioned emotional responses are established through the functioning of the cortical association areas, which allow for highly organized and integrated use of symbols—just one example of the physiological basis necessary for man's complex adjustment activities.

Recommended readings

THE FOLLOWING BOOKS are listed for students who wish to undertake further general reading in areas of psychology which are of special interest to them. The list of footnote references on pages 746-763 serves as a bibliography for specific topics discussed in the text.

Part One: Introduction

BIRD, C. and BIRD, D. *Learning More by Effective Study.* New York: Appleton-Century, 1945.

CARMICHAEL, LEONARD and DEARBORN, WALTER F. *Reading and Visual Fatigue.* Boston: Houghton Mifflin, 1947.

CONANT, JAMES B. *On Understanding Science.* New Haven: Yale University Press, 1947.

FLÜGEL, J. C. *A Hundred Years of Psychology.* New York: Macmillan, 1940.

GARRETT, H. E. *Great Experiments in Psychology* (rev. ed.). New York: Appleton-Century, 1941.

GUILFORD, J. P. (ed.). *Fields of Psychology.* New York: Van Nostrand, 1940.

HEATON, K. L. and WEEDON, V. *The Failing Student.* Chicago: University of Chicago Press, 1939.

HEIDBREDER, EDNA. *Seven Psychologies.* New York: Appleton-Century, 1933.

LEWIS, NORMAN. *How to Read Better and Faster.* New York: Crowell, 1944.

NORTHROP, F. S. C. *The Logic of the Sciences and the Humanities.* New York: Macmillan, 1947.

PRESCOTT, D. A. *Emotion and the Educative Process.* Washington: American Council on Education, 1938.

SMITH, S. STEPHENSON. *How to Double Your Vocabulary.* New York: Crowell, 1947.

VALENTINE, W. L. *Experimental Foundations of General Psychology* (rev. ed.). New York: Farrar & Rinehart, 1941.

Part Two: Endowment and Environment

ARLITT, ADA HART. *Psychology of Infancy and Early Childhood* (New third edition). New York: McGraw-Hill, 1946.

BAKER, HARRY J. *Introduction to Exceptional Children.* New York: Macmillan, 1944.

CANNON, W. B. *The Wisdom of the Body.* New York: Norton, 1939.

CARMICHAEL, L. (ed.). *Manual of Child Psychology.* New York: Wiley, 1946.

GERARD, R. W. *The Body Functions.* New York: Wiley, 1941.

ISAACS, S. *The Intellectual Growth in Young Children.* New York: Harcourt, Brace, 1930.

JERSILD, ARTHUR T. *Child Psychology.* New York: Prentice-Hall, 1947.

KLINEBERG, O. *Social Psychology.* New York: Henry Holt, 1940. Chapters 5 and 6.

LINTON, RALPH. *Cultural Background of Personality.* New York: Appleton-Century, 1945.

MORGAN, C. T. *Physiological Psychology.* New York: McGraw-Hill, 1943.

MUNN, N. L. *Psychological Development.* Boston: Houghton Mifflin, 1938.

SCHEINFELD, AMRAM. *You and Heredity.* New York: Lippincott, 1939.

TERMAN, LEWIS M. and ODEN, MELITA H. *The Gifted Child Grows Up.* Stanford: Stanford University Press, 1947.

WORTIS, S. BERNARD, *et al.* "Physiological and Psychological Factors in Sex Behavior," *Annals, The New York Academy of Sciences,* Volume XLVII, Article 5, pp. 603-664.

Part Three: Knowing Our World

BARTLETT, F. *Remembering.* New York: Macmillan, 1932.

BRANDT, HERMAN F. *The Psychology of Seeing.* New York: Philosophical Library, 1945.

CHURCHMAN, C. W. *Elements of Logic and Formal Science.* Philadelphia: Lippincott, 1940.

HARTMANN, GEORGE. *Gestalt Psychology.* New York: Ronald Press, 1935.

HILGARD, E. R. *Theories of Learning.* New York: Appleton-Century, 1948.

HILGARD, E. R. and MARQUIS, D. G. *Conditioning and Learning.* New York: Appleton-Century, 1940.

HUXLEY, ALDOUS. *Words and Their Meaning.* Los Angeles: Ward Ritchie Press, 1940.

KINGSLEY, H. L. *The Nature and Conditions of Learning.* New York: Prentice-Hall, 1946.

LUCKIESCH, M. W. and MOSS, F. K. *The Science of Seeing.* New York: Van Nostrand, 1937.

MCGEOCH, J. A. *The Psychology of Human Learning.* New York: Longmans, Green, 1942.

THOULESS, R. H. *How to Think Straight.* New York: Simon & Schuster, 1939.

TOLMAN, E. C. *Purposive Behavior in Animals and Man.* New York: Appleton-Century, 1932.

VERNON, M. D. *Visual Perception.* New York: Macmillan, 1937.

WRIGHT, W. D. *The Perception of Light.* Brooklyn: Chemical Publishing Company, 1938.

Part Four: Emotional Adjustment

ADAMSON, E. *So You're Going to a Psychiatrist.* New York: Crowell, 1936.

ALEXANDER, FRANZ; FRENCH, THOMAS MORTON; *et al. Psychoanalytic Therapy.* New York: Ronald Press, 1946.

BARKER, ROGER G.; WRIGHT, BEATRICE A.; and GONICK, MILLIE R. *Adjustment to Physical Handicap and Illness.* A Survey of the Social Psychology of Physique and Disability. Washington: Social Science Research Council, Bulletin No. 55.

DOLLARD, J., *et al. Frustration and Aggression.* New Haven: Yale University Press, 1939.

DUNLAP, KNIGHT. *Religion—Its Function in Human Life.* A Study of Religion from the Point of View of Psychology. New York: McGraw-Hill, 1946.

ENGLISH, O. SPURGEON and PEARSON, G. H. J. *Emotional Problems of Living.* New York: Norton, 1945.

FARROW, E. PICKWORTH. *Psychoanalyze Yourself.* With a foreword by Sigmund Freud. New York: International Universities Press, 1945.

FROMME, ERICH. *Escape from Freedom.* New York: Farrar & Rinehart, 1941.

GESELL, A. *The Infant and Child in the Culture of Today.* New York: Harper, 1943.

GILLESPIE, R. D. *Psychological Effects of War on Citizen and Soldier.* New York: Norton, 1942.

GUTHRIE, EDWIN R. *The Psychology of Human Conflict.* New York: Harper, 1938.

HORNEY, K. *The Neurotic Personality of Our Time.* New York: Norton, 1937.

————. *Our Inner Conflicts.* New York: Norton, 1945.

————. *Self-Analysis.* New York: Norton, 1942.

HUNT, J. McV. (ed.). *Personality and the Behavior Disorders.* New York: Ronald Press, 1944.

ISAACS, S. *The Social and Emotional Growth of Children.* New York: Harcourt, 1933.

KINSEY, ALFRED C. *Sexual Behavior of the Human Male.* Philadelphia: Saunders, 1948.

KRAINES, S. H. and THETFORD, E. S. *Managing Your Mind.* New York: Macmillan, 1944.

LARSON, JOHN A. *Lying and Its Detection.* Chicago: University of Chicago Press, 1932.

LEWIN, KURT, *et al. Authority and Frustration.* Studies in Topological and Vector Psychology III, University of Iowa Studies, Studies in Child Welfare, Vol. XX, 308 pp. Iowa City: 1944.

MENNINGER, K. A. *Love Against Hate.* New York: Harcourt, Brace, 1942.

MORGAN, JOHN J. B. *How to Keep a Sound Mind* (rev. ed.). New York: Macmillan, 1946.

MYERS, C. ROGER. *Toward Mental Health in School.* Toronto: University of Toronto Press, Canada.

RICHARDS, T. W. *Modern Clinical Psychology.* New York: McGraw-Hill, 1946.

STRECKER, EDWARD A. and APPEL, KENNETH E. *Psychiatry in Modern Warfare.* New York: Macmillan, 1946.

STRECKER, EDWARD A. and CHAMBERS, FRANCIS T. *Alcohol, One Man's Meat.* New York: Macmillan, 1938.

SYMONDS, PERCIVAL M. *The Dynamics of Human Adjustment.* New York: Appleton-Century, 1946.

WATSON, J. B. *Psychology from the Standpoint of a Behaviorist.* Philadelphia: Lippincott, 1929.

ZACHRY, C. *Emotion and Conduct in Adolescence.* New York: Appleton-Century, 1940.

Part Five: The Individual and the Group

ALEXANDER, FRANZ. *Our Age of Unreason.* Philadelphia: Lippincott, 1942.

BEAN, L. H. *Ballot Behavior.* Washington: American Council on Public Affairs, 1940.

BENEDICT, RUTH. *Race: Science and Politics* (rev. ed.). New York: Viking Press, 1945.

BINGHAM, W. VAN DYKE. *Aptitudes and Aptitude Testing* (rev. ed.). New York: Harper, 1945.

CANTRIL, HADLEY, and associates. *Gauging Public Opinion.* Princeton, New Jersey: Princeton University Press, 1944.

HARTMANN, G. W. *Educational Psychology.* New York: American Book Co., 1941.

HEALY, WILLIAM. *Personality in Formation and Action.* New York: Norton, 1938.

KAPLAN, OSCAR J. *Vocational Guidance.* New York: Philosophical Library, 1948.

KARDINER, A. *The Individual and His Society.* New York: Columbia University, 1944.

LASSWELL, H. *Democracy Through Public Opinion.* Menasha, Wisconsin: George Banta Publishing Co., 1946.

LAZARSFELD, PAUL F., et al. *The People's Choice.* New York: Duell, Sloan and Pearce, 1944.

MAIER, NORMAN R. F. *Psychology in Industry.* Boston: Houghton Mifflin, 1946.

MERRILL, MAUD A. *Problems of Child Delinquency.* Boston: Houghton Mifflin, 1947.

MERTON, ROBERT K. *Mass Persuasion*. New York: Harper, 1946.

MURPHY, GARDNER. *Personality*. New York: Harper, 1947.

MURPHY, G.; MURPHY, L. B.; and NEWCOMB, T. M. *Experimental Social Psychology*. New York: Harper, 1937.

OSBORN, F. *Preface to Eugenics*. New York: Harper, 1940.

PRESSEY, S. and ROBINSON, F. *Psychology and the New Education*. New York: Harper, 1944.

RYAN, T. A. *Work and Effort*. New York: Ronald Press, 1947.

SMITH, B. L.; LASSWELL, H. D.; and CASEY, R. D. *Propaganda, Communication, and Public Opinion*. Princeton, N. J.: Princeton University Press, 1947.

TANNENBAUM, F. *Crime and the Community*. Boston: Ginn, 1938.

TERMAN, L. M., *et al*. *Psychological Factors in Marital Happiness*. New York: McGraw-Hill, 1938.

TIFFIN, JOSEPH. *Industrial Psychology*. New York: Prentice-Hall, 1947.

TYLER, LEONA E. *The Psychology of Human Differences*. New York: Appleton-Century, 1947.

WATSON, GOODWIN. *Action for Unity*. New York: Harper, 1947.

WILLIAMS, ROBIN M., JR. *The Reduction of Inter-Group Tensions:* A Survey of Research on Problems of Ethnic, Racial, and Religious Group Relations. New York: Social Science Research Council, 1947.

YEAGER, W. HAYES and UTTERBACK, WILLIAM E. *Communication and Social Action*. Philadelphia: The Annals, The American Academy of Political and Social Science, 1947.

YOUNG, KIMBALL. *Social Psychology* (rev. ed.). New York: Crofts, 1944.

Part Six: The Brain and Nervous System

FULTON, J. F. *Physiology of the Nervous System* (2nd ed.). New York: Oxford University Press, 1943.

GERARD, RALPH WALDO. *Body Functions; Physiology*. New York: Wiley, 1941.

HALSTEAD, WARD. *Brain and Intelligence*. Chicago: University of Chicago Press, 1947.

MORGAN, C. T. *Physiological Psychology*. New York: McGraw-Hill, 1943.

References

Following are complete citations for names appearing in parentheses within the text. This system of removing names from the main body of the text was adopted to concentrate students' attention on principles rather than names. Yet names are easily available for reference if desired. When a name appears *within* a sentence, it indicates the source for that one statement only. When a name appears *outside* a sentence, it indicates the source of the paragraph or sentences immediately preceding.

Chapter 1. Psychology as Science

1. Moll, Albert. *Hypnotism: Including a Study of the Chief Points of Psycho-Therapeutics and Occultism.* (Trans. by A. J. Hopkirk from the Fourth Enlarged Edition.) The Walter Scott Publishing Co., Ltd., 1909, p. 173.
2. Husband, R. W. "Human Learning on a Four-Section, Elevated, Finger Maze." *Journal of General Psychology*, 1928, 1: 15-28.
3. From *The Psychology of Personality* by English Bagby. Copyright, 1928, by Henry Holt and Company, Inc. Reprinted by permission of the publishers.
4. Cox, C. M. "The Early Mental Traits of Three Hundred Geniuses." *Genetic Studies of Genius*, Volume II. Stanford University Press, 1926.
5. Doll, E. A., in David Shakow et al., "Graduate Internship Training in Psychology." *Journal of Consulting Psychology*, 1945, 9: 244.
6. Brimhall, D. R. "Family Resemblances among American Men of Science." *The American Naturalist*, 1923, 57: 74-88.
7. Walter, H. E. *Genetics.* The Macmillan Co., 1938, p. 317.
8. Scheinfeld, A. "The Kallikaks After Thirty Years." *Journal of Heredity*, 1944, 35: 259-264.

Chapter 2. The Management of Learning

1. Bird, Charles and Dorothy M. *Learning by More Effective Study.* D. Appleton-Century Co., 1945, p. 24.
2. Pressey, S. L. *Research Adventures in University Teaching.* Public School Publishing Co., 1927.
3. Edmiston, R. W. "The Effects of Emphasizing 'How to Learn' upon Knowledge of Course Content and Course Marks." *Journal of Educational Psychology*, 1937, 28: 371-381.
4. Gifford, W. S. "Does Business Want Scholars?" *Harper's Magazine*, 1928, 156: 669-674.
5. Nicholson, F. S. "Success in College and in After Life." *School and Society*, 1915, 2: 229-232.
6. Tunis, J. R. *Was College Worth While?* Harcourt, Brace & Co., 1936.
7. Young, C. W. "Scholarship and Social Adjustment." *School and Society*, 1936, 43: 607-608.
8. Bills, A. G. "The Influence of Muscular Tension on the Efficiency of Mental Work." *American Journal of Psychology*, 1927, 38: 227-251.
9. Stauffacher, J. C. "The Effect of Induced Muscular Tension upon Various Phases of the Learning Process." *Journal of Experimental Psychology*, 1937, 21: 26-46.
10. Lauer, A. R. "An Experimental Study of the Improvement in Reading by College Students." *Journal of Educational Psychology*, 1936, 27: 655-662.
11. Ferree, C. E., and Rand, G. "Lighting in Its Relation to the Eye." *Proceedings of the American Philosophical Society*, 1918, 57: 440-478.
12. Tinker, M. "Cautions Concerning Illumination Intensities Used for Reading." *American Journal of Optometry*, 1935, 12: 43-51.
13. Ferree, C. E., and Rand, G. "Good Working Conditions for Eyes." *Personnel Journal*, 1936-1937, 15: 339.
14. Ferree, C. E., and Rand, G. "Some Experiments on the Eye with Different Illuminants." *Transactions of the Illuminating Engineering Society*, 1919, 14: Part II, 107-132.
15. Metfessel, M. "The All-or-None Nature of Thinking." *Journal of Psychology*, 1940, 9: 323-326.
16. Bates, Ralph. *Scientific Societies of the United States.* John Wiley & Sons, 1945.
17. Lund, F. H. "The Psychology of Belief." *Journal of Abnormal and Social Psychology*, 1925, 20: 63-81, 174-196.
18. Coffin, Thomas E. "Some Conditions of Suggestion and Suggestibility: A Study of Certain Attitudinal and Situational Factors Influencing the Process of Suggestion." *Psychological Monographs*, 1941, 53: No. 4.

19. Orwell, George. "Politics and the English Language." *New Republic*, 1946, 114: 873.
20. Wilkins, M. C. "The Effect of Changed Material on Ability to Do Formal Syllogistic Reasoning." *Archives of Psychology*, 1928, 16: No. 102.
21. English, H. B.; Wellborn, E. L.; and Killian, C. D. "Studies in Substance Memorization." *Journal of General Psychology*, 1934, 11: 233-260.
22. Waters, R. H. "The Influence of Tuition upon Ideational Learning." *Journal of General Psychology*, 1928, 1: 534-547.
23. Harris, L. H. "A Study in the Relation of Latin to English Composition." *School and Society*, 1915, 2: 251-252.
24. Rugg, H. O. *The Experimental Determination of Mental Discipline in School Subjects*. Warwick & York, Inc., 1916.
25. Hamley, H. R. "Formal Training: A Critical Survey of Experimental Work." *British Journal of Educational Psychology*, 1936, 6: 233-249.
26. Bird and Bird, *op. cit.*, pp. 137-138.
27. *Ibid.*, p. 134.
28. Gates, A. I. *Psychology for Students of Education*. The Macmillan Co., 1924, p. 270.
29. Peterson, H. A. "Recitation or Recall as a Factor in the Learning of Long Prose Selections." *Journal of Educational Psychology*, 1944, 35: 220-228.
30. Starch, D. "Periods of Work in Learning." *Journal of Educational Psychology*, 1912, 3: 209-213.
31. Henry L. K., and Wasson, R. "The Repetition of Classical Experiments: I. Starch's Distribution of Practice." *Journal of Applied Psychology*, 1939, 23: 503-507.
32. Cook, T. W. "Massed and Distributed Practice in Puzzle Solving." *Psychological Review*, 1934, 41: 330-355.
33. Boswell, F. P., and Foster, W. S. "On Memorizing with the Intention Permanently to Retain." *American Journal of Psychology*, 1916, 27: 420-426.
34. Eurich, A. C. "Retention of Knowledge Acquired in a Course in General Psychology." *Journal of Applied Psychology*, 1934, 18: 209-219.
35. Sones, A. M. "A Study in Memory, with Special Reference to Temporal Distribution of Reviews." *University of Iowa Studies, Aims and Progress in Research*, 1943, No. 72, pp. 65-72.
36. Meyer, G. "An Experimental Study of the Old and New Types of Examination. I. The Effect of the Examination Set on Memory." *Journal of Educational Psychology*, 1934, 25: 641-661.
37. Meyer, G. "An Experimental Study of the Old and New Types of Examination. II. Methods of Study." *Journal of Educational Psychology*, 1935, 26: 30-40.
38. Bird and Bird, *op. cit.*, p. 194.

Chapter 3. Nature and Nurture: How We Develop

1. Scheinfeld, Amram. *You and Heredity*. J. B. Lippincott, 1939, pp. 298-299.
2. Burks, Barbara. "Mental and Physical Developmental Pattern of Identical Twins in Relation to Organismic Growth Theory." *Thirty-ninth Yearbook of the National Society for the Study of Education*, 1940, 39: Part II, 85-96.
3. Conrad, H. S., and Jones H. E. "A Second Study of Familial Resemblance in Intelligence: Environmental and Genetic Implications of Parent-Child and Sibling Correlations in the Total Sample." *Thirty-ninth Yearbook of the National Society for the Study of Education*, 1940, 39: Part II, 97-141.
4. Merriman, C. "The Intellectual Resemblance of Twins." *Psychological Monographs*, 1924, 33: No. 5, 58.
5. Lauterback, C. E. "Studies in Twin Resemblance." *Genetics*, 1925, 10: 525-568.
6. Minkowski, M. "Uber fruhzeitige Bewegungen, Reflexe und muskulare Reaktionen beim menschlichen Fotus und ihre Beziehungen zum fotalen Nerven und Muskelsystem." *Schweizerische medizinische Wochenschrift*, 1922, 3: 721-724, 751-755.
7. Hooker, D. "Fetal Behavior." *Research Publications of the Association for the Study of Nervous and Mental Diseases*, 1939, 19: 237-243.
8. These motion pictures were taken by an American anatomist, Davenport Hooker, and are described in "Reflex Activities in the Human Fetus," in *Child Behavior and Development* (ed. by Roger G. Barker; Jacob S. Kounin; and Herbert F. Wright). McGraw-Hill Book Co., Inc., 1943, pp. 17-28.
9. These pictures, and fresh material as well, have been carefully studied by Arnold Gesell, *The Embryology of Behavior*. Harper & Bros., 1945.
10. Spelt, David. "Conditioned Responses in the Human Fetus in Utero." *Psychological Bulletin*, 1938, 35: 712-713.
11. Morgan, J. J. B. *Child Psychology*. Farrar & Rinehart, 1934, p. 53.
12. Stubbs, E. M. "The Effect of the Factors of Duration, Intensity and Pitch of Sound Stimuli on the Responses of Newborn Infants." *University of Iowa Studies in Child Welfare*, 1934, 9: No. 4, 75-135.
13. Aldrich, C. A. "A New Test for Hearing in the New-Born: The Conditioned Reflex." *American Journal of Diseases of Children*, 1928, 35: 36-37.
14. Sherman, M., and Sherman, I. C. "Sensori-Motor Responses in Infants." *Journal*

of *Comparative Psychology*, 1925, 5: 53-68.

15. Sherman, M.; Sherman, I. C.; and Flory, C. D. "Infant Behavior." *Comparative Psychology Monographs*, 1936, 12: No. 59.

16. Chase, W. P. "Color Vision in Infants." *Journal of Experimental Psychology*, 1937, 20: 203-222.

17. Disher, D. R. "The Reaction of New-Born Infants to Chemical Stimuli Administered Nasally." *Ohio State University Studies: Contributions to Psychology*, 1934, No. 12, pp. 1-52.

18. Pratt, K. C.; Nelson, A. K.; and Sun, K. H. "The Behavior of the New-Born Infant." *Ohio State University Studies: Contributions to Psychology*, 1930, No. 10.

19. Sherman, Sherman, and Flory, op. cit.

20. Sherman and Sherman, op. cit., pp. 53-69.

21. Jensen, Kai. "Differential Reactions to Taste and Temperature Stimuli in Newborn Infants." *Genetic Psychology Monographs*, 1932, 12: 361-479.

22. Halverson, H. M. "Infant Sucking and Tensional Behavior." *Journal of Genetic Psychology*, 1938, 53: 365-430.

23. Jensen, op. cit., pp. 361-479.

24. Wolowik, A. B. "Uber die gegenseitige Wirkung der Schmerz- und Nahrungs-reflexe bei Kindern." *Jahrbuch fur Kinderheilkunde*, 1927, 115: 185-193.

25. Halverson, H. M. "Studies of the Grasping Responses of Early Infancy. I, II, and III." *Journal of Genetic Psychology*, 1937, 51: 371-449.

26. Peiper, A. *Die Hirntatigkeit des Sauglings*. Springer, 1928.

27. Wenger, M. A. "Conditioned Responses in Human Infants," in *Child Behavior and Development* (ed. by Roger G. Barker; Jacob S. Kounin; and Herbert F.

Wright). McGraw-Hill Book Co., Inc., 1943, pp. 67-86.

28. Kantrow, R. W. "An Investigation of Conditioned Feeding Responses and Concomitant Adaptive Behavior in Young Infants." *University of Iowa Studies in Child Welfare*, 1937, 13: No. 3.

29. Morpurgo, B. "Über Activitats-Hypertrophie der willkurlichen Muskeln." *Archiv fur pathologische Anatomie*, 1897, 150: 522-554.

30. Carmichael, L. "The Development of Behavior in Vertebrates Experimentally Removed from the Influence of External Stimulation." *Psychological Review*, 1926, 33: 51-58.

31. Stone, C. P. "The Congenital Sexual Behavior of the Young Male Albino Rat." *Journal of Comparative Psychology*, 1922, 2: 95-153.

32. Strayer, L. C. "Language and Growth: The Relative Efficacy of Early and Deferred Vocabulary Training Studied by the Method of Co-Twin Control." *Genetic Psychology Monographs*, 1930, 8: 209-319.

33. Dennis, W., and Dennis, M. G. "The Effect of Cradling Practices upon the Onset of Walking in Hopi Children." *Journal of Genetic Psychology*, 1940, 56: 77-86.

34. McGraw, Myrtle. *Growth: A Study of Johnny and Jimmy*. D. Appleton-Century Co., 1935.

35. McGraw, Myrtle. "Later Development of Children Specially Trained during Infancy. Johnny and Jimmy at School Age." *Child Development*, 1939, 10: 1-19.

36. Wells, F. L. "The Relation of Practice to Individual Differences." *American Journal of Psychology*, 1912, 23: 75-88.

37. Anastasi, Anne. "Practice and Variability: A Study in Psychological Method." *Psychological Monographs*, 1934, 45: No. 5.

Chapter 4. Motivation: Biological and Social

1. Cannon, W. B. "Hunger and Thirst." A *Handbook of General Experimental Psychology* (Carl Murchison, ed.). Clark University Press, 1934, Chapter 5.

2. Carlson, A. J. *The Control of Hunger in Health and Disease*. University of Chicago Press, 1916.

3. Tsang, Y. C. "Hunger Motivation in Gastrectomized Rats." *Journal of Comparative Psychology*, 1938, 26: 1-17.

4. Bash, K. W. "Contribution to a Theory of the Hunger Drive." *Journal of Comparative Psychology*, 1939, 28: 137-160.

5. Morgan, C. T., and Morgan, J. D. "Studies in Hunger: II. The Relation of Gastric Denervation and Dietary Sugar to the Effect of Insulin upon Food-Intake in the Rat." *Journal of Genetic Psychology*, 1940, 57: 153-163.

6. Luckhardt, A. B., and Carlson, A. J. "Contributions to the Physiology of the Stomach. XVII. On the Chemical Control of the Gastric Hunger Mechanism." *American Journal of Physiology*, 1915, 36: 37-46.

7. Tschukitschew. *Contributions of the Timiriazer Institute*, 1929, p. 36, as cited in R. D. Templeton and J. P. Quigley, "The Action of Insulin on Motility of the Gastric Intestinal Tract." *American Journal of Physiology*, 1930, 91: 467-474.

8. Davis, C. M. "Self-Selection of Diet by Newly-Weaned Infants." *American Journal of Diseases of Children*, 1928, 36: 651-679.

9. Wada, T. "An Experimental Study of Hunger in Its Relation to Activity." *Archives of Psychology*, 1922, 8: No. 57.

10. Elliott, M. H., and Treat, W. C. "Hunger-Contractions and Rate of Conditioning." *Proceedings of National Academy of Science*, 1935, 21: 514-516.
11. Pack, G. T. "New Experiments on the Nature of the Sensation of Thirst." *American Journal of Physiology*, 1923, 65: 346-349.
12. Bellows, R. T. "Time Factors in Water Drinking in Dogs." *American Journal of Physiology*, 1939, 125: 87-97.
13. Adolph, Edward F. *Physiological Regulations*. Jaques Cattell Press, 1943, pp. 27-32.
14. Carpenter, C. R. "Psychobiological Studies of Social Behavior in Aves." *Journal of Comparative Psychology*, 1933, 16: 25-57.
15. Stone, C. P. "The Retention of Copulatory Behavior in Male Rats Following Castration." *Journal of Comparative Psychology*, 1927, 7: 369-387.
16. Wiesner, B. P., and Sheard, N. M. "Sex Behavior in Hypophysectomized Male Rats." *Nature*, 1933, 132: 641.
17. Davis, K. B. *Factors in the Sex Life of Twenty-two Hundred Women*. Harper & Bros., 1929.
18. Benedek, Therese, and Rubenstein, Boris B. "The Sexual Cycle in Women." *Psychosomatic Medicine Monographs*, 1942, 3: Nos. 1 and 2.
19. Rosanoff, Aaron. *Manual of Psychiatry and Mental Hygiene*. John Wiley & Sons, 1938.
20. Glass, S. J., and Johnson, Roswell H. "Limitations and Complications of Organotherapy in Male Homosexuality." *Journal of Clinical Endocrinology*, 1944, 4: 540-554.
21. Staples, R. "The Responses of Infants to Color." *Journal of Experimental Psychology*, 1932, 15: 119-141.
22. Peterson, F., and Rainey, L. H. "Beginnings of Mind in the New-Born." *Bulletin of the Lying-in Hospital of the City of New York*, 1910, 7: 99-122.
23. Smith, K. U. *The Acquisition of the Token-Reward Habit in the Cat* (film), 1937.
24. Wolfe, J. B. "Effectiveness of Token-Rewards for Chimpanzees." *Comparative Psychology Monographs*, 1936, 12: No. 60.
25. Kohler, W. *The Mentality of Apes*. Harcourt, Brace & Co., 1927, p. 286 ff.
26. Nissen, H. W., and Crawford, M. P. "A Preliminary Study of Food-Sharing Behavior in Young Chimpanzees." *Journal of Comparative Psychology*, 1936, 22: 383-419.
27. Tolman, Edward C. "Motivation, Learning and Adjustment." *Proceedings of the American Philosophical Society*, 1941, 84: 543-563.
28. Gesell, Arnold. *Wolf Child and Human Child*. Harper & Bros., 1940, pp. 39-40.
29. Klineberg, Otto. *Social Psychology*. Henry Holt & Co., Inc., 1940, pp. 89-101.
30. *Ibid.*, pp. 78-89.

Chapter 5. Emotions: Inner Springs of Action

1. Smith, W. W. *The Measurement of Emotion*. Kegan Paul, Trench, Trubner & Co., Ltd., 1922.
2. Ruckmick, Christian. *Psychology of Feeling and Emotion*. McGraw-Hill Book Co., Inc., 1936, p. 402.
3. Hastings, J. T. "Tensions and School Achievement Examinations." *Journal of Experimental Education*, 1944, 12: 143-164.
4. Shaffer, L. F. "Fear and Courage in Aerial Combat." *Journal of Consulting Psychology*, 1947, 11: 137-143. Table reprinted by permission of the American Psychological Association.
5. Meltzer, H. "Students' Adjustments in Anger." *Journal of Social Psychology*, 1933, 4: 285-309.
6. Gates, G. S. "An Observational Study of Anger." *Journal of Experimental Psychology*, 1926, 9: 325-336.
7. Dysinger, W. S., and Ruckmick, C. A. *The Emotional Responses of Children to the Motion Picture Situation*. The Macmillan Company, 1933.
8. Springer, N. N., and Roslow, S. "A Study of the Estimation of Feelings." *Journal of Applied Psychology*, 1935, 19: 379-384.
9. Cason, H. "General Curves and Conditions of Feeling." *Journal of Applied Psychology*, 1931, 15: 126-148.
10. Hersey, R. B. "Rate of Production and Emotional States." *Personnel Journal*, 1932, 10: 355-364.
11. Weiss, E. "The Study of the Emotional Life in the Practice of Medicine." *Medical Record*, 1935, 141: 68-71.
12. Perry, J. S. "Emotions as Functional Factors in the Etiology and Prognosis of Disease." *Medical Record*, 1934, 1939: 643-645.
13. Kaplan, B. "Can Emotions Produce Organic Lesions in the Digestive Tract?" *Medical Record*, 1936, 143: 379-382.
14. Chappell, M. N.; Stefano, J. J.; Rogerson, J. S.; and Pike, F. H. "The Value of Group Psychological Procedures in the Treatment of Peptic Ulcer." *American Journal of Digestive Diseases and Nutrition*, 1937, 3: 813-817.
15. Wolf, Stewart, and Wolff, Harold G. "Evidence on the Genesis of Peptic Ulcer in Man." *Journal of the American Medical Association*, 1942, 120: 670-675.

16. Weiss, Edward, and English, O. S. *Psychosomatic Medicine*. W. B. Saunders Co., 1943, p. 10.
17. Reprinted by permission of the publishers from Stanley Cobb, *Borderlands of Psychiatry*. Harvard University Press, 1943, pp. 6-8.
18. Margolis, H. M. "The Psychosomatic Approach to Medical Diagnosis and Treatment." *Journal of Social Casework*, 1946, 27: 291-299.
19. Hinsie, Leland, E. "A Clinical Description of Psychosomatic Medicine." *Medical Clinics of North America*, 1944, 28: No. 3, 525-552.
20. Sherman, M., and Sherman, I. C. *The Process of Human Behavior*. W. W. Norton & Co., 1929, p. 114.
21. Goodenough, Florence L. "The Expression of the Emotions in Infancy." *Child Development*, 1931, 2: 96-101.
22. Landis, C. "The Expression of the Emotions." *Foundations of Experimental Psychology* (Carl Murchison, ed.). Clark University Press, 1929.
23. Davis, R. C. "The Specificity of Facial Expressions." *Journal of General Psychology*, 1934, 10: 42-58.

24. Munn, Norman L. "The Effect of Knowledge of the Situation upon Judgment of Emotion from Facial Expressions." *Journal of Abnormal and Social Psychology*, 1940, 35: 324-338.
25. Dunlap, K. "The Role of Eye Muscles and Mouth-Muscles in the Expression of the Emotions." *Genetic Psychology Monographs*, 1927, 2: 195-233.
26. Hanawalt, N. G. "The Role of the Upper and the Lower Parts of the Face as a Basis for Judging Facial Expressions: II. In Posed Expressions and 'Candid-Camera' Pictures." *Journal of General Psychology*, 1944, 31: 23-36.
27. Sherman and Sherman, *op. cit.*, p. 138.
28. Tiffin, J., and Seashore, R. H. "Summary of Established Facts in Experimental Studies on the Vibrato up to 1932." *University of Iowa Studies in Psychology: Studies in the Psychology of Music*, 1932, 1: 344-382.
29. Gaskill, H. V. "The Objective Measurement of Emotional Reactions." *Genetic Psychology Monographs*, 1933, 14: 177-281.
30. Arnold, Magda B. "Physiological Differentiation of Emotional States." *Psychological Review*, 1945, 52: 35-48.

Chapter 6. Intelligence

1. Anonymous. "Superkid." *Time*, 1943, 41: No. 11, p. 40. Courtesy of *Time*, copyright Time, Inc., 1943.
2. Files of Veterans' Guidance Center, University of Southern California.
3. From H. H. Woodrow, *Brightness and Dullness in Children*, 1923, pp. 11-12. By permission of J. B. Lippincott Co.
4. Roberts, A. Dudley. "Case History of a So-Called Idiot-Savant." *Journal of Genetic Psychology*, 1945, 66: 259-265.
5. Binet, A., and Simon, T. "La mesure du developpement de l'intelligence chez les jeunes enfants." *Bulletin de la societe libre pour l'etude psychologique de l'enfant*, 1911, pp. 187-248.
6. Terman, L. M. *The Measurement of Intelligence*. Houghton Mifflin Co., 1937.
7. Terman, L. M., and Merrill, M. A. *Measuring Intelligence*. Houghton Mifflin Co., 1937.
8. Arthur, Grace. *Arthur Point Scale of Performance Tests*, Revised Form II, Psychological Corporation, 1946.
9. Cornell, E. L., and Coxe, W. W. *Cornell-Coxe Performance Ability Scale*, Examination Manual. World Book Co., 1934.
10. Wechsler, D. *The Measurement of Adult Intelligence*. Williams & Wilkins Co., 1944.
11. Stern, W. L. *The Psychological Methods of Testing Intelligence*. (Trans. by G. M. Whipple.) Warwick & York, 1914.

12. Terman, L. M. "Psychological Approaches to the Biography of Genius." *Science*, 1940, 92: 293-301.
13. Graves, K. "The Influence of Specialized Training on Tests of General Intelligence." *Contributions to Education*, No. 143, Teachers College, Columbia University, 1924.
14. Binet, A., and Simon, T. *The Development of Intelligence in Children*. (Trans. by Elizabeth S. Kite.) Williams & Wilkins Co., 1916.
15. Spearman, C. *Abilities of Man*. The Macmillan Co., 1927.
16. Thurstone, L. L. "Primary Mental Abilities." *Psychometric Monographs*, 1938, 1: No. 1.
17. Minogue, B. M. "The Constancy of the I.Q. of Mental Defectives." *Mental Hygiene*, 1926, 10: 751-758.
18. Cattell, P. "Constant Changes in the Stanford-Binet I.Q." *Journal of Educational Psychology*, 1931, 22: 544-550.
19. Hirt, Z. I. "Another Study of Retests with the 1916 Stanford-Binet Scale." *Journal of Genetic Psychology*, 1945, 66: 83-105.
20. Mann, C. W., and Mann, H. P. "An Analysis of Results Obtained by Retesting Delinquents." *Journal of Psychology*, 1939, 8: 133-141.
21. Terman, "Psychological Approaches to the Biography of Genius," *op. cit.*
22. Goodenough, F. L., and Maurer, K. M. *The Mental Growth of Children from*

Two to Fourteen Years. University of Minnesota Press, 1942.

23. Bradway, K. P. "Predictive Value of Stanford-Binet Preschool Items." *Journal of Educational Psychology,* 1945, 36: 1-16.

24. Newman, Horatio H.; Freeman, F. N.; and Holzinger, Karl J. *Twins: A Study of Heredity and Environment.* University of Chicago Press, 1937.

25. Freeman, F. N., et al. "The Influence of Environment on the Intelligence, School Achievement, and Conduct of Foster Children." *Twenty-seventh Yearbook of the National Society for the Study of Education,* 1928, 27: Part I, 103-217.

26. Skodak, M. "Children in Foster-Homes: A Study of Mental Development." *University of Iowa Studies in Child Welfare,* 1939, 16: No. 1, 1-156.

27. Skodak, Marie, and Skeels, H. M. "A Follow-Up Study of Children in Adoptive Homes." *Journal of Genetic Psychology,* 1945, 66: 21-58.

28. Wellman, B. L. "The Effect of Pre-School Attendance upon the I. Q." *Journal of Experimental Education,* 1933, 1: 48-69.

29. Goodenough, F. "A Preliminary Report on the Effect of Nursery School Training upon the Intelligence Test Scores of Young Children." *Twenty-seventh Yearbook of the National Society for the Study of Education,* 1928, 27: Part I, 361-369.

30. Barrett, H., and Koch, H. "The Effect of Nursery-School Training upon the Mental Test Performance of a Group of Orphanage Children." *Journal of Genetic Psychology,* 1930, 37: 102-122.

31. Skeels, H. M.; Updegraff, Ruth; Wellman, B. L.; and Williams, Harold. "A Study of Environmental Stimulation. An Orphanage Pre-School Project." *University of Iowa Studies in Child Welfare,* 1938, 15: No. 4, 191.

32. McHugh, G. "Changes in I.Q. at the Public School Kindergarten Level." *Psychological Monographs,* 1943, 55: No. 2.

33. Reymert, M. L., and Hinton, R. T. "The Effect of Change to a Relatively Superior Environment upon the I.Q.'s of One Hundred Children." *Thirty-ninth Yearbook of the National Society for the Study of Education,* 1940, 39: Part II, 255-268.

34. Burks, B. "The Relative Influence of Nature and Nurture upon Mental Development; a Comparative Study of Foster Parent-Foster Child Resemblance and True Parent-True Child Resemblance." *Twenty-seventh Yearbook of the National Society for the Study of Education,* 1928, 27: Part I, 219-316.

35. Leahy, A. M. "Nature-Nurture and Intelligence." *Genetic Psychology Monographs,* 1935, 17: 236-308.

36. Freeman et al., *op. cit.*

37. Saltzman, Sara. "The Influence of Social and Economic Background on Stanford-Binet Performance." *Journal of Social Psychology,* 1940, 12: 71-81.

38. Steckel, M. L. "Intelligence and Birth Order in Family." *Journal of Social Psychology,* 1930, 1: 329-344.

39. Held, Omar C. "The Influence of Month of Birth on the Intelligence of College Freshmen." *Journal of Genetic Psychology,* 1940, 57: 211-217.

40. Goodenough, F. "Intelligence and Month of Birth." *Psychological Bulletin,* 1940, 37: 442.

41. Roberts, J. A. "Intelligence and Season of Conception." *British Medical Journal,* 1944, 1: 320-322.

42. Klineberg, O. "An Experimental Study of Speed and Other Factors in Racial Differences." *Archives of Psychology,* 1928, 15: No. 93. Also *Race Differences.* Harper & Bros., 1935.

43. From S. L. Pressey, *Psychology and the New Education.* Harper & Bros., 1933, p. 237.

44. Brigham, C. C. *A Study of American Intelligence.* Princeton University Press, 1923.

45. Brigham, C. C. "Intelligence Tests of Immigrant Groups." *Psychological Review,* 1930, 37: 158-165.

46. Klineberg, Otto. *Social Psychology.* Henry Holt & Co., Inc., 1940, p. 301.

47. Benedict, Ruth. *Race: Science and Politics.* Viking Press, 1943, p. 119.

48. Freeman, F. S. *Individual Differences.* Henry Holt & Co., Inc., 1934, p. 159.

49. Terman, L. M., et al. "Genetic Studies of Genius." *Mental and Physical Traits of a Thousand Gifted Children.* Vol. I. Stanford University Press, 1925.

50. Schwesinger, G. C. *Heredity and Environment.* The Macmillan Co., 1933, p. 313.

51. Bronstein, I. P., and Brown, A. W. "Hypothyroidism and Cretinism in Childhood." *American Journal of Orthopsychiatry,* 1934, 4: 413-420.

52. Brown, A. W.; Bronstein, I. P.; and Kraines, R. "Hypothyroidism and Cretinism in Childhood: VI. Influence of Thyroid Therapy on Mental Growth." *American Journal of Diseases of Children,* 1939, 57: 517-523.

53. Schott, E. L. "Superior Intelligence in Patients with Frohlich's Syndrome." *Journal of Applied Psychology,* 1938, 22: 395-399.

54. Rogers, M. C. "Adenoids and Diseased Tonsils: Their Effect on General Intelligence." *Archives of Psychology,* 1922, 7: No. 50.

55. Lowe, G. M. "Mental Changes after Removing Tonsils and Adenoids." *Psychological Clinic,* 1923, 15: 92-100.

Chapter 7. The Special Senses

1. Chapanis, A. "Night Vision—A Review of General Principles." *The Air Surgeon's Bulletin*, 1945, 2: 279-284.
2. Jones, M. C. "The Development of Early Behavior Patterns in Young Children." Here quoted from H. L. Hollingworth, *Mental Growth and Decline*. D. Appleton-Century Co., 1927, p. 113.
3. Boring, E. G. (ed.). *Psychology for the Armed Services*. Infantry Journal, 1945, p. 39.
4. Kisker, George W. "Watch Those Sunglasses!" *Hygeia*, 1946, 24: 485.
5. Dimmick, H. L., and Hubbard, M. R. "The Spectral Components of Psychologically Unique Red." *American Journal of Psychology*, 1939, 52: 348-353.
6. Viteles, Morris S. "Postlude to the Application of Psychology in Industry." *Journal of Consulting Psychology*, 1944, 8: 182-185.
7. Boring, *op. cit.*, p. 117.
8. Michael, W., and Crawford, C. C. "An Experiment in Judging Intelligence by the Voice." *Journal of Educational Psychology*, 1927, 18: 107-114.
9. Guilford, J. P., and Lovewell, E. M. "The Touch Spots and the Intensity of the Stimulus." *Journal of General Psychology*, 1936, 15: 149-159.
10. Laird, D. A., and Breen, W. J. "Sex and Age Alterations in Taste Preferences." *Journal of American Dietetic Association*, 1939, 15: 549-550.
11. Sinnot, J. J., and Rauth, J. E. "Effect of Smoking on Taste Thresholds." *Journal of General Psychology*, 1939, 17: 151-153.

Chapter 8. Perception, Attention, and Report

1. Stevens, S. S., and Davis, H. *Hearing: Its Psychology and Physiology*. John Wiley & Sons, Inc., 1938, p. 173.
2. Fuchs, W. "Experimentelle Untersuchungen uber die Anderung von Farben unter dem Einfluss von Gestalten." *Zeitschrift fur Psychologie*, 1923, 92: 249-325.
3. Leeper, R. "A Study of a Neglected Portion of the Field of Learning—The Development of Sensory Organization." *Journal of Genetic Psychology*, 1935, 46: 41-75.
4. Sinclair, J. G. "The Lens in Accommodation." *American Journal of Ophthalmology*, 1945, 28: 38-39.
5. Francois, M. "Contribution a l'etude du sens du temps: la temperature interne comme facteur de variation de l'appreciation subjective des durees." *L'Annee psychologique*, 1927, 28: 186-204.
6. Terman, L. M. *Record Booklet for the Stanford Revision of the Binet-Simon Tests*. Houghton Mifflin Co., 1922, pp. 2-3.
7. Elkine, D. "De l'orientation de l'enfant d'age scolaire dans les relations temporelles." *Journal de psychologie normale et pathologique*, 1928, 25: 425-429.
8. Wyatt, S.; Fraser, J. A.; and Stock, F. G. "The Effects of Monotony in Work." *Industrial Health Research Board Report*, 1929, No. 56.
9. Harton, J. J. "The Influence of the Difficulty of Activity on the Estimation of Time." *Journal of Experimental Psychology*, 1938, 23: 428-433.
10. Harton, J. J. "An Investigation of the Influence of Success and Failure on the Estimation of Time." *Journal of General Psychology*, 1939, 21: 51-62.
11. Pratt, J. G., et al. *Extra-Sensory Perception after Sixty Years*. Henry Holt & Co., Inc., 1940, 9: 463.
12. Kennedy, J. L. "A Methodological Review of Extra-Sensory Perception." *Psychological Bulletin*, 1939, 36: 59-103.
13. Collier, R. M. "An Experimental Study of the Effects of Subliminal Stimuli." *Psychological Monographs*, 1940, 52: No. 5.
14. Coover, J. E. *Experiments in Psychical Research*. Stanford University Press, 1917.
15. Leuba, Clarence. "An Experiment to Test the Role of Chance in E.S.P. Research." *Journal of Parapsychology*, 1938, 2: 217-221.
16. Warner, Lucien, and Clark, C. C. "A Survey of Psychological Opinion on E.S.P." *Journal of Parapsychology*, 1938, 2: 296-301.
17. Laird, D. A. "Experiments on the Physiological Cost of Noise." *Journal of the National Institute of Industrial Psychology*, 1929, 4: 251-258.
18. Freeman, G. L. "Changes in Tension-Pattern and Total Energy Expenditure during Adaptation to 'Distracting' Stimuli." *American Journal of Psychology*, 1939, 52: 354-360.
19. Harmon, F. L. "The Effects of Noise upon Certain Psychological and Physiological Processes." *Archives of Psychology*, 1933, 23: No. 147.
20. Elliott, F. R., and Louttit, C. M. "Auto Braking Reaction Times to Visual vs. Auditory Warning Signals." *Proceedings Indiana Academy of Science*, 1939, 47: 220-225.
21. Froeberg, S. "The Relation Between the Magnitude of Stimulus and the Time of Reaction." *Archives of Psychology*, 1907, 1: No. 8.
22. Davis, R. C. "Set and Muscular Tension." *Indiana University Publication. Science*

Series, No. 10, 1940.

23. Pearson, K. "On Our Present Knowledge of the Relationship of Mind and Body." Annals of Eugenics, 1925, I: 382 ff.

24. De Silva, H. R. Research on Driving Skill. Massachusetts FERA Project XS-FZ-U25, 1935.

25. McFarland, R. A. "Psychophysiological Studies at High Altitudes in the Andes: IV. Sensory and Circulatory Responses of the Andean Residents at 17,500 Feet." Journal of Comparative Psychology, 1937, 24: 189-220.

26. Kleitman, N., et al. "The Effect of Body Temperature on Reaction Time." American Journal of Physiology, 1938, 121: 495-501.

27. Gilliland, A. R., and Nelson, D. "The Effects of Coffee on Certain Mental and Physiological Functions." Journal of General Psychology, 1939, 21: 339-348.

28. Henmon, V. A. C. The Time of Perception as a Measure of Difference in Sensation. Science Press, 1906.

29. Husband, R. W., and Godfrey, J. "An Experimental Study of Cigarette Identification." Journal of Applied Psychology, 1934, 18: 220-223.

Chapter 9. Learning: Its Basic Nature

1. Lashley, K. S., and Ball, J. "Spinal Conduction and Kinesthetic Sensitivity in the Maze Habit." Journal of Comparative Psychology, 1929, 9: 71-105.

2. Lashley, K. S. "Studies of Cerebral Function in Learning. VI. The Theory that Synaptic Resistance Is Reduced by the Passage of the Nerve Impulse." Psychological Review, 1924, 31: 369-375.

3. Crespi, Leo. "Quantitative Variation of Incentive and Performance in the White Rat." American Journal of Psychology, 1942, 55: 467-517.

4. Menzies, R. "Conditioned Vasomotor Responses in Human Subjects." Journal of Psychology, 1937, 4: 75-120.

5. Lashley and Ball, op. cit.

6. Kohler, W. The Mentality of Apes. Harcourt, Brace & Co., 1925.

7. Alpert, A. "The Solving of Problem Situations by Preschool Children." Contributions to Education, No. 323, Teachers College, Columbia University, 1928.

8. Crawford, A. B. Incentives to Study. Yale University Press, 1929.

9. Spence, K. "The Role of Secondary Reinforcement in Delayed Reward Learning." Psychological Review, 1947, 54: 1-8.

10. Lorge, I., and Thorndike, E. L. "The Influence of Delay in the After-Effect of a Connection." Journal of Experimental Psychology, 1935, 18: 186-194.

11. Lashley, K. S. "The Mechanism of Vision: I. A Method for Rapid Analysis of Pattern Vision in the Rat." Journal of Genetic Psychology, 1930, 37: 453-460.

12. Lashley, K. S. "The Mechanism of Vision: XV. Preliminary Studies of the Rat's Capacity for Detail Vision." Journal of General Psychology, 1938, 18: 123-193.

13. Lashley, K. S. "An Examination of the 'Continuity Theory' as Applied to Discriminative Learning." Journal of General Psychology, 1942, 26: 241-265.

14. Bunch, M. E., "Certain Effects of Electric Shock in Learning a Stylus Maze." Journal of Comparative Psychology, 1935, 20: 211-242.

15. Thorndike, E. L. The Psychology of Wants, Interests and Attitudes. D. Appleton-Century Co., Inc., 1935, pp. 71-80.

16. Brown, Warner. "The Positive Effect of Punishment." Journal of Comparative Psychology, 1939, 28: 17-22.

17. Hull, Clark. "Differential Habituation to Internal Stimuli in the Albino Rat." Journal of Comparative Psychology, 1933, 16: 255-273.

18. Leeper, R. "The Role of Motivation in Learning: A Study of the Phenomenon of Differential Motivational Control of the Utilization of Habits." Journal of Genetic Psychology, 1935, 46: 3-40.

19. Dunlap, Knight. Habits: Their Making and Unmaking. Liveright Publishing Corporation, 1932.

20. Thorndike, E. L. Adult Learning. The Macmillan Co., 1928.

21. Kendler, H. H. "The Influence of Simultaneous Hunger and Thirst Drives upon the Learning of Two Opposed Spatial Responses of the White Rat." Journal of Experimental Psychology, 1946, 36: 212-220.

22. Tolman, E. C., and Honzik, C. H. "Introduction and Removal of Reward, and Maze Performance in Rats." University of California Publications in Psychology, 1930, 4: 257-275.

23. Haney, G. W. "The Effect of Familiarity of Maze Performance of Albino Rats." University of California Publications in Psychology, 1931, 4: 319-333.

24. Becker, F. C., and Olsen, H. "Metabolism during Mental Work." Skandinavisches Archiv fur Physiologie, 1914, 31: 81-197.

25. Ibid.

26. Rounds, G. H.; Schubert, H. J. P.; and Poffenberger, A. T. "Effects of Practice upon the Metabolic Cost of Mental Work." Journal of General Psychology, 1932, 7: 65-79.

27. Thorndike, Adult Learning.

28. Ruch, F. L. "The Differentiative Effects of Age upon Human Learning." Journal of General Psychology, 1934, 11: 261-286.

29. Brown, R. W. "The Relation between Age (Chronological and Mental) and

Rate of Piano Learning." *Journal of Applied Psychology*, 1936, 20: 511-516.

30. Gray, W. S. "Reading." *Encyclopedia of Educational Research* (W. S. Monroe, ed.). The Macmillan Co., 1941, pp. 891-926.
31. Menke, F. G. *All-Sports Record Book*, Inc., 1936.
32. Lehman, H. C. "The Most Proficient Years at Sports and Games." *Research Quarterly of the American Association of Health and Physical Education and Recreation*, 1938, 9: 3-19.
33. Ruch, F. L. "The Differential Decline of Learning Ability in the Aged as a Possible Explanation of Their Conservatism." *Journal of Social Psychology*, 1934, 5: 329-337.

Chapter 10. Remembering and Thinking

1. Ebbinghaus, H. *Memory*. (Trans. by H. A. Ruger.) Teachers College, Columbia University, 1913.
2. Cain, L. F., and Willey, R. "The Effect of Spaced Learning on the Curves of Retention." *Journal of Experimental Psychology*, 1939, 25: 209-214.
3. Ebbinghaus, H. *Grundzuge der Psychologie*, Verlag, 1902.
4. Warren, Howard C. "Two Cases of Long Latent Memory." *Psychological Bulletin*, 1918, 15: 207-209.
5. Martin, G. R. "Reminiscence and Gestalt Theory." *Psychological Monographs*, 1940, 52: No. 4.
6. *Ibid.*
7. Buxton, Claude E. "Level of Mastery and Reminiscence in Pursuit Learning." *Journal of Experimental Psychology*, 1943, 32: 176-180.
8. Leavitt, H. J. "The Relation of Speed of Learning to Amount Retained and to Reminiscence." *Journal of Experimental Psychology*, 1945, 35: 134-140.
9. Jenkins, J. G., and Dallenbach, K. M. "Obliviscence during Sleep and Waking." *American Journal of Psychology*, 1924, 35: 605-612.
10. Van Ormer, E. B. "Retention after Intervals of Sleep and Waking." *Archives of Psychology*, 1932, 21: No. 137.
11. McGeoch, J. A., and McDonald, W. T. "Meaningful Relation and Retroactive Inhibition." *American Journal of Psychology*, 1931, 43: 579-588. (Table used by permission of the American Journal of Psychology.)
12. Newman, E. B. "Forgetting of Meaningful Material during Sleep and Waking." *American Journal of Psychology*, 1939, 52: 65-71.
13. Snygg, D. "The Relative Difficulty of Mechanically Equivalent Tasks: II. Animal Learning." *Journal of Genetic Psychology*, 1935, 47: 321-336.
14. Meltzer, H. "The Present Status of Experimental Studies on the Relationship of Feeling to Memory." *Psychological Review*, 1930, 37: 124-139.
15. Gilbert, G. M. "The New Status of Experimental Studies on the Relationship of Feeling to Memory." *Psychological Bulletin*, 1938, 35: 26-35.
16. Shaw, F. J. "Two Determinants of Selective Forgetting." *Journal of Abnormal and Social Psychology*, 1944, 39: 434-445.
17. Erickson, M. H. "Negation or Reversal of Legal Testimony." *Archives of Neurology and Psychiatry*, 1938, 40: 548-553.
18. Tolman, E. C. *Purposive Behavior in Animals and Men*. Century Co., 1932.
19. Hull, Clark. *Principles of Behavior*. D. Appleton-Century Co., 1943.
20. Lashley, K. S. "The Mechanism of Vision: XV. Preliminary Studies of the Rat's Capacity for Detail Vision." *Journal of General Psychology*, 1938, 18: 123-193.
21. Kluver, H. *Behavior Mechanisms in Monkeys*. University of Chicago Press, 1933, pp. 258-292. See also H. Kluver, "Reexamination of Implement-using Behavior in a Cebus Monkey after an Interval of Three Years." *Acta Psychologica*, 1937, 2: 347-397.
22. Crosland, H. "A Qualitative Analysis of the Process of Forgetting." *Psychological Monographs*, 1921, 29: No. 1.
23. Bartlett, F. C. *Remembering: A Study in Experimental and Social Psychology*. Cambridge University Press, 1932.
24. Hanfmann, E.; Rickers-Ovsiankina, M.; and Goldstein, K. "Case Lanuti: Extreme Concretization of Behavior Due to Damage of the Brain Cortex." *Psychological Monographs*, 1944, 57: No. 4.
25. Hanawalt, N. G., and Ruttiger, K. F. "The Effect of an Audience on Remembering." *Journal of Social Psychology*, 1944, 19: 259-272.
26. Ziegarnik, B. "Uber das Behalten von erledigten und unerledigten Handlungen." *Psychologische Forschung*, 1927, 9: 1-86.
27. Marrow, A. J. "Goal Tensions and Recall: I." *Journal of General Psychology*, 1938, 19: 3-35.
28. Marrow, A. J. "Goal Tensions and Recall: II." *Journal of General Psychology*, 1938, 19: 37-64.
29. Zener, Karl. "The Significance of Behavior Accompanying Conditioned Salivary Secretion for Theories of the Conditioned Responses." *American Journal of Psychology*, 1937, 50: 384-403.
30. Humphreys, L. "The Effect of Random Alternation of Reinforcement on the Acquisition and Extinction of Conditioned Eyelid Reactions." *Journal of Experimental Psychology*, 1939, 25: 141-158.

31. Humphreys, L. "Extinction of Conditioned Psychogalvanic Responses Following Two Conditions of Reinforcement." *Journal of Experimental Psychology*, 1940, 27: 71-75.

32. Dunlap, Knight. *Habits: Their Making and Unmaking*. Liveright Publishing Corp., 1932.

33. Dewey, J. *How We Think*. D. C. Heath & Co., 1933, p. 92.

34. Patrick, Catharine. "Creative Thought in Artists." *Journal of Psychology*, 1937, 4: 35-73.

35. Galton, Sir Francis. *Inquiries into Human Faculty*. The Macmillan Co., 1883.

36. Fox, C. "The Conditions Which Arouse Mental Images in Thought." *British Journal of Psychology*, 1914, 6: 420-431.

37. Allport, G. W. "The Eidetic Image and the After-Image." *American Journal of Psychology*, 1928, 40: 418-425.

38. Karwoski, T. F., and Odbert, H. S. "Color-Music." *Psychological Monographs*, 1938, 50: No. 2.

39. Weinstein, B. "The Evolution of Intelligent Behavior in Rhesus Monkeys." *Genetic Psychology Monographs*, 1945, 31: First Half.

40. Jacobson, E. "Electrophysiology of Mental Activities." *American Journal of Psychology*, 1932, 44: 677-694.

41. Totten, E. "Eye-Movements during Visual Imagery." *Comparative Psychology Monographs*, 1935, 11: No. 3.

42. Thorson, A. M. "The Relation of Tongue Movements to Internal Speech." *Journal of Experimental Psychology*, 1925, 8: 1-32.

43. Max, L. W. "Experimental Study of the Motor Theory of Consciousness; IV. Action-Current Responses in the Deaf during Awakening, Kinaesthetic Imagery and Abstract Thinking." *Journal of Comparative Psychology*, 1937, 24: 301-344.

Chapter 11. Emotional Development: Experimental Findings

1. Miller, James Grier, *Unconsciousness*. John Wiley & Sons, 1942, pp. 1-16.

2. *Ibid.*, p. 3.

3. Watson, J. B., in *Psychologies of 1925* (Carl Murchison, ed.). Clark University Press, 1926, pp. 1-81.

4. *Ibid.*

5. Bridges, K. M. B. "Emotional Development in Early Infancy." *Child Development*, 1932, 3: 324-341.

6. Dennis, W., and Dennis, M. G. "The Effect of Cradling Practices upon the Onset of Walking in Hopi Children." *Journal of Genetic Psychology*, 1940, 56: 77-86.

7. Hunt, W. A. "Body Jerk as a Concept in Describing Infant Behavior." *Journal of Genetic Psychology*, 1939, 55: 215-220.

8. Ribble, Margaret. *The Rights of Infants*. Columbia University Press, 1943.

9. Bridges, *op. cit.*, p. 334.

10. Jones, H. E. "The Retention of Conditioned Emotional Reactions in Infancy." *Journal of Genetic Psychology*, 1930, 37: 485-498.

11. Watson, *op. cit.*, pp. 51-54.

12. Jones, M. C. "The Elimination of Children's Fears." *Journal of Experimental Psychology*, 1924, 7: 382-390.

13. *Ibid.*, p. 387.

14. *Ibid.*, pp. 388-390.

15. *Ibid.*, pp. 385-386.

16. Jones, M. C. "A Laboratory Study of Fear: The Case of Peter." *Pedagogical Seminary*, 1924, 31: 308-315.

17. Bayley, N. "A Study of the Crying of Infants during Mental and Physical Tests." *Journal of Genetic Psychology*, 1932, 40: 306-329.

18. Washburn, R. W. "A Study of the Smiling and Laughing of Infants in the First Year of Life." *Genetic Psychology Monographs*, 1929, 6: 397-537.

19. Gesell, Arnold. "The Individual in Infancy," in *The Foundations of Experimental Psychology* (Carl Murchison, ed.). Clark University Press, 1929, p. 656.

20. Jones, H. E., and Jones, M. C. "Fear." *Childhood Education*, 1928, 5: 138-139.

21. *Ibid.*, p. 142.

22. Valentine, C. W. "The Innate Bases of Fear." *Journal of Genetic Psychology*, 1930, 37: 394-420.

23. Bregman, E. O. "An Attempt to Modify the Emotional Attitudes of Infants by the Conditioned Response Technique." *Journal of Genetic Psychology*, 1934, 45: 169-198.

24. Diven, Kenneth. "Certain Determinants in the Conditioning of Anxiety Reactions." *Journal of Psychology*, 1937, 3: 291-308.

Chapter 12. Emotional Development: Clinical Findings

1. From *The Psychology of Personality* by English Bagby. Copyright, 1928, by Henry Holt & Co., Inc.

2. Erikson, E. H. "Problems of Infancy and Early Childhood." *Cyclopedia of Medicine, Surgery, and Specialities*. F. A. Davis, 1940, pp. 714-730.

3. Roheim, Geza. "The Origin and Function of Culture." *Psychoanalytic Review*, 1942, 29: 162.

4. Ribble, Margaret. *The Rights of Infants*. Columbia University Press, 1943, p. 4.

5. Ribble, Margaret. "Infantile Experience in Relation to Personality Development." *Personality and the Behavior Disorders* (J. McV. Hunt, ed.). The Ronald Press,

1944, pp. 628-637.

6. Ribble, *The Rights of Infants*, pp. 4-7.
7. Levy, David M. "Fingersucking and Accessory Movements in Early Infancy." *American Journal of Psychiatry*, 1928, 7: 881-918.
8. Levy, David M. "Experiments on the Sucking Reflex and Social Behavior of Dogs." *American Journal of Orthopsychiatry*, 1934, 4: 203-224.
9. Lewis, Samuel J. "Undesirable Habits Influencing the Deciduous Dentition." *Journal of the American Dental Association*, 1931, 18: 1766-1778.
10. Lewis, Samuel J. "Effect of Thumb and Finger Sucking on the Primary Dental Arches." *Child Development*, 1937, 8: 93-98.
11. Symonds, Percival. *The Dynamics of Human Adjustment*. D. Appleton-Century Co., 1946, pp. 140-147.
12. Bergler, Edmund. *Unhappy Marriage and Divorce*. International Universities Press, 1946.
13. Frank, Lawrence. "Cultural Control and Physiological Autonomy." *American Journal of Orthopsychiatry*, 1938, 8: 622-626.
14. Gesell, Arnold, and Ilg, Frances L. *Infant and Child in the Culture of Today*. Harper & Bros., 1943.
15. Aldrich, C. A., and Aldrich, M. M. "Habits Belong to Children." *Child Study*, 1939, 16: 111-113.
16. Huschka, Mabel. "The Child's Response to Coercive Bowel Training." *Psychosomatic Medicine*, 1942, 4: 301-308.
17. Murphy, Gardner; Murphy, Lois Barclay; and Newcomb, Theodore. *Experimental Social Psychology*. Harper & Bros., 1937, p. 588.
18. Levy, David M. *Maternal Overprotection*. Columbia University Press, 1943.
19. Dollard, John. *Frustration and Aggression*. Yale University Press, 1939.
20. Healy, William, and Bronner, August F. *Delinquents and Criminals: Their Making and Unmaking*. The Macmillan Co., 1926.
21. Bowler, Alida, and Bloodgood, R. S. *Institutional Treatment of Delinquent Boys, Part II*. United States Department of Labor, Children's Bureau, Publication No. 230, 1936.
22. Wilson, Margaret. *The Crime of Punishment*. Harcourt, Brace & Co., 1931.

23. Rogers, Carl R. *The Clinical Treatment of the Problem Child*. Houghton Mifflin Co., 1939, pp. 237-238.
24. Rosenszweig, Saul. "A Dynamic Interpretation of Psychotherapy Oriented Toward Research." *Psychiatry*, 1938, 1: 521-526.
25. Klein, Melanie. *The Psychoanalysis of Children*. Hogarth Press, 1932, pp. 276-277.
26. Blanton, M. G. "The Behavior of the Human Infant During the First Thirty Days of Life." *Psychological Review*, 1917, 24: 456-483.
27. Halverson, H. M. "Genital and Sphincter Behavior of the Male Infant." *Journal of Genetic Psychology*, 1940, 56: 95-136.
28. Levy, D. M. "Fingersucking and Accessory Movements in Early Infancy," op. cit., p. 889.
29. Wolf, Anna W. M. *The Parents' Manual*. Simon & Schuster, 1946, pp. 179-180.
30. Kinsey, Alfred C. "Homosexuality: Criteria for a Hormonal Explanation of the Homosexual." *Journal of Clinical Endocrinology*, 1941, 1: 424-428.
31. Terman, L. M., and Cox, C. M. *Sex and Personality*. McGraw-Hill Book Co., Inc., 1936.
32. Glass, S. J., and Johnson, Roswell H. "Limitations and Complications of Organotherapy in Male Homosexuality." *Journal of Clinical Endocrinology*, 1944, 4: 540-544.
33. Seward, Georgene. *Sex and the Social Order*, McGraw-Hill Book Co., Inc., 1945, p. 179.
34. Henry, G. W. "Psychogenic Factors in Overt Homosexuality." *American Journal of Psychiatry*, 1937, 93: 889-908.
35. Willoughby, R. R. "Sexuality in the Second Decade." *Monographs of the Society for Research in Child Development*, 1937, 2: 57.
36. Ferguson, L. W. "Correlates of Women's Orgasm." *Journal of Psychology*, 1938, 6: 295-302.
37. Hamilton, G. V., and Macgowan, K. *What Is Wrong with Marriage?* Albert & Charles Boni, 1929.
38. Dickinson, R. L., and Beam, Lura. *A Thousand Marriages: A Medical Study of Sex Adjustment*. Williams & Wilkins Co., 1931, p. 129.

Chapter 13. Reactions to Frustration

1. Hovland, C. I., and Sears, R. R. "Minor Studies of Aggression: VI. Correlation of Lynchings with Economic Indices." *Journal of Psychology*, 1940, 9: 301-310.
2. Minz, Alexander. "A Re-Examination of Correlations Between Lynchings and Economic Indices." *Journal of Abnormal and Social Psychology*, 1946, 41: 154-160.
3. Wechsler, I. *The Neurologist's Point of View*. L. B. Fischer, 1945, pp. 84-102.
4. Menninger, Karl A. *Man Against Himself*. Harcourt, Brace & Co., 1938, p. 76.
5. Hart, B. *The Psychology of Insanity*. The Macmillan Co., 1931, p. 118.
6. Kraines, Samuel H. *The Therapy of the Neuroses and Psychoses*. Lea & Febiger, 1943, p. 80.

7. Cory, Charles E. "A Divided Self." *Journal of Abnormal Psychology*, 1919, 14: 281-283. Reprinted by permission of the American Psychological Association.
8. Phillips, Robert. *American Government and Its Problems*. Houghton Mifflin Co., 1941.
9. Shaffer, L. F. *The Psychology of Adjustment*. Houghton Mifflin Co., 1936, pp. 193-195.
10. Kimmins, C. W. "Children's Dreams." *Handbook of Child Psychology* (Carl Murchison, ed.). Clark University Press, 1931, pp. 527-554.
11. Masserman, Jules. *Principles of Dynamic Psychiatry*. W. B. Saunders Co., 1946. (Case from Dr. John Romano.)
12. Landis, C., and Cushman, J. F. "The Relation of National Prohibition to the Incidence of Mental Disease." *Quarterly Journal of Studies in Alcohol*, 1945, 5: 527-534.
13. Masserman, J. H. "Biodynamics of Experimental Neuroses and Alcoholism." *Transactions of the New York Academy of Science*, 1945, 7: 61-71.
14. McDougall, Wm. *Outline of Abnormal Psychology*. Charles Scribner's Sons, 1926, p. 245.
15. Maslow, A. H., and Mittelmann, Bela. *Principles of Abnormal Psychology*. Harper & Bros., 1941, pp. 418-419.
16. From the author's files.
17. This and the following material is taken from *Instructor's Guide* to the film by Dr. Margaret E. Fries, "The Life History of Mary; A Psychoneurosis with Compulsive Trends in the Making." (Film obtainable through New York University Film Library, Washington Square, New York.)

Chapter 14. Psychotherapy and Readjustment

1. Statistics furnished the author by James C. Coleman, University of New Mexico.
2. Erickson, M. Y., and Kubie, L. S. "The Successful Treatment of a Case of Acute Hysterical Depression by a Return under Hypnosis to a Critical Phase of Childhood." *Psychoanalytic Quarterly*, 1941, 10: 583-609.
3. Jenness, Arthur. "Hypnotism," in *Personality and the Behavior Disorders* (J. McV. Hunt, ed.). Ronald Press Co., 1944, Vol. I, Chapter 15.
4. Dorcus, Roy M., and Shaffer, G. Wilson. *Textbook of Abnormal Psychology*. Williams & Wilkins Co., 1945, p. 459.
5. Napoli, P. J. "Finger-Painting and Personality Diagnosis." *Genetic Psychology Monographs*, 1946, 34: 129-231.
6. Levy, David. "Trends in Therapy. III. Release Therapy." *American Journal of Orthopsychiatry*, 1939, 9: 736.
7. Moreno, J. L. *Psychodrama*. Beacon House, 1946, Vol. I.
8. Sarbin, T. R. "The Concept of Role-Taking." *Sociometry*, 1943, 6: 274-275.
9. Horsley, J. S. *Narco-Analysis*. Oxford University Press, 1943.
10. Grinker, R. R., and Spiegel, J. P. *Men under Stress*. Blakiston, 1945.
11. Landis, Carney, and Bolles, M. Marjorie. *Textbook of Abnormal Psychology*. The Macmillan Co., 1946, p. 523.
12. Horney, K. *Our Inner Conflicts*. W. W. Norton & Co., 1945, p. 13.
13. Sward, Keith. A review of *Our Inner Conflicts* by K. Horney. *Journal of Abnormal and Social Psychology*, 1946; 41: 496-499.
14. Rogers, Carl R., and Wallen, J. L. *Counseling with Returned Servicemen*. McGraw-Hill Book Co., Inc., 1946.
15. Rogers, Carl R. *Counseling and Psychotherapy*. Houghton Mifflin Co., 1942.
16. Morgan, John J. B. *The Psychology of Abnormal People*. Longmans, Green & Co., 1936, p. 577.
17. Knight, R. P. "Evaluation of the Results of Psychoanalytic Therapy." *American Journal of Psychiatry*, 1941, 98: 434-446.
18. Landis, C. "A Statistical Evaluation of Psychotherapeutic Methods." *Concepts and Problems of Psychotherapy* (Hinsie, ed.). Columbia University Press, 1937.
19. Knight, *op. cit.*
20. Wilder, Joseph. "Facts and Figures on Psychotherapy." *Journal of Clinical Psychopathology and Psychotherapy*, 1945, 7: 311-347.
21. *Ibid.*

Chapter 15. Individual Differences and Their Measurement

1. Rice, S. A. "Contagious Bias in the Interview." *American Journal of Sociology*, 1929, 35: 420-423.
2. Rugg, H. O. "Is the Rating of Human Character Practicable?" *Journal of Educational Psychology*, 1921, 12: 425-438, 485-501; 1922, 13: 30-42, 81-93.
3. Rice, S. A. "Stereotypes." *Journal of Personal Research*, 1926, 5: 267-276.
4. O'Rourke, L. J. *A New Emphasis in Federal Personnel Research and Administration*. U. S. Government Printing Office, 1930.
5. Scott, W. D. "The Scientific Selection of Salesmen." *Advertising and Selling Magazine*, 1915, 25: 5-6, 94-96.
6. Hovland, C. I., and Wonderlic, E. F. "Prediction of Success from a Standardized Interview." *Journal of Applied Psychology*, 1939, 23: 537-546.

7. McMurry, R. N., and Johnson, D. L. "Development of Instruments for Selecting and Placing Factory Employes." *Advanced Management*, 1945, 10: 113-120.
8. Strong, E. K. *Vocational Interest Blank for Men (Revised) Form M.* Stanford University Press, 1938.
9. Strong, E. K. *Vocational Interest Blank for Men (Revised)—Scoring Stencils.* Stanford University Press, 1938.
10. Woodworth, R. S. *Personal Data Sheet.* C. R. Stoelting Co., 1918.
11. Ruch, Floyd L. "A Technique for Detecting Attempts to Fake Performance on the Self-Inventory Type of Personality Test," in *Studies in Personality.* McGraw-Hill Book Co., Inc., 1942, Chapter 12.
12. Ellis, Albert. "The Validity of Personality Questionnaires." *Psychological Bulletin,* 1946, 43: 385-440.
13. Frank, L. K. "Projective Methods for the Study of Personality." *Journal of Psychology,* 1939, 8: 403.
14. Carter, H. D. "Emotional Factors in Verbal Learning: IV. Evidence from Reaction Time." *Journal of Educational Psychology,* 1937, 28: 101-108.
15. Crosland, H. "The Psychological Methods of Word-Association and Reaction-Time as Tests of Deception." *University of Oregon Publications (Psychology Series),* 1929, 1: No. 1.
16. Munroe, Ruth. "An Experiment in Large Scale Testing by a Modification of the Rorschach Method." *Journal of Psychology,* 1942, 13: 229-263.
17. Munroe, Ruth. "Use of the Rorschach in College Counseling." *Journal of Consulting Psychology,* 1943, 7: 89-96.
18. Swift, Joan W. "Relation of Behavioral and Rorschach Measures of Insecurity in Preschool Children." *Journal of Clinical Psychology,* 1945, 1: 196-205.
19. Morgan, C. D., and Murray, H. A. "A Method of Investigating Fantasies: the Thematic Apperception Test." *Archives of Neurology and Psychiatry,* 1935, 34: 289-306.
20. Rapaport, David. "The Clinical Application of the Thematic Apperception Test." *Bulletin of the Menninger Clinic,* 1943, 7: 106-113.
21. Dr. William E. Henry of the University of Chicago is the author of this interpretation of the Thematic Apperception Test.
22. The case report on this patient (including her reactions to the Thematic Apperception Test) was provided by Dr. Helen Sargent of Northwestern University, through the cooperation of Dr. Henry. Dr. Sargent is the author of the Rorschach interpretation in this case.
23. Hull, C. L. *Aptitude Testing.* World Book Co., 1928.
24. Spearman, C. E. *The Abilities of Man.* The Macmillan Co., 1927.
25. Staff of the Test and Research Section, Bureau of Navy Personnel. "Psychological Test Construction and Research in the Bureau of Naval Personnel. V. Navy Radio Technical Training Program." *American Psychologist,* 1946, 1: 83.
26. Paterson, D. G.; Elliott, R. M.; Anderson, L. D.; Toops, H. A.; and Heidbreder, E. F. *Minnesota Mechanical Ability Tests.* University of Minnesota Press, 1930.
27. *Ibid.*
28. Seashore, R. H.; Buxton, C. E.; and McCollom, I. N. "Multiple Factor Analysis of Five Motor Skills." *American Journal of Psychology,* 1940, 53: 251-259.
29. Seashore, C. E., and Mount, G. H. "Correlation of Factors in Musical Talent and Training." *Psychological Monographs,* 1918, 25: No. 2.
30. Tracker, C. C., and Howard, V. M. "Correlations between Intelligence and Musical Talent among University Students." *Psychological Monographs,* 1928, 39: 157-161.
31. Hartshorne, H., and May, M. A. *Studies in Deceit.* The Macmillan Co., 1928.
32. Hartshorne, H.; May, M. A.; and Shuttleworth, F. K. *Studies in the Organization of Character.* The Macmillan Co., 1930.

Chapter 16. Problems in Human Relations

1. Hamilton, G. V., and Macgowan, K. *What Is Wrong with Marriage?* Albert & Charles Boni, 1929.
2. Hall, C. "The Instability of Post-War Marriages." *Journal of Social Psychology,* 1934, 5: 523-530.
3. Terman, L. M., et al. *Psychological Factors in Marital Happiness.* McGraw-Hill Book Co., Inc., 1938.
4. Burgess, E. W., and Cottrell, L. S. *Predicting Success or Failure in Marriage.* Prentice-Hall, 1939.
5. Maslow, A. H. "Self-Esteem (Dominance Feeling) and Sexuality in Women." *Journal of Social Psychology,* 1942, 16: 259-294.
6. Kelly, E. L. "Marital Compatibility as Related to Personality Traits of Husbands and Wives as Rated by Self and Spouse." *Journal of Social Psychology,* 1941, 13: 193-198.
7. Terman, L. M., and Buttenweiser, P. "Personality Factors in Marital Compatibility." *Journal of Social Psychology,* 1935, 6: 143-171, 267-289.
8. Burgess and Cottrell, *op. cit.*
9. Hamilton and Macgowan, *op. cit.*
10. Terman and Buttenweiser, *op. cit.,* p. 163.

11. *Ibid.*, p. 164.
12. *Ibid.*, p. 169.
13. Terman, *op. cit.*, pp. 142-166.
14. Winch, Robert F. "The Relation Between Neurotic Tendency and Adjustment in Engagement." Master of Arts Thesis, University of Chicago, 1939.
15. Terman and Buttenweiser, *op. cit.*
16. Bernreuter, R. G. *The Personality Inventory.* Stanford University Press, 1931.
17. Landis, Paul H., and Day, Katherine. "Education as a Factor in Mate Selection." *American Sociological Review*, 1945, 10: 558-560.
18. Terman, *op. cit.*, pp. 319-355.
19. Kelly, E. L. "Concerning the Validity of Terman's Weights for Predicting Marital Happiness." *Psychological Bulletin*, 1939, 36: 202-203.
20. Burgess, E. W., and Wallin, Paul. "Predicting Adjustment in Marriage from Adjustment in Engagement." *American Journal of Sociology*, 1944, 49: 324-330.
21. Baldwin, Alfred L.; Kalhorn, Joan; and Breese, Fay H. "Patterns of Parent Behavior." *Psychological Monographs*, 1945, 58: No. 3.
22. Symonds, Percival M. *The Psychology of Parent-Child Relationships.* D. Appleton-Century Co., 1939, pp. 18-24.
23. Burt, C. *The Young Delinquent.* University of London Press, 1925.
24. Kvaraceus, W. C. *Juvenile Delinquency and the School.* World Book Co., 1945.
25. Shaw, C. R. *Delinquency Areas.* University of Chicago Press, 1929.
26. From *Social Psychology* by Otto Klineberg. Copyright, 1940, by Henry Holt & Co., Inc. Reprinted by permission of the publisher.
27. Robinson, Reginald. "Beneath the Surface." *Survey Midmonthly*, 1947, 83: 42-52.
28. Zachry, Caroline. *Emotion and Conduct in Adolescence.* D. Appleton-Century Co., 1940, pp. 210-211.
29. Robinson, *op. cit.*, p. 47.
30. Burt, *op. cit.*
31. Slawson, J. "Marital Relations of Parents and Juvenile Delinquency." *Journal of Delinquency*, 1923, 8: 278-286.
32. Healy, W., and Bronner, A. F. *New Light on Delinquency and Its Treatment.* Yale University Press, 1936.
33. Blumer, H., and Hauser, P. M. *Movies, Delinquency and Crime.* The Macmillan Co., 1933, p. 198.
34. Healy and Bronner, *op. cit.*, p. 72.
35. Pintner, R. *Intelligence Testing.* Henry Holt & Co., Inc., 1923, p. 285.
36. Yerkes, Robert M. (ed.). "Psychological Examining in the United States Army." *Memoirs of the National Academy of Sciences*, 1921, 15: 799-802.
37. Murchison, C. "American White Criminal Intelligence." *Journal of Criminal Law and Criminology*, 1924, 15: 435-494.
38. Kuhlmann, F. "Biennial Report for Period Ending June 30, 1926." *Division of Research of the State Board of Control*, Minnesota, pp. 10 ff.
39. Klein, Philip. "Next Steps in Dealing with Delinquency." *Bulletin of the New York School of Social Work*, 1945, 38: No. 4, 1-41.
40. Healy, Wm., and Bronner, Augusta F. *Delinquents and Criminals, Their Making and Unmaking.* The Macmillan Co., 1926.
41. Bowler, A. C., and Bloodgood, R. S. *Institutional Treatment of Delinquent Boys, Part II.* United States Department of Labor, Children's Bureau, Bureau Publication No. 230, 1936.
42. Wilson, Margaret. *The Crime of Punishment.* Harcourt, Brace & Co., 1931.
43. Lewin, K.; Lippitt, R.; and White, R. K. "Patterns of Aggressive Behavior in Experimentally Created 'Social Climates.'" *Journal of Social Psychology*, 1939, 10: 271-299.
44. Klineberg, *op. cit.*, pp. 340-341. Reprinted by permission of Henry Holt & Co., Inc.
45. Bavelas, Alex. "Morale and the Training of Leaders," in *Civilian Morale* (Goodwin Watson, ed.). Houghton Mifflin Co., 1942, pp. 143-165.
46. Mead, M., et. al. *Cooperation and Competition among Primitive Peoples.* McGraw-Hill Book Co., Inc., 1937.
47. Vaughn, James, and Diserens, Charles M. "The Experimental Psychology of Competition." *Journal of Experimental Education*, 1938, 7: 76-97.
48. Sims, V. M. "The Relative Influence of Two Types of Motivation on Improvement." *Journal of Educational Psychology*, 1928, 19: 480-484.
49. Maller, J. B. "Co-operation and Competition." *Contributions to Education.* No. 384. Teachers College, Columbia University, 1929.
50. Whittemore, I. C. "The Influence of Competition on Performance." *Journal of Abnormal and Social Psychology*, 1924, 19: 236-253.
51. Watson, J. B. "Do Groups Think More Efficiently Than Individuals?" *Journal of Abnormal and Social Psychology*, 1928, 23: 328-336.
52. Elkine, D. "De l'influence du groupe sur les fonctions de la memoire." *Journal de psychologie*, 1927, 24: 827-830.
53. Gates, G. S., and Rissland, L. Q. "The Effect of Encouragement and of Discouragement upon Performance." *Journal of Educational Psychology*, 1923, 14: 21-26.
54. Sears, R. R. "An Experimental Test of One Phase of the Hypothecated Repression Sequence." *Psychological Bulletin*, 1936, 33: 744.

55. Horney, K. *The Neurotic Personality of Our Time.* W. W. Norton & Co., 1937.
56. Pennington, L. A. "Shifts in Aspiration Level after Success and Failure in the College Classroom." *Journal of General Psychology,* 1940, 23: 305-313.

Chapter 17. Psychology in Industry

1. Mayo, Elton. *Social Problems of an Industrial Civilization.* Harvard University, Division of Research, 1945.
2. Hartmann, G. W., and Newcomb, T. (eds.). *Industrial Conflict: A Psychological Interpretation.* The Cordon Co., 1939, pp. 118-119. Copyright, 1940, by the Society for the Psychological Study of Social Issues.
3. Mayo, op. cit., p. 76.
4. Roethlisberger, F. J., and Dickson, W. J. *Management and the Worker.* Harvard University Press, 1939.
5. Fox, John B., and Scott, Jerome F. "Absenteeism: Management's Problem." *Harvard University, Business Research Studies,* No. 29, 1943.
6. Borsook, Henry. "Nutritional Status of Aircraft Workers in Southern California. III. Effects of Vitamin Supplementation on Absenteeism, Turnover and Personnel Ratings." *Milbank Memorial Fund Quarterly,* 1945, 23: 113-160.
7. Roethlisberger and Dickson, op. cit.
8. Mayo, op. cit., p. 81.
9. Vernon, H. M.; Bedford, T.; and Warner, C. G. "A Study of Absenteeism in a Group of Ten Collieries." *Industrial Fatigue Research Board Report No. 51,* 1928.
10. Luckiesh, M., and Moss, F. K. *The Science of Seeing.* D. Van Nostrand Co., 1937.
11. Vernon, H. M. *Health of Munitions Workers Committee,* Memo. No. 21. 1918, p. 24.
12. Hersey, Rexford B. "Emotional Factors in Accidents." *Personnel Journal,* 1936, 15: 59-65.
13. Stockford, LeBaron. "Chronic Absentee and Good Attendant." *Personnel Journal,* 1944, 23: 202-207.
14. American Institute of Public Opinion, News Release, May 20, 1943.
15. Viteles, M. S. "Selecting Cashiers and Predicting Length of Service." *Journal of Personnel Research,* 1924, 2: 467-473.
16. Harrell, T. W., and Harrell, M. S. "Army General Classification Test Scores for Civilian Occupations." *Educational and Psychological Measurement,* 1945, 5: 231-232.
17. Hemmelweit, H. T., and Whitfield, J. W. "Mean Intelligence Scores of a Random Sample of Occupations." *British Journal of Industrial Medicine,* 1944, 7: 224-226.
18. Elwood, R. H. "The Role of Personality Traits in Selecting a Career: The Nurse and the College Girl." *Journal of Applied Psychology,* 1927, 11: 199-201.
19. Bingham, Walter V. *Aptitudes and Aptitude Testing.* Harper & Bros., 1937, pp. 367-368.
20. Counts, G. S. "Social Status of Occupations: A Problem in Vocational Guidance." *School Review,* 1925, 33: 16-27.
21. Deeg, M. E., and Paterson, D. G. "Changes in Social Status of Occupations." *Occupations,* 1947, 25: 205-208.
22. Davis, J. "Testing the Social Attitudes of Children in the Government Schools in Russia." *American Journal of Sociology,* 1927, 32: 947-952.
23. Bills, M. A. "Relation of Scores on Strong's Interest Analysis Blanks to Success in Selling Casualty Insurance." *Journal of Applied Psychology,* 1938, 22: 97-104.
24. Strong, E. K. *Vocational Interests of Men and Women.* Stanford University Press, 1943, p. 491.
25. Thurstone, L. L. "A Multiple Factor Study of Vocational Interests." *Personnel Journal,* 1931, 10: 198-205.
26. Marquis, Donald G. "Post-War Reemployment Prospects in Psychology." *Psychological Bulletin,* 1944, 41: 653-663.
27. Landis, C., and Phelps, L. W. "The Prediction from Photographs of Success and of Vocational Aptitude." *Journal of Experimental Psychology,* 1928, 11: 313-324.
28. Viteles, M. S. *Industrial Psychology,* W. W. Norton & Co., 1932, p. 186.
29. Kurtz, A. K. "Evaluating Selection Tests." *Manager's Magazine,* 1939, 14: 10-16.
30. Steward, Verne. *Analysis of Sales Personnel Problems.* Verne Steward and Associates, 1943, p. 47.
31. Grimsley, Glen. "Draftsmen—Aptitude Tests Cut Turnover." *Western Industry,* 1944, 9: No. 1, 32-36.
32. "Psychological Activities in Training Command, A.A.F." *Psychological Bulletin,* 1945, 42: 46.
33. Viteles, Morris. "Getting Results from a Program of Testing for Sales Ability," in *The Value of Psychology in Selecting Salesmen.* Market Series, No. 45. American Management Association, 1941.
34. Viteles, Morris S. "The Aircraft Pilot: Five Years of Research; A Summary of Outcomes." *Psychological Bulletin,* 1945, 42: 489-526.
35. Russell, W., and Cope, G. D. "A Method of Rating the History and Achievement of Applicants for Positions." *Public Personnel Studies,* 1925, 3: 202-219.

36. Phoenix Mutual Life Insurance Company. *Selecting the Successful Salesman.* 1937.
37. Guilford, J. P., and Lacey, J. I. (eds.). "Army Air Forces Aviation Psychology Program." *Printed Classification Tests,* 1947, Report No. 5, pp. 767-795.
38. Stockford, *op. cit.*
39. Palmer, D. L.; Purpus, E. R.; and Stockford, L. O. "Why Workers Quit." *Personnel Journal,* 1944, 23: 111-119.

40. McMurry, R. N. "The Knack of Interviewing Applicants." *Industrial Relations Magazine,* 1945, 2: No. 11, 8-9, 26; "The Interview Pattern." *ibid.,* 1945, 3: No. 1, 13-14, 34-36; "Following Thru on the Interview." *ibid.,* 3: No. 3, 9-11; "Interviewing the Veteran." *ibid.,* 3: No. 5, 11-13.
41. McMurry, R. N., and Johnson, Dale. "Development of Instruments for Selecting and Placing Factory Employees." *Advanced Management,* 1945, 10: 113-120.

Chapter 18. Psychology and Social Issues

1. Lentz, T. "Relation of I.Q. to Size of Family." *Journal of Educational Psychology,* 1927, 18: 486-496.
2. Sewell, W. H. "Differential Fertility in Completed Oklahoma Farm Families." *American Sociological Review,* 1944, 9: 427-434.
3. Conrad, H. S., and Jones, H. E. "A Field Study of the Differential Birth-Rate." *Journal of the American Statistical Association,* 1932, 27: 153-159.
4. Dawson, S. "Intelligence and Fertility." *British Journal of Psychology,* 1932, 23: 42-51.
5. Scheinfeld, A. *You and Heredity.* J. B. Lippincott Co., 1939, p. 378.
6. Harris, Daniel. "Factors Affecting College Grades: A Review of the Literature." *Psychological Bulletin,* 1940, 37: 125-166.
7. Woodrow, H. H. "Practice and Transference in Normal and Feeble-minded Children." *Journal of Educational Psychology,* 1917, 8: 85-96.
8. Aikin, Wilford M. "The Story of the Eight-Year Study." *Adventure in American Education,* Vol. I. Harper & Bros., 1942.
9. Gibson, James J. (ed.). "Motion Picture Testing and Research." Army Air Forces Aviation Psychology Program Research Reports, 1947, Report No. 7, pp. 241-254.
10. *Opinion News,* August 6, 1946.
11. Lasswell, Harold. *Democracy Through Public Opinion.* George Banta Publishing Co., 1941, pp. 29-32.
12. Marple, C. H. "The Comparative Susceptibility of Three Age Levels to the Suggestions of Group versus Expert Opinion." *Journal of Social Psychology,* 1933, 4: 176-186.
13. Roslow, S.; Wulfeck, W. H.; and Corby, P. G. "Consumer Opinion Research: Experimental Studies on the Form of the Question." *Journal of Applied Psychology,* 1940, 24: 334-336.
14. Ruch, Floyd L. "The Problem of Measuring Morale." *Journal of Educational Sociology,* 1941, 15: 221-228.
15. Ruch, Floyd L. "A New Test of the Suggestibility-Negativism Dimension of Personality." A paper read before Section I of the American Association for the Advancement of Science, St. Louis, Missouri, December 30, 1935.
16. Hartmann, G. W. "The Contradiction Between the Feeling-Tone of Political Party Names and Public Response to Their Platforms." *Journal of Social Psychology,* 1936, 7: 336-357.
17. Lasswell, *op. cit.,* p. 40.
18. Kris, Ernst. "Mass Communication Under Totalitarian Governments." *Print, Radio and Film in a Democracy* (Douglas Waples, ed.). University of Chicago Press, 1942, p. 31.
19. Dunlap, K. *Civilized Life.* Williams & Wilkins Co., 1934, pp. 360-361.
20. Ruch, Floyd L., and Young, Kimball. "Penetration of Axis Propaganda." *Journal of Applied Psychology,* 1942, 26: 448-455.
21. Annis, A., and Meier, N. C. "The Induction of Opinion through Suggestion by Means of 'Planted Content.'" *Journal of Social Psychology,* 1934, 5: 65-81.
22. Collier, R. M. "The Effect of Propaganda upon Attitude Following a Critical Examination of the Propaganda Itself." *Journal of Social Psychology,* 1944, 20: 3-17.
23. Allport, F. H., and Lepkin, M. "Wartime Rumors of Waste and Special Privilege: Why Some People Believe Them." *Journal of Abnormal and Social Psychology,* 1945, 40: 3-36.
24. Cahalan, Don, and Meier, N. C. "The Validity of Mail-Ballot Polls." *Psychological Record,* 1939, 3: 3-11.
25. Shuttleworth, F. K. "Sampling Errors Involved in Incomplete Returns to Mail Questionnaires." *Psychological Bulletin,* 1940, 37: 437.
26. Jenkins, John G. "Characteristics of the Question as Determinants of Dependability." *Journal of Consulting Psychology,* 1941, 5: 164-169.
27. Cook, Stuart W., and Welch, Alfred C. "Methods of Measuring the Practical Effects of Polls of Public Opinion." *Journal of Applied Psychology,* 1940, 29: 441-454.
28. Boas, Franz. *Anthropology and Modern Life.* W. W. Norton & Co., 1932.
29. Guthe, C. E. "Notes on the Cephalic Index of Russian Jews in America." *Journal*

of *Physical Anthropology*, 1918, 1: 213-223.

30. Boas, Franz (ed.). *General Anthropology*. D. C. Heath, 1938.

31. Spier, L. "Growth of Japanese Children Born in America and in Japan." *University of Washington Publications in Anthropology*, III, 1929-1930, 1: 1-30.

32. Kroeber, A. L. *Anthropology*. George G. Harrap & Co., Ltd., 1923, p. 37.

33. Hogben, Lancelot. *Genetic Principles in Medicine and Social Science*. Alfred Knopf, 1932, pp. 133-141.

34. Woodworth, R. S. "Racial Differences in Mental Traits." *Science*, 1910, 31: 171-186.

35. Pasamanick, B. "A Comparative Study of the Behavioral Development of Negro Infants." *Journal of Genetic Psychology*, 1946, 69: 3-44.

36. Lasker, Bruno. *Race Attitudes in Children*. Henry Holt & Co., Inc., 1929, p. 55.

37. Allport, Gordon, and Murray, Henry A. (eds.). *ABC's of Scapegoating*. Central YMCA College, n.d., p. 33.

38. Bettelheim, Bruno. "Individual and Mass Behavior in Extreme Situations." *Journal of Abnormal and Social Psychology*, 1943, 38: 417-452.

39. Horowitz, E. L. "The Development of Attitude Toward the Negro." *Archives of Psychology*, 1936, No. 194.

40. Smith, F. T. "An Experiment in Modifying Attitudes Toward the Negro." *Contributions to Education*, No. 887, Teachers College, Columbia University, 1943.

41. DuBridge, L. A. "Science and National Policy." *American Scientist*, 1946, 34: 228.

42. Shapley, Harlow, quoted in "Survival of Man Assured." *Science News Letter*, 1947, 51: No. 1, 2.

43. McDougall, Wm. *An Introduction to Social Psychology*. Methuen & Co., Ltd., 1918, p. 281.

44. May, Mark. *A Social Psychology of War and Peace*. Yale University Press, 1943, pp. 6-8.

45. Bernard, L. L. *War and Its Causes*. Henry Holt & Co., Inc., 1944, p. 379.

46. Diggins, E. "A Statistical Study of National Prejudice." Master's Essay. Columbia University, 1927. Cited in Murphy, G.; Murphy, L. B.; and Newcomb, T. M. *Experimental Social Psychology*. Harper & Bros., 1937, pp. 993-995.

47. Britt, S. H. *Social Psychology of Modern Life*. Farrar & Rinehart, Inc., 1941, p. 462.

Chapter 19. Illustrated Reference Manual: The Brain and Nervous System

1. Wendt, G. R. "An Interpretation of Inhibition of Conditioned Reflexes as Competition between Reaction Systems." *Psychological Review*, 1936, 43: 258-281.

2. Ruch, T. C. "Cortical Localization of Somatic Sensibility." *Proceedings of the Association for Research on Nervous and Mental Diseases*, 1935, 15: 289-330.

3. Ruch, T. C.; Fulton, J. F.; and German, W. "Sensory Discrimination in the Monkey, Chimpanzee, and Man after Lesions of the Parietal Lobe." *Archives of Neurology and Psychiatry*, 1938, 39: 919-937.

4. Hecht, S. "On the Binocular Fusion of Colors and Its Relation to Theories of Color Vision." *Proceedings of the National Academy of Science*, 1928, 14: 237-241.

5. Marquis, D. G. "Phylogenetic Interpretation of the Functions of the Visual Cortex." *Archives of Neurology and Psychiatry*, 1925, 33: 807-815.

6. Bornstein, W. S. "Cortical Representation of Taste in Man and Monkey. I. Functional and Anatomical Relations of Taste, Olfaction and Somatic Sensibility." *Yale Journal of Biology and Medicine*, 1940, 12: 719-736.

7. Lashley, K. S. *Brain Mechanisms and Intelligence*. University of Chicago Press, 1929.

8. Culler, E. A. *The Decerebrate Dog, A Demonstrational Film*. Animal Hearing

Laboratory, University of Illinois.

9. Jacobsen, C. F. "Studies of Cerebral Function in Primates." *Comparative Psychology Monographs*, 1936, 13: No. 3.

10. German, W., and Fox, J. C., et al. "Observations Following Unilateral Lobectomies." *Proceedings of the Association for Research in Nervous and Mental Disease*, 1932.

11. "Localization of Function in the Cerebral Cortex." *Proceedings of the Association for Research in Nervous and Mental Disease*, 1932.

12. Lovell, H. W.; Waggoner, R. W.; and Kahn, E. A. "Critical Study of a Case of Aphasia." *Archives of Neurology and Psychiatry*, 1932, 28: 1117-1181.

13. Travis, Lee E. *Speech Pathology*. D. Appleton-Century Co., 1931.

14. Berger, H. "Uber das Elektrenkephalogramm des Menchen." *Archives fur Psychiatrie und Nervenkrankheit*, 1929, 87: 527-570.

15. Lindsley, D. B. "A Longitudinal Study of the Occipital Alpha Rhythm in Normal Children; Frequency and Amplitude Standards." *Journal of Genetic Psychology*, 1939, 55: 197-213.

16. Travis, Lee E., and Knott, John R. "Brain Potentials from Normal Speakers and Stutterers." *Journal of General Psychology*, 1936, 2: 137-150.

17. Travis, Lee E. "Brain Potentials and the Temporal Course of Consciousness." *Journal of Experimental Psychology*, 1937, 24: 534-535.
18. Gibbs, F. A.; Gibbs, E. L.; and Lennox, W. G. "Epilepsy: A Paroxysmal Cerebral Dysrhythma." *Brain*, 1937, 60: 377-388.
19. Gottlober, A. B. "The Relationship between Brain Potentiality and Personality." *Journal of Experimental Psychology*, 1937, 25: 67-74.
20. Hudgins, C. V. "Conditioning and the Voluntary Control of the Pupillary Light Reflex." *Journal of General Psychology*, 1933, 8: 351.
21. Culler, op. cit.
22. Bard, Philip. "On Emotional Expression after Decortication with Some Remarks on Certain Theoretical Views: Part II." *Psychological Review*, 1934, 41: 424-449.
23. Fulton, J. F. "Levels of Autonomic Function with Particular Reference to the Cerebral Cortex." *Research Publications of the Association for the Study of Nervous and Mental Diseases*, 1939, 19: 219-236.
24. Harlow, Harry F., and Stagner, Ross. "Psychology of Feelings and Emotions." *Psychological Review*, 1932, 39: 570-589; 1933, 40: 184-195.
25. Masserman, J. H. *Behavior and Neurosis*. University of Chicago Press, 1943.

Subject index

Baby, behavior of unborn, 92-95; conditioned plantar reflex in, 96-97; depression and grief in, 444-447; early emotional development in, 410-416; eliminating conditioned fear in, 421-429; emotional conditioning in, 416-421; emotional needs of, 443-452; facial expression of emotion in, 178; instinctive fears in, 407-410; levels of muscular coordination in, 454-455; response of newborn, 100-103; response of, to restraint, 412-413, 431; sensitivity of newborn, 96-100; taste buds in, 275; vocal expression of emotion in, 183-184

Balancing movements, 94, 104
Bali, derived motives in, 154-155
Band-wagon vote, 672-673
Behavior, -al development in different races, 679-680; of fetus, 92-95; of newborn child, 95-103; pattern, 12-14; sampling, 542, 554-555; social, 152-158; study of, 37-38, 39

Behavioristic, school of psychology, 37-38, 39, 407; theory of emotional life, 421

Belief, and desire to believe, 666; and pleasantness, 52; source of, 388
Bi-modal theory of types, 572
Binet's intelligence tests, 197-198, 204
Biographical, method, 24, 25-26; inventory, 647-648
Biological, basis for social motives, 150-151, 156; significance of pain, 133
Blindness, 248; types of, 720-722
Blind spot, 241, 250-251
Blood, as conecting mechanism, 11-12; chemistry and sexual urge, 135; effect of fatigue on, 131; flow during emotion, 107; in different races, 677; pressure in emotion, 165, 185, 187; role of, in temperature sensitivity, 132-133
Body, cells, 81, 88; changes during emotion, 107, 109; changes in relations between parts of, 78-79; -sensitivity area in the brain, 718-720; structure of lemur, gorilla, and man, 8; temperature and reaction time, 308; temperature and time perception, 293
Brain, anatomy of, color plate; association areas of, 723-728; auditory area of, 264-265, 722; body-sensitivity area of, 718-720; cancer, 89; centers of emotion in, 737-740; degeneration in old age, 724; gustatory and olfactory areas in, 723; incomplete in infant, 448; inhibition of reflexes by, 713; -injured person, 377-378; localization of function in, 716-728; methods of study of,

715-716; motor area of, 717-718; new-, 700; old-, 700, 715, 719, 723; relation of, to autonomic nervous system, 733; role of, in habit, 328-329; size of, 9, 103-104; somesthetic area of, 718-720, 722-723; stem, 700, 735; topography of, 714-715; visual area of, 242, 243, 248, 250-251, 720-722; waves, 2, 716, 730-732

Brightness, 253-255; 257
Broca's area, 724, 729

Cafeteria experiments, 128
Capacity to learn, changes in, with age, 119, 355-359; in fetus, 94-95; in infant, 102; relation of, to maturation and performance, 111-120
Case-history method, 24-25
Castration, 107; and sexual appetite, 135-136
Catharsis, 519-527, 536; in industry, 626, 629; methods of, 520-527
Cats, fear-conditioning and use of alcohol by, 498, 500; sham rage in, 739; token-reward experiment with, 146
Centile scores, 567
Central nervous system. See Nervous system
Central tendency, measures of, 564-567
Cephalic index, 676
Cerebellum, 104, 698, color plate
Cerebrum, 698, 714-715; role of, in emotional response, 737-738, color plate
Chemical conditions in body, as origin of hunger drive, 127-128; causing sleepiness, 132; effect of, on heredity, 82; in emotion, 165; in fatigue, 131
Chicago Area Project, 601-602
Children, conditioned emotions in, 418-421; daydreaming by, 494; early emotional development of, 410-416; effect of exciting movies on, 171; eliminating fear response of, 421-429; instinctive fears of, 407-410; maturation of fears in, 430-432; meeting emotional needs of, 437-439, 442-452; observation of, at Yale Clinic, 24; play therapy for, 521-523; socialization of, 452-460; study of insecurity in, 558; testing intelligence of, 197-205, 210
Chimpanzees, social behavior of, 150
Chromosomes, 82-83; selection of, 86-88
Chronological age, relation of to I.Q., 204-205
Chronoscope, 2, 305
Cigarette identification test, 312-313
Clinical psychology, approach of, to study of emotion, 2, 404-406; findings of, concerning emotional development,

436-471; typical day's cases in, 28; use of mental tests in, 199, 201

Closure reflex, 101

Cluster, 574-576; of interests, 637-638

Cochlea, 264-265

Coefficient of correlation. See Correlation coefficient

Cold, as a drive, 132-133; sensitivity, 270-271

College students, anger in, 169-170; choice of vocation by, 630-631, 638-639; conversation among, 23; daydreams of, 493; effects of propaganda on, 668-669; emotional stability of, 634; evidences of stereotypes in, 545; from progressive schools, 658-660; hypochondria in, 502-503; hysteria in, 501; intelligence of, 208; learning experiments with, 371, 379; prejudice of, toward foreign countries, 691; psychograph of, 563; reaction of, to competition, 609-610, 612-613; Rorschach given to, 558; social suggestibility of, 663-664; study difficulties in, 41-43

Color, -blindness, 89, 258-261, 634; mixing in the brain, 721; mixture, laws of, 256-258; red-green, 15-16, 21, 259-261; sensitivity in infants, 98; solid, 253, color plate; vision, 239, 252-258, 261-262; wheel, 254, color plate

Compensation, 480, 481

Competition, between stimuli, 123; instinct of, 608-609; vs. cooperation, 608-614

Complementary hues, 256-258, 261

Compulsions, 504-507

Concepts, 395-397

Condensation in dream work, 529-530

Conditioning experiments, developing fear response, 418-421; experimental extinction in, 380-384; first, 322; logic of, 94-95; of plantar reflex in infants, 96-97; reinforcement in, 380-384; to show stimulus-response connections, 328; with symbolic rewards, 146-147

Conditioned reflex, 322-323, 732-733

Conditioned response, 94; as a type of, habit, 322-324; emotional, below the level of consciousness, 434-435; emotional, in relation to gland responses, 104; extinguishing, 380-384, 421-429; in infant, 96-97; in racial prejudice, 685-686; in unborn child, 94-95; limitations of, in explaining emotional development, 433; showing sensory generalization, 373-375; to words and subject's own thinking, 732-733

Conditioned stimulus, 322, 429

Cones in retina, distribution of, in retina, 261; functioning of, 243-244, 247, 252-253; lack of in color-blindness, 260

Conflict frustration, 473-474; in cats, 500; in rejected child, 586-587; resulting from competition, 611-612

Connecting mechanisms, in the nervous system, 238, 695-700, 707-708; kinds of, 11-12

Contrast effects, in taste, 275; in vision, 257-258, 261

Control, group, 33-34, 221, 223; of variables, in experiments, 95; subject, use of, in experiments, 97

Convergence, 283-284

Cooperation, as adaptive behavior, 478-479; in industry, 621-626; in marriage, 581-582; vs. competition, 608-614

Core curriculum, 658

Cornea, 241, 250

Cornell-Coxe Performance Test, 201

Corpus, callosum, color plate; luteum, 137, 139

Correlation, between intellectual abilities, 574-575; between intelligence and athletic ability, 575-576; between intelligence and mechanical ability, 575; between intelligence and musical abilities, 576; between intelligence and school marks, 653; between intelligence, interests, and special aptitudes, 637-638; between musical abilities, 576; coefficient, 84-85, 568-572; mistaking for causation, 55; of I.Q. and other factors in real and foster homes, 223-225; of I.Q.'s of siblings, 225

Cortex, areas of cerebral, 717-728, 737-740; cerebral, 175, 700, 715, 719, color plate; of adrenal glands, 106-107, 109; role of, in habit, 328

Crime, and social approval, 156; causes of, 593-600; ways of dealing with, 600-604

Criterion, in experimental method, 29-30

Critical period for learning, 115-117; 120, 357

Culture, effect of on test scores, 230; relation of, to derived motives, 150-158

Curiosity, as a motive, 144-145

Dark adaptation, 244, 261

Daybook method, 24

Daydreaming, as autistic thinking, 386-387; as healthy adjustment, 476; as unhealthy reaction to frustration, 490; of college students, 493-495; of factory workers, 618. (See also Fantasy)

Deafness, intensity, 267; tested by conditioning, 96-97; tone, 267-268

Deconditioning of emotional habits, 434, 534-536

Deduction, as a primary ability, 214-215

Defense, movements in infants, 99; reflexes, 101, 710

Delayed response, effect of brain lesions on, 726-727

Delight, as early emotion, 411, 412, 414-415; substituted for fear, 427

Democratic, homes, 591-592; leadership, psychological effects of, 604-608; living, childhood training for, 437-439; opportunity for higher education, 652-653

Dendrites, 701-702, 708-709, 715

Dependent variable, 29-30

Derived motives, 123; development of, 143-153, 156-158; in Bali, 154-155; lists of, 149-150

Desensitization in psychotherapy, 534-536

Detour behavior, 479-481

Dexterity, development of, 454-455; manual, tests of, 3, 633

Dichromatic color vision, 260. (See also Color-blindness)

Diencephalon, 738-739

Differences, allowing for, in education, 653-656; among relatives, 84-89; among siblings, 86-87; between sexes, 118; in maturational status, 118-120; in opportunity to learn, 118; individual, 541

Digestion, 126; stopped during emotion, 736

Diminishing returns, curve of, 355

Diplopia, 250

Discrimination, effects of brain lesions on, 718-719, 722, 726; in infant, 96-100; -learning situations, 339, 341-342, 373-374; reactions and reaction time, 308-309

Disease, and emotions, 172-177, 501-504, 513; and heredity, 82

Disgust, as an early emotion, 412, 413

Displacement, in dream work, 530; of aggression, 483-484; of fear, 504

Dissociation, 487-490

Distraction of attention, 302-304

Distress, as an early emotion, 411-414

Disuse, method of, 423-424

Dogs, behavior of, after brain lesions, 725, 738; experimental extinction in, 380-381; in original conditioning experiment, 322; in thirst experiment, 130-131; sensory generalization in, 374-375; sham rage in, 738

Dominance, cerebral, 728-730; in heredity, 86, 88-89, 90-91; relation of, to

happy marriage, 581; -submission factor in parent-behavior, 592-593

Drawings, as tests of children's intelligence, 201

Dream, analysis, 529-531; manifest and latent content of, 529; work, 529-531

Drive, 122, 123; air hunger, 131; fatigue, 131-132; frustration of, 473; hunger, 125-129; pain, 133-134; sleepiness, 132; thirst, 130-131; visceral tensions as, 134; warmth and cold, 132-133

Drugs, addicts, incidence of, 510; and sleep, 132; escaping frustration through, 497, 499, 612; used in brain study, 716

Dwarfism, 89, 105

Ear, structure of, 264-265

Economic, insecurity and scapegoating, 687; status and I.Q., 208-210, 226-227

Education, adjustment of, to individual differences, 653-656; as cure for scapegoating, 686-687; democratic opportunity for, 652-653; progressive, 658-660; project method in, 655-656; related to instincts and needs, 657-661; sectioning of students in, 654-655

Effectors, 318; maturation of, 103; relation of, to nervous system, 695, 696, 709, 734

Ego-blocking games, 474-475

Eidetic imagery, 196, 393-394

Elation, 168, early development of, 412, 415; physiological patterns in, 185

Electric, -al resistance in skin, 383-384, 403, 416-418; currents in brain, 716, 730-732; currents in muscles, 397-398; phenomena in nerve impulses, 703, 705-706, 709; -shock therapy, 511, 518-519, 523

Emotion, and maturation, 430-432; as conscious experiences, 162-163; as drive, 165-166; as motive, 159-160; as unconscious experiences, 163; bodily changes during, 107, 736; brain centers of, 737-740; breathing rate in, 185-187; clinical and laboratory approaches to, 404-406; control of, 188-191; detecting, from visceral changes, 185-188; early development of, 410-416; everyday, 168-172; external responses in, 163-165; facial expressions in, 177-183; functions of nervous system in, 732-740; in relation to thyroids, 106; internal response in, 165; interpreting, from vocal expression, 183-185; -provoking stimulus situations, 160-162; pulse changes during, 107, 165, 185; results of, 166-168; role of, in disease,

result of repression, 371-372, 487

Foster home, effect of, on I.Q., 220, 222-226; to aid emotional development, 447

Fovea, 241, 243, 247-248, 260

Frequency, of light waves, 252; role of in learning, 348-349

Frequent application of stimulus, method of, 424

Frigidity in women, 469-470

Frontal lobe of brain, 714-715, 723, 724, 725-727, 729, color plate

Frustration, -aggression hypothesis, 461-462, 681, 687; and alcoholism, 497-500; as cause of scapegoating, 681-684; conflict, 473-474, 500, 586-587, 611-612; emotional reaction to, 170; environmental, 472-473; healthy reactions to, 476-481; illnesses, 501-504, 513; in factory workers, 618, 621; necessity of, 452; of sucking behavior, 450; personal, 473; relieving, in play therapy, 474-475, 522; repression of, 486, 490; sexual, 464, 470-471; tolerance, 463; unhealthy reactions to, 481-507

Functionalists, 37, 39

"G" factor in intelligence, 211

Galvanic response, 186-187, 384, 416-418, 557

Galvanometer, 402-403, 417

Ganglia, 734; basal, 700; spinal, 707; vertebral, 698-699

Gastric physiology, effect of emotion on, 173-175; in infants, 448

Genes, 83-84, 88-89, 651, 675

Genius, 25, 193-194

Germ cells, 81-82, 88

Gestaltists, 39

Giantism, 105

Gifted group, studies of, 208-209

Glands, 11-12, 695, 699; always involuntary, 732; conditioning of secretion, 322-324; controlled by automatic nervous system, 733, 736; functioning of sex, 135-140; maturation in, 104-109; overactivity of, 105, 106, 107

Glandular functioning, 105-109; and intelligence, 232-233; determined by heredity, 84; in female sexual appetite, 136-139; in male sexual appetite, 135-136

Goal, in learning, 47, 316, 345; in motivation, 123

Graphic, aids in measuring learning, 350; representation of syllogism, 57

Gregariousness, 150, 151, 620-626

Grief, 164; in infancy, 444

Guilt, as cause of scapegoating, 681-684; detection, 186-188, 557; overcoming, 478, 514, 535-536; remaining in substitution behavior, 480; repression of, 484, 487, 504

Gustatory area of the brain, 723

Habit(s), as adjustment techniques, 326-327; as redintegrative mechanisms, 329-331; changes within, 331, 365-366; conditioned, 322-324; definition of, 320, 360; effect of, on test performance, 230; emotional and motivational, 324-326; modifying, 380-385; factors in the use of, 372-380; interpretive, 326-327; kinds of, 320-327; motor, 321-322; nature of, 327-331; perceptual, 320-321; symbolic, 327; -ual attention, 301

Hair, color, determined by heredity, 84; texture of racial groups, 677

"Halo effect," 544, 545, 550

Handedness, 728-730

Health, and emotional disturbance, 501-504; and intelligence, 232-234; -y modes of adjustment, 476-481

Hearing, 262-268; defects, 89, 267-268; in infants, 96-97; perceiving space through, 290-292

Hemianopia, 721

Heredity, 79; control of through eugenics, 650-652; influence of, on basic abilities, 82; influence of, on intelligence, 218-226; influence of, on traits and attitudes, 82; mechanics of, 82-83, 86-89; operative by maturation throughout life, 80; role of, in development, 32-33; role of, in racial differences, 231, 674-675

Hippocampus, 723

Homosexuality, and endocrines, 139-140; causes of, 468-469; description of, 467-468

Hormone(s), 11-12, 104-109; and homosexuality, 468-469; growth, 105; in sexual functioning, 135-140; "mother-love," 106

Hostility, and gastric changes, 174; as reaction to repression, 587; between labor and management, 624; frequency in clinical cases, 460; in inferiority complex, 441; in response to autocratic leadership, 605; underlying overprotectiveness, 586

Hue, 252-261

Humor, role of in emotional control, 190-191

Hunger drive, effects of, 129; origin of,

125, 127-128; specific hungers, 128; visceral sensations in, 736-737

Hyperopia, 249

Hypnosis, used in clinical work, 487, 514, 515-518

Hypochondria, 502-503

Hypothalamus, 175, 700; in emotion, 738-740; in temperature sensitivity, 132

Hypothesizing as a factor in learning, 343-344

Hysteria, 501-502; 503-504; faith-healing of, 515; produced and banished in hypnosis, 516

Identical twins, 87; brain waves in, 731; different training given to, 114-115; effect of differing environments on, 218-220

Identification, 495

Idiocy, amaurotic family, 89; behavior in, 207; example of, 196; pain sensitivity as test for, 99

Illness as reaction to frustration, 501-504

Imbeciles, 207

Implicit movements in thinking, 398-400

Impotence, 469-470

Improvement, as criterion of learning, 315-316

Inborn, emotions, 407-412; motives, 150-151; preferences, 141-142

Incomplete tasks, memory of, 379-380

Increasing returns, curve of, 354

Independence, early need for, 438-439, 478

Independent variable, 29-30

Individual tests, 546, 548

Induction as a primary ability, 214

Infant. See Baby

Inferiority complex, case of, 24-25, 440-442; compensation for, 481; overcoming, 534-536; overcompensation for, 481-482

Inhibition of motor neurons, 712-713

Insanity, 89, 510; combatting, by eugenics, 651; in gifted group, 209

Insecurity in children, case of, 586-587; study of, by Rorschach test, 558

Insensitivity, in infants, 96; to pain in idiocy, 99

Insight, in learning, 332-335; emotional, 475

Inspiration-expiration ratio, 185

Instinct, 108; in animals, 110-111; in man, 111, 120; of race prejudice, 680; of war, 689; theory of human nature, 151

Institution, effect of, on intelligence, 216; effect of, on mental cases, 536

Intelligence, and emotional maladjustment, 441; and hunger, 129; and race, 229-231; and scholarship, 653, 654; and use of habits, 375-376; as factor in delinquency and crime, 207-208, 598-600; Binet's early tests of, 197-198, 204; definition of, 192; distribution of, in population, 206; G factor in, 211, 574; levels of, 193-196; lowering of, in syphilis, 234; needed for various vocations, 631-633; primary abilities comprising, 211-215; resemblance in, among relatives of varying closeness, 84-85; roles of heredity and environment in, 218-227; social, 633-634; studies of superior, 208-209; tests, 193, 197-203

Intelligence quotient (I.Q.), 198, 201, 655; and birth order, 227; and diseased tonsils and adenoids, 233-234; and glandular imbalance, 232-233; and health, 232-234; and malnutrition, 232; and month of birth, 228-229; and occupational group, 208-210, 632-633; and race, 229-231; constancy of, 215-227; distribution of, in population, 206; effect of coaching on, 210-211; meaning and computation of, 203-209

Intensity, deafness, 267; of sensation, 704-705, 717; of sound, 262

Interests, as factor in learning, 46-48; as factor in vocational success, 636-638; development of, 148-149; education related to child's, 657-660; role of, in perception, 282, 300; testing, 637-638

Interference material, in experiment, 356, 368, 369

Interpretive habits, 326-327

Interviewing, 542, 550-552; sources of error in, 543-546; standardized, 550-551, 646, 648-649

Introspective method, 16-17, 39; combined with objective method, 19-20; used in study of emotion, 162-163; used to study units of sensation, 36-37

Introversion, 572-573, 576-577; brain waves in, 731; in certain vocations, 633

Iris, 240, 241

Irradiation, 93, 710

Ishihara test for color-blindness, 259, 261

Jealousy, 168, 170-171; early development of, 412, 413-414

Jensen, grids to test visual acuity, 246-247; test for color-blindness, 259, color plate

Job, families, 643; -testing, 642-646

Joy, early development of, 412

Juvenile delinquency, and intelligence, 207; and lack of family protection, 457-458; broken homes and, 597; causes of, 593-600; incidence of, 510; increased by punishment, 462-463; reduced by working off aggressions, 463; ways of dealing with, 600-604

Kinesthesis, 99; affected in brain injury, 727
Kinesthetic, sensitivity, 272-273; stimulation, 321-322

Laboratory psychology, study of emotion in, 404-406
Labyrinthine sense, 273
Laissez-faire leadership, effects of, 605-607
Language differences, effect of on test performance, 200, 230
Leadership, effect of different systems of, 604-607; training of, 606-608
Learning, 81; and age, 355-359; conditions necessary for, 336-349; definition of, 315-318; effect of, on gland responses, 104; graphic representation of, 350; in fetus, 94-95; in infant, 96-97, 102; in modern schools, 657-661; in monkeys and apes, 332-334; measuring, 349-355; of habits, 319-331; of ideas, 68, 70; organizing processes in, 336-337; prerequisites to, in studying, 43-50; relation of, to performance, 111, 351-353, 365, 379; retention of, 360-372; situation, deficiencies in, 342; spacing of, 66-68; transfer of, 62-64; verbatim, 66, 67-68, 70; ways of, 331-336
Learning ability. See Capacity to learn
Lens of eye, 240-242, 721; accommodation of, 286; defects of, 248-250
Level(s) of development, examples of, 454-455; formula for, 79
Lie detectors, 186-188
Life-history methods, 23-26
Light waves, 252-253, 255
Limen, 9
"Little man," baby as a, 442; concept, 7, 36
Logic-tight compartments, 491

Maladjusted, old and new treatment of, 26-27; students, 558; study of the, 436; workers, 618, 621, 626, 629-630, 640-641
Male sex drive, 135-136
Mammary glands, 105, 106
Manual dexterity test, 3, 634, 643
Marasmus, 443-447

Marital incompatibility as factor in maternal overprotection, 459
Marriage, factors in success and failure of, 579-585; predicting compatibility in, 585; sexual compatibility in, 469-471
"Masculine" traits, 140; in our culture, 468; relation of to adrenals, 107
Mass action, 93
Masturbation, 465-466
Maternal activity and "mother-love hormone," 106; effected by pineal, 107
Maturation, after birth, 80; and emotion, 410-416, 430-432; and environment in learning, 114-120; and socialization, 443, 453-455; before birth, 92-95; during first year, 448; importance of, in certain skills, 111; in nervous system, 103-104; in rats, 110-111; in relation to performance, 111-117; in sexual development, 140; in tadpoles, 110; limited by heredity, 89, 120; of appetites and aversions, 134; of cortex, 740; of glands, 104-108; of muscles, 103; of nerve fibers, 702; rate of, 89
Maze, tests for intelligence, 203; use of in experiments, 19-20, 127, 324
Mean, arithmetic, 564-567, 632
Meaningfulness, as a factor in retention, 369-370, 657; in learning, 58-62, 68, 70; in motivation, 376
Measuring, individual differences, 541-561; intelligence, 197-205; learning, 349-355; personality, 543-561; results of, dependent on methods, 54-55; visual acuity, 246-247
Mechanical ability, 574, 575; tests for, 634, 643
Median, 565-567
Medulla, of the adrenal glands, 106-107; of the brain, 175, 698, 699 color plate
Membrane theory of nerve impulses, 705-706
Memory, as a primary ability, 213; study of, by Gestaltists, 39
Menstrual period, 137; and psychological cycle, 138-139
Mental, abnormality, incidence of, 510; age, 197-201; age in relation to I.Q., 204-205, 216; age as basis of sectioning school children, 654, 655; development, 193-196; deterioration due to inadequate mothering, 444-447; deterioration due to syphilis, 234; disease and pituitary disorder, 105; fatigue, 56; growth, rate of, 205; patients, old and new treatment of, 26-27, 508; states, study of, 36-37; telepathy, 295-297;

tests, 542, 546-548; tests of intelligence, 193, 197-203, 205

Mental set. See Set

Mesmerism, 515

Midbrain, 699, 738

"Middle man" hormones, 105, 109; and mother-love, 106; in male sexual appetite, 135

Migraine, 251

"Mind-body" medicine, 165. (See also Psychosomatic medicine)

Minnesota Tests, 3, 575, 634, 643

Mode, 565-566, 572-573

Monkey, intelligence of, 375-376; learning and insight in, 332-334; study of brain localization in, 719, 725-727; use of concepts by, 396-397

Monotony in industrial work, 618; counteracting effects of, 619-620

Moods, 172

Morale of employees, 616, 629; improving, 619-620, 621-626

Morality, studies of, in children, 577; variability in, 577-578

Morons, 207-208

Mother, babies' need for, 443-452; overprotective, 458-460, 586

Motion sickness, 273

Motivation, -al habits, 324-326; as factor in learning, 46-48, 317, 338-339; competition as, 609-610; influence of, on our perception, 124; role of, in performance, 351-352, 376, 379; social, 145, 147-158; supplied in modern education, 657-660

Motives, 123; derived, 123, 145, 149-156; emotions as, 159-160; reinterpreting one's, 479-481; social, 9, 152, 153

Motor, areas of the brain, 716, 717-718; basis of thought, 397-400; coordination, development of, 454-455; fibers, 701, 707, 710, 712-713, 715, 736; habits, 321-322; method in learning maze, 20; skills taught to young children, 115-117, 318; tasks in learning experiment, 356

Mouth vs. eyes as revealers of emotion, 181-183

Movements, eye, 49-50, 245; infant sensitivity to, 99; in unborn child, 92-95

Movies, and delinquency, 598; as excessive emotional stimulation, 171

Muscle cells, 696, 697, 707; before and after contraction, 711; size and number of, 103

Muscles, as responding mechanisms, 12, 695, 699; electric current in, 397-398; eye, 240-242, 283-284; inhibition and

reciprocal innervation in, 711-713; maturation of, 103; sensitivity in, 272-273; used in facial expression, 179; voluntary and involuntary, 732-733

Muscular, activity and external temperature, 133; basis in thinking, 397-400; coordination in motor habits, 104, 321-322; coordination, levels of, in infants, 454-455; exercises to improve vision, 250; response, meaning of, in infants, 96; skills developed in one twin, 114-117; troubles, 89

Musical ability, 576, 634

Myelin sheath, 702, 715

Myelination of axons, 702

Myopia, 248-249

Narco-analysis, 520, 526-527

Nationalism, 690-692

Navy, General Classification Test, 205; Standard for visual acuity, 246

Near-sightedness, 248-250

Negative, after-sensations, 257; practice method, 349, 385, 534-536

Negativism, 148, 455

Nerve (s) arrangement of, in spinal cord and ganglia, 734; cells, 103, 696, 697, 700-709, 715, 717; cervical, 698; cranial, 698; correlating, 702, 734; impulses, 696, 702-709, 715, 717, 718; lumbar, 698; motor, 701, 707, 710, 712-713, 715, 736; pathways, 697, 709; sacral, 698; sensory, 701, 707, 710, 715, 717, 736; specificity of, 717, 722; thoracic, 698; trunks, 696

Nervous system, autonomic, 384, 699-700, 732-737; central, 697-700, 702, 732-733; change of, in learning, 329-331; functioning of, 702-713; functioning of, in emotion, 732-740; incomplete in infant, 448; in conditioning, 382, 384; injury to portions of, 716; maturation in, 103-104; peripheral, 697, 698-700, 702; role of, in air hunger, 131; role of, in fatigue, 131; role of, in perception, 238, 247-248, 278-280; stimulated by visceral tensions, 134; units of, 695-702

Neural, functioning, 700-713; impulses, 702-709; pathways, 697, 709; patterns, 11, 13, 104, 697

Neurasthenia, 501, 502, 503; produced and banished in hypnosis, 516

Neurologist, 511

Neuron. See Nerve cell

Neutral stimulus, 94, 96-97

Night vision, 243-245

Noise, 141, 263, 303-304

Nomadism, 472, 495-496

Nondirective therapy, 531-533
Nonsense material, in learning experiments, 356, 365, 368
Non-verbal intelligence tests, 200-203, 546, 548; used to study effect of environmental factors, 226-227
Nordic superiority theory, 231
Normal adjustment to frustration, 476-481
Nose shape, as criterion of racial groups, 677
Number series, learning of, 335
Nursery school, effect of on I.Q., 221

Observation, by introspective, 16-17, 19-20, 39; objective, 16, 17-20, 37-38, 39
Obsessions, 504-505
Occipital area, 243, 714-715, 720-722; brain waves of, 731; color plate
Occupational, disease, 267; opportunity, 638-639; requirements, 631-635; success and interest pattern, 636-637; therapy, 536
Odors, inborn preferences in, 142; infant sensitivity to, 98
Old age, and loss of taste sensitivity, 275-276; in relation to learning ability, 119, 355-359
Olfactory, area of brain, 723; bulb, 698; response, in infants, 98
Old-sightedness, 249-250
Optic chiasm, 698, 720, color plate
Optic nerve, 241, 243, 250-251, 306, 703, 720-721
Optical illusions, 245, 279
Organic lesions, in ulcers, 173-175
Organism, man as an, 7-8
Organizing process, in learning, 336-337, 369-370, 385-386; in perception, 278-283, 313, 337, 378
Ovaries, 104, 108, 109, 136
Overcompensation, 481-482, 612
Overprotection, case of, 586-587; maternal, 458-460, 478
Overtones, 263, 266, 292
Oviduct, 136
Ovulation, 136-139
Oxygen starvation, 131

Pain, as a drive, 133-134; impulses in sympathetic nerves, 736; in decorticate animal, 737; infant sensitivity to, 99; recognition of, from facial expression, 178; repression of, 484; role of thalamus in, 719, 738-739; sensitivity, 269-270
Paired comparisons, method of, 548-549
Paradoxical, cold, 271; warmth, 271

Paralysis, 89; from air hunger, 131; hysterical, 501-502; following a "stroke," 718; spastic, 196
Parasympathetic nervous system, 734-737, 738-739
Parathyroids, 104, 106, 109
Parent behavior, and crime, 596-597; example of harmful, 586-587; factors in successful, 588-589; patterns of, 589-593
Parent-child relationship, 457; and socialization of child, 451-452; determining emotional development, 470-471; faulty, where mother is overprotective, 458-460; ideal point in, 592-593; improving, 477; in controlling aggressive feelings, 463-464; role of, in child's sexual expression, 464; types of, 589-593
Parietal lobe of brain, 714, 715, color plate
Part-whole relationship, 278-283
Peptic ulcers. See Ulcers
Perception, ambiguity in, 279, 281-283, 320; habits in, 320-321; of movement, 289-290; of parts as a whole, 278-283; of space, 283-289, 290-292; of time, 292-295; organizing processes in, 278-283; reorganization of, in learning, 333-335; role of interest in, 282, 300; selectivity of, 297-304; study of, by Gestaltists, 39
Perceptual, conditions in learning, 340-342; conditions in use of habit, 375; speed as a primary ability, 214
Perceptual-motor habits. See Motor habits
Performance, as indicator of learning, 349-355, 365; curves, 325, 350, 352, 354-355; factors governing, 372-380; relation of, to capacity and practice, 111-120; role of motivation in, 325-326; tests, 200-203; under competition, 610-611
Peripheral nervous system, 697, 698-700, 702
Periphery of retina, 247-248
Perseveration, in word-association tests, 556
Personal frustration, 473
Personality, development in modern schools, 657-660; effect of competition on, 611-613; in relation to various glands, 106-109; measurement, 543-561, 646-649; requirements for vocations, 633-635; subjectivity in measuring, 543-544
Phobias, 504

Photographs, use of in judging applicants, 642; use of in studying facial expression, 180-183

Physical, development and glands, 105-108; differences between races, 675-679; requirements for vocations, 633

Physiological processes and time perception, 293

Picture-completion tests, 201, 202

Pilot aptitude test, 645

Pineal gland, 104, 107, 109, color plate

Pitch, 262-263, 265; deafness to, 267-268

Pituitary gland, 104-106, 109, color plate; disorders of, and intelligence, 233; in response to emotion, 165; in sexual activity, 135-136

Placebo, 514, 518-519

Plantar reflex, 96-97

Play-therapy, 2, 520, 521-523

Pleasantness, and desire to believe, 52-53; as factor in retention, 52, 365, 370-371

Point of origin, 564

Pons, 698, 699, color plate

Positive after-sensations, 258

Post-hypnotic suggestion, 516

Poverty as factor in delinquency, 594-595, 600

Power tests, 546

Practice, and reaction time, 306, 307-308; distributed, 66, 67; group, example of, 112; massed, 66, 68; of self-recitations, 64-66; period, 350, 354-355; relation of, to performance and capacity, 111-120; spacing of, 66-68, 70

Prediction, 20-22; from correlation coefficients, 570-572; of job stability, 648-649; of marital success, 583-584, 585; of vocational success, 637, 644, 645

Pregnancy, 136-137; hormone, 139

Prejudice, against foreign countries, 691-692; created by newspapers, 668; racial, 680-688; reducing, 686-688; sources of, 680-686

Prenatal maturation, 92-95

Preparatory response, 323

Prematurely delivered fetus, behavior of, 92-95

Presbyopia, 249-250

Preschool. See Nursery School

Pressure front, 262, 264-265; sensitivity, 268-269, 718

Primary, abilities, 211-215; colors, 255-256

Prime of life, 119, 120

Problem-solving, in monkeys with brain lesions, 725-726; thinking, 386-388, 390-392

Production, industrial, 622-624, 627-628

Progestin, 108, 136-139

Progressive education, 658-660

Project method, 655-656

Projective techniques, 542, 555-561

Propaganda, 665-669; and desire to believe, 52-53; combatting, 669; power of, 667-669; techniques of, 665-667

Psychiatrist, 511

Psychoanalysis, 527-531; efficacy of, 537-538

Psychoanalyst, 38, 39, 511

Psychodrama, 520, 523-525

Psychogenic illness, 501-504

Psychograph, 562-563, 567, 573, 643

Psychological, differences among races, 679-680; factors in productive efficiency, 622-624; needs, 615-618, 620-621, 626, 629-630

Psychological, profile. See Psychograph

Psychological tests. See Tests

Psychology, clinical, approach of, to study of emotion, 404-406; definition and objectives of, 4-7, 36-40; employment, 639-649; industrial, 616-630; laboratory, approach of, to study of emotion, 404-406; nationalist, 690-692; operations and methods in, 15-35; schools of, 35-40; vocational, 630-639

Psychoneurotics, incidence of, 510, 526; reassurance of, 514

Psychopathic personality, incidence of, 510; possible cause of, 739

Psychosomatic, disorders distinguished from frustration illness, 503-504; medicine, 165, 172-177

Psychotherapy, 324, 371-372; client-centered, 519-533; counselor-centered, 512-519; description of, 509; eclectic methods of, 533-537; facts and figures on, 537-538; in cure of various disorders, 177; in curing compulsions, 505; in curing ulcers, 173; in treating alcoholism, 499; information giving, as a form of, 513; practitioners of, 510-512

Psychotics, incidence of, 510

Public opinion, effect of propaganda on, 665-669; factors molding, 661-665; measuring, 669-674

Punishment, in learning, 339-340, 345-348; of aggression, 461-462; of crime and delinquency, 602-603

Pupil of eye, 240, 241, 736; nerves to, 699; pupillary reflex, 251, 721, 732-733

Purkinje effect, 244, 253

Puzzle box, used in experiment, 324, 725-726

Rabbits, eliminating fear of, 423, 426-429; in thirst experiment, 130

Race, and intelligence, 229-231; continuity of, 678; development of differences, 674-675; physical differences, 675-679; prejudice, 680-688; psychological differences, 679-680

Rage, in decorticate animals, 737-738, 739; in young child, 412, 740

Rate of learning, and delayed reward, 339-340; and stomach contractions, 129; with insight, 332-335

Range, as measure of variability, 567-568; interquartile, 568

Rating scales, 542, 546, 548-550

Rationalization, 492

Rats, anticipatory behavior in maze, 324, 325; behavior of, after brain lesions, 725; conditioned fear of, 418-419, 428-429; response to punishment in learning situation, 347-348; role of "set" in learning, 343; rote vs. meaningful learning in, 370; sensory generalization in, 373-374; visual discriminations of, 341-342

Reaction time, 305-309; as clue in word-association tests, 556; caffein and, 308; neural basis of, 710

Reading, skill in, 48-50

Rearrangement, method of, 362

Reasoning, 387-388; ability, testing, 546; correlation of, with intelligence, 574

Recall, method of, 362; when learning with intent to remember, 70

Receptors, 11, 103; for temperature, 132; functioning of, 695, 696-697, 707, 709, 734; in color vision, 253, 261-262; in hearing, 264-265; in kinesthesis, 272; in retina, 242-244, 247-248, 306; in touch senses, 269-271; to taste, 275-276

Recessiveness, 86, 88-89, 90-91, 651

Reciprocal innervation, 711-713

Recognition, method of, 362

Reconditioning, 427-429

Redintegrative mechanisms, 329-331, 375, 395

Reduction division, 86-88, 209

Reflexes, conditioned, 96-97, 322-323, 732-733; in infants, 96-97, 101; neural functioning in, 709-713; protective, 710, 713; pupillary, 251, 721, 732-733

Refractory period, 704-706

Regression, 496-497; established in hypnosis, 516-517, 612

Reintegrative. See Redintegrative

Rejection, case of, 586-587; patterns in parent behavior, 590-593

Relatives, resemblances and differences among, 84-89

Relearning, 362-363

Reliability, 542, 543; of interviews, 543-546, 551-552

Reminiscence, 364-365

Report, accuracy of, 309-313; speed of, 305-309

Repression, 163, 612; as factor in forgetting, 371-372; compared with forgetting, 485-486; dissociation as a form of, 487-490; of dreams, 530; of hostility, 460, 568-587; of unpleasant things, 52, 484-490; produces fear and hostility, 462; revealed in release therapy, 522

Resistances in psychoanalysis, 528

Response, as criterion of sensitivity, 96-97; changed by learning, 317-318; conditioned, 94-95, 97; in emotion, 163-165; mechanism of, 12, 238, 695, 700, 707-713, 732-740; of infant, 95-102; of unborn child to stimulation, 92-95; preparatory, 323-324

Rest, need for, 131-132

Restraint, infants' reaction to, 412-413, 431

Retention, of learning, 360; course of, 363-364; curve of, 367; factors governing, 365-372; measuring, 361-363

Retina, 240-244, 245, 247-251; of color-blind eye, 260, 261

Retinal, disparity, 283, 284-285; pictures, 283, 284, 721

Retroactive inhibition, 364-369, 485

Review, 71-74

Reward, in learning, 316-317, 339-340, 341, 344-345; symbolic, in conditioning, 146-147

Ridicule, method of, 425-426

Rods in retina, 243-244, 252-253; in color-blind eye, 260, 261

Rorschach tests, 27, 555, 557-558, 561, color plate

Rote memory, 335, 370. (See also Verbatim learning)

Rumor, acceptance of, 52, 667-669

Safety in industry, 626-629

Saturation, 252-258, 259-260

Scapegoat mechanism, 483; appearance of, under autocratic leadership, 605; history and origin of, 680-686; reducing, 686-688

Schizophrenia, shown by Rorschach test, 557; treatment of, by psychodrama, 523-525

Scotoma, 250-252

Security, need for psychological, 437-439, 443-452, 621

Self-feeding, learning, 455

Stereoscope, 284-286
Stereotypes, 544-545, 550, 664-665
Sterilization of unfit, difficulties of, 89, 651
Stimulated movement in fetus, 92-95
Stimulus, internal, 95, 122-123, 134; meaning of, 9; -response behavior, 37, 39, 709-713; -response cycle, 238, 328-331; -response theory of learning, 328-329, 330-331; summation of, 711; threshold, 704-705, 737
Stimulus situation(s), evoking emotion in babies and children, 407-415, 418-433; emotion-provoking, 160-162, 432-433; role of, in learning, 335-336; selectivity of organism toward, 297-304; used as cue to emotion, 178-184
Stomach, 175; condition and thirst, 130-131; condition in emotion, 107, 173-175, 736; contractions, 125-127, 129
Structuralists, 36-37, 39
Study, difficulties, 41-43; efficient procedures for, 58-76; for examinations, 68-76; prerequisites for efficient, 43-50; schedule, 43-46
Stuttering, brain waves during, 731; case of, 24-25; causes of, 729-730
Sublimation, 480
Submissiveness, 478, 592-593
Substitution, 480
Sucking, conditioned, responses, 102; in fetus, 94; in infants, 100
Suggestion, 514-515; indirect, 518-519; posthypnotic, 17, 516; self-, in treating ulcers, 173
Suicide, as self-aggression, 483-484; incidence of, 510; rate in gifted group, 208
Summation of stimuli, 711
Syllogism, 57-58, 214-215
Symbolic, compulsions, 505; habits, 327; rewards, 145-148
Symbols, in dreams, 529, 530; in thinking, 386, 389, 394-395; use of, dependent on association areas in brain, 724-727; use of, in learning, 334-335
Sympathetic nervous system, 734-736, 738
Synapse, 708-709, 710; outside central nervous system, 699, 733-734
Synesthesia, 394
Syphilis, and mental deterioration, 234; discovering treatment of, 387-388

Taste, -blindness, 89, 90-91; organs and sensitivity in newborn, 98-99; sense of, 275-276
Teaching, opportunities for, 638-639; techniques of, 656-661

Teamwork, in industry, 621-625
Temperament, and climate, 132; relation of, to pituitary, 106; requirements for vocations, 633-634; scales, 646-647
Temperamental traits, influence of heredity on, 82
Temperature sensitivity, 132-133, 270-271, 718; in infants, 100
Temporal lobe, 714, 723
Termination rate, 640, 644
Testes, 104, 107-108, 109, 135
Testimony, unreliability of, 310-312
Tests, classification of, 546-548; for color-blindness, 259-261; for personality, 555-561; for special abilities, 633-635; for visual acuity, 246-247; intelligence, 193, 197-203, 230-231; of manual dexterity, 3; performance, 200-203; predicting marital happiness by use of, 585; sometimes not comparable for differing groups, 230-231; value of, in selecting employees, 642-649
Thalamus, 699, 700; role of, in emotion, 738-740; in hearing, 265; in lower animals and men, 719
Thematic-Apperception Test, 555, 558-561
Therapy. See Psychotherapy
Thinking, autistic, 386-387, 561; avoiding cloudy, 50-58; checking, 56-58; muscular basis in, 397-400; problem solving, 386-388, 390-392; procedures in, 389-392; tools of, 392-397; use of symbols in, 386, 389, 394-395; values of, 387-389
Thirst, 125, 130-131
Thumb-sucking, 449-450
Thymus gland, 104, 107, 109
Thyroid glands, 104, 106, 109; deficiency of, and intelligence, 232-233; role of, in adjustment to external temperature, 133; role of in emotion, 165
Timbre, 263, 266
Time, perception, 292-295; relations, in learning, 339-340
Toilet-training, 453-455; regression in, 496
Token-reward habits, 146-147
Tone deafness, 267-268
Tonsils, and intelligence, 233-234
Touch senses, 268-271; brain area controlling, 718-720, 723, 727
Transfer of learning, 62-64
Transference to psychoanalyst, 528-529
Trial and error, and insight, 333-335; in apes, 334; learning, 324, 331-332, 477; theory, 316-317; use of symbolic, 334-335; vicarious, 344
Tunnel vision, 21-22, 250-252

Tweenbrain, 738-739

Twins, brain waves in identical, 731, heredity in identical, 87; influence of heredity and environment on intelligence of, 219-220; maturation and learning in, 114, 115-117

Ulcers, development of, 173-175

Unborn child. See Fetus

Unconditioned reflex, 322

Unconscious, emotion, 163; guilt as cause of scapegoating, 683; process, 16-17, 38, 39, 372 (See also Repression)

Uneven mental development, 196; role of environment in, 226-227

Unpleasantness, as factor in retention, 52, 365, 370-372; role of in repression, 485

Vagus nerve, 175, 699

Validity, 542-543; of Rorschach technique, 557-558

Values, development of, 149-150

Variability, measures of, 567-568

Variable, dependent, 29; independent, 29

Vasomotor response, 330

Ventricles of the brain, color plate

Verbal, ability of slum vs. middle-class children, 226-227; ability as a primary ability, 212; appeal in eliminating fears, 427; intelligence, 200, 202, 212; method in learning maze, 20; tasks in learning, 356; tests, 199-200, 546, 548

Verbatim learning, 66, 67-68, 70, 657

Vibrato, 184-185

Virilism, 107

Visceral, changes used to detect emotion, 185-188; musculature, neural control of, 700; nervous system, 732-737; responses in emotion, 165, 169, 736; sensation, 736-737; tensions as drives, 134

Vision, 239-262, 634; mechanics of, 239-245

Visual, acuity, 246-248; area of brain, 243, 248, 720-722; defects, 89, 248-253; imagery, 213, 392-394; images, mechanics of receiving, 240-245; method for learning maze, 20; sensitivity in infants, 98; space perception, 283-289

Visualizing, as primary ability, 213; testing, 643

Vitamins, and color-blindness, 260; and industrial morale, 623

Vocabulary training, of identical twins, 114-115

Vocational psychology. See Psychology

Voice change, 80

Walking, development of, 78, 79; in Indian babies, 115; movements in infant, 103

War, and "aggressive instinct," 153, 689; theories of causes of, 688-690

Warmth, as a drive, 132-133; sensitivity, 270-271

Water level of body, 130-131

Wernicke's center, 724

Wisdom of the body, 128-129

Withdrawal reflex to pain, 133

Wolf-child, 151-152

Word-association tests, for studying personality, 555-557

Work, as aid in emotional crisis, 190, 477; -sample tests, 547

Workers, emotional needs of, 615-630

Worry, 168-169